PHOENIX RISING:
COLLECTED PAPERS ON HARRY POTTER,
17–21 MAY 2007

PHOENIX RISING:
COLLECTED PAPERS ON
HARRY POTTER,
17–21 MAY 2007

EDITED BY

Sharon K. Goetz

Narrate Conferences, Inc.   *Sedalia, Colorado*

Published by Narrate Conferences, Inc.
P.O. Box 149
Sedalia, Colorado, USA 80135

http://www.narrateconferences.org/

Cover design: Emily Balawejder
Internal layout and formatting: Sharon K. Goetz

ISBN 978-0-6151-9524-7

CONTENTS

Phoenix Rising received a wide variety of programming proposals in many fields. These submissions were meant to address the diversity of study about *Harry Potter* as literature, art, a teaching tool, a cultural phenomenon, a springboard for creativity, and various other areas of scholarship. To facilitate the selection, Phoenix Rising depended on the decisions of several independent review boards, whose members evaluated presentations based on relevance, representation of the widest possible variety of topics, and quality of scholarship. The review boards, in turn, represented the various areas in which Phoenix Rising received the majority of its submissions; thus, each proposal could be evaluated by those most qualified to do so. We are grateful to the following board members for lending their time and expertise to Phoenix Rising.

PHOENIX RISING VETTING BOARDS

The Academic Peer Review Board examined proposals that were presented as scholarly studies or analyses in academic fields.

Anne Hiebert Alton, a professor of English at Central Michigan University, earned her Master of Arts in Children's Literature from the University of Calgary and her Doctor of Philosophy, with a specialization in Victorian Literature, from the University of Toronto. Her research and publication interests include children's literature, Victorian literature, fantasy, and the novel; and Dickens, the Brontës, Robert Louis Stevenson, Diane Duane, Jean Little, L. M. Montgomery, Anthony Browne, Maurice Sendak, P. L. Travers, E. L. Konigsburg, John Marsden, and J. R. R. Tolkien. Dr. Alton has also written "Generic Fusion and the Mosaic of *Harry Potter*" (in *Harry Potter's World: Multidisciplinary Critical Perspectives*) and presented "Here's…Harry!: The Popular Genres of *Harry Potter*."

Annalee Newitz is the author of *Pretend We're Dead: Capitalist Monsters in American Pop Culture* (Duke University Press, 2006) and co-editor of *White Trash: Race and Class in America* (Routledge, 1997). A freelance writer in San Francisco, she is a contributing editor at *Wired* magazine and publishes regularly in *Popular Science* and *New Scientist*. She has a Ph.D. in English and American Studies from the University of California, Berkeley.

Suzanne Scott is a doctoral student of Critical Studies at the University of Southern California's School of Cinema–Television. In addition to presenting works on fan cultures and cult media at various conferences and working as a staff writer for the New York-based film magazine *Reverse Shot*, Ms. Scott is preparing to begin work on her dissertation, a study of the convergence between new media and fan narratives, focusing exclusively on *Harry Potter* fandom and multimedia texts. She was the Chair of Programming for Phoenix Rising.

Gwen Tarbox, Associate Professor of English at Western Michigan University, specializes in youth culture, women's literature, and literary modernism. Her publications include *The Clubwomen's Daughters: Collectivist Impulses in Progressive-era Girls' Fiction*, a forthcoming book entitled *Feminist Dialogues in Contemporary Girls' Fiction*, and a number of articles on adolescent literature. An ardent fan of both literary and pop culture approaches to the *Harry Potter* phenomenon, Dr. Tarbox teaches a course that brings the two perspectives together.

Catherine Tosenberger is a Ph.D. candidate in children's literature and folklore at the University of Florida. Her dissertation "Potterotics: *Harry Potter* Fanfiction on the World Wide Web," under the direction of Dr. Kenneth Kidd, is an in-depth study of *Potter* fanfic and fandom from both literary and ethnographic perspectives. She has presented papers on fan cultures, folklore, and adolescent literature at a number of conferences, and is a contributor to the National Public Radio program *Recess!* Catherine is a longtime member of the *Harry Potter* fandom and will read anything that involves Weasleys.

Karin Westman (M.A., Ph.D. Vanderbilt University) is Associate Professor of English at Kansas State University, where she teaches courses in modern and contemporary British literature, including a course on *Harry Potter*. Her areas of interest include narrative studies, gender, performance and technology. She has presented and published most recently on J. K. Rowling and Philip Pullman, among other contemporary British writers. She is currently completing *J. K. Rowling's Library: Harry Potter in Context*, a book-length study of the series within British literary history.

L. Rene Wright has an M.F.A. in Creative Writing from Bowling Green State University and a Ph.D. in English from the University of Nebraska, where she also teaches courses in the English Department. Her dissertation is titled "Re-imagining Genre: Comics, Literature, and Textual Form," and her academic interests include 20th-Century American Poetry and Fiction, Visual Culture, Literary Theory, and Women's Studies.

The Creative Review Board received submissions that addressed craft and scholarship specific to writing and the visual and performing arts, as well as those that examined the creative process.

Michael C. Bolton received his M.A. from the University of Southern California's School of Cinema–Television. He currently works in television post-production.

Rachel Caine is the author of the Weather Warden series. Book five, *Firestorm*, was released in September 2006, with a sixth book arriving in 2007. She also writes the contemporary fantasy/action series *Red Letter Days* for Silhouette Bombshell, and has recently sold a new young adult series, whose first title, *Glass Houses*, was published in 2007. Additionally, she wrote *Sacrifice Moon* for the new line of *Stargate SG-1* media tie-in books as Julie Fortune. As Roxanne Longstreet Conrad, her essays are included in several BenBella Books anthologies, including *Seven Seasons of Buffy*, *Five Seasons of Angel*, *Stepping Through the Stargate*, *What Would Sipowicz Do?*, *Finding Serenity*, *Alias Assumed*, and *Mapping the World of Harry Potter*. Her previous novels (as Roxanne Longstreet and Roxanne Conrad) include *Stormriders*, *The Undead*, *Red Angel*, *Cold Kiss*, *Slow Burn*, *Copper Moon*, *Bridge of Shadows*, and *Exile, Texas*. She and her husband, fantasy artist R. Cat Conrad, live in Texas with their iguanas Popeye and Darwin, a *Mali uromastyx* named (appropriately) O'Malley, and a leopard tortoise named Shelley (for the poet).

Christine Lee Gengaro holds a Ph.D. in Music History from the University of Southern California. Dr. Gengaro teaches classes in music appreciation, theory, education, and research methods at three community colleges and at USC. She has presented scholarly papers at conferences in England, France, and the United States. Dr. Gengaro was also a presenter at The Witching Hour and a member of the vetting team. An attendee of Nimbus–2003, The Witching Hour, and Lumos: 2006, Dr. Gengaro has been involved in the *Harry Potter* fandom since 2003. She recently finished her first novel.

Glockgal loves fanart and has been illustrating for almost ten years. She's jumped between various fandoms but still sticks with *Harry Potter* due to the great canon, entertaining fandom and especially the fantastic fanart community on LiveJournal. She's finally doing something professional about her love for art and getting an education in video game art and design. Her fanart website can be found at twinners.org.

Marjorie Cohee Manifold is an assistant professor of art education at Indiana University–Bloomington, and teaches undergraduate and graduate level courses in curriculum development and the instruction of visual art. Her interests include the relationship between aesthetic experience and learning, philosophy in art education, patterns of expression, and the aesthetic expression of grief. Her present research explores the art-making activities (fanart and cosplay) of youth involved in various participatory fan cultures, including *Harry Potter* and *The Lord of the Rings*.

Nystana has been enamored with *Harry Potter* and the fandom since 2001. She works as a freelancer in film and television productions.

L. Rene Wright has an M.F.A. in Creative Writing from Bowling Green State University and a Ph.D. in English from the University of Nebraska, where she also teaches courses in the English Department. Her dissertation is titled "Re-imagining Genre: Comics, Literature, and Textual Form," and her academic interests include 20th Century American Poetry and Fiction, Visual Culture, Literary Theory, and Women's Studies.

The Fandom Review Board received submissions that addressed fan perspectives, and were charged with selecting proposals that represented current trends and issues across the diversity of the on- and offline fan community.

BeccaFran has been a fan of *Harry Potter* ever since her husband dragged her kicking and screaming to see *Harry Potter and the Chamber of Secrets* at the movie theater. He didn't know what he was getting himself into (the poor man)—she's been a part of the fandom ever since. An avid fan of Ginny Weasley (among other characters), BeccaFran led a roundtable discussion on Ginny's character development at The Witching Hour in 2005.

Sarah Benoot is a member of species *cubicus dwellerus* in Arizona. Her current position allows little usage of her A.A.S. in Video Production from the Art Institute of Phoenix, but she practices constant vigilance for that script writing, lighting, or editing emergency that is sure to come up any time now. Her wide-ranging fandom activities have included serving as a Coder Elf for FictionAlley's Fic Intake Team and as Assistant Chair of Formal Programming for The Witching Hour, but mostly just being amazed and impressed by the stories and art she sees produced every day. Ms. Benoot was the Exploratory Programming Secretary for Phoenix Rising.

Casey Fiesler is a graduate of the Georgia Institute of Technology, where she studied human-computer interaction, focusing on online communities. Her thesis was on weblog communities, roleplaying, and the *Harry Potter* fandom, and she presented on these topics at The Witching Hour in 2005. Casey also writes young adult fantasy and attended Clarion East in the summer of 2006. She is currently a first-year law student at Vanderbilt University and has a particular interest in how copyright laws apply to fanfiction.

Cleolinda Jones is a graduate student in the creative writing program at the University of Alabama, Birmingham. Her parody "Harry Potter and the Prisoner of Azkaban in Fifteen Minutes" first appeared on LiveJournal in 2004, and a parody of the first *Harry Potter* movie appeared in her 2005 book *Movies in Fifteen Minutes*.

McKay earned a Bachelor of Arts degree after double-majoring in English and History and a master's degree in English Literature. She has presented papers at such professional conferences as the International Association for the Fantastic in the Arts. Currently, she teaches composition and literature at the university level. McKay has been an active member of fandom since the early 1980s, of the online fandom since 1997, and of the *Harry Potter* fandom since 2001. She helped found the Snape Slash Fleet and was one of the original editors of the Daily Snitch newsletter. These days, she is most active in the Snape/Lupin ship, editing the Snupin Prophet newsletter and running the Pervy Werewolf community.

Richard is a 24-year-old market researcher living in London. He's been in the Harry Potter fandom since 2001. He's organized many "t00bages"— weekend get-togethers for fandomers — as well as a two-week fandom vacation in 2003. He also served on the fandom review board for The Witching Hour. His favorite character is Barty Crouch Jr. Really.

Starrysummer is a confused twentysomething graduate of a Southern California liberal arts college. Originally from the New York area and possibly living there again, she vacillates between plotting to rule the world and just wanting to go back to bed. She enjoys shiraz, black coffee, film noir, and pretending to be vegan. When immersed in the Potterverse, she particularly likes darkfic, Blackcest and the giant squid, and enjoys being alternately needlessly pretentious and just plain silly. Her OTP is het/slash, and her dog is cuter than yours.

The Professional Review Board selected proposals in specialized areas, such as education, library studies, business, law, and other fields and professional development areas.

Colette Drouillard is a doctoral student at Florida State University's College of Information. In addition, she is also the instructor librarian for the Goldstein Library at the College of Information. Ms. Drouillard is preparing to begin work on her dissertation, a study of the response of young readers to the *Harry Potter* series, what they believe they are responding to in the stories, and their perceptions of how this reading experience has impacted their future reading choices.

Doris Herrmann is an English/Language Arts teacher from Texas. She uses *Harry Potter* in her classroom to provide high-interest lessons to at-risk students. Along with her teaching career she is the Project Coordinator for The Leaky Cauldron website, appears on Pottercast, and is a forum administrator for The Leaky Lounge. Doris has three boys who eat as much in one day as most people do in a week. She loves surfing, the beach, and having long lunches with her friends at The Kemah Boardwalk.

Jan Kent is a licensed massage therapist living in beautiful central New York. In previous incarnations she held positions from women's clothing buyer to chamber of commerce administrator to self-employed upholsterer. Her long history of introducing children to sci-fi and fantasy began in 1977 when she loaded her young nieces and nephews into a station wagon and took them to see *Star Wars* at a drive-in theatre. Her adult daughter Lauren is responsible for Ms. Kent's current addiction to the *Harry Potter* universe. Jan possesses an affinity for spirituality, alternative healing, and esoteric subjects and has attended numerous expos and conferences as attendee and vendor. She coordinates WizardTies.com's day-to-day operations.

Bonnie Kunzel is an acknowledged expert on the subjects of young adult literature and science fiction and fantasy. She regularly presents on a national basis, including such topics as science fiction and fantasy for adults and teens, graphic novels, the best of the best in young adult fiction, *Harry Potter* read-alikes, and adult books for young adults. Ms. Kunzel is a past president of the Young Adult Library Services Association and has served on numerous committees, including the prestigious Best Books for Young Adults committee, the Margaret A. Edwards Award Committee and the ALEX committee, which is charged with selecting the best adult books for young adults each year. She is a regular reviewer for the journal *VOYA* (*Voice of Youth Advocates*), specializing in the areas of science fiction and fantasy, and she is a science fiction and fantasy editor for NoveList, an online reader's advisory service. Her publishing credits include: *First Contact: A Reader's Selection of Science Fiction and Fantasy* and *Strictly Science Fiction*, which she co-authored with Diana Tixier Herald.

Kimberly Lowe, a business attorney, is a shareholder in the Corporate, Cooperatives, Securities, and Mergers & Acquisitions groups at Fredrikson & Byron. She has substantial experience advising private and public companies and cooperatives on acquisitions, mergers, periodic reporting obligations, corporate governance and securities compliance issues. Ms. Lowe represents issuers, investors, and lenders in connection with public offerings, venture capital investments, commercial lending transactions and private placements of debt and equity securities. She also assists tax-exempt and nonprofit organizations with obtaining and maintaining tax-exempt status, corporate governance issues, tax-exempt financings, joint ventures between for-profit and nonprofit organizations, mergers and consolidations. In addition, she assists charter schools with formation, IRS compliance and financings.

Vannessa McClelland is an environmental permitting engineer working for regional government in Washington State and focusing in the air media. She works with other environmental permitting engineers throughout the state government on joint projects to reduce emissions from major industrial facilities. She also leads fellow volunteers in projects to remove invasive plant species and replant the area with native plants. Reading is a passion for her, and *Harry Potter* has been an obsession for the last few years. She enjoys discussing character goals and influences as well as speculating about the final outcome with local fans.

JoSelle Vanderhooft is a Utah-based poet, novelist and freelance writer. Her published or forthcoming books include *10,000 Several Doors, The Tale of the Miller's Daughter, Vice of Kings, Enter, Elsinore,* and *Desert Songs,* among others. Her poetry and short stories have appeared or will appear online and in print in *Star*Line, Cabinet des Fées, Sybil's Garage, Mythic Delirium, Reflection's Edge, The Seventh Quarry,* and others. She is an editor for the spec literary magazine *Crow's Nest,* which she co-founded in 2005. She holds honors degrees in English and Theatre Studies from the University of Utah.

CONTRIBUTORS

Layla A. Abuisba holds an M.F.A. in Creative Writing from the University of Missouri–St. Louis. She teaches developmental writing and composition at St. Louis Community College in St. Louis, Missouri. She still trusts Severus Snape.

lyric apted spends a good deal of time trying to figure out exactly what's going on in life. To this end she has been trained in various intuitive arts and reads runes, tarot and medicine cards. A longtime *Harry Potter* fan, she discovered the joys of fanfiction, both reading and writing, which she spends an extraordinary amount of time doing. lyric was involved in The Witching Hour and Lumos and loved both experiences. An American ex-pat, she now lives with her beloved cat in New Zealand.

Veronica Atkins, a student, has been an avid *Harry Potter* fan since 2002. She is a member of AtlantaHP (Georgia), and she reads and writes cross-generation fanfiction. As she tells her friends, "I will read anything—and I mean anything—in fandom."

Karen M. Bayne is a doctoral student at Indiana University. Her dissertation investigates how the experience of city spaces affects the construction of female self-identity in late nineteenth-century British novels. Her interest in the relationship between spaces and the development of identity led her to think about the Gothic heritage of J. K. Rowling's *Harry Potter* novels; she is interested in considering how the spaces of the wizarding world fit between, beneath, and beside those of the Muggle world and how Harry Potter's coming-of-age story is influenced by access to the Gothic spaces of the magical world.

Brandy Blake is currently a Ph.D. student at the University of Georgia, where she studies Romantic, Victorian, and Fantasy Literature, examining connections between fantasy and more traditional literature. She plans to write her dissertation on the *Harry Potter* series. She received an M.A. from Georgia State University and a B.A. from Emory University; at Emory her honors thesis addressed shadow imagery in J. R. R. Tolkien's *The Lord of the Rings*, and her master's thesis, entitled "Am I a Monster? Jane Eyre: A Fairy in Victorian England," examined supernatural elements in Charlotte Brontë's novel.

Gina Burkart teaches English courses at the University of Northern Iowa, where she is a doctoral student in Special Education. She recently published *A Parent's Guide to Harry Potter* (InterVarsity Press). Some of her other writings include *Christian Lessons from the Half-Blood Prince, Why Harry Potter Should Go to School, Meeting at the Lamp Post: A Family's Journey Through Narnia*, and *Classics Like Narnia Offer Lenten Lessons for Kids*. She presented at Nimbus–2003 and the Art and Soul conference at Baylor University, and has been interviewed by numerous radio and television stations across the country. She also conducts workshops and delivers presentations on using *Harry Potter* to foster moral development in children.

Katherine Calore is a mother of three, who she occasionally allows to borrow her *Harry Potter* books.

Yolanda R. Carroll has a Bachelor of Arts degree in English and Political Science from Baylor University. Besides *Harry Potter*, she has contributed to several fandoms for various anime series. Yolanda has attended several *Harry Potter* conferences and enjoys getting together with other fans. She loves to travel and is learning Japanese, and she is the proud aunt of one niece and two nephews.

Paula Christensen is an associate professor at Northwestern State University of Louisiana in Natchitoches. She teaches graduate courses at NSU in both gifted education and counseling. She is a National Certified Counselor with a strong background in counseling with gifted children and adults and teaching middle-school gifted students. Dr. Christensen has also engaged in research studies regarding the processes of gifted students reaching their potential. Her passion for the *Harry Potter* novels and for gifted students has led to a wonderful blend of studying both.

Vivienne D'Avalon is an Eclectic Goth Wiccan who founded Snape's Grove, a discussion group for Pagan Snape fans. She has studied metaphysical subjects all her life, has taught many classes at venues across central Florida, and is the author of *The Patriot's Spell*

Book. Vivienne is also the founder of Persephone's Haven, a business that serves Goths, Pagans, and all others who walk between worlds and need a safe place to be themselves. In 2003 she was crowned Goth Princess of Orlando. She has a degree in Music and Theatre from Hunter College, and another in Anthropology from Rollins.

Katherine DelGiudice is a second-year graduate student in the University of Central Florida's Human Factors and Experimental Psychology Ph.D. program. She is an active researcher in the area of Web usability and hopes to eventually make the Internet equally accessible by all. She has been sorted into the House of Hufflepuff, but her husband is decidedly Slytherin. In her spare time she spends way too much time online.

Cherie M. del Rio is the founder and Headmistress of the Filipino community of *Harry Potter* fans, Hogwarts Philippines, which has more than 3,500 registered members and is the largest *Harry Potter* fanbase in the Philippines. She works as the Public Relations Officer of De La Salle Lipa, Philippines. Cherie is also a M.F.A. student in the Creative Writing program at De La Salle University; her thesis is titled "Destierro and Other Stories." Her many hobbies and interests include poetry, creative non-fiction, charcoal painting, music and movies.

Tracy Douglas is a copy editor at the *Southern Illinoisan* in Carbondale, Illinois. She graduated with a Journalism degree and English minor from the University of Illinois in May 2006, where she studied postcolonial theory and popular culture. She loves popular culture and theorizing *Harry Potter*. She hopes to be a student of literature and popular culture continually.

Valerie Estelle Frankel teaches creative writing for all ages and composition at San Jose State University. Her many short stories have appeared in over seventy magazines and anthologies. Valerie is very excited about her new book, *Henry Potty and the Pet Rock: An Unauthorized* Harry Potter *Parody*, now in paperback.

Michelle K. Gardner, if sorted, would be designated to the noble House of Ravenclaw. Michelle's research areas include all things *Harry Potter*, fan cultures, and various forms of media interaction. She is constantly perusing the dusty shelves of bookstores to locate a copy of *Hogwarts, A History*. Michelle is the mother of a beautiful and inventive seven-year-old girl, wife of a very tolerant and loving husband, and located in the world's largest destination for theme-park entertainment.

Amy Goetz has been reading and interpreting various forms of oracles her entire life. Her obsession with oracle work began in junior high, when she secretly bought her first tarot deck and studied it under her blankets at night. She currently works as a body worker and Faery doctor. Amy is trained in shamanism, oracle work, Faery doctoring, energy work and tarot. She teaches classes on reflexology and intuition in her hometown of Seattle, Washington. Amy also leads retreats for women in the Pacific Northwest based in Celtic wisdom.

Jacqueline Goodenow, a believer in magic of all kinds, especially the subtle and everyday kinds of magic, studied film and screen writing at the University of Miami and the University of California–Santa Barbara. She thinks that poet Gwendolyn Brooks said it best: "Books are meat and medicine / and flame and flight and flower / steel, stitch, cloud and clout / and drumbeats on the air."

Jessica Gray is a Ph.D. candidate studying Theatre at Louisiana State University. She is also Director of Religious Education at the Unitarian Church of Baton Rouge. As Headmistress Iris Imaginoria of the Louisiana-based "Hogwarts School of Magic and Fun," she enjoys bringing the magic of *Harry Potter* to children's lives.

Skyler Hijazi has a master's degree in Women's Studies from the University of Arizona. His thesis, "Bodily Spectacles, Queer Re-Visions: The Narrative Lives of *Harry Potter* Slash Online," explores the issues of collective memory, queer reading, trauma, and embodiment which become salient in fan-produced texts in the *Harry Potter* fandom.

Victoria Hippard, Ph.D., M.S.W., L.C.S.W., completed her doctorate in 2007 at Pacifica Graduate Institute in Santa Barbara, California, in Mythological Studies with an emphasis in Depth Psychology. Her dissertation, "Who Invited Harry?: A Depth Psychological Analysis of the *Harry Potter* Phenomenon," examines Harry's place within the hero genre as well as the themes of evil and shadow, childhood loss and grief, and alchemy and individuation within Rowling's work. She has a private practice in psychotherapy in New Orleans, Louisiana, where she teaches as an adjunct professor in social work and religious studies.

Tilia Klebenov Jacobs earned her Bachelor of Arts at Oberlin College, where she majored in Religion and English with a concentration in Creative Writing. She went on to Harvard Divinity School, where she graduated with a Master of Theological Studies and a secondary school teaching certification, which she earned from the Harvard Graduate School of Education. She has taught religion and literature at the middle school, high school, and college levels. Her most recent academic position was at Framingham State College in Framingham, Massachusetts, where she resides with her husband, two young children, and psychotic poodle.

Nancy K. Jentsch is Instructor of German and Spanish at Northern Kentucky University in Highland Heights. Her essay, "Harry Potter and the Tower of Babel," was published by the University of Missouri Press in *The Ivory Tower and Harry Potter* and in *Multilingual Matters in the Translation of Children's Literature: A Reader.* She has given papers on the *Harry Potter* novels and their translation at meetings of the Kentucky Philological Association and the Popular Culture Association.

Hilary K. Justice is Associate Professor of English and Publishing at Illinois State University. She is author of *The Bones of the Others*, a book-length study of the creative process, and of *A Walking Shadow*, a novel-length book seven fanfiction. She serves on the Board of the Hemingway Society and as Senior Admin Staff for the On-line Wizarding Library fanfiction archive. Her academic essays have appeared in *Resources for American Literary Study, The Hemingway Review, North Dakota Quarterly*, and as chapters in several collections; her fanfiction is archived on the On-line Wizarding Library and The Petulant Poetess. She teaches courses in Publishing, Drama in Performance, and Twentieth Century Literature.

Annette Doblix Klemp teaches courses in fantasy and science fiction at the University of Wisconsin, River Falls. Her interests include revisionist fairy tales, eco-feminism, C. S. Lewis, and Philip Pullman.

Katherine E. Krohn earned her doctorate in Old English Literature (Folklore minor) at Texas A & M University. She presented "The Silver Hand Motif: Peter Pettigrew in Its Grasp" at Lumos 2006. She has presented work on folklore, pedagogy, disability studies, and Renaissance theater at numerous conferences. Her entry on the Old English *Judith* appears in the *Dictionary of Literary Biography*.

Donna Lafferty resides in Indiana. She's happily married, a small business owner (day spa), a fairly decent trombonist, and a better than average vegetarian cook. She spends way too much time reading and thinking about the *Harry Potter* series, writing *Harry Potter* trivia questions, and arguing with her friends about Horcruxes. Along with Jen214 and Amberigo, Donna administers Knockturn Alley, a *Harry Potter* message board for grown-ups.

Nancee Lee-Allen holds a bachelor's degree in Communications from Brooklyn College and a Master of Arts in Psychology from Antioch University. Nancee redesigned the Children of the Night School to better meet the needs of sexually victimized teens. She has taught Shakespeare, British History, and Human Sexuality. Nancee has also guest-lectured on such varied subjects as "Human Sexuality and the Law" at Northeastern University School of Law and "*Harry Potter* as a Teaching Tool" at the LA Department of Mental Health. She currently works at The Violence Intervention Program in Los Angeles, California.

Alison Luperchio has worked in Web development for ten years and moonlights as an amateur party planner. In her professional capacity, she worked on a team to design user personas and interaction scenarios, as well as to create and execute usability tests for her company's Web site—in addition to actually developing the site. As part of the process, she had the opportunity to work closely with usability expert reviewers. Alison is a Girl Scout leader and Sunday School workshop teacher. She has also taught drama workshops and has run a Triwizard Tournament birthday party and a "Hogwarts Day" for a group of local elementary kids.

Joanne Macgregor is a counseling psychologist in private practice in Johannesburg, South Africa. After completing degrees in English Literature and Education, she taught high school English and then joined the corporate worlds of training, business consulting and change management. Joanne earned her Honors and Master's degrees (*cum laude*) in psychology: her thesis was on criminal victimization and the victim's experience of hijacking (carjacking). She works mainly with adults, especially in the field of trauma, using a holistic approach, including hypnotherapy and EMDR. She enjoys drama and reading, and may often be found *Harry Potter*-quizzing her husband, two children and beagle, Hermione.

Sister Magpie has been a children's book editor and writer of over a dozen books for young readers, including original novels for the *Dexter's Laboratory* and *Malcolm in the Middle* series. She is currently a writer and staff editor at a national bi-monthly magazine. She received a B.A. in English from Smith College and an M.F.A. in Writing from Columbia University.

Marjorie Cohee Manifold is an assistant professor of Art Education at Indiana University. Her research has focused on learning through aesthetic experiences. She explores aesthetic learning among youth who engage in online (global) fandom communities of popular culture, such as *Harry Potter*, anime, manga, and comics; and RPGs. Her publications have appeared as book chapters and in national and international journals. She has given presentations at state, regional, national and international levels and is active in several professional art educational organizations, including the National Art Education Association (NAEA), the United States and the International Society for Education Through the Arts (USSEA/InSEA).

Robin Martin, a graduate student and composition instructor at Texas A&M University–Corpus Christi, is working towards a Master of Arts in English with an emphasis in Rhetoric and Composition. Her academic interests include cultural literary criticism, literacy theory, Palestinian culture, and *Harry Potter* fandom. Her previous conference experience includes presentations relating to cultural literary criticism and Palestinian literature. As a very active member of the fandom, Robin tries to use the *Harry Potter* series in her writing classroom as often as possible.

When not stuck in Southern California traffic, **Susan Miller** is a software consultant with over twenty years' experience in all things digital. With bachelor's degrees in Music and Computer Science and a master's in E-commerce, she knows she really should get out more. She attended Nimbus–2003, Convention Alley, and Accio 2005, and was on the senior staff at Lumos as head of Site and Tech.

Vincent Moore, Ph.D., has been at Tiffin University since fall 2002; he became chair of the English Department in the spring of 2005. He founded and instructs the Tiffin University Martial Arts Club and the Association for College Martial Arts Programs, and is a faculty advisor for the English Enthusiasts, which produces the *TU Review*. His teaching interests are composition, creative writing, modern and postmodern literature, and film. A former competitive martial artist, he enjoys travel, exercise, cooking, movies, reading, juggling, and writing, and is a big fan of New Orleans.

Phyllis D. Morris holds a Bachelor of Arts degree in English and History from the University of Notre Dame and a Master of Public Administration degree from George Washington University. Phyllis served as chair of programming for the 2004 Convention Alley conference, and led the wildly unsuccessful effort to convict Severus Snape at the Accio 2005 conference. She delivered presentations on the Heir of Gryffindor theory at Convention Alley, on Arthurian-*Harry Potter* connections at Accio 2005, and on the role of fear in the series at Lumos. In what the non-wizarding world refers to as "real life," Phyllis lives in Albany, New York, and directs policy for three New York State public assistance programs.

Diana Patterson has a Ph.D. from the University of Toronto in English, and a subsequent M.A. in the history of the book from the University of London. She teaches English language and literature, with emphases on rhetoric and print & manuscript culture, at Mount Royal College in Calgary, Alberta, Canada. She has presented and published several papers on *Harry Potter*, the most recent in the *Edinburgh Bibliographical Society Journal* (Sept. 2006).

Hilary Pollack has been an educator for thirty-five years, progressing from first grade to college education. Reading is her passion, and she feels fortunate to spend her professional life helping children to learn to read and to love reading. She is also an ardent gardener, cross-country skier, and kayaker.

Amanda Pommer, a.k.a. generalmanda or PyrateM, is a world-famous hopscotch champion who spends her time drawing squares on various horizontal surfaces. She likes a wide variety of things, including but not limited to the color green. When she is not daydreaming or prodding solid objects with sticks, she likes to sew, draw, write and consider the finer points of aerospace-grade carbon composites.

Martha Young-Rhymes (Ed.D. Georgia Southern University), a 24-year veteran of both regular and gifted education classrooms, is currently Assistant Professor of Reading in the College of Education at Northwestern State University in Natchitoches, Louisiana. She instructs undergraduates in the teacher education program and alternative certification candidates in the Master of Arts in Teaching program. Her areas of interest include critical literacy and cultural studies involving the influence of popular children's literature on how young readers perceive themselves and others in relation to gender, race, and class.

FOREWORD

The essays and roundtable overviews in this volume were presented at Phoenix Rising, a conference devoted to all things *Harry Potter*, which took place May 17–21, 2007, in New Orleans, Louisiana. The conference's three core days of educational and academic programming encompassed papers, panels, workshops, roundtable discussions, and combinations of multiple elements of these. Recorded here are approximately one-third of the many voices who presented their analyses of J. K. Rowling's creations and the surrounding phenomenon, two short months before the release of *Harry Potter and the Deathly Hallows*, the series' seventh and final book. Though *Deathly Hallows* opens avenues for further thought as much as it closes Rowling's canon, the essays herein were conceived without its benefit.

Throughout this volume the following abbreviations are used to cite the titles of Rowling's books and their film adaptations: *PS* and *SS* for *Philosopher's Stone* and *Sorcerer's Stone*, *CoS* for *Chamber of Secrets*, *PoA* for *Prisoner of Azkaban*, *GoF* for *Goblet of Fire*, *OotP* for *Order of the Phoenix*, *HBP* for *Half-Blood Prince*, and *DH* for *Deathly Hallows*. Each contributor's reference system is allowed to stand, be it *Chicago Manual*, APA, or MLA, to reflect something of the diversity of approaches their papers represent.

As Phoenix Rising's Academic Programming Coordinator, I am grateful foremost to the volume's contributors and to all who participated at the conference. In particular, I would like to thank our Chair of Programming, Suzanne Scott, and the many on-site volunteers who monitored rooms, ran audio-visual equipment, and generally helped presentations to proceed smoothly. I also thank the members of our four vetting boards, who gave their time generously to review and select the conference's presentations; their biographies appear towards the end of the present volume, as do biographies of our contributors. Special acknowledgments are due to all who helped to proofread the essays included here: Renee L. Antoine,

Jennifer Boxerman, Sabrina Chin, Amy Tenbrink, Amy Wilson, and especially Hallie Tibbetts.

S.K.G.

About Phoenix Rising

Phoenix Rising, a conference on all things *Harry Potter*, was held May 17–21, 2007, in New Orleans, Louisiana. The conference included around 1,000 attendees from the United States, Canada, the United Kingdom, Australia, New Zealand, South Africa, England, the Philippines, Trinidad and Tobago, Austria, France, Norway, and Germany. More than 175 scholars, educators, librarians, professionals in business and law, parents, students, and fans presented approximately 200 hours of educational, analytic, and often interactive programming over the course of the conference.

The call for papers requested that presenters examine the *Harry Potter* books, films, and surrounding phenomenon, encouraging final thoughts on an incomplete series. The resulting presentations— many multi- or inter-disciplinary—ranged from educated speculation on the architecture of Hogwarts to analysis of the books as Gothic literature, from roundtable discussions for parents to a critique of the books' economic issues, and from scientific takes on the genetic heritability of magic to studies of the online fan community.

The conference Web site may be found in archival mode at <http://www.thephoenixrises.org>. Phoenix Rising was produced by Narrate Conferences, Inc., and is not endorsed, sanctioned or any other way supported, directly or indirectly, by Warner Bros. Entertainment, the *Harry Potter* book publishers, or J. K. Rowling and her representatives.

ABOUT NARRATE CONFERENCES

Narrate Conferences, Inc., a 501(c)(3) charitable organization, produces dynamic, innovative events for scholars, students, professionals and fans. A driving purpose of the organization is to educate through both traditional and non-traditional interactions, including promoting collaboration among diverse groups, regardless of education or background. Narrate Conferences, Inc. aims to challenge and inspire both the seasoned academic and the literary enthusiast. By combining elements drawn from academic, professional, media, and other types of conferences, Narrate Conferences, Inc. creates forward-thinking, multi- and inter-disciplinary educational events.

At the time of publication, Narrate Conferences was producing Terminus, a conference designed to address the completed *Harry Potter* series, and developing conferences that include an exploration of women fantasy writers and their work; a series on teen literature targeted at teens, parents, educators and librarians; and a conference focusing on the cutting edge in multimedia studies and education.

For more information about Narrate Conferences and its events, please visit its Web site at <http://www.narrateconferences.org> or e-mail info@narrateconferences.org. You may also write to Narrate Conferences, P.O. Box 149, Sedalia, CO, 80135.

OF HORCRUXES, ARITHMANCY, ETYMOLOGY & EGYPTOLOGY: A LITERARY DETECTIVE'S GUIDE TO PATTERNS AND PARADIGMS IN *HARRY POTTER*

Hilary Kovar Justice
Illinois State University

The central mystery confronting both Harry Potter and readers as we await the publication of *Harry Potter and the Deathly Hallows* is, according to the plot, "What are the remaining Horcruxes?"[1] According to the fandom (and Borders bookstore), the real question is "Where do Severus Snape's loyalties really lie?" If Rowling has written *Deathly Hallows* according to her usual orderly, logical standards, and doesn't actively subvert her own paradigms and pull the rug out from under what she's constructed so carefully in nearly two decades of writing, those are questions to which we already have answers—and not just any answers, *hers*—buried somewhere in the first six books.

All readers of the series are familiar with the "Eureka!" moments for which Rowling has carefully prepared us. Part of the tremendous enjoyment of reading a new book in the series lies in the many fleeting "So that's what that was about!" moments that register in our minds, consciously or un-, as we read. One of the earliest seemingly "throw-away" moments in the series involves Hagrid's arrival at Privet Drive on Sirius Black's motorcycle. "Flying motorcycle... shiny," we think, and read on. Only in the third book,

---

1   Following the tradition of fanfiction writers, I must gratefully acknowledge the help of my research assistants and beta-readers: Erin Bales, Rhonda Nicol, Pam Coleman, Michele Budden, Minuet99, Anicée Dowling, PotionMistress, Annie Tarbuck, and Peter Nelson Rose. A special thanks to Taryn Marie Zarrillo for her invaluable critique of an earlier version of this essay.

Prisoner of Azkaban, do we learn that Sirius Black is actually important. Another early instance also involves Hagrid, explaining who Voldemort is to Harry: "Some say he died. Codswallop, in my opinion. Dunno if he had enough human in him left to die" (*SS* 57). Well, no; we all know now that he didn't die. He keeps showing up, and in *Order of the Phoenix*, we learn the truth behind Hagrid's statement: "He" split his "human" into seven pieces explicitly so he wouldn't die.

Examples of Rowling's seed-planting technique abound in the series. By *Chamber of Secrets*, wary readers are already on the alert for such Rowlingisms, and are afforded many opportunities for feeling clever themselves—"So that's why Myrtle haunts the U-bend!"—and much of the series' success may lie in the simple fact of Rowling's sheer cleverness with this technique, which is less foreshadowing than hiding things in plain sight. Like Salome in the Dance of the Seven Veils, Rowling rewards the alert reader with an ego stroke as she satisfies multiple desires, both intellectual curiosity and self-esteem, as the veil of each mystery, no matter how small, is drawn aside, revealing what we seem to have known already.

She's taught us well. Six books in, we've all learned to trust J. K. Rowling, and we're breathlessly close to the seventh veil—breathless in no small part because we want to learn if "our" theories are correct. Given Rowling's care in planting the apparent "throw-away" seeds and her reliance on parallels (for instance, the foil relationships between Harry and Voldemort and Harry and Snape), it is extremely likely that the answers to the "questions" everyone is asking are available via a close examination of the information she has provided thus far.

Of Horcruxes and Arithmancy

I'll begin to reconstruct the deep structural logic of Rowling's work by examining the Horcruxes and the murders Voldemort committed to create them. The first Horcrux is the diary; the first victim, Moaning Myrtle. The second is the ring; the second victim (or victims), Tom Riddle, Sr. (and Voldemort's paternal grandparents). What raises a flag here is that the destruction of these Horcruxes involves a sacrifice of someone who embodies many of the qualities of the original victims: Ginny Weasley, a young schoolgirl like Myrtle before her, is very nearly lost to the diary, and Dumbledore, who is very nearly the Platonic ideal of a father figure, is seriously injured for (or maybe by) the ring. Whether in Rowling's mind the destruction of a Horcrux intrinsically involves some kind of necessary sacrifice (or magical indemnity) or whether the logic of her narrative extrinsically requires juxtaposing Horcrux destruction with extreme risk to some character cannot be ascertained from a data set of two; either way, the extant text has taught us to expect one sacrifice per Horcrux.

The exact order in which the third and fourth Horcruxes, Slytherin's locket and Hufflepuff's cup, were created has yet to be revealed in canon. Dumbledore tells Harry:

"He seems to have reserved the process of making Horcruxes for particularly significant deaths. You would certainly have been that. He believed that in killing you, he was destroying the danger the prophecy had outlined." (*HBP* 508)

Although no obviously significant murders are ascribed to Voldemort in the interim between killing his father and killing the Potters, what is interesting is that there are only two named murders identified in canon as having happened during the relevant period: that of Hepzibah Smith, who owned both objects, and that of Marlene McKinnon and her family.

Given that these are the only two murders specified for this period in the text, and given that the *modus operandi* for the Smith murder matches that of the murder of Tom Riddle, Sr., exactly (including the memory modifications by which Morphin Gaunt and Poky the house-elf are proven guilty), it seems psychologically likely that Voldemort would follow the murder pertaining to the object most closely associated with fatherhood with that most closely associated with motherhood—the locket that once belonged to Voldemort's mother, Merope Gaunt—and that the victim was Hepzibah Smith.

How the old witch Hepzibah Smith embodies the concept of motherhood poses a bit of a problem. However, the word used to describe Merope Gaunt's path toward motherhood is "slut"—a label applied to her by her family, who blame her for sullying the purity of their line. Although the moniker is undeserved, its judgmental evocation of female sexuality begins to suggest why Smith is a likely victim for the Horcrux most closely associated with Merope.

Rowling's description of Smith tells us she is overly made up and titillated by the parody of romantic courtship enacted by young Tom Riddle, who brings her flowers and flattery. Readers are invited to judge Smith as an aged caricature of female sexuality, as her success as a borderline-comic character depends on a deliberately evoked "squick" factor in her fantastic insistence that Tom Riddle behave as a "suitor": she is old enough to be his mother. The more we laugh, though, the further we are implicated in an unjust system—we are tainted by parallel with a shadow of the Gaunts' unjust castigation of Merope. Both Merope Gaunt and Hepzibah Smith are figures deserving of pity, rendered bankrupt merely by virtue of class and age in the sexual economy in which they wish to participate. Further, both seek escape in self-consciously constructed fantasy—Merope by brewing a love potion for Tom Riddle, Sr., and Hepzibah by carefully scripting interactions with Tom Riddle, Jr., a script from which neither he nor her dutiful house-elf will deviate.

If the concept that relates Merope's locket and Smith's murder is motherhood in its sexual sense, the obvious candidate for the role of "likely sacrifice" for this Horcrux is Molly Weasley—who, by simple arithmetic, enjoys an extremely fertile sexual existence. She is abundantly rich in the very economic arena in which Merope and Smith are unjustly but inarguably impoverished.

Further, Rowling has shown readers that Molly fears for everyone in her family except herself. From the family clock to the Boggart Molly faces in number twelve, Grimmauld Place, who assumes the dead form of all her family members and Harry, to the unfortunate mathematical reality that "Half the family's in the Order, it'll be a miracle if we all come through this" (*OotP* 161), we have been set up to fear for a Weasley, but because we've participated in that fear from Molly's point of view, the person we least fear for is Molly herself.

I hope I'm wrong, but Molly Weasley appears to be a very likely candidate for one of the major character deaths Rowling has promised in book seven. Having taken the head of the Order with Dumbledore's death, the next best strategic (and narrative) move is to take its heart with Molly's.

This brings us to the next Horcrux—very likely the cup—and the other named murder from the relevant period in Voldemort's history: that of Marlene McKinnon and her family.

Marlene who?

In *Order of the Phoenix*, at the party at number twelve, Grimmauld Place, Mad-Eye Moody shows Harry a photograph of the original Order, identifying each person by name, including the Longbottoms, Harry's parents, and "Marlene McKinnon, she was killed two weeks after this was taken, they got her whole family..." (*OotP* 173). In the absence of McKinnons amongst the current staff and students of Hogwarts, or the denizens of Hogsmeade or Diagon Alley, identifying Marlene McKinnon would seem a fool's errand were it not for one additional clue.

In the movie, *Harry Potter and the Sorcerer's Stone*, Hermione leads Harry to a trophy case in which rests a plaque celebrating his father's Quidditch team. Another name on the plaque is "M. G. McGonagall." Minerva McGonagall is, in both books and films, too old to have played Quidditch with James. She is, in fact, old enough to be his mother. As J. K. Rowling's licensing agreement universally grants her approval over all written text (Bilson 2007), and as a camera lens will show much more of a trophy than must a narrative description, the inclusion of a McGonagall on the plaque must have been at Rowling's insistence. Another "throw-away" moment that really isn't one? Perhaps. In the absence of any other likely contenders, the initial "M." and the Scottish surname "McKinnon" seem to point to a Marlene McGonagall McKinnon—and "her family"—which, if logic holds, would mean that Minerva McGonagall lost her daughter, son-in-law, and at least one grandchild, and perhaps her husband in the last war with Voldemort.

And how easily a cup could be Transfigured into a trophy, to be hidden by Voldemort during his last visit to Hogwarts—a visit made on the obviously trumped-up excuse of requesting employment. Although Dumbledore speculates that Voldemort might have been there to try to steal an object (perhaps Gryffindor's sword), it seems more likely that he was there to hide one. As Hagrid tells Harry, "Gringotts is the safest place in the world fer anything yeh want ter keep safe—'cept maybe Hogwarts" (*SS* 63). If, in fact, Voldemort did sequester one of the Horcruxes at Hogwarts, it would be most satisfying if it were in the guise of his Special Services to the School award—which Ron spent hours polishing in what is, at least thus far in publication, another throw-away moment. This would, I think, satisfy that sense of egotistical irony peculiar to evil overlords.

Voldemort tells Dumbledore, "I could show and tell your students things they can gain from no other wizard" (*HBP* 443); even in his fictive purposes, he is at Hogwarts to offer his special services to the school.

For Ron to have spent hours polishing a piece of Voldemort's soul suits Rowling's tendency to conceal things in open view. And how satisfying for Ron to have vomited slugs all over it.

The conceptual link amongst victim and object for Hufflepuff's cup and Marlene McKinnon's family would appear, again, to be motherhood, but differently nuanced than the sexuality signified by the locket. We know from the Sorting Hat's song that Helga Hufflepuff embodied the Earth Mother—accepting and nurturing all those children rejected elsewhere, embracing all, regardless of specific talent, character, or birth. This would seem, on the surface, to point us toward Molly Weasley (and it may, in fact, play out this way; the details are too sparse to be entirely certain). However, if one factors in Minerva McGonagall's loss, and the guilt she must yet endure for being unable to protect her child and grandchild (perhaps grandchildren), then she, too, encompasses an element of motherhood, one less associated with fertility and more associated with protection—specifically, the failure of protection through abandonment and absence.

Voldemort's—and Harry's—primary focus when it comes to Merope is her death. Young Tom mutters, "My mother can't have been magic, or she wouldn't have died" (*HBP* 275); Harry asks Dumbledore, "She wouldn't even stay alive for her son?" (*HBP* 262). Both statements imply a failure of nurturing, a failure to be there to protect a child; in other words, absence—the very absence that may have saved Minerva McGonagall's life but also probably torments her in the long hours of darkness between patrolling the corridors and overseeing breakfast from the High Table. To judge Merope as Harry and (probably) Voldemort do, were it possible, Merope somehow should feel guilt for abandoning her child by dying; Minerva probably feels the inverse of that guilt—that she abandoned her family by not dying.

The above reasoning combined with the at least plausible Transfiguration factor render Minerva McGonagall the likeliest character to pay a magical or narrative sacrifice for the destruction of the cup Horcrux.

For the sake of argument, and in the absence of better information in canon, I will invoke Dumbledore's reasoning regarding the identification of the fifth Horcrux (although chronologically speaking it was the sixth one created) and assume that Harry's seeing through Nagini's eyes during the attack on Arthur is intended to parallel Voldemort's connection to Harry, to which Rowling and Dumbledore both refer throughout *Order of the Phoenix* and *Half-Blood Prince*.

If Nagini is a Horcrux, the murder required for her creation as such must be Frank Bryce, the Muggle caretaker of the abandoned Riddle estate, and the combination of "caretaker" and "magical creature" (not to say "violent monster") points rather obviously to Hagrid as the character most at risk in this instance. However, because this particular Horcrux is contained in an animate creature which, as Dumbledore points out, is mortal, the risk to Hagrid seems far less than that in the more arcane situations which have already risked Ginny, quite possibly killed Dumbledore (at the very least, his arm), and seem to implicate Molly Weasley and Minerva McGonagall.

Begging, for now, the question of what really killed Dumbledore (to which I will return momentarily), there remains the final Horcrux. Although readers know that Emmeline Vance was probably killed by Voldemort personally, a far more significant murder in everyone's mind (including Voldemort's) is his murder of the Potters and his attempted murder of Harry. Given the similarities Dumbledore implies between the connection between Voldemort and Nagini and that between Voldemort and Harry (as well as that between Harry and Nagini in his "dream" of the attack on Arthur), why Harry hasn't yet figured out that his scar is almost definitely the result of a Horcrux spell gone seriously awry is, as he says of Dudley, "A bit stupid, really." Presumably, the timing of the revelation of the sixth Horcrux is subservient to the requirements of Rowling's narrative arc (personally, my money's on Hermione to figure it out); again, an early remark by Hagrid may prove retrospectively illuminating: "That's what yeh get when a powerful, evil curse touches yeh" (*SS* 55). "Avada Kedavra" may be an evil curse, but it, at least, is mentioned in Hogwarts textbooks; the far more evil Horcrux curse (presumably a different spell, else for every murder there would be a Horcrux) is hardly even mentioned in the entire school library.

The debate surrounding the status of Harry's scar in the list of six Horcruxes has raged since the publication of *Half-Blood Prince*. Everyone has a pet theory, but by now the original vibrancy of this debate seems to have devolved into an endless round of "Is not/Is too."

Of Etymology

One extremely fertile angle for inquiry in settling the question is etymology, especially given Rowling's penchant for multilingual wordplay that is often much more connotationally subtle than it seems. One example is the name Draco Malfoy—"draco" being Latin for "dragon"; "Malfoy" from the French "mal foi," meaning "bad faith"—a linguistic condemnation of the whole Pureblood question, to be sure. With a bit of wordplay, "Mal foi" resonates homonymically with "mal fois" (bad times), "mal fait" (badly made), and "mal faix" (oppressive burdens)—all of which offer shades of insight into Rowling's perspective on the family, and perhaps a nuance of "nurture" to the "nature" side of the equation in the sad case of the Malfoy boy. A bit of creative thought, and one sees that Rowling does not blame only his blood, but his parents: he is not only born bad, but made that way, a character deserving not only of harsh judgment, but also mercy. With Rowling, the first answer is almost never the full answer; the more creative a reader's thought, the richer the experience of the text.

"Horcrux," a word she coined, poses a rich ground for etymological investigation and wordplay consideration. The syllable "-crux" carries with it obvious meaning; the phrase "the crux of the matter" applies very obviously to the Horcruxes and to their importance in the series: thereon hinge the resolution of Harry's tasks, his destiny, and the seven-book plot.

It would be easy to stop with "crux," especially since an obvious homonym for "Hor-" is "whore," which seems a little heavy-handed (and age-inappropriate) for Rowling. It may not be much of a stretch to say that Voldemort has prostituted his soul in service of his inhuman desire for a kind of immortality: his promiscuity with the pieces of his soul would certainly shock Professor Slughorn;

even the notion that a wizard might split his soul into more than two pieces sends Slughorn into apoplexy.

However, this feels rather "thin" for Rowling; one usually does not have to push beyond etymology into outright literary speculation to discern what she is up to with her coined phrases and names, so having gone a bit down that path, I'll back up and go another way. Readers have suggested several directions to go with "Hor-": the homonym "hoar" (implying advanced age, in keeping with Voldemort's goal of immortality), the Greek prefix "hor-" (having to do with time), and the French "hors" (implying "outside," consistent with Voldemort's housing bits of his soul outside his body).[1] The rich diversity of approaches to the syllable "Hor-" marks another of Rowling's invisible veils beyond which may lurk the key to the structure of the series (and, pushed a bit further, a likely answer to the question of what form Snape's Patronus will take).

Among Harry's few sources of information on Horcruxes is Horace Slughorn, whose first name has one homonym in the matrix that comprises Anglophone culture: Horus, an Egyptian sky-god among whose symbols is an eye. This detail seems almost trivial, even given Rowling's stated interest in world mythology (a thus-titled book appears on the bookshelf on her website). However, the Egyptian angle proves a worthwhile line of inquiry regarding not only the word "Horcrux" but also the series as a whole.

Most of us don't have a working knowledge of Ancient Egyptian, in which the word "Hor" means "face," which Rowling combines with "crux," Latin for "cross," the Christian symbol of Christ's burden and sacrifice. If Harry can be said to be a savior, as countless readers have argued, he bears that burden on his face in the shape of his scar.

Of Egyptology

Delving further into the Egyptian angle opens a thus-far unexplored area of Rowling's contribution to the cultural monomyth of "orphaned boy comes of age under tutelage of wise, white-bearded mentor, and, after some adolescent self-pity and whinging, embraces his destined responsibility and defeats evil, thereby saving the world." The story has been told and re-told in Western culture

---

1   I am indebted to Taryn Marie Zarrillo, Emma Crew, and Lorrie Kim for their insights on the "Hor-" question.

for centuries; the similarities of Rowling's plot to the Arthurian legends, to *The Lord of the Rings*, and to *Star Wars* are so obvious as to scarcely bear mention (one might also add *Hamlet* to the list, but that is a topic for another time).

Although references to Egypt in *Harry Potter* are scanty, they are present—the Weasleys' vacation to visit Bill, and the location of a missing Quidditch referee. Thus far, these are more throw-away moments. But the myth of Horus—more precisely, that of Isis, Osiris, Horus, and Set—resonates so strongly with Rowling's work that it's somewhat surprising that it's not received critical attention before now. In microcosm, the stories are strikingly similar.

In the myth, Horus is born to Isis and Osiris. The evil god Set murders Osiris and divides him into several pieces (the number varies depending on version: the inscription on the Temple of Denderah [Zarrillo 2007]; this number is sometimes simplified to seven pairs or, further, seven pieces). Set hides these pieces in various locations along the banks of the Nile. Horus, being far too young to avenge his father, is kept hidden, under his mother's protection, until he reaches maturity. In some versions of the myth, Horus reassembles the pieces of Osiris, who remains dead but ascends to the sky (in other versions, this task is performed by Isis); in all versions, Horus meets Set in a final aerial battle. For this battle, Set assumes the form of a serpent, and Osiris assumes the form of a winged beast with the body of a lion and the head of a hawk—in other words, a gryphon. In the Ancient Egyptian battle of Gryffindor and Slytherin, Gryffindor wins.

The correlations thus far are obvious (Horus = Harry, Set = Voldemort, Osiris and Isis = James and Lily, particularly in the matter of maternal protection for the maturing hero), although they are not strict (Osiris and not Set is divided in the myth). There is another character in the myth who bears more than cursory scrutiny: Anubis.

Anubis was the faithful companion of Isis in her efforts to protect Horus (and, in the version where she reassembles Osiris, during that task as well, either as baby-sitter or errand-boy). Anubis' animal form is that of the black jackal; he is one of the gods of the dead, the guardian of the underworld and the protector of lost (or fatherless) souls. He is, most evocatively, the patron of orphans in Egyptian mythology.

Although an obvious choice for an Anubis analog in Rowling's tale is Sirius Black, whose Animagus form is a black dog, and a slightly less obvious (but still canine) choice would be the werewolf Remus Lupin,[1] there may be a third—who, like Black and Lupin, may prove another patron-protector of the orphaned Harry: Severus Snape. If Rowling is indeed reinscribing elements of this myth toward her own narrative ends, we are already well-prepared for a third dog-like guardian by the figure of Fluffy, the three-headed guard dog in *Sorcerer's Stone*.

Unlike Sirius' Animagus form, which proves to be playful, and Lupin's lycanthropic one, which proves dangerous, Anubis, like all jackals, is a fairly unpleasant creature, being associated with funeral rites (including the evisceration of the body prior to mummification), graveyards, night-time, and carrion. His canine form is the equivalent of the greasy git of the dungeons of Hogwarts, living for neither good nor ill but right on the line, with one foot in this world (Hogwarts) and one in the world of the lifeless immortal spirit (the Death Eaters). Anubis is unpleasant, to be sure, but he also embodies loyalty and faithfulness—not to an ideal, not to one world or the other, but to Isis.

Readers who have picked up the trail of clues Rowling has left regarding a possible attachment (whether mutual or unrequited) between Severus Snape and Lily Evans need look no further. The question of "Does Snape hate Harry or not?" is thus far unanswerable; I offer the position that it is neither that simple nor really the point. Harry, who would say Snape does hate him, is an unreliable narrator, and the one time we see Snape outside of Harry's vicinity, in the "Spinner's End" chapter of *Half-Blood Prince*, he is in the presence of Narcissa and Bellatrix, before whom he must maintain the façade of the perfect Death Eater (if his loyalties lie with the Order) or before whom he is behaving authentically (if his loyalties lie with the Death Eaters). A third possibility that has been argued (some would say to death) on countless internet discussion boards is that he is playing both sides, waiting to see who wins. In any of the above cases, he plays the scene with the Black sisters perfectly, but can we with any accuracy accept his behaviour as genuine or dismiss it as a brilliant act?

---

1   I am again grateful to Taryn Marie Zarrillo, whose conversations on this issue provided the opportunity to articulate "the Fluffy theory."

No.

But we can discern his motivations if we consider his character in light of the various patterns Rowling has both constructed and borrowed.

Because there is a fourth possibility regarding the character of Severus Snape: that he is loyal, and unfailingly so, not to Dumbledore's Order nor to Voldemort, nor to whichever side wins, but to Lily's child. Not Harry, per se, but to whatever child Lily Evans was carrying when she and James went into hiding after Snape betrayed them to Voldemort.

I would go so far as to say his life depends on it.

Rowling doesn't give readers too much to go on when it comes to Snape, and even making allowances for the fact that nearly all of what we see of him is filtered through the unreliable Harry and the maddeningly vague Dumbledore, his every action can with equal likelihood stem from two equal and opposite motivations—especially since *Half-Blood Prince*. He is almost the perfect empty signifier—a walking shadow, signifying nothing.

Almost. But in that "almost," he may, in fact, come to signify nearly everything.

Does he hate Harry? I would argue that his feelings for Harry are much more complicated than that, that they are intensely personal, and that if he has any sense at all he fears Harry above all else. I would wager that he fears Harry so intensely that his Boggart assumes Harry's guise, yet that what he sees in the Mirror of Erised is Harry's victory over Voldemort. I would also argue, as is probably obvious by now, that his Patronus is likely to be a jackal.

The logic underlying this position is suggested by the patterns in which Rowling's mind has thus far proven itself to work. As there are seven pieces of Voldemort's soul, there are six Horcruxes, six relevant identifiable murders, and six aspects of human relationships that describe the psychological logic by which Voldemort appears to be working (seven, including the relationship with one's own soul). Just as this suggests seven likely at-risk characters (those who most readily signify whichever kind of connection Voldemort was severing in his soul-fragmenting progress), it also provides a pattern by which to examine what we do know for sure about Severus Snape's history.

We have his memories, ranging from childhood to adult experiences. We know that his trust in the world was broken when, as a child, as he witnessed his mother's abuse at his father's hands, which matches the conceptual aspect of childhood trust in the Diary/Myrtle/Ginny Horcrux. We know that while at school he was in Lily's Advanced Potions class and that he endured mistreatment by the Marauders, mistreatment that almost killed him and may have resulted in his taking the Dark Mark. We do know he took the Dark Mark, rejecting the story's uber-father, Dumbledore, swearing loyalty instead to its anti-father, Voldemort, which matches the conceptual aspect of fatherhood in the Ring/Tom Riddle, Sr./Dumbledore Horcrux. We know that he overheard the Prophecy (at least part of it), thereby setting Voldemort on the Longbottoms and Potters, both of which families were at that time expecting babies, which conceptually matches the sexual/fertility aspect of motherhood suggested by the Merope's locket/Hepzibah Smith/(Molly?) Horcrux. We know that he made an Unbreakable Vow with Narcissa Malfoy to serve as Draco's caretaker, and to act in his stead should he fail—thus, given the "dragon" definition of Draco's name, completing the conceptual pattern of subservient caretaking and magical creatures in the Nagini/Frank Bryce/(Hagrid?) Horcrux. And we know that he cast the Killing Curse on Dumbledore, which was either the biggest betrayal of, or the greatest proof of, love in the entire series—by killing Dumbledore, he signed his own death warrant—if that was love, it's the kind of love you're willing to die for: Lily's sacrifice for Harry.

Any of these, it seems, could easily stand as "Snape's Worst Memory."

We also know that Dumbledore trusted him absolutely, yet we don't know why. We also know that Lupin doesn't know why, that McGonagall doesn't know why—and therewith a veil falls over the path to an answer until the publication of *Deathly Hallows*.

But we know that Harry has his mother's eyes—no one in the series will let us forget that. We know that in all other aspects he resembles his father—no one will let us forget that, either. And love—we know a lot about love.

We know that Lily's love saved Harry and has protected him for sixteen years. We know that Dumbledore's faith in the transformative, even cataclysmic power of love is so extreme that it is tempting to dismiss him (as Harry and many readers have done) as a barmy old codger, despite his clarity on the darker side of love: "Of course, it is also possible that [Merope's] unrequited love and the attendant despair sapped her of her powers; that can happen" (*HBP* 262). Even Horace Slughorn—of all people—has something to say on the subject of love: "When you have seen as much of life as I have, you will not underestimate the power of obsessive love..." (*HBP* 177).

Huh.

In other words, considered in chronological order, Snape's worst memories—he seems to have no other kind—map perfectly onto the framework of Rowling's established chronological and conceptual patterns. But according to Rowling's established pattern, there's one memory missing, and it may very well involve love.

Although there is no explicit evidence for this in canon, the mysteries surrounding the character of Severus Snape, in all its dark ambiguity, can be explained by supplying one more significant memory. What if, as Anubis's was to Isis, Snape's loyalty to Lily is unimpeachable—unquestionable—unbreakable? What if, after realizing he'd signed her death warrant (Anubis in his aspect of a god of death), he vowed to protect her child in her absence (Anubis in his aspect of the protector of orphans)? What if the vow was an Unbreakable one, with Dumbledore as their Bonder?

Not only would this would complete the pattern (both conceptually and chronologically standing in parallel to the Cup/McKinnon/McGonagall Horcrux, with its quality of failure of protection by the absent mother), not only is it consistent with the Egyptian mythological framework underlying the story, but—which is much more satisfying—it would explain why Severus Snape always shows up when Harry is about to do something terminally stupid. Snape appears out of nowhere not because, as Harry thinks, he's a greasy git with impeccably bad timing, but because he's responding to an Unbreakable Vow. Even leaving the problem of Lily's eyes in James's face aside, given Harry's penchant for courting (and being courted by) life-threatening situations, Snape's antipathy is thus explained perfectly: his own life may very well depend on the rash judgments and actions of a half-trained teenaged boy.

Based on Rowling's very ordered structuring and fondness for parallels (*i.e.*, those between Harry's character and Voldemort's, which Dumbledore articulates for Harry [who has reached the same conclusion himself but is unwilling to say it]; also, those between Harry's childhood and Snape's, which are no less evocative), the mysteries surrounding Snape's character—from how he feels about Harry to why Dumbledore trusted him—would dissolve in the face of an Unbreakable Vow made with Lily Potter, along the same lines as that he made with Narcissa Malfoy:

> "Will you, Severus, watch over my son, Draco, as he attempts to fulfill the Dark Lord's wishes?"
> "I will," said Snape.
> …
> "And will you, to the best of your ability, protect him from harm?"
> "I will," said Snape.
> …
> "And, should it prove necessary…if it seems Draco will fail…" whispered Narcissa (Snape's hand twitched within hers, but he did not draw away), "will you carry out the deed that the Dark Lord has ordered Draco to perform?"
> There was a moment's silence. Bellatrix watched, her wand upon their clasped hands, her eyes wide.
> "I will," said Snape. (*HBP* 35–36)

"Watch over my son…protect him from harm…carry out the deed…"—all are pertinent to how he has been behaving toward Harry since *Sorcerer's Stone*, and possibly prophetic for the climax of *Deathly Hallows*.

If Snape did make such a Vow with Lily, Dumbledore would have been their most likely Bonder. This would explain why Dumbledore trusts Snape so thoroughly (and exonerate Dumbledore from the popular theory that his trust is misplaced). If that Vow happened, then his absolute trust is very well placed indeed: every time Dumbledore saw Snape alive, he would know that Snape was fulfilling the Vow to protect Harry. Finally, such a Vow would explain why Snape is always in the vicinity when Harry is doing something life-threatening.

He saves Harry's life twice in the first book alone—first from Quirrell's broomstick curse (his eyes go immediately to Harry and he begins the countercurse without, apparently, even checking to see who might be doing it—which would be far more in character), and second, he appears just as Harry is deciding to go after the Sorcerer's

Stone and is the one who finds him collapsed after the confrontation. He oddly speaks up for Harry when the Chamber of Secrets is open, appears in time to save Harry from the werewolf and Peter Pettigrew (although he may believe he is there to save him from Sirius Black), and probably spends the entire year of *Goblet of Fire* having heart failure. He rousts the Order to the Ministry at the end of *Order of the Phoenix*. In the *Half-Blood Prince* duel with Draco, Harry is in as much danger as, if not more than, the Slytherin boy; protecting one means protecting the other. And, in a strange way, the best way for him to protect Harry long-term is to kill Professor Dumbledore once Harry has had time to learn what he needs to go on the offensive against the Horcruxes. What better way to protect him than to be standing right next to Voldemort during the final confrontation? Killing Dumbledore guarantees Snape whatever passes for "trust" in Voldemort's Inner Circle. To cast a successful Killing Curse, one must mean it; for Snape to want to kill Dumbledore, if he is, in fact, on the Order's side, extenuating circumstances must exist: he must want something else more—with such intensity that he is willing to kill to achieve it. Perhaps Dumbledore is already dying (which is quite likely; whether from the potion in the cave or from the Horcrux destruction the previous summer—Snape can, after all, "stopper death," and how better for Harry to finally forgive Snape than to fear for a while that it was his own hand—Harry's—that killed Dumbledore, when he forced him to drink?). We already know that Snape's life is at stake; he is required to complete Draco's mission for him by the terms of his Vow to Narcissa. How convenient if the murder of Dumbledore hinges with another, earlier Vow to protect Harry, to aid him in his mission, and, if he dies, to complete it for him; how better to place himself at Voldemort's side for a final confrontation—and where better to stand to protect Harry during that confrontation?

We have Snape's worst memories—five of them. But what if he has a "best" memory? Best in the knife-twisting, dark, bitter Snapeian sense of "incredibly painful and not nearly enough to expiate loss, regret, and guilt, but not without what remains for me of honor." Best in the sense of Dickens' Sydney Carton, who goes to the guillotine to save the husband of the woman he loves, thinking: "It is a far, far better thing I do, than I have ever done…" (*A Tale of Two Cities* 404).

I hope that, after all of this, Severus Snape is the character to whom J. K. Rowling decided to grant a last minute reprieve—certainly the first time an author's decision regarding a character made the CNN crawler. It would be refreshingly original, a break in a pattern that would not otherwise affect its overall clarity, and it would give Hermione a chance to grow up, forget about Ron, and apply her tremendous energies for saving the downtrodden to saving the one who most deserves it.

Lest you dismiss that as the nutter rambling of She-who-sails-a-squicky-'ship, I offer you a final tidbit from Egypt: as the ancient Egyptian pantheon was influenced by that of ancient Athens, the god Anubis became so closely associated with the god Hermes that both became known as Hermanubis.

But that is a fantasy.

In all probability, July 21, 2007, will mark the death of Severus Snape in the service of his lost love's son with his schoolboy nemesis. As his character is nearly forty in canon, perhaps it is enough just to let him rest; perhaps the best we can wish for him is that his missing "best" memory leads him to "a far, far better rest... than [he has] ever known" (*A Tale of Two Cities* 404), since his childhood trust was broken by his abusive father. If it must be, then, "Goodnight, sweet Prince/ And flights of Angels sing thee to thy rest" (*Hamlet* ll. 3849–50).

1st Parchment (recto): Of Horcruxes & Arithmancy

*Horcruxes (in order of creation)	*Relevant Murders committed by V. (chrono. order)	§ Conceptual Link	**Sacrifice (Indemnity)	*Snape's Memories (chrono. order)
*1: Diary	*Myrtle	§ Childhood/Innocence?; Trust (Exploitation of) (Hogwarts)	*Ginny (almost)	*Witnesses abuse of mother
*2: Ring (worn by grandfather & uncle; taken from uncle)	*Paternal Family—esp. father	§ Fatherhood; Loyalty (Rejection of) (Tom Riddle, Sr.)	*Dumbledore (arm / delayed death?)[4]	*(Mistreatment by Marauders / Calling Lily "Mudblood" leads to(?) → Taking Dark Mark[5] (Voldemort = really skewed father figure)
*3 or 4: Locket (worn by mother; stolen from Hepzibah Smith)[1]	*Hepzibah Smith	§ Motherhood; Female Sexuality / Fertility; Protection (Failure to) (Merope)	§ (Unknown: Molly Weasley?)[6]	*Hearing prophecy; betraying pregnant Lily to D.E.
*3 or 4: Cup (stolen from Hepzibah Smith)[1,3]	‡(Unknown: Marlene McKinnon & family?)[2]	§ Family; Protection (Failure of) (Minerva)	§ (Unknown: Minerva McGonagall?)[2,6]	**(Unknown: Vow to protect Lily's child?)[7]

**5: (Unknown: Scar?)	*Potters	*Love (the kind you're willing to die for); Protection (Success of) ([James +] Lily Potter)	§ (Unknown: Snape?)	**(Promise to?) Kill Dumbledore
†6: Nagini (? Posited by Dumbledore)	*Frank Bryce (caretaker of father's estate)	§ Guardianship/Caretaking; (Failure of) (Frank Bryce)	§ (Unknown: Hagrid?)[6]	*Vow to protect Draco

Probable Order of Horcrux Destruction
(where different from order of creation)

†5: Nagini (? Posited by Dumbledore)	*Frank Bryce (caretaker of father's estate)	§ Guardianship/Caretaking; (Failure of) (Frank Bryce)	§ (Unknown: Hagrid?)[6]	*Vow to protect Draco
**6: (Unknown: Scar?)	*Potters	*Love (the kind you're willing to die for); Protection (Successful) ([James +] Lily Potter)	§ (Unknown: Snape?)	*Murder of Dumbledore

Key:

* Source = Confirmed Explicitly in Canon	† Source = Dumbledore's Speculation	** Source = Formal Literary Analysis	‡ Source = Formal Analysis + Movie Clue	§ Source = Logic (Arithmancy)

1st Parchment (verso): Of Horcruxes & Arithmancy

Notes

1   Canon does not specify whether the cup or the locket was first made a Horcrux; I argue that the locket was first, but either possibility can work.

2   Marlene McKinnon family: Who?! It is likely that Marlene McKinnon (mentioned by Moody when discussing the photo he shows Harry of the former Order) was Minerva McGonagall's daughter; Marlene McKinnon is the only name given in canon that satisfies certain conditions, including one clue dropped in the movie version of *Sorcerer's Stone*.

3   The location of the cup is a mystery, but it is quite possibly in the Trophy Room at Hogwarts.

4   What really killed Dumbledore?

   a)   The *Avada Kedavra* cast by Snape.—Logical, on the surface.
   b)   The liquid he drank in the cave, with the assistance (later, force) of Harry.
   c)   Whatever destroyed his arm (rings go on fingers, which are attached to arms, after all).

If the destruction of the Horcrux in the ring is what killed his arm (which seems logical), then it is possible that Snape had been keeping Dumbledore alive all year—the speech given on the first day of first-year Potions class comes to mind: "Even stopper death." Rowling doesn't throw anything away.

5   That Snape took the Dark Mark isn't in question, and for good or ill it would stand as one of his most important memories.

6   The list of probable sacrifices (or near-misses) for the remaining Horcruxes is conjectural, based on a) the fact that the destruction of each Horcrux thus far has required a sacrifice (or a near miss) and b) the logic given in the rest of the table.

7   Unfortunately for loyal Snape fans, this probably means that Snape will die in book seven, but there may be a way around that....

Works Cited

Bilson, Danny. Keynote Address: "From Text to Technology." Phoenix Rising Conference. Sheraton Hotel, New Orleans, La. 18 May 2007.

Dickens, Charles. *A Tale of Two Cities.* Ed. George Woodcock. New York: Penguin, 1989.

Rowling, J. K. *Harry Potter and the Sorcerer's Stone.* New York: Scholastic, 1998.

—. *Harry Potter and the Chamber of Secrets.* New York: Scholastic, 1999.

—. *Harry Potter and the Prisoner of Azkaban.* New York: Scholastic, 1999.

—. *Harry Potter and the Goblet of Fire.* New York: Scholastic, 2000.

—. *Harry Potter and the Order of the Phoenix.* New York: Scholastic, 2003.

—. *Harry Potter and the Half-Blood Prince.* New York: Scholastic, 2005.

Shakespeare, William. *Hamlet.* Folio 1, 1623.

Zarrillo, Taryn Marie. E-mail with author (24 May 2007).

THE GRAND UNIFIED HORCRUX THEORY

Donna Lafferty (mongoluehring)

When J. K. Rowling introduced the concept of the Horcrux in *Harry Potter and the Half-Blood Prince*, she opened a whole new area of mystery and speculation for fans of the series.

What are Horcruxes? How are they created? How, specifically, do they operate? What is their nature? Which objects did Tom Riddle use for his Horcruxes, and where are they hidden? How can a seventeen-year-old wizard possibly hope to find and destroy these repositories of Lord Voldemort's fragmented soul?

In this presentation, I hope to clarify what we already know about this "wickedest of magical inventions." I will analyze the prior interactions that Harry and others have had with known Horcruxes to understand specific details about how they function. Given what we know of Lord Voldemort's goals, habits and nature, I will extrapolate what (and where) the remaining Horcruxes might be. Finally, I will give Harry a bit of advice on how he might succeed in his seemingly impossible goal of destroying Lord Voldemort through the elimination of his remaining Horcruxes.

First, let's review what we know, from canon, about Horcruxes. According to Horace Slughorn in Chapter 23 of *Half-Blood Prince*,

"A Horcrux is the word used for an object in which a person has concealed part of their soul...you split your soul...and hide part of it in an object outside the body. Then, even if one's body is attacked or destroyed, one cannot die, for part of the soul remains earthbound and undamaged."

When Tom Riddle presses him further, Slughorn replies, "the soul is supposed to remain intact and whole. Splitting it is an act of violation, it is against nature."

Riddle insists on being told how to accomplish this, to which Slughorn replies,

"By an act of evil—the supreme act of evil. By committing murder. Murder rips the soul apart. The wizard intent upon creating a Horcrux would use the damage to his advantage: He would encase the torn portion —"

Riddle interrupts—"Encase? But how—?"

And Slughorn reluctantly continues, "There is a spell, do not ask me, I don't know."

Subsequent discussions between Dumbledore and Harry reveal other details about Voldemort's creation of Horcruxes, including these:

- Voldemort was determined to do everything in his power to make himself immortal.
- He was willing—even eager—to create multiple Horcruxes.
- Voldemort's cavalier treatment of the diary Horcrux indicated that he had, or would soon have, other Horcruxes on which he might rely.
- For the most part, Voldemort preferred to use important and/ or valuable objects to store his soul fragments.
- Voldemort reserved the creation of Horcruxes for murders of "special significance" (the murder of his father, for example).
- Once the Horcrux had been encased in its intended object, Voldemort distanced himself from it physically, and (with the exception of the diary) took great pains to protect each object from detection/harm.
- Voldemort tended to hide completed Horcruxes in places that had held some earlier significance in his life (e.g., the ruins of the Gaunt hovel, the cave where he terrorized fellow students, etc.).

More specific information on the nature of Horcruxes comes from Harry's interaction with a very early Horcrux in his second year at Hogwarts. The diary in which Tom Riddle had stored a fragment of his seventeen-year-old soul gives us our first glimpse into the "life" of a Horcrux.

Clearly, this Horcrux can interact, respond, learn and grow. Once the soul fragment is freed from its physical container, it immediately begins thinking and acting independently. It has a clear sense of self and is motivated by self-interest. It sets goals, then takes action to achieve those goals. Although at first the soul fragment did not have physical form, it was still able to manipulate people, and (to some extent) its environment: "The pages of the diary began to blow as though caught in a high wind, stopping halfway through the month of June" (*CoS*, Ch. 13, "The Very Secret Diary"). It is important to note that this early Horcrux was only aware of events that had taken place at or before the time when it was separated from Lord Voldemort. All of the information it learned about Harry Potter and the events surrounding Voldemort's earlier defeat were obtained from Ginny Weasley. This was a "young" Horcrux—derived from a comparatively unskilled, inexperienced Voldemort. Harry is able to destroy it by accident and/or instinct.

As time progresses, Voldemort's abilities and knowledge grow; therefore, the soul fragments that become detached later in his life have more advanced skills and knowledge than those soul fragments which were shed early on.

Now contrast Harry's relatively easy defeat of the diary to Dumbledore's off-screen battle with the second Horcrux (the Gaunt family ring). Four years after Harry's encounter with Riddle's diary, the "greatest sorcerer of all time" loses the use of his arm (and very nearly his life) in battling the terrible curse placed on the ring.

If the ring was only the second Horcrux created, and if Voldemort protected each subsequent Horcrux with even deadlier obstacles to its discovery, Harry has an incredibly dangerous journey ahead of him. And, as he reveals each Horcrux, he will be facing much deadlier and more advanced foes.

By the end of *Half-Blood Prince*, two of the six Horcruxes have been destroyed. What, then, are the most likely candidates for the remaining Horcruxes?

Dumbledore has his own ideas, yet he freely admits that he is guessing. He suggests Salazar Slytherin's locket, Helga Hufflepuff's cup, something belonging to either Rowena Ravenclaw or Godric Gryffindor, and Nagini as the most likely remaining Horcruxes.

Notice that the first Horcrux (diary) is not an "important" or valuable object; it is merely a common paper diary which was purchased in a Muggle shop. Later on, the vessels chosen to encase Voldemort's soul are of greater significance or value—family heirlooms, golden lockets, rings, etc.

Each successive Horcrux represents another step in the evolution of Tom Riddle into Lord Voldemort, both spiritually and physically. Given his growing sense of self-importance, the relative importance and value of each object (and each associated murder) increase over time.

Object	Voldemort's Connection	Significance in the Riddle → Voldemort "Evolution"
Diary	Muggle birth—orphanage	Powerlessness; obscurity; this object is easy to let go, since it represented his despised "common" beginnings
Ring	Gaunt family	Voldemort's growing self-knowledge and confidence, and his ties to the wizarding world on his mother's side
Locket	Salazar Slytherin	Reinforce Voldemort's pride by confirming his connection with "the greatest of the Hogwarts Four"
Cup+*	Hogwarts—Four Founders	Voldemort compares himself to his peers and decides that his place is among the great and powerful
Other	Ultimate supremacy of self	Voldemort is convinced that he is above all others, and he alone deserves immortality

"Cup+" here means both the golden cup taken from Hepzibah Smith's collection and an object that could be traced back to Rowena Ravenclaw. We can assume that, given Voldemort's prior actions/attitudes, he would feel entirely justified in claiming one object from each of the Founders to ensure his own immortality.

While I agree with the first items on Dumbledore's list, I believe Nagini is a red herring.

Dumbledore suggests that, having been unable to create all six of his Horcruxes before his unexpected defeat in Godric's Hollow, Voldemort may have used the murder of Frank Bryce to implant one last soul fragment in Nagini. While this is theoretically possible, it seems highly unlikely. In the first chapter of *Harry Potter and the Goblet of Fire*, Lord Voldemort reminds Wormtail that he is "no

stronger, and a few days alone would be enough to rob me of the
little health I have regained."

Was Voldemort in any condition at this point to do what is
assuredly a very complex, advanced bit of magic? He has taken great
care in creating and storing his Horcruxes up to this point. There is
no way he could have known that Frank Bryce would appear at that
moment, so how could he have been prepared to create this last, and
most significant, Horcrux? Would Voldemort risk his little remaining
strength, plus 50% of his remaining humanity, to take advantage of
this chance encounter? I don't think so.

Why would Rowling plant the notion of Nagini as a Horcrux,
then? I believe she wants her readers to entertain the notion of a
living Horcrux vessel, and Nagini is a convenient way to introduce
this concept. If it's possible for a Horcrux to exist inside a sentient
being (i.e., Nagini), then less of a leap of faith will be required when
she reveals the true nature of the final Horcrux.

Given the pattern established with the previous Horcruxes,
Voldemort would have reserved the creation of his final Horcrux
for the most significant murder of all—the death of "the one with
the power to vanquish the Dark Lord" *(OotP*, Ch. 37, "The Lost
Prophecy"). In Voldemort's mind, there could be no more
"important" murder than the killing of the child who was foretold
to be his downfall.

Voldemort would have put everything in order to create his final
Horcrux on the night of Lily and James Potter's deaths. The spell(s)
required to encase the soul fragment would be prepared. The chosen
vessel would have been secured and at hand. Voldemort would have
left nothing to chance in this, his final step toward achieving
immortality.

Yet something unexpected *did* happen. The murders of the Potter
family did not go as planned. Lily's sacrifice not only saves her son;
it also robs her murderer of his body and his power.

Let's imagine the events of that night in sequence—

1   Voldemort prepares the spell(s) and intended vessel (knowing
Voldemort, this was probably something of Gryffindor's) for his
final Horcrux.

2   With the help of Wormtail, he hunts down and murders James
Potter.

3   As a result of this murder, Voldemort's soul splits.

4   Lily pleads for Harry's life, sacrificing herself instead.

5   As he murders Lily, Voldemort splits off another portion of his soul.

6   Lily's sacrifice makes it impossible for Voldemort to kill Harry.

7   Voldemort's curse rebounds, destroying both his body and his powers.

Clearly, one or more fragments of Voldemort's soul were already detached by the time his body and powers were destroyed. After being hit by the rebounding Killing Curse, Voldemort was in no condition to perform the necessary spell-work to encase the soul fragment in his intended vessel.

So, if you were a detached bit of evil soul floating around amidst a pile of wreckage and dead bodies, what would *you* do?

In keeping with the behavior of the other known Horcruxes, this fragment of Voldemort's soul would be intent on self-preservation. It would still be sentient, and would do everything it could to ensure its survival.

But, how best to survive? What protection was left, after the destruction of the house in Godric's Hollow?

At this point, Voldemort's own existence became dependent on his ability to possess the bodies of others (*GoF*, Ch. 33, "The Death Eaters"). He was desperate to survive, and by extension, so was the part of his soul that became detached through these murders.

To my mind, it makes sense that the toddler represented the safest place for the isolated bit of soul to hide. A toddler would be cared for by others. It would not be buried, rejected or discarded, as was likely to happen to the dead bodies and bits of debris from the ruined house. Hiding inside of Harry's scar would be the surest way of surviving that the soul fragment would have after the death of Voldemort's original body.

Very early in the series (*CoS*, Ch. 18, "Dobby's Reward"), Dumbledore and Harry have a conversation which, at first glance, seems innocuous enough, given the events that precede it:

"Unless I'm very much mistaken, he transferred some of his own powers to you the night he gave you that scar. Not something he intended to do, I'm sure…"

"Voldemort put a bit of himself in *me?*" Harry said, thunderstruck.

Initially, we assumed that this refers to things like Harry's inherited ability to speak Parseltongue. However, if we take Harry's response literally, it explains many otherwise incomprehensible events, including the many visions Harry has later in the series and his odd behavior (particularly in *Order of the Phoenix*). If we assume that Harry's scar really *does* contain a bit of Voldemort himself, we may also be able predict the outcome of the single biggest remaining conflict in the series.

The fact that it is "no ordinary scar" has been well established in canon. In *Harry Potter and the Philosopher's Stone*, Harry has very early indications of just how odd his scar is. Whenever he is in proximity to Voldemort, Harry's scar burns or causes stabbing pains. In the final confrontation with the parasitic Voldemort/Quirrell, "his head felt as though it was about to split in two" (Ch. 17, "The Man with Two Faces").

As we have already established, each Horcrux is self-aware and motivated to ensure its own survival. I believe these searing and splitting pains in Harry's scar are the result of his resident Horcrux recognizing the proximity of Voldemort, then trying to escape so it can rejoin its host body.

While he was never a true Horcrux, it is interesting to note that Quirrell represents a very early example of how a piece of Voldemort's soul could survive inside another human. Voldemort's parasitic existence within Quirrell differs substantially from Harry's unwilling custody of a Horcrux, yet it is significant that Harry's very first battle in the series involves someone who shares this common burden.

Because Voldemort is inactive for the next two books, little is said about the scar's behavior again until *Goblet of Fire*. In this book, not only does Harry's scar subject him to frequent bouts of searing pain, it also begins feeding him glimpses into Voldemort's current existence.

Chapter Two ("The Scar") begins with a vision:

Harry lay flat on his back, breathing hard as though he had been running. He had awoken from a vivid dream with his hands pressed over his face. The old scar on his forehead, which was shaped like a bolt of lightning, was burning beneath his fingers as though someone had just pressed a white-hot wire to his skin.

He then recalls very specific elements of the encounter between Voldemort, Pettigrew, Nagini and Frank Bryce, despite the fact that the encounter takes place hundreds of miles away.

Voldemort's growing strength throughout the course of *Goblet of Fire* corresponds to a marked increase in the intensity and frequency of Harry's visions. In Chapter 29, "The Dream," Harry is transported back to the Riddle House:

"You are in luck, Wormtail," said a cold, high-pitched voice from the depths of the chair in which the owl had landed. "You are very fortunate indeed. Your blunder has not ruined everything. He is dead."

And later—

Wormtail screamed, screamed as though every nerve in his body were on fire, the screaming filled Harry's ears as the scar on his forehead burned with pain; he was yelling too. ... Voldemort would hear him, would know that he was there. ...

Notice that the eagle owl Harry has been riding in his vision lands on Voldemort's chair and that we do not see Voldemort himself. At this point, Harry shares Voldemort's physical point of view, as he does repeatedly in *Order of the Phoenix*. Harry is drawn in by Voldemort's emotional state at the time of these incidents— Voldemort's rage at the failure of Wormtail, his perverse pleasure in inflicting punishment—all clearly communicated to Harry through their link.

The argument has been made that, if Harry's scar really were a Horcrux, Voldemort would never have attempted to kill Harry in the earlier books. I agree that this would be a valid argument, *if* Voldemort had knowingly turned Harry's forehead into a repository for a fragment of his soul.

I have already suggested that Voldemort was unaware of the eventual disposition of this particular soul fragment. For all Voldemort knew, it perished along with most of his own magical powers after the Killing Curse backfires. He is unaware of this inadvertent Horcrux until after his rebirth in *Goblet of Fire*.

However, once Voldemort finally recognizes the significance of Harry's scar, his instructions to his Death Eaters change drastically:

"Do nothing!" Voldemort shrieked to the Death Eaters, and Harry saw his red eyes widen with astonishment. ... "Do nothing unless I command you!" (*GoF*, Ch. 34, "Priori Incantatem")

Later, as Harry tries to escape, Voldemort instructs his Death Eaters to stun Harry, not to kill him. By this time Voldemort has recognized the presence of another Horcrux, and he is therefore determined to be the only one to confront Harry. He cannot risk losing another soul fragment to the sloppy brutality of his minions, nor can he risk telling them about his creation of Horcruxes.

By the first chapter of *Order of the Phoenix*, Voldemort has already learned to direct Harry's thoughts and actions through their link. Harry initially believes that the "unsettling dreams about long dark corridors, all finishing in dead ends and locked doors" have something to do with the "trapped feeling he had when he was awake" (Ch. 1, "Dudley Demented"). The fact that Voldemort is actively using his knowledge of the scar's true nature to manipulate Harry becomes clear much later.

The very first scene in *Harry Potter and the Order of the Phoenix* contains another interesting clue as to the nature of Harry's scar. When Vernon Dursley attacks Harry,

...as the pain in the top of Harry's head gave a particularly nasty throb, Uncle Vernon yelped and released Harry as though he had received an electric shock. Some invisible force seemed to have surged through his nephew, making him impossible to hold.

If Harry's scar is a Horcrux, this passage takes on special meaning. Horcruxes are interested in self-preservation—the one in Harry's scar perceives a physical threat from Vernon and responds aggressively. Harry is as surprised by this as Vernon; clearly, this bit of self-defensive magic is not something Harry intends or controls.

Throughout the book, the mental link between the Horcrux in Harry's forehead and Voldemort himself is explored from a variety of perspectives. The link appears to work both ways—not only is Voldemort able to show Harry what he wanted him to see, but Harry continues to have unexpected (and frequently very useful) glimpses of Voldemort's activities, emotions, and motivation. It is also clear that Harry's unusually antisocial behavior (especially towards Dumbledore) is primarily due to the influence of the

Horcrux. From Chapter 22, "St. Mungo's Hospital for Magical Maladies and Injuries":

> ...Dumbledore's clear blue gaze moved from the Portkey to Harry's face.
>
> At once, Harry's scar burned white-hot, as though the old wound had burst open again—and unbidden, unwanted, but terrifyingly strong, there rose within Harry a hatred so powerful he felt, for that instant, that he would like nothing more than to strike.

The Horcrux in Harry's scar responds to the presence of Dumbledore by instinct. Now that its master is back, it becomes correspondingly stronger, more active, and highly malevolent. Harry's rage and petulance at the beginning of the book also seem exaggerated, as if the soul fragment were influencing his subconscious and asserting its own personality.

During the confrontation between Dumbledore and Voldemort in the Ministry of Magic (*OotP*, Ch. 36, "The Only One He Ever Feared"), Voldemort makes the leap from merely influencing Harry through the scar to actively possessing him:

> And then Harry's scar burst open.... he was locked in the coils of a creature with red eyes, so tightly bound that Harry did not know where his body ended and the creatures began. They were fused together, bound by pain, and there was no escape.

The surge of emotion that flows through Harry is enough to scare his possessor off, not only in the short term, but for an extended period afterwards.

In *Half-Blood Prince* (Ch. 4, "Horace Slughorn"), Harry asks Dumbledore why his scar ceased to burn after the battle at the Ministry of Magic. Dumbledore replies that Voldemort has recognized the danger of allowing Harry access to his thoughts and feelings, and that he has started to employ Occlumency against Harry. This continues for the duration of the book.

So, hopefully everyone is now convinced that Harry's scar is the final Horcrux. While we can't be absolutely sure about anything until July 21st, it is possible to make some fairly educated guesses as to the location of the other remaining Horcruxes.

Horcrux #3—Slytherin's Locket

We've been told that there was a "heavy golden locket" in the china cabinet at the drawing room of number twelve, Grimmauld

Place. Assuming that this locket is the actual Horcrux removed by R.A.B., it should be fairly easy to locate. Kreacher, in his efforts to save the family heirlooms from Sirius's attempts to purge them, may have hidden it or turned it over to his preferred branch of the Black family. Alternatively, Mundungus Fletcher's pilfering of the house might have resulted in the removal of the locket to a buyer's private collection, a shop (possibly Borgin and Burkes again), or his own stash. It is also possible (although unlikely) that the locket from the Black household is not the Horcrux at all, and is merely mentioned as another red herring.

On the American cover of *Harry Potter and the Deathly Hallows*, Harry is wearing a locket. If this is *the* locket (not the false one he and Dumbledore retrieved), has it been neutralized? Is Harry wearing it as a reminder to Voldemort that he can be defeated? The locket is still a locket—not visibly damaged. Is this a good sign for Harry, since previously the other Horcruxes had to be damaged to remove the soul fragment, yet this one seems intact?

Horcrux #4—Hufflepuff's Cup

Until the release of the book covers for *Deathly Hallows*, I was leaning towards the belief that Hufflepuff's cup was hidden somewhere at Hogwarts, either in the trophy room or transfigured into something else, like the House Cup. However, the British children's version of the book cover shows Harry, Ron and Hermione stumbling into a pile of treasure. Some say that this could be a vault at Gringotts Bank.

While that might be one possibility, I think it is far more likely to be Hepzibah Smith's collection of treasures. Remember that Voldemort has a habit of hiding his Horcruxes in locations that were of significance earlier in his life, and that he committed a murder at her house that secured him two of his Horcrux vessels. I believe that Voldemort stored one of his Horcruxes (probably the cup) in Hepzibah Smith's home.

Horcrux #5—Ravenclaw Object

Now the situation becomes murkier. If Voldemort stuck to his pattern of stealing and then using objects from the Four Founders to create his Horcruxes, what object would he have that originated with Rowena Ravenclaw? And where would it be stored? I think the latter question is easier to answer than the former, since we know of one remaining place that has a special significance in Voldemort's past.

In *Half-Blood Prince*, we learn that Voldemort made repeated efforts to return to Hogwarts after his graduation. Neither Armando Dippet nor Albus Dumbledore was willing to let him return, yet he persisted in his efforts. Dumbledore assumed this was because he was hoping to find another object from the Four Founders, or because he hoped to recruit additional Death Eaters.

If, contrary to Dumbledore's theory, Voldemort already had an object of Ravenclaw's, could his attempts to return to Hogwarts have indicated his intention of storing that Horcrux in the school itself? While we know the adult Voldemort never regained access to Hogwarts, it might have been possible for him to plant a Horcrux on the school grounds via a surrogate. There is one Death Eater who has been on staff at Hogwarts since just before Voldemort's defeat at Godric's Hollow. Could Severus Snape have placed a Horcrux at Hogwarts at Voldemort's request?

The nature of the Ravenclaw object is harder to guess. If we extrapolate from the commonly held theory that the title "Deathly Hallows" has its source in Arthurian legend's four hallows, does this give us a clue as to the possible nature of the Ravenclaw Horcrux? We've seen the stone, the chalice (cup) and the pendant (locket). The remaining object might therefore be the last, unseen hallow, namely a wand or scepter. Of course, the "Deathly Hallows" might have nothing whatsoever to do with the four hallows of Arthurian legend, or even if they do, it does not mean they correlate directly with the Horcruxes.

Of course, it's entirely possible that Dumbledore was correct, and Voldemort never found anything of either Ravenclaw's or Gryffindor's to use. In that case, we either have to assume that Voldemort never made a total of six Horcruxes, or that there is another object out there which has yet to be identified. To me, this is still quite a mystery.

As I suggested earlier, the destruction of each succeeding Horcrux will very likely become increasingly difficult. Dumbledore lost the use of his arm in fighting the soul fragment stored in the Gaunt family ring. Harry has an incredibly difficult task ahead of him, both in finding the Horcruxes and destroying them. Luckily for

Harry and the rest of the wizarding world, he has three things going for him.

First, he is not working alone. As proven repeatedly, both Ron and Hermione have qualities which make them valuable in a fight. While Harry will ultimately have to face Voldemort alone, it is clear that his two best friends will be a great help to him in the earlier parts of his quest.

Harry's second advantage is his growing magical strength. While he feels himself to be nothing particularly extraordinary, we know that he has grown dramatically in his abilities since first discovering his powers. His Patronus is strong enough to consistently repel Dementors, and he has repeatedly survived attacks by both Death Eaters and Voldemort himself. Harry is becoming a formidable wizard in his own right.

The third (and most significant) advantage that Harry has is the strength and purity of his soul. As Dumbledore says in *Half-Blood Prince* (Ch. 23, "Horcruxes"),

> "You are protected…by your ability to love!" said Dumbledore loudly. "The only protection that can possibly work against the lure of power like Voldemort's! In spite of all the temptation you have endured, all the suffering, you remain pure of heart…
>
> "You have flitted into Lord Voldemort's mind without damage to yourself, but he cannot possess you without enduring mortal agony… I do not think he understands why, Harry, but then, he was in such a hurry to mutilate his own soul, he never paused to understand the incomparable power of a soul that is untarnished and whole."

Given these advantages, I believe Harry will ultimately succeed in his goal of finding and destroying the remaining Horcruxes.

However, several of my friends have varying opinions on what this all means for Harry's future. If the Horcrux inside his scar is removed and destroyed, how can he possibly survive? If he does survive, will the departing Horcrux take all of his remaining magical powers with it? Will Harry be left in the unenviable position of having to live as a Squib or Muggle?

For several reasons, I feel that Harry will survive the series.

First, we know that Quirrell dies when Voldemort chooses to leave his body. While this might not seem like good news for Harry, I would argue that the two circumstances are very different. Quirrell was admittedly weak; he did not possess the strength to continue on his own once the parasite was removed. Harry has never consciously ceded control to Voldemort; he retains mastery of himself and his mind. Harry is, in all respects, stronger than Quirrell ever was.

We have seen the remnants of both the diary and the ring; they were mutilated beyond repair upon the removal of their respective soul fragments. Does this mean that Harry will be mutilated beyond repair when the Horcrux inside of his scar is destroyed? We have already established that this particular Horcrux is different than the others. We know that it behaves differently from those deliberately placed in inanimate objects. There are no "rules" for what happens with a Horcrux that exists within a sentient being, since there is no precedent for such a thing. It is therefore entirely possible that the removal of the Horcrux will merely result in the destruction of the scar alone, and not Harry himself.

Ultimately, Harry's capacity for love, coupled with the purity of his soul, will ensure both his own survival and the defeat of Lord Voldemort. As Dumbledore says in *Order of the Phoenix*, Chapter 37, "The Lost Prophecy":

"There is a room in the Department of Mysteries," interrupted Dumbledore, "that is kept locked at all times. It contains a force that is at once more wonderful and more terrible than death, than human intelligence, than forces of nature. It is also, perhaps, the most mysterious of the many subjects for study that reside there. It is the power held within that room that you possess in such quantities and which Voldemort has not at all. That power took you to save Sirius tonight. That power also saved you from possession by Voldemort, because he could not bear to reside in a body so full of the force he detests. In the end, it mattered not that you could not close your mind. It was your heart that saved you."

Harry on the Couch: A Psychologist's Reading of *Harry Potter*

Joanne Macgregor

1. Introduction

As a practising Counselling Psychologist, I have found it fascinating to read and analyse the *Harry Potter* books from a psychological perspective. Naturally, this does not happen on the first reading, when I gallop at top speed through the story like any other addicted Muggle! But on closer inspection, it adds a great deal to my understanding and enjoyment of the books to consider the characters, creatures and magical inventions in terms of the various branches of psychological theory and practice.

2. Developmental Psychology

Developmental psychology is that field of psychology which examines the age-related maturational changes that happen to an individual across his or her entire lifespan, from birth to death. It examines our physical, mental, social and identity development in key life stages.

Erikson's Stage Theory of Psycho-Social Development

One of the best known theories of the personality development is Erik Erikson's theory of psychosocial development. According to Erikson, the individual's *ego identity*, or conscious sense of self, develops through social interaction, across the whole lifespan, in a series of stages. In each age-related developmental stage we face a particular crisis. If we master the conflict, we develop an important new part of our identity. If we fail to resolve the crisis positively, we emerge with a sense of inadequacy or failure.

It adds to our understanding of Harry Potter as a character if we examine his progression through these stages, and the impact that his life experiences have had on his development. It is also worth noting how some of the other key characters have negotiated these stages.

Stage 1—Infancy (Trust versus Mistrust)

Stage	Basic Conflict	Important Events	Outcome
Infancy (birth to 18 months)	Trust vs. Mistrust	Feeding, being mothered	Children develop a sense of trust when caregivers provide reliability, care and affection. Positive outcome = hope, faith, trust Negative outcome = withdrawal, mistrust

The first stage of Erikson's theory of psychosocial development occurs between birth and 18 months old. In this critically important stage, the utterly dependent baby is ideally taken care of by loving, reliable and nurturing parents who meet his needs for food when he is hungry, comfort when he is distressed, amusement when he is bored, and so on. The child begins to learn that his needs are met by relatively constant, predictable carers, and so he develops a sense of trust in others and safety in the world. Later in his life, this will enable him to form relationships with friends and an intimate relationship with someone very special. His faith in others will allow him to be able to rely on others, to work in teams and to have a sense of hope in the future.

Where the infant's care is inconsistent, where he is neglected or abandoned, he develops a profound sense of mistrust. He may later be unable to form good relationships, or to trust others enough to rely on them or work with them well.

What implications does this hold for Harry? It seems that baby Harry received about a year's worth of love and consistent care from Lily and James Potter, and so would have developed a basic sense of trust. This is what has enabled him to make such deep and trusting relationships with Ron and Hermione, even though he had very little practice in his childhood at making or keeping friends (since Dudley would always scare off potential friends of Harry's).

However, when Harry was about 15 months old, his parents were killed, and he lost the two most important people in his life, with whom he had already formed a deep, trusting attachment. He heard maniacal laughter and his mother screaming, and then he was struck with a powerful, painful curse, amidst blinding jets of light and the collapse of the house around him. He was then taken by a giant and left with strangers, the Dursleys, who, from their later behaviour, we can only surmise would have been rather more neglectful of Harry, inattentive to his needs, rejecting of him emotionally, and more unpredictable in their care.

This attack, the "abandonment" by his parents (a baby cannot distinguish between voluntary abandonment and involuntary death; all he knows is that his parents are gone), and the patchy care he received afterwards, would have scarred Harry deeply. Perhaps this is why he often prefers to work alone and to wander about the castle alone, and is why, ultimately, he believes he needs to face Voldemort alone. Moreover, as he discovered later in his life, his parents were killed largely because Voldemort wanted to get to him, and this has made him determined not to expose others, such as Ginny, to danger. He is reluctant, in *OotP*, to take the others (Ginny, Luna and Neville) to the Ministry, and needs to be talked into the teamwork of Dumbledore's Army.

In short, Harry is primarily independent and self-sufficient. He has both the fundamental ability to be able to trust, but also the degree of loneliness that comes from not being able to trust wholly. He has enough of a sense of hope and faith in the future to enable him to get through his losses and crises.

Interestingly, Tom Riddle was abandoned by his father before he was even born, and his mother died in childbirth. He was an orphanage baby from the start, and was exposed, we must surmise, to a succession of carers and not nearly enough one-on-one loving, nurturing and meeting of his emotional needs. It seems Voldemort had a negative outcome to this first developmental crisis. True to what Erikson's theory would predict, he withdraws from others and has developed a suspicious, mistrusting nature, with paranoid and psychotic tendencies. Because these individuals cannot trust others, they tend to be loners and are incapable of making true friendships or intimate relationships later in life. These malignant outcomes certainly seem true of our villain!

As an interesting aside, it seems appropriate that when her two chief protagonists suffer in their earliest stage of development, J. K. Rowling should be concerned enough to draw the world's attention to Eastern European orphans who are incarcerated in cage-like cots.

Stage 2—Toddler Years (Autonomy versus Shame and Doubt)

Stage	Basic Conflict	Important Events	Outcome
Early Childhood (18 months to 3/4 years)	Autonomy vs. Shame and Doubt	Toilet Training	Children need to develop a sense of personal control over physical skills and a sense of independence. Positive outcome = willpower, determination, autonomy Negative outcome = shame, self-doubt, impulsivity, compulsion

Between 18 months and three or four years, the child develops a greater sense of personal control, particularly over his own body. He learns toilet training, gets more adept at walking, running, speaking, and riding tricycles, and chooses what food and toys he prefers. He emerges, hopefully, with a feeling of control, and a sense of autonomy and independence, rather than a sense of shame and self-doubt.

We know little of Harry's life during this period. We know that the Dursleys did not provide Harry with great love or a wide variety of choices, but they were probably good enough. Left to his own devices much of the time, toddler Harry would have explored his environment and grown rather self-sufficient. Harry emerged with a strong will, and is confident in his physical and athletic abilities. We see later that he is a natural when it comes to flying; he has no doubts that when he says, "Up!", the broomstick will leap into his hand. Certainly, however, he did not emerge feeling "special" or overly confident—he is surprised to hear that he is a wizard, and believes that if he has a gift, like the ability to speak Parseltongue, then it cannot be a unique or special ability.

His development in this stage contrasts widely with that of Dudley's. Dudley is over-indulged, given too wide a range of choices and too little in the way of discipline and limits. As a result he develops an imperious will and a determination to remain the spoilt favourite. He does not learn self-control.

We can guess that Neville must have suffered during this stage, since he has an abiding sense of self-doubt, and feelings of inadequacy and inferiority. Perhaps his austere and dominating grandmother undermined his choices, or criticized his potty-training efforts! Or perhaps it was Uncle Algie always dropping him off piers and out of windows in an attempt to force some magic out of him!

Stage 3—Preschool (Initiative versus Guilt)

Stage	Basic Conflict	Important Events	Outcome
Preschool (3 to 5 years)	Initiative vs. Guilt	Exploration	Children need to begin asserting control and power over the environment. Success in this stage leads to a sense of purpose. Positive outcome = a sense of purpose, courage. Negative outcome = ruthlessness due to lack of conscience, inhibition due to excess of guilt

During this third stage, pre-schoolers begin to assert their power and control over the world, usually through playing with others and objects in the environment. Children who are given the opportunity and encouragement to do so, within reasonable limits, wind up feeling capable, confident and believe they are able to lead others. Those who do not succeed in this stage are left with a sense of guilt over their desires and actions, self-doubt, and lack of initiative. The beginnings of moral judgment, of knowing the difference between right and wrong, take root in this stage.

Again, we know little of Harry's life at this stage. We can probably assume that Harry is left alone much of the time, and this gives him a chance to explore and play and probably to develop a rich imagination. In his interactions with Dudley and the Dursleys, he is probably not given much encouragement or recognition. We are told that, at Dudley's fifth birthday party, Aunt Marge beats Harry about the shins with a walking stick to prevent him from beating Dudley at musical statues. So already Harry is physically confident, competent and courageous, but we must assume that he developed some doubt in himself. This is what, later in his life, keeps him humble and perhaps what makes him abhor the limelight and public adulation. Certainly, by the time we meet Harry, he has a sense of initiative and purpose; he is willing to take on responsibilities and believes he can learn new skills. He has developed courage—a capacity for action despite knowing his limitations and remembering his past failings.

Both Dudley and Voldemort appear to receive way too little discipline and limit-setting at this stage of development; through over-indulgence and through over-sight, they are never made to feel appropriately guilty for their unkind or wrong actions. They are allowed to "get away with murder", and in both, this leads to an under-developed conscience and little empathy with others. An inherent ruthlessness, the determination to get their own way at all costs, begins to take root. Their capacity for moral judgment is impaired and sociopathy begins to grow.

Again, poor Neville does not seem to have mastered this stage— he is inhibited in his actions, and doubts his own abilities. "Nothing ventured, nothing lost" seems to be his guiding motto when we first meet him.

Stage 4—School Age (Industry versus Inferiority)

Stage	Basic Conflict	Important Events	Outcome
School Age (6 to 11 years)	Industry vs. Inferiority	School	Children need to cope with new social and academic demands. Positive outcome = sense of competence Negative outcome = sense of inferiority, or narrow virtuosity or inertia

In this fourth stage, which lasts roughly from when Harry would have started school until we meet him at age eleven years, the focus is on schooling and being industrious, getting things learned and achieved. Children who achieve well enough at school, and who are encouraged and praised by parents and teachers, develop a sense of pride in their accomplishments and abilities and a sense that they are competent and skilled.

We think here of Hermione who would have come into her own at this time, and who has developed a healthy sense of pride and in her academic abilities. In fact, she probably goes too far to the healthy extreme, developing what Erikson called "a narrow sense of virtuosity", focusing more or less exclusively on academic achievement and neglecting the learning of important social skills. Certainly, when we meet her, she is a swotty academic who struggles to interact with her peers without annoying them. Like many child prodigies, she has forgotten how to have fun.

Contrast this with Dudley, who would have "hit the wall" when confronted with the more objective ratings of teachers and tests. Although Aunt Petunia persists in thinking of him as an unrecognized genius, his experiences in the classroom would have left Dudley with a deep-seated sense of inadequacy. He masks this, as many bullies do, with a veneer of superiority and pushes others around to try and make himself feel adequate.

Neville, by contrast, would have received little in the way of encouragement or commendation from his dominating grandmother—the person who was probably in charge of his home-schooling. She would undoubtedly already have begun her horrible habit of comparing him unfavourably to his talented parents. As a consequence, he doubts his own ability to be successful and has a strong inferiority complex.

Ron, too, may have had a hard time of it—one can imagine him feeling inferior to talented Bill, Charlie and Percy, and we can picture Fred and George giving him a difficult time, belittling his efforts as they frequently do. Perhaps this is why he underrates his abilities and has a tendency to lack a sense of industry. He procrastinates when he can and likes to copy Hermione's work when he can no longer put off the inevitable!

Voldemort, a truly intelligent child, additionally gifted with the initially inexplicable talents that being magic brings, simply develops an increasing sense of his own importance and superiority. The other children at the orphanage offer no real competition and he quickly discovers he is able to manipulate the adults to his advantage. He is eager and ripe to discover, at age eleven, at the end of this period, that he *is* special—a wizard, no less!

What of Harry in this stage? He is an intelligent boy and so, despite the playground bullying and lack of support on the home front, he probably did well enough at school—probably rather better than Dudley, which would have fuelled the latter's sense of inferiority. Harry generally feels competent (except in Potions!), but sensibly humble. One wonders, however, what Harry could have achieved with more encouragement and praise. I believe he has always underachieved academically—notice how the Sorting Hat rated him as "very bright". This is probably at least partly due to the fact that he is so often distracted by his various adventures and the ongoing threats to his life! But it is also surely a consequence of his not appreciating how potentially talented he actually is!

During this time, he endures some humiliating experiences at the hands of Dudley and Aunt Marge, but perhaps these are balanced out by the delight of some of the magical experiences—when he manages to regrow his hair overnight following a severe haircut by Aunt Petunia, perhaps, or when he turns a teacher's hair blue, or escapes Dudley and gang and incredibly finds himself sitting on top of the school kitchens (perhaps apparition?). He discovers, a month before his eleventh birthday, that he is able to talk with snakes!

Although Harry has a strong sense of humility and often ascribes his successes to good luck and the help of friends, he also has a sense of competency and even at age eleven, he does not doubt his ability to confront Voldemort. He achieves much in his first year at Hogwarts: he discovers his significant flying talent, he succeeds academically, he defeats a troll and triumphs over Quirrell-Voldemort. He emerges from this stage confident in his ability to face challenges. But then adolescence happens!

Stage 5—Adolescence (Identity versus Confusion)

Stage	Basic Conflict	Important Events	Outcome
Adolescence (12 to 18/19 years)	Identity vs. Role Confusion	Social Relationships	Teens need to develop a sense of self and personal identity. Positive outcome = fidelity (true to self), loyalty. Negative outcome => fanaticism, role confusion, weak sense of self

The primary task of adolescence is for the individual to investigate different facets of their identity, and to decide who they are and what they believe—to find an answer to the question: "Who am I?" During this stage, teenagers explore political beliefs, spiritual systems, career choices, and sexual role identity and orientation, until, hopefully, they emerge with a clear sense of self and a feeling of independence and control. Those whose self-exploration is curtailed in this stage will remain unsure of their beliefs and desires; they will therefore feel insecure and confused about themselves and their role in society in the future. In short, they develop what is called an "identity crisis".

Teens typically seem rebellious, but what they are actually doing is "trying on for size" beliefs and practices which are different from their own. By kicking against the authority of the adults in their lives, they learn who they are and who they aren't. This is partly why Harry seems so angry and defiant in *OotP*, and why his mutiny against the tyranny of the Ministry and Dolores Umbridge's teaching inadequacies is so typical of the teenage years. It is also the time when he increasingly begins to defy the Dursleys.

Harry is exploring his future career identity when he considers becoming an auror and chooses his subjects for the more senior grades. We see the development of his political identity in his increasing rejection of the values and practices of the Ministry of Magic. He begins exploring his sexual identity in his relationships with Cho Chang and Ginny Weasley. We see the progressive development from the rather innocent infatuation with Cho, in which a kiss is "wet", to the more sexualized relationship with Ginny when Harry is two years older, in which he is driven by an inner "beast".

He also searches for a sense of familial identity. We see this longing reflected in the Mirror of Erised, and in his search for father-figures in the characters of Sirius, and to a lesser degree, Lupin and Dumbledore. By the end of his adolescence, as is typical of most teenagers, he has transferred his primary attachment from parental figures to his friends, who become his true family. It is *their* advice he seeks, their counsel he values most.

Harry's parents and parent figures were removed suddenly and often violently, but all teens (if they ever intend to leave home and forge their own lives and families) must go through the process of realizing that their parents are fallible human beings and that some problems in the world are beyond the parents' ability to solve for their child. We see this very poignantly when Harry discovers that his father (and Sirius) were a couple of conceited, bullying prats at school. This is a necessary step for Harry, who until now, has idealised James and who needs to move to a more realistic and mature acceptance of his father, warts and all, before he can truly become himself.

As in many societies, there are rites of passage in the wizarding world which demonstrate to the community that children are now accepted and respected as adults—hence wizards come of age at 17 years, and the licence to apparate may be earned at the same time. In the wizarding world, there is apparently no *moratorium*, a term used by Erikson to describe the late adolescent meanderings, explorations and delays that often occur in Western societies where young adults "take a break" before settling down to the business of assuming adult responsibilities.

In Harry, we definitely see the move from the carefree, irresponsible world of childhood to the more powerful position and responsible duties of adulthood. He takes increasing responsibility by leading the DA, initiating rescue missions, and even giving orders, at the end of *HBP*, to other members of the Order of the Phoenix. His increasing authority and trustworthiness is recognized by others who entrust him with secret information (Sirius in *OotP*, Dumbledore with his memories of Riddle and the Horcruxes in *HBP*).

In the search for political identity and social affiliation, adolescence is often a time of idealism and activism—thus we see Hermione forming an essentially political party (the Society for the Promotion of Elfish Welfare) and trying to recruit followers. She is also the driving force behind the formation of Dumbledore's Army, which is really an underground resistance organisation in political opposition against the perceived tyranny and censorship of the ruling power. She becomes fired up about all forms of discrimination and grows adept at using the rules of the ministry against itself. I predict that Hermione is a great candidate for a future Minister of Magic!

Those individuals who over-identify with one or another cause at this stage often become fanatics about a particular cause (Umbridge, anyone?) or fanatical about a certain aspect of self (Voldemort, anyone?). A fanatic believes his way is the only way, and will go to extremes to achieve it.

Another maladaptive outcome is to develop a "negative identity"—as Voldemort does—deciding that being spectacularly bad is better than being a nobody. Some might choose to emulate a particular person or system (as Percy does) or to fuse with a group that defines choices and identity, such as a cult or militaristic group, and adopt its slogans, uniforms, beliefs and rituals. Perhaps this is what happens with Tom Riddle's friends who form the core of the original Death Eaters, and what Draco and his fellow Slytherins find appealing about being part of Umbridge's Inquisitorial Squad—they do not have to do the hard work of thinking critically and forming their own identities, taking responsibility for their own choices. They can have decisions made for them, and then shift blame by saying they were only "following orders".

Stage 6—Young Adulthood (Intimacy versus Isolation)

Stage	Basic Conflict	Important Events	Outcome
Young Adulthood (19 to 35/40 years)	Intimacy vs. Isolation	Relationships	Young adults need to form intimate, loving relationships with other people. Positive outcome = love, strong relationships. Negative outcome => loneliness and isolation, promiscuity

This stage of early adulthood (from the end of adolescence to between roughly 35 and 40 years) is the time when the individual is exploring personal relationships. Hopefully, he is able to form a committed intimate relationship with a chosen person and have children. To do this, he needs all the positive outcomes from previous stage-crises, such as the ability to trust others, confidence in the self, and a strong sense of personal, gender and sexual identity.

Our chief protagonist trio are not yet in this phase, but we see others who are grappling with its issues—consider Tonks and Lupin, and Bill Weasley and Fleur Delacour, as well as those who have already mastered the challenge of the stage, such as Arthur and Molly Weasley. Harry's parents—James and Lily Potter—were killed while in this phase.

Those who are unable to build close, trusting, committed relationships are more likely to suffer emotional isolation, loneliness, and depression. Here, two characters pop into mind—Snape and Sirius. Snape, if some of the theories out there are to be believed, has been disappointed in love, perhaps with Lily. He has not developed the ability to trust others and form close bonds, and he remains in his adulthood as he was in his adolescence—a loner, single, and apparently friendless. Remarkably, it is these very qualities which make him an ideal double-agent. Unlike Harry, there is no-one in his life who could be held hostage to force his hand, no-one with whom he is emotionally close enough to risk exposure. He is a free agent, though not a happy one.

Sirius, incarcerated in the isolation of Azkaban for almost all of this phase, has sadly not had the opportunity to explore love relationships. Indeed, his development seems fixated at the adolescent stage—perhaps this is why he is so rash, reckless and immature at times.

Voldemort, of course, had lost significant parts of his soul both before and during this phase and is not capable of forming close, trusting relationships. He remains the ultimate self-absorbed, isolated loner. As we see in his exchanges with Dumbledore, he cannot even intellectually understand the *concept* of love, or imagine its transformative and redemptive power. Perhaps this is what ultimately will be his downfall.

Stage 7—Middle Adulthood (Generativity versus Stagnation)

Stage	Basic Conflict	Important Events	Outcome
Middle Adulthood (35/40 to 55/65 years)	Generativity vs. Stagnation	Work and Parenthood	Adults need to create or nurture things that will outlast them, often by having children or creating a positive change that benefits other people. Success leads to feelings of usefulness and accomplishment, while failure results in shallow involvement in the world. Positive outcome = sense of

usefulness, accomplishment, capacity
for caring

Negative outcome = overextension /
burnout, rejectivity

Very briefly, the work of middle adulthood lies in the areas of career and parenthood, and the goal is to remain generative—in other words, capable of being creative and generating new ideas, inventions, goals, accomplishments, work projects and artistic endeavours, and, especially, of mentoring younger people and guiding the next generation. Generativity is an extension of love into the future—consider Lily's self-sacrificial gift, Dumbledore's mentoring of Harry, Arthur and Molly's focus on raising their children, and many of the Hogwarts teachers' goals of transferring their knowledge to the pupils.

Failure to master this task results in stagnation—a sterile, bitter, self-absorbed existence where the individual ceases to be a productive member of society. We see this in characters such as Wormtail.

Voldemort, of course, embarked on a type of false Generativity —he attempted to achieve immortality by procreating *himself*— storing multiple parts of his soul in the Horcruxes. This is a "creativity" which serves no-one but himself, and the last book is likely to show us that it is ultimately unsatisfying and unsuccessful in addressing the need to leave a legacy for future generations.

Stage 8—Old Age (Integrity versus Despair)

Stage	Basic Conflict	Important Events	Outcome
Maturity (60/65 to death)	Ego Integrity vs. Despair	Reflection on Life	Older adults need to look back on life and feel a sense of fulfilment. Positive outcome = wisdom. Negative outcome = regret, bitterness, presumption (false wisdom), despair

The goal of this stage, which lasts from the end of middle adulthood until death, is to develop a sense of self in which you feel your existence has been meaningful.

If you fail to master this stage, you are left with regrets and despair, rather than the satisfaction of a life well-lived. You are increasingly ruled by a fear of your own approaching death or declining powers. Voldemort, clearly, has not mastered the crisis of this stage—he still believes that death is the worst thing that can happen to anyone. This is exacerbated by the fact that he has built no lasting legacy (he has raised no children, he has contributed no lasting legacy to society), and so his sole means of achieving immortality is by remaining physically alive at all costs, even at the cost of his soul and integrity.

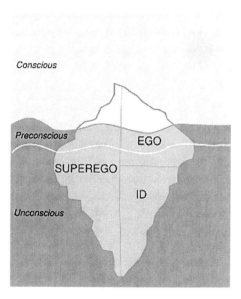

For Dumbledore, who has a strong sense of ego integrity, and whose imprint will long remain on the wizarding world, death is "but the next great adventure". It is simply the next step in, and not the end of, life.

Source:
<http://commons.wikimedia.org/wiki/
Image:Structural-Iceberg.svg>

His satisfactory negotiation of all the stages, especially the last of his life, has left him with great wisdom.

3. Freud's Id-Ego-Superego Construct Applied to *Harry Potter* Triads

Sigmund Freud was another of the great thinkers in terms of psychological development. He proposed that the human psyche is composed of three interconnected and interacting parts—the id, the ego and the superego. It is worth getting a basic understanding of the nature and function of these parts before seeing how a variety of character triads in the *Harry Potter* series can be understood in terms of this structure.

The id is the only part of personality that is present from birth. It is the completely unconscious and instinctive drive in an individual to satisfy his needs. The id is pleasure-seeking and wants immediate gratifications of all wants, needs and desires, with no consideration for others or the realities of the situation. The id tries to ensure the survival of the individual, and of the species, by propelling the individual to seek survival (primarily via food and sex), and getting rid of opposition with direct aggression. The lib-id-inal, primitive impulses of the id are often therefore socially unacceptable! They are squashed down, or "repressed", by the ego and the superego.

The second part of the personality is **the ego**. More grounded in reality, the ego helps the individual understand that others, too, have needs and desires, and that allowing the id to dictate our behaviour can have serious negative consequences in the long run. The ego's job is to help the self meet the needs of the id in socially appropriate ways, while working within the realities and moralities of the situation. The word "ego" comes from the Latin personal pronoun meaning "I, myself".

The last part of personality to develop is the highly evolved **superego**. This is the moral part of us, the internalised voice of authority, religion, schooling—the voice of restraint and conscience which guides our judgement. For the civilised superego, most of the desires and impulses of the id are taboo, and it tries to suppress these urges. This is the part of ourselves which tells us when we have done wrong, and punishes us with guilt and shame.

Because of their strong differences and competing goals, there tends to be a great deal of conflict between the id, ego and superego. The individual needs a great deal of ego-strength to manage and balance the competing pressures. If the id becomes too strong, the individual gives in to impulse and self-gratification at the expense of others and the future. If the superego dominates the personality, however, the person can become rigidly moralistic, judgemental and unquestioningly obedient to the dictates of authority, religion and government.

A triad is a trio, a group of three, interacting in some form of unit. In the *Harry Potter* series, there are quite a few triads that can be viewed in terms of the id-ego-superego structure.

Ron—Harry—Hermione

The most obvious triad is that of the trio—Harry, Ron and Hermione. In this group, Ron is surely the voice of the id. He is more impulsive and less clear-sighted than the other two, and he loves to gratify his basic urges. How often don't we see a pairing of Ron and food—he is always stuffing his mouth (and talking with it full!), filling his pockets with sweets, admiring Fred and George's ability to extract extra food from the Hogwarts kitchen house-elves. He is also the first of the trio to develop libidinal urges. While Harry's infatuation with Cho is an idealised romantic crush, Ron is swayed by lust—think of his reactions to Madam Rosmerta, the Veela Fleur Delacour, and eventually Lavender, whom he snogs for the sake of experiencing the act of snogging, rather than out of true love. He has a healthy sense of fear which propels him to seek pleasure and avoid pain, he curses frequently, and he is not above growling at juniors and evicting first-years out of comfortable spots for his own pleasure.

Hermione, of course, is the voice of the superego in the trio. She has the most evolved conscience, a clear sense of right and wrong, and, when first we meet her, she is conscientious and obedient to the point of being rule-bound and judgemental. She is horrified, especially initially, by rule-breaking and tries to restrain the others from rash and impulsive action. She also is the first to warn of potential consequences. She consults established authority for permission and guidance and urges Ron and Harry to do the same —be it in the form of Dumbledore, a teacher, or the "written authority" of her beloved books. She is passionate about justice and seeks to challenge institutionalised injustice, such as the censorship and dictatorship of Umbridge and her educational decrees, or discrimination against house-elves, giants and werewolves. She protects and assists junior pupils, rather than bullying them, and is cautious and considered in her actions.

Harry may be considered to be the core self, or ego, of the triad and the reader's primary point of identification. Just as the ego has to mediate continually between the dictates of the superego and the demands of the id, so Harry is often "piggy-in-the-middle" between Ron and Hermione, trying to smooth their differences and end their bickering. The choices the triad makes, and the action it engages in, are usually Harry's because he represents the midpoint between

Ron's and Hermione's choices. He is neither overly conscientious nor rash, and has strong regard for the feelings of others. Hermione is the voice of reason and conscience, Ron the voice of instinct, while Harry is the voice, often, of compassion and empathy.

Interestingly, Harry, Ron and Hermione start out quite polarized in these positions, but, as they mature, they become much more well-rounded, integrated and realistic personalities—more like characters and less like caricatures. Thus, our obedient, rule-loving Hermione who would rather be dead than expelled (*PS*), begins over time to lighten up and break rules, and is not above indulging in some good old-fashioned spite and manipulation (with Rita Skeeter in *GoF* and *OotP*), though still in the service of a higher purpose (truth). Already in *CoS*, Hermione begins breaking rules by brewing Polyjuice potion; she justifies this to herself because what the three friends are attempting to do is in the greater good; morality takes precedence over letter-of-the-law rules. She says: "*I* don't want to break rules, you know. I think threatening Muggle-borns is far worse than brewing up a difficult potion" (*CoS*, Ch. 10).

Essentially-id Ron begins to develop more of a conscience and more ego-strength. Contrast the Ron of *PS* who believes that fame and glory on the Quidditch pitch can somehow be magically delivered without effort, to the Ron of *OotP* and *HBP* who has a real appreciation of the hard work and sacrifice that go into success.

As Harry matures, he begins to develop a stronger superego. He starts to look before he leaps; he exerts moral authority (a superego function) over Lupin and Sirius in *PoA* to stop them exacting summary revenge on Pettigrew; he analyses his own motives and begins to understand that defeating Voldemort is less about revenge (an aggressive id instinct) and more about the need to preserve the good in society for the future.

Voldemort—Harry—Dumbledore

Another of the triads which can be understood in terms of the id-ego-superego construct is that of the Voldemort-Harry-Dumbledore triad.

Here, Voldemort represents the id—out for its own survival at all costs. Voldemort is pure id, determined to meet his own needs for power and immortality with none of the considerations of conscience that are the domain of the superego. He enjoys the pain and humiliation of others because this makes him feel more powerful. In *PS* (Ch. 17) he has persuaded Quirrell that "[t]here is no good and evil, there is only power, and those too weak to seek it!". He has no empathy for others, no concern for the welfare of the broader society. Interestingly, given the Latin root of the word "id", Voldemort, dehumanised by the splitting of his soul, has become an "it" or a "thing" who no longer even appears human.

Dumbledore is surely the superego of this triad. He embodies the far-sighted voice of consequence and conscience. He has a strong sense of right and wrong, and understands the value and importance of love, compassion and wisdom. He tries to guide Ministers of Magic away from self-serving vainglory, attempts to steer young Tom Riddle down a more moral path, and introduces Harry to the superego domain of learning, restraint and good judgement. He is able to make Harry feel guilty simply by using a mildly disappointed voice, and Harry finds this much more agonising than even the fiercest rants of Snape, Dursley or McGonagall.

Harry is the ego, more inclined to action and error than Dumbledore, not at all evil like Voldemort. Just as the ego must mediate between the id and superego, so Harry is often the pivotal point of connection between Dumbledore and Voldemort. It will be fascinating to discover whether, in his final confrontation with the character of Voldemort, Harry is loyal to the dictates of his superego (or Dumbledore impulse) and destroys Voldemort with love, pity and compassion, or whether he gives in to his id (or Voldemort impulse) and tries to destroy Voldemort with sheer power, hatred and vengeance in his heart.

The Voices in Harry's Head

A third, fascinating triad which threads itself throughout the *Harry Potter* books is that of the set of voices in Harry's head, those parts of himself which try to govern his actions. The most dominant part of self of which Harry is aware is that of his own voice—the clever, compassionate, adventure-seeking hero whom we all know and love. This is the ego voice.

There are many theories in the fan kingdom and some, like the Harry-as-Horcrux theory, posit that there is a Voldemort voice in Harry—the voice that bids him resist Mad-Eye Moody's Imperius curse. To me, this is most unlike Voldemort. It seems rather to be a typically Harry voice, ever questioning blind obedience to authority and wanting to know "why?". It feels a little disembodied because most of his mind is free-floating in the carefree, dreamy state which the Imperius curse induces.

There certainly is a more primitive, impulsive, id-like voice which appears at times in Harry's head. We hear the id voice in Harry's encounters with Dudley in *OotP*, where he goads and taunts, apparently in the hope of provoking a violent clash.

It is perhaps most clear in *HBP*, where it is described as a slumbering beast which raises its head in the presence of Ginny. When Ginny fights with Dean, the "drowsing creature in Harry's chest suddenly raised its head, sniffing the air hopefully" (*HBP*, Ch. 20). When Harry walks in on Ginny and Dean kissing, this primal, animalistic part rears as a sudden madness: "It was as though something large and scaly erupted into life in Harry's stomach, clawing at his insides. Hot blood seemed to flood through his brain, so that all thought was extinguished, replaced by a sudden urge to jinx Dean into a jelly." The aggressive id voice tempts Harry to beat off her suitors, making him "want to rip Dean limb from limb for kissing her" (*HBP*, Ch. 14). This id-self does not only have violent impulses; it also has libidinal, or sexual, ones. It is this part which propels Harry to kiss Ginny very thoroughly, heedless of onlookers, and then "roars in triumph" (*HBP*, Ch. 24).

The third very clear voice in his head is the one Harry calls "a most Hermione-like voice". This is the superego voice, which urges caution, and restraint and persuades Harry to look before he leaps.

There are, of course, many other triads in the series, such as that of the Marauders, where rash, bold, vengeful Sirius may be seen as the id, talented but fallible James as the ego, and wise, prefect Lupin as the superego.

And we can have fun in the world of fan sites, too. Consider the PotterCast Trio—Melissa Anelli, Sue Upton and John Noe. Which of these is id—focused on appetite (Chipotle anyone?) and always pushing the limit of the envelope in terms of rude jokes? (John.) Which of the three is superego—always rapping John on the knuckles, leaving notes for the PotterCast elves to edit out the rude bits, bringing the conversation back on topic? (Melissa.) And which is the joyous, caring ego—our favourite Hufflepuff, Sue!

4. Psychopathology

Abnormal psychology, or psychopathology, is that branch of psychology that deals with mental and emotional illness. In the *Harry Potter* books, many of these conditions can be seen to be represented by various creatures and manifested in the characters.

Psychopathology—Creatures and Beings

Dementors

When viewing the creatures and beings through a psychological lens, it seems reasonably clear that Dementors in the *Harry Potter* books represent *major depression*. These foul creatures immobilise their victims by sucking joy, warmth and vitality out of them, leaving them with the feeling that they will "never be cheerful again" and sucking out all positive thoughts. While under the Dementor's spell, you relive the worst times and memories of your life, and forget that things ever were good, or could ever be so again. You feel deadened. Dementors are even capable of leaving you in a state of living death by sucking out your soul through the "Dementor's Kiss". The state induced by a Dementor is very similar to the state of being in clinical, or major, depression. There, too, you have no energy, no hope and no joy (what is called "anhedonia", or the loss of pleasure); you are immobilised and tend to dwell on all the negative feelings and experiences in your life.

Jo Rowling has in fact confirmed this interpretation. In a 2000 interview (*The Times* [London]), Jo was asked if Dementors are a description of depression. She replied, "Yes. That is exactly what they are. It was entirely conscious. And entirely from my own experience. Depression is the most unpleasant thing I have ever experienced."

The way to repel a Dementor is to think of a very happy memory and say the incantation *"Expecto patronum"*, presumably as the expectation of help from some patron protector or what Rowling has called a "spirit guardian" (ITV interview, 17 July 2005). This is very interesting because recovery from depression also requires you to remember that you are capable of being happy, and usually requires assistance from some sort of helper who can hold onto

hope and protect you from the worst of your depression—be that
helper a counsellor, therapist, or special friend.

Boggarts

Boggart seem to divine our deepest fears and then assume the
appearance of that thing.

To me, Boggarts seem to represent anxiety in general, and
specific phobias in particular.

When we worry about our worst fear coming true, we bring
about anxiety in ourselves. When we have anxiety, we are
experiencing an excessive fear reaction (the fight-or-flight response)
to something which is, in fact, not real or life-threatening. Thus
many of the class in *PoA* are scared of silly things—mummies and
spiders, for example, or unrealistic things. Hermione is scared, in her
Defence Against the Dark Arts examination, by a Boggart
pretending to be Professor McGonagall and telling her that she has
failed all her exams. Even Harry responds with real fear to the
Boggart-Dementor, which is not real.

Specific phobias are when we have a strong fear and avoidance
reaction to something not immediately or realistically dangerous—
such as the fear of spiders, of heights or the fear of flying.

To cut a Boggart back down to size, a wizard must make it appear
ridiculous, say the incantation *"Riddikulus"* and then finish it off
with laughter. This is much the same way to deal with anxiety. When
we stop avoiding what we fear and instead confront it directly, we
often see how absurd it is and can stop worrying about it.

For phobias, the most effective treatment, taken from the school
of Cognitive Behavioural Therapy, is similar to what occurs in
Lupin's DADA classroom. Clients are taught to change their
unrealistic thinking or fearful view of what they fear. Then, in a
process called *systematic desensitization*, clients directly confront the
feared thing (spiders, or heights, for example) in increasingly real
approximations of the real thing, until they can endure full exposure
without fear.

By forcing his pupils to see, approach, and interact with a very
realistic approximation of what they fear, Lupin is using a process
called "flooding"—what amounts to a rapid systematic
desensitization session. The relaxation brought about by laughing at
the ridiculously altered Boggart is mutually incompatible with the

tension which results from fear, and so fear is driven out. Anxiety, like the Boggart, is defeated by laughter and a sense of perspective.

Nifflers

Nifflers seem to me to be furry little kleptomaniacs! *Kleptomania* is classified in the standardised psychiatric diagnostic system (DSM–IV) as an Impulse-Control Disorder. Individuals with kleptomania find themselves compelled to steal little treasures for themselves, and, like Nifflers, they are very difficult to control. Nifflers are specifically drawn to small shiny objects, even when these might not actually be valuable (as is the case when they niffle out Leprechaun gold in Hagrid's Magical Creatures lesson in *GoF*). They are quite prepared to take shiny objects which belong to others. In the same way, kleptomaniacs tend to have a preference for certain types of objects (batteries, small ornaments or remote controls, for example), many of which have little real value. It is this lack of profit motivation, lack of premeditation and the compulsive nature of the urge to steal which sets them apart from ordinary thieves.

Werewolves

Werewolves are truly interesting and complex magical creatures. J. K. Rowling herself, speaking of Lupin, has said: "He's a damaged person, literally and metaphorically. I think it's important for children to know that adults, too, have their problems, that they struggle. His being a werewolf is a metaphor for people's reactions to illness and disability" (J. K. Rowling, Scot, 2002).

If we examine the condition of being a werewolf as being a metaphor for *mental* illness and disability, the comparison still holds true. As is the case with werewolves in the *Harry Potter* books, Muggles with mental and emotional disorders are often stigmatized, discriminated against in the workplace, and may avoid seeking treatment out of shame and embarrassment. As with lycanthropy (the condition of being a werewolf), many psychiatric conditions are chronic, they flare up from time to time in the individual's life. Like the transformed werewolf, the acutely affected Muggle has impaired control over his own thoughts, feelings and actions, and may behave in ways that later bring him remorse and guilt.

Psychiatric disorders need to be managed, with a combination of symptom-minimising medicine (like good old Wolfsbane potion!), plus social support (like the Marauders) and helpful strategies in the person's environment, behaviour and lifestyle. As with lycanthropy, there is usually no "cure", if by that we mean that the problem can be totally solved and just go away, never to reappear.

Psychological disorders result from an interacting combination of nature and nurture. Genetics predispose an individual to developing a certain condition, while aspects of the individual's life experiences may trigger the actual development of the disorder. With alcoholism, for example, this might include watching a parent model the use of alcohol to relax or avoid dealing with problems, or being part of a group of friends who drink heavily.

Because of the nature-nurture double-whammy, many psychological disorders, such as depression, alcoholism, anxiety and childhood abuse, repeat themselves over generations. It is as if the individual, like the young boy Lupin, gets "bitten" in childhood, and spends the rest of his life trying to master and manage his condition. Thus the *Harry Potter* werewolf may be viewed as symbolising the inter-generational transmission of dysfunction, and/or the intermittent manifestation of childhood trauma.

Specifically, when we examine Lupin's monthly transformations, the werewolf conditions seems to closely parallel a group of problems known as *Impulse-Control Disorders*. The individual with an impulse-control disorder periodically feels an overwhelming urge to commit some negative, and often self-destructive, act. This may range from shoplifting, fire-setting or gambling, to pulling out one's own hair (a condition known as trichotillomania) or exploding in rage (*intermittent explosive disorder*). They feel unable to resist the compulsion to commit the deed and often seem disassociated, or separated from their "right mind" when they do it. It is interesting to note that Wolfsbane potion appears to work by helping the individual retain their mind while in the lunar state, and so preventing him from committing harmful actions even though transformed. Muggle medications aim to achieve the same goal.

There is a long-established and fascinating connection between aberrant behaviour and phases of the full moon. We are not sure how this works, but certainly if the human body is composed mostly of water, it is not unreasonable to assume that the moon exerts a pull on us, in much the same way as it does on the world's oceans. When the moon is full, hospitals know to have extra doctors on duty in their Emergency Rooms, midwives know their pregnant clients are more likely to go into labour and psychologists often notice an upsurge in "loony" behaviour. In fact, the origins of the words "lunacy", "lunatic" and Lupin's nickname "loony", all derive from the Latin *luna*, meaning *moon*, and from the observation or belief that lunar cycles influence madness.

Thestrals

Thestrals, the skeletal black horses which draw the Hogwarts carriages, seem to symbolize what you know and what you can perceive once you've experienced death. Individuals who have witnessed death and experienced grief are perhaps left with a greater sensitivity and more empathy for the pain of others. It is this which allows Luna to be the only friend who is able to comfort Harry after the loss of Sirius (*OotP*). Being able to see Thestrals, then, is a marker of the loss of childhood innocence brought about by experiencing the losses of the adult world.

Ghosts

The ghosts in the *Harry Potter* books seem to represent "unfinished business". This term is taken from Gestalt Psychology and refers to unresolved issues from the past which have not yet been fully dealt with, or "finished", and so they continue to haunt us in the present. We need to make peace with our losses, fears and selves before we can move on. In the *Harry Potter* books, happy people, or those who have accepted their lives as full and who have the courage to move on to what the "well-organised mind" of Dumbledore calls the "next great adventure" of death, do not choose to become ghosts.

Traditionally, the spirits of those who were murdered are "unquiet"; their souls linger until the murderer is found and justice is meted out. There is a long literary tradition of this, reaching back from *Hamlet* and *Macbeth* until the modern-day film *Ghost*, in which Whoopi Goldberg channels the spirit of a murdered man to his wife.

Moaning Myrtle has unfinished business both because she died a premature, unnatural death (killed by the Basilisk) and because she never quite finished her fight with a schoolmate. She stays on in spirit form to haunt and taunt Olive Hornby. Never having felt loved and accepted in life, she lingers on miserably in the neither-here-nor-there state between life and death, and tries to make connections with the living, from Harry to Draco.

Nearly Headless Nick also died a gruesome death, but his unfinished business is with the life beyond. Not having had the courage to leave this life and accept the inevitable fact of death, he has chosen (like other ghosts, he tells us) a half-life, in limbo between life and death. The same is presumably also true of the other Hogwarts ghosts—the Fat Friar, the Grey Lady and the Bloody Baron.

Peeves is a poltergeist, not a ghost. In Rowling's own words (http://www.jkrowling.com), "Peeves isn't a ghost; he was never a living person. He is an indestructible spirit of chaos." Traditionally, poltergeists are found in houses where there are adolescents and it is believed, by those who believe, that the poltergeist is a visible manifestation of all that adolescent angst, intense feelings and libidinal energy. It is not surprising, then, that one should be found in Hogwarts, with all its teenage turbulence, and that it should take the form of this curious little man who behaves like an immature brat. Half-adult, half-child is very much the condition of adolescence!

Psychopathology—Characters

A psychologist based at Hogwarts would have a fully booked diary, as we can hypothesize that many of the characters in the wizarding world are suffering from one or another type of psychological disorder.

Harry Potter

Our hero Harry is in fact remarkably well-adjusted, given his years at the mercy of the Dursleys and the number of traumatic experiences which he has subsequently endured! He is exposed to neglect, bullying from Dudley and his cronies, and what might even be called emotional abuse at the hands of the Dursleys, but still turns out to be quite a hardy, good-hearted character. Still, in the Muggle world of psychology, Harry would most certainly be diagnosed as suffering from *post-traumatic stress disorder* (PTSD), a grief reaction and survivor guilt.

Following a traumatic experience in which the individual experienced both extreme terror and profound helplessness, combined with a threat to life or limb, most survivors show symptoms of PTSD (or of acute stress disorder). These symptoms include nightmares, flashbacks, difficulties with concentration and short-term memory, amnesia for parts of the original traumatic event, insomnia or disturbed sleep, irritability and short-temperedness, emotional numbing, hyper-vigilance and the inability to relax, and emotional distress in response to reminders of the trauma. Feelings of intense guilt at surviving when others did not, and anger over one's powerlessness at the time are often common.

Harry demonstrates many, if not all of these symptoms. Already from the first book he is described as having flashbacks to a green light, which he assumes to be of the car accident which allegedly killed his parents, but which turns out to be the Avada Kedavra spell which Voldemort cast on his parents and Harry himself. Later, he starts having nightmares of his "parents disappearing in a flash of green light while a high voice cackled with laughter" (*PS*, Ch. 13). Weeks after his encounter with Quirrell-Voldemort, Harry still has flashbacks and nightmares: "Harry kept waking in the night, drenched in cold sweat, wondering where Voldemort was now, remembering his livid face, his wide, mad eyes" (*CoS*, Ch. 1). After the gruesome graveyard events at the end of *GoF*, Harry suffers even more from flashbacks, nightmares which relive Cedric's death, and guilt over having survived. After Sirius's death, this survivor guilt is intensified. He feels especially guilty because he believes himself to be partly responsible for the deaths since he persuaded Cedric to touch the cup, and it was his mad dash to the Ministry in *OotP* that drew Sirius to the battle.

His grief reactions at the loss of his parents, and following the deaths of Cedric, Sirius and Dumbledore are normal, not pathological, responses to the loss of significant others and demonstrate that, despite all, Harry is still capable of loving, and thereby willing to risk losing, even with the pain that this entails.

On many of the fan sites, the idea that Harry is "depressed" is casually and frequently tossed around. Harry is certainly sad and angry, but he is most definitely not depressed. Remember the symptoms of depression: exhaustion, listlessness, lack of energy, weight gain or loss, lack of pleasure and joy, withdrawal from friends, suicidiality and feelings of worthlessness. The person with true depression is more numb or emotionally "flatline" than sad, and struggles even to get out of bed in the morning. Their ability to function in the world is significantly impaired and the condition continues for months and years at a time. This is *not* a description of Harry's psychological functioning.

Ron Weasley

Ron Weasley suffers from a specific phobia of spiders. This fear was triggered by an initial traumatic experience, called the "sensitizing event", with a spider. When Ron was just three years old, his brother Fred turned Ron's teddy bear into a "dirty great spider" as revenge for Ron's having broken Fred's toy broomstick. Ron was holding the spider at the time and was terrified by the transformation. The fear and shock that the little boy felt at the time, became associated with the object that was present at the time (the spider), and now Ron has what is called a *conditioned* response of fear to any spider he sees. It is a measure of Ron's courage that he goes with Harry into the dark forest on the trail of spiders.

We might also hypothesize that Ron suffers from feelings of inferiority. He has consistently been overshadowed by the talents and achievements of his older brothers (and, in the later books, even by his talented younger sister), and he often compares himself unfavourably to his best friend, Harry, whose successes are the stuff of legend. Like many of those who feel insecure about themselves and who have low self-esteem, Ron vacillates between moments of excruciating self-doubt (wanting to quit the Gryffindor Quidditch team after his hopeless performances, for example), and unjustified self-aggrandizing (as, for example, when Ron exaggerates his role in the *GoF* underwater task). When Ron starts believing in himself, and stops listening to the criticism of the crowd and his brothers, he is able to perform really well. This is largely the treatment for feelings of inferiority—to reach a place of self-acceptance, and realistically placed self-confidence.

Neville Longbottom

Neville suffers from a severe *inferiority complex*. He has a very low self-esteem; he doubts his own abilities and suffers from a severe lack of confidence, which makes him easy prey for bullies such as

Snape and Malfoy. Happily, it seems that with the progression of each year, Neville is slowly but surely developing more confidence and I think we may yet expect even greater things from him.

Neville also possibly suffers from *psychogenic amnesia*, meaning that he may well have distressing traumatic memories which he has unconsciously repressed (pushed down out of awareness). More than once, we see him having a strong negative reaction to screaming noises, such as the Mandrake roots being re-potted (*CoS*) and the noise which screeches out from Harry's golden egg in *GoF*. He says that this noise sounds like "someone being tortured". We may guess that Neville has subconscious memories of the torture of his parents by Bellatrix Lestrange. Intriguingly, he may yet reclaim these memories.

His reactions to the screaming noises represent "distress to similar sensory cues"—one of the symptoms of PTSD—as do his inattentiveness and memory problems, but from the limited amount we know of the inner workings of Neville's mind and heart, he does not appear to present with sufficient of the other symptoms to qualify for a diagnosis of PTSD.

More will be said of Neville's memory and physical coordination problems in the section on neuropsychology.

Ginny Weasley

Ginny, Ginny, Ginny! She was very lucky that no Muggle healer got hold of her in her first year at Hogwarts, when she was possessed at times by the part of Voldemort's soul that was stored in the Horcrux diary. In the Muggle world of psychiatry, Ginny would most likely have been diagnosed as suffering from the extremely serious disorder called *schizophrenia,* complete with visual hallucinations (the writing appearing by itself in the diary) and auditory hallucinations (hearing voices telling her what to do). Her violent behaviour towards roosters would have ensured that she be incarcerated until such time as she was no longer considered dangerous!

Much the same would have happened to Harry, incidentally, had a Muggle healer gotten hold of him—hearing voices, seeing mysterious writing and spirit manifestations of past pupils, believing himself capable of speaking a special language which snakes could understand. These constitute the psychotic break with reality, and would have earned Harry a chemical straight-jacket (anti-psychotic medication) for sure!

Professor Dolores Jane Umbridge

Sadism is the abnormal derivation of pleasure or gratification from inflicting pain on others, or watching others endure it. Those with *Sadistic Personality Disorder* have a pervasive pattern of cruel, demeaning behaviour and use violence or physical cruelty to achieve dominance over others. They often discipline those under their control (such as children, pupils or junior work colleagues) harshly and enjoy the resulting humiliation. They are frequently paranoid and untrusting, manipulative, deceitful, and may be highly ambitious, power-seeking authoritarians with a rigid loyalty to their work or cause. This sounds remarkably like the *Harry Potter* character we most love to hate, none other than, *"hem hem"*, Professor Dolores Jane Umbridge.

Lord Voldemort

Harry's arch-enemy, Lord Voldemort, definitely qualifies for a diagnosis of *Anti-social Personality Disorder* (APD). Those with APD, who in the past have been called *psychopaths* and *sociopaths*, show a deep disregard for society's norms and rules, and are indifferent to the feelings and rights for others. Indeed, they seem to lack both a conscience and the ability to empathise with others and do not suffer from guilt. They may feel themselves superior to others, or special in some way which excludes them from having to conform to rules and regulations.

More common in men than women, APD appears to have its roots both in genetics (and remember what stock Tom Riddle derives from—the inbred and violent Gaunts, and the charming but negligent, self-serving Riddle) and in environment (especially maternal deprivation in the first five years of life). They are deceitful con-men whose superficial facade of charm makes them able to deceive and manipulate others for personal gain, but they have a very limited range of sincere feelings and battle to maintain enduring deep relationships. This description certainly fits the charming Tom and loner Voldemort. They are frequently in conflict with the law because they continue to violate it. Muggle prisons, like, one presumes, Azkaban, are filled with APD individuals.

Their short tempers and aggressiveness mean that they are frequently involved in violence. They often steal—as Tom Riddle does from the children at the orphanage, and later from the Gaunts and Hepzibah Smith. They lack remorse and will shift the blame onto others if they can—as Tom does when he uses memory-modifying charms to ensure that Morfin Gaunt and Hokey the house-elf take the blame for the deaths of Marvolo Gaunt and Hepzibah Smith, respectively. For an individual to receive a diagnosis of APD, he needs to have begun such behaviour (called, in childhood and adolescence, *conduct disorder*) before the age of fifteen. Tom, with his torturing of children, killing of animals, and petty thefts at the orphanage, certainly meets this criterion.

Intriguingly, those with APD do not tolerate frustration well and are usually reckless and impulsive, and it is often this failure to plan ahead that leads to their downfall and capture by the authorities. Although we can hardly accuse Voldemort of a failure to plan ahead, perhaps he had not thought through all the permutations of his decision to use Harry's blood to regenerate his body, and the as yet unexplained "gleam of something like triumph" in Dumbledore's eye when told of this act (*GoF*, Ch. 36) possibly points to this being a weak spot in Voldemort's planning, which may yet lead to his undoing.

The Dursleys

"Mr and Mrs Dursley, of number four, Privet Drive, were proud to say that they were perfectly normal, thank you very much" (*PS*, Ch. 1). Apart from their horrible treatment of their nephew, the Dursleys are disturbingly normal, from their choice of car to their deficient parenting skills.

Although many folks consult psychologists in order to discover what is "normal", this is actually not a psychological term. "Normal" or norm-al is a concept from the field of statistics, where all variations of something, all possible scores, are pooled together and a average or a midpoint, the so-called "norm", is calculated. The norm may well be a version or a score that no-one, in fact, has. For example, the "normal" amount of children for married couples to have may be 2.4, but no-one actually has two and four-tenths of a child—therefore, no-one is normal!

Psychologist Erich Fromm was the first to speak of "the pathology of the normal", a determination to be so average and to avoid standing out in any way that one actually becomes very narrow and bland, and lacks individuality. Psychologist Abraham Maslow said that healthy individuation requires us to resist unhealthy enculturation—in other words, that we need to be a little different from, and questioning of, our culture in order to be healthy individuals.

In their preoccupation with what is "normal", in their obsession that nobody (especially not the neighbours!) discover anything unusual about them, the Dursleys actually lead a very unhealthy life. Happiness and health are more than just the absence of disease, and by trying to eliminate every element of what is not strictly "normal", of what may be considered strange or mysterious, they also eliminate life, spontaneity, joy, creativity, growth and uniqueness. Sometimes our eccentricities of taste and style, our quirks of character, are what give us our magic and our uniqueness.

5. Neuropsychology

Neuropsychology is that field of psychology which aims to explain the structure and function of the brain and examines the impact on emotions, thinking and behaviour of damage to the brain through injury, infection or lack of oxygen. In the *Harry Potter* series, there are a couple of characters suffering from what, in the Muggle world, would be understood as neuropsychological disorders.

Memory Impairments

At least two key characters—Gilderoy Lockhart and Neville Longbottom—have serious impairments in their short-term memory systems—that part of our memory which stores records of what has happened in our immediate and recent past. Long-term memory systems (what happened in the distant past) often remain intact when old age, dementia or brain injury damage short-term systems because there is a failure in the brain's ability to store new experiences as memories. This is why old folks can reminisce in accurate detail about their youth, while being unable to remember what happened yesterday.

When Lockhart, who himself had been obliviating very specific sections of the memories of many talented wizards, attempts to cast a memory charm with Ron's broken wand, the spell backfires catastrophically. Lockhart receives his own, more widespread brain damage, leaving him with almost no ability to form new memory traces. In the world of Muggles, he would be diagnosed as suffering from *anterograde amnesia* (the inability to make new memories), together with some degree of *retrograde amnesia,* since his memory of events before the injury is also fuzzy.

Lockhart exists in a transient world where anything beyond his immediate attention-span disappears permanently from his consciousness. He lives in the eternal now. Motor skills, such as walking or Gilderoy's ability to sign autographs, are typically not affected by this disorder. Those who suffer from this awful damage have great difficulty in acquiring new information or skills, lack insight into their condition and believe they are functioning normally. They often invent stories, or *confabulate*, to cover their lapses, and exhibit repetitive and talkative behaviour—this is certainly true of the Lockhart we meet in St. Mungo's Hospital in *OotP*.

When Muggles sustain a brain injury, such as that left by a stroke or accident, they generally make some recovery within the first two years following the accident, as the brain finds new ways of rerouting its messages and relocating its storage systems. We see, too, from his appearance at St Mungo's, that Gilderoy has made some improvement but, as is the case with brain-damaged Muggles, it is likely that some, perhaps unfortunately even most, of the damage to his brain will be permanent.

In the backfiring spell, there was probably damage to Gilderoy's brain in the regions of the fornix, diencephalons, mamillary bodies, and/or *hippocampus*. Yes, the hippocampus does in fact exist! In the wizarding world it may well be a mer-horse, with the head and forequarters of a horse, and the hindquarters and tail of a giant fish, but in human brains, the hippocampus is a small seahorse-shaped structure involved in memory and emotion.

Memory Impairments—Neville

The more subtle memory impairments of Neville Longbottom are perhaps even more interesting. He is constantly described as extremely forgetful. He never remembers to pack all his belongings when travelling to Hogwarts; he forgets about trick-steps, can never remember where he left Trevor the Toad, and has even written down the common room passwords so that he does not forget them. Like many patients with memory impairments, he needs to rely on mnemonics (a memory-helping device or strategy), such as a Remembrall (the wizarding world's version of post-it notes?) to help him, but then forgets what it is trying to remind him of!

Like many with concentration and memory problems, Neville gets worse when he is stressed, such as in the classrooms of cruel Snape or severe McGonagall, but improves when he is in a non-stressful environment, such as that provided by the kindly Professor Sprout and the predictable plants in Herbology.

It is (remotely) possible that Neville's patchy memory is psychogenic—that is, a forgetfulness having its origin in the traumatic torture and loss of his parents—but it is much more likely that these problems originate in the biology of Neville's brain. It is possible that, in attempt to protect Neville and help him forget what he might have witnessed of his parents' torture, Neville's grandmother performed a powerful memory obliviation charm on him which damaged other memory systems as a side effect, leaving him with lingering problems. He also seems to be inordinately clumsy, and many patients with brain damage have difficulties with fine and gross motor control.

There is another possible explanation for Neville's condition, however. *Dyspraxia* (sometimes called *apraxia*) is the general term used to cover a wide range of disorders affecting the initiation, organization and performance of action. The word "dyspraxia" comes from the Greek words "dys", meaning bad, and "praxis", meaning action or deed. It is more common in males than in females, occurring (in varying degrees of severity) in up to 8% of all children. It seems to be caused by an immaturity in the way the brain processes information, resulting in messages not being fully transmitted between the brain and the body.

It can be present from birth (developmental dyspraxia), or as a result of brain damage suffered from a stroke or accident (acquired dyspraxia). Remember that Neville nearly drowned when his uncle Algie pushed him off the end of Blackpool Pier in an attempt to force some magic out of him. This may have caused some damage due to *anoxia* (oxygen deprivation). Additionally, he was dropped from an upstairs window by the same uncle and "bounced", possibly occasionally on the head, all the way down the garden and into the road, which may also have caused damage.

Individuals with dyspraxia have poor physical coordination, they struggle to get their bodies to do what they want. They have problems in *gross motor control*—large-body movements such as walking and running, climbing, jumping, flying on a broomstick, and throwing and catching. They trip, stumble, fumble catches and appear slow, hesitant and awkward in their movements. How often have we not seen Neville stumble, trip and misstep?

They have difficulties in spatial awareness, and so physical skills are hard to learn, and difficult to retain. They therefore tend to avoid sports and, like Neville, loathe flying lessons! Because of their poor balance, they often trip over their own feet. These folks tend to be rather clumsy—always knocking things over and bumping into other people. They can be quite annoying to others!

Dyspraxia also causes problems in fine motor control—the coordination of fine movements, such as would be involved in writing, and in executing the movement patterns in waving wands and preparing potions ingredients. Objects are always falling through their fingers—remember Neville's struggle to hold onto the prophecy ball in *OotP*? They do not "catch on" to movements instinctively, but must learn by practising sequences over and over again—remember determined Neville in the DA lessons?

In addition, dyspraxia affects speech and language—and Neville stutters and struggles to remember words. Concentration is also usually impaired, and most people with dyspraxia have short-term memory problems; they may forget instructions, passwords and deadlines, and constantly misplace items.

Their difficulties with integrating sensory information means that these folks are often extremely sensitive to sensory stimulation such as sound, light and touch. Neville faints when the screaming Mandrakes are re-potted and is very disturbed by the screeching noise from inside the golden egg in *Goblet of Fire*. This may be due to the fact that these sounds remind him unconsciously of the torture of his own parents, but the effect may well be exacerbated by the aversion to loud noises found in dyspraxics.

Because of these difficulties in managing their bodies and in interacting with the environment, dyspraxics can be prone to anxiety and low self-esteem; this is certainly true of Neville!

Emotion and Memory in the Neurology of Lie-Detection and Legilimency

Occlumency is the magical defence of the mind against external penetration. It is a skill which allows the individual to seal the mind against magical intrusion and influence, while Legilimency is the art of sensing the emotions and memories of another in such a way as to be able to tell the thoughts of the other, particularly when he is lying.

Legilimency seems to incorporate both *emotion and memory* in its lie detection. Snape implies that the way to occlude is to empty oneself of emotion. According to Snape, "The Dark Lord, for instance, almost always knows when somebody is lying to him. Only those skilled at Occlumency are able to shut down those feelings and memories that contradict the lie, and so can utter falsehoods in his presence without detection" (*OotP*, Ch. 24).

Legilimency also uses memory in lie-detection. A Legilimens knows others are lying when their statements are at odds with their foremost memories. When Voldemort confronts Harry in *PS*, although Harry shows no outward sign of guilt or deception, Voldemort can see into Harry's memory (the memory of himself receiving and holding the stone) and therefore knows "he lies". In the same way, in *HBP*, Snape knows that Harry's knowledge of the Sectumsempra curse derives from his copy of *Advanced Potion Making*, even when Harry denies this, because Harry cannot block the memory of the book swimming "hazily to the forefront of his mind" (*HBP*, Ch. 23).

Lacking the magical skill of Legilimency and the very useful Veritaserum potion, Muggles have developed rather crude methods of lie-detection. Typical lie-detection instruments, called polygraphs, do not actually detect lying behaviour, but rather measure the *emotion* of anxiety a typical person automatically experiences when telling a lie. They measure physiological variables of the sympathetic nervous system such as heart rate or blood pressure, pulse, respiration and skin conductivity. Most people get stressed and feel guilty when consciously lying and so these measures increase when they tell an untruth but stay relatively constant when telling the truth. We could say that most people are unable to *occlude* their emotions and so respond with a physiological response.

Unfortunately, truly adept liars, including (usually) those with Antisocial Personality Disorder, are, in a sense, accomplished Occlumens since they can easily fool a polygraph. Having no conscience, and being less emotional than the average person, they do not feel guilty or anxious when telling a lie, and no deviation may be shown on their polygraph tests. In short, they are able to "occlude". Snape and Voldemort would have no problems fooling a polygraph! It is for this reason, and also because normally anxious, though innocent, people also show a heightened arousal during polygraph tests, that polygraphs are notoriously unreliable and tend not to be admissible as evidence in courts of law.

There are exciting new developments in the field of Muggle lie-detection, however, which seem to approximate the wizarding technique of Legilimency. Just as Legilimency detects lies by honing in on key *memories*, so too do the modern methods of lie detection, sometimes called the "Guilty Knowledge Test" because they rely on incriminating recognition. Distinct patterns of brain activation occur when someone *recognizes* a previously seen piece of information, compared to when they do not. Functional magnetic resonance imaging scans of the brain show that parts of the brain involved in memory, specifically recognition, light up when the subject sees or hears something familiar that he recognises from personal experience—such as the scene of the crime, or the weapon used. If this is something which the subject has never before seen, then different areas of the brain will be activated.

The neuroscience of brain-scan lie-detection is still in its infancy, and there are concerns about both ethics and reliability. Once again, the wizarding world is ahead of the Muggle world.

6. Psychometrics

Psychometric devices are instruments and methods that allow psychologists to "see inside" their clients. We use pen and paper, or computerised tests which ask specific questions. Then we score the individual's results and compare their "raw score" against the average scores (or "norms") for people in roughly the same population group (the same age, language, level of schooling, etc.). This gives us a "normed score" which tells us if an individual is significantly higher or lower on the aspect or ability being measured compared to others in his age, educational and social group. We can then tell if an individual's ability or trait is significantly stronger or weaker than those of his peers.

Some psychometric devices are "projective". We present an individual with an inkblot (as in the Rorschach test) and ask him to tell us what he sees, or we show a picture (in the Thematic Apperception Test) and ask the client to tell a story about this picture, or we may ask the client to draw a person, or a tree, or tell us what animal they identify with. When you see a form in a graphic, or when you make up a story, you project aspects of yourself, your personality and your problems into the neutral picture or inkblot. By carefully analyzing the responses, psychologists are able to form hypotheses about aspects of the client's life, values and personality. These are not certainties—unlike the Sorting Hat, we *are* sometimes wrong.

Psychometric tests are a relatively quick and more objective way of measuring aptitude, personality, and pathology (what's wrong with you, psychologically speaking), and they also help to predict future behaviour. A high score on an IQ test, for example, predicts, though it does not guarantee, that you will find academic study easier than the average person. Psychometric tests are psychologists' attempts to venture into the realm of divination, though I do not think that they are a method of which Professor Trelawney would approve!

In the *Harry Potter* books, there are a number of objects which behave as magical psychometric devices, including the Sorting Hat, the Mirror of Erised, Boggarts and Patronuses. Of these, the Sorting Hat is the most widely used personality and aptitude assessment instrument.

The Sorting Hat

When first-years arrive at Hogwarts School of Witchcraft and Wizarding, the Sorting Hat is placed on their heads where, presumably, it investigates their minds and personalities before announcing the name of the house into which they will be placed. It classifies students into houses which, as McGonagall tells the first-years, will be "like your families within Hogwarts" (*PS*, Ch. 7).

It seems that there is a familial, possibly even genetic, predisposition for the traits on which the Hat sorts, to be transmitted across generations within families—thus Malfoy, Crabbe and Goyle all follow their fathers into Slytherin, while Harry and the Weasley children follow their parents into Gryffindor. There are exceptions—for example, the Patil twins are sorted into two different houses (Ravenclaw and Gryffindor), and Sirius did not get sorted into Slytherin like the rest of his family—but most families tend to aggregate in certain houses, such as the Weasleys and the Creevey boys.

The Sorting Hat may be considered to be a psychometric device in two ways: it sorts on aptitude and on personality. Your *aptitude* is your ability to do something. Psychometric tests such as IQ or intelligence tests are an example of aptitude tests. In *Harry Potter*, the Sorting Hat chooses only those with high intelligence and academic aptitude for Ravenclaw.

Personality traits are those characteristic ways of being and interacting which an individual favours and practices. There are hundreds of psychological tests which assess different personality types and place individuals in groups according to their particular combination of character traits. For example, based on your inclination and preferences regarding interacting with others in social contexts, you might be assigned the label "introvert" or "extrovert" on a test called the Myers-Briggs Type Inventory, which is based on Jungian theory.

In much the same way in *Harry Potter*, the Sorting Hat allocates people into personality types which are also given labels. Thus "Gryffindor" describes a set of people who show courage, daring, chivalry and strong nerve. Those who are primarily just, loyal, honest, patient and hard-working are called "Hufflepuffs". We call "Ravenclaws" those people who value intelligence, quick-wittedness and academic pursuits. And finally, we assign the label of "Slytherin" to those who prioritise cunning, who put themselves first and believe that the end justifies the means.

As with psychometric tests, being given a label or a typology does not mean that you *cannot* behave in different ways; it simply registers your preferred or habitual way of being. Of course, introverts can stand up and given speeches and even become the life and soul of the party; it's just that they usually choose not to, and may find it exhausting or a little "unnatural". If you are right-handed, then with a great deal of effort and concentration, you *can* form letters with your left hand, but usually, you simply automatically take your pen with your right hand and start writing. In the same way, these primary personality traits are what "come naturally" for those sorted into these houses. Thus in *GoF*, Cedric, a Hufflepuff, is able to display courage and nerve, while Harry, not a Ravenclaw by nature, is nevertheless able to use his brains to figure out the Sphinx's riddle.

Our preferences also tend to reflect what we, as individuals, value. The Sorting Hat also assesses what *value* the students assign to the assessed traits. Thus, although Harry has, according to the hat, "a nice thirst to prove (him)self" (*PS*, Ch. 7), he values integrity and courage more highly and so is sorted into Gryffindor.

This also helps us understand the puzzle of Hermione. Measured on aptitude and even on preferred habitual ways of behaving and engaging with the world, she should, by rights, be sorted into Gryffindor. But Hermione tells us later in *PS* what she values even higher than intelligence. Having cracked Snape's fiendish logic puzzle with the different potion and poison bottles, Hermione tells Harry: "You're a great wizard, you know." An embarrassed Harry replies that he is not as good as she is, to which Hermione retorts: "Me!... Books! And cleverness! There are more important things— friendship and bravery" (*PS*, Ch. 16). We see here that Hermione assigns a higher value to courage than to cleverness, and it is for this reason that the Hat sorts her into Gryffindor.

Good, reliable psychometric devices also measure *traits* (enduring personality characteristics and abilities) rather than *states* (temporary states of feeling). The Sorting Hat does well in this regard—it measures the permanent trait of courage in Harry, rather than his acute, but temporary, state of nervous fear and anxiety when the Hat is plonked on his head in front of the assembled crowd.

The Sorting Hat has told Harry that it is never wrong| in psychological jargon it has *reliability* (it is accurate) and *validity* (it measures what it aims to measure). This would seem to imply that it also has *predictive validity*—in other words, that it can predict future behaviour based on the abilities and personality characteristics it has measured in the present or past. Certainly, the Hat itself does not hesitate to make predictions, saying to Harry, "You could be great, you know, it's all here in your head."

This predictive ability is interesting, particularly when we think about it in relation to Peter Pettigrew and Severus Snape. Pettigrew's strongest, most prominent or most highly valued trait was courage;

that is presumably why he was sorted into Gryffindor. Does this mean that we can still expect some courageous behaviour in a good direction from Pettigrew? Or has he already demonstrated his courage by being the only Death Eater brave enough to seek out his evil master and face the repulsive abomination that is the bodiless Voldemort? If the Sorting Hat has measured Snape and found him to be first and foremost a self-serving Slytherin, then does this lend weight to the theories that Snape is bad, or at least playing both sides against the middle to serve his own interests?

The Mirror of Erised

In some ways, the Mirror of Erised may also be understood as a diagnostic psychometric device. When a character looks into this Mirror, he sees not his reflection but his heart's deepest desire. Thus when Harry looks into the mirror, he sees his parents and long-gone members of his extended family, which tells us that Harry's deepest longing (certainly at the time of the first book) was to have some sense of family and belonging. We know, however, that Ron's most heartfelt desire is to outshine all his brothers (and Harry) in achieving the glory and recognition that being head boy and Quidditch champion would bring.

We could infer a great deal about certain characters' personalities, motivations and ultimate loyalties if only we knew what they would see when standing before the mirror. Some we can infer—that Voldemort, for example, would see himself as immortal and powerful. Indeed, Rowling has confirmed this in interview (The Leaky Cauldron and MuggleNet interview, *The Leaky Cauldron*, July 2005), where she also refused to confirm what Dumbledore would see (we can only guess it is not more socks!). But of other characters —Malfoy, Kreacher, Lupin, Fawkes—we can only speculate wildly. And what, oh what, would Snape see?

Boggarts

Boggarts can also be used as psychometric devices to ascertain the person's deepest fear. They can be considered to be projective, rather than objective, tests, since the individual's worst fear is projected onto the shape-shifter. It tells us an enormous amount about the individual—because of Boggarts, we know that Hermione is strongly (though unrealistically) terrified of academic failure, that

Harry is scared of what fear does to him, that good-hearted Lupin fears lycanthropic transformation much more than he fears detection and exposure, and that Molly's love for her children is so strong that she fears their death more than her own.

Again, we are denied a deeper knowledge of Snape through the Boggart. When the pupils arrive in the staffroom (*PoA*) to practice on the Boggart, Snape excuses himself from the room. Is this because Snape does not want to have knowledge of Harry's deepest fear, for fear that the Dark Lord will divine this and use it against Harry? *(Trust Snape!)* Or is it so that Harry (and the reader) cannot learn his worst fear? (*Snape is a very bad man!*)

Patronuses

We can also use Patronuses as projective psychometric devices because they reveal aspects of the character's personality. Thus Hermione's Patronus is an industrious otter always preparing for the future, while Cho Chang's Patronus is a graceful, beautiful, but largely decorative swan. Dumbledore's Patronus, a phoenix, embodies the essence of good that cannot be destroyed, that will be reborn from the ashes of death and destruction.

Patronuses also reveal the individual's perceived sources of inner strength—thus Harry's is a powerful animal which resembles aspects of his father (since James's Animagus form was a stag), and Tonks's Patronus takes the form of Lupin.

W.O.M.B.A.T.s

In her online Wizards' Ordinary Magic and Basic Aptitude Test, Rowling has actually given us Muggles a psychometric test which assesses both our acquired knowledge of canon and the wizarding world, as well as our probable aptitude based on our responses to questions for which we can have no definitive answers, only educated guesses.

7. Psychopharmacology

Psychopharmacology refers to the use, under a medical doctor's supervision, of medications which target the brain and nervous system to improve mood, control aberrant behaviour and minimise negative and distressing symptoms. Common types of psychiatric medications used in the Muggle world include anti-depressants (such as Prozac), anti-anxiety medication (tranquilisers), mood stabilisers (such as lithium) and anti-psychotics (such as Haldol).

In the wizarding world, there are many potions to cure (or induce!) *physiological* ailments, but there are also a variety of potions and other substances which seem to be psychoactive. When imbibed, they lead to an improvement in mood and psychological well-being.

Madam Pomfrey's calming draught, which she sometimes administers to pupils overwrought with examination anxiety, seems to be the wizard equivalent of a tranquiliser, as does the Draught of Peace, which calms anxiety and soothes agitation. Sleeping draughts appear to work in much the same way as Muggle sleeping tablets, and without any of the side effects!

There is, sadly, no Muggle equivalent of the truly marvellous potions: the *Amortensia* Love Potion, the Elixir to Induce Euphoria and fabulous Felix Felicis, which not only tweaks opportunity in favour of the drinker but also induces a marvellous sense of self-confidence and a tremendous sense of opportunity. We see, though, that even in the world of magic, there can be nasty side effects—if an individual takes too high a dose of Felix Felicis, he suffers from giddiness, recklessness and overconfidence.

There are quite a few potions which affect the cognitive (or thinking) abilities of the brain, including Memory Potions (which seemingly work to enhance the drinker's memory), Wit-sharpening Potion (which presumably makes a person think more clearly) and Dr Ubbly's Oblivious Unction, which helps to heal the scarring left by damaging thoughts. This is what Madam Pomfrey gives to Ron after his encounter with the brain tentacles at the Ministry of Magic. That would be a really useful potion in my work, as a lot of my time is spent trying to help those with low self-esteem erase the scars left by negative beliefs about themselves.

Hate Potion (presumably the opposite of *Amortensia*) would also come in useful for those who persist in believing themselves in love with people who are uninterested, already in a relationship with someone else, or abusive by nature. This potion helps the drinker see the worst faults and habits of the target person. This potion seems to be a sort of "He's just not that interested in you" elixir!

Wolfsbane potion seems to work as a sort of mood-stabilizer, preventing the werewolf from succumbing to the extremes of his urges by helping him keep his mind during full moon phases.

Veritaserum is a potion which forces the witch or wizard who drinks it to tell the truth. We see Dumbledore using it on Barty Crouch Jr in *GoF*, and Harry narrowly escapes getting it from both Professors Umbridge and Snape. There are some Muggle approximations of Veritaserum. A variety of drugs, including sodium amytal and sodium pentothal, seem to loosen the tongue by weakening the inhibiting resolve to withhold information. Unlike with Veritaserum, however, these Muggle drugs often cause problems. The subject may fill in the gaps with invented material, or may form false memories in response to suggestive or leading questions. In short, with Muggle truth serums, we are still not completely sure how much of what the subject says is actually true.

As any wizard healer knows, the way to cure the depression left by an encounter with a Dementor is to immediately eat some chocolate. It seems that chocolate is therefore a wizard anti-depressant! Happily, this is one aspect of magic that Muggles *do* seem to have discovered—many of us Muggles turn to chocolate when we are feeling blue, and it turns out that there may well be a psychopharmacological basis to why we feel better afterwards.

There are a number of substances in good-quality chocolate which, taken in moderation, can improve our mood and overall feeling of wellbeing. Phenylethylamine is a chemical in the body that is similar to an amphetamine, and it can produce both emotional highs and lows. Researchers believe that our body releases phenylethylamine when we are in love, thus producing the emotional highs associated with romance, though whether any of the phenylethylamine in chocolate actually reaches the brain has not yet been determined.

Theobromine, also found in chocolate, is an alkaloid; like caffeine, it is a stimulant and can be addictive, but it works as an anti-depressant in the body. On a side note, theobromine is toxic to dogs and other animals, so it's just as well Harry never gave chocolate any to Snuffles, but a pity he did not give any to Scabbers!

Another psychoactive substance found in chocolate is anandamide, which might act in the brain similarly to tetrahydrocannabinol (THC), which is found in marijuana. Don't expect chocolate to be on a list of banned substances anytime soon, though; you would need to eat about 25 pounds of chocolate to feel effects similar to marijuana!

Chocolate also contains caffeine, which acts as a stimulant, perhaps speeding up and warming up the body weakened by a Dementor attack, and helping to focus the disoriented mind.

The sugar in chocolate would cause a rapid, but short-lived, boost in energy and might improve mood by raising serotonin levels in the body. Seratonin is a neurotransmitter, or chemical messenger in the nervous system. Where we have too little serotonin, we suffer from the constellation of symptoms which are collectively known as "depression". Most modern anti-depressants work by boosting the amount of serotonin available to the brain, and therefore work to alleviate these symptoms. Chocolate (like many refined carbohydrates) contains tryptophan, which is the mother substance of serotonin and may therefore boost the mood for a very short while. This is why, when suffering an attack of the blues (or should that be "an attack of the Dementors"?), most Muggles reach for chocolate, ice-cream and cake, rather than for celery and salad!

I can imagine Jo Rowling smiling when she decided to make chocolate the treatment to counteract the after-effects of a Dementor attack. She has publicly admitted to having suffered from depression in her own life, and may have found a block or three of strictly medicinal chocolate more than a little helpful in giving her a lift. I wonder if she knew how close to the medical mark she actually was?

8. Psychotherapy

Psychotherapy is that branch of psychology which deals with the actual help that a client receives to help him or her get better. Therapy includes the usual "talk therapy", plus more active counselling where the client is taught ways of managing their problems, cognitive behavioural therapy—which challenges dysfunctional ways of thinking and behaving—while specific methods such as dream analysis and hypnotherapy help the client at deeper, less conscious levels.

In the wizarding world, psychoactive help comes not only from potions and chocolate, but also from charms, such as the Cheering Charm, which makes one feel temporarily happy and giggly, and memory-modifying charms such as *Obliviate* which can help the traumatised person forget distressing memories.

EMDR (Eye Movement Desensitization and Reprocessing) is one Muggle psychological treatment which may work a little like memory-modifying charms. Although this technique will not make the subject completely forget the trauma suffered, it will help to make the memory much less distressing. This is one treatment for trauma that *does* work just like magic! Even better, EMDR does not cause brain damage!

In the *Harry Potter* books, the Imperius Curse is described almost as most people would imagine hypnosis to work. One powerful person magically puts another, presumably feeble-minded or weak-willed person into a trance with the aim of dominating him. The spell-caster can then control and manipulate his subject, who surrenders to the oblivious bliss of having another control his mind. Just to set the record straight—hypnotherapy is nothing like this!

Hypnosis is not mind-control. All hypnosis is in fact self-hypnosis, and when in trance, the mind is conscious and alert. If hypnosis were powerful enough to control another's behaviour with mere suggestion, then we would all have instant cures for our bad habits, our depression, our relationships, and all our problems! There would be no need for any other type of therapy, or for medications. As a psychologist who practises hypnotherapy, I find it very useful as an adjunct therapy, merely one more method in my toolbox of techniques, to help my clients. It does perhaps utilise the subconscious mind and the brain's right hemisphere more than conventional "talk therapy", but it is no *Imperius*!

In the Muggle world, skilled psychologists are able to use dream analysis to help the client access the wisdom of their subconscious mind, but this method is a far cry from Professor Trelawney's "cookbook approach", where she advocates a one-to-one correlation between certain symbols and specific meanings or predictions for the future.

As an interesting aside, Trelawney's prescribed textbook for dream analysis is "The Dream Oracle" by Inigo Imago. The term *Imago* is in fact one from the world of psychology, but it has nothing to do with dreams. Imago Therapy (pioneered by Harville Hendrix) is a type of relationship therapy which focuses on your *imago*, which is the individualised unconscious template or image of the ideal life partner we all devise based on our parents and childhood experiences.

The Phoenix

It seems to me that the most powerful symbol of hope and healing in the *Harry Potter* books is Fawkes, the Phoenix. At times when Harry is a state of pain or despair—when, for example, Harry lies dying from the poisonous bite of the Basilisk in the Chamber of Secrets, or when he is duelling Voldemort in *GoF*, the cry or song of the Phoenix brings a rebirth of hope and strength in his heart and he is able to continue his fight: "It was the sound of hope to Harry… the most beautiful and welcome thing he had ever heard in his life… and it was almost as though a friend was speaking in his ear" (*GoF*, Ch. 34).

After Dumbledore's death, Fawkes the Phoenix sings a sad song of lament which lightens the hearts of the despairing and devastated members of the Order of the Phoenix:

Somewhere out in the darkness, a phoenix was singing in a way Harry had never heard before: a stricken lament of terrible beauty. And Harry felt, as he had felt about phoenix song before, that the music was inside him, not without: it was his own grief turned magically to song … it seemed to ease their pain a little to listen to the sound of their mourning. (*HBP*, Ch. 29)

This is one of the key processes of therapy, too—for the client to speak his inner pain and hear himself doing so, and for the therapist to turn the pain into a healing song and reflect this back to the client.

It is as if Fawkes' compassion (his ability to feel *for* others) as well as his empathy (his ability to feel *with* others, to himself feel what they are feeling) provides healing. This, really, is what psychologists attempt to do in therapy, to understand and empathise with the client's suffering. When another person truly understands and validates our pain, it is as if we share it, and the load becomes lighter to carry.

There is another way in which Fawkes heals through compassion and empathy. When he is moved by Harry's emotional pain, his physical injuries, and his unswerving loyalty to Dumbledore, Fawkes cries tears which land on Harry's wounds (from the Basilisk in *CoS* and from the Acromantula in *GoF*) and heal these otherwise deadly and incurable injuries. In the same way, in the world of psychotherapy, the therapist must have the courage to hear her client's pain with the non-judgemental understanding and true empathy that can help a client to heal wounds which have long caused them suffering and have impaired their ability to function in the world.

Phoenixes also help in more practical ways. They are able to help carry very heavy loads, and this certainly mirrors how therapists attempt to help lighten the load which their clients have to carry, by means of encouragement, advice, validation, and helping clients to find meaning in their life experiences. In *CoS*, Fawkes brings Harry the Sword of Gryffindor in the Sorting Hat—a very practical and useful tool which helps Harry defeat the Basilisk. In therapy, too, counselling psychologists like to equip their clients with very practical coping skills and "tools" to manage their lives and conditions more effectively.

The Phoenix's Birth-Death-Rebirth Cycle as a Metaphor for Therapy

The most unusual characteristic of the phoenix is its magical ability to be reborn from the ashes of its own fiery death. It seems to me that this birth-death-rebirth cycle can be viewed as a metaphor of the therapeutic process. Clients are individuals who have developed dysfunctional patterns of feeling, thinking and behaving at least partly in an attempt to deal with some difficult aspect of development or distressing life experience. They need to release the symptom and the function which the symptom serves, to grow and become stronger. They need to replace the symptom with a healthier, more functional way of behaving or thinking.

In short, the dysfunctional symptom or aspect of the individual's character needs to "die" and be reborn in a new, revitalised and healthier form. The old you needs to pass away in order to make way for the new you.

Many clients, surprisingly, cling tenaciously to their dysfunction and would often prefer to continue suffering than risk changing and relinquishing their disorder. One client recently told me, "I don't know how much of me is me and how much of me is the depression. Who would I be without it? How would I get my family's sympathy and attention if I was healthy?" This client needs to allow her depression to wither and die in order that she can be reborn to health and vitality, and to do so, she needs to find healthy new ways of defining her identity and getting the nurturance she requires, since these are the functions which the depression serves in her life.

Unlike the Phoenix's resurrection from the ashes, when he redevelops into the same bird, we want our clients to be birds of a slightly different, healthier feather after the transformative process of therapy.

It is with great caution and tentativeness that I respectfully suggest these similarities between Phoenixes and therapists, and between the life-death-rebirth cycle and therapy, since I know we psychologists are nowhere in the Phoenix's league! I do wish we were as strong and powerful as these magical birds, but I am afraid to say that we Muggle therapists must muddle along as best we can without the help of magic, although I am convinced that the core of our wands would almost certainly be Phoenix feathers!

9. Conclusion

I am fairly sure that, with a couple of exceptions, J. K. Rowling did not consciously *intend* many of the parallels between her characters and inventions, and aspects of psychology. How much more remarkable, then, that her stories and characterizations are true to the essence of so much in the world of psychology. For me, it strengthens the reality and integrity of the books that they stand up to the analysis of psychological theory and practice. These little nuggets of psychological truth stud their way through the stories and are there to be mined, adding to our *Harry Potter* riches.

I hope that this paper has added another layer to your understanding and appreciation of the *Harry Potter* books, and that it will deepen your awareness as you read the conclusion to the series.

LOSS AND GRIEF IN *HARRY POTTER*

Victoria Hippard

"It was cruel," said Dumbledore softly, "that you and Sirius had such a short time together. A brutal ending to what should have been a long and happy relationship."

—J. K. Rowling, *Harry Potter and the Half-Blood Prince*

Witnessing death in the wizarding world becomes a rite of passage, a trauma that enables one to see winged thestrals, the black horses that pull the carriages entering Hogwarts. From the opening chapter of J. K. Rowling's *Harry Potter and the Sorcerer's Stone*, we learn that Harry faces the aftermath of the death of his parents, an attempt on his life, an interesting but disfiguring scar, mistreatment and loneliness. I begin my observations on loss and grief in the *Harry Potter* novels with some relevant comments from author J. K. Rowling. I will then explore some of the images of the underworld in Harry's adventures. Experiences beneath and between are metaphors for psychological growth and individuation, images enjoyed by both Rowling and C. G. Jung. There is no image that depicts the yearning of loss more poignantly than Rowling's description of Harry standing in front of the Mirror of Erised. In this presentation I include a film clip of this, as well as scenes from other *Harry Potter* films to illustrate my comments.

There is, however, another traumatized child in addition to Harry Potter worthy of our reflections. In the sixth book, *Harry Potter and the Half-Blood Prince*, Rowling describes the life of Tom Marvolo Riddle, also known as Voldemort, Harry's antagonist. In addition to other atrocities, we learn in *Goblet of Fire* that Voldemort kills his father, along with the rest of the Riddles seated at dinner with his father one fateful night. His childhood, however imaginary, provides food for thought about emotional deprivations in early childhood.

Merely demonizing the villain Voldemort limits the possibilities of a deeper knowledge about the evil of which wizards, Muggles, and humans are capable. The past, a focus of Jungian depth psychology, yields important information about Voldemort and Harry. I will explore both Harry's and Voldemort's reactions to losses within the context of some theories about mourning in childhood, including mirroring and reflection, identification and internalization, and alchemy. In conclusion, I will comment on Rowling's messages about vulnerabilities.

Childhood experiences of upheaval and trauma often find their way into artistic images and literature. Although Joanne Rowling was in her early twenties when her mother died, she was twelve when her mother was diagnosed with multiple sclerosis. As an adolescent, Joanne watched as her mother's health and abilities rapidly declined. In an interview she has said that death and bereavement, and what death means, are central themes in all seven books (Jones, "Why Harry's Hot"). Rowling reports that much of *Sorcerer's Stone* was planned and written before 1993, before the birth of her first daughter and the death of her mother. She acknowledges that, in retrospect, her mother's death exerted the more significant influence in her subsequent writing. She explains: "I think that the only event in my own life that changed the direction of *Harry Potter* was the death of my mother. I only fully realized upon re-reading the book how many of my own feelings about losing my mother I had given Harry" (Weir). Rowling's realization that feelings of loss and grief guide her in writing *Harry Potter* is a valuable insight about how unknown, unconscious processes work in the psyche. Loss of a loved one conjures up attendant feelings of abandonment and loneliness, especially in childhood.

Harry Potter visits the underworld, as all heroes must. He endures losses and sorrows that usher him into the depths geographically and intrapsychically as he travels within the realms in and under Hogwarts. Such subterranean travels offer lasting legacies. The realities of trauma for Harry combine with the metaphor of child as pilgrim as he descends into the depths of his unconscious.

C. G. Jung writes in "Psychology and Alchemy":

The myth of the descent as universally exemplified in the myth of the hero is to show that only in the region of danger (watery abyss, cavern, forest, island, castle, etc.) can one find the 'treasure hard to attain' (jewel, virgin, life-potion, victory over death). The dread and resistance which every natural human being experiences when it comes to delving too deeply into himself is, at the bottom, the fear of the journey to Hades. (*CW* 12: 439)

Depth psychology is the term used when referring to Jung's theories as well as the ideas of James Hillman and other contemporary Jungian analysts. In a nutshell, achieving sufficient self-knowledge requires the exploration of the depths of one's personality. This includes the shadow, which refers to our unknown and often less than desirable characteristics. Harry's similarities to Voldemort cause horror and, more importantly, self-reflection. In Rowling's novels, the action that takes place underneath is of more lasting importance than all of the flying around on broomsticks that occurs during a Quidditch match. As each year passes, Harry gains more trust and relies more on the assistance of others. His defensive "loner" stance is replaced by connections with others more trustworthy than those in his past. New growth and increasing consciousness comes from such compost as Harry finds within and below Hogwarts.

Moaning Myrtle is a ghost who "lives" in the girl's bathroom at Hogwarts. Killed by whatever lurks below the bathroom, an important part of the plot in the second book, *Chamber of Secrets*, Moaning Myrtle cries and sobs from her perch on the tank of a toilet. We find ourselves in the underworld goddess Hekate's realm, a place of howling, hysteria, and waste. Like the shades with unfinished business in M. Night Shyamalan's film *The Sixth Sense*, Myrtle searches for release, as well as harboring a childish revenge towards Olive Hornby for laughing at her (299). When the boys find the secret passageway in Moaning Myrtle's bathroom, Rowling writes: "it was like rushing down an endless, slimy, dark slide … [Harry] knew that he was falling deeper below the school than even the dungeons." Littered with small animal bones, "the tunnel was quiet as the grave" (301–2). [Discussion of film clip (Scene 29: *Harry Potter and the Chamber of Secrets*)].

How do we distinguish between healthy grief and pathological mourning? Should we worry about Harry's mental health? As Ron Weasley wisely counsels his friend, "hearing voices no one else can hear isn't a good sign, even in the wizarding world" (*CoS* 145). In *Order of the Phoenix*, Harry realizes that Luna Lovegood and Neville Longbottom have also lost parents. Sherwin Nuland, physician and author, tells us that the death of his mother when he was eleven

shaped his life. He writes that "all that I have become and much that
I have not become, I trace directly or indirectly to her
death" (Nuland xviii). Many who lose parents at an early age can
only describe their memories and feelings at a later time when
adulthood allows expression. The ways in which the characters
Harry, Luna, Voldemort, and Neville react to their losses reflect
Rowling's insightful ideas about childhood psychology.

Feelings of depression and sadness are understandably associated
with loss and grief. Rowling admits to her own feelings of emptiness
and depression that intentionally show up in her creations, the
Dementors. Described as a type of witchery and evil, these icy soul
suckers "drain peace, hope, and happiness out of the air around
them" (*PoA* 140). Coldness equated with evil is consistent with the
icy barrenness in the seventh circle of Hell described in Dante's
Inferno. Rowling describes depression as the "absence of hope. That
very deadened feeling, which is so different from feeling sad. Sad
hurts but it's a healthy feeling ... Depression is very
different" (Treneman 7). The distinction between sadness and
depression is as important for Rowling as it is in the lives of her
characters. Holding on to destructive thoughts can also leave scars.
In *Order of the Phoenix*, Harry notices that "there were still deep welts
on his forearms where the brain's tentacles had wrapped around
him. According to Madam Pomfrey, thoughts could leave deeper
scarring than almost anything else" (847). [Film clip and discussion
of Harry's encounter with a Dementor (Scene 7: *Harry Potter and the
Prisoner of Azkaban*)].

Harry and Voldemort share the tragedy of early parental loss with
Sartre, Friedrich Nietzsche, and Edgar Allan Poe (Harris 47, 83,
191). The popular film star, James Dean, whose persona remains
alive in spite of his early death, lost his mother at nine years of age
(58). Rock star and astute business woman Madonna lost her mother
when she was six, setting the stage for the "necessity" that Madonna
"create herself" (125). The knowledge of death came early to the
melancholy Abraham Lincoln, whose mother died when he was nine
(196). Of particular interest is the background of Adolf Hitler, who
had lost both parents by seventeen (196). Like Hitler, Voldemort
tries to take over the world, the fictional world of wizards and
Muggles. Voldemort sums up his grandiose worldview when he tells
Dumbledore in *Order of the Phoenix* that "greatness inspires envy,

envy engenders spite, spite spawns lies" (443). His psychological defenses repel consciousness and prevent his acceptance of responsibility.

Voldemort's family history, as pieced together from Dumbledore and Harry's trips down memory lane in *Half-Blood Prince*, suggests a dysfunctional, tragic environment in which to raise a child. His mother's death and absence of supportive caregivers predispose Voldemort to overwhelming feelings of loss and abandonment. Mastering his legacies of catastrophe, along with the resultant emptiness and insecurity, proves impossible. Harry suffers some neglect, to be sure, during his days living under the cupboard at the Dursleys', but he is not psychologically overwhelmed, even as additional traumas occur.

Earl Grollman writes about the differences between normal reactions of bereavement and more complicated, distorted reactions, often a difficult judgment call. Suggesting that concern is not so much with the symptom as with the intensity of the symptom, Grollman specifies that pathological mourning "is a *continued* denial of reality even many months after the funeral, or a *prolonged* bodily distress, or a *persistent* panic, or an *extended* guilt, or an *unceasing* idealization, or an *enduring* apathy and anxiety, or an *unceasing* hostile reaction to the deceased and others" (21). Although Harry reports a variety of unpleasant sensations that emanate from the scar on his forehead, we know that these are not symptoms of unresolved mourning. On the other hand, Voldemort harbors several of the symptoms mentioned by Grollman. The intensity is there as well, but it is the apathy, the absence of feeling, that is most disturbing and dangerous.

At the end of *Order of the Phoenix*, Rowling depicts Harry's powerful feelings of loss. In his acute state of mourning for his godfather Sirius, Harry "felt the white-hot anger lick his insides, blazing in the terrible emptiness, filling him with the desire to hurt Dumbledore for his calmness and his empty words" (823). When Dumbledore assures him that his suffering is part of being human, "Harry roared, and he seized one of the delicate silver instruments from the spindle-legged table beside him and flung it across the room. It shattered into a hundred tiny pieces against the wall" (824). More illustrative of the mourning of a sudden loss than the volatile nature of adolescence, Harry strikes out in his powerlessness and desolation at yet another loss, and Dumbledore accepts all of Harry's feelings. Although dramatic, his actions are understandable and indicate signs of healing.

As created by Rowling, Voldemort's situation is the more complicated and extreme. Having killed his father and lacking any memory of his deceased mother, he exists with no empathy for others. When Harry asks Dumbledore about Voldemort's ability to feel the loss of his parts when under the Horcrux spell, Dumbledore sums up the extent of Voldemort's alienation. He tells Harry that "these crucial parts of himself have been detached for so long, he does not feel as we do" (507). Identification with feelings of loss and grief and the struggle for individuation in *Harry Potter* are deep areas of resonance for readers.

In his effort to evade death, as well as to gain immortality, Voldemort splits his soul into seven parts, hiding six pieces in cleverly selected objects that become quests for Dumbledore and Harry. The magical spell of fracturing one's soul into a Horcrux, or in Voldemort's case, Horcruxes, is a carefully guarded and dangerous process. Each time Voldemort splits off a part of himself into a Horcrux, the greatest act of evil, murder, is required. Rowling makes it clear that killing claims the soul of the murderer as well as the life of the victim. Six people die to complete his spells, but in the process Voldemort fractures his spirit. These detached parts represent Voldemort's emotionally fractured psyche and soul. His "split soul" remains alive but requires the blood and often the host bodies of others. Voldemort keeps one part, "the seventh part of his soul, however maimed, resides inside his regenerated body… without that, he has no self at all" (*HBP* 503).

This is not the split personality of pop psychology, which suggests that one part is unaware of another part. Voldemort's dissociations occur at an early age, and eventually lead to his complete disregard of others. This type of psychological splitting is common in those diagnosed with anti-social personality disorder. Voldemort displays the characteristics of one commonly referred to as a psychopath. He has failed to develop a conscience or inner consciousness. Dumbledore tells Harry that "it is the unknown we fear when we look upon death and darkness, nothing more" (566). Voldemort fears the darkness, as Dumbledore explains, the place where the shadow resides as well as the place wherein consciousness is discovered.

Dumbledore does not fear darkness or death. As Dumbledore reassures Harry in *Sorcerer's Stone*, "After all, to the well-organized mind, death is but the next great adventure" (297). At the end of the sixth book, *Half-Blood Prince*, Severus Snape kills Dumbledore with the Killing Curse. Harry and his friends barely escape Voldemort and the Death Eaters and, in shock, manage to tend to their wounded. Devastated, they listen when "in the darkness, a phoenix was singing in a way Harry had never heard before: a stricken lament of terrible beauty" (613–14). For many readers, mourning for Dumbledore continues even after the cover of the sixth book is closed.

It is Harry who requests that the assembled Hogwarts faculty allow the students to remain for Dumbledore's funeral in order that they may say good-bye. However, not until the funeral is underway is Harry overwhelmed with feelings all too familiar to mourners everywhere: "and then without warning, it swept over him, the dreadful truth, more completely and undeniably than it had until now, Dumbledore was dead, gone" (644). But the apprenticeship between Harry and Dumbledore does not end with Dumbledore's death. In alchemy, the archetypes of wizard and apprentice, *senex* and *puer*, wise old man and divine child, survive in the unconscious.

Mourning, too, is included as a part of the alchemical process that produces the philosopher's stone, as well as psychological consciousness. Referred to as the greening of the stone, mourning contributes to the individuation of the ego. Comparing an intense period of mourning in his life to a greening process, Robert Romanyshyn "recalls the sound of my own soul becoming green" (60). As part of the soul-making darkness of the *nigredo*, Romanyshyn describes the "green consciousness" as a "force which drives the flower and runs deeply and silently in our veins, plunges into the dark soil of the earth, where all is night" (60). These alchemically inspired comparisons gently move tragedy and loss to a re-integration of psyche. The reality of pain and suffering merges with the metaphorical meanings of death and rebirth. Even Dumbledore's death, the death of the ruler or king, can be understood metaphorically as the removal of the old in preparation for the new. Edward Edinger mentions that "dragon, toad, king, sun, and lion" are often subjects of *mortificatio*, along with the "figure of purity and innocence" (155). Of course, until the final book is read, we cannot be sure that Dumbledore has yielded the throne.

Mirroring and reflection in childhood aid in the identification with and internalization of lost parents, important aspects of the healing process. Because of a concrete level of understanding in the younger child, mirroring can be quite literal, as when the wicked queen in *Snow White* asks, "Mirror, mirror on the wall, who is fairest of all?" However, interest in mirroring and reflection existed in the time before Disney popularized the queen's self-serving question. The queen received more than she bargained for, as do we all when we truly seek our reflections.

Something happens to Harry Potter when he finds the Mirror of Erised in *Sorcerer's Stone*. Large and ornate, the following words are carved on top of the mirror: "I show not your face but your heart's desire" (206). Of course Harry has seen other mirrors at the Dursleys'. But those mirrors only reflected his rapidly growing and unruly head of hair, which always seems to need cutting. Of course, this rapid growth of hair, and the underlying power it promises, bothers the Dursleys more than it does Harry. The reflection he sees in this mirror surprises and strangely comforts him. [Film clip and discussion of Scene 23, *The Sorcerer's Stone*)].

In his comments to Harry about the seduction of unrequited desires, Dumbledore gives warning that an idealized, two-dimensional memory of Harry's parents will not serve him in his pursuits or enhance his emerging individuation. For Harry, information about his parents at different levels of development proves helpful. It provides a sort of catching up for him. As an eleven-year-old, Harry "sees" his parents and can identify with the tangible similarities he observes. The psychological defense of identification is defined as

an automatic, unconscious mental process whereby an individual becomes like another person.... [I]t is a natural accompaniment of maturation and mental development and aids in the learning process.... Separation from a loved person becomes more tolerable as a result of identification with him. (Moore and Fine 50)

Identification provides Harry with the opportunity to internalize previously unknown and unavailable aspects of his deceased mother and father. The more he is able to internalize images of his parents, the better he can tolerate the inevitable tasks of separation and individuation. Rowling provides a good example of the older Harry's struggle with separation from the image of his father in *Prisoner of Azkaban* when he realizes, reluctantly and with help from Hermione, that the Patronus he conjures is himself and not his father.

Harry and Voldemort are equally challenged in how each might resolve their respective struggles in regard to absent parents, especially their fathers. Considered by many as an important aspect of developing identity, identification with the parent of the same sex is negotiated differently by Harry and Voldemort.

Harry has a tricky situation in which he must discern as accurate a picture as possible of his father, James Potter, based upon the negative information he gleans from Snape, as well as the somewhat idealized recollections from Hagrid, Sirius, and others. Voldemort, however, lacks the benefit of available parents of either sex. There is little information available to him on which to base impressions, desirable or undesirable, about his parents. Like the tragic hero, Oedipus, Voldemort kills his father, but unlike Oedipus, Voldemort is clear about his intention. He relies upon fantasies and distortions that he has created during an isolated childhood. The psychoanalytic view suggests that he seeks retaliation for abandonment; for Voldemort this is not the ancient call of a primeval abandonment, but an all too real emotionally empty life.

Harry's experiences of inadequate fathering or parenting occur at the hands of the Dursleys, a split, in psychological terms, which can lead to idealizing the absent, unknown father or parents. In *Order of the Phoenix*, fifteen-year-old Harry learns that his father could be a cruel tease, especially toward the younger Severus Snape. Daring detection by a nearby Snape, Harry takes a look into Snape's memories by means of the Pensieve. Harry sees the fifteen-year-old Snape, his godfather, Sirius, as well as his father, in Professor Flitwick's class. Harry revels in the fact that James Potter looks just like him, unruly hair and all. Then he watches as his father taunts the unpopular Snape with spells from his wand, until stopped by a girl standing nearby. His mother, the youthful Lily, tells an immature James, "You think you're funny... But you're just an arrogant, bullying toerag, Potter. Leave him *alone*" (647).

Rowling implies that Harry gains empathy for how it feels to be humiliated. He has now witnessed the arrogant, unkind side of his father. Integrating the knowledge that his father lacks perfection offers Harry, or any child, a more authentic and realistic internalization of his missing parent. With a more balanced inner image of the parent, one is able to accept oneself more honestly. With this knowledge, however, comes the pain of separation. In "The Psychology of the Child" Jung writes that "identity does not make consciousness possible; it is only separation, detachment, and agonizing confrontation through opposition that produces consciousness and insight" (*CW* 9.1: 289). In contrast, Voldemort never acquires insight and the much needed human quality of empathy. He cannot give what he himself has never received.

Harry is presented with another mirror in *Order of the Phoenix*, Rowling's fifth novel. Grief-stricken after the death of his godfather, Harry finds a forgotten package from Sirius at the bottom of his trunk. He recalls his friend's words: "Use it if you need me, all right?" When Harry unwraps the small package, "Out fell a small, square mirror. It looked old; it was certainly dirty. Harry held it up to his face and saw his own reflection looking back at him" (857). Instructions scribbled on the back of the mirror explain that this is a two-way mirror that will summon Sirius, just as it did when Harry's father used it during his days at Hogwarts. When he calls out the name of his departed mentor and confidant, "His breath misted the surface of the glass. He held the mirror even closer...but the eyes blinking back at him through the fog were definitely his own" (858). In disappointment, Harry throws the mirror into his trunk and it breaks. Older now than when he experienced the reunion with his parents in the Mirror of Erised, he still longs for a real connection with his departed godfather.

Gone is the Mirror of Erised, broken is the reflection of Sirius, but, for Harry, the mirroring of the diviner remains. As he matures and accepts his wizard world responsibilities, his mirroring becomes that of "many reflections of [his] soul" (Miller 398). Unlike Voldemort, Harry is capable, psychologically, of mourning and integrating the broken pieces and losses in his life, rather than enduring a fractured existence.

Rowling highlights the age-old vulnerability and powerlessness of children. In *Sorcerer's Stone*, Harry and Hermione listen as the centaur

Ronan issues a mysterious warning: "'Always the innocent are the first victims,' he said. 'So it has been for ages past, so it is now.....
The forest hides many secrets'" (253). Interestingly enough, Rowling selects a centaur as spokesperson, a highly intuitive and knowledgeable mythological animal that, according to Hagrid, does not trust human beings. Her empathy for the feelings of children, whether wounded by loss, neglect, inadequate parenting or all of the above, does not extend to adults, especially superficial and unthinking types. The vulnerability of children who lack adult protection is a major theme in her books.

Child and adult readers relate to situations in which she describes children who suffer great sadness and loneliness, as do Harry and Luna Lovegood, Voldemort, and Neville Longbottom, and who deal in their own ways, with these traumas. On a deeper level, however, she also reveals the fallibility of those who are supposed to be in charge. Although criticized for writing scenes in her adventures in which children disobey teachers, (especially Harry, Hermione and Ron) and ignore their parents (for example, Fred and George Weasley), Rowling provides a way out for the child who reaches for it, even if they must ignore uninformed adults. She also suggests, "Listen to the children; perhaps they have some things of great importance to say."

On a deeper level, Rowling writes about the metaphor of the child, an archetype of the collective unconscious. She raises questions about the future of the individual soul and the attendant plight of humankind. If the child represents the future, then Rowling has tapped into our anxieties about the future of the world. Although the last book will satisfy curiosity and speculation about whether Harry and his world survive, and I'm betting both do, it will also provide necessary closure to a busy time of growth for Harry, Hermione, and Ron. Childhood and adolescence ends chronologically, and Rowling enlists the magical number of seven to weave her story about love, support from friends, and innocence lost.

Works Cited

Edinger, Edward F. *Anatomy of the Psyche: Alchemical Symbolism in Psychotherapy*. Chicago, Illinois: Open Court, 1985.

Harris, Maxine. *The Loss That Is Forever: The Lifelong Impact of the Early Death of a Mother or Father.* New York: Plume, 1995.

Harry Potter and the Sorcerer's Stone. Dir. Chris Columbus. Perf. Daniel Radcliffe, Rupert Grint, and Emma Watson. Warner Bros. Pictures, 2002.

Harry Potter and the Chamber of Secrets. Dir. Chris Columbus. Perf. Daniel Radcliffe, Rupert Grint, and Emma Watson. Warner Bros. Pictures, 2003.

Harry Potter and the Prisoner of Azkaban. Dir. Alfonso Cuarón. Perf. Daniel Radcliffe, Rupert Grint, and Emma Watson. Warner Bros. Pictures, 2004.

Jones, Malcom. "Why Harry's Hot." *Newsweek,* 17 July, 2002: 52–56. 2 Mar 2005. newsweek@newsbank.com.

Jung, Carl Gustave. "Psychology and Alchemy." Trans. R. F. C. Hull. *Collected Works of C. G. Jung.* Vol. 12. Bollingen Series 20. Princeton: Princeton UP, 1953.

—. "The Psychology of the Child Archetype." Trans. R. F. C. Hull. *Collected Works of C. G. Jung.* Vol. 9.1. Bollingen Series 20. Princeton: Princeton UP, 1959. 151–81.

Miller, David L. "Through a Looking Glass: The World as Enigma." *Eranos* 55 (1986): 349–402.

Moore, Burness E. and Bernard D. Fine. *A Glossary of Psychoanalytic Terms and Concepts.* 2nd ed. New York: The American Psychoanalytic Association, 1968.

Nuland, Sherwin. *How We Die.* New York: Knopf, 1994.

Romanyshyn, Robert. *The Soul in Grief: Love, Death and Transformation.* Berkeley, CA: North Atlantic Books, 1999.

Rowling, J. K. *Harry Potter and the Sorcerer's Stone.* New York: Scholastic, 1997.

—. *Harry Potter and the Chamber of Secrets.* New York: Scholastic, 1999.

—. *Harry Potter and the Prisoner of Azkaban.* London: Bloomsbury, 1999.

—. *Harry Potter and the Goblet of Fire.* New York: Scholastic, 2000.

—. *Harry Potter and the Order of the Phoenix.* New York: Scholastic, 2003.

—. *Harry Potter and the Half-Blood Prince.* New York: Scholastic, 2005.

The Sixth Sense. Dir. M. Night Shyamalan. Perf. Bruce Willis and Haley Joel Osment. Hollywood Pictures and Spyglass Entertainment, 2002.

Treneman, Ann. "That is exactly." *The Times*, 30 June 2000. 28 Aug 2006. <http://www.quick-quote-quill.org/articles/2000/0600-times-treneman.html>.

Weir, Margaret. "Of Magic and Single Motherhood." *Salon*, 31 Mar 1999. <http://www.salon.com/mwt/feature/1999/03/cov_31featureb.html>.

"A POWER HE WILL NEVER KNOW": LOVE, PUBLIC SPACE, AND (NATIONAL) SALVATION IN HARRY POTTER

Skyler James Hijazi
University of Arizona

"These are not your books. These are JKR's books. They're heterocentric because the world is heterocentric, but that's not important because they're about wizards and such and not sex. The sexual bits are more about growing up than anything else."

—Anonymous fan comment

"Romance is such a small part of Harry Potter, that there is no reason to make it any larger by creating homosexual characters. [Rowling] never once goes into sexuality. Why should she?"

—Anonymous fan comment

"[I]ntimacy builds worlds; it creates spaces and usurps places meant for other kinds of relations."

—Lauren Berlant, "Intimacy: A Special Issue"

I want to respond to a certain insidious and persistent attitude among particular fans of the *Harry Potter* novels, an attitude that presumes that sexuality, as a matter of solely "private" concern, enters into the *Harry Potter* series only tangentially if at all and, moreover, that a series of "children's books" can and should be insulated from all inflections of sexuality in the first place. For those fans with whom this argument resonates, the story of an orphaned boy who goes to wizarding school and must eventually fight a megalomaniacal Dark Lord, a boy whose greatest strength lies in his capacity to love, who is protected from harm by the power of his dead mother's self-sacrifice, and whose greatest desire is to see himself surrounded by his family—this story, the train of thought implies, hasn't the least bit to do with arrangements of sexuality.

But it is only from an absurdly narrow understanding of the domain of the sexual that such an argument could begin to make sense. If sexuality is understood as having any meaning at all beyond (or even within) the performance of the sex act, it must be because the signifying power of sexuality does not cease at any discrete and predictable border, not the spatial boundaries of the bedroom (or of the body/ies involved), or the temporal boundaries of an orgasmic release. As Kath Weston points out, "because sexuality brings people into relationship, its implications can never be contained within the parameters of identity or some ideally privatized sphere" (68). Sex, in other words, is never simply private, never simply equivalent to the sex act itself. It is always inflected with concerns over arrangements of kinship, intimacy, citizenship, and nation, just to name a few. As Lauren Berlant and Michael Warner write, "although the intimate relations of private personhood appear to be the realm of sexuality itself, allowing 'sex in public' to appear like matter out of place, intimacy is itself publicly mediated" (172). So too in the *Harry Potter* novels.

What is particularly notable about the *Harry Potter* series is not just the way that sexuality figures implicitly as a matter of key public concern within the diegesis,[1] but the way that the text manages to obfuscate this very publicity through its deployment of alternate discourses: discourses of kinship, consanguinity,[2] and love work within the text to decenter sexuality so that it appears to be consistently outside the domain of "the real story"—material that is either tangential or superfluous to the conflict between the forces of good and the forces of evil. My goal here is twofold. First, I hope to map the ways in which the epic Manichaean battle told in the *Harry Potter* series, rather than being removed from the domain of the

---

1 "Diegesis" or "diegetic" (terms often used by film scholars) denote the world within the narrative, as opposed to "extra-diegetic," which denotes the world outside of the narrative, the world that readers inhabit.

2 That is, relations of ancestry and descent that are based in blood lineage rather than on marriage or other contractual bonds.

sexual, is in fact staged on a terrain that is indivisible from sexuality, a terrain that becomes comprehensible and coherent through its reliance on a heteronormative field of social relations, and a terrain which at once invokes and dispels the specter of nation. Second, by offering a brief consideration of one fan text, Stray's Harry/Draco story "Into the West," I hope to consider how the magical technologies of canon may be redeployed to interrogate this heteronormativity through a queering of bodies: by making liminal bodies, abject bodies, unintelligible bodies, and impossible bodies, fan texts, I will suggest, can make salient that which not only canon but modern Western nation-states seek to hide.

Heteronormativity. I've now used this word twice, so before we go on, I'd like to pause and define just what I mean by using it. Heteronormativity is *not* just a simple shorthand way of saying that most people in modern Western cultures "are," or at least live and identify as, straight. Rather, as Berlant and Warner note, heteronormativity is a concept distinct from heterosexuality; it is the

tacit sense of rightness and normalcy...embedded in things and not just in sex... Heteronormativity is more than ideology, or prejudice, or phobia against gays and lesbians; it is produced in almost every aspect of the forms and arrangements of social life: nationality, the state, and the law; commerce; medicine; and education; as well as in the conventions and affects of narrativity, romance, and other protected spaces of culture. (173)

By the same token, in the *Harry Potter* series, "rightness" and magical power are conferred together in ways that are both central to the text and constitutive of the very existence and viability of the "wizarding world": the protective power of consanguinity conferred upon Harry by his mother's blood allows him to survive to adulthood, while Harry's own capacity to love despite the brutality and trauma of his childhood provides him with the prophesied power to defeat Voldemort and save the wizarding world.

Mother's ~~Milk~~ Blood

Harry Potter is, from the moment at which the reader first meets him as an infant on the night of his parents' murder, a boy whose life is a site of sustained public attention and concern. When he is only a year old, Harry has "people meeting in secret all over the country ... holding up their glasses and saying in hushed voices: 'To

Harry Potter—the boy who lived!'" (*SS* 17). Harry's subsequent
placement with the Dursleys—paragons of normalcy, who take it as
their mission to stamp any hint of magical "abnormality" out of
their foster son—is clearly not dependent on the quality of their
care. Rather, as we learn in book five, it is based on the magical
power the text attributes to consanguinity relations. As Dumbledore
explains to Harry,

> "Your mother died to save you. She gave you a lingering protection…a
> protection that flows in your veins to this day. I put my trust, therefore, in
> your mother's blood. I delivered you to her sister, her only remaining
> relative…. She may have taken you grudgingly, furiously, unwillingly,
> bitterly, yet she still took you, and in doing so, she sealed the charm I
> placed upon you. Your mother's sacrifice made the bond of blood the
> strongest shield I could give you…. While you can still call home the place
> where your mother's blood dwells, there you cannot be touched or harmed
> by Voldemort. He shed her blood, but it lives on in you and her sister. Her
> blood became your refuge." (*OotP* 836)

The paradox involved in this formulation of kinship sets up one
of the fundamental tensions of the series: in the *Harry Potter*
universe, consanguinity is the axis upon which "good" and "bad"
kinship relations revolve. The inhumane and abusive treatment
Harry receives at the Dursleys' hands is apparently trumped by the
power of "blood ties," and the enduring, almost transcendental
power of blood figures biological kinship relations as "real" in a way
that elective families (as the Weasleys are for Harry) can seemingly
never be. Implicitly, this formulation works to narrow the domain of
what counts as legitimate (here read magically—i.e., *materially*—
potent) kinship relations: Harry must suffer the Dursleys' abuse
because the enduring power of blood is stronger than any other
bond.

But consanguinity functions in the novels in another register as
well. The ideological agenda of Voldemort and his followers is
centered on lineage and biological descent: "purebloods" against
"Mudbloods" or Muggle-borns. This is the conflict which proves
central to the series as a whole. As Ron says,

> "Mudblood's a really foul name for someone who is Muggle-born—you
> know, non-magic parents. There are some wizards—like Malfoy's family—
> who think they're better than everyone else because they're what people call
> pure-blood…. [Mudblood is] a disgusting thing to call someone…. Dirty

blood, see. Common blood. It's ridiculous. Most wizards these days are half-bloods anyway. *If we hadn't married Muggles we'd have died out.*" (*CoS* 115–16, emphasis mine)

Ron and his family are, as we all know, what Malfoy calls "blood traitors," their treachery being their lack of prejudice against wizards of Muggle descent. But while this diegetic discourse is certainly inflected with a recognizably racist xenophobia, it is not simply coterminous with it. Instead, the rhetoric of pure-bloods and Mudbloods simultaneously cuts across and redraws the axis of traditional understandings of race, ethnicity, and nation.

Racial and national heritage, it is worth noting, becomes legible for many *Potter* characters (for example, Cho Chang and the Patil twins) through conventions of naming. Only in the cases of Dean Thomas and Blaise Zabini does Rowling specify ethnicity in the text, and while the multiracial makeup of Hogwarts is clearly implied, the text instantiates a sort of race blindness in the form of several interracial student romances. Cho is Harry's first crush, he takes Parvati as his date to the Yule ball, and when Ginny Weasley begins dating Dean Thomas in book six, no mention is made of the interracial dynamics of the relationship. Racial tensions appear instead as (dis)placed onto the question of blood purity, and a discourse of blood purity becomes the regulatory grammar around which both the spaces and the relationships of the wizarding world are organized. Of course, considered historically, this clear distinction between discourses of blood and race is a fabrication. As many feminist and postcolonial scholars have demonstrated, rhetoric about the former often functions as code for policing the boundaries of the latter—for making regulatory claims about citizenship, national belonging, and the legality (and legitimacy) of particular intimate relationships.

In the *Harry Potter* series there is a territorial boundary at stake as well, but it is not one that could be mapped by any of the conventional means by which states mark geopolitical borders. The wizarding world is within, underneath, and between the spaces of the Muggle world—platform nine and three-quarters is inside King's Cross station; the Knight Bus drives down the streets of London squeezing between pedestrians and traffic; number twelve, Grimmauld Place seems to shove neighboring buildings aside when it appears—and yet the Muggles never know that these spaces exist because wizards keep them from knowing. The borders of the wizarding world are tirelessly guarded and defended; the Other is kept out relentlessly, kept not only from entering the spaces of the wizarding world but from knowing that these spaces exist. And yet there are some for whom the border between Muggle and wizarding worlds is still too permeable, some for whom the most unconscionable breaching of that border is one enacted through desire, through sexuality, intermarriage, and reproduction. Blaise Zabini makes the stakes of this contested border particularly salient when, confronted with his belief that Ginny Weasley is attractive, he responds, "I wouldn't touch a filthy little blood traitor like her whatever she looked like" (*HBP* 150).

This regulatory grammar—this patrolling of the wizard-Muggle border—transcends national boundaries and discourses in a way that is perhaps most readily apparent in the Minister of Magic's meeting with the (British?) Prime Minister in book six. Cornelius Fudge tells the (Other) Prime Minister (notably addressed as the Prime Minister *of Muggles*) that there are "witches and wizards still living in secret *all over the world.*" Fudge then offers "his reassurances that [the Prime Minister] was not to bother his head about [these wizards and witches] as the Ministry of Magic took responsibility for the whole *Wizardingcommunity) and prevented the non-magical population from getting wind of them" (HBP 5, emphasis added).*

However, it is not that nation is simply illegible in the wizarding world—the Triwizard Tournament was historically, we are told, "generally agreed to be a most excellent way of establishing ties between young witches and wizards *of different nationalities*" (*GoF* 187, emphasis added), though considering it was "first established some seven hundred years ago" (*GoF* 187), well before the advent of "nations" in the modern sense, it is hard to say just what this means. Nation, in this sense, becomes a present absence, a specter which haunts the *Harry Potter* series, continually disappearing from view at the very moment in which it is invoked. Diegetically, nation (especially in book four) provides a framework that signifies characters' loyalties, affiliations, and proximities, but that dissolves like a mirage before the "real" topography of the *global* threat presented by Voldemort. At the Quidditch World Cup, for example, in the lead-up to the match between Ireland and Bulgaria, nationalist iconography rules, but what frames the match (and what is most important to the larger unfolding conflict of the series) is a tension not over national identities, but over points of contact between Muggle and wizarding worlds that transcend nation. The Muggle campsite owner who "needs a Memory Charm ten times a day to keep him happy" (*GoF* 78) (i.e., to keep him from noticing that there are wizards all around him), is the same man later assaulted by Death Eaters who dangle him *and his family* upside down in the air while they terrorize the camp site. The projection of Voldemort's Dark Mark in the sky above the camp cuts across nationalist sentiment altogether and reconfigures loyalty on the supposedly planetary axis of good and evil.

"We Fools Who Love"

"Intimacy," writes Berlant, is "formed around threats to the image of the world it seeks to sustain" (7). For Harry, the intimate fantasy is (familial) love, and the threat presented by Voldemort is most directly encountered by Harry as a threat to *family*. Harry's dream of his parents is what sustains him again and again—in the shape of his Patronus and the power to summon it, under the folds of his father's invisibility cloak, when he gazes into the Mirror of Erised and sees himself surrounded by relatives, in his graveyard duel with Voldemort at the end of book four. If the image in Harry's intimate fantasy is of (heteronormative) familial love, the ever-present threat to that image is the force of a world-destroying evil in the form of Voldemort, who has murdered Harry's parents, and Voldemort's followers, who cause the death of Harry's godfather.

Just as consanguinity is figured in the novels as having a real and palpable power, so too is Harry's love. When Harry is possessed by Voldemort just moments after witnessing Sirius's death, it is his love for Sirius that saves him: "*Let the pain stop*, thought Harry. *Let him kill us... Death is nothing compared to this... And I'll see Sirius again...* And as Harry's heart filled with emotion, the creature's coils loosened, the pain was gone" (*OotP* 816). As Dumbledore explains, "In the end, it mattered not that you could not close your mind. It was your heart that saved you" (*OotP* 844). Dumbledore takes great pains to explain that Harry's capacity to love, even "given everything that has happened to [him]" (*HBP* 511), is his greatest strength. Love, suggests Dumbledore, is "a force that is at once more wonderful and more terrible than death, than human intelligence, than forces of nature" (*OotP* 843); it is "the only protection that can possibly work against the lure of power like Voldemort's" (*HBP* 511).

While the redemptive power of heteronormative love may not be a new theme, the *Harry Potter* canon situates that redemption as public and collective. And given the way "the wizarding community" is figured as transnational, the salvation promised by Harry's love and Voldemort's defeat is salvation on a *global* (or at the very least a pan-European) scale.

Intimacy may indeed, as Berlant says, build worlds, but in Harry's case its task is to save a world that already exists, a world that implicitly understands and authorizes particular inscriptions of heteronormativity (i.e., particular inscriptions of *intimacy and love*) as the foundation for legitimate relationships and connectivity. What is ultimately at stake in these formulations of kinship, love, and (trans)national public space is a construction of the wizarding world *as* a global community that transcends national boundaries through a romanticized extrapolation from local to global. The wizarding world is a space in which national, racial, and ethnic differences are no longer situated as the key sites of contest. By (dis)placing these tensions onto configurations of consanguinity, Rowling's text imagines those wizards fighting "the good fight" as a globalized, transnational, and multiracial "community."

But community is never simply a neutral construction. As Miranda Joseph argues, "rather than simply referring to an existing collectivity, invocations of community attempt to naturalize and mobilize such a collectivity: on both the left and right community is deployed to lower consciousness of difference, hierarchy, and oppression within the invoked group" (xxvi). It is worth thinking here of the radically racialized Others *within* the wizarding world— goblins, house-elves, centaurs, giants—and the ways they are situated in the text, the ways in which we as readers are encouraged to alternately see and to dismiss them, the ways in which concerns over social hierarchy and oppression are *marginalized* by a narrative that imagines a *global* community which can be saved by the power of (heteronormative) love.

Harry Potter's Vagina, or Sex Publics in the Wizarding World's Dark Tomorrow

Given this canon topography of a sex public so deeply (and yet so stealthily) invested in the triumph of the heteronormative love script, I want to briefly consider one fan text which departs from, counter-reads, and queers the *Potter* canon's understanding of heteronormative love as not just benevolent but *transnationally redemptive*. That fic, "Into the West" by Stray, tells a queer love story against a dystopic, nightmarish backdrop by projecting a postwar future in which all non-reproductive wizards—all those with the "degenerative deformity" that causes their homosexual desire—are forced, first, to undergo a process of magical sex reassignment, then exiled to an island where their corporeal contact with other (straight, reproductive) wizards will be forever severed.

A Harry/Draco fic, "Into the West" is set on the ship which bears the exiles to their new home. The narrative unfolds to reveal Draco's role in the framing of exile as the best possible alternative available under the Ministry of Magic's postwar totalitarianism which

had all started with a half-official decree from the Ministry to re-populate the wizarding world after the war with Voldemort had decimated it. They had called upon every witch and wizard to start a family and have children. There had even been a reward system for those who complied and it seemed to work.... Homosexuality had not really been a great issue in the wizarding world. It had certainly not been something to be proud of, but it had been tolerated, as it had been assumed that, regardless of one's preferences, wizards and witches would get married to procreate and then practice their sexuality outside of wedlock. It had almost been like a tradition. But then, with the influx of Muggle-born and half-blood wizards and witches, morals slackened and it became more and more common for someone preferring their own gender to settle down with his or her partner and shirk their responsibilities. The Ministry had tried several ways to coerce obedience before the readjustment programme, such as new decrees and taxes. *The Daily Prophet* had found more and more creative or just plain disgusting ways to discredit same-sex relationships and the people involved in them. The culmination of all this, though, had been an article about the alleged fact that He-Who-Must-Not-Be-Named had been a homosexual— which was the most ridiculous lie if there ever was one, since Voldemort's only concern had been power and immortality, he had cared nothing about the pleasures of the flesh—and from then on, the word homosexual equaled evil. (Stray Ch. 1)

The mandatory "readjustment programme" to which both Harry and Draco have, to varying degrees, been subjected in "Into the West" is a magical modification of both the bodies and the identities of gay male wizards. While lesbian witches' compliance with the doctrine of mandatory reproduction necessitates only "an injection of sperm from a generous wizard" (Stray Ch. 1), the Ministry finds it harder to enforce compulsory procreation in the gay male population. Thus, apparently presuming a "gender inversion" style conception of same-sex desire, the wizarding world's government institutionalizes a program to magically modify the bodies of gay male wizards with the goal of making them sexually reproductive: "contrary to myths and legends, there was no way for a male to become pregnant—a wizard's magic would try to 'heal' him if he suddenly obtained a uterus—except if the male in question was transfigured entirely into a woman. That's why later—in addition to being transfigured—wizards would have to go through a gender identity-readjustment: to prevent their magic from fighting their new female biology" (Stray Ch. 1).

The Ministry of Magic in "Into the West" proffers a bald-faced revelation of their investment in the particularly gendered and sexed bodies of their citizenry. To adapt Judith Butler here, we might say that they have unmasked the politics whereby some bodies come to *matter* and some bodies (here, non hetero-reproductive bodies) do not. Writing of Butler's work on the matter of bodies, Nan Alamilla Boyd notes that, in the eyes of the modern Western nation-state, "abject bodies—bodies transgressive of borders and boundaries— do not matter. They do not function intelligibly as matter, and they do not have value.... How do bodies that do not matter become bodies that matter?" (136). "Into the West," I would argue, is a narrative about the way that the state (in this case, a state which has, at its disposal, magical technologies that enable the "impossible") attempts to force bodies to conform to a preexisting heteronormative valuation of *what matters*—the Ministry of Magic attempts to alter what bodily matter *is* in order to make it *do* what (in its view) matter that "matters" *does*.

Thus, by altering the inflections of the Ministry's already-present domination of bodies in canon, "Into the West" marks that which remains unmarked in both diegetic and extra-diegetic formulations of state authority over bodies: the state's investment in the gendered and sexed bodies of its subjects, specifically *as* reproductive bodies. The particular modality of this investment at the intersection of gender, sexuality, and reproduction appears in Stray's text as the spectacle of the magically altered "in-between" body. Draco, for example, when Harry first meets him as an unrecognized stranger on board the ship, appears not just as androgynous but hybridized:

the carefully positioned left thigh combined with the tight cut and the thin, almost translucent fabric of the trousers did nothing to hide the distinct shape of a half erect penis. In fact, they were designed to do the exact opposite.... [Harry] knew that [this dress code] had become fashionable within the wizarding gay community after the beginning of the readjustment program. Not everyone followed it, of course, only those most desperate to prove that they had not yet been turned completely into a witch, or those who were less self-conscious about revealing so much of their anatomy.... The shockingly casual exhibit of masculinity diverted his attention from noticing something equally shocking: the slightly raised mounds of breasts flaunted just as casually by the open neckline. (Stray Ch. 1)

Harry's body, too, is a magically crafted hybrid, though his experience of its hybridity is markedly different from Draco's: Harry binds his magically created breasts, anxiously waiting for his body's innate magic to assert itself and make them disappear (as it has apparently already done in response to other elements of the "readjustment;" as Draco observes: "'I don't remember you having such a monster in your pants while we were at Hogwarts.' ... 'Let's just say, my magic tried to compensate,' Harry said, slightly breathless" [Stray Ch. 2]). But while Harry and Draco both expect that their magically enlarged breasts will gradually shrink and disappear over time, and while neither of them have undergone the final phases of the readjustment which would have rendered all its alterations permanent, Harry's body *has* been rendered permanently and literally hermaphroditic by the magical modification—his body has become a site of liminality, abject and unintelligible.

Harry's vagina—created by a totalitarian state as a bodily ingress for the purpose of procreation but unable, as Stray notes in a comment, to actually achieve conception (Harry "doesn't have a uterus and has no ovaries either. His breasts aren't permanent. He only has a vagina he cannot get rid of" [Stray Ch. 2])—renders his body at once an abject and also a (diegetically) unintelligible body.

Harry's vagina is, for him, a hypermateriality from which dangerous emanations of fluid (the "unexpected stickiness between [Harry's] thighs" [Stray Ch. 2]) and odor leak: "Harry thought he would die of shame—Draco lowered his head until his nose was digging under Harry's balls and sniffled once, twice" (Stray Ch. 2). The Ministry's readjustment program seeks to make maternal bodies in the service of the wizarding (transnational) nation-state, but in Harry's vagina we see only the spectacle of the Ministry's failure, a spectacle of Harry's body, his magically altered genitals now made a fetish object —Harry's vagina is a materiality without the attendant reproductive power with which that symbolic location is most often associated.

It is specifically through such fetishizing of spectacularized and queer(ed) bodies that the already-public character of sex—the role which sex plays in organizing multiple manifestations of intimacy between subjects in places beyond the confines of the bedroom— may be unmasked by a queer re-reading (and writing) of canon. For through an affectively invested and unabashedly *shared and public* watching of those sex acts and those bodies which modern heteronormative culture tells us should be hidden, a text like "Into the West" backlights and emphasizes the traces of bodies left by privatized sex culture. To quote Berlant and Warner, "The sex act shielded by the zone of privacy is the affectional nimbus that heterosexual culture protects and from which it abstracts its model of ethics, but this utopia of social belonging is also supported and extended by acts less commonly recognized as part of sexual culture: paying taxes, being disgusted, philandering, bequeathing, celebrating a holiday, investing for the future, teaching, disposing of a corpse, [etc.]" (173).

Thus, although Harry and Draco certainly do become spectacularized in "Into the West," the spectacle offered by the text is not just the characters' bodies but also the (wizarding) state which, in its desperate fervor not just to impel but to micromanage "life" through the reproductive bodies of its citizens, takes normative bodies and legible (if perhaps not sufficiently docile) desires and *makes them unintelligible*. In the process, the regulatory apparatus of the state makes a spectacle of itself through its acts of tyranny: the purported aim of the regime's readjustment program is to create *maternal bodies* and thereby to increase (re)productivity, to shore up the population under its control. But with its usual ineffectiveness, all the Ministry in fact manages to do, in this queered reading of the Potterverse future, is to unmask itself as the sham it has been from the outset: what the creating of unintelligible bodies in "Into the West" does best is to illuminate, despite any claims the regime might make to the contrary, that (and I'm adapting Achille Mbembe here) "to exercise authority is, above all, to tire out the bodies of those under it, to disempower them not so much to increase their productivity as to ensure the maximum docility" (110).

In canon, we are bombarded with instances in which the Ministry not only manipulates infomation but also enacts extreme and baseless punishments upon the bodies of its subjects; indeed, this often appears to be the Ministry's *modus operandi* for domination. (I'm thinking here of Harry's trial at the beginning of book five, of Umbridge forcing Harry to carve "I will not tell lies" into his own hand, of Stan Shunpike's imprisonment, of the Ministry sending Hagrid to Azkaban, however temporarily, in *CoS* so that the Ministry can be "seen to be doing something.") These are all cases in which, as Mbembe says in a different context, "the power of the state seeks to dramatize its importance and to define itself in the very act" (115) of exacting punishment on the bodies of its subjects. But in canon, these punishments, more often than not, appear disjoined from any overt politics of gender, sexuality, and desire. Insofar as the Ministry of Magic is intelligible as the governing body of a modern state, however, *this disjunction is a fabrication.* The workings of state power in the modern West—what Michel Foucault has called *biopower*—do not work that way.

Biopower, as Foucault conceptualizes it, is contrasted to the power held by a sovereign (i.e., a king) in the premodern West. Here's how it works: in the premodern (preindustrial) West the power of the sovereign was framed as a power to *take life* (among other things it could take, like bodies, material possessions, etc.). In the modern world, on the other hand, the mechanics of power have shifted, and under this system, the state's power asserts itself as a power not to *take*, but to *impel, foster*, and *regulate* life, or "to *disallow* it to the point of death" (138). In the modern era of biopower, regulatory controls which shape docile bodies and self-policing subjects form a *politics of populations.* And the nexus at which these twin goals—to regulate bodies and to regulate populations—come together is *sex.* As Foucault writes, "sex became a crucial target of a power organized around the management of life rather than the menace of death" (147).

I want to suggest that we read "Into the West" as a narrative in which biopower meets magic at the site of a vulgar and absurd bureaucracy, creating a spectacle not just of non-normative bodies but of the state apparatus that seeks to script and compel their (heteronormative sexual) performance. In the process, what the narrative dramatizes (and explodes) is the investment not just of *Potter* canon but of the modern nation and the modern state in the sexual bodies and sexual selves of its citizens—the very qualities of sexed and gendered bodies, *desiring bodies*, that are *always present* in public, but that modern popular discourse constantly seeks to render as only private or "personal" concerns.

Dreaming Queer Dreams (of Public Sex)

The fantasy contextualizing Harry and Draco's romance in "Into the West" may not be one in which desire is freed from coercion, or in which the opening of possibilities liberates subjects, but it is a fantasy nonetheless—one in which even the most coercive forms of gendered and sexed violence (violence that is made possible, like the bodies it creates in the text, only through magic's ability to enable the impossible) cannot ultimately stand in the way of subjective connectivity, expressions of desires, faithfulness to the self, and enduring love. If, as Boyd argues, "Bodies that inhabit or enact naturalized states of being remain culturally intelligible, socially valuable, and as a result, gain and retain the privilege of citizenship and its associated rights and protections…[while] less intelligible or unintelligible…bodies undermine in many different ways the recognition or comradeship central to nationalism's purpose" (135–36), then the contact Harry and Draco forge upon the terrain of Harry's hybridized body—a touching of bodies and an iteration of desire that remains fundamentally unintelligible to both the Ministry and, I would say, to any reader who is not socialized in *Potter* slash fandom, carries with it an epistemically transformative potential. Not only is the heteronormativity of canon unmasked as a potential forerunner to explicitly gendered violence, but the very shape and materiality of *which bodies matter* is (at least potentially) reframed.

In this sense, and because it is specifically through their (diegetically) unintelligible bodies that Harry and Draco *meet*, "Into the West" is a text which dramatizes how "the embodied relation to the norm exercises a transformative potential. To posit possibilities beyond the norm or, indeed, a different future for the norm itself, is part of the work of fantasy when we understand fantasy as taking the body as a point of departure for an articulation that is not always constrained by the body as it is" (Butler, *Undoing Gender* 28). Harry and Draco's hybridized bodies—trans-gendered, trans-sexed, hermaphroditic, or at least, to adapt Butler, allegorizing those categories—(and in Harry's case, not coincidentally, also the body traumatized by its hybridity) become, in this fic, the site of such a fantasy.

"Into the West" maintains the encounter between bodies which is archetypal in slash fic (male/male anal penetration), but reframes it: Harry's offer to penetrate Draco anally appears as his defense against Draco's discovery of the female genitals which the Ministry's "readjustment program" has left him with, while his post-orgasmic euphoria (in which Draco *does* discover Harry's magically created vagina) becomes the occasion for Draco's admission of his arousal by the hybridized quality of Harry's body. Draco's attempt to articulate his sexual self to Harry—a passage in which Draco tries to press an articulation of his desire into already-intelligible categories and language—points to the text's tacit questioning of the very categories around which it is staged: "What counts as a person? What counts as a coherent gender? What qualifies as a citizen? Whose world is legitimated as real?" (Butler, *Undoing Gender* 58). And these questions are *always*—whether they appear in a fantasy narrative, in a "children's book," in a fan text, a canon text, or in one's "real-life" world that seems radically separate from fandom— questions about sex as a public matter, about the sexual matter of bodies in public and about all of the exfoliating implications a given sex act might have: implications for love, for intimacy, for identity, for blood kinship, for desire, for scripts of normative life, and for an individual's "place" in a world still divided into nations and still governed by states.

While extreme xenophobia and paranoia over the policing of boundaries is figured as a mark of "evil" in the *Harry Potter* novels, blood ties are simultaneously recentered, affirmed, and legitimized through use of a discourse centered on the redemptive power of love. Clothed in this discourse of (heteronormative) love as (transnational) salvation, consanguinity is reified as a source of power—the most enduring power—and a deep abiding valuation of "traditional" familial ties is invoked as that thing which will enable "good" to triumph over "evil." Harry's battles with Voldemort and their eventual inevitable showdown thus dress a traditional Western configuration of heteronormative familial love in the guise of transnational salvation and a romanticized fantasy of global community. As much as we may love the *Harry Potter* texts, their characters, their conflicts, and their magic, we must also be attentive to the work that they do, not just to *un*mask particular iterations of power and disempowerment, prejudice and discrimination, but also to *mask* some of the more troubling investments of heteronormative culture, like the masking of the public character of sex which makes some bodies, some desires, and some loves matter... and some *not*.

Works Cited

Berlant, Lauren. "Intimacy: A Special Issue." Ed. Lauren Berlant. *Intimacy*. Chicago: University of Chicago Press, 2000. 1–8.

Berlant, Lauren, and Michael Warner. "Sex in Public." Eds. Robert J. Corber and Stephen Valocchi. *Queer Studies: An Interdisciplinary Reader*. Malden, MA: Blackwell, 2003. 170–86.

Boyd, Nan Alamilla. "Bodies in Motion: Lesbian and Transsexual Histories." *A Queer World: The Center for Lesbian and Gay Studies Reader*. Ed. Martin Duberman. New York: New York University Press, 1997. 134–52.

Butler, Judith. *Bodies That Matter: On the Discursive Limits of "Sex"*. New York: Routledge, 1993.

—. *Undoing Gender*. New York: Routledge, 2004.

Foucault, Michel. *The History of Sexuality, Volume 1: An Introduction*. New York: Vintage, 1978.

Joseph, Miranda. *Against the Romance of Community*. Minneapolis: University of Minnesota Press, 2002.

Mbembe, Achille. *On the Postcolony*. Berkeley: University of California Press, 2001.

Rowling, J. K.. *Harry Potter and the Chamber of Secrets.* New York: Scholastic, 1999.

—. *Harry Potter and the Goblet of Fire.* New York: Scholastic, 2000.

—. *Harry Potter and the Half-Blood Prince.* New York: Scholastic, 2005.

—. *Harry Potter and the Order of the Phoenix.* New York: Scholastic, 2003.

—. *Harry Potter and the Sorcerer's Stone.* New York: Scholastic, 1997.

Stray. "Into the West." 19 Oct 2006. <http://grey-hunter. livejournal.com/38470.html>.

Weston, Kath. *Families We Choose: Lesbians, Gays, Kinship.* New York: Columbia University Press, 1991.

Evil and the Loss of Identity in the Harry Potter Series

Annette Doblix Klemp
University of Wisconsin–River Falls

Three of the first four books of the *Harry Potter* series by J. K. Rowling end in climactic and unexpected revelations. In *Sorcerer's Stone,* the seemingly harmless and weak Professor Quirrell is revealed as the unwilling host to the parasitic, returned Lord Voldemort; in *Prisoner of Azkaban,* the despised Scabbers is revealed as the traitorous Peter Pettigrew, former trusted friend of James and Lily Potter; in *Goblet of Fire,* Alastor Mad-Eye Moody is revealed as the convicted Death Eater Barty Crouch, Jr., dosed heavily with Polyjuice potion. All three revelations come as a surprise even to the discerning reader and attest to the skill with which Rowling manipulates her characterization and plot structure. But in addition to creating an exciting story, each revelation presents an important illustration of the effects of evil in the *Harry Potter* world. Far from romanticizing evil, Rowling presents all three of Voldemort's followers as weak-willed, pitiful individuals. In each case their devotion to Lord Voldemort leads, not to greater power, but to a servile enslavement that eventually robs them of free will and of their own identities. Significantly, this loss of power and identity present in Voldemort's victimized followers is also present in the seemingly powerful and terrifying Voldemort himself.

The climactic revelation scene in *Sorcerer's Stone* dramatically illustrates the grotesque weaknesses of both Voldemort and Quirrell. Successfully breaking through all obstacles to reach the Sorcerer's Stone, Harry confronts a stammering and extremely nervous Professor Quirrell. In describing his encounter with Voldemort, Quirrell claims, "'A foolish young man I was then, full

114

of ridiculous ideas about good and evil.... There is no good and evil, there is only power and those too weak to seek it"" (*SS* 191). While praising power and condemning weakness, Quirrell, unlike the reader, is unable to perceive the irony inherent in his assertions. Enslavement to the parasitic and evil Voldemort has led to the ultimate weakness: because Quirrell no longer has power over his own decision-making or even his own body, he has lost his own identity.

The same generalization about loss of identity can be applied to Voldemort himself, who has been robbed of a body and reduced to a mere snakelike and grotesque face protruding from the back of Quirrell's head. Significantly, this dependent parasitic situation is Voldemort's first appearance in the novel and allows Rowling to portray evil as inherently ugly and grotesque. Moreover, in her treatment of Voldemort, Rowling has proven herself to be a master of suspense as she keeps her major villain, the embodiment of evil, hidden from the reader. *Sorcerer's Stone* opens with rejoicing among the wizarding community over Voldemort's supposed defeat at the hands of the infant Harry. The lack of detail about Voldemort and his defeat and the use of the phrase "He-Who-Must-Not-Be-Named" suggest an image of evil that is powerful precisely because it is so devoid of details. Prior to Harry's confrontation, the reader, like Harry, knows only that Voldemort was a powerful evil wizard responsible for a reign of terror and for the death of Harry's parents. Voldemort is intriguing and terrifying precisely because, for most of the series, he is unseen and unknown. Even after his reappearance at the conclusion of *Sorcerer's Stone*, Voldemort is surrounded in mystery. Quirrell dies in his confrontation with Harry, but Voldemort's fate remains unclear until his reappearance in *Goblet of Fire*.

Voldemort's follower/victim Quirrell is a powerful illustration of the dangers of a commitment to evil. As Voldemort's sadistic exploitation of Quirrell illustrates, evil, because it is inherently selfish, is dangerous to both foes and followers. This selfishness illustrates one of evil's inherent weaknesses. While the opposition of Harry, Dumbledore, and the other good characters helps to keep evil in check, there is strong evidence that the evil characters may also be a force for destroying themselves. Simply stated, a collection of inherently selfish individuals cannot be relied upon to stand together or protect each other in the way that the novels' heroes do. Voldemort's willingness to sacrifice his own followers and his indifference to their welfare are prime indications of this tendency.

While Voldemort is motivated by selfish desires for eternal life and power, many of his followers are also motivated by fear. At a climactic moment in *Prisoner of Azkaban,* Sirius Black confronts Peter Pettigrew/Scabbers about his betrayal of Lily and James Potter. In response to Pettigrew's defense that "He [Voldemort] would have killed me," Sirius responds, "THEN YOU SHOULD HAVE DIED!… DIED RATHER THAN BETRAY YOUR FRIENDS, AS WE WOULD HAVE DONE FOR YOU!" (*PoA* 375). This exchange highlights several of the important aspects of J. K. Rowling's treatment of good and evil in the *Harry Potter* series. Sirius articulates one of the principles underlying the actions of the good characters: they are willing to die, not just for abstract principles but also but for each other's protection. In other words, they are often motivated by their love for others. The death of Harry's parents prior to the opening of the first book is the prime example of this self-sacrifice, but the deaths of Sirius and Dumbledore and Rowling's promise of the deaths of other major characters in the concluding novel also support this concept. In contrast, in the figure of Scabbers/Pettigrew, Rowling makes one of her most compelling arguments about the nature of evil: through Pettigrew and other characters who seem minor at first, Rowling shows that a commitment to evil is prompted often by weaknesses and cowardice and that it leads not to greater power but to servitude and ultimately a loss of identity. Importantly, this generalization applies not only to Voldemort's weak followers, notably Scabbers, Quirrell, and Barty Crouch, but also to Voldemort himself. Like Pettigrew, Voldemort is motivated primarily by his fear of death.

In her treatment of Peter Pettigrew, Rowling deliberately misleads the reader. Present from the first novel of the series, Pettigrew is seen only as the pathetic rat Scabbers throughout *Sorcerer's Stone* and *Chamber of Secrets,* as well as for most of *Prisoner of Azkaban.* While Rowling distracts reader attention away from Quirrell by presenting the hateful Snape as a likely villain, she distracts attention away from Scabbers as a possible villain by using him as extensive comic relief. For most of his appearances, Scabbers performs largely as a comic expression of Ron's frustration with the poverty of the Weasley family. He even appears as a catalyst for a dispute between Ron and Hermione for most of *Prisoner of Azkaban*, due to the animosity of Hermione's cat Crookshanks.

When Pettigrew reappears at the opening of *Goblet of Fire*, he is presented as totally dependent upon the goodwill of the unseen Voldemort. However, the helpless Voldemort is also dependent upon Pettigrew and manipulates his servant largely through threats of punishment. In many ways *Goblet of Fire* serves as a transition novel for the projected seven-book series. Unlike the previous two novels, *Goblet* does not begin with scenes of Harry chafing at his mistreatment by the Dursleys. Instead, the reader is given a brief history of the deaths of the Riddle family before moving to the introduction of Voldemort and Pettigrew. Prior to *Goblet*, each novel had ended with victory for the heroes: Quirrell is defeated in *Sorcerer's Stone*; the diary version of Tom Riddle is defeated in *Chamber of Secrets*; Sirius and Buckbeak are rescued in *Prisoner of Azkaban*. However, starting with *Goblet*, the balance of power begins to shift. The innocent Cedric Diggory dies at the conclusion of *Goblet*; Sirius falls into the veil of spirits in *Order of the Phoenix*; Dumbledore dies at the conclusion of *Half-Blood Prince*. In each case, Voldemort is directly or indirectly responsible for the deaths. In his interactions with Pettigrew and later with his own Death Eaters, Voldemort reveals that their relationship to him is primarily one of sacrifice. The Death Eaters who renounced him are threatened for their supposed abandonment of him, while Pettigrew is forced to be a "willing" sacrifice for the potion that will restore Voldemort to a body.

Due to his interaction with Voldemort, Pettigrew loses his own identity, first in his masquerade as Scabbers the rat and later in his transformation into Wormtail, Voldemort's servant. Like Quirrell before him, Pettigrew is even required to sacrifice his own body. Voldemort was a parasite for Quirrell, but his relationship with Pettigrew carries suggestions of cannibalism as he forces his servant to "willingly" cut off his own hand for the potion that will restore Voldemort. This loss of identity is also seen in another seemingly minor character in *Goblet*, Barty Crouch, Jr. In fact, for most of the novel the reader and the major characters believe that Barty is dead. The reader and Harry hear of him in conversations about his father, and Harry watches his trial in Dumbledore's Pensieve. Viewed by

Harry through the Pensieve, young Crouch appears terrified and repentant when he is sentenced to Azkaban, where he supposedly dies. What the conclusion of *Goblet* reveals is that Crouch, years earlier, had escaped Azkaban by exchanging places with his dying mother. For years afterward, he lived hidden in the Crouch home and cared for primarily by Winky. When he does emerge from captivity, it is to assume the role of Alastor Moody in order to manipulate Harry into the Triwizard Tournament.

Like Quirrell and Scabbers before him, Crouch is presented largely as a character who has sacrificed his own identity. After his capture, he is briefly restored to his true identity only to have his return abruptly cut short by a Dementor's Kiss, a process by which they suck out their victims' souls. As Lupin tells his students, "You can exist without your soul, you know, as long as your brain and heart are still working. But you'll have no sense of self anymore, no memory, no... anything. There's no chance at all of recovery. You'll just—exist. As an empty shell. And your soul is gone forever... lost" (*PoA* 247). Lupin's description of the Dementor's soul-stealing suggests a parallel to Voldemort's treatment of his followers, particularly in his reference to the loss of sense of self. This parallel between Voldemort and the Dementors is further strengthened by a statement made by Dumbledore when warning the students of Hogwarts: "It is not in the nature of a Dementor to understand pleading or excuses. I therefore warn each and every one of you to give them no reason to harm you" (*PoA* 92). Dumbledore himself also recognizes the affinity between the Dementors and Voldemort: because of their similarity, the two are natural allies, and the Dementors do eventually defect to the Dark Lord.

Using Crouch/Moody as the new Defense Against the Dark Arts Instructor for Year Four at Hogwarts also allows Rowling to develop her concept of what constitutes evil. In his lessons with the students, the supposed Mad-Eye Moody introduces them to the three Unforgivable Curses: Imperius, Cruciatus, and the Killing Curse. Imperius robs its victims of free will; Cruciatus causes pain, and *Avada Kedavra* kills. It seems hardly coincidental that all three of these actions—the deprivation of free will, torture, and murder—are associated primarily with Voldemort in his treatment of both enemies and followers. Ironically, by teaching Harry about these curses, Crouch (in his guise as Moody) prepares Harry to withstand future encounters with Voldemort.

As this brief survey of three of Voldemort's followers has indicated, loyalty to Voldemort usually ends in disaster: Quirrell loses control of his body and will to Voldemort and is eventually compelled to cause his own torment and death, when he is forced to physically struggle with Harry; Pettigrew lives for ten years as a rat, only to live in fear as Voldemort's continually threatened servant; Barty Crouch lives hidden in his father's house, only to emerge briefly as Alastor Moody before he loses his soul to a Dementor's Kiss. All three men are clear illustrations of the fact that to be a follower of Voldemort means, in effect, to be his victim. Voldemort himself shares several of the important characteristics of his unfortunate followers. Like them, he is motivated by fear—but in his case it is fear of death. Voldemort reveals this fear when he recounts his experiences after his defeat by Harry. Claiming that he was "less than spirit, less than the meanest ghost," Voldemort continues, "I remember only forcing myself, sleeplessly, endlessly, second by second, to exist" (*GoF* 653).

While he does rightfully inspire terror, Voldemort, despite his obvious power, is thus depicted as a man who has wilfully chosen to be less than human. Illustrating the concept that evil is ultimately self-destructive, Voldemort is primarily responsible for his own diminishment, first by severing his own soul and later by attempting to confound the prophecy made by Sibyll Trelawney and remove the infant Harry Potter. In his joyless existence and obsessions with death and revenge, Voldemort thus becomes an object lesson illustrating not only that evil is self-destructive but that it also creates its own punishments.

Voldemort's belief that he can "conquer death" and his willingness to sacrifice all others, both friends and foes, to this end, links him to one of the classic archetypal figures of horror fiction: the vampire. Although many readers and viewers today are familiar with the romanticized vampire presented in early films or in the novels of Anne Rice, the most well-known use of this creature/villain is in Bram Stoker's *Dracula* (1897). Stoker firmly establishes the figure of the vampire as a predator and as an illustration of the paradox "living dead." In Stoker's novel, the vampire is not truly dead or alive and depends upon the blood of victims. This parallel to the vampire is even directly presented to the reader in the first novel. Hagrid, introducing Professor Quirrell, offhandedly attributes Quirrell's nervousness to previous experience with vampires in the Black Forest, the location where Quirrell met the disembodied Voldemort and was subjugated.

However, unlike a vampire, whose condition is caused by the bite of another, Voldemort has created his own condition. In *Half-Blood Prince,* the reader learns that Tom Riddle has not only recreated himself as Lord Voldemort but, in his fear of death, has actually severed his own soul and deposited fragments in objects and in the snake Nagini. In so doing, he has reduced himself to "existence" or a "living death," governed only by his fears of mortality and of Harry Potter. He and the Dementors also resemble vampiric figures in that both deprive their victims of selfhood: Voldemort through the use of fear and the Imperius curse, the Dementors through the action of actually sucking out their victims' souls. Like Stoker's Dracula, Voldemort also despises his victims or followers, and much like the vampire dependent upon blood, the diminished Voldemort is dependent upon them, particularly upon Wormtail, who prior to Voldemort's restoration is responsible for "feeding" his "master" from the snake Nagini.

Voldemort blindly refuses to recognize his own diminishment, and in *Goblet of Fire* he proudly announces to the unfortunate caretaker, Frank Bryce, "But I am not a man, Muggle… I am much, much more than a man" (*GoF* 15). This boast is highly ironic coming from a man who had earlier asked his own servant, "How am I to survive without you, when I need feeding every few hours?" (*GoF* 9). In addition, Voldemort's claim to be "much, much more than a man" links him to another archetypal literary figure, the overreacher. In British literature the primary example of this figure, one which shares many traits with Voldemort, is the title character from Christopher Marlowe's *Doctor Faustus.* Faustus, wishing to be more than man, makes a bargain with the devil and exchanges his soul for twenty-four years of power.

Unfortunately for Faustus, the bargain turns out badly; instead of becoming greater than man, he spends most of his allotted twenty-four years playing stupid pranks and entertaining the nobility. Like Voldemort, his bargain has diminished him, and his pride has brought about his own destruction. He accomplishes nothing of value during his allotted time and during his final night on earth is reduced to pleading to become less than man. Reasoning that animals have no souls, he voices the desire to be an animal, or even an inanimate object like a water drop. Although I am not arguing for direct influence, I believe the parallels between the two cases are striking. Both men voice a desire to be greater than man; both are diminished by their own actions. While one relinquishes his soul in a worthless bargain, the other willingly severs his soul and distributes the fragments among things less than a man, namely material objects and a snake.

Unlike the consuming fear of death experienced by both Faustus and Voldemort, Dumbledore at the conclusion of *Sorcerer's Stone* articulates a much more philosophical position. Reassuring Harry that destruction of the stone is really for the best, Dumbledore states, "After all, to the well-organized mind, death is but the next great adventure" (*SS* 297). Later, in a direct confrontation, Dumbledore tells Voldemort, "your failure to understand that there are things much worse than death has always been your greatest weakness—" (*OotP* 814). In addition to his acceptance of death as a necessity, Dumbledore possesses many qualities that make him Voldemort's polar opposite. Unlike Voldemort, who subjugates his followers, Dumbledore allows his cohorts and students freedom to make their own decisions. This willingness to respect the individuality of others is especially apparent in his treatment of the young Tom Riddle. As his memories held in the Pensieve reveal, Dumbledore is suspicious of Tom from a very early age. However, he allows the boy the freedom to make his own choices and determine his own path, merely refusing to help him in the process.

Another overreacher from literature who provides a parallel to Voldemort is the title character from Mary Shelley's *Frankenstein*. While the early film version and later popularizations have demonized the Creature and frequently portrayed Victor Frankenstein in a heroic light, the original novel presents a far more critical portrayal of Frankenstein the creator. Like Voldemort, Frankenstein is motivated by pride and an obsessive desire to defy death. Also, like Voldemort's treatment of his followers, Frankenstein's treatment of the creature is characterized by selfishness and cruelty. Revolted by the ugliness of the being he has created, Victor abandons the creature and then becomes a helpless witness to the creature's murder of all those whom Victor loves. Seeking to be a creator or a being greater than man who can master death, Victor becomes the unintentional means for bringing death to the members of his immediate family. Like Voldemort, Frankenstein becomes less because he had tried pridefully to become more. He spends the latter portion of the novel and of his life in hopeless pursuit of his creature in order to fulfill his obsessive desire for revenge. His focus on destroying his creature in many ways parallels Voldemort's relationship to Harry. Both men live joyless existences consumed by thoughts of destroying an adversary that they themselves have created. As Dumbledore tells Harry, "Voldemort himself created his worst enemy... He heard the prophecy and he leapt into action, with the result that he not only handpicked the man most likely to finish him, he handed him uniquely deadly weapons" (*HBP* 510).

This comparison to Victor Frankenstein also highlights Voldemort's fundamental cowardice. Unlike Frankenstein, who hopelessly pursues an adversary who is bigger and stronger than he is, Voldemort brings about his own downfall by attempting to kill an infant. In *Goblet of Fire,* he decides to display his power by staging a "duel" that he mistakenly assumes he can win easily, and the confrontation at the Ministry near the conclusion of *Order of the Phoenix* depicts the disconcerting spectacle of Lucius Malfoy and a band of adult Death Eaters taunting and attempting to destroy a group of adolescents. It seems highly fitting that Rowling has postponed the final confrontation between Harry and Voldemort until Harry reaches the age of adulthood in the wizarding world.

Throughout his appearances, Rowling presents Voldemort as obsessed with avoiding death but unable to enjoy life. This characteristic of joylessness is another important attribute in Rowling's depiction of evil as Voldemort and his followers live lives totally devoid of joy or pleasure of any sort. His followers live in fear of reprisals from a demanding master; Voldemort lives in fear of death and of a prophecy about Harry. Their misery is in marked contrast to Rowling's depiction of her "good" characters. While the novels have progressively become darker and more preoccupied with Voldemort, the early novels and major portions of even the later works depict Harry and his friends as leading full and frequently satisfying adolescent lives. Harry, Ron, Hermione, and their friends do not spend every waking hour of their six years at school worrying over Voldemort. They quarrel, make up, take lessons, break rules, play games, and fall in love. Unlike Voldemort, who merely exists, they actually live.

It is interesting to note that most critical work thus far has been devoted to Harry and to Rowling's skillful creation of a magical world. In three early anthologies devoted to the series—*The Ivory Tower and Harry Potter: Perspectives on a Literary Phenomenon, Reading Harry Potter: Critical Essays,* and *Harry Potter's World: Multidisciplinary Critical Perspectives*—Voldemort is discussed in passing in some of the essays, but in none of the three anthologies is there an essay focusing entirely upon him. One obvious explanation is that Harry and the "good" characters appear a great deal more than the largely absent Voldemort; however, they are also more interesting characters than he is. They share dynamic and changing relationships and show a potential for growth and development. In contrast, Voldemort recognizes only relationships in which he is either the master or the antagonist. It is perhaps one of Rowling's greatest accomplishments that she has made good a great deal more interesting and attractive than evil.

In addition, a quality which is frequently ignored in her novels and which contributes greatly to their success is their extensive and effective use of humor. Because evil takes itself totally seriously, it is unable to laugh. In contrast, Dumbledore frequently exhibits a sly sense of humor, and Remus Lupin teaches his Defense Against the Dark Arts class that the way to defeat a boggart taking on the shape of their deepest fears is to laugh at it. The action of the early books is often dominated by the Weasley twins, who become the beneficiaries of Harry's winnings from the Triwizard Tournament. Insisting that they open their planned joke shop, Harry asserts, "We could all do with a few laughs. I've got a feeling we're going to need them more than usual before long" (*GoF* 733). I have chosen to end with this particular quotation because it illustrates one of the significant but neglected differences between good and evil: good is characterized by generosity and a willingness to laugh at itself; evil is markedly devoid of both qualities.

Works Cited

Anatol, Giselle Liza, ed. *Reading Harry Potter: Critical Essays.* Westport, Conn.: Praeger, 2003.

Heilman, Elizabeth E., ed. *Harry Potter's World: Multidisciplinary Critical Perspectives.* New York and London: RoutledgeFalmer, 2003.

Marlowe, Christopher. *Doctor Faustus.* In *The Works of Christopher Marlowe.* Ed. C. F. Tucker Brooke. Oxford: Clarendon Press, 1966. 139–229.

Rowling, J. K. *Harry Potter and the Chamber of Secrets.* New York: Scholastic, 1999.

—. *Harry Potter and the Goblet of Fire.* New York: Scholastic, 2000.

—. *Harry Potter and the Half-Blood Prince.* New York: Scholastic, 2005.

—. *Harry Potter and the Order of the Phoenix.* New York: Scholastic, 2003.

—. *Harry Potter and the Prisoner of Azkaban.* New York: Scholastic, 1999.

—. *Harry Potter and the Sorcerer's Stone.* New York: Scholastic, 1997.

Shelley, Mary. *Frankenstein.* 2nd ed. Ed. Johanna M. Smith. Boston and New York: Bedford/St. Martin's, 2000.

Stoker, Bram *Dracula.* Ed. John Paul Riquelme. Boston and New York: Bedford/St. Martin's, 2002.

Whited, Lana A., ed. *The Ivory Tower and Harry Potter: Perspectives on a Literary Phenomenon.* Columbia and London: University of Missouri Press, 2002.

Turban Legend: A Different Perspective on P-p-poor P-p-professor Quirrell

Susan Miller

Professor Quirrell is the Rodney Dangerfield of the Potterverse.

He is teaching the most dangerous course in the curriculum and apparently has a good handle on his subject matter, but his classes are derided as being "a joke." He doesn't even get the courtesy of a verifiable first name. He rarely has any screen time in the one book where he is the star and is dramatically disposed of in the story climax. It's about time we gave him his due.

His name comes up in every book. And for a minor character, we actually know quite a bit of his backstory. Why are we constantly reminded of such a minor and disposable character?

This presentation will attempt to resurrect the stuttering professor from the dustbin of forgotten plot points into his rightful place as an important piece of the *Potter* saga.

First, let's see if we can give the poor guy a first name.

Quirrell has a trading card in the Wizards of the Coast™ game, where his name is listed as Quirinus. The makers of the game claim that their information came from J. K. Rowling herself. Their information has tended to be reliable, since they also provided the first names of professors Pomona Sprout and Filius Flitwick. These names have since been confirmed by Rowling on her Web site on their respective birthdays.

As we know, Rowling gives much thought to the names she chooses. Pomona is the name of a Roman goddess of fruit trees. Filius means "son of." It is also a type of umbrella, so maybe that's why his drink of choice is cherry syrup and soda with ice and an umbrella.

Why might she have chosen the name Quirinus for Quirrell?

The Men With Two Faces

Janus Quirinus

Quirinus Quirrell

God of Beginnings and Endings

Anti-hero of the beginning of a saga

Figure 1 (coin source:
<http://affordablehousinginstitute.org/blogs/us/
2005/11/fixing_french_h.html>)

He is known as The Man with Two Faces.

In Roman mythology, the god with two faces is Janus Quirinus. He was the god of gates, doors, doorways, beginnings and *endings*.

Janus Quirinus was one of the most important deities of the Roman state. In later years, he became known by another name: Romulus, the twin brother of Remus, who together were raised by wolves. For everyone who has been wondering whether Lupin has a brother, here you go. A fanfic is in there somewhere. It's also interesting to note that Janus Quirinus is associated with the myrtle plant.

There was a real person named Quirinus, who became a Catholic martyr. The Catholic Online site calls him an "outstanding hero." (Remember that "hero" part. It may come back in regards to another Quirinus.)

St. Quirinus is the patron saint of protection against evil spirits, obsession and possessed people. St. Quirinus' supposed last words were, "God is always with us and can help us. He was with me when I was taken and He is with me now." Compare that to Quirrell's remark that Voldemort "is with me wherever I go. I have served him faithfully."

As Quirrell was possessed by an evil spirit, was obsessed, was a man with two faces and was instrumental in the beginning of the saga, Quirinus is a perfect name for this character on several levels, and as usual, Rowling thought carefully when she selected this name.

Naturally, the movie gives him the first name of Slatero. That's only one of many things the movie got wrong about this character. We will get to that later.

Now that he has a full name, let's examine the stuttering professor and why he is so important to the story.

Like the Potter saga itself, Quirrell's story can be broken down into...books.

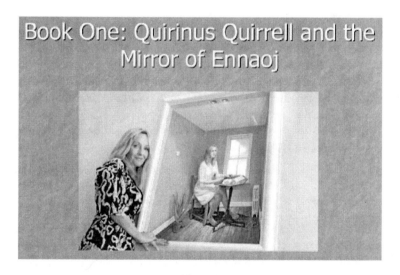

Figure 2

Book One: Quirrell and the Mirror of Ennaoj

This is a great picture of J. K. Rowling. She is standing, smiling, in front of a painting that shows something of what her life was like at the time she was writing *Harry Potter and the Philosopher's Stone*. In the painting, she is alone in a bare room with only her papers and the barest of necessities. I don't know the history of this painting, but is apparent that she loves it. She is not afraid to remember and explore her life when she was at a very different place than she is now.

Rowling has often said that she identifies with the character of Hermione. That is true—Jo and Hermione were both bookish know-it-alls when they were children. But alone, impoverished and downtrodden as she was when she was writing *Harry Potter and the Philosopher's Stone*, she wrote herself into the character of Quirrell.

Prior to beginning the writing of the *Harry Potter* saga, Rowling was an impressionable young teacher who went to a foreign country to gain experience and teach. She fell in love, married and bore a daughter to a man who became an abusive and controlling master. She fled back to Scotland, and the rest is history.

Prior to the beginning of *Sorcerer's Stone*, Quirrell was an impressionable young teacher who went to a foreign country to gain experience to improve his teaching. He was seduced by a dynamic stranger who became an abusive and controlling master. He returned to Hogwarts in Scotland, and the rest is history.

In the Potterverse, Quirrell represents the abused spouse archetype. As a young man, his idealism caused him to leave his secure job to gain practical experience and improve his teaching. He wandered the world, until he crossed paths with Voldemort. Voldemort began his control over Quirrell by confusing him with questions of morality:

"A foolish young man I was then, full of ridiculous ideas about good and evil. Lord Voldemort showed me how wrong I was. There is no good and evil, there is only power, and those too weak to seek it."

Voldemort is creating dependence by making Quirrell question his values and removing him from his normal circle of friends and influences. After this point, we have no indication that Quirrell has any friends at all at Hogwarts.

Voldemort is successful in convincing Quirrell to bring him home and set up house. The seduction is complete. Quirrell is completely dependent upon Voldemort for companionship. This is the way of the abuser: Remove all avenues of support. Close off all outside influences and shut down critical thinking. Establish a pattern where the victim lives in a world of loneliness and fear. The victim will then begin to do whatever it takes to please the abuser and avoid punishment.

Figure 3

In Figure 3, the movie got it right. Here the teachers are at a fun school activity. But Quirrell is isolated. He is alone in the crowd, invisible to his neighbors. Sadly, this is often true for abuse victims in their surroundings. People instinctively withdraw from one who seems different or seems under stress.

With his victim isolated, the controller begins to make demands. He starts small. The first tiny task will be to rob a bank. And not just any bank or any vault. This particular vault is especially secure. Accessing this vault in this bank without the help of a goblin will cause you to get sucked into the vault, where they might find your bones in ten years. In his need to please his master, Quirrell is willing to attempt the impossible, even at great personal cost.

After the robbery failure, the demands become greater and the punishments more severe. Voldemort moves permanently into Quirrell's body against his will, completing the rape metaphor. The symptoms are there for all to see—Quirrell begins to behave differently. He begins to dress oddly. He stutters and appears to be afraid. His work goes downhill. His personal hygiene suffers. He smells. Certainly, part of this is for show, part of the act, but we hear him weeping when he is in private. This is surely true suffering.

In the dungeon, he tells Harry:

"[My master] has had to be very hard on me. He does not forgive mistakes easily. When I failed to steal the stone from Gringotts, he was most displeased. He had to punish me."

This is typical speech from an abuse victim: "My master *has had* to be hard on me." It is *their own* fault that the master has to punish them.

Quirrell tries to get in the master's good graces by trying to knock Harry off his broom at the Quidditch match, but fails. This is sort of a feeble effort in any event as people seem to survive falls from brooms easily. Quirrell tries desperately to make points without much forethought about the likely results. This is a pattern that we see repeated in *Half-Blood Prince*, when Draco is in the same position. Attempting to please his new master, Draco tries first a cursed necklace, then poisoned wine. Neither is very well thought out, but Draco, like Quirrell, is willing to try anything to please Voldemort. Voldemort is a serial abuser.

Voldemort's demands against Quirrell escalate, and Quirrell complies. Kill unicorns? Okay. Murder Harry? Okay. His entire personality is displaced by that of his abuser.

This is how an abuser works—get the victim into a state of learned helplessness, where they no longer have any personal will other than that of the abuser. It takes a very special strength to be able to break out of that kind of bind. Rowling was that type of special person. She broke free from her abuser and fled.

Figure 4

She built her pain and her experience into the character of Quirrell. She gave him a name that expresses weakness and pain, "Quirrell"—small "I" in the middle of a quarrel. This is how a victim of an abusive relationship feels—diminished and surrounded by quarrelling.

This is how she must have felt at the time. It is so clearly a reflection of her that she even puts a mirror in the scene. It is a special mirror that doesn't reflect the truth, but reflects what the viewer wants to see. No victim wants to look at things the way they are, so this mirror shows things the way they should be.

Figure 5 (source:
<http://www.bbc.co.uk/london/content/articles/
2005/09/06/portrait_painting_revival_feature.shtml>)

I think that is why Rowling is smiling in the photograph above. She is standing in front of a reverse Mirror of Erised. This mirror shows the way things were and might have remained, except for her personal strength, her creativity and a lot of very good luck.

And that is the whole point of the story. This is a story about choice and consequences. And that is going to be the message of the final book in the series.

With the realization that Quirrell is Jo, let's see how it could possibly play out. And since there is only a little time left for speculating, let's take advantage of it and make some guesses!

Book Two: Quirrell and the Celluloid Fanfic

Quirrell is most famous for two things: He wears a turban, and he is dead.

We'll get to the turban and what it contained in a moment. Let's first examine his "death."

In the book, whatever happened in the dungeon happens outside our view. Let's see what we know for certain.

> Quirrell raised his hand to perform a deadly curse, but Harry, by instinct, reached up and *grabbed Quirrell's face*—
> "AAAARGH!"
> Quirrell rolled off him, his face blistering, too, and then Harry knew: Quirrell couldn't touch his bare skin, not without suffering terrible pain.
> Hrary jumped to his feet, *caught Quirrell by the arm*, and hung on as tight as he could. Quirrell screamed and tried to throw Hrary off—the pain in Harry's head was building—*he couldn't see*—he could only hear *Quirrell's terrible shrieks* and Voldemort's yells of "KILL HIM! KILL HIM!" and *other voices*, maybe in Harry's own head, crying "Harry! Harry!"
> He felt Quirrell's arm, wrenched from his grasp, knew all was lost and fell into blackness, down… down… down… (emphasis added)

This is the text of what happened in the dungeon. There are several items of note in the narrative here, which I've italicized.

First, Harry may have touched Quirrell's face, but at the time Voldemort leaves, Harry only has hold of Quirrell's *arm*. Furthermore, Quirrell is *alive* when Harry loses consciousness. Quirrell is shrieking when the rescuers are arriving. And notice, it's *rescuers*—plural. Harry hears *other voices*.

Secondly, just after Harry grabs Quirrell, Harry is blinded.

The narrative says "the pain in Harry's head was building—he couldn't see—he could only hear." This is the last thing he is to see for the next three days. What is going on that Rowling doesn't want Harry, or us, to see?

Then there is a gap of three days before the narrative resumes with Harry waking up in the hospital wing. If you listen closely to Dumbledore's speech to Harry, he clearly makes the case that Quirrell did not die in the dungeon. Let's review:

In the hospital wing, Dumbledore speaks:

"Professor Quirrell did not manage to take [the stone] from you. I arrived in time to prevent that, although you were doing very well on your own, I must say.

"I arrived in time to pull Quirrell off you."

Quirrell must have still been alive when Harry was blacking out. Dumbledore had to pull Quirrell off him.

And what does Dumbledore say about the end of Quirrell? "[Voldemort] left Quirrell to die; he shows just as little mercy to his followers as his enemies." Notice the "left to die" phrasing. It is clear that when Voldemort left, Quirrell was not yet dead.

What else does Dumbledore say about Quirrell?

"...[T]o have been loved so deeply, even though the person who loves us is gone, will give us some protection forever. It is in your very skin. Quirrell, full of hatred, greed, and ambition, sharing his soul with Voldemort, could not touch you for this reason. It was agony to touch a person marked by something so good."

Dumbledore says it was "agony" for Quirrell to touch Harry, not that it was fatal.

And then, there's the unicorn blood.

"[I]t is a monstrous thing, to slay a unicorn," said Firenze. "*The blood of a unicorn will keep you alive, even you are an inch from death*, but at a terrible price..."

"But who'd be that desperate?" [Harry] wondered aloud. "If you're going to be cursed forever, death's better, isn't it?"

"It is, Firenze agreed, "unless all you need is to say alive long enough to drink something else—something that will bring you back to full strength and power—something that will mean you can never die." (emphasis added)

As Firenze tells us, drinking a unicorn's blood will keep you alive even if you are an inch from death. And Quirrell had at least a double-dose of unicorn blood in him. In fact, if you think about it, the whole unicorn subplot here serves very little purpose. We are introduced to the Forbidden Forest and the centaurs, but there is very little reason otherwise to introduce the unicorn blood device. Either we will see unicorn blood being put to some use in the final book, or it was already used to bring back one who was close to death and to leave everyone believing otherwise.

Furthermore, as Firenze tells us, the unicorn blood only needs to keep the drinker alive until they can drink something else with more power. An elixir whose prime ingredient is right there in the room with them along with a wizard who knows how to make it! Is it a coincidence?

Flint? Or Something Else?

In *Half-Blood Prince*, Dumbledore makes a problematic statement. He says that he has *never* been able to keep a Defense Against the Dark Arts teacher for more than one year. But Quirrell would have to have taught at Hogwarts more than just one year. If he were a new teacher, or new to the position of Dark Arts, Dumbledore would have said something in the welcoming feast of Harry's first year. Other evidence also suggests that Quirrell had the post for at least two years, and probably more.

Is it a Flint? Is Dumbledore mistaken, or is it something else? If it were a Flint, Rowling would have made a correction as she did with the Marcus Flint error, where she mistakenly had him stay at Hogwarts for too many years.

I don't think this is a Flint. I think Dumbledore's statement is deliberate. There is something so important that Dumbledore must break his promise to Harry and tell an outright lie. He is an inexpert fibber and the whopper he tells doesn't sit right. What could he be hiding?

Perhaps it's that Quirrell did not die as everyone thinks, and is off doing important and very secret work for a man who is known to employ spies and double agents?

There is no doubt that Voldemort believes that Quirrell is dead. Let's skip ahead to the graveyard scene in *Goblet of Fire* and see what Voldy himself says about the incident and about possession in general (emphasis added):

"Only one power remained to me. I could possess the bodies of others.... I sometimes inhabited animals—snakes, of course, being my preference—but *their bodies were ill adapted to perform magic*...and my possession of them shortened their lives; none of them lasted long...

"Then...four years ago...the means for my return seemed assured. A wizard—young, foolish, and gullible—he wandered across my path in the forest I had made my home. Oh, he seemed the very chance I had been dreaming of...for he was a teacher at Dumbledore's school... he was easy to bend to my will. I took possession of his body, to supervise him closely as he carried out my orders. But my plan failed. I did not manage to steal the Sorcerer's Stone. I was not to be assured immortal life. I was thwarted...thwarted, once again, by Harry Potter.

"The servant died when I left his body, and I was left as weak as ever I had been."

On this last, Voldemort is wrong. Voldemort assumes that leaving a possessed body causes the host to die because it always happened with the animals. But note—the animals died because their bodies were ill-adapted to perform magic. The animals died because they weren't wizards. And it's a good thing that wizards can survive a possession because Harry is possessed in the battle at the Ministry of Magic. There is no reason to assume that Quirrell would have died because of the possession by Voldemort.

In fact, there is no reason at all why Quirrell could not have survived the face-off in the dungeon. At worst, he has a blistered face, a sore arm, and a cursed half-life.

I know what everybody is thinking. The movie couldn't have been that wrong. Doesn't Rowling have script approval?

Now, yes. But back at the time of the first film, here is what she was saying.

"I have been allowed to make my views felt. You know, that's not to say they're going to take my views on board, but the conscience rests easy, if you like, knowing that I was able to sit in the meeting and say what I would not be comfortable with. But it's not my call.... All I can really say on that is that I've, I've been allowed to say what I would be happy with, whether that happens or not, it's not in my control." (Nigel Ballard, Interview, BBC Bristol, 12 Nov 2001)

"When I actually sat down to see the film, I was terrified. Because it was way too late if bits were wrong. But at the end of the film, I was happy." (*BBC Newsround*, 2 Nov 2001)

And there's this from the Rowling Thunder interview in August of 2000:

Jeff Jensen: "Do you have kind of control over what Warner Bros. does with Harry Potter?"

Rowling: "Can I prevent it in terms of what's in my contract? No. But they have been very gracious in allowing my input; and I have been asked a lot of questions I never expected to be asked." (*Entertainment Weekly*, 4 Aug 2000)

At the time of the first movie, she did not get to see the script beforehand. She sat in at only one meeting to discuss the script. She could respond only to questions they asked her during production. She saw the movie for the first time at the premiere along with the rest of us. If they made a huge mistake, what was she going to say —"Oops, they shouldn't have killed off that character, since he will be important later on"? No, she could only keep quiet and demand more input in future films—which she now has, and I feel confident that it was because of this one major blunder in the first film.

And besides—so he's dust. Are we certain that in this magical world of Rowling's creation, he can't be reconstituted into a living being again? It's magic.

Book Three: Quirrell and the End of the Saga

We left Quirrell in the dungeon with an unconscious Harry, Dumbledore and unknown others, a sore arm and a headache.

This is a story about choice and consequences. If Rowling is Quirrell, could she really kill off her own avatar without redeeming him first?

Let's speculate what happened next, in the missing three days and afterwards.

Dumbledore pulls Quirrell off Harry and Voldemort leaves, believing that Quirrell has died. The first priority is Harry, who is near death. It is likely that someone conjured a stretcher and took him off to the hospital wing, where he remained for the next three days, collecting sweets, get-well cards and toilet seats.

And Quirrell? Is it possible that, free from Voldemort's influence, Quirrell's head literally cleared and was able to make the choice to return to the good side?

Let's examine what else we know about Quirrell, and draw some conclusions on how it might have gone.

It's all about "The Philosopher's Stone."

Quirrell flies under the radar throughout the whole book. His importance only shows up in association with the Philosopher's Stone. And this is vital.

Typically, the first book of a series is simply named after the protagonist. We would expect the first book to be called simply "*Harry Potter*," with sequels being named "*Harry Potter and the....*" But Rowling didn't do it that way. The first book is called *Harry*

Potter and the Philosopher's Stone. The Philosopher's Stone has equal billing with the star, and I think that is by design. It is the Philosopher's Stone that encapsulates what the whole series is about.

The Philosopher's Stone does two things. It turns base metals into precious ones and it is a key ingredient in the Elixir of Life.

Rowling is fond of hiding things in plain sight and then leading us in the completely wrong direction in the narrative. We have spent the last six books talking about immortality, which is one of the powers of the Stone. But I believe that the real power of the stone —and the message of the book—is about turning baseness into purity. I believe that the whole immortality thing is a giant red herring. The story isn't about Voldemort's search for immortality at all. It's really about the other side of the Philosopher's Stone. It's really about the transmutation of the base into the pure.

The story is about looking in the mirror and making a choice.

Quirrell looks in the mirror and sees himself serving his master. Harry looks in the mirror and sees himself amidst his family or sees himself saving the stone from Quirrell. Contrast this. Quirrell has no "self" left. He is nothing more than a conduit for another. Harry, on the other hand, has his own concept of love and valor. In this situation, Harry is the adult and Quirrell is the child. The mirror shows us the truth.

But this was Quirrell under the influence of Voldemort. When he was free of his parasitic master, Quirinus Quirrell, god of beginnings and endings, patron saint of possessed people, looked in the mirror and chose to become—what? This is what we don't know. But knowing what we now know, we might be able to do some theorizing.

Quirrell needed a dragon's egg to fool Hagrid. He could have gotten a handy Welsh Green or Hebridean Black, which are local to the neighborhood. Instead, he got a Norwegian Ridgeback. We are told this is a rare dragon. Surely, Rowling is hinting that this dragon lives only in northern Scandinavia and is rarely or never found elsewhere.

Why did Quirrell choose to get this particular egg when any one would do? Is it because he is familiar with Norway and has connections there? And how did he get there and back without missing any classes or allowing the egg to cool? There is not enough time to fly on a broomstick or thestral. The Knight Bus can't go over water. Apparate? Perhaps, but we don't see wizards Apparating over long distances. Even when traveling to London, Dumbledore doesn't Apparate.

Did Quirrell have someone get it and deliver it to him? Unlikely. He has no confederates and is operating in stealth. Besides, the messenger would have the same time travel—and time—problems as Quirrell himself.

But there is one other way into and out of Hogwarts—the lake portal to Durmstrang. Could this have been his shortcut to Norway?

There is evidence that Quirrell is familiar with Scandinavia. He is good with trolls. Trolls are Scandinavian. Some types of trolls are known to herd dragons. Quirrell must have spent some time in Norway or Scandinavia to become familiar with beings and dragons that are native there. Did he learn this at Durmstrang?

Quirrell knows the Dark Arts well enough to be hired as the teacher of Defense Against the Dark Arts at Hogwarts. Where did he learn it? How about at the wizarding school that teaches the Dark Arts to students from around the world? Is Quirrell an alumnus of Durmstrang? He shows no apparent affiliation with any of the houses of Hogwarts. And where did he get skilled with animals and beings that are native to Scandinavia?

Is Durmstrang in Norway? Experts in fandom have argued this for years. The mountainous terrain and long cold winters agree with Norway as a location. The only thing that does not agree with Norway is the name of the school and names of the students and faculty.

But as noted by Draco Malfoy, Durmstrang attracts students from many countries. There could easily be Bulgarian students and Russian teachers at such a school.

And what about the German-sounding name of the school itself? Rowling has told us that major events in the Muggle world do affect those in the wizarding world. For example, wizards participated in World War II. What was happening in Norway during World War II? It was occupied by the Germans. The name "Quirrell" reminds us of Quisling, the Norwegian milquetoast who cooperated with the Nazis during World War II. Quisling allowed evil to come to Norway because of his weakness. Quirrell allowed evil to come to Hogwarts because of his weakness.

Finally, Rowling gave a reading in Glasgow for the Maggie's Cancer Caring Centre on December 9, 2000, where she was quoted as saying that she believed Durmstrang was in northern Scandinavia —the very north of Sweden or Norway—but that since it was secret, she was not certain.

So, why is all this noise about Durmstrang important in a presentation about Quirrell? It provides a clue as to what we might expect in the last book.

In 1945, Dumbledore defeated the evil wizard Grindelwald. What was happening in 1945, and does it have anything to do with our story?

Q: Is Grindelwald dead?

A: Yeah, he is.

Q: is he important?

A: [regretful] Ohhh....

Q: You don't have to answer but can you give us some backstory on him?

A: I'm going to tell you as much as I told someone earlier who asked me.... Is it coincidence that he died in 1945? And I said no. It amuses me to make allusions to things that were happening in the Muggle world, so my feeling would be that while there's a global Muggle war going on, there's also a global wizarding war going on.

Q: Does he have any connection to—

A: I have no comment to make on that subject.

Q: Do they feed on each other, the Muggle and wizarding wars?

A: Yeah, I think so. Yeah. Mmm.

Q: You've gone very quiet.

[All laugh, Rowling maniacally]

Q: We like when you get very quiet, it means—

Q: You've clearly hiding something. (Interview with Melissa Anelli and Emerson Spartz, 16 July 2005)

So, 1945 is important. Wizards went to war with the Nazis. Grindelwald is important. Now, make the next leap with me.

I think we will find that during the occupation of Norway, Nazi wizards took over an existing Norwegian school of magic and renamed it with a German name. The purpose was to create a school whose main focus is to teach the Dark Arts, which it does to this day. Durmstrang Institute is the child of Wizard World War II.

Did Dumbledore use or create the lake portal between Hogwarts and Durmstrang as part of the battle that defeated Grindelwald?

And is that how Quirrell got to Norway and back with Norbert's egg so quickly?

And to think, it all started with a simple Norwegian dragon egg.

Is all this a hint of what could be coming in the end of the saga?

Let's look at Dumbledore's lie: "I have never been able to keep a DADA teacher…"

I think it is part of Dumbledore's plan. Everybody thinks Quirrell is dead. Rowling makes a point of reminding us in every book. He makes a perfect agent. He can return to Durmstrang and work to recruit students for the final battle. He could even work on the trolls. Voldemort has giants, in the last battle; maybe Hogwarts' side will have trolls.

I think that Quirrell left Hogwarts secretly by using the plumbing pipes to get from the dungeon to the lake. At that point, he took a first-year's boat and went on a mission from Dumbledore to Durmstrang. And that is where he has been for the last five years while everybody thinks he is dead.

Janus Quirinus Quirrell is the Man with Two Faces, the god of beginnings and *endings*. And I think the p-p-poor stuttering p-p-professor will be the big surprise of the final book.

And anyway, if I'm wrong, then there is a heck of a great fanfic to be written by somebody.

THE PRISONER AND THE PATRIARCHY: FAMILY SECRETS IN *HARRY POTTER AND THE PRISONER OF AZKABAN*

Brandy Blake
University of Georgia

J. K. Rowling's *Harry Potter* series draws on a variety of literature genres, but only one novel in this series emphasizes many of the traditions of the Gothic novel. *Harry Potter and the Prisoner of Azkaban* utilizes Gothic traditions in order to emphasize the novel's focus on fear, on family, on the patriarchal line. More importantly, however, it allows her to introduce her focus on tearing down the patriarchal line in order to force Harry to take the place of those who came before him—to stop relying on father figures, step up, and become the hero.

In general, *Prisoner of Azkaban* uses many Gothic conventions and motifs. Some of these appear in the entire series—the haunted house, ghosts, occult phenomena, and monstrous creatures. However, others are specific to *Prisoner*. Sirius Black alone embodies several Gothic conventions. As far as Harry knows at the beginning of the novel, Black is an escaped prisoner, a murderer, and a madman, three characteristics that appear often in Gothic novels. Even the name "Black" emphasizes the evil nature of this character. Gothic literature also depicts imprisonment and madness, both of which are represented through dementors, which guard Azkaban, the wizard prison, by "'suck[ing] the happiness out of a place'" and making most of the prisoners mad (*PoA* 97). Gothic literature also emphasizes repetition, "the constant recurrence of the same thing" (Freud 234)—one of Freud's concepts of the uncanny. And both this repetition and the concept of doubling are apparent when

Harry and Hermione go back in time and relive the past three hours of their lives. Finally, according to Anne Williams in her critical work on Gothic literature, *Art of Darkness*, "Male Gothic plot and narrative conventions also focus on female suffering" (104). Throughout the novel, Harry and Ron ignore Hermione, make her cry, and generally make her suffer—all because she is defending her pet, attempting to protect Harry from being harmed by Sirius Black, and overall, just being too virtuous (or more of a goody-two-shoes) than Harry and Ron want her to be.

While *Prisoner of Azkaban* does conform to general Gothic traditions, according to critics, the Gothic has two particular foci important to the overall ideas of this essay: its relationship to family (in general) and to patriarchy (specifically). In *Art of Darkness*, Anne Williams writes: "family stories, especially those involving exclusion and repression, are somehow intimately connected with 'Gothic'" (11). All of the major Gothic novels revolve around the family: *The Castle of Otranto*, *The Mysterious Mother*, *The Monk*, *Frankenstein*, etc. More specifically, these Gothic plots that focus on "exclusion and repression" often attempt to keep secrets.

Resolution of the conventional Gothic mystery coincides with the revelation of a particular family secret, usually a hitherto unrecognized aspect of family relationship: that Emily's aunt has been murdered by Laurentini di Udolpho; that Manfred's claim to the throne is illegitimate; that Jane is not only [Jane] Eyre but an heir. Indeed, despite the length and narrative complexity of many early Gothics, they yield surprisingly precise information about the family trees of the characters involved, information that is not trivial, given the importance of the family as basic organizing principle in the narratives (Williams 45). Thus, secrets that explicitly involve the family recur constantly in the Gothic, and as a way to build suspense, they make the audience wait until the end for the twist.

Williams also emphasizes the Gothic's use of patriarchy. Because families are traditionally patriarchal structures, the Gothic must emphasize this structure: "[F]amily structure ... generates the plots that occur within Gothic, for it imposes a certain balance of power, both personal and political: power that may redound through the generations as surely as fortunes—or family curses—may be inherited" (22). Power is inherited through the patriarchal line. However, while Gothic literature is shaped by notions of and focus on the family, it also emphasizes the weaknesses of the patriarchal line and with manhood in general. According to Cyndy Hendershot in *The Animal Within: Masculinity and the Gothic*, Gothic works "frequently reveal the fragility of traditional manhood. While reactions to this fragility vary, the Gothic is preoccupied with the precarious alignment of the whole male subject and the fragile, individual men who attempt to represent the male subject" (4). The patriarchy seems to structure and define everything, but it is paranoid about falling apart. And it is falling apart: "[f]rom Ambrosio's loss of his position as a whole and untainted monk to the depletion of the vampire hunters' blood supply to Kurtz's loss of his European ego to Rochester's maimed body, the Gothic continually reveals the gulf between the actual male subject and the myth of masculinity" (4). Whether taken apart by outsiders or destroyed from within, the patriarchy in Gothic literature is at risk and in danger of collapse.

Prisoner of Azkaban, unlike the other books in the *Harry Potter* series, focuses on Harry's family. Up until this point in the series, Rowling has provided little information on Harry's parents, Lily and James. However, in this novel, Rowling reveals information on the patriarchal line. Harry learns about his father's years at school, meets his father's closest friends (his symbolic "uncles"), and learns that he has a godfather. The entire plot of *PoA* revolves around these characters. Harry's discovery of this information leads to the revelation of the family's secrets and to his knowledge of the instability of this patriarchy, which becomes the central anxiety of the story.

Along with patriarchal anxiety, Gothic novels generally present a mood of fear, and the plot of *PoA* emphasizes fear with two creatures in particular—the boggart and the dementors. A boggart, according to Hermione, "'can take the shape of whatever it thinks will frighten us most'" (*PoA* 133). Dementors are Harry's greatest fear, which we know because throughout the novel Harry's boggarts turn into dementors, but the relevant question is: Why are dementors Harry's greatest fear? The audience might think, as Professor Lupin does, that Harry's worst fear would be Voldemort. However, Harry's fear of dementors is complex, and it emphasizes the Gothic categories of horror and terror. First, dementors are undoubtedly figures of horror. Horror "is conveyed through the devices of the grotesque" (MacAndrew 156), such as bloody body parts and wormy corpses. The description of the dementor emphasizes the grotesque: "There was a hand protruding from the cloak and it was glistening, grayish, slimy-looking, and scabbed, like something dead that had decayed in water" (*PoA* 83). When Harry first realizes that his boggart will turn into a dementor, he remembers this hand. Ann Radcliffe, whose definitions of horror and terror originally defined the differences in the two ideas, "associated horror with physical symptoms—contraction, freezing, a threat that the faculties will be annihilated" (Williams 73). Harry's experiences with the dementors focus on this freezing physicality: "An intense cold swept over them all. Harry felt his own breath catch in his chest. The cold went deeper than his skin. It was inside his chest, it was inside his very heart" (*PoA* 83). Thus, part of the fear inspired by the dementors comes from their grotesque Otherness, their monstrosity as gross, vampiric creatures. However, that is the most simplistic aspect of the dementors, and Harry's fear of them goes far beyond their simple monstrosity, more closely illustrating terror, which Radcliffe "[associates] with the Burkean sublime" (Williams 73). According to *A Glossary of Literary Gothic Terms*, "Works of terror create a sense of uncertain apprehension that leads to a complex fear of obscure and dreadful elements" (Rigdon). Harry fears the dementors because they make him remember. They force him to see negative aspects of himself and of his patriarchal line, showing him who is to blame for the death of his mother, and it is this fear, linked more to the idea of terror than that of horror, which I will trace through the rest of the book.

Unlike in most novels, the plot of *PoA* slowly unveils the past rather than focusing on a progression to the future. At this point in the series, Harry knows very little about his parents, and he possesses no actual memories of either of them. His only memory before the Dursleys is of the spell that failed to kill him: "Sometimes, when he strained his memory during long hours in his cupboard, he came up with a strange vision: a blinding flash of green light and a burning pain on his forehead.... He couldn't remember his parents at all" (*PoA* 29). Harry's first memory of his parents, particularly his mother, emerges because of the dementors. Dementors don't simply make people feel cold and experience a gut reaction; they make people relive bad experiences. Lupin explains, "Get too near a dementor and every good feeling, every happy memory will be sucked out of you.... You'll be left with nothing but the worst experiences of your life" (187). Thus, when Harry gets close to a dementor, he remembers this worst experience, reliving his mother's death: "And then, from far away, he heard screaming, terrible, terrified, pleading screams. He wanted to help whoever it was, he tried to move his arms, but couldn't" (84). However, since he does not know anything about dementors at this time, he does not understand the significance of this experience. According to Lupin, Harry's fear of dementors "suggests that what [he fears] most of all is—fear" (155). If that is the case, then the dementors represent Harry's fears, which can be seen through this worst experience. It begins vague, but as Harry progresses through the novel, his memories of the event become stronger, as does his realization that those memories indicate his great fear and the great fear of all men in western society: the weakness of the patriarchal line—represented by the death of Harry's mother.

Until this point in the story, all Harry knows about his mother's death is that she died to save him. In *Harry Potter and the Sorcerer's Stone*, both Voldemort (294) and Dumbledore (299) confirm this. Once Harry knows that this is a memory of his mother's death, he feels helpless. He could not do anything to stop his mother's murder, and she died only because she would not "stand aside" and give him to Voldemort. Thus her death is his fault, and when Harry wakes up, he remembers this "scariest thing" (*PoA* 179) and begins to obsess over it: "Because Harry knew who that screaming voice belonged to now. He had heard her words, heard them over and over again during the night hours in the hospital wing while he lay awake, staring at the strips of moonlight on the ceiling" (184). This death scene haunts him for the rest of the novel.

As the title of the novel indicates, the action of the story is dictated by the presence of one particular character—Sirius Black. As the novel progresses, Harry learns that Black worked for Voldemort and wants to kill Harry, but since Harry's life has always been in danger from Voldemort, he does not concern himself about Black until he accidentally learns Black's connection to his patriarchal line and to the death of his mother. First, he discovers Black's relationship to his father and to himself when he overhears

Cornelius Fudge, the Minister of Magic, explain that "Potter trusted Black beyond all his other friends. Nothing changed when they left school. Black was best man when James married Lily. Then they named him godfather to Harry" (204). Not only is this man one of his father's closest friends, he is a replacement for Harry's father. However, Harry's relationship with Black becomes more complicated when Harry learns that this best friend and godfather betrayed his parents, bringing about their deaths. When Harry's parents went into hiding, Sirius Black became their Secret-Keeper, so the only way Voldemort could have found them was if he betrayed their secret. While this betrayal by a friend and godfather shows great weakness in the patriarchal line, Harry believes it alleviates the guilt he has been feeling: his mother did not die because of him but because of Black. Harry further links this new information about Black to his fears, represented by the dementors:

> "D'you know what I see and hear every time a dementor gets too near me? … I can hear my mum screaming and pleading with Voldemort. And if you'd heard your mum screaming like that, just about to be killed, you wouldn't forget it in a hurry. And if you found out someone who was supposed to be a friend of hers betrayed her and sent Voldemort after her —" (214)

Harry connects the dementors to his mother's death and his mother's death to Black. Thus, Harry shifts all of the blame off of himself and places it on his "bad" father-figure.

Harry cannot shift all of the blame to Black, unfortunately. During his lessons on fighting off dementors, he discovers information about his father's death that makes him uncomfortable. In *Sorcerer's Stone*, as noted, both Voldemort (294) and Dumbledore (299) tell Harry that his mother was virtuous and died to save him. However, Harry's information about his father is less certain. People seem to have liked him, but his death is still suspect. When Voldemort first tries to intimidate Harry, he claims that Harry's parents were weak and "died begging [him] for mercy" (294). However, after Harry stands up to Voldemort, he changes his story: "I killed your father first, and he put up a courageous fight" (294). During one of his dementor-induced flashbacks, Harry hears his father's death:

> …then came a new voice, a man's voice, shouting, panicking—

"Lily, take Harry and go! It's him! Go! Run! I'll hold him off—"
The sounds of someone stumbling from a room—a door bursting open—a cackle of high-pitched laughter— (PoA 240)

His father had tried to fight off Voldemort; he had not, as Voldemort said, "died begging...for mercy" (294). Nor, however, does he seem to have been as valiant as Harry had hoped. After all, Harry hears "stumbling" and "panicking." There is no sound of a struggle, just Voldemort's laughter.

At first, this may not seem like a terrible crime, but to Harry it shows what Williams describes as "the gradual recognition that one's parents are not the omnipotent beings they seemed when one was extremely young, but flawed, real, and perfectly ordinary human beings" (Williams 89). Until the beginning of this book, Harry's image of his father had been strong and good, but in this story, several people actively try to destroy his concept of his father. While at the Dursleys', Harry's Aunt Marge comes to visit, and during her stay, she insults Harry's father, calling him a "wastrel," a "drunk," and a "no-account, good-for-nothing, lazy scrounger who—" (PoA 28), at which point Harry becomes so angry that he loses control of his magical powers and fills her full of hot air. Later in the novel, Harry and Professor Snape have a confrontation during which Snape also deflates Harry's opinion of his father. In *Sorcerer's Stone*, Harry learns that the reason Snape hates him so much is that he actually hated James, in part because Harry's "father did something Snape could never forgive...saved his life" (300). This statement by Dumbledore helps Harry to develop an image of his father as a hero, an image which Snape attempts to destroy in *Prisoner of Azkaban*:

"I would hate for you to run away with a false idea of your father, Potter," he said, a terrible grin twisting his face. "Have you been imagining some act of glorious heroism? Then let me correct you—your saintly father and his friends played a highly amusing joke on me that would have resulted in my death if your father hadn't got cold feet at the last moment. There was nothing brave about what he did. He was saving his own skin as much as mine." (PoA 285)

Thus, Harry's image of his father seems to be breaking down, foreshadowing the more complete breakdown in *Order of the Phoenix*, and Harry's anxieties about his patriarchal line increase. At this point in the story, his father, his godfather, and Harry himself have demonstrated weakness.

All of this information builds to a climax, the discovery of the family secret. According to Williams, "[t]he imposing house with a terrible secret is surely one—possibly *the*—'central' characteristic of the category 'Gothic' in its early years" (39). Hogwarts is such a house, even though it is also a school that has accommodated many families throughout its long history. Though it is a school and not the ancient home of some fatal man's family, the school emphasizes patriarchy. The only school of witchcraft and wizardry in England, Hogwarts passes down all magical knowledge and rules, just as the patriarchy passes down fortunes, curses, and power. Additionally, the castle itself fits descriptions of the gothic house. Hogwarts is old, huge, and isolated; the exact location of the castle is hidden (*GoF* 166). However, the inside of the castle, first described in *Sorceror's Stone*, most resembles the frightening structure of the Gothic novel.

> There were a hundred and forty-two staircases at Hogwarts: wide, sweeping ones; narrow, rickety ones; some that led somewhere different on a Friday; some with a vanishing step halfway up that you had to remember to jump. Then there were doors that wouldn't open unless you asked politely, or ticked them in exactly the right place, and doors that weren't really doors at all, but solid walls just pretending. (131–32)

Sounds like a fun place—and it is. This description comes from book one, which is more like a fairy tale than a Gothic novel. The emphasis is much different, but it still gets the point across. Hogwarts is large and confusing, a maze that keeps changing: "It was also very hard to remember where anything was, because it all seemed to move around a lot. The people in the portraits kept going to visit each other, and Harry was sure the coats of armor could walk" (132). The paintings and the armor are both Gothic stereotypes. Usually, the hero or heroine believes that someone may be watching them from the painting or out of the suit of armor, but at Hogwarts, the paintings and armor are as active as the ghosts. Thus, the Gothic tradition that the castle provokes "claustrophobia, loneliness, a sense of antiquity" (Williams 40) is true, but with a sense of fun. However, one other characteristic of the Gothic house, the "recognition that this is a place of secrets" (40), is exceptionally important to the story.

Harry has already discovered several secrets of Hogwarts. In *Sorcerer's Stone*, he and his friends traverse the forbidden third-floor corridor where the stone is hidden, passing numerous "traps" along the way. In book two, Harry finds the aptly named Chamber of Secrets. Harry's exploration of this castle has been well established before he enters book three, the Gothic novel. However, in this novel, Harry receives a tool that opens up all of the castle's secrets to him—the Marauder's Map: "It was a map showing every detail of the Hogwarts castle and grounds. But the truly remarkable thing were the tiny ink dots moving around it, each labeled with a name in minuscule writing" (*PoA* 193). With this map, not only can Harry examine every aspect of the castle and its grounds, but he can also watch all the people within it. He knows the secrets of the castle and its people, simultaneously gaining the ability to act as a voyeur and gaze at everyone inside.

The main point of the castle, however, is to contain a secret chamber, which houses the family's secrets, and in this novel, such a room exists. Harry's actual goal, then, corresponds to the main purpose of the male Gothic tradition, which "represent[s] the male protagonist's attempt to penetrate some encompassing interior" (Punter 279). However, since the patriarchal line both holds the map and has the secrets, they would have made sure to leave the secret room off the map—otherwise, anyone who happened to get hold of the map could penetrate their secrets. The entrance to this secret chamber does appear on the map, as one of the secret passages that Harry notes, the one that Fred and George Weasley "'don't reckon anyone's ever used…because the Whomping Willow's planted right over the entrance" (*PoA* 193). Because of the danger at the entrance, the Marauders do not believe anyone would choose to explore the passage and thus find the secrets. This passage leads to the secret chamber so hidden within Hogwarts that it does not even remain on Hogwarts' grounds, the Shrieking Shack. The Shrieking Shack is in itself a haunted house, "supposed to be the most severely haunted building in Britain" (77), but it also houses the Potter family's secrets, the "truth" about this patriarchy.

Once all of the important figures gather in this secret room— Harry, Black, Lupin, and (perhaps most importantly of all) Scabbers the rat—all of the secrets of the patriarchy come out in a rush: Lupin is a werewolf, James and his friends are both the Marauders and Animagi, Black used his abilities as an Animagus to escape from jail and to enter Hogwarts, Black was not the Potters' Secret-Keeper nor did he betray them, and (finally) Scabbers the rat is Peter Pettigrew, the dead friend who turns out to be the disguised traitor. At this point in the story, the audience realizes that the entire plot has quietly (though not subtly) focused on the patriarchal line from the beginning. The Grim that has haunted Harry's footsteps since he left the Dursleys turns out to be his godfather in disguise. The side story that focuses so intently on Scabbers the rat, which seemed so childish at the time, suddenly takes on whole new significance.

All of these secrets have been terribly well kept and are very exciting to discover. However, the most important secret learned in the Shrieking Shack reinforces Harry's great fear, for he finally learns the entire truth about how his parents died—and every single member of this male line is implicated. Peter Pettigrew is the true traitor and the secret-keeper, but he should not have been. He was only made secret-keeper because Sirius convinced Lily and James to change (369), thinking that Lupin was the traitor—a mistake probably based on the prejudice against werewolves and their reputation for being untrustworthy and duplicitous. The second misconception, choosing Peter as a substitute, is also a mistake. Sirius, thinking they needed to change secret-keepers so that Lupin would not know who it was, chooses Peter because "Voldemort would be sure to come after me, would never dream [the Potters would] use a weak, talentless thing like you" (369). After all, Peter "[h]ero-worshipped Black and Potter" (207), thus feeding both of their egos and making them think that he would never betray them. Sirius's arrogance, Lupin's identity as a werewolf, and the assumption of James, Sirius, and Lupin that Peter was too weak and too obsessed with pleasing them to be a threat—all of these working together cause the death of Harry's mother. The entire patriarchal line is to blame. They have shown great weakness because of their arrogance, their duplicity, and their distrust. And worse—since their weakness has also caused the death of his father, Harry sees that the patriarchal line is destroying itself.

Harry tries to fix the problem, to reassert order and structure into the patriarchy, but it backfires. Harry stops Lupin and Black from killing Pettigrew "'because—I don't reckon my dad would've wanted them to become killers—just for you" (376). By stopping them from murdering Pettigrew, Harry keeps them from transgressing even worse than they already have by committing murder. However, he has forgotten that keeping the patriarchal line from becoming weaker does not make it strong. When they leave the confines of the secret passage to go back to the castle, Lupin unfortunately transforms into a werewolf, Black ignores Pettigrew (again) to go after Lupin, and "Harry stood, transfixed by the sight, too intent upon the battle to notice anything else" (381), including Pettigrew making his escape. Rather than improving, the patriarchal line emphasizes its weakness and failure.

Thus, Harry's fear progresses, grows worse because the magnitude of the crime increases; the weakness is not in one individual but in the entire patriarchal line. The psychological terror that he feels when he realizes that the whole patriarchy is in danger —the "paralyzing terror [that] filled Harry so that he couldn't move or speak" (384) that has been building in Harry since the beginning of the story—is symbolized by a massive dementor attack: "And then Harry saw them. Dementors, at least a hundred of them, gliding in a black mass around the lake toward them" (383). Harry's fear, multiplied to encompass the entire patriarchal line, comes not only to kill Harry and his godfather (the male line), but to destroy them utterly by sucking out their souls. And just to reiterate the point, Harry hears his mother screaming one more time, knowing that "[s]he was going to be the last thing he ever heard" (384).

Harry does not die. He, Sirius, and Hermione are saved by a Patronus, a symbol of good feelings and the only defense against the dementors. However, the key question is: whose Patronus was it?

Something was driving the dementors back.... It was as bright as a unicorn.... Fighting to stay conscious, Harry watched it canter to a halt as it reached the opposite shore. For a moment, Harry saw, by its brightness, somebody welcoming it back...raising his hand to pat it...someone who looked strangely familiar...but it couldn't be... (385)

When Harry and Hermione go back in time to save Sirius, Harry has an additional desire: he wants to see who rescued them at the lake. He believes that the man he saw across the lake, the one who conjured the powerful Patronus, was his father.

He was thinking about his father and about his father's three oldest friends...Moony, Wormtail, Padfoot, and Prongs.... Had all four of them been out on the grounds tonight? Wormtail had reappeared this evening when everyone had thought he was dead.... Was it so impossible his father had done the same? (407)

If Harry's father lives and if he saved him, then Harry can regain confidence in the strength of the patriarchy and in his father. Hermione reiterates this idea, saying that "it must have been a really powerful wizard, to drive all those dementors away" (406–7). However, when Harry reaches the bank, he makes an important realization: "And then it hit him—he understood. He hadn't seen his father—he had seen *himself*—" (411). Harry is the one who conjures the powerful Patronus and saves himself, Sirius, and Hermione. In the uncanny, "the subject identifies himself with someone else, so that he is in doubt as to which his self is, or substitutes the extraneous self for his own. In other words, there is a doubling, dividing and interchanging of the self" (Freud 234). In this situation, Harry has been divided; when he is attacked by dementors, he thinks he sees both himself and his father, whereas he actually sees his double. MacAndrew indicates that the double can be "a good aspect of the character" (211). Harry is divided into the original failing Harry on the bank and the successful, good Harry, the savior of the patriarchal line. In this respect, through doubling, Harry erases his earlier defeat by the lake.

More importantly, Harry overcomes the hundreds of dementors, the symbol of his fears in the weakness of the patriarchal line. Hendershot explains: "Thus while the Gothic frequently reveals male lack and hence subverts dominant notions of masculine plenitude, it also frequently demonizes this lack and dispels it by the end of the work" (3). The "male lack" symbolized by the dementors is dispelled by Harry, who both conquers his own fears and reasserts the strength of the patriarchy. When Harry sees the form of his Patronus, the stag, he realizes that his Patronus, his hope and good feelings, are represented by his father: "It stopped on the bank. Its hooves made no mark on the soft ground as it stared at Harry with its large, silver eyes. Slowly, it bowed its antlered head" (Rowling *PoA* 411). By bowing to Harry, Prongs acknowledges Harry's role in reaffirming the patriarchy and places its future in his hands. As Dumbledore says later, "You know, Harry, in a way, you did see your father last night.... You found him inside yourself" (428). Harry awakens the former strength of the patriarchy within himself and takes that with him through the rest of the series.

J. K. Rowling chooses to make *Harry Potter and the Prisoner of Azkaban* a Gothic novel because it fits the points she needs to make in book three. The Gothic plot allows her to reveal information about Harry's family, particularly about Harry's father's closest friends. She introduces the vital characters Peter Pettigrew, who helps to bring about Voldemort's return, and Sirius Black, who acts as a father figure towards Harry. And finally, by using the Gothic plot and the fears that it emphasizes, she begin to tear down the patriarchal line and force Harry to rise with self-sufficiency and strength. In order to be a true hero, Harry must stop relying on father figures, step up, and act on his own. While the novel does not end particularly happily for Black, Lupin, or Harry, Harry at least has taken the next step in becoming the hero he needs to be to defeat Voldemort.

Works Cited

Freud, Sigmund. *The Standard Edition of the Complete Psychological Works of Sigmund Freud.* Ed. and trans. James Strachey. Vol. 17. London: Hogarth Press and the Institute of Psycho-Analysis, 1955.

Hendershot, Cyndy. *The Animal Within: Masculinity and the Gothic.* Ann Arbor, MI: U of Michigan P, 1998.

MacAndrew, Elizabeth. *The Gothic Tradition in Fiction.* New York: Columbia UP, 1979.

Punter, David, and Glennis Byron. *The Gothic.* Malden, MA: Blackwell, 2004.

Rigdon, Betty. "The Literature of Terror vs. the Literature of Horror." *A Glossary of Literary Gothic Terms.* Georgia Southern. 15 May 2007 <http://personal.georgiasouthern.edu/~dougt/goth.html#lit>.

Rowling, J. K. *Harry Potter and the Chamber of Secrets.* New York: Arthur A. Levine, 1998.

—. *Harry Potter and the Goblet of Fire.* New York: Arthur A. Levine, 2000.

—. *Harry Potter and the Prisoner of Azkaban.* New York: Scholastic, 1999.

—. *Harry Potter and the Sorcerer's Stone.* New York: Scholastic, 1997.

Williams, Anne. *Art of Darkness: A Poetics of Gothic.* Chicago: U of Chicago P, 1995.

ARRESTO MOMENTUM?:
HARRY, SIRIUS, AND LUPIN

Jacqueline Goodenow

Phoenix Rising took place in May 2007, about two months before the release of the seventh and final book, *Harry Potter and the Deathly Hallows*. So, as I write this paper, we don't yet know how Harry's story will end. The sixth book, *Harry Potter and the Half-Blood Prince*, ended with Dumbledore's funeral. Amidst his grief, Harry has a deeply moving epiphany:

> And Harry saw very clearly as he sat there under the hot sun how people who cared about him had stood in front of him one by one, his mother, his father, his godfather, and finally Dumbledore, all determined to protect him; but now that was over. He could not let anybody else stand between him and Voldemort; he must abandon forever the illusion he ought to have lost at the age of one, that the shelter of a parent's arms meant that nothing could hurt him. There was no waking from his nightmare, no comforting whisper in the dark that he was safe really, that it was all in his imagination; the last and greatest of his protectors had died, and he was more alone than he had ever been before. (*HBP* 645)

Following this realization, Harry breaks up with Ginny, and he scornfully turns down Scrimgeour's offer to place a couple of Aurors in Harry's service. Of course, Harry quickly learns that he won't be *completely* alone, as Ron and Hermione reaffirm their solidarity and pledge to be with him, "whatever happens." But Harry realizes that he must now proceed without the guidance of a mentor or parental figure. Displaying the fierce self-reliance of any classical literary orphan, Harry decides that it is time to go forward as an *adult*.

On the eve of the publication of the final book, in which Harry will come of age, I think it is important to look back on the adult influences Harry has had in the preceding books. There are the Dursleys, and Mr. and Mrs. Weasley, Hagrid, and Dumbledore, but I'd like to focus on Harry's relationships with Sirius Black and Remus Lupin, the two strongest links to Harry's actual parents. How has having Sirius and Lupin in his life, no matter how briefly or incompletely, changed Harry as a person, and ultimately helped shape him into the hero he will become? As we speculate on the outcome of Harry's endeavors in *Deathly Hallows*, let's examine what Sirius and Lupin have meant to him. What can he learn from them that might help him to defeat Voldemort? Let's consider how Harry's evolving relationships with them have already—and undoubtedly *will*—affect Harry's coming of age.

Before we begin, I'd like to explain why I refer to Sirius by his first name and Lupin by his last. It's because that's what Harry does, and this practice also reinforces the very different meanings they have to him.

In researching Sirius's and Lupin's relationships with Harry, I formulated a list of questions to explore the three characters' similarities and differences. My first question revealed some notable similarities in their backgrounds. *How have their families and childhoods affected who they are today?* Harry's childhood with the Dursleys is fraught with misery. His aunt and uncle don't love him; they don't even understand him. They don't care to. They are horrified by the things that make him different from them. They lie to him about his parents—his very origins—and they become enraged if he asks any questions or uses the "M" word (magic). Uncle Vernon tells Harry that he is "abnormal," and to the Dursleys, "having a wizard in the family is a matter of deepest shame" (*CoS* 4). As Harry explains to Dobby, he just doesn't *belong* with the Dursleys; Hogwarts becomes his true home, the place where he can truly be *Harry*. Indeed, before the Triwizard Tournament, when Harry is almost overcome with a despairing sort of nervousness, Rowling writes that "somehow, the knowledge that he would rather be here and facing a dragon than back on Privet Drive with Dudley was good to know" (*GoF* 339). Now that is saying something!

What have been the lasting effects of Harry's childhood, which, in Dumbledore's words, was filled with cruelty, neglect, and misery? In an essay entitled "Orphans in the Literary Tradition," T. Ritchie writes that, prior to Hogwarts, "Harry has never had any strong moral guidance. We can only assume he has learned his values by pitting himself against everything that the Dursleys stand for."[1] Dumbledore emphatically tells Harry that the reason Harry can defeat Voldemort is that despite the hardships of his childhood, and the temptations and losses he has endured, Harry has remained good and pure, and has a uniquely remarkable ability to love. Unlike Tom Riddle and (so far) Draco Malfoy, Harry has overcome his upbringing. He *chooses* to be as un-Dursley-like as he can be!

Of Sirius Black, J. K. Rowling said in her July 16, 2005, interview with MuggleNet and the Leaky Cauldron that "like Harry, he is a displaced person without a family." True, Sirius did grow up with two living parents, but he was so miserable at home, and he rejected his family's world view so utterly, that he essentially "orphaned" himself by leaving them. In describing his departure from Grimmauld Place and the severing of his family ties at the age of sixteen, Sirius uses—not coincidentally—the same words that Harry uses when he storms away from the Dursley home after blowing up Aunt Marge: "I've had enough." Teenage Sirius had had enough of number twelve, Grimmauld Place, which was oppressively dark and severe, and full of nasty artifacts. Sirius had had enough of his family's "pure-blood mania," their snobbery and elitism. Like Harry, who (in the Dursleys' eyes) suffered by comparison to his cousin Dudley, Sirius too had to endure his parents' reminders that his brother Regulus was a "much better son" and "a right little hero" (*OotP* 112).

We can extrapolate from the behavior of Mrs. Black's portrait that she was a demanding, viciously tempered mother, but Sirius has barely anything to say about his father. Nevertheless, I'd like to offer a bit of speculation. Consider the energy and bitterness that Sirius devotes to describing the dynamics within the Crouch family. Sirius tells Harry, Ron, and Hermione that Barty Crouch, Senior, "should have spent a bit more time at home with his family, shouldn't he? Ought to have left the office early once in a while…gotten to know his own son" (*GoF* 528). Sirius says that after Crouch, Junior, was thrown into Azkaban, "the conclusion was that his father never

---

1 T. Ritchie, "Orphans in the Literary Tradition." Editorial posted on MuggleNet, 14 May 2005.   <http://www.mugglenet.com/editorials/editorials/edit-tritchie01.shtml>.

cared much for him" (*GoF* 529–30). My guess is that Mr. Black was also distant and lacking in what Sirius terms "fatherly affection."

In his lengthy evaluation of the Crouches, Sirius also says that Crouch, Senior, didn't even try to get his son exonerated, because "anything that threatened to tarnish his reputation had to go" (*GoF* 528). Is there any doubt that when young Sirius went off to Hogwarts and was sorted not into Slytherin, but into Gryffindor, his family began to think him just as freakish and "abnormal" as the Dursleys thought Harry to be? Both Harry and Sirius seem to be the black sheep of their families, and it is significant that they are just as contemptuous of their bigoted families as their families are of them.

Furthermore, Harry and Sirius's lives take similar trajectories after they leave their families. Harry quite often finds refuge at the Burrow and becomes a sort of unofficial Weasley. In addition to the fun he has there, Harry likes being with the Weasleys because they like to be with *him*, and unlike the Dursleys they are interested in what he has to say (*CoS* 42). Similarly, teenage Sirius found refuge during school holidays at the house of *his* best friend, James Potter. Just as Molly Weasley says that Harry is "as good as a son" to her, Sirius says that the Potters "sort of adopted me as a second son." When Sirius came of age at seventeen, he got a place of his own, and after that he pretty much looked after himself. Such a move toward further independence is very similar to Harry's situation at the end of *Half-Blood Prince*. He too is about to turn seventeen and set off on his own without adults to watch over him.

Both Harry and Sirius's rejection of the bigotry espoused by their families (the Dursleys' anti-magic stance and the Blacks' pure-blood racism) fuel their desires in adulthood to fight against Voldemort, the very symbol of bigotry.

We know much less about Remus Lupin's family and childhood, but it is clear that his early years also had great influence on the man he is today. Lupin was bitten as a very small boy by the werewolf Fenrir Greyback, who had somehow been insulted by Lupin's father. He says his parents tried everything they could to help him, but in those days there was no cure and no Wolfsbane. So, Lupin's childhood was marked by month after month of terrifying, wrenchingly painful transformations. Lupin doesn't describe his parents, but even if they were loving and supportive, the very fact that Lupin was *the only one* in his family to be infected with lycanthropy would have set him apart from them in some way. Young Lupin likely had no one to talk to who knew what he was experiencing. He feared that he would *never* have any friends: "I became a fully-fledged monster once a month. It seemed impossible that I would be able to come to Hogwarts. Other parents weren't likely to want their children exposed to me" (*PoA* 353). Lupin learned at a very early age that he was likely to be an object of fear and bigotry for the rest of his life. Like Harry and Sirius, Lupin's childhood introduction to prejudice would influence his choices in adulthood. He too would join the Order of the Phoenix, a response to bigotry in all forms.

Lupin shares another similarity to Harry, in that the misery they experienced as children leaves a particular mark on them. Harry was a victim of Dudley's bullying, and he remains particularly sensitive to other victims of bullying. He is very sympathetic towards Luna Lovegood when she tells him that other students like to hide her belongings. And he angrily derides Dudley for picking on Mark Evans and other defenseless kids. Similarly, Lupin displays a particular sympathy towards others who might be feeling some of the isolation he felt as a child: he makes an effort to encourage the unpopular Neville Longbottom, and he reaches out to the newly infected werewolf he encounters at St. Mungo's, no doubt to reassure him that he *can* learn to deal with their condition's isolating nature.

One more note about a similarity between Harry's and Lupin's childhoods: how do they view the people responsible for "rescuing" them from their hopeless situations? In Harry's case, that's Hagrid, the one who comes seemingly out of nowhere and tells Harry that he is a wizard; that he isn't, in fact, abnormal or worthless; and that Hagrid is taking him to a wonderful place where he *does* belong. Hagrid is the one who rescues Harry from his childhood, who tells Harry the truth for the first time in Harry's life. Consequently, Harry maintains a deep affection and loyalty towards Hagrid, who delivered him from his life with the Dursleys. For young Lupin, this "deliverer" role is filled by Dumbledore. It is Dumbledore who makes it possible through special accommodations for Lupin to come to Hogwarts, which, quite frankly, alters the very course of Lupin's life. Like Hagrid for Harry, Dumbledore is the first bringer of *hope* to Lupin. And Lupin loves and appreciates his "deliverer" as much as Harry does, even into adulthood.

Because all three characters share the childhood trait of being very different from their families, my next consideration was the degree to which their friends become their substitute families. *Why are their friends so very vital to them?* Even the most casual reader can't fail to notice how much Harry, Sirius, and Lupin treasure their friends, who provide them with the acceptance and "family" they so desperately yearn for. I think we can even say of all three of them that their friendships make life worth living, and help to take some of the sting from the miseries they must suffer.

Lupin's deep appreciation of his friends is palpable in his retelling of how his life completely changed upon entering Hogwarts:

My transformations in those days were—were terrible. It is very painful to turn into a werewolf…. But apart from my transformations, I was happier than I had ever been in my life. For the first time ever, I had friends, three great friends…. I was terrified they would desert me the moment they found out what I was. But of course, they, like you, Hermione, worked out the truth…. And they didn't desert me at all. Instead, they did something for me that would make my transformations not only bearable, but the best times of my life. They became Animagi. (*PoA* 353–54)

Not only were Sirius, James, and Peter *not* scared or revolted when they learned that Lupin was a werewolf, but they worked diligently for three years (and risked expulsion) to become Animagi, all to make Lupin's life more bearable. His normally terrifying and lonely transformations then became "highly exciting" opportunities for adventure and lighthearted mischief-making. Lupin says that "under their influence, I became less dangerous. My body was still wolfish, but my mind seemed to become less so while I was with them" (*PoA* 355). His friends taught him that he was worth knowing, and worth being cared about, despite the danger he presented. Instead of shunning him, they embraced him, and Lupin felt not only relieved, but profoundly grateful.

As for Sirius, consider the qualities that are traditionally associated with his Animagus form, a dog: loyal, protective, faithful, "man's best friend." J. K. Rowling said in a FAQ on her own Web site that "Sirius's great redeeming quality is how much affection he is capable of feeling" (http://www.jkrowling.com). And in her July 16, 2005, interview, she said that "Harry and Sirius were very similar in that both of them were craving family connections with friends. So, Sirius with James wanted a brother, and Harry has nominated Ron and Hermione as his family." James Potter became Sirius's best friend, as close as a brother. (Even the Hogwarts staff and Madam Rosmerta noticed how inseparable they were!) The Potters effectively welcomed Sirius into their family when he broke away from his own. Sirius's friends—especially James—became so dear to him that he would have given up his own life to save theirs. Indeed, when Peter says that Voldemort would have killed him if he hadn't divulged the Potters' hiding place, Sirius roars back, "THEN YOU SHOULD HAVE DIED! DIED RATHER THAN BETRAY YOUR FRIENDS, AS WE WOULD HAVE DONE FOR YOU" (*PoA* 375). Rowling confirmed in that July 16, 2005, interview that Sirius was telling the truth:

> Sirius would have done it. He, with all his faults and flaws, he has this profound sense of honor, ultimately, and he would rather have died honorably, as he would see it, than live with the dishonor and shame of knowing that he had sent those three people [James, Lily, and Harry] to their deaths, those three people that he loved beyond any others.

In the Shrieking Shack scene from *Prisoner of Azkaban*, it is Sirius's simple and earnest plea for Harry to believe that he would *never* have betrayed James and Lily which finally and utterly convinces Harry that Sirius is innocent (*PoA* 372).

I'd also like to include two non-human characters in this discussion of Sirius's friendships: Crookshanks and Buckbeak. Crookshanks's relationship with Sirius (which occurs mostly when Sirius is in dog form and unable to have any human contact because he is still in hiding during Harry's third year) is worth noting because it illustrates the devotion that Sirius inspires others to feel for *him*. Normally a cat would be too afraid of a big black dog, but something in Sirius's very nature is able to kindle a fierce loyalty in Crookshanks, and so cat befriends dog. Crookshanks steals Neville's Gryffindor password list for Sirius, and he even leaps onto Sirius's chest to stop anyone from killing him in the Shrieking Shack. Now that's devotion! (And Harry seems to be quite able to inspire it in *his* friends, too.)

Sirius's empathetic relationship with Buckbeak is also important. In Gwynog'srabbit's essay entitled "Sirius and Buckbeak: A Hero's

Journey," Sirius's first encounter with Buckbeak (in which he climbs onto Buckbeak's back without even needing to bow first to gain the hippogriff's acceptance) is described thus: "They became one, refugees together on a quest for freedom." That author goes on to eloquently describe the relationship that develops between Sirius and Buckbeak as they are forced to hide out at number twelve, Grimmauld Place:

Since Buckbeak and Sirius shared a common transformation, we can understand that Buckbeak must also be suffering. To realize the potential of his wings, then be forced to live in one room of a dark, moldy house, must have been unbearable for him.... On Sirius's darkest days, he shuts himself up alone with Buckbeak, the only one who understands, and shares in the misery of his spirit.[1]

Sirius and Lupin both find acceptance, comfort, and strong familial bonds in their friendships. So too does Harry form a "family" with his friends, Ron and Hermione. They help him to endure his life—his history (and future) with Voldemort. As Sirius and Lupin do, Harry risks his life many times over to save his friends. He admires and appreciates them, and sticks up for them if anyone dares to disparage them. Like Sirius, he feels immense guilt whenever he believes that he's put his friends in danger. When Hermione is struck down in the battle at the Ministry of Magic in book five, Harry pleads, "Don't let her be dead, don't let her be dead, it's my fault if she's dead" (*OotP* 593). And when he returns to Hogwarts near the end of book six and sees the Dark Mark looming above it, Rowling writes of his fear: "Would he be responsible, again, for the death of a friend?" (*HBP* 583).

Like Lupin, Harry is deeply grateful that his friends choose to stick by him, no matter what. When Lupin, Tonks, Moody, and Mr. and Mrs. Weasley show up at King's Cross to warn the Dursleys not to mistreat Harry, his gratitude is clear to the reader: "He somehow could not find the words to tell them what it meant to him, to see them all ranged there, on his side" (*OotP* 870). Another example also illustrates how vital Ron's and Hermione's friendship is to Harry. Dumbledore, understanding how critical their support will be to Harry, urges him to divulge to his friends the full content of the

---

1 Gwynog'srabbit, "Sirius and Buckbeak: A Hero's Journey." Editorial posted at The Leaky Cauldron, date unknown. <http://www.the-leaky-cauldron.org/ #scribbulus:essay:172>.

Prophecy. Harry does tell Ron and Hermione his secret at the Burrow, and Rowling's description of how he feels about their reaction is very striking:

A warmth was spreading through him that had nothing to do with the sunlight; a tight obstruction in his chest seemed to be dissolving. He knew that Ron and Hermione were more shocked than they were letting on, but the mere fact that they were still there on either side of him, speaking bracing words of comfort, not shrinking from him as though he were contaminated or dangerous, was worth more to him than he could ever tell them. (*HBP* 99)

Due to Rowling's word choices here ("contaminated or dangerous"), we can imagine that this is quite similar to the relief that Lupin felt when he learned that *his* friends wouldn't reject him despite the danger and that they would be, as Ron says to Harry, "with [him] whatever happens."

For all three characters—Harry, Sirius, and Lupin—their friendships transcend the usual definition of mere school-time pals; their friends become their families. Their friends give them strength. Aside from the causes they believe in, their friendships give them something to fight for, something to live for, even something to die for.

Now that I've reviewed some of the similarities in their childhoods (isolation from / rejection of family, and the importance their friendships take on), I'd like to turn to the effects that Sirius and Lupin have on Harry's life. How does teenage Harry interact with adult Sirius and adult Lupin? What do they *mean* to him?

First, I'd like to briefly explore the third question on my list: *What are Sirius's and Lupin's general temperaments? How easy are they for Harry to relate to?* This includes their differences in expressiveness, sense of humor, and maturity level. In short, how would we describe their personalities? J. K. Rowling wrote in the FAQ section of her Web site that

Sirius is brave, loyal, reckless, embittered and slightly unbalanced by his long stay in Azkaban. He has never really had the chance to grow up; he was around 22 when he was sent off to Azkaban, and has had very little normal adult life. Lupin, who is the same age, seems much older and more mature.

In his youth, Sirius was cocky, mischievous, and extremely bright, and we often see glimpses of that in Sirius as an adult. However, the twelve years of daily physical and emotional torture by the Azkaban dementors, not to mention the limitations and isolation forced on him even after his prison escape, leave their mark on Sirius's general temperament. He is sometimes bitter and sarcastic, with a dark sense of humor (especially about Kreacher, and his mother's portrait). Unlike Lupin, Sirius usually has no hesitation in saying exactly what he means; he is much more expressive, and his emotions are generally right on the surface for everyone to see. It's easy for Harry (and everyone) to "read" Sirius. Harry knows when Sirius is depressed or angry, or feeling lighthearted and affectionate. Remember the joyful "dog hug" that Sirius gives Harry on the train platform (*OotP* 183)? Unlike Lupin, Sirius makes no effort to contain his emotions. This is good for his relationship with Harry when his openness and youthfulness encourage their rapport, but it can also be a hindrance. One example occurs in *Order of the Phoenix*, when the Christmas break is drawing to a close, and Sirius knows that all his guests—Harry in particular—will be leaving him again:

> [Sirius] became more and more prone to what Mrs. Weasley called "fits of the sullens," in which he would become taciturn and grumpy, often withdrawing to Buckbeak's room for hours at a time. His gloom seeped through the house, oozing under doorways like some noxious gas, so that all of them became infected by it. (*OotP* 516)

Sirius's moods have a great effect on Harry's ability to communicate with and relate to him. In *Goblet of Fire*, when Sirius is worried about Harry and the Triwizard Tournament, but is still able to enjoy some relative freedom and improving mental health, Harry feels quite free to talk things over with Sirius, to be reassured by an adult he trusts. But when Sirius is once again "imprisoned" (at number twelve, Grimmauld Place) in *Order of the Phoenix*, he gradually becomes more temperamental, his moods darker. Harry has noticeably more difficulty in talking to Sirius, and the progress we had seen in their relationship in the previous book actually starts to regress.

Lupin's general temperament is very different from Sirius's, and also has some positive and negative aspects when it comes to how Lupin and Harry interact. On the positive side, Lupin is exceedingly kind, empathetic, and an attentive listener. Most of the Hogwarts students consider him to be their best teacher, as his methods involve the plentiful (and somewhat unique to Hogwarts) use of encouragement and praise. He controls his temper, and his moods and behavior, unlike Sirius's, are generally very consistent and predictable. Furthermore, he is perceptive and often seems to understand exactly what is troubling Harry, such as when he perceives that Harry needs to be reassured that that his dad was not the Half-Blood Prince—and therefore not capable of inventing such nasty spells ("Lupin's smile was a little too understanding" [*HBP* 336]). However, while Lupin's qualities make him an even-keeled, reliable (when present) resource for Harry, other aspects of his personality make it hard for Harry to get to know him on a deeper level. Lupin can be much harder to "read" than the more expressive Sirius. Harry often has only Lupin's body language, self-halted gestures, and subtle shifts in tone of voice to guess at what Lupin is thinking and feeling. It's hard for the emotionally constrained Lupin to talk about subjects which are personally painful to him, including the lives and deaths of Harry's parents (though he does loosen up a bit on that subject as the books go on). He internalizes his grief and sadness, not wanting to "inflict" them upon others. That can be good for Harry, who doesn't need any extra burdens, since he already has (in Dumbledore's words) quite "enough responsibility to be going on with." But by not allowing himself to share any of his grief or troubles with Harry, not even a little, Lupin misses out on some chances for them to bond and heal together.

Another factor that influences Harry's relationships with Sirius and Lupin brings me to my fourth question: *How much information is each willing to give to Harry?* Do they tend to treat him as a child, an adolescent, or an adult in terms of what they think he can handle? And from that, what level of confidence does Harry infer that they have in him? We know that Harry—like most literary orphans—is very self-reliant. Because the adults in his life aren't always around (for example, think of Dumbledore's frequent absences from school throughout the entire series), he tends to want to make his own decisions, to act independently. And at age sixteen, he's already faced more trials and tragedies than most adults. Because he bears so much responsibility, he believes he's entitled to know everything the adults know, especially where it concerns Voldemort and the Order of the Phoenix. Harry becomes *very* angry and resentful at the beginning of *Order of the Phoenix* when he's trapped at Privet Drive with no information. He wonders how Dumbledore and his friends can treat him like some helpless child who hasn't already proven himself many times over.

Harry wants people to feel they can trust his ability to handle difficult information, and their openness (or reticence) with him signals to Harry how much faith they have in him. One can "earn points" in Harry's estimation by telling him everything he wants to know, the instant he demands to know it. Of course, this is a trait typical of most adolescents (or all people, in fact); nobody appreciates being kept in the dark. But to Harry, given the magnitude of his role in the wizarding world, having the implied confidence of the adults around him is vital, not just to his own self-image but to his ability to make well-informed, mature decisions.

An important incident early in *Order of the Phoenix* illustrates the positions that Sirius and Lupin generally take when it comes to giving Harry "adult" information. An argument occurs between Sirius and Molly Weasley over how much to tell Harry about Voldemort's current endeavors. Sirius and Molly fall at opposite ends of the spectrum, and Lupin, who sort of moderates the argument, falls somewhere in the middle. Sirius wants to tell Harry everything. In fact, it is Sirius who prompts Harry to question the adults in the first place! As everyone starts to head off to bed, Sirius says to Harry, "You know, I'm surprised at you. I thought the first thing you'd do when you got here would be to start asking questions about Voldemort" (*OotP* 87). Sirius insists that Harry has the *right* to be informed, that Harry has already dealt with as much or more than the adults, that Harry is not a child. (This is pretty much Harry's own position on the matter.) Molly insists that since Harry is still school-aged, and since Dumbledore has told them that there are certain things Harry shouldn't know yet, Harry should be informed of basically nothing. (And he certainly shouldn't be allowed to ask whatever he likes!) Sirius and Molly have a rather intense argument, debating about which of them is more responsible for Harry, and which of them has his best interests at heart. All of this plays out in Harry's presence, and as he states, "I want to know what's been going on," it's clear that Harry sides with Sirius and no doubt appreciates Sirius's vote of confidence in Harry's ability to handle the information. While Harry is touched by Molly's concern for him, Rowling writes that he grows "impatient at her mollycoddling.... Sirius was right, he was *not* a child" (*OotP* 90).

Lupin quite handily quells the squabbling between Sirius and Molly and suggests a more balanced approach to answering Harry's questions about Voldemort. He believes that Harry should "get the facts—not all the facts, Molly, but the general picture—from us, rather than a garbled version from...others" (*OotP* 89). Lupin mostly agrees with Sirius, saying, "I think Harry ought to be allowed a say in this. He's old enough to decide for himself" (*OotP* 90). He assists Sirius in answering most of Harry's questions and explaining what the Order is doing to fight Voldemort. But when Harry then asks to join the Order, Lupin leans towards more temperance in his answer: "The Order is comprised only of overage wizards. Wizards who have left school. There are dangers involved of which you can have no idea, any of you.... I think Molly's right, Sirius. We've said enough" (*OotP* 97). Harry accepts Lupin's response, but considers it a defeat to be barred from joining the Order. Nevertheless, he is glad that the two men argued against Molly on his behalf and allowed him to learn as much as he did, even if Lupin did place a few limitations on the scope of that information. Also, he notices and is heartened by the fact that both Sirius and Lupin refer to Voldemort by name (not the childish "You-Know-Who" moniker), just as Harry does (*OotP* 99).

Sirius's desire to tell Harry as much as he wants to know applies generally throughout the books. There is a wonderful example of this in *Goblet of Fire*, during Sirius's meeting with Harry, Ron, and Hermione in his cave hideout near Hogsmeade. He has a very thoughtful conversation with them about the chaos that occurred at the Quidditch World Cup, and goes over various clues with them. He clearly shows that he thinks they are capable of helping him figure out some of the puzzling things that have been happening. He listens to their input and thinks deeply about the mysteries they're trying to solve. When he has a momentary lapse and starts to say that Harry, Ron, and Hermione are too young to understand the atmosphere of fear and uncertainty that existed during the first "war" with Voldemort, Ron calls him on it. Irritated, Ron says, "That's what my dad said at the World Cup. Try us, why don't you?" Sirius grins and instantly replies, "All right, I'll try you" (*GoF* 526).

He devotes an hour and a half to explain thoroughly—and without any condescension—what he means, to recount the story of Barty Crouch and his son's trial, to evaluate Moody's abilities, to discuss (with some semblance of objectivity) Dumbledore's trust in Snape, and to suggest that they try to follow up on Bertha Jorkins' disappearance. He treats Harry and his friends as capable and worthy participants in a give-and-take discussion about things that others might consider too "adult" for them to understand.

Another example, this one from the Shrieking Shack scene in *Prisoner of Azkaban*, has Lupin taking the initiative to make sure Harry knows everything he needs to. The instant that Peter Pettigrew is forced to transform from a rat into human form, Sirius moves impulsively to kill him. (Sirius is, after all, in a state of extreme emotional turbulence, and still in the throes of what he himself admits is his "obsession" to avenge the Potters and protect Harry.) Lupin physically restrains Sirius, insisting that Sirius can't just kill Peter before Harry truly knows what's going on. Lupin gives Sirius several reasons why they must take the time to explain themselves: that Harry, Ron, and Hermione need to understand why a wizard is being killed right in front of them, that Ron has thought of "Scabbers" as his pet for many years, that Lupin himself needs more information, and, most importantly, that Sirius "owes Harry the truth" (*OotP* 350). Note the words that J. K. Rowling uses to describe Lupin's demeanor during this scene: quietly, calmly, coolly. He masters his emotions in large part to ensure that he and Sirius take the time to help Harry understand what's happening.

Of course, there is also a glaring example in *Prisoner* of Lupin's failure to provide Harry with vital information. Before it is revealed that Sirius is innocent, and everyone thinks that he's been breaking into the castle in order to murder Harry, Lupin fails to tell Harry that not only did he know Sirius, but that he had been very good friends with him, and that Sirius was an Animagus who could now be exploiting that ability to sneak into Hogwarts. In fact, during his numerous Patronus lessons with Harry, Lupin has multiple opportunities to tell him about *all* of the "Marauders," including Harry's very own father. But Lupin says nothing. It is clearly painful for him to talk about Harry's parents. As for his failure to tell Harry that Sirius is an Animagus, which could have eliminated some of Harry's wrong thoughts about the "Grim," this is due less to a belief

that Harry is unable to handle such information, and more to the
nature of Lupin's relationship with Dumbledore. This leads us to my
next line of inquiry.

What does Dumbledore represent to them, and do they accept his authority?
Are they willing to trust Dumbledore and follow his orders, even if
it's very difficult or they disagree? I think it's important to examine
Sirius's and Lupin's feelings about Dumbledore, because he is an
authority figure to all of them. Also, Sirius and Lupin are role-
models to Harry, and through their relationships with Dumbledore
they teach Harry how to respond to authority in general, in both
positive and negative ways.

Let me reiterate what I said earlier about Dumbledore and Lupin.
Dumbledore is the one who made it possible for Lupin to come to
Hogwarts, which enabled Lupin to get an education and to have
friends. Dumbledore's effort to accommodate Lupin essentially
changed the course of his life. Because Lupin admires Dumbledore
so much and is so grateful for all the opportunities he has given him,
Dumbledore's faith in him is very precious to Lupin. These are
Lupin's own words: "Dumbledore's trust has meant everything to
me. He let me into Hogwarts as a boy, and he gave me a job when I
have been shunned all my adult life, unable to find paid work
because of what I am" (*PoA* 356). I believe that Lupin's willingness
to take on such an extreme and dangerous Order assignment (to
infiltrate the werewolves) is due not only to Lupin's sense of duty
and wanting to do what is right, but also to a desire to "re-pay"
Dumbledore and make him proud. He doesn't ever want to let
Dumbledore down. Consider the guilt and outright self-disgust he
feels when explaining that the reason he didn't tell Dumbledore (in
Harry's third year) that Sirius is an Animagus is because doing so
"would have meant admitting that I'd betrayed [Dumbledore's] trust
while I was at school, that I'd led others along with me" (*PoA* 356). I
get the impression that aside from Lupin's fear of being a potential
danger to children, his ungrudging willingness to resign his post at
Hogwarts—without any complaint—is in part attributable to a need
to "punish" himself for betraying Dumbledore's trust over the past
year.

Until Lupin learns that it is Snape who has killed Dumbledore at
the end of *Half-Blood Prince*, Lupin never questions Dumbledore's
absolute trust of Snape. When Harry asks Lupin and Mr. Weasley

how they know for sure that Snape isn't double-crossing them, Lupin replies:

It isn't our business to know. It's Dumbledore's business. Dumbledore trusts Severus, and that ought to be good enough for all of us.... People have said it, many times. It comes down to whether or not you trust Dumbledore's judgment. I do; therefore I trust Severus. (*HBP* 332)

But is Lupin's absolute faith in Dumbledore's position on Snape reasonable? Isn't it at least a little bit childish? Yes, it's good for Lupin to accept the word of a person as wise as Dumbledore, but to do it so uncritically, so absolutely, reveals a small spot of immaturity in Lupin's otherwise mature character. Is it right for Lupin to expect that Dumbledore's opinion "ought to be good enough for all of us"? I am of the persuasion that Snape *is* working for the same aims as the Order, and *does* want to see Voldemort defeated (and not from any desire to take Voldemort's power for himself). I think that Dumbledore was right to trust Snape, but I do have qualms about Lupin's unquestioning faith in Dumbledore's infallibility. I think that all authority figures need to be questioned from time to time. I wonder if Lupin would have been as certain about Dumbledore's judgment of Snape if Lupin had known how cruelly Snape has treated Harry over the years.

However, Lupin does seem to experience some disillusionment about Dumbledore after the headmaster's death. At last, some doubt creeps into Lupin's mind about Dumbledore's trust in Snape. When Harry tells everyone in the hospital wing that Snape killed Dumbledore, and that Dumbledore had believed that Snape was remorseful about the part he had played in the Potters' deaths, Lupin is incredulous: "And Dumbledore believed that? Dumbledore believed Snape was sorry James was dead? Snape *hated* James" (*HBP* 644). Dumbledore's death is a defining moment in Lupin's life, not just because of Dumbledore's importance to the wizarding world, but specifically because of his meaning to Lupin. Indeed, Lupin's reaction to Dumbledore's death is the first time Harry is allowed to see some cracks appear in Lupin's façade of emotional control: "Lupin collapsed into a chair beside Bill's bed, his hands over his face. Harry had never seen Lupin lose control before; he felt as though he was intruding upon something private, indecent" (*HBP* 614).

Sirius admires Dumbledore's wisdom and experience. Despite his own personal hatred for Snape, Sirius is willing to take Dumbledore's word that Snape is truly working for the Order (though he is unwilling to be as magnanimous to Snape as Lupin is). After Voldemort's rebirth at the end of *Goblet of Fire* and Dumbledore's decision to re-establish the Order of the Phoenix, Sirius readily accepts that Dumbledore is the one in charge, that Dumbledore is their leader. He reveals himself to Snape (transforming from a dog) and shakes Snape's hand upon Dumbledore's request. He hastily departs to perform Dumbledore's first assignment (though I suspect that this is also due to Sirius's eagerness to leap into action). Despite his own desire to let Harry go to bed immediately after the horrible conclusion of the tournament's third task, he acquiesces to Dumbledore's insistence that it would be better for Harry to recount everything now, rather than put off the pain for later. And it turns out that Dumbledore is right, because Rowling writes that as Harry tells his story, "It was even a relief; he felt almost as though something poisonous were being extracted from him.... He sensed that once he had finished, he would feel better" (*GoF* 695).

I think that in his younger days, Sirius was somewhat less obedient to Dumbledore as an authority figure. After all, he was quite a mischief-maker in school, and Sirius, unlike Lupin, was probably just less impressed by authority figures in general. One of the occasions that he chose *not* to follow Dumbledore's advice turned out to be disastrous. Dumbledore had wanted to be the Potters' Secret-Keeper, but Sirius had said no, that he wanted to do it himself. (James was his best friend, after all.) Furthermore, Sirius even decided to switch being the Secret-Keeper with Peter Pettigrew, and neglected to inform Dumbledore of the switch. We all know what that mistake led to.

Still, in the two years after Sirius escaped from Azkaban, he shows himself to be more pliant to Dumbledore's authority. In *Order of the Phoenix*, he obediently follows Dumbledore's order to stay put at number twelve, Grimmauld Place, even though it's excruciatingly difficult for Sirius to be stuck back in a place he hates, with no one but Buckbeak and the wretched Kreacher for company, and unable to do anything "useful" for the Order. The fact that Sirius is willing to endure such misery for so many months—to be, essentially, his own jailer—is evidence of his respect for Dumbledore as their leader. He does let some resentment towards Dumbledore creep into his speech (which strengthens Harry's affection for Sirius because Harry at the time is feeling the same resentment towards Dumbledore!), but the fact remains that Sirius does what Dumbledore has told him to do. He stays put, and he leaves only when he feels there is no other choice—he must help Harry battle the Death Eaters at the Ministry of Magic.

Harry's relationship with Dumbledore also goes through a sort of evolution in the books. In general, Harry views Dumbledore as incredibly wise, in control, and powerful. Whenever Harry is in trouble and Dumbledore appears (or Harry hears the uplifting phoenix song, which he associates with Dumbledore), Harry thinks, "We're saved!" After all, Dumbledore is known to be the only one Voldemort has ever feared. In general, Harry listens to Dumbledore, and follows his advice. Dumbledore is usually a very heroic figure to Harry (and to most of the wizarding world, too). Like Lupin, Harry looks up to Dumbledore and wants to please him. When Harry must admit to Dumbledore in *Half-Blood Prince* that he has so far put little effort into obtaining the complete Horcrux memory from Horace Slughorn, Harry feels very guilty: "A hot, prickly feeling of shame spread from the top of Harry's head all the way down his body. Dumbledore had not raised his voice, he did not even sound angry, but Harry would have preferred him to yell; this cold disappointment was worse than anything" (*HBP* 428). Harry apologizes and earnestly promises to get the job done.

Despite Harry's high esteem for Dumbledore, there are some times when Harry is critical of him—certainly more so than Lupin ever seems to be. Harry is angry and resentful (and hurt, too, I think) when Dumbledore doesn't talk to Harry at all during Harry's *entire* fifth year of school. He thinks that Dumbledore is ignoring him, taking him for granted, treating him like a baby, or perhaps that Dumbledore just doesn't care about him any more. There are many times in *Order of the Phoenix* when Harry could have used Dumbledore's help (like dealing with Umbridge, or Snape's Occlumency lessons), but when Hermione suggests that Harry talk to Dumbledore, Harry refuses. When I talked earlier about how much information Sirius and Lupin are willing to give Harry, I could have pointed out that Dumbledore seems to be the worst offender in this area. He admits it himself after Sirius is killed. He finally tells Harry all the things he has been keeping from him for so long, about the Prophecy and Voldemort, and even things about Harry himself. Keeping Harry in the dark has had some tragic consequences, but Dumbledore says that he has done it out of love for Harry; he didn't want to burden Harry with so much terrible knowledge. Finally, however, Dumbledore admits that this has been a huge error on his part, and that Harry deserves to know—and *needs* to know, in order to be successful—everything that Dumbledore can tell him about Voldemort. We see the results of Dumbledore's decision in *Half-Blood Prince*, when he makes a conscious effort to mentor Harry more actively, to discuss the Pensieve scenes of Voldemort's past, and to treat Harry like a more mature, active participant in his own destiny.

The other issue over which Harry has had major disagreements with Dumbledore is Snape. Harry generally accepts Dumbledore's judgments and opinions, because Dumbledore is so incredibly wise and experienced. But the issue of Snape's trustworthiness is something that Harry just can't take Dumbledore's word for, unlike Lupin and Hermione. (And really, who can blame him, considering how nasty Snape has been to him, and the fact that Dumbledore refuses to explain his reasons for trusting Snape?) Book six is full of Harry's indignation on this subject. When Harry asks Dumbledore about Snape, and Dumbledore shuts down Harry's questioning, Harry is said to feel "mutinous" (*HBP* 359). When Dumbledore tells Harry that he decided to give young Tom Riddle a clean slate at Hogwarts (and just keep an eye on him), even after witnessing Riddle's creepy behavior at the orphanage, Harry thinks to himself, "Here, again, was Dumbledore's tendency to trust people in spite of overwhelming evidence that they did not deserve it!" (*HBP* 361). In the sad days following Snape's killing of Dumbledore, Rowling writes that Harry still can't "stop himself dwelling upon Dumbledore's *inexcusable* trust in Snape" (*HBP* 637; emphasis mine). All along, the issue of Snape's loyalty has been the major area in which Harry refuses to blindly accept Dumbledore's word without some kind of evidence.

Nevertheless, despite some mistakes and disagreements in the history of their relationship, Harry clearly loves and admires Dumbledore, and is devastated after his death. Indeed, it is

Dumbledore's death (as I cited at the very beginning of this essay) which prompts Harry to discard some of his "childish illusions" and start to see himself as an adult. Harry's feelings for Dumbledore are clear when he is looking at the headmaster's body at the bottom of the Astronomy Tower:

…there was still no preparation for seeing him here, spread-eagled, broken; the greatest wizard Harry had ever, or would ever, meet…. [H]e gazed down at the wise old face and tried to absorb the enormous and incomprehensible truth: that never again would Dumbledore speak to him, never again could he help. (HBP 608–9)

Having reviewed the three characters' relationships with Dumbledore (the ultimate authority figure), I'd like to return to Severus Snape, and their relationships with him as an adversarial figure, an enemy. Learning to deal with one's enemies is an important part of growing up, and Harry is influenced by the attitudes and behaviors that Sirius and Lupin display towards Snape. So my next question is: *How do Harry, Sirius, and Lupin interact with Snape, an antagonist?* Do they try to understand him? How do they respond to his taunts and provocations? How do they seem to expect Harry to deal with him?

Snape is such an important and complex character in the books that to perform a thorough study of his interactions with *any* of the main characters would take quite a while, and is therefore beyond the scope of this essay. Instead, I'd like to select a few scenes of interaction between Sirius and Snape, and between Lupin and Snape, and examine the effects they have on Harry.

Sirius's interactions with Snape are *always* bitter and contentious. It is very clear to Harry that Sirius hates Snape and Snape hates Sirius. They have hated each other since at least the age of eleven; no amount of maturing has softened their views of each other. The consistency of Sirius's attitude toward Snape gives Harry the message that it is okay to write Snape off completely as a permanent enemy. Sirius sees no need to re-examine his relationship with Snape, and he certainly never implies to Harry that Harry should adjust his attitude, either! During the Shrieking Shack scene in *Prisoner of Azkaban*, Sirius shows that even as an adult, he feels no remorse for the prank he tried to play on Snape when they were fifteen: "It served [Snape] right. Sneaking around, trying to find out what we were up to...hoping he could get us expelled" (*PoA* 356). Furthermore, Sirius frequently talks derisively about Snape in Harry's presence. He refers to the teenage Snape as a "slimy, oily, greasy-haired kid," a petty characterization that nevertheless makes Harry and Ron grin at each other (*GoF* 531).

There is a very illustrative scene in *Order of the Phoenix*. Snape has come to number twelve, Grimmauld Place, to inform Harry that Dumbledore wants him to give Harry Occlumency lessons. It turns into a very heated argument between Sirius and Snape, in which they rehash all their old grudges. They provoke each other into a nasty temper and trade childish insults. It is *Harry* who has to act like a mature adult here and step in to prevent them from having a duel. Harry, a teenager, has to physically push the two adults apart! When the Weasley family enters the room and unwittingly interrupts the confrontation, Sirius and Snape lower their wands, but continue to glare at each other with "utmost contempt" (*OotP* 521).

J. K. Rowling considers Sirius's absolutist attitude toward Snape to be a weakness. She wrote in the FAQ section of her Web site that "Sirius claims that nobody is wholly good or wholly evil, and yet the way he acts toward Snape suggests that he cannot conceive of any latent good qualities there" (http://www.jkrowling.com). I wonder—if Sirius would try instead to be more magnanimous toward Snape, or at least try to control his own temper, would Harry follow his lead?

Will Harry ever be able to view Snape the way Lupin always has (before Dumbledore's death)? Lupin unwaveringly accepts Dumbledore's certainty that Snape is on their side. Furthermore, Lupin adopts a stance of neutrality and tolerance toward Snape that is very unlike Sirius's position. Lupin lets any insults that Snape might hurl at him slide right off his back. A conversation at the Burrow between Harry and Lupin offers a summary of how Lupin chooses to deal with Snape (*HBP* 332–33). Lupin tells Harry the following: "I neither like nor dislike Severus"; that he and Snape will never be "bosom friends," due to the bitterness that still lingers from the long-ago feuds between Snape and the other Marauders; that Lupin appreciates the Wolfsbane Potion that Snape made for him in Harry's third year because it alleviated some of his suffering ("I must be grateful"); and that he holds no grudge against Snape for revealing his lycanthropy because the news would have come out anyway. Lupin always refers to him as either "Professor Snape" or "Severus," not some insulting nickname (like Sirius's "Snivellus"). In all, Lupin tries to handle Snape as maturely as possible.

Lupin models extreme equanimity for Harry in his attitude toward Snape, but he recognizes that Harry does not feel the same way he does. He tells Harry, "You are determined to hate him. And I understand; with James as your father, with Sirius as your godfather, you have inherited an old prejudice" (*HBP* 333). I think that Lupin's attitude toward Snape is quite evolved and admirable, but I sometimes wonder if Lupin couldn't take it a step further, and try to help *Harry* deal with Snape better, perhaps to give Harry some tips on how to control his temper during the Occlumency lessons. Lupin takes Harry aside and says, "Harry, I know you don't like Snape, but he is a superb Occlumens and we all—Sirius included—want you to learn to protect yourself, so work hard, all right?" (*OotP* 527). Why not offer Harry some practical advice on how to do that?

As for Harry's own relationship with Snape (which, as I said, could take up another whole essay!), despite the unyielding suspicion and hatred Harry feels, particularly after Snape has killed Dumbledore, I do find some signs of hope that Harry could maybe one day find a speck of goodness in Snape. I'm writing this before *Deathly Hallows* has been published, but if Snape will indeed play some vital role in Harry's defeat of Voldemort, it might be necessary for Harry to find some way to relent in the hatred he feels for Snape —to consider that Snape could have, in Rowling's words, some "latent good qualities." Harry has shown some ability to feel a tiny bit of sympathy or understanding for his other enemies. For example, at the end of *Half-Blood Prince*, Harry comes to feel some pity for the previously despised Draco Malfoy, and he recognizes that Draco would not have killed Dumbledore (*HBP* 640). Also, Harry feels a tiny twinge of sympathy for Tom Riddle (of all people!) because Riddle's mother didn't seem to care enough to, in Harry's words, "stay alive for her son" (*HBP* 262). There is even an example of Harry being able to feel some empathy for *Snape* when he views the "Snape's Worst Memory" Pensieve scene. Harry experiences some disillusionment about his father's character, and judges James's behavior toward Snape to be pretty despicable. Thanks to Dudley, Harry has some experience being a victim of bullying. Rowling writes:

What was making Harry feel so horrified and unhappy was…that he knew how it felt to be humiliated in the middle of a circle of onlookers, knew exactly how Snape had felt as his father had taunted him, and that judging from what he had just seen, his father had been every bit as arrogant as Snape had always told him. (*OotP* 650)

As of this writing, it remains to be seen whether these examples of Harry's ability to empathize with his enemies will ever evolve into a willingness to forgive Snape for killing Dumbledore. Will Harry take a Lupin-like approach, and try to find *some* good in Snape, or will he follow Sirius's lead and curse Snape as his enemy forever?

Due to space limitations, unfortunately, I won't be able to fully discuss the next set of questions on my list. However, I believe these are important questions about some of the indicators typically used to mark the progress and development a person experiences on the way to adulthood. Therefore, I would like to list these questions here, in the hope that they will inspire other readers to come up with some of their own answers. I believe that these questions would be profitable lines of inquiry for anyone wishing to study Sirius's and Lupin's effects on Harry at greater length…

1. *Accepting loss.* How do Harry, Sirius, and Lupin differ in the way they deal with the loss of loved ones? How do they deal with grief, and the things that cannot be changed?

2. *Rebelliousness.* How do the three characters take action and stand up for what they believe in, even if it means opposing authority and it involves risk to themselves?

3. *Disillusionment.* Which incorrect impressions does Harry have of Sirius and Lupin, and for that matter, his own father? How is Harry affected by learning the truth about them? Is Harry disappointed, or does the disillusionment merely provide him a more rounded, and less idealized, picture of them?

4. *Mastering impulses.* What are the similarities in Harry's and Sirius's tendencies toward reckless behavior? In which situations do they act impulsively, and in which do they pause to consider the consequences? Has Harry shown progress in his ability to act with appropriate caution and forethought?

5. *Recognizing and applying one's talents.* How do Harry and Lupin both find purpose and enjoyment in being teachers? Why is this role so seemingly uplifting to both of them?

6. *Entering into romantic relationships.* How open are they to dating and forming romantic attachments? If they feel that the relationship is a danger to their partner (Harry/Ginny, Lupin/Tonks), are they able to overcome the fear and find some way to make it work? Why doesn't Harry turn to Sirius or Lupin for advice on dealing with girls?

7. *Role-reversal.* What are the ramifications of any instances of role-reversal in Harry's relationships with Sirius and Lupin, in which Harry has to be the mature one, or has to worry for *their* safety? How does Harry judge *their* actions? When does he feel they are being hypocritical?

8. *Self-awareness.* Do they recognize their own flaws and weaknesses? Do they learn from their mistakes? What do they regret?

I would like to share some of the notes from my research into the last item: self-awareness. I think this is a critical topic because Harry's developing capacity for introspection will be absolutely vital to his ability to defeat Voldemort. Therefore, I think it is worthwhile to examine some instances of Sirius and Lupin demonstrating self-awareness (and in some cases, the lack of it), and to see whether this skill is reflected in Harry's own development.

A study of Lupin reveals some good examples of his ability as an adult to look back on some of the mistakes he made in his youth (and even some mistakes from recent adulthood) and recognize that he should have done better. He is able to see his flaws for what they are—areas for improvement. One example is the self-evaluation he provides during *Prisoner of Azkaban*'s Shrieking Shack scene. Hermione points out that it was very dangerous for school-age Lupin to have run around as a werewolf with his Animagus friends because he could have bitten his friends unintentionally, or anyone else that they ran into. Lupin responds with honesty:

[That] is a thought that still haunts me. And there were near misses, many of them. We laughed about them afterwards. We were young, thoughtless —carried away with our own cleverness. I sometimes feel guilty about betraying Dumledore's trust... he had no idea I was breaking the rules he had set down for my own and others' safety.... But I always managed to forget my guilty feelings every time we sat down to plan our next month's adventure. (*PoA* 355–56)

Lupin goes on to admit that he hasn't changed, and Harry picks up on the self-disgust in Lupin's voice. Lupin calls himself "cowardly" for not having told Dumbledore all year that Sirius could be using his Animagus ability to sneak into Hogwarts: "I convinced myself that Sirius was getting into the school using dark arts he learned from Voldemort, that being an Animagus had nothing to do with it...so, in a way, Snape's been right about me all along" (*PoA* 356). In a 2003 interview at Royal Albert Hall, J. K. Rowling described another one of Lupin's flaws:

Lupin's a wonderful teacher and a very nice man but he has a failing and his failing is that he does like to be liked and that's where he slips up because he has been disliked so often that he's always so pleased to have friends, so he cuts them an awful lot of slack.

Is Lupin self-aware enough to recognize this weakness in himself? Consider this statement made by Lupin in book five: "I think Dumbledore might have hoped [in making Lupin a prefect] that I would be able to exercise some control over my best friends. I need scarcely say that I failed dismally" (*OotP* 170). And when Harry later asks Lupin and Sirius about the "Snape's Worst Memory" Pensieve scene, Lupin is critical of his own behavior back then, and he says to Sirius, "Did I ever tell you to lay off Snape? Did I ever have the guts to tell you I thought you were out of order?" (*OotP* 671). Although Lupin was unwilling then to call his friends out on their bad behavior because he feared rejection, in the present Lupin seems a bit more secure, and there are numerous instances of Lupin's willingness in adulthood to rein in Sirius's behavior. (See the previously discussed Sirius/Molly/Lupin argument, and Lupin's forcing Sirius to explain himself to Harry in the Shrieking Shack scene, for two examples.)

There is, however, a particular area in which Lupin still seems to be lacking some self-awareness: his tendency toward extreme containment of his emotions, and his reluctance to open up to others about what troubles him. Does he recognize that it would probably be healthier for him to open up to other people a little more? There are two occurrences in book six which might indicate he's moving in that direction; namely, his opening up to Harry about how hard it's been for him to live among the werewolves as a spy (*HBP* 334–35), and his apparent change of mind about denying himself Tonks's affection (*HBP* 624, 641). But Lupin's emotional reservedness is so ingrained in his character that I think we won't know whether Lupin is going to be *consistently* more open with others until the seventh book comes out. Will Lupin be more communicative with Harry about Sirius's and Dumbledore's deaths? Will he allow himself to grieve *with* Harry?

Now let's look at Sirius's ability to look within himself and examine his own flaws. He shows himself able to look back on his teenage behavior with some regret when responding to Harry's distaste for what he witnessed in the "Snape's Worst Memory" Pensieve scene. Sirius says that he's not proud of his role in attacking and embarrassing Snape. He admits that he and James were "sometimes arrogant little berks" (*OotP* 670). However, while he recognizes the flaws in his past behavior toward Snape, it doesn't seem that Sirius puts this insight to any use when he's an adult; he continues to follow the same old pattern with Snape, scornfully trading childish insults with him. J. K. Rowling points out another fault of Sirius's in the FAQ section of her Web site:

Sirius is very good at spouting bits of excellent personal philosophy, but he does not always live up to them. For instance, he says in *GoF* that if you want to know what a man is really like, "look how he treats his inferiors, not his equals." But Sirius loathes Kreacher, the house-elf he has inherited, and treats him with nothing but contempt. (http://www.jkrowling.com/)

What does Harry think of Sirius's treatment of Kreacher? Right after Sirius has died, and Harry is raging against Dumbledore in his office, Harry can't bear to hear Dumbledore say that Sirius should have been kinder to Kreacher, and should have taken more seriously Dumbledore's warning that Kreacher could present a danger to them. Harry is outraged, and yells at Dumbledore, "DON'T TALK ABOUT SIRIUS LIKE THAT!" Harry says that Kreacher was a foul little liar, and the house-elf deserved any ill-treatment he might have received from Sirius (*OotP* 832).

In another example, Sirius seems unable to live up to one of his own ideals. In the fourth book, while giving an assessment of

Alastor Moody's character, Sirius has this to say to Harry, Ron, and Hermione:

"He takes his Defense Against the Dark Arts seriously, Moody. I'm not sure he trusts anyone at all, and after the things he's seen, it's not surprising. I'll say this for Moody, though, he never killed if he could help it. Always brought people in alive where possible. He was tough, but he never descended to the level of the Death Eaters." (*GoF* 532)

Does Sirius recognize that he himself did not live up to this ideal the year before, when he was so hell-bent upon *killing* Peter Pettigrew (rather than merely capturing him)? Or does Sirius excuse himself because he had a *personal* score to settle with Peter, whereas Moody presumably would have had the luxury of no personal stakes to interfere with his judgment when capturing Death Eaters?

While I'm on the subject of the almost-killing of Peter Pettigrew in the Shrieking Shack scene (*PoA*), I'd like to point out again that it is Harry who steps in to stop Sirius *and* Lupin from killing their former friend. (Remember, Lupin too had seemed perfectly okay with killing Peter in front of three teenagers once Lupin had made sure that all of the backstory was explained!) Harry despises Peter for betraying his parents, but here he shows a remarkably mature and insightful ability to reason. He actually steps in front of Peter, blocking him from Sirius and Lupin's upraised wands. When he tells them not to kill Peter, Sirius and Lupin both "look staggered" (*PoA* 375–76). Here they are, being reined in by a thirteen-year-old and forced to pause for a bit of self-reflection. Harry tells them that his father wouldn't have wanted them to become murderers. Lupin and Sirius look at each other and seem to engage in some soul-searching. They realize that Harry is right about what James would have wanted, so they submit to Harry's request. Throughout this essay, I have been highlighting some of Sirius and Lupin's effects on Harry, but I wanted to include this incident as a wonderful example of some of the effect Harry has on *them*.

Before I leave the subject of Sirius's ability to be self-reflective, I'd like to include an example in which he is successfully self-aware and shows signs of progress. Hermione asks Sirius how he managed to be the first wizard ever to escape from Azkaban. Not knowing for sure himself, he takes the time to really "ponder his answer" and reflect on how his mental state factored into his escape (*PoA* 371–

72). He realizes that his desire to track down Peter became an "obsession." I think this moment of self-examination plays itself out a bit later, after Sirius and Buckbeak have flown off from Hogwarts together and Sirius is a bit freer to think back on everything that he has done since Azkaban. Perhaps he comes to realize how recklessly he had been acting all year, and how his various methods of getting at Peter (slashing the Fat Lady's portrait, hovering over Ron's bed with a knife) didn't help to change the public's misconception that he was a bloodthirsty and insane criminal. He at least has some awareness of how his wild behavior might have affected *Harry.* Consider this bit from the letter Sirius sends to Harry on the departing Hogwarts Express: "I would also like to apologize for the fright I think I gave you that night last year when you left your Uncle's house. [Sirius had appeared in Little Whinging as a big, black dog.] I had only hoped to get a glimpse of you before starting my journey north, but I think the sight of me alarmed you" (*PoA* 433).

Now I'd like to point out a few examples of Harry demonstrating some mature self-awareness, followed by one example in which he fails to be self-reflective, and in which if he doesn't learn to make some improvement, could have disastrous results in *Deathly Hallows.* First, there is Harry's insightful inner discussion with himself concerning his bitter feelings about Ron being selected as a prefect rather than Harry. Harry is able to recognize some of the unfairness in his initial feelings, and overcomes them and decides to be supportive to his friend (*OotP* 166–67). Second, he gives himself a bit of a wake-up call following the troubling incident of Molly's encounter with her boggart at number twelve, Grimmauld Place: "[Harry] felt older than he had ever felt in his life, and it seemed extraordinary to him that barely an hour ago he had been worried about a joke shop and who had gotten a prefect's badge" (*OotP* 178). Third, when he and his friends arrive at the Ministry to find that Sirius is not being tortured there, he admits to himself that maybe Hermione had been right, that maybe this is all just a trap set by Voldemort. He feels embarrassed about the rashness of his mistake and worries that, due to his "saving people thing," he might actually have put his friends in danger (*OotP* 779, 782). Fourth, in the devastating aftermath of Sirius's death, Harry expresses deep regret for not having practiced his Occlumency more: "I didn't practice, I didn't bother, I could've stopped myself having those dreams, Hermione kept telling me to do it, if I had, [Voldemort would] never have been able to show me where to go, and—Sirius wouldn't —Sirius wouldn't [have died]" (*OotP* 829).

As for the area in which Harry desperately needs to learn some self-awareness, there is his penchant, after witnessing the death of a loved one, to immediately and impulsively go after the perpetrator and get some revenge. It happens in the fifth book after Bellatrix Lestrange has killed Sirius. Harry is so enraged that he storms after her towards the Atrium and hurls spells at her, including an attempt at the "Unforgivable" Cruciatus curse (*OotP* 809–11). In pursuing his vengeance, Harry effectively abandons his friends in the Department of Mysteries, all of whom are suffering from some degree of injury! And, not having reflected on his recklessness, Harry repeats the same mistake in *Half-Blood Prince*. After seeing Snape kill Dumbledore, Harry furiously rushes down from the Astronomy Tower in pursuit of Snape. Even the chaos of the battle taking place in the corridor between some Death Eaters and his friends doesn't cause Harry to stop and help them; he is too fixated on punishing Snape (and again, tries to perform some Unforgivable Curses). Rowling writes,

Harry scrambled up from the floor and began to sprint along the corridor, ignoring the bangs issuing from behind him, the yells of the others to come back, and the mute call of the figures on the ground whose fate he did not yet know. (*HBP* 599–600)

It is not until later, after Snape has escaped, and Ginny is catching him up on the status of all their friends as she leads him up to the hospital wing, that Harry finally is woken up to the fact that he failed to do the right thing: "Fear stirred in Harry's chest again: He had forgotten the inert figures he had left behind" (*HBP* 612). As of this writing, it remains to be seen whether or not Harry will learn to be more aware of this flaw he has. If something happens in *Deathly Hallows* which enrages Harry to such a degree, will he be able to master his impulse to hurl himself into vengeance, and instead maintain the self-control to stay with and help his injured friends?

The remainder of this essay will focus on the different *roles* that Sirius and Lupin fill for Harry, and the corresponding expectations that Harry has for each of them.

First, let's compare Sirius's status as Harry's godfather to Lupin's status as teacher (and subsequent role as friend-among-the-adult-crowd). Aside from the fact that Sirius cares about Harry for his own sake, the fact that he is Harry's *godfather* inspires him to make concerted efforts to be involved in Harry's life as much as he can. Having failed, in his own eyes, to protect James and Lily by suggesting that Peter be their Secret-Keeper, Sirius feels honor-bound to do a "better job" in protecting their son. Furthermore, Sirius likes and admires Harry as a person. He is deeply proud of Harry's track record of surviving against tremendous odds, over and over again, and of the fact that Harry managed to spoil what Voldemort expected to be his own triumphant comeback at the end of *Goblet of Fire*. As stated earlier, Sirius feels that Harry is competent enough to handle information that others might consider too troubling for a teenager to deal with. Sirius seems to find great purpose in being Harry's godfather. In *Goblet*, when he is asked why he has risked exposing himself by hanging around Hogsmeade as a dog, Sirius replies that he wants to be closer to Harry to help him cope with the tension of being in the Triwizard Tournament; in Sirius's own words, he is "fulfilling my duties as godfather" (*GoF* 522).

In my opinion, the fourth book illustrates what great potential there is for Harry and Sirius to have a solid and mutually beneficial relationship. It forms a beautiful portrait of "what could have been," had the events of book five turned out differently. In Harry's fourth year, Sirius is still on the run from the Ministry of Magic, but in comparison to his torturous imprisonment in Azkaban, Sirius is at least free to move about, and to keep informed on everything that is happened in the wizarding world. He seems to be enjoying some emotional healing after his long Azkaban stint, and he is quite eager to establish a relationship with Harry.

He keeps in contact with Harry by owl post in order to give him moral support and to advise him to be cautious. Indeed, just before the third task of the Triwizard Tournament, Sirius is sending Harry *daily* letters with godfatherly advice! Harry's happiness at receiving letters from his friends and adult supporters is a running theme through the books. Whenever he is stuck in a demoralizing situation, Harry is usually heartened to receive their letters, to know that there is someone out there who cares about him. And Harry is always eager to receive Sirius's letters in particular. For example, in the beginning of the fourth book, Harry is indecisive about whom to ask for answers and reassurance about his new scar pain. He is comforted by the fact that he now has Sirius to write to:

What he really wanted...was someone—someone like a *parent*: an adult wizard whose advice he could ask without feeling stupid, someone who cared about him, who had experience with Dark Magic…. And then the solution came to him. It was so simple, and so obvious, that he couldn't believe it had taken so long—*Sirius*. (*GoF* 22)

Consider some of the things that Sirius has brought into Harry's life aside from guidance and father-like affection. He is the giver of what Harry considers to be his "pride and joy" possession, the Firebolt. His "dangerous" reputation (and the threat that he will be checking up on his godson) forces the Dursleys to lighten up on Harry. They allow him to keep his wizarding paraphernalia in his room for a change, and they let him go to the Quidditch World Cup, all so as not to anger Sirius. Additionally, in Sirius's first-ever letter to Harry after escaping with Buckbeak, Sirius thoughtfully provides a signed Hogsmeade permission note, which Sirius knows will "make your next year at Hogwarts more enjoyable" (*PoA* 433).

Sirius is clearly a very important person in Harry's life. Harry often identifies with Sirius, and is able to discern some of the many things they have in common. After his feelings of resentment and helplessness from being stuck at Privet Drive with no information at the beginning of *Order of the Phoenix*, Harry has great sympathy for Sirius when he arrives at Grimmauld Place to discover that Sirius is similarly "imprisoned," and dealing with some of the same frustrated feelings. After Sirius's death, Harry even goes so far as to yell at Dumbledore for keeping Sirius stuck in his gloomy ancestral home. Indeed, when Sirius had remarked to Harry that he hated being back at Grimmauld Place, Rowling writes that "Harry understood completely. He knew how he would feel if forced, when he was grown up and thought he was free of the place forever, to return and live at number four, Privet Drive" (*OotP* 114–15).

In addition to identifying with Sirius, and viewing him as a source of affection and guidance, Harry can't help but be influenced by what Sirius's godfather role implies. The fact that James and Lily selected Sirius to be Harry's godfather probably has many implications to Harry. First, that his parents admired Sirius and trusted him specifically to be Harry's protector if they should be killed. Harry must feel that his parents hoped and intended for him to turn to Sirius for parental support. Perhaps Harry even infers that his parents would have desired for Harry to be *like* his godfather.

Despite all of these good things that develop in the relationship between Harry and Sirius (mostly in *Goblet of Fire*), we cannot forget that their relationship changes drastically over the course of *Order of the Phoenix*. Sirius has once again lost his freedom, and the chance to feel useful to anybody. He becomes bitter and moody, and there is regression in the emotional health he had been developing after his Azkaban escape. He withdraws from Harry, and allows Harry to know that he disapproves of him for not being as "daring" as James (*OotP* 305). Hermione opines that Sirius is desperately lonely, and becoming increasingly apt to do something reckless. In fact, Harry starts to experience a sort of role reversal in his relationship with Sirius, in that Harry has to become the "worrying parent." Hermione tells him that he has enough to worry about without having to worry about Sirius too.

There is an incident that occurs during Year Five's Christmas holiday which I think illustrates the deterioration in Harry and Sirius's relationship rather well. The Weasleys have just found out from Molly that Arthur is going to recover from his snake attack. Everyone is relieved, but Harry is still profoundly distressed and confused about what he thinks was his own role in the attack. (He feels responsible because he had seen the attack through the snake's eyes, as if he had been an active participant in it.) As Harry rides with the others on the Underground after visiting Arthur at St. Mungo's, Rowling describes Harry's inner turmoil:

He felt dirty, contaminated, as though he were carrying some deadly germ, unworthy to sit on the underground train back from the hospital with innocent, clean people whose minds and bodies were free of the taint of Voldemort.... He had not merely seen the snake, he had *been* the snake, he knew it now. (*OotP* 492)

Harry is consumed by a terrible fear that he is a danger to everyone around him, and is going mad. He takes Sirius aside and confesses his fears to him, but Sirius essentially dismisses him. He says that Harry is just suffering from shock and needs to get some sleep. Harry needs to "just stop worrying." Eager to get back to enjoying the Weasleys' company and the happy atmosphere at the breakfast table, "he clapped Harry on the shoulder and left the pantry, leaving Harry standing alone in the dark" (*OotP* 480–81).

Still, although there have been regressions and communication barriers in their relationship, Harry is frantic when he thinks that Sirius is being tortured at the Ministry of Magic. He rushes to Sirius's aid with no thought for his own safety. When Sirius is killed, Harry is devastated. It is the fact that Harry loves Sirius which renders Voldemort unable to possess Harry's body in the Ministry atrium (*OotP* 816). Later, in Dumbledore's office, Harry is so filled with guilt and rage and despair that he doesn't even want to be human anymore, to suffer the pain of it. Dumbledore himself recognizes that Harry has lost the "closest thing to a parent [he] has ever known" (*OotP* 824).

Finally, we come to Lupin's meaning to Harry. They have a generally healthy and productive relationship, and Lupin himself is for the most part very highly regarded in the *Harry Potter* fandom. Harry truly likes Lupin. In a chat on the Barnes & Noble website, Rowling said, "I was looking forward to writing the third book from the start of the first because that's when Professor Lupin appears, and he is one of my favorite characters in all seven books" (B&N chat, 8 Sept 1999). As I stated earlier, Lupin is a well-loved teacher, and he is kind, empathetic, and an attentive listener.

However, there are some definite barriers that (so far) prevent Lupin from being as important and close to Harry as Sirius is. First, there is the fact that Lupin is introduced to Harry as his teacher. Even after Lupin is no longer Harry's Defense Against the Dark Arts professor, the teacher/student, or adult/adolescent, barrier seems a little difficult to overcome. As I pointed out in the beginning of this essay, Harry never comes around to calling Lupin by his first name, as he does with Sirius. Then there's the simple fact that Lupin is not Harry's godfather, and after he resigns from Hogwarts, he just doesn't have as much contact with Harry as Sirius does. (He is noticeably absent from Harry's fourth year altogether.)

There are two major barriers in the relationship between Harry and Lupin: Lupin's extreme emotional restraint and reticence, and the way that Lupin perceives his own meaning to Harry.

First, as discussed earlier, Lupin is very reserved. Due to his lifelong fear of being a danger to others because he is a werewolf (and also due, I think, to the fact that he internalizes his negative emotions and grief in order to survive the difficulties in his life), Lupin wants to remain very much in control of his emotions and behavior. He doesn't ever want to slip up and hurt someone, physically or emotionally. Therefore, instead of opening up to Harry, he keeps things to himself. He doesn't want to burden other people, or "inflict" his own pain on them. The result has been that Lupin has denied himself some opportunities to bond more deeply with Harry. Harry mentions his parents several times during the numerous Patronus lessons he has with Lupin, but Lupin painfully clams up on the subject. He could be a great wealth of information about Harry's father, but he is unable to talk about James and Lily; perhaps he even believes that it would be too painful for *Harry* to hear about them. However, as Harry grows a little older, and Lupin sees that Harry can indeed handle some very adult things (Harry survives the loss of Sirius, after all), Lupin starts to loosen up in book six on the subject of Harry's parents, to the point where it makes him happy to share his memories with him (*HBP* 335). The other area in which Harry and Lupin could improve their bond is their shared grief over the death of Sirius and Dumbledore. Harry and Lupin were unable in book six to help each other deal with Sirius's death. My hope is that in the final book they will find a way (and the time!) to at least talk about Sirius and Dumbledore, even if only to acknowledge that they both suffered and survived these severe losses. Will Lupin continue to be a "lone wolf," or will he (perhaps under the influence of Tonks) realize that shared joy is double joy, but shared sorrow is half a sorrow?

The second thing that impedes Lupin's becoming more important to Harry is the way that Lupin seems to perceive his role. He seems to think that Harry just doesn't *need* him as much as he needs Sirius. While in *Prisoner of Azkaban* Lupin is perhaps the primary adult influence in Harry's life, and is a great source of comfort to him (by very patiently teaching him the Patronus Charm), once Sirius enters the picture, Lupin steps back to allow Sirius to become the primary influence. Lupin can't fail to notice that when Harry is troubled about what he viewed in the "Snape's Worst Memory" Pensieve scene, it is specifically *Sirius* whom Harry seeks out for explanations and reassurance (*OotP* 669). Conversely, Lupin knows how important it is to Sirius to be Harry's godfather. When Sirius has an argument with Molly over how much they should tell Harry about Voldemort, Lupin *stares* at Sirius while Sirius is making his case (for two pages, in fact!). I think that Lupin is thoughtfully studying Sirius's demeanor, and taking full measure of the great care and interest for Harry that is evident in Sirius's position. He understands how much it means to Sirius to be Harry's godfather.

I think it's therefore possible that Lupin might feel a bit of survivor's guilt after Sirius's death. Sirius had been Harry's *godfather*, and now he is dead, while he, Lupin, survives. Perhaps Lupin feels that he can never mean as much to Harry as Sirius did. I do think that Harry would welcome a more intense relationship with Lupin. After all, Harry has always had a very favorable opinion of him, and has always seemed to take careful notice of any changes in Lupin's shabby appearance or apparent health. Harry feels sympathy for the great difficulties Lupin's lycanthropy imposes on Lupin's life. (Harry's hatred for Professor Umbridge increases even more when he learns that she is responsible for passing some very hurtful anti-werewolf legislation, for example). But still, until the final book is released, we must consider that J. K. Rowling never intended Lupin to be anything more to Harry than what he already is. She has explained in interviews that she has killed off the primary adult influences in Harry's life, Sirius and Dumbledore, in order to follow the literary tradition that necessitates Harry's going forward now as an autonomous adult, with no all-powerful protectors to shield him from danger. Harry must become his own man.

In my study of Harry's relationships with Sirius and Lupin—their similarities and differences, the meanings they have to each other, and the signs of maturity and progress that the two men have inspired in Harry by their examples and influence—I hope to have demonstrated the profound impact that they will have on Harry's coming of age. No matter how briefly or incompletely they have been in Harry's life, there is no doubt that they have left their mark on him and have helped to shape the hero Harry will become.

Jacqueline Goodenow can be contacted at jacmargoo@yahoo.com.

Sirius Black:
The Face of Eleggua in the Potterverse

Vivienne D'Avalon

Sirius Black: unpredictable, unstable, and very popular. He's been compared to various mythological tricksters, but I think Sirius has the most in common with the trickster from the African Ifa tradition, Eleggua. The Yoruban faith called Ifa is from the West Coast of Africa. Because of forced immigration caused by the slave trade, Ifa blended in the New World with Catholicism and Native American beliefs. The preferred name for this blended religion in Cuba and Mexico is Lukumi, but since most people are unfamiliar with this name I will use the better-known term, Santería. It is also known as Voudon in Haiti and New Orleans, as Candomble in Brazil, and by many other names.

In the various Ifa traditions there is only one God, but this God is served by many spirits or "mysteries," called orishas in Santería and lwa in Voudon. The orishas act as intermediaries, carrying out God's orders and communicating human wishes back to His ears. These spirits are more likely to grant their favor to people who are grateful and make offerings to them. The orisha that must always be addressed and "fed" first is known as Eleggua in Santería. In New Orleans, he is known as Papa Legba, and I will point out some of the differences between Eleggua and Papa Legba as I draw my comparison to Sirius Black.

Eleggua is the spirit in charge of all communications. Without Eleggua's help, no prayers can reach any of the other spirits in the pantheon. No matter which orisha someone wishes to contact, they must always propitiate Eleggua first to ensure that their message is communicated correctly to the proper spirit. This is because Eleggua is a Trickster with a highly mischievous nature. If he is

189

insulted, he might cause miscommunications that lead to substantial trouble. Eleggua is thus an immensely important spirit. But he is unpredictable, has a twisted sense of humor, and delights in dangerous pranks. Sirius Black shares many of these attributes, and we may be able to predict plot points in the final book based on these comparisons.

Sirius is a trickster, like Eleggua, and known for his dangerous pranks, such as luring Snape to a meeting with a werewolf. Eleggua is a shape-shifter, like Sirius, and the animal associated with both is a black dog. Eleggua is one of Three Warriors—important protective spirits who associate with a fourth, Osun, who warns them of danger. Each of these Warriors, including Osun, shares traits with the Marauders. Eleggua is also associated with divine twins called the Ibeyi. They share many characteristics with the Weasley twins, who convey the Marauder's Map to Harry.

Sirius is an important source of information for Harry, and the two-way mirror Sirius gives him to communicate is a tool associated with Eleggua. Part of Eleggua's importance as a communicator is the link he provides to the ancestors. Sirius is Harry's most valued link to his parents. Finally, Eleggua's avatars sometimes die, and he stands astride the world of the living and the dead. Sirius's death may allow him to help Harry, by bridging the gap between Harry in this world, and his parents and other allies in the next. The manner of his death is significant, as well: Eleggua is the orisha of crossroads, doors, and gateways, particularly cemetery gates, as the barrier between worlds. Sirius "dies" by falling through just such a gateway, the veil in the Department of Mysteries.

Eleggua's most important job is facilitating communications. Sirius warns Harry of danger, gives him hints and advice, and runs messages to the Order of the Phoenix for Dumbledore. Sirius gets his information however he can, whether by getting newspapers out of the garbage, where Eleggua is often found, or "from inside the Ministry" itself.[1] Sometimes his sources even mystify his own godson. "How did you know about that?" Harry demands in *Order of the Phoenix.* "You want to choose your meeting places more carefully," Sirius says cryptically. "The Hog's Head, I ask you…"[2]

---

1   J. K. Rowling, *Harry Potter and the Order of the Phoenix* (New York: Scholastic, 2003 [pbk rpt. 2004]), 302.
2   *OotP* 369.

But because he's a trickster, Eleggua sometimes changes messages. Though Ron's mother uses Sirius to convey a message to the children, apparently she fears he won't pass it all on. Despite Eleggua's tendency to twist messages around, however, Lupin still thinks Harry's better off getting the skinny from Sirius than from rumor-mongers. Harry is thus willing to go to great lengths to talk to Sirius, even when it seems impossible to do so. Distance is usually no object, for Sirius frequently writes letters. The only distance Sirius cannot overcome is reaching from the land of death. "It's just hard," poor Harry admits in *Half-Blood Prince*, "to realize he won't write to me again."[1]

However, we know that one form of communication Sirius has with Harry is the Marauder's Map, and the Map is evidence of the possibility of communication after death. The map is an interactive tool. When Harry is unable to figure out how to work it, speech bubbles appear with instructions. It doesn't communicate as a single "mind," either. Each of the Marauders can speak independently, and Harry sees his dead father's and his godfather's words appear to insult Snape almost as if they were present—as, in a way, they were.

Indeed, one of Eleggua's most important communications functions is connecting us to our ancestors. In Ifa, ancestors are considered part of the family, as if still present, just on another level; oral tradition keeps them alive in memory. The ancestors look after their legacy by watching over their descendants, in much the same way the portraits in Dumbledore's office lend him advice. This is clearly visible in Harry's relationship to his parents and even his grandparents. Their memories are kept alive by friends who knew and loved them, especially Sirius.

But Sirius's relationship with his own ancestors is less cordial. Haskins tells us the worst thing someone can do is "sell...ancestral lands.... In such cases the family face[s] certain ruin;" nothing "could restore them to the good graces of the ancestors, and little help could be offered by outside intermediaries."[2] Could Sirius's treatment of his family home be the reason for his death? Kreacher would say so, as would Sirius's deceased mother: "*How dare you befoul the house of my fathers*," her portrait shrieks. "*Blood traitor, abomination,*

---

1   J. K. Rowling, *Harry Potter and the Half-Blood Prince* (New York: Scholastic, 2005 [pbk rpt.]), 77.

2   Jim Haskins, *Voodoo and Hoodoo: the Craft as Revealed by Traditional Practitioners* (Chelsea, MI: Scarborough House/Publishers, 1978, 1990), 34.

shame of my flesh!"[1] Compare this to an Eleggua story: He "decided to test" his friend Obi by inviting "all the beggars and derelicts…he could find" to his party. "When Obi saw his beautiful house full of poor…people…in dirty, smelling rags…he almost choked with rage… [H]e threw them all out…[and] Eleggua…left with them."[2]

But crossing such lines is Eleggua's favorite pastime. He thinks outside the box, whether that box is social custom, the duality of life and death, or the laws of physics. Eleggua adopts those who share this proclivity as his godchildren. "Don't go blaming Dumbledore for Potter's determination to break rules," Snape says of Sirius's godchild. "He has been crossing lines ever since he arrived here."[3]

Eleggua gives his godchildren many gifts; however, the recipient must be cautious about accepting such presents because they might be dangerous. There are three prominent gifts Sirius gives Harry. Each one is the sort of gift Eleggua gives. The broomstick represents freedom (from the law of gravity). Yet when it was first delivered, it had to be checked for booby traps. Another gift is a knife that can open any lock—and Eleggua can break any lock. A third gift is a mirror that allows two-way communication. Mirrors are sacred to Eleggua, since he is "on both sides of the mirror,"[4] because he stands at the crossroads between worlds. Harry receives one more gift, but from the Weasley twins—the map that Sirius and friends created. It shows all the secret ways in and out of Hogwarts, allowing Harry to "manage mischief" when he is "up to no good." It is "a very dubious magical object" we are told, "and… incriminated not only him, but his own father, Fred and George Weasley, and Professor Lupin."[5]

There is a price to pay for Eleggua's gifts, however. Eleggua can throw a tantrum worse than a toddler in his "terrible twos," and his "jokes" can be nasty—like leading an enemy to a deadly werewolf just for fun. Eleggua must be fed, and he becomes very jealous if he is not fed first. Harry and his friends make a point of sending Sirius food on a regular basis when he visits. Sirius as a teenager is the

---

1   *OotP* 78.
2   Migene Gonzalez-Wippler, *Santería: African Magic in Latin America* (New York: Original Publications, 1987), 102.
3   J. K. Rowling, *Harry Potter and the Goblet of Fire* (New York: Scholastic, 2000 [pbk rpt. 2002]), 276.
4   Author unknown, <http://www.co.uk.lspace.org/books/apf/witches-abroad.html>.
5   *GoF* 477.

epitome of the spoiled child, and Eleggua is "the king of mischief."[1] Perhaps it was Sirius's idea to make "mischief managed" the spell to erase the Marauder's Map. "You're less like your father than I thought," says Sirius petulantly, when his idea for a meeting is nixed as too dangerous. "The risk would've been what made it fun for James."[2] His past and his torture in Azkaban combine to give him a reputation of outright insanity. "Black is mad. He's a danger to anyone who crosses him," Fudge says.[3] Sirius displays a terrible temper when he fails to get into Gryffindor Tower. Eleggua is, after all, accustomed to being able to get through any door. And when Eleggua becomes "very angry," someone can end up dead. Lupin acknowledges that Sirius's little "prank" of luring Snape to a potentially lethal meeting with a werewolf "nearly killed" Snape— and would have if James Potter hadn't rescued him "at great risk to his life."[4]

Sirius's reputation for dark moods finally lands him in wizarding prison, albeit in error. But as a trickster used to crossing lines and making possible the impossible, Eleggua is also adept at opening locks and overcoming insurmountable barriers. It should come as no surprise, then, that he is an escape artist. He is equated with St. Anthony in his role as "Liberator of Prisoners."[5] "Sirius Black escaped from them," says Harry in *Prisoner of Azkaban*. "He got away."[6] Later, Fudge says, "We had Black cornered and he slipped through our fingers yet again!" But it was only possible because Harry and Hermione defy the rules of linear time. Nevertheless, Harry worries. "Made it so far, though, hasn't he?" Ron reminds him.[7]

One of the reasons Sirius has "made it so far" is the distinct advantage of being a shape-shifter, one of Eleggua's many deceptive skills. This ability allows Sirius to escape from Azkaban. "They could tell that my feelings were…less human, less complex when I was a dog," he says to Harry of the Dementors. "[W]hen they opened my

---

1 Gonzalez-Wippler 110–11.
2 *OotP* 302.
3 J. K. Rowling, *Harry Potter and the Prisoner of Azkaban* (New York: Scholastic, 1999 [pbk rpt. 2001]), 38.
4 *PoA* 356–57.
5 Author unknown, "Anthony of Padua," <http://www.catholic-forum.com/ saints/sainta01.htm>.
6 *PoA* 188.
7 *GoF* 510.

door to bring food, I slipped past them."[1] Dogs are important to
Eleggua because they eat offerings left for the orisha, and he uses
them as messengers. And it is specifically a black dog that is
associated with Eleggua. In both the Old and the New World, the
black dog is an omen of death. Eleggua's association with that
animal is related to his role as a psychopomp, one who guides souls
in the underworld, can travel between the world of the living and
the dead with ease, and who guards cemetery gates. "The Grim!"
Professor Trelawney names it. "The giant, spectral dog that haunts
churchyards!"[2] A book on death omens shows "a black dog large as
a bear, with gleaming eyes" on the cover[3]—just the form in which
Harry first meets Sirius.

Eleggua's colors are red and black, representing life and death, the
beginning and the end. In his form as Ghede or death, however, his
color is black. Another name for him is "The Black Man," and in
this form he determines who will and won't be able to shape-shift. It
is also through this aspect that one contacts the ancestors in the land
of the dead. Haskins tells us this "divine trickster could also be the
ancestor who had most recently died. New to the afterworld and…
closer to the living, he might be…more in sympathy with their
problems."[4] But to be an ancestor, one must first be dead.

"[Eleggua] is eternal," Canizares tell us, "but many of his avatars
have experienced birth and death."[5] Just as Rowling's characters are
grief stricken when Sirius dies, so Eleggua's people grieved for him:
"[A]n inconceivable tragedy befell the village when their beloved
prince Eleggua fell ill and died suddenly. Everyone felt the loss of
the handsome youth." But Eleggua's spirit is transformed through
magic: "They then understood that they had not lost their son, who
had become an orisha and would now be protecting them from his
divine realm.… Since that day everyone in the community enjoyed
great prosperity [because of]…Eleggua, the magical prince who
became a god."[6] Do we not wish the same when we lose Sirius,
seemingly forever?

---

1   *PoA* 371.
2   *PoA* 107.
3   *PoA* 54.
4   Haskins 32.
5   Baba Raul Canizares, *Eshu-Eleggua Elegbara: Santeria and the Orisha of the Crossroads*
    (Plainview, New York: Original Publications, 2000), 3.
6   Canizares 4–5.

Of course, the veil of death is just one more threshold, and Eleggua lives at crossroads and stands in doorways, existing in both worlds at once. Here we see why a vibrant, virile figure like Eleggua would be depicted in New Orleans Voudon as the crippled Papa Legba, an old man who walks with a cane and limps. You would probably limp a bit too if you had to keep one foot in the grave, and make of your body a bridge to span the chasm between life and death. Eleggua is also linked to St. Anthony in his role as "Reviver of the Dead,"[1] and Ghede is the "Lwa of death and resurrection."[2] Let us have hope, then, that Sirius still has one foot in the world of the living.

If Sirius does manage to come back, it will most likely be because his godson Harry is in desperate need. Another of Eleggua's jobs is to protect his godchildren, and Ghede also protects children. Sirius stays by his godson in the hospital wing; he writes Harry scathing letters, chastising him for dangerous escapades; he gives Harry warnings; he threatens people on Harry's behalf, offering to "see to Amelia Bones,"[3] and tells Snape, "If I hear you're using these Occlumency lessons to give Harry a hard time, you'll have me to answer to."[4]

Compare this to an Eleggua story: "'Are you trying to cheat Orunmila?'... Eleg[g]ua...put his powerful warrior's hand around the Babalawo's neck.... 'Tell me...are you looking for trouble...? You'd never do anything to make me angry, would you?'" he growls.[5] But Sirius does not only protect Harry. Like Eleggua, he defends his ancestral home, once it becomes the headquarters for the Order of the Phoenix, though he chafes at being homebound, especially after being imprisoned for many years already. Eleggua is used to being able to pass freely through doors, not to being trapped inside.

This theme becomes important when Harry dreams about a door in the Hall of Mysteries that he desperately wants to open. Finally, in his dream, he succeeds. When he arrives at the Ministry, he faces

---

1   "Anthony of Padua" (*op. cit.*).
2   Bob Corbett, "Introduction to Voodoo in Haiti, The most basic concepts of Voodoo," *African Religion: Syncretism*, "Descriptions of Various Loa of Voodoo" (March 1988), <http://bonney.org/keystrokestudios/portfolio/myAyiti/Voodoo.htm>.
3   *OotP* 123.
4   *OotP* 520.
5   Author   unknown,   <http://w3.iac.net/~moonweb/Santeria/Chapter5.html#Elegua>.

numerous unmarked doors. Harry realizes, "I'll know the right way when I see it."[1] He uses Sirius's knife in an unsuccessful attempt to overcome the most difficult of them. Hermione wisely decides it must not be the one because "Harry could get through all the doors in his dream."[2]

But opening doors is just the first step. An initiate to Santería receives Eleggua first, but usually receives all Three Warriors together. Eleggua opens the path; Ogun, the warrior, removes obstacles from the path; and Ochosi, the tracker, navigates the path.[3] In the Potterverse they correspond to Padfoot, Moony, and Prongs. Osun warns the Three Warriors of danger.

Together, the Three Warriors are almost unstoppable. Gonzalez-Wippler tells us they are "very close friends. They work together sometimes to create the most fearful [evil spells]."[4] The Marauders attacked Snape because they were bored and entertained themselves by being cruel. Lupin is finally given a prefect's badge to rein his friends in. "I need scarcely say that I failed dismally,"[5] he tells Harry. "*James Potter and Sirius Black. Apprehended using an illegal hex upon Bertram Aubrey. Aubrey's head twice normal size. Double detention.*"[6] Harry finds the names of James and Sirius frequently in the school records, occasionally coupled with those of Remus and Peter.

Ochosi the hunter is beautiful, and wears stag's horns, just like the ones the handsome James Potter had once he transformed. Harry becomes proficient at hunting Dementors with his stag Patronus. But it is the moral compass that Ochosi provides that comes through most clearly with Harry. "James wouldn't have wanted me killed," Wormtail begs; "he would have shown me mercy."[7] "[M]y dad wouldn't've wanted [Sirius and Lupin] to become killers—just for you,"[8] Harry agrees. "[James] would have saved Pettigrew too," Dumbledore tells Harry. "I am sure of it."[9]

---

1   *OotP* 771.
2   *OotP* 775.
3   rafh Tzeenj, "Eleggua," <http://www.spiralnature.com/spirituality/deities/eleggua1.html>.
4   Gonzalez-Wippler 111.
5   *OotP* 170.
6   *HBP* 532.
7   *PoA* 374.
8   *PoA* 376.
9   *PoA* 427. For more information about Ochosi, see: Fatunmbi, Awo Fá' Lokun. *Ochosi: Ifá and the Spirit of the Tracker.* Plainview, NY: Original Publications, 1992.

Lupin is the only Marauder who does not willingly transform. He was bitten and infected by a werewolf. Ogun, spirit of war and iron, is also a spirit of blood, so petitioners turn to him for assistance with "blood diseases," such as lycanthropy. He is also "Lord of... wild beasts."[1] Ogun and Eleggua are very tight, and Ogun frequently helps him out of trouble.[2] Harry and his friends are shocked at first, when they see Prof. Lupin "embrace Black like a brother."[3] But Snape saw the danger: "It seems—almost impossible—that Black could have entered the school without inside help. I did express my concerns when you appointed—"[4] The name "Lupin" is left unspoken. Métraux tells us that in Voudon, "[t]he 'werewolf [spirit]'...confers the power of being able to turn into an animal. Many sorcerers use it to walk about at night as black" animals, to commit cruel acts.[5] It is no coincidence that Lupin's condition inspires his three closest friends to learn how to become Animagi.

But what of Osun? One story calls him a traitor: "And you, Osun, because you have betrayed me for food, will only eat the scraps Eleggua throws your way, and you will live only to serve him."[6] "You returned to me, not out of loyalty," Voldemort chastises, "but out of fear of your old friends."[7] Nevertheless, Wormtail may be of use to Harry. "Pettigrew owes his life to you," Dumbledore tells him. "When one wizard saves another...it creates a certain bond between them.... [T]he time may come when you will be very glad you saved [him]."[8] Perhaps, like Osun, Wormtail will warn Harry of danger at a crucial moment.

The Three Warriors are not the only other spirits associated with Eleggua. The Ibeyi are mischievous identical twins linked to him. "The presence of twins in a family involves its members in constant attentions and a thousand precautions," Métraux says.[9] "No ambition," Molly Weasley says in discouragement, "unless you count making as much trouble as they possibly can."[10] When first

---

1 Author unknown, <http://www.hauntedamericatours.com/voodoo/7AFRICANPOWERS/>.
2 Gonzalez-Wippler 116.
3 *PoA* 344.
4 *PoA* 166.
5 Alfred Métraux, *Voodoo in Haiti* (New York: Schocken Books, 1959), 299.
6 Canizares, 6.
7 *GoF* 649.
8 *PoA* 427.
9 Métraux 146.
10 *GoF* 58.

presented with the blank Marauder's Map, Harry thinks it's "one of Fred and George's jokes." "Moony, Wormtail, Padfoot, and Prongs," George says reverently. "Noble men, working tirelessly to help a new generation of lawbreakers," Fred adds.[1] Corbett describes the Ibeyi as "[a] mysterious set of…contradictions: good and evil, happy and sad etc. If honored…they will…help you have the better side of life."[2] Harry takes this into account, whether he realizes it or not, when he gives Fred and George his Triwizard earnings for their joke shop. "I could do with a few laughs," he tells them. "We could all do with a few laughs. I've got a feeling we're going to need them."[3]

The Twins leave a long record of misdeeds behind them: They try to trick the Goblet of Fire; they blackmail a Ministry official; they feed their friends joke candies; they invent "Extendable Ears," steal doxies to experiment for their Skiving Snackboxes, put Bulbadox Powder down someone's pajamas, tried to make an Unbreakable Vow with five-year-old Ron, and challenged that same little brother, as prefect, to keep them in line. When Fred misremembers a prank, he says, "Hard to keep track sometimes, isn't it?"[4]

Finally they plan their grand exit:

"We've always known where to draw the line," said Fred.
"We might have put a toe across it occasionally," said George.
"But we've always stopped short of causing real mayhem," said Fred.
"But now?" said Ron tentatively.
"Well, now—" said George.
"—what with Dumbledore gone—" said Fred.
"—we reckon a bit of mayhem—" said George.
"—is exactly what our dear new Head deserves," said Fred.
…"[P]hase one is about to begin. I'd get in the Great Hall for lunch if I were you, that way the teachers will see you can't have had anything to do with it."[5]

It makes you almost agree with Kreacher: "and there's its twin, unnatural little beasts they are."[6]

---

1   *PoA* 191–93.
2   Corbett (*op. cit.*).
3   *GoF* 733.
4   *OotP* 226.
5   *OotP* 627.
6   *OotP* 108.

But we have not heard the last of Fred and George Weasley, nor, I suspect, of the Marauders, living or dead. Whether Rowling meant to arrange it or not, Sirius has many similarities with Eleggua, so many that there is not room to list them all here. I believe that, like Eleggua, Sirius Black will be a vital connection for Harry when he most needs the help of heroes on the other side of the veil of death, and that Sirius will make that communication possible. There is an Eleggua for just about everything and every job in the universe, and Sirius is the face of Eleggua in the Potterverse.

Anything's Possible: An Examination of the Trickster Archetype in J. K. Rowling's Harry Potter Series

Layla A. Abuisba
St. Louis Community College

In mythology, the trickster as archetypal hero often crosses boundaries of acceptable human behavior. Lewis Hyde, author of *Trickster Makes This World*, asserts that not only does the trickster cross boundaries, but at times he or she sets new boundaries between "right and wrong, sacred and profane, clean and dirty, male and female, young and old, living and dead" (7). A trickster, as described by Hyde, is the ambivalent "god of the threshold" who blurs the distinction of specific boundaries. The trickster's main function is mischief or the desire to disrupt the status quo, but this disruption serves an important task, which is to release an important person, element, or idea into the world (Hyde 8). Regarding these mythic tales, Hyde says that "the motif of freeing some needed good from heaven is found all over the world" (6).

Trickster themes permeate J. K. Rowling's *Harry Potter* series. Certain characters, such as James Potter and his Marauders' group, Peeves the Poltergeist, the Weasley twins, Luna Lovegood, and Rita Skeeter embody the core of what a trickster is about: challenging, existing on, and at times creating boundaries of human behavior and understanding (Hyde 7–8). These characters are important to the movement of the plot of each of the *Harry Potter* books. When tricksters act, the resulting events reveal important information and create new challenges for Harry and the wizarding world. In addition, trickster behavior inspires Harry and his young friends to mature as they examine and adjust their ideas about right and wrong.

Harry is the primary beneficiary of trickster behavior, which has an important influence on his actions and what may ultimately be the outcome of the series. It is also clear that Rowling's writing style and the series' effect on readers demonstrate the trickster's role of crossing boundaries.

As readers, we learn about Harry, his friends, and the wizarding world due to trickster behavior. However, a trickster can also be caught in traps of his or her own making (Hyde 19). Rowling does not allow her trickster characters to run amok without their being occasionally restrained in some way. When Peeves the Poltergeist taunts Professor Lupin in *Harry Potter and the Prisoner of Azkaban*, Lupin performs a spell that forces a wad of chewing gum into Peeves' nostril, forcing him to retreat. This is an event that Peeves himself would have enjoyed, if it had happened to someone else. However, in this case, the joke was on him (*PoA* 131). The twins may have sold Draco Malfoy Peruvian Darkness powder, not realizing that he would use it against members of Dumbledore's Army and bring Death Eaters into the castle (*HBP* 618). Even Luna, a sweet, dreamy, and mild-tempered trickster, attracts negative attention due to her unusual fashion sense and her frank habit of stating unusual ideas and uncomfortable truths (*OotP* 262). However, trickster characteristics are important elements of Rowling's work, especially in relation to character development and plot.

Peeves the Poltergeist is a trickster who plays a significant role in the *Harry Potter* series because Peeves' actions often are precursors to important plot developments. Rowling describes Peeves as "an indestructible spirit of chaos." This definition corresponds to Hyde's description of a trickster as one who enlivens silent places with mischief (6). In *Harry Potter and the Sorcerer's Stone*, it is because of Peeves that Harry, Ron, Hermione, and Neville find Fluffy, Hagrid's three-headed dog. Peeves creates a disturbance in order to attract Argus Filch to the location of the four, who are out of bed and wandering the castle. After Peeves shouts that they are out of bed and in the Charms corridor, the four rush into the room where Fluffy is and discover him. Meanwhile, when Filch arrives, he asks Peeves for help:

> "Which way did they go, Peeves?... Quick, tell me."
> "Say 'please.'"
> "Don't mess with me, Peeves, now *where did they go?*"

"Shan't say nothing if you don't say please," said Peeves in his annoying singsong voice.

"All right—*please.*"

"NOTHING! Ha haaaa! Told you I wouldn't say nothing if you didn't say please!" (160)

With this exchange we see Peeves the trickster in full form. He acts merely for the sake of causing mischief. He is ambivalent regarding the concerns of either Filch or the students.

We gain insight into Neville's character because of Peeves. Although Neville often seems to be timid and inept, he actually possesses a great amount of determination. In *Harry Potter and the Half-Blood Prince*, when Peeves jams a door shut and refuses to let anyone pass until he sets fire to his own pants, Neville, not having any alternative, goes ahead and does so (387–88). While others either stay where they are or, like Harry and Ron, find a way around Peeves, Neville faces the obstacle head-on and does what he must in order to get past Peeves. This makes Neville appear gullible, but the scene also demonstrates his single-minded determination to achieve his goal. In either case, Rowling uses Peeves' actions as a device for giving the reader more insight into Neville's character. It is a light, funny moment in the book, too.

Important events surrounding the vanishing cabinet in *Chamber of Secrets* are set in motion by Peeves. It is Peeves, persuaded by Sir Nick, who first breaks the vanishing cabinet. Sir Nick suggests the idea to Peeves so that Filch will be distracted and leave Harry alone. Peeves, we can assume, agrees to do it purely for the sake of mischief (*CoS* 126–29). Later, in *Harry Potter and the Order of the Phoenix*, another set of tricksters, Fred and George, push Montague into the cabinet and trap him there when he tries to take points from Gryffindor (627). Montague later is found trapped in a toilet that he Apparated into to escape the cabinet (*HBP* 637–38). When Snape is called away to help Montague, Harry takes advantage of his absence to enter the Pensieve and view Snape's memory of his father and Sirius. This leads Harry to develop a more mature understanding of his father. The memory also gives readers a new dynamic to consider in the progression of the plot: that James and Sirius were not always as perfect as Harry believed, and that Snape may have a good reason to have hated James and Sirius. Montague's experience allows Draco to realize the potential of the cabinet. He then repairs the cabinet and uses it to bring Death Eaters into Hogwarts, as previously mentioned, which leads to Dumbledore's downfall (*HBP* 587).

Peeves' actions also lead to Hermione's discovery that house elves work at Hogwarts. Sir Nick casually mentions a disturbance that Peeves causes in the Hogwarts kitchens, and explains that the house elves were in an uproar. As a result, readers observe Hermione's indignation and we gain an understanding of Hermione as a person who idealistically seeks justice for the downtrodden (*GoF* 181–82).

Tricksters bring opportunity to Harry. One of the most significant tricksters in relation to Harry, and to the plot, is James Potter. Harry inherits much from James: his physical appearance and facial features (except for his eyes), his unruly hair that seems to defy gravity, the invisibility cloak, and the Marauder's Map. The last two clearly are trickster items, as they enable Harry to exist along the boundary of the seen and unseen. The Marauder's Map allows Harry to view almost all areas of the castle, and it allows him to see where individuals are within the castle. With the help of the invisibility cloak and the map, Harry is able to roam the castle and surrounding grounds unseen.

According to Lupin, Harry also inherits an old prejudice against Snape as well as Snape's prejudice against him (*HBP* 333). When Harry sees Snape's memory of James in the Pensieve, we learn that James had an arrogant streak, and Snape must be thinking of James as much as he is of Harry when he tell Cornelius Fudge that Harry has been "crossing lines" since he came to Hogwarts (*GoF* 276). In addition, we know that James was a risk-taker, somewhat along the lines of Fred and George, who believe, according to Ginny, that "anything's possible if you've got enough nerve" (*GoF* 305; *OotP* 655). Snape may be correct. Arrogance and risk-taking apparently were part of James's character, but this is not entirely a bad attribute to have when you are fighting the most evil wizard of the age. Perhaps James felt that anything *was* possible, even the defeat of Voldemort, if he, Lily, and others used their wits and nerve. The inheritance of the prejudice prevents Harry and Snape from understanding each other, however.

Harry also inherits the remainder of the Marauders: a trickster group led by James. As a group, the Marauders existed on and crossed several boundaries. The first is that of social expectations, since James, Sirius, and Wormtail befriended and supported Lupin the werewolf. None of the three, apart from James, is a trickster in his own right, yet together they formed the group of mischief-makers. They also existed on the boundary between human and animal, given that each Marauder could transform into an animal. James and the others learned to transform themselves into animals in order to keep Lupin company when he became a werewolf at the full moon (*PoA*).

James could transform into a stag, which has important symbolic implications for the *Harry Potter* story. The legend of St. Hubertus features a stag-fairy who is "an avatar of Christ," according to author Philippe Walter (49). St. Hubertus was the son of a duke who was so passionate about hunting that he even hunted on Good Friday. A stag he was chasing turned on Hubertus and warned him to pay heed to his salvation. An image of Christ was on the stag's forehead (48). Walters also notes that the stag "can influence the destiny of the person who encounters it by converting the sinner to the Faith or by revealing to the young, innocent man the truths of love" (49). In addition, the stag "symbolizes the temporary liaison [the holiday] Samhain allows between the human world and the enchanted world of the fairies" (48). This is important information in relation to what we know of the *Harry Potter* story. Because Harry's parents were killed on Halloween, and his link with Voldemort was solidified then, there is a significance to a connection between James' ability to transform into a stag and the trickster festival of Halloween. According to the History Channel, "Halloween's origins date back to the ancient Celtic festival of Samhain.... The Celts...celebrated their new year on November 1. This day marked the end of summer and the harvest and the beginning of the dark, cold winter, a time of year that was often associated with human death. Celts believed that on the night before the new year, the boundary between the worlds of the living and the dead became blurred." Remember, as Hyde says, that a trickster blurs the lines between boundaries (7). Walters also notes that a white stag was the mediator between these worlds at Samhain (49). Evidently, the stag could exist on that blurred boundary. Harry's Patronus is a silvery stag, and James could transfigure himself into a stag. Harry, using his Patronus or another inheritance from James, may be able to cross the boundary between the living world and the spirit world before the series comes to an end.

What Harry does with this inheritance seems to be closely connected to the main core of the book; in fact, I believe that the true meaning of this information is not yet fully revealed. We must wait for *Harry Potter and the Deathly Hallows* in order to understand it fully. Harry must use all of these trickster influences in his quest to defeat Voldemort.

Harry is helped by James's legacy, but he can also count tricksters among his contemporaries. As previously mentioned, the Weasley twins, Fred and George, are tricksters. In *Harry Potter and the Sorcerer's Stone*, Harry's first encounter with the wizarding world comes when he meets Hagrid. Albus Dumbledore has sent Hagrid to fetch Harry from the Dursleys'. Harry is swept up in the idea of belonging to the wizarding world, and he likes Hagrid, who is to become an important influence in his life. When Hagrid takes him to Diagon Alley for the first time, Harry is amazed and delighted with all that he finds there. But when Harry meets Draco Malfoy in Diagon Alley, he is disconcerted with Draco's behavior, which reminds him of his bullying cousin Dudley (*SS* 77–78). Draco's comments leave Harry worried about how little he knows of the wizarding world (79). He does not experience an emotional connection with Draco.

Harry's third opportunity to connect emotionally with the wizarding world occurs upon boarding the Hogwarts Express, where he is aided by the Weasley twins, Fred and George. Fred and George Weasley display classic trickster attributes. They pursue disruption and mischief purely for its own sake. They are skillfully drawn characters with very human qualities, but they nevertheless demonstrate a pure form of mischief that does not seek to work for good or evil. Instead, at times they seem to act merely to see what will happen. For example, in *Harry Potter and the Chamber of Secrets*, they feed a fire-dwelling salamander a firework to "find out what would happen" (130). The lizard flies about the room emitting sparks in a scene that would make any animal-lover cringe, and although the fire lizard survives to go and hide in the fire, little remorse is shown by the pair as their brother Percy "bellows" at them to cut it out (131).

By the time the twins help Harry onto the Hogwarts Express, they have already signaled their identity as tricksters by playing a joke on their mother. Their appearance is so similar, and Mrs. Weasley so harried by the effort of getting all of her children onto the train, that she mistakes one for the other, with their encouragement (*SS* 92). In another scene, the twins refer to that most important attribute of the trickster, the ability to exist on, and at times create, a boundary (Hyde 7). In *Harry Potter and the Order of the Phoenix*, Hermione asks whether they have ever cared about getting into trouble:

> "Course we have," said George. "Never been expelled, have we?"
> "We've always known where to draw the line," said Fred.
> "We might have put a toe across it occasionally," said George. (627)

Mrs. Weasley, the mother of Fred and George, gives Harry directions to get onto the platform, but then it is the twins who offer him assistance onto the train and identify him as Harry Potter. It is also the twins who give Harry an opportunity not only to join the wizarding world and take his rightful place on the train, but to make his first emotional connection—the first real friend of his life —Ron (*SS* 94–95).

Throughout the books, the twins continue to bring opportunities to Harry. When Harry has been locked in his room by Uncle Vernon, it is the twins who fly their father's car to Privet Drive, and even pick the lock on Harry's bedroom door (using Muggle skills) to retrieve his Hogwarts supplies from under the stairs (*CoS* 25–26). In *Harry Potter and the Prisoner of Azkaban*, they bestow the Marauder's Map on him. The Marauder's Map is a trickster artifact that is rightfully Harry's, since one of its authors is James Potter, yet it is significant that the twins were able to decipher the code of the Marauder's Map when Filch could not (192–93). Their ability to work the map signifies that they are on a similar wavelength to the Marauders. This is important to the overall theme of the *Harry Potter* story, for as the story unfolds, we learn that James Potter and his gang were tricksters in their own right, and Harry, although not a trickster himself, benefits from the legacy of his father's group. As Harry matures, his father's old school friends, Lupin and Sirius, become his mentors. And Wormtail, while Harry reviles him as a traitor, may ultimately benefit Harry in his quest to vanquish Voldemort. Harry saved Wormtail's life by not allowing Lupin and Sirius to kill him, thus creating a life debt that Wormtail owes Harry. The twins offer Harry a link to his own past, and in fact Harry compares them to James after observing Snape's memory of James in the Pensieve. Harry reminds himself that the twins would never hang someone upside down just "for the fun of it" (*OotP* 653). When Harry compares James to the twins, we understand that Harry's father and Sirius had an arrogant side that that Harry does not like and that the twins do not display.

We gain insight into Harry's compassionate personality through this information, and we also gain an insight into the overall plot of the story. Harry's comparison of the twins to his father reinforces the subject of James and his overconfidence. It was James who did not tell Dumbledore that he and Sirius had switched their Secret-Keeper to be Wormtail, apparently not taking Dumbledore's offer to be the Secret-Keeper himself (*PoA* 205). As for the trickster legacy that Harry inherits from James, Harry continues his relationship to trickster practices when, in *Harry Potter and the Goblet of Fire,* he gives the twins his Triwizard winnings so that they can open a joke shop, thereby investing in the continuation of trickster practices (733).

In *Harry Potter and the Order of the Phoenix,* the joke shop merchandise that Fred and George are preparing, and that Harry has invested in, becomes useful toward disrupting the oppressive oversight of the Ministry of Magic when the twins use one of their products to conjure a swamp in a school corridor and exit the school on a note of mayhem (675). Again, trickster actions fuel an important plot point. This diversion gives Harry an opportunity to use Umbridge's fire and talk to Sirius about James' behavior (*OotP* 671).

After Fred and George are gone, their joke products remain, and other Hogwarts students and Peeves continue to create mayhem. In fact, it is Peeves who most diligently follows the twin's instructions to give Dolores Umbridge "hell" (*OotP* 675). When she at last makes her exit from the castle, Peeves follows her out, alternately whacking her with Professor McGonagall's walking stick and a sock full of chalk (*OotP* 857). Symbolically, this is the trickster triumphing over the status quo. The twins' joke products and Peeves have made a mess, but the result is valuable to wizard and Muggle society. The twins' actions provide fuel for an emerging rebellion by Hogwarts students and staff, and more people begin to believe Harry's warnings of Voldemort's return instead of believing the ministry's denials. Dumbledore is reinstated as Headmaster of Hogwarts. Those working for the forces of good begin to gain ground.

The joke products contribute to the discomfort of Dolores Umbridge, but they may play a role in the outcome of the series as well. In *Harry Potter and the Half-Blood Prince*, Fred and George give Harry joke shop merchandise, in case it becomes useful as he embarks on his quest to find Horcruxes (20). However, the twins also apparently sell Peruvian Darkness Powder to Draco Malfoy (*HBP* 618). This illustrates the double-edged sword that trickster practices can be. As Hyde states, "trickster can also get snared in his own devices" (19). This happens when Draco uses the powder to make everything go black and to delay members of Dumbledore's Army as they keep watch near the Room of Requirement. Draco and several Death Eaters are able to slip past them with the use of Draco's Hand of Glory, which gives light only to the one holding it (*HBP* 618). The Peruvian Darkness Powder is another trickster artifact. Its uses are the same for whoever has it, and it can be used for good or ill. In the case of Draco and the Death Eaters, like the vanishing cabinet, the powder is a trickster-related item whose use contributes to the downfall of Albus Dumbledore.

Hyde says that "in the invention of traps, trickster is a technician of appetite and a technician of instinct" (19). This element is apparent when the twins test the Ton-Tongue Toffees on Dudley (*GoF* 51). They trust his appetite to trap him. However, another trickster who more deservedly is caught in a trap of her own making is Rita Skeeter. She toys with the appetite of the public for salacious gossip with her talent for writing sensational stories. She also qualifies as a trickster due to her identity as an unregistered Animagus.

Tricksters in mythology are rarely women, according to Hyde, both because trickster mythology springs mainly from patriarchal polytheistic religions and because mythological tricksters pursue their appetites, sexual and otherwise—a complicating factor for women, who run the risk of pregnancy due to promiscuity (Hyde 8). However, women may act as tricksters in Rowling's work because in a "children's" story, most sexual references are muted and in fact are unimportant to most of the storyline. In the *Harry Potter* series it is love of a spiritual and mental kind that takes center stage.

Rita's main trickster function is to search ambivalently for dirt, or "matter out of place" (Hyde 165). Hyde says that what tricksters in general like to do, is erase or violate that line between the dirty and the clean. As a rule, trickster takes a god who lives on high and debases him or her with earthly dirt, or appears to debase him, for in fact the unusual consequence of this dirtying is the god's eventual renewal. (177)

Rita writes for *The Daily Prophet*, and she looks for and sometimes invents mischievous stories, regardless of the moral and even regardless of whether the information she writes is entirely true. This is because she has a desire to create a dust cloud of sorts at the boundary where truth and untruth collide. She is a purveyor of shameless speech, another trickster quality. Hyde says, "Those who work the edge between what can and cannot be said do not escape from shame but turn toward it and engage with it" (165). Rita repeatedly succeeds in reporting troublesome stories for and about respected figures and institutions, especially Harry, whose life story she sensationalizes to his embarrassment. She also defames Dumbledore, who she calls an "obsolete dingbat," and she does not refrain from revealing embarrassing information about the Ministry of Magic (*GoF* 307). After the trouble at the Quidditch World Cup, she starts a rumor that several bodies were taken from the forest, which causes a headache for the Ministry and Mr. Weasley (*GoF* 148).

However, Rita gets caught in her own trap when she focuses on Hagrid and then Hermione in two separate news articles. Hermione is incensed, and she begins to wonder how Rita is getting private information about the various individuals she features in her articles. Rita's actions have a positive side, however, in terms of the plot and our understanding of the characters' personalities. The aggravation that Harry, Ron and Hermione face, as they endure the ridicule that her articles create, allows them to develop a mature understanding of others' motivations; we have an opportunity to see Hermione's personality at work as she tries and succeeds to trap Rita and turn the tables on her. Hermione works quietly and patiently to discover Rita's secret that Rita is an unregistered Animagus (*GoF* 728). In addition, Albus Dumbledore's reaction to Rita's criticism is patient and amused, which demonstrates his personality as well (*GoF* 307).

Luna Lovegood is also a trickster. Where Rita Skeeter may embody the negative of Hyde's point that "they're all the same, these tricksters; they have no shame and they have no silence" (7), Luna is a sweeter, positive trickster force. Luna rides the boundary where faith parts from skepticism, and she also clearly defines a boundary of truth. Luna states plainly what others are afraid to (or unable to) declare. She does this unconsciously, yet she plays the role of trickster by churning up emotion, recognition, dismay and discomfort. For example, in this scene from *Harry Potter and the Half-Blood Prince*, Luna speaks plainly about Ron:

> "He says very funny things sometimes, doesn't he?... But he can be a bit unkind. I noticed that last year."
> "I s'pose," said Harry. Luna was demonstrating her usual knack of speaking uncomfortable truths; he had never met anyone quite like her. (310–11)

While Harry feels uncomfortable with her statements about Ron, it is Luna's faith that brings comfort to Harry when nothing else does. In this scene from *Harry Potter and the Order of the Phoenix*, Luna gives comfort to Harry as he grieves for Sirius. Harry learns that Luna's mother died when she was nine years old, and that she is sure she will see her again. Luna says:

> "Oh, come on. You heard them, just behind the veil, didn't you?"
> "You mean..."
> "In that room with the archway. They were just lurking out of sight, that's all. You heard them."
> They looked at each other. Harry did not know what to say, or to think. Luna believed so many extraordinary things...yet he had been sure he had heard voices behind the veil too. (863)

Harry offers to help Luna find the things others have taken from her, but she declines and wishes him a good holiday. The scene ends this way:

> She walked away from him, and as he watched her go, he found that the terrible weight in his stomach seemed to have lessened slightly. (864)

Luna's knack for plainly stating her beliefs, whether provable or not, both astonishes and comforts Harry. Her trickster personality gives Harry a new and valuable perspective. A great scene comes in *Harry Potter and the Order of the Phoenix* when Hermione, a representative of facts and truth, brings together the two female tricksters, Luna and Rita, to help Harry tell the truth of Voldemort's return (566–67). Rita writes the story Harry tells her, and Luna's father publishes it in his newspaper, *The Quibbler* (579). This article helps Harry find supporters as the rebellion against Umbridge and the Ministry begins at Hogwarts.

Luna and Rita, arguably minor in relation to the larger plot line, play an important role in Harry, Ron and Hermione's development into mature individuals. As I mentioned above, Rita teaches the trio lessons about the motivations of others and about how public opinion can vacillate. In addition, we see Harry, Ron and Hermione mature as they adjust their reactions to Luna. They begin to offer Luna respect as they understand the value of the contributions she makes to the group and their cause. For example, after the fight at the Ministry, Hermione is much nicer to Luna. She refrains from challenging Luna about the existence of Crumple-Horned Snorkacks. After Luna says that she and her father planned to travel to Sweden to look for one, Hermione "seemed to struggle with herself...then said, 'That sounds lovely'" (*OotP* 848). Later, Ron comments, "You know, she's grown on me, Luna" (*HBP* 425). Harry even invites Luna to Slughorn's Christmas party "just as friends" (*HBP* 311). Luna is at first an unsettling trickster force, but as Harry, Ron and Hermione realize her value, their emotional responses mature.

J. K. Rowling's writing style utilizes qualities of the trickster. As readers, we are repeatedly surprised and delighted with the plot twists in the series. When we suspect Severus Snape of nefarious intentions in *Harry Potter and the Sorcerer's Stone,* it is our first experience with Rowling's trickster style. Our defined boundaries of human understanding (or of children's fiction) are challenged. Snape dislikes Harry, and we are as sure as Harry is that Snape is after the Stone, yet we learn later that Snape has been protecting Harry all along. Something in our reader's experience is released and expanded: a deepening sense of the complexity of human personalities and behavior.

As I have shown, trickster practices are significant to the plot of the *Harry Potter* series, and to the development of the characters. Crossing lines and boundaries is a very important part of the outcome of the series. Whether these boundaries relate to the night of Halloween, when the line between our world and the spirit world grows thin, to the veiled archway in the Department of Mysteries, or to each character's (and reader's) emotional and intellectual awakening, it seems that the trickster theme fuels and binds the plot of the entire *Harry Potter* series. The series, however, is only the latest in a long tradition of trickster tales. A trickster provides an important purpose in mythology, and the myths are more than just humorous stories to the giver and receiver of the tales. Trickster stories teach the reader or listener important truths; a trickster brings useful knowledge to humanity. Rowling's work reminds us that, like her characters, we are complex beings. She has released a deeper understanding of human behavior and spiritual awareness into the world.

Works Cited

"The History of Halloween." *History*. 17 Mar 2007. <http://history.com/minisites/halloween/view>.

Hyde, Lewis. *Trickster Makes this World*. New York: North Point Press, 1998.

Rowling, J. K. *Harry Potter and the Chamber of Secrets*. New York: Scholastic, Arthur A. Levine Books, 1999.

——. *Harry Potter and the Goblet of Fire*. New York: Scholastic, 2000.

——. *Harry Potter and the Half-Blood Prince*. New York: Scholastic, 2005.

——. *Harry Potter and the Order of the Phoenix*. New York: Scholastic, 2003.

——. *Harry Potter and the Prisoner of Azkaban*. New York: Scholastic, 1999.

——. *Harry Potter and the Sorcerer's Stone*. New York: Scholastic, 1997.

Walter, Philippe. *Christianity: the Origins of a Pagan Religion*. Rochester: Inner Traditions, 2003.

DIVINATION:
USEFUL TOOL OR WOOLLY SCIENCE?

Amy Goetz and lyric apted

"Know Thyself"
Temple at Delphi

Intuition: The ability to know without words, and sense truth without explaining. Intuition operates knowing the past, present, future is simultaneous, and speaks through insight, revelation, and urges.
Adapted from *Personal Power Through Awareness,* by Sanaya Roman

Intuition—noun

1   Direct perception of truth, fact, etc., independent of any reasoning process; immediate apprehension.

2   A fact, truth, etc., perceived in this way.

3   A keen and quick insight.

4   The quality or ability of having such direct perception or quick insight.

[Origin: 1400–50; Middle English *intuicioun*, insight, from Late Latin *intuitiō, intuitiōn-*, a looking at, from Latin *intuitus*, a look, from past participle of *intuērī*, to look at, contemplate : *in-*, on; see in-2 + *tuērī*, to look at.]
Adapted from *dictionary.com*

"The soul never thinks without a picture."
~ Aristotle

Since language can be limiting and it is sometimes difficult to articulate spiritual journey in linear form, we are now seeing a resurgence of symbol as expression in the western world. As people

213

delve into new experiences, many are finding that our current languages lack words to describe these events. To be able to communicate the "unspeakable," people are turning to and rediscovering systems of symbolic language such as the I Ching, the Tarot, runes and astrology. "To the imagination the sacred is self-evident," Nietzsche said. It is to the imagination that symbols speak; our focus should be learning to play again as we discover new ways to communicate with each other.

Symbols are rich channels of information. Determining the meaning held within them is a journey of personal discovery. No two people ever view the same symbol in quite the same way. We each have our own life story behind us that adds to our experience and interpretation. Mythologist Joseph Campbell once remarked that those who do not know that symbols hold hidden meaning are "like diners going into the restaurant and eating the menu rather than the meal it describes." The soul thinks in symbols. It is not literal-minded. It is play-minded.

We sense that metaphor and symbol are a pathway to discovering, really discovering, ancient archetypes that hold the keys to personal transformation. Tools like the labyrinth, the Tarot, and others can help you walk a path of deeper understanding, linking you to the collective unconscious and leading you to rediscover a life with more play and less "reality."

Adapted from *Walking a Sacred Path*, by Lauren Altress

> *"The formulation of the question is far more important than the answer."*
> ~ Albert Einstein

Oracle and Tarot cards are meant to give insight, to inform and aid in decision-making. These tools are designed to help reveal options and possibilities about the individual and the predicaments we find ourselves in. By centering, asking directed questions and interpreting the answers that come, we can become empowered to make better decisions. More importantly, we can harness the ability to make decisions from our own power. Oracle or Tarot readings are not meant to "tell" or "predict"; these words make the questioner a victim, enslaved to the reader, the outcome, and a bystander to fate. I believe the aim of any reading is to create a person informed about possibility and able to utilize all forms of resources to make wise decisions. The ultimate goal in working with a symbolic language is learning to listen to, and trust, your inner knowledge.

Tarot and Oracle cards are tools to tap your intuitive genius. There are guidelines, books and vast amounts of resources to help you interpret meanings. Ultimately each of us must intuit (decide) what each card means to us in any given situation. As we begin to play with any form of symbol, we quickly see that each card, stone, or drawing holds many meanings. There is no set meaning for anything; you must look inside yourself and find which meaning holds truth in the now. Although this can cause some discomfort at first, with practice reading becomes easier because you discover it is all about play and none of it is about being right.

It is our belief that there is no good or bad in the Tarot or in any oracle. Any negative meaning a card might portray can be seen as a warning or an offer for potential for change. It is the compost that fertilizes new growth, or the weed that must be pulled.

The Key to Finding Your Intuition Is ACID

✓ **Awareness**: Breathe, find your center and open to the vast amounts of information you hold hidden in your mind—and tap into universal wisdom.

✓ **Connection**: Trust that you "know" more and that you are a divine being.

✓ **Intention**: Why are you seeking information? Have a specific focus agreed upon by all people involved in the reading.

✓ **Detach**: Let It Go. Do not be connected to the outcome; speak the information and be done; the other person will decide what to do with it.

"The more faithfully you listen to the voice within you, the better you will hear what is sounding outside. And she who listens can speak."
~ *Dag Hammarskjöld*

The following is a possible way to begin utilizing Oracle or Tarot:

➢ If you are reading for someone, have them shuffle the cards, all the while thinking of their question. This infuses the question into the cards and hopefully makes the reading easier.

➢ Have the Questioner cut the deck or fan the cards and pick some. You can decide the number and layout, or you can wing it.

➢ When you first begin to read the cards, try going through a reading intuitively, speaking what comes to you from the images on the cards. Then, if you wish, go back and check the "traditional" meaning of the cards. Know that as you do more and more readings, you will develop your own sense of what a card means. Remember that each card holds many meanings. If you find yourself getting stuck while interpreting, and you are using a book, put the book down. While books will set you on the right track for learning the basics of Tarot, they need to be used in conjunction with your intuition. The best way to start this process is to define what you think each card means, then go to the book to see what else is there. This will keep you an active participant in the process of learning the cards, and it will take away the fear of "Did I memorize these keywords correctly? Do I have this card down pat?" Your readings will flow because you will have developed a personal connection with the cards.

➢ If you find you need more information for the Questioner, pull more cards. There are several traditional ways to read Tarot and other oracles and I advocate finding the way that works best for you. This may be a traditional way or it may be a whole new way known only to you. Play!

➢ Above all, remember a reading is a snapshot of the Questioner's life at a specific place in time. It is a reflection of the energies in their life, and it shows where their opportunities and challenges are. This is *their* story—a story that will unfold, as it should, from card to card, each card gaining meaning from the others. Each card holds some basic (traditional) meanings, but each card also holds a meaning that it gains from the cards around it. Nothing exists in isolation, and any reading should reflect the whole.

➢ There should be no pressure to get it "right." Everyone will get out of the reading exactly what they need; you are here to play with your own soul, learning to interpret its language.

Guidelines to Interpretation

"The Unknown can be a disconcerting place, especially when we realize our
place in it. In that moment the Universe becomes much, much bigger.
And, therefore, so do we."
~ Unknown

Suites/ (Elementals)

➢ **Wands/Clubs** (Fire):   passion   and   self-discovery   or expression

➢ **Cups/Hearts** (Water):   emotional and intuitive awareness or interaction

➢ **Swords/Spades** (Air):   thinking and cognitive expression

➢ **Pentacles/Diamonds** (Earth):   physical   experience   and manifestation

The Arcana
Definition: mystery or secrets

Minor Arcana hold the daily secrets of the universe (56 cards)

➢ **Aces:** beginning, conceiving, starting, initiating

➢ **Twos:** confirming, affirming, choosing, deciding

➢ **Threes:** planning, preparing, projecting, detailing

➢ **Fours:** doing, manifesting, solidifying, creating

➢ **Fives:** adapting, adjusting, challenging, changing

➢ **Sixes:** cycling, repeating, maintaining, patterning

> ➤ **Sevens:** expanding, varying, experimenting, stimulating

> ➤ **Eights:** contracting, organizing, structuring, limiting

> ➤ **Nines:** flowing, moving, integrating, processing

> ➤ **Tens:** hesitating, waiting, taking time out, pausing

> ➤ **Page/Princesses:** risking, daring, jumping in, naivety

> ➤ **Knight/Princes:**   focusing,   concentrating,   fixating, intensifying

> ➤ **Queens:** maturing, fulfilling, ripening, arriving

> ➤ **Kings:** releasing, completing, sharing, letting go

"Perhaps the myths are telling us that these [quests] are not so much voyages of discovery as of rediscovery; that the hero is seeking not for something new but for something old, a treasure that was lost and has to be found, his own self, his identity."
~ P. L. Travers

Major Arcana hold the more momentous/greater secrets of the universe, including major life lessons, the archetypes and the hero's journey (22 cards)

0 The Fool: Faith

Having faith in others or the world, having faith in self or spirit, innocence

*XI Justice: Equilibrium

Creating balance or harmony in the world or self

I The Magician: Discernment

Discerning what is happening in the world or in self, alchemy

XII The Hanged Man: Waiting

Waiting for external cues, waiting for internal readiness

II The High Priestess: Spirituality

Keeper of wisdom, pursuing a spiritual path or life of contemplation

XIII Death: Transformation

Transforming something in the world or internally. Letting go

---

*   In some decks Strength and Justice are switched.

III The Empress: Nurture

Nurturing other or self, abundance

IV The Emperor: Power

Demonstrating worldly power, experiencing personal power

V The Hierophant: Morality

Publicly demonstrating moral, living by moral, teaching

VI The Lovers: Cooperation

Cooperation with others or self. Combining opposites.

VII The Chariot: Control

Controlling external action, directing inner experience

***VIII Strength:** Survival

Holding on to or maintaining physical or psychological survival. Love conquers all.

IX The Hermit: Knowledge

Finding truth about life or self. Withdrawal

X Wheel of Fortune: Cause / Effect

Setting things into motion, surrendering to fates/universe

XIV Temperance: Creativity

Creating something tangible, having an internal experience

XV The Devil: Structure / Materialism

Establishing worldly structure or limits, finding personal boundaries

XVI The Tower: Catalyst

Shattering the internal or external structures or foundation

XVII The Star: Resources

Directing and/or receiving abundance

XVIII The Moon: Guidance

Receiving guidance/ sign from the world, dreams, within

XIX The Sun: Rebirth

Redoing, rebirthing the self, joy

XX Judgment: Graduation

Graduating to the next level, psychologically moving on

XXI The World: Choice

Recognizing the infinite options, opening doors within

---

*　In some decks Strength and Justice are switched.

"One does not become enlightened by imaging figures of light,
but by making the darkness conscious."
~ Carl Jung

Suggested Uses for Tarot Cards and Journeys:

Daily Draw: Shuffle cards focusing on an intention, ask a question or ask for guidance, pull as many cards as you desire. Sit with them for a few moments and interpret them based on your present outlook. After taking this moment you may refer to a book for further guidance and clarity.

Meditation: You can simply pull a card to meditate on or ask a question and then draw. The intention behind meditation is to engage in a dialogue with this archetype presented in the card. Sit or lie quietly allowing this mentor to teach you.

Dream Time: Before going to bed, ask a question or simply pull a card, and ask to receive clarity or an understanding of this card in your dreams tonight. Make sure to have something to write with by your bed so that you can write immediately upon awakening.

Rubbish Oracle: Wandering through your day, hone in on the images, creatures, and sounds that draw your attention or focus. It is often fascinating to "see" in this open way, and many words or potential treasures may draw your attention. Make a collage or journal your findings if they feel significant to you.

Intuition Journal: Find a blank book and begin collecting images, quotes and words that speak to you. Paste them in the book and begin a visual diary of your life.

"The truth is a beautiful & terrible thing, and it should therefore be
treated with great caution."
~ Albus Dumbledore

During a reading, remember that this could be a vulnerable experience for both people. A suggestion is to speak in "I" statements when reading (e.g., "I see a lot of blue. To me this means…"). Asking "Does this resonate?" can help solicit feedback and involve the questioner in the process. Remember to detach and not take it personally if things are not resonating at that moment. Clarity may come at a later time.

It is suggested that you not read for anyone if you are in conflict with them or could have any harmful intentions (conscious or unconscious). These could transfer or be spoken out during the reading. The consequences of this could be lack of energy, headache, or other things that deplete your ability to function with ease.

Bibliography

Andrews, Ted. *Animal Speak*. St. Paul, MN: Llewellyn, 2003.

Arcarti, Krystyna. *Runes for Beginners*. London: Hodder & Stoughton, 1994.

Arrien, Angeles. *The Tarot Handbook*. Sonoma, CA: Arcus, 1987.

Artress, Lauren. *Walking a Sacred Path*. New York: Penguin, 2006.

Bennet, Hal Zina. *Zuni Fetishes*. San Francisco: HarperCollins, 1993.

Beren_writes. "Gold Tinted Spectacles." 11 Feb. 2004. Beren's Fanfic/Art. 23 Oct 2004. <http://beren-writes.livejournal.com/5307.html>.

Bierlein, J. F. *Living Myths*. New York: Ballantine Wellspring, 1999.

Bunning, Joan. *Learning the Tarot*. Nov. 2006.

Campbell, Joseph. *Pathways to Bliss*. Novato, CA: New World Library, 2004.

Campbell, Joseph. *The Power of Myth*. New York: Doubleday, 1988.

Choquette, Sonia. *The Psychic Pathway*. New York: Three Rivers, 1995.

Cumming, Robert. *Annotated Art*. New York: DK Publishing, 1995.

Fairfield, Gail. *Choice-Centered Relating and the Tarot*. York Beach, ME: Weiser, 2000.

Feldman, Edmund Burke. *Varieties of Visual Experience*. Engelwood Cliffs, NJ: Prentice Hall, 1992.

Fontana, David. *Teach Yourself to Dream*. San Francisco: 1997.

Grant, Russell. *The Illustrated Dream Dictionary*. New York: Sterling 1991.

Greer, Mary. *Tarot for Yourself*. North Hollywood, CA: Newcastle, 1984.

a 2007 beltane fic exchange. May 2007. `<http://hds-beltane.`
`livejournal.com>`.

Linn, Denise. *The Secret Language of Signs.* New York: Random House, 1996.

Lupin, Olivia. "Solstice." 20 Dec 2004. `<http://lovely-slyth.`
`livejournal.com/10618.html>`.

Pollack, Rachel. *The Complete Illustrated Guide to Tarot.* Boston: Element Books, 1999.

Potter, Frances. "Resolution." 15 April 2007. `<http://dragon-charmer.`
`livejournal.com/242884.html>`.

Steffens, Kimberly. Personal interview. Oct.–Nov. 2005.

Tzu, Lao. *Tao Te Ching.* New York: Random House, 1997.

Zander, Benjamin, and Rosamund Stone. *The Art of Possibility.* Boston: Harvard Business School, 2000.

The Dread of Opals:
What Folklore Reveals About
the *Harry Potter* Septology

Katherine E. Krohn

Three sets of opals appear within the first six volumes of J. K. Rowling's novels: the cursed necklace at Borgin and Burkes, Mme. Maxime's rings and necklace, and the opal-stoppered vial in the Black mansion. This presentation uses folklore methodology to trace associations of opals, to predict what may next befall the wizarding community. Opals, said to keep one's vision clear, while clouding that of others (cf. "Hand of Glory"), turn pale when near poison. They also change their appearances to indicate whether illness or injury looms over their owners, confer prophetic power if used for good, and may protect children from predatory beasts.

As recently as the 1960s, the study of Folklore and Folk Life has had a reputation for being "a bit of a wooly discipline." People dismissed such studies as being about "things people believe that are wrong." Modern folklorists examine what people believe and do when they are not being controlled by one or more institutions, such as the church, a school, the state, or a corporation. Modern folkloristics seeks to track and document what people do when out from under the watchful eye of organizational control. I offer this preamble to explain why the primary method of this study will be to compile accounts of what average people believe about opals and luck, both good and bad, as a way of appreciating the spectrum of possibilities the appearance of these stones gives the *Harry Potter* septology. These first-hand accounts, carefully not identified by request of the archive, were compiled over forty years by student folklorists for the Folklore Archives, University of California, Berkeley.

I will offer historical background that may have contributed to "what everyone knows," even though how people come to believe certain things is at some level unknowable. It is enough to know what leaps to most people's minds in certain situations. I offer these stories on the understanding that we will be examining what people tell each other are the root causes of these beliefs—not at all the same as knowing what the actual causes are—but these beliefs-within-beliefs hold interest for what they are, even if that is not what they purport to be.

The goal of the present paper is not to offer scientific explanations of what opals can and cannot do in the physical world, but to explore what reactions an author might reasonably expect to evoke in readers by deploying opals in various situations. It would, for example, have been quite clear which responses would have been forthcoming had Rowling had one character present another with a red rose after the Yule Ball (or a yellow one during it).

Opals As Gemstones

While opals come in many types, the sort most familiar to people living in North America and Europe show play-of-color against a white background. The play-of-color—flashes of violet, blue, green, yellow, orange, and/or red—comes from light being refracted by tiny silica spheres and microscopic droplets of water embedded in the stones, in exactly the same way that prisms break up white light into the visible spectrum.

Opals differ from all the other precious and semi-precious gemstones. Aside from the organics (amber, coral, and pearl, which are made of plant or animal secretions), other stones are crystalline, whereas opal is amorphous. Other stones show their distinctive colors by filtering, where opals refract light. That means that a red ruby captures all the light which enters the crystal structure, allowing only the red light to bounce back to the eye. Opals, by contrast, split up white light into spectral colors, then bend them out of the stone.

Beautiful Stone, Ugly Reputation

D. Douglas Graham speaks so eloquently about emotions and opals that I must quote from his essay, "Fatal Attraction," at some length:

While many stones were prized for their positive magical qualities, others were denounced as vessels of evil. No gem was more vilified than the poor opal. Witches and sorcerers supposedly used black opals to increase their own magical powers or to focus them like laser beams on people they wanted to harm. Medieval Europeans dreaded the opal because of its resemblance to "the Evil Eye" and its superficial likeness to the optical organs of cats, toads, snakes, and other common creatures with hellish affiliations.

Biologists call the reflective layer on the inside backs of the eyeballs of nocturnal animals the "tapetum." Much like a telescope, the tapetum gathers and concentrates light to enable night-going creatures to see in near-darkness. These reflective membranes appear to glow in the dark when one catches the family cat or a foraging raccoon in the automobile-headlights at night. Graham continues:

The opal's nasty reputation has troubled folklorists for centuries. Fantastic legends have grown up around this harmless stone, cautionary tales designed to discourage those who might otherwise find themselves mortally attracted by its fiery brilliance. To this day, the odd prejudice against opals remains alive and well in some corners of the world, especially in the backwaters of southern Europe and the Middle East, where jewelers won't carry opals and customers won't buy them.

Opals...are also thought to have teleportation powers. A piece of opal jewelry might suddenly disappear from some obvious place, only to turn up weeks or months later in a refrigerator freezer, the breast pocket of a T-shirt, the glove compartment of the family car, or some other absurd location.

Fear of the Evil Eye, common to cultures the world over, was and remains especially acute in the Mediterranean. Simply defined, the term signifies a covetous or malicious glance meant to bring harm. Witches were thought to possess this awful power in great abundance, though common people with unrealized magical talents could also wield it, albeit unconsciously. [This schema sounds very like Harry Potter's early life with the Dursleys.] The Eye did its stuff directly and indirectly. It could strike its intended victim sick or dead on the spot; it might kill family members, blight crops, sicken livestock, or summon a storm with the muscle to level a house, village, or an entire town.

The Evil Eye's association with the opal probably originated in Elizabethan England. There the stones were called "ophals," a shortening of the word "ophthalmos," which referred to the human eye. The Evil Eye was accepted as fact in sixteenth-century Britain, as was belief in omens and auguries. In the minds of the superstitious Elizabethans, the occult link between ophals and ophthalmos was both obvious and ominous.

There is one other source almost universally blamed for ruining opal's reputation, which I will save for last, because the tale carries a twist for *Harry Potter* readers never intended by the original author.

Wearing / Giving

Variants on the basic belief include "It's bad luck to buy an opal for someone if it's not that person's birthstone," "It's bad luck to wear someone else's opal / borrow opals" and "It's bad luck to buy your own opals." One folklorist reported, "My informant used the analogy that it is just like getting bad luck if you buy your own Tarot cards."

Another variant holds, "If your birthstone is an opal, it's bad luck to buy yourself one. Only accept those given to you." A Filipina student reported hearing this bit of wisdom from a friend whose mother shared it when the daughter "wanted to buy an opal ring for herself. She told me that the opal was a precious and rare stone, which held special magic. The magic is only activated through the act of giving. Therefore, buying it [for oneself] is considered bad luck." A 1985 informant states that "they can only be given to you by someone who truly loves you.... They are called 'The Eye of the Cat,' and you'll have nothing but bad luck if you receive them improperly."

A 1991 account says, by contrast, "You don't ever want your love to give you opals. This signifies that the love between you will dry up, so it is bad luck." "Lorin[, the informant,] explained that opals contain a lot of water. Over a long period of time, the water evaporates. The opals then shrink, and often fall out of their settings. So if your love gives you opals, it is a sure sign that your love, like the stones, will dry up, shrink, and be lost forever."

Another informant tells us that an opal is "too powerful to possess on purpose. She said that if someone gives it to you, it isn't like you are trying to get its power; it is somehow less threatening and more honest." This statement brings to mind how it came to be that Harry was able to retrieve the Philosopher's Stone when he gazed into the Mirror of Erised; he did not want to use it for himself. (Professor Quirrell, although apparently not desiring gold or the Elixir of Life for himself, wanted to profit from using the Stone as a means of currying favor with, or least appeasing, Him Whom We Must Not Name (HWWMNN).)

Note that even where the belief is stated as "It's bad luck to buy an opal for someone else," the bad luck always devolves upon the recipient, never the giver. While Katie Bell was intended to give the Cursed Necklace to Professor Dumbledore, she inadvertently harmed herself with it. This event differs from traditional opal gift-giving in that this necklace was officially pronounced "Cursed," meaning that it could have been a Cursed Eggplant and it would still produce deadly results. This may be why the unwitting giver of the "gift" was harmed.

Why would Rowling "gild the lily" by producing a cursed opal strand, when garden-variety opals can carry more than sufficient "bad *gris-gris*" for any number of people? Did Tom Riddle deliberately mislabel the necklace so no one would buy it? (See *Who Killed Albus Dumbledore?* for one scenario.) It may also matter that to date, if the card in Borgin and Burkes may be relied upon, the necklace had brought harm only to Muggle owners before it was handed to Ms. Bell (*CoS* 44). Note that many "bad luck" beliefs have to do with the stones' association with witches. Might that suggest that "uncursed" opals only harm Muggles?

Howard Pyle's version of King Arthur furnishes an example of opals that bear an enchantment, rather than a curse. The collar made of gold, and emeralds, and "opal-stones" belonging to Nimue, the Lady of the Lake, was enchanted so that whosoever wore it would be irresistible to everyone else. She lent the collar to Sir Pelleas, who, unfortunately, was persuaded by the sorceress Vivienne to surrender the collar to her. She immediately, by this means, had the otherwise virtuous knight in her thrall (Book 2, Part 2, Chs. 1, 3, & 6). Still, the fact that the collar had to be enchanted suggests that it would not have exercised such power on its own, unless it could have been enchanted only by virtue of the numinous quality of its component parts.

In one of the rare reports in the University of California Folklore Archives from a male informant, a first-generation Irish-American father told his daughter on her October 19 birthday almost thirty years ago that "the opal is supposed to guard the wearer's life and keep people with blonde hair forever blonde." (Is that just a beauty tip, or could opals alter the efficacy of Polyjuice?) He said that she "should get an opal ring because of that," which seems to indicate that he did not seem to find it necessary to give her an opal himself.

This may be explained by yet another informant, mother to the folklore student who collected the information. She told her daughter that "if you wear opals and they were not given to you as a gift, they will bring you bad luck." I pause to consider the status of opals inherited in the absence of a will, meaning not deliberately left to the heir, but passed down according to intestacy laws. The mother also said that "if the opal is your birthstone, you are exempt from this rule, you may purchase them for yourself and wear them as you please." She also noted, contrary to what we have heard earlier, that some people believe that you must only wear opals that were given to you by your spouse or fiancé(e)....

Another anthropologist reports that her close friend reminds her of the unwisdom of opal-wearing for those not born in the tenth month every time she sees the anthropologist wearing an opal ring, which happens fairly frequently, since the informant was, as is well-known to the friend, born in October. Interestingly, the friend does not mention the flip side of the belief, that opals bring especially good luck to October's child.

An official list formalizing birthstones with birth months was published in 1912 by the American National Retail Jewelers' Association. While based on "traditional birthstones," probably derived from the twelve stones of the *Hoshen* or Breastplate given to the High Priest in Exodus 28:19 and 39:12, some alterations were made, favoring commercially advantageous stones. In addition, the exact identities of these gems still occasion spirited debate among scholars. "Ligure," associated with the tribe of Ephraim, is thought by many to be that which we now call "opal," but it is not clear that the order in which the stones were named ties ligure to October.

The same friend remembers her mother warning her against opals because the friend had two siblings born in October but was herself born in May. She notes that "my husband wears opals that people have given him, but that is okay because he was born in October and is a Libra, but I cannot wear the stone at all, even though people have given them to me also."

The notion of gift-giving brings us back to Chapter Twelve of *Half-Blood Prince*, "Silver and Opals." Is the link uniting silver and opals that they are both precious substances, or the "yin and yang" notion that one is a stolen stuff that both owner and thief desire to keep, and the other a "gift" that no one wants?

Changeability / Inconstancy

Shakespeare's *Twelfth Night* (ii.4) contains a reference that his original audience would have recognised as pointing to the opal's appearance linking the stone with inconstancy. The Clown says to the Duke, regarding his tendency to fall in and out of love so frequently:

> Now the melancholy God protect thee
> and the Tailor make thy garment of changeable taffeta,
> For thy mind is a very opal.

Another folklore student's informant reports,

I think that the unreliability of the stone as valuable leads people to believe it was bad luck. It is made up of common elements, sand and water, which deceive the person into thinking it is colorful. This deception is even worse when a buyer of the stone one day finds that it has cracked and become useless. This superstition is teaching people not to trust appearances.

[It's] not as durable as hard stones like emeralds and diamonds. Thus, opals are never worn as wedding rings since the softness and nondurability of the stone could represent the future marriage. It is much better to have a hard stone like a diamond for a wedding ring since it symbolizes everlastingness and durability. As opposed to the opal, the diamond represents a strong, long-lasting marriage.

A Mrs. [S.] told one folklorist in 1965 that she had first heard the warnings about opals when she was a child, in 1925.

It was told her by her mother, who was born in Vienna, Austria, in 1891. "Opals change color with changes in body temperature. During the Bubonic Plague, when a person died, he would become colder, and if he were wearing an opal, it would change color. Therefore, it became a bad luck symbol to wear an opal. People associated it with death." Mrs. [S.] still thinks of an opal as meaning bad luck, even though she owns several herself.

The folklorist did not ask the informant about the month of the latter's birth.

October

"It is bad luck to wear an opal ring unless it is your birthstone."

One other woman in the room, about 50 [this in 1969], said that her son had found an opal ring when he was a little boy and that she thought that was the reason behind his problems today. (Her son was one of the first to go "hippie" and ended up in jail and mental hospitals. The lady wished to remain anonymous.) She felt very strongly about the subject.

Another report states that

This superstition probably originated from the idea that a birthstone belonged to the people who were born in that month, and if anyone else tried to assume something that "naturally" was a characteristic of something else, i. e. another month, then it would be bad luck for you. This idea makes me see the superstition as "Don't try to be something you're not." [Or, for the close reader of the Septology, "No good comes of Things Not Being What They Seem."] (From an informant born in October)

An especially astute young folklorist had this to say in 1978:

There are two symmetrical and balanced aspects of this superstition: the first is the negative power of the gem; the second is the opal's beneficence toward people born in October.... Thus, the stone seems to exude equal amounts of good and evil, which are released according to the time of birth of the wearer. Although this folk belief does not state explicitly that the evil of the stone can be changed to good by changing its owner, this kind of magical prescription lies implicitly in the informant's phrasing of the superstition.

Note that "wearer" and "owner" appear to be used interchangeably here.

The escape clause is restricted to those people born in October. October is a month when plants die, leaves crumble into dust and animals prepare for winter. It is a month that symbolizes death and dying—with the act one of deception, the leaves turning brilliant colors before they die. This is also a time when the weather may become warm for a while instead of colder. Thus, I think that the omen or bad luck was one of a fear of death. The appearances of the stone masked a sudden change with beauty. Those born in the month of these changes are somehow considered exempt from the "spell."

Other "escape clauses" have been mentioned: the bad luck may be avoided by anyone, by wearing opals with diamonds or by wearing two opals. A significant amount of nineteenth- through twenty-first-century fiction, prose and poetry casually opposes opals to diamonds, as if the stones neutralize each other or are polar opposites.

A somewhat less articulate informant, who had first heard of the dangers in 1942, said she

had once heard that opals were associated with witches (and witches are born in October due to Halloween, the opal's month), but she was not positive whether this was a correct explanation.

In Harry's world, witches are the norm. If anyone, the Muggle-born excite suspicion here. If opals were truly emblematic of witchery, Hogwarts Castle would be fairly ablaze with flashing rainbow hues.

Another informant offers,

I think this superstition came about because the sparkle of opals makes people think that the stone is possessed by a spirit or soul. [Does this suggest anything, Gentle Reader?] This would make the stone unlucky to most people, except those born in October, because October is associated with witches, spirits, and Hallowe'en.

———————

Perhaps it is the fact that the stone itself can change from whatever angle you look at it ["moral relativism"?], symbolizes the power October babies have, and non-October people are not cosmic enough to handle it...a difference between October people and other people.

We cannot forget what the Prophecy told us about a child "born as the seventh month dies." Could something important be embedded here concerning someone born in the tenth month as well? Two of the three opal-bearing-objects we have seen in the first six books have unclear provenances—that is, we do not know with certainty where they came from, or who owned them, although technically Harry now owns, through inheritance-by-will (a specific gift from someone who truly loves him), the "ornate crystal bottle with [the] large opal in its stopper." The other opals, those called "magnificent" and "superb," grace the neck and "thick fingers" of Olympe Maxime. Was she born in the tenth month? If not, does bad luck loom? If so, has she then the gift of prophecy? Were those opals gifts from someone who truly loves her? Perhaps she offsets any bad luck by wearing multiple opals. Our attention was certainly drawn to them repeatedly, even when she was putting her arm protectively around her pupil's shoulders, upon learning that Harry was to be a fourth competitor in a field of three (*GoF* 106; Chs. 15, 22).

Returning to the theme of not wearing opals if they are not one's birthstone, a folklorist working in 1991 reports:

Mrs. [G.] learned this superstition from her mother while growing up in East Flatbush, Brooklyn, New York in the early 1950's [*sic*]. Opal is not her birthstone. One day she borrowed her mother's opal ring. She was washing dishes with the ring on, and it fell off and was lost down the drain. This story is evidence of the validity of the superstition, according to Mrs. [G.]. She does not know the meaning of it, just that wearing opals if its [*sic*] not one's birthstone is bad luck.

Interestingly this informant does not register either the injunction against wearing borrowed opals, or the "common knowledge" that opals tend to wander, which might just as easily explain the mishap.

Margaret [Z.] took a contrary position to the last-cited informant, Mrs. [G.], in 1987, reporting that "it's bad luck to buy an opal for someone if the opal is not that person's birthstone." Here the fault lies in making an ill-conceived gift, rather than in the wearing of it of by the recipient. The example offered was of the informant's mother, who refused Ms. [Z.]'s childhood request for a gift of an opal ring when the mother took a trip to Australia, citing the belief just mentioned. The mother, however, herself not an October baby, felt no compunction about purchasing such a bauble for her own use:

Bernice has no idea why the opal is unlucky for those born the other eleven months of the year but she does not question it. She also believes that it exercises its power for good 'especially on those who are unselfish and generous.' Bernice has since learned that the opal is a symbol of hope because of its rainbow hues [presumably suggesting a fresh start, like a rainbow after the rain].

I think that Juliet was trying to make her daughter feel special [by giving her an opal], because she is one of the few who can wear opals. Her other daughter was born in May, which has the emerald as a birthstone. Juliet did not give this daughter jewelry with an emerald in it, most likely because emeralds are very expensive, but also because there is not the same exclusive meaning about wearing them.

Another lady whose mother taught her to be wary of wearing opals said,

They are somewhat mysterious. I assume that people thought that they had special powers and only some special people were capable of controlling the power of the opals. (Collected 1980, Berkeley, CA)

When I wear pearls, no one has ever asked me if I were born in June. Pearls are, in fact, my birthstone, but no one has ever asked. Nor have I found traces of the equivalent behavior around other months' birthstones. No one ever says, "Oh, dear, is that turquoise? That's very unlucky to wear if you weren't born in December!"

Gender-related Issue

The superstition seems to be passed from women to female children, at least in our family. [My mother] stated that she never recalled any of her brothers (she has three brothers and three step-brothers) knowing it and she does not think she ever told my only brother. (I asked my brother and he knew nothing of it.) She was positive that all of her five sisters do know this superstition. At least two of my female cousins know it, one of my [aunts-in-law] knows it for sure, and my paternal grandmother.... Of all the men in my family, only my own step-father had any knowledge of the tradition (he adheres to it strictly and because my mother loves opals, buys them for her so that she feels comfortable wearing them).

In 1975 another informant remarked, "It is amazing how many females ask me if I was born in October when they see the opal." (She was not.) In point of fact, out of over 150 accounts I read in the Folklore Archives at U. C. Berkeley, only two had been collected by men, and even those recorded the responses of female informants. One of these noted that

"It's definitely more prevalent among women than men," Carla [a "jewelry consultant"] says. "I've never had a man say anything about an opal." She says many men have bought opals, but never has a man said anything about the superstition. It also seems to cut across all cultural and economic lines, according to Carla.

Color

The only interpretation I can think of for this superstition has to do with the opal's color. Perhaps since its color is not distinguishable ["distinctive"?], it could signify a deceptive personality. One who wears an opal is not true to others, thus the bad luck association. The opal as someone's [rightful] birthstone, however, could never be associated with bad luck.

In *Popular Beliefs and Superstitions*, the changing color of opals is associated with the devil, according to a seventeen-year-old black student from Cleveland (1959): "If you wear an opal, it reflects your soul because the devil lives in it and changes the colors."

A young woman who asked her English grandmother about her beliefs was told, "Opals are not clear and they have many colors":

She said the fact that they are not clear is bad because it is a sign that a girl cannot trust her love. My grandmother said a clear stone, like a diamond, is a sign of a faithful love because it has nothing to hide. She added that an opal implies a man with confused emotions. The many colors of the stone are also bad luck because she believes they represent thoughts about other women. She commented,

> Elizabeth, you want a boy that is true blue and only devoted to you. Too many colors shows a confused mind. If he likes you he'll spend the money and give you a sapphire or a diamond, or something people know. An opal is an inferior stone. (Collected in 1994.)

Marriage

The Frank C. Brown Collection of North Carolina Folklore (cited by numerous Folklore Archive contributors) documents a widespread belief that "if you have an opal engagement ring, you will have ill fortune during your married life." For some, that may not be a problem for long. *A Dictionary of Superstitions*, edited by Iona Opie and Moira Tatem, explains that opals are associated with "widowhood and tears (*s.v.*)"

There is a superstition that wearing an opal, if it is not your birthstone, will cause you bad luck. This is especially true if this is your engagement ring.... This superstition is probably related to opals' fragility; if they undergo moderate to extreme changes in temperature, they can shatter like glass. This shattering is taken as symbolic of one's bad luck....

It's also related to the degree of anxiety women may feel towards marriage. Many these days seem to "shatter easily"; they may be displacing their fears into the physical metaphor for their coming marriage, their engagement ring [*sic*].

Newbell Niles Puckett, writing in *Popular Beliefs and Superstitions*, specifies that "it is bad luck to have an opal as an engagement ring" and that "opals in an engagement ring will bring an unhappy marriage."

We must note one of the few situations where we receive specific information as to what the bad luck might actually be in this context. One authority states that widowhood (a premature end to the marriage) comes about because of opal engagement rings, another that the marriage itself will be unhappy (otherwise the lady might welcome widowhood), the last informant suggests that a readily shatterable opal suggests a marriage breaking up likewise, and to this collection of calamities I have anecdotal evidence to add: my close friend was prevented from venturing into the wedded state with her intended. They picked out an opal engagement ring against the advice of the very jeweler who stood to profit from the sale, and not long after, her intended died following a surgical operation, before the young couple could marry. Indeed, that there are four points at which wedded bliss may be thwarted suggests that the object of the bad luck—in this case, destroying someone's hopes for a happy wedded life—seems more important than the actual form in which it manifests.

Most people learn not say unpleasant or worrisome things to others at a point where "the deed was already done," as it were. In other words, if a friend asked whether she should buy an opal ring or a ruby ring, then that would be the time to share any concerns about birthdates and birthstones. If, on the other hand, she had already bought the opal or been given one, then one should make some pleasant but neutral remark and keep helpful hints about "what everyone knows" to oneself. The concern about opals bringing bad luck, however, seems to be so urgent that it transcends the normal bounds of propriety.

The Evil Eye

An informant named Adrienne told her collector in 1990 that she has an opal ring that is her lucky ring, which she

does not wear all the time, but only when she "has something important to do." She wears it more to bring good luck than to prevent bad luck, even though she knows that the stone in the ring, an opal, is traditionally known for bringing bad luck. I would guess that Adrienne, who I should mention is Jewish, is—consciously or unconsciously—following a pattern of behavior seen in many Jewish superstitions: doing the opposite to achieve the intended affect. In this case, wearing something that is meant to be the opposite of good luck (an unlucky opal) guarantees that good luck will result. This probably stems from the "like against like" principle of homeopathic magic (as explained in Alan Dundes's *Wet and Dry, the Evil Eye*), in which some form of a dangerous object is employed as a "prophylactic counteragent."

Along the same lines, another informant pointed out that many opals have a bluish background color—blue, in particular, blue eyes, being the color associated with the *Malocchio* ("Evil Eye"). The medical doctrine of *similia similibus* dictates that one needs something similar to the ailment one suffers from to effect a cure. In this way, plants with yellow spots are used against liver disease, and powdered rubies for blood disorders. This idea is related to taking "a hair of the dog that bit you" to cure a hangover.

Eye of the World

One peculiar type of opal demands closer inspection. Hydrophane opal looks like an ordinary pebble when dry, but becomes transparent and full of fire when soaked in water. When removed from the water, it slowly dries out, loses its play of color, and looks again like an uninteresting ordinary rock. Popular belief spreads that within such a remarkable opal resides an eye which can see everything. The ancient Romans dub it *oculis mundi* ("eye of the world") and the Germans, *Weltauge*. George Kunz also lists *lapis mutabilis* ("changeable stone") amongst its names in *Curious Lore of Precious Stones*. Allan W. Eckert's *World of Opals* explains that

[b]y 5 A.D. it has been nicknamed *ophthalmis lapis* ("the eye stone"), the stone that sees all, knows all, and imparts to its owner the power of generally foretelling the immediate future. Some decades earlier this belief in opal-

induced prognostications has expanded to endow the opal's owner [note: not wearer] with the specific ability to warn of impending disaster, natural or man-made, and opal has become so highly esteemed in the Roman Empire that it is virtually all but priceless.

In addition to these useful qualities, the stone is also regarded as turning pale in the presence of poison (Brewer, *s.v.*).

By the year 1020, stipulations are being attached to the mythology of the opal. Instead of it simply being a stone that brings good luck to its owner, this is deemed true only if the owner is possessed of high ideals and purity of soul. To such a person, the opal is believed to induce visions that are valuable guides in decision-making when faced with a dilemma. If, however, the owner of the opal is a person whose character is low and whose intentions are evil, then such visions will be deliberately misleading.

Note that this distinction differs markedly from that of a neutral object which may be used either for good or for evil. This belief, both as stated above, and in the somewhat mutated form of "good luck for October 'babies,' and bad luck for those born in the other eleven months," remains active in twenty-first-century parlance.

In 1075, in an important volume titled *Lapidarium*, the stone is referred to as *patronus furum*, "protector of thieves." A slightly earlier verse elucidates:

> Though from the eyes each ail th' Opthalmius chase
> Yet 'tis the guardian of the thievish race;
> It gifts the bearer with acutest sight
> But clouds all other eyes with thickest night;
> So that the plunderers bold in open day
> Secure from harm can bear their spoil away.

Lapidarium notes that the stone must be wrapped in a bay leaf to work. In 1280, Alfonso X, Spanish King of Castile and Leon, wrote in his *Lapidario del Rey* that the opal-induced blindness was called "Amentia" (Eckert 62).

People desperate to escape the Bubonic Plague in 1348–49 blamed the opal. Eckert tells us that

the notion is not so outlandish as one might believe today: those experiencing this harrowing time soon notice that an opal worn by a victim is quite brilliant up to the point of death, but then it quickly loses much of its brilliance. They deem this to be evidence of the opal having malignant influence on the victim's fate, and do not understand that it is the demise of the victim that alters the stone, due to the relatively rapid change from the warmth of the fever the victim was experiencing to the chill of death. Within a few short months the dire malady kills fully ⅔ the population of major European cities. Though to this time opal has always been a highly favored gemstone with European jewelers, following the plague they regard it as a badge of dread. (62)

Alfred, Lord Tennyson, writing centuries later, invokes this belief about opals' temperature sensitivity in "Idylls of the King": "The pale blood of the wizard / Took gayer colors, like an opal warm'd." Could this useful quality lead an opal to be used, subtly, as later people would a mirror, to see if an apparently dead person still lives? A pity that Mme. Maxime was not available to slip one of her superb stones on Professor Dumbledore's still finger.

Some 500 years after the Black Death, during the Crimean War, British soldiers bought Hungarian opal in quantity in Slovakia. These well-meant souvenirs were found in the pockets of many soldiers killed on the battlefield, or when they fell victim to war-related disease. Such sad discoveries meant that the stones failed in their intended role of lovingly bestowed keepsake, instead reviving their earlier reputation as a bringer of ill-fortune. At least in the latter situation, one can understand how so many fallen soldiers came to have opals in their pockets. Why so many Europeans should be opal-bedight during the Black Death is less clear.

Those who tie opals' own bad fortunes to the 1829 publication of *Anne of Geierstein* may not be wrong; Tilley's exhaustive *Dictionary of Proverbs in England in the Sixteenth and Seventeenth Centuries* contains no hint of opals; Stith Thompson's *Motif-Index of Folk Literature* lists many motifs containing diamonds, rubies, sapphires, and emeralds, but not a single opal association. Earlier works favor positive traits. Two other tales are much offered as explaining away the opal's unpopularity. One concerns five royal French coaches named for the precious stones (opal was once regarded as precious, on par with diamonds, rubies, sapphires, and emeralds, but is now considered semi-precious). The coachman responsible for the one called Opal was much given to drink, and because of the drink, caused more than a few accidents, and ladies began requesting that that particular carriage not be sent for them, as "Opal is so unfortunate, you know."

The other tale concerns Alfonso XII, King of Spain. Graham tells the story engagingly:

> In the late 19th Century, Alfonzo XII [*sic*] fell madly in love with a beautiful aristocrat named Comtesse de Castiglione. The Comtesse reciprocated the King's affection, but months before the pair were to wed, the faithless Alfonzo married another woman, the Princess Mercedes. Vowing to get even, the Comtesse sent the couple a wedding present in the form of a magnificent opal set in a huge ring of the purest gold. The princess was immediately smitten by the gift, and insisted that her husband slip it on her finger. He obliged, and two months later the princess mysteriously died.
>
> After the funeral Alfonzo gave the ring to his grandmother, Queen Christina, who almost immediately thereafter also expired. After that the ring passed to Alfonzo's sister, the Infanta Maria del Pilar. Maria died as well, apparently victim to the same weird illness that had taken the other two women. The ring was up for grabs yet again, and when Alfonzo's sister-in-law expressed an interest, he let her have it with the usual result.
>
> Deeply depressed by then, the King decided to end it all by slipping the ring on his own finger, just as Cleopatra had embraced the asp to terminate her own misery. In little over a month, the ring did to Alfonzo what the snake had done to the Egyptian Queen. (3–4)

Cholera swept all over Spain at that time, killing more than 100,000 people by the fall of 1885. Traders visiting the Spanish court may have brought the disease to the nobles first.

At this point I would like to offer a seriously abridged selection from Sir Walter Scott's *Anne of Geierstein*, a misreading of which most people blame for savaging the opal's reputation. "Misreading" here really means a failure to finish reading the three-volume novel. The third book contains a conversation which sheds much light on the actions in the first. It features a cast of characters who hold a more than passing interest for *Potter* scholars.

This story, the last of the Waverly Novels, whose publication began in 1814, tells of a certain baron who faces the loss of his much-esteemed tutor:

> "Be not discouraged, my son," answered the sage; "I will bequeath the task of perfecting you in your studies to my daughter, who will come hither on purpose. But remember, if you value the permanence of your family, look not upon her as aught else than a helpmate in your studies; for if you forget the instructress in the beauty of the maiden, you will be buried with your sword and your shield, as the last male of your house; and farther evil,

believe me, will arise; for such alliances never come to a happy issue, of which my own is an example. —But hush, we are observed."

...[T]here stood...a most beautiful female figure in the Persian costume, in which the color of pink predominated. But she wore no turban or head-dress of any kind, saving a blue ribbon drawn through her auburn hair, and secured by a gold clasp, the outer side of which was ornamented by a superb opal, which, amid the changing lights peculiar to that gem, displayed, internally a slight tinge of red like a spark of fire.

The figure of this young person was rather under the middle size, but perfectly well formed. The Eastern dress, with the wide trousers gathered round the ankles, made visible the smallest and most beautiful feet which had ever been seen, while hands and arms of the most perfect symmetry were partly seen from under the folds of the robe. The little lady's countenance was of a lively and expressive character, in which spirit and wit seemed to predominate; and the quick dark eye, with its beautifully formed eyebrow, seemed to presage the arch remark, to which the rosy and half smiling lip appeared ready to give utterance.

———————

"I am come as I have been commanded," she said, looking around her. "You must expect a strict and diligent mistress, and I hope for the credit of an attentive pupil."

After the arrival of this singular and interesting being in the castle of Arnheim, various alterations took place within the interior of the household. A lady of high rank and small fortune, the respectable widow of a Count of the empire, who was the Baron's blood relation, received and accepted an invitation to preside over her kinsman's domestic affairs, and remove, by her countenance, any suspicions which might arise from the presence of Hermione, as the beautiful Persian was generally called.

The Countess Waldstetten carried her complaisance so far, as to be present on almost all occasions, whether in the laboratory or library, when the Baron of Arnheim received lessons from, or pursued studies with, the young and lovely tutor who had been thus strangely substituted for the aged Magus. If this lady's report was to be trusted, their pursuits were of a most extraordinary nature, and the results which she sometimes witnessed were such as to create fear as well as surprise. But she strongly vindicated them from practising unlawful arts, or overstepping the boundaries of natural science.

———————

Meantime a marked alteration began to take place in the interviews between the lovely tutor and her pupil. These were conducted with the same caution as before, and never, so far as could be observed, took place without the presence of the Countess of Waldstetten, or some other third person of respectability. But the scenes of these meetings were no longer the scholar's library, or the chemist's laboratory;— the gardens, the groves, were resorted to for amusement, and parties, hunting and fishing, with evenings spent in the dance, seemed to announce that the studies of wisdom were for a time abandoned for the pursuits of pleasure. It was not difficult to guess the meaning of this…and no one was surprised to hear it formally announced, after a few weeks of gayety, that the fair Persian was to be wedded to the Baron of Arnheim.

…[W]hen her eyes sparkled, her cheeks reddened, and her whole frame became animated, it was pretended that the opal clasp amid her tresses, the ornament which she never laid aside, shot forth the little spark, or tongue of flame, which it always displayed, with an increased vivacity. In the same manner, if in the half-darkened hall the conversation of Hermione became unusually animated, it was believed that the jewel became brilliant, and even displayed a twinkling and flashing gleam which seemed to be emitted by the gem itself, and not produced in the usual manner, by the reflection of some external light. Her maidens were also heard to surmise, that when their mistress was agitated by any hasty or brief resentment (the only weakness of temper which she was sometimes observed to display), they could observe dark-red sparks flash from the mystic brooch, as if it sympathized with the wearer's emotions.

The women who attended on her toilet farther reported that this gem was never removed but for a few minutes, when the Baroness's hair was combed out; that she was unusually pensive and silent during the time it was laid aside, and particularly apprehensive when any liquid was brought near it. Even in the use of holy water at the door of the church, she was observed to omit the sign of the cross on the forehead, for fear, it was supposed, of the water touching the valued jewel.

These singular reports did not prevent the marriage of the Baron of Arnheim from proceeding as had been arranged. It was celebrated in the usual form, and with the utmost splendor, and the young couple seemed to commence a life of happiness rarely to be found on earth.

In the course of twelve months, the lovely Baroness presented her husband with a daughter, which was to be christened Sybilla…. [M]any were invited to be present on the occasion, and the castle was thronged with company.

It happened, that amongst the guests was an old lady, notorious for playing in private society the part of a malicious fairy in a minstrel's tale. This was the Baroness of Steinfeldt, famous in the neighborhood for her insatiable curiosity and overweening pride. She had not been many days in the castle, ere, by the aid of a female attendant, who acted as an intelligencer, she had made herself mistress of all that was heard, said, or suspected concerning the peculiarities of the Baroness Hermione. It was on the morning of the day appointed for the christening, while the whole company were assembled in the hall, and waiting till the Baroness should appear, to pass with them to the chapel, that there arose between the censorious and haughty dame whom we have just mentioned, and the Countess Waldstetten, a violent discussion concerning some point of disputed precedence. It was referred to the Baron von Arnheim, who decided in favor of the Countess. Madame de Steinfeldt instantly ordered her palfrey to be prepared, and her attendants to mount.

"I leave this place," she said, "which a good Christian ought never to have entered; I leave a house of which the master is a sorcerer, the mistress a demon who dares not cross her brow with holy water, and their trencher companion one, who for a wretched pittance is willing to act as matchmaker between a wizard and an incarnate fiend!"

She then departed with rage in her countenance, and spite in her heart.

…[S]aid the Baron of Arnheim[,] "only, all who are here this morning shall be satisfied whether the Baroness Hermione doth or doth not share the rites of Christianity."

The Countess of Waldstetten made anxious signs to him while he spoke thus; and when the crowd permitted her to approach near him, she was heard to whisper, "O, be not rash! try no experiment! there is something mysterious about that opal talisman; be prudent, and let the matter pass by."

The Baron, who was in a more towering passion than well became the wisdom to which he made pretence—although it will be perhaps allowed that an affront so public, and in such a time and place, was enough to shake the prudence of the most staid, and the philosophy of the most wise, answered sternly and briefly, "Are you, too, such a fool?" and retained his purpose.

The Baroness of Arnheim at this moment entered the hall, looking just so pale from her late confinement, as to render her lovely countenance more interesting, if less animated, than usual…. [H]er husband made the signal for the company to move forward to the chapel, and lent the Baroness his arm to bring up the rear. The chapel was nearly filled by the splendid company, and all eyes were bent on their host and hostess….

As they passed the threshold, the Baron dipt his finger in the font stone, and offered holy-water to his lady, who accepted it, as usual, by touching his finger with her own. But then, as if to confute the calumnies of the malevolent lady of Steinfeldt, with an air of sportive familiarity which was rather unwarranted by the time and place, he flirted on her beautiful forehead a drop or two of the moisture which remained on his own hand. The opal, on which one of these drops had lighted, shot out a brilliant spark like a failing star, and became the instant afterwards lightless and colorless as a common pebble, while the beautiful Baroness sunk on the floor of the chapel with a deep sigh of pain. All crowded around her in dismay. The unfortunate Hermione was raised from the ground, and conveyed to her chamber; and so much did her countenance and pulse alter, within the short time necessary to do this, that those who looked upon her pronounced her a dying woman. She was no sooner in her own apartment then she requested to be left alone with her husband. He remained an hour in the room, and when he came out he locked and double locked the door behind him. He then betook himself to the chapel, and remained there for an hour or more, prostrated before the altar.

...[U]pon opening the door of the chamber in which the Baroness had been deposited little more than two hours before, no traces of her could be discovered, unless that there was about a handful of light gray ashes, like such as might have been produced by burning fine paper, found on the bed where she had been laid. A solemn funeral was nevertheless performed, with masses, and all other spiritual rites, for the soul of the high and noble Lady Hermione of Arnheim; and it was exactly on that same day three years that the Baron himself was laid in the grave of the same chapel of Arnheim, with sword, shield, and helmet, as the last male of his family.

Following the publication of *Anne of Geierstein*, opal sales in Europe plummeted more than 55%, and remained crippled for decades. Si and Ann Frazier's article for *Lapidary Journal*, "Lore, Lies, and Misinformation," explains that a careful reading of the third volume of *Anne* reveals that this Hermione, here mother of Sibylla, and Anne's grandmother, was poisoned (331). Scott has Anne explain to her suitor that "that noble stone" had simply done its job, which was to turn pale to warn the wearer of the poison. Her death was reflected, not caused, by the opal. Readers not hardy enough to finish all three volumes of the novel would have missed Hermione's granddaughter's exculpation of the opal. More likely, large numbers of people formed firm opinions without the benefit of having read any of Scott's novel at all, as have the many convinced that the *Harry Potter* books promote devil-worship.

Hermione must not have been concerned about being poisoned, for wearing such a warning device in one's hair would not seem to be the way to get the greatest possible notice of impending danger. It would, however, telegraph such an event to anyone skilled enough to read the signs.

Her father, the Baron's original tutor, warned him against forming a romantic alliance with Hermione. He, too, it would seem, was a man without male issue, as a result of such a marriage. The mortal-fey marriage bears resemblance to folktales wherein a man weds a selkie or other supernatural being. They live happily for a time, until some trouble-maker tempts the husband to burn his wife's periodically doffed skin or fur-pelt. Inevitably, he listens to the trouble-maker and goes against his wife's clear warnings to the contrary. His burning the skin or pelt forces her to leave him forever and return to her people.

Might J. K. Rowling be drawing inspiration from *Anne of Geierstein*? Will the Hermione we know so well, or Professor Trelawney, engage with any of the opals in their world? Another telling coincidence concerns a sub-heading in the Fraziers' article, which reads "Cloak of Invisibility," a reference to the opal's somewhat less unsavory, Hand-of-Glory-like talents. Did Harry's invisibility cloak get its start here? The realization that three different "disappearing devices" may be in play here elevates "nothing is what it appears to be" to new heights.

While Scott's Hermione, although a Persian, explicitly does not wear the expected turban, Henrik Ibsen's Peer Gynt dons an opal-decorated turban in Act Four, Scene Six of the play that bears his name. A lovely girl named Anitra catches his eye, but laments, tellingly for Rowling readers, that she has no soul:

> PEER
> You are tempting, my daughter! The Prophet is touched.
> If you don't believe me, then hear the proof;—
> I'll make you a Houri in Paradise!
>   ANITRA
> Impossible, Lord!
>   PEER
> What? You think I am jesting?
> I'm in sober earnest, as true as I live!
>   ANITRA
> But I haven't a soul.
>   PEER
> Then of course you must get one!
>   ANITRA
> How, Lord?
>   PEER
> Just leave me alone for that;—
> I shall look after your education.
> No soul? Why, truly you're not over bright,
> as the saying goes. I've observed it with pain.
> But pooh! for a soul you can always find room.

Come here! let me measure your brain-pan, child.—
There is room, there is room, I was sure there was.
It's true you never will penetrate
very deep; to a large soul you'll scarcely attain-
but never you mind; it won't matter a bit;-
you'll have plenty to carry you through with credit—
    ANITRA
The Prophet is gracious—
    PEER
You hesitate? Speak!
    ANITRA
But I'd rather-
    PEER
Say on; don't waste time about it!
    ANITRA
I don't care so much about having a soul;—give me rather—
    PEER
What, child?
    ANITRA
[pointing to his turban]
That lovely opal.
    PEER
[enchanted, handing her the jewel]
Anitra! Anitra! true daughter of Eve!
I feel thee magnetic; for I am a man.
And, as a much-esteemed author has phrased it:
"Das Ewig-Weibliche ziehet uns an!"

This play concerns itself largely with a man's soul and its ultimate disposition. Peer Gynt worries about the Button Molder, a figure familiar to Ibsen's contemporaries from Nordic folklore, who collects the souls of those who have been not good enough to go to Heaven but not wicked enough to deserve Hell, and melts them down into buttons. So much does he fear his soul being molded into something utterly inconsequential that he lobbies ferociously to be sent to Hell. He even pleads with his long-neglected wife to explain how evil he has been.

    Anitra and Peer continue their discussion in Scenes Six and Eight:

    ANITRA
[lies down at his feet]
All thy words are sweet as singing,
though I understand but little.
Master, tell me, can thy daughter

catch a soul by listening?
     PEER
Soul, and spirit's light and knowledge,
all in good time you shall have them.
When in east, on rosy streamers
golden types print: Here is day,—
then, my child, I'll give you lessons;
you'll be well brought-up, no fear.
But, 'mid night's delicious stillness,
it were stupid if I should,
with a threadbare wisdom's remnants,
play the part of pedagogue.—
And the soul, moreover, is not,
looked at properly, the main thing.
It's the heart that really matters.
     ANITRA
Speak, O Master! When thou speakest,
I see gleams, as though of opals!

———

Act Four, Scene Eight (end):
     PEER
Oh, listen;—
you shall have the soul that I promised you once—
     ANITRA
Oh, thank you; I'll get on without the soul.

Ultimately, she robs Peer of his purse and his steed, keeps the opal, and rides off, never to be seen again. His earlier assessment of her as a stupid woman would seem to have been disproven. Are her lack of soul and affinity for opal connected? Perhaps opals inherently possess Horcrux potential.

The *patronus furum*, "protector of thieves," a warning against poison, protection from, if not the invocation of, the Evil Eye, the gift of prophecy—surely all those opals in so few books portend serious insight for someone. Even if *Harry Potter and the Deathly Hallows* were not to pick up the clues surrounding four mentions of three groups of opals in six previous books, an appreciation of the intriguing body of folklore surrounding these entrancing stones should, nevertheless, embue the wizarding world with a richness of color that no other stone could.

Works Cited

Brewer, E. Cobham. *Dictionary of Phrase and Fable.* London: [n.p.], 1898.

Brown, Frank C. *The Frank C. Brown Collection of North Carolina Folklore.* Durham: North Carolina UP, 1952–64.

Casetta, Anna, Wayland Hand and Sondra Thiederman, eds. *Popular Beliefs and Superstitions: A Compendium of American Folklore.* Boston: G. K. Hall, 1981.

Eckert, Alan W. *The World of Opals.* John Wiley: New York, 1997.

Folklore Archives. University of California at Berkeley. 110 Kroeber Hall, Berkeley CA 94720. Superstitions III. J4 06. [The Archive explicitly requests that researchers not cite the work of individual folklorists, as requesting written permission to do so, and addressing rights to privacy, were not part of the collecting work when the Archive was begun.]

Frazier, Si and Ann. *Lapidary Journal.* "Lore, Lies, and Misinformation." June 1994, 48.6, pp. 48 *et* p.

Graham, D. Douglas. "Fatal Attraction: the History and Folklore Behind Opal." *Colored Stone.* September / October 2001. Accessed 1 June 2007. <http://www.colored-stone.com/stories/sep01/opal.cfm>.

Granger, John, ed. *Who Killed Albus Dumbledore?* Wayne, PA: Zossima, 2006.

Ibsen, Henrik. *Peer Gynt.* Accessed 1 June 2007. <http://home.c2i.net/espenjo/home/ibsen/peergynt/pg_4f_e.htm>.

Kunz, George Frederick. *The Curious Lore of Precious Stones.* New York: Lippincott, 1913.

Leechman, Frank. *The Opal Book: A Complete Guide to the Famous Gemstone.* Sydney: Ure Smith, 1961.

Opie, Iona, and Moira Tatem, eds. *A Dictionary of Superstitions.* New York: Oxford UP, 1989.

Puckett, Newbell Niles. Essay in *Popular Beliefs and Superstitions.* Boston: G. K. Hall, 1981.

Pyle, Howard. *The Story of King Arthur and His Knights.* 1902. New York: Dover, 1965.

Rowling, J. K. *Harry Potter and the Chamber of Secrets.* London: Bloomsbury, 1998.

—. *Harry Potter and the Goblet of Fire.* New York: Scholastic, 2000.

Scott, Walter. *The Waverly Novels.* Part Three. New York: Peter Fenelon Collier, [1831].

Tennyson, Alfred. "Idylls of the King." Accessed 1 June 2007. <http://gutenberg.org/etext610>.

The Magic and the Profane

Tilia Klebenov Jacobs

J. K. Rowling's creation of a compelling magical world relies on the careful construction of magical spaces in both Muggle and wizarding settings. She has formed a quasi-sacred universe that permeates and overlaps with ours. Her magical spaces and objects are ripe with meaning and ultimately describe an Otherworld defined by ongoing clashes between darkness and light. Access to this world is possible only by extraordinary means: the use of enchanted objects or portals whose existence is known to only the enlightened few. At its heart is a great stage on which battles between good and evil are eternally waged. These concerns—sanctified or enchanted objects; thresholds to the Other; and moral concerns of a sometimes cataclysmic nature—are also the interests of religion, so that a hermeneutic of religious scholarship is instructive in understanding Rowling's construction of space and its ethical dimensions.

The great religious scholar Mircea Eliade posits a world in which the sacred and the profane can on occasion intrude on each other, so that our world, the profane, contains at certain key physical points access to the sacred. He goes on to expound upon his central thesis: that the religious human, *homo religiosus*, is unceasingly driven by a constant search for contact with the sacred, that which has been touched by the gods. As a result, most if not all archaic societies are physically and ritually structured to create points of access to that sacred realm. He describes the function of myth in relation to this underlying belief:

[T]he myth describes the various and sometimes dramatic irruptions of the sacred into the world.... It is the irruption of the sacred into the world, an irruption narrated in the myths, that *establishes* the world as a reality. (Eliade, *Sacred* 97)

The job of the fantasy writer is much the same: to create a primary world defined by its contact with the Other, and subsequently a "Secondary World" that becomes the locus for the main action of the story. This term first appeared in J. R. R. Tolkien's seminal essay, "On Fairy-Stories":

[T]he story-maker proves a successful "sub-creator." He makes a Secondary World which your mind can enter. Inside it, what he relates is "true": it accords with the laws of that world. You therefore believe it, while you are, as it were, inside. (Tolkien 37)

The *Harry Potter* series describes a richly imagined Secondary World, with its own internal rules and limitations. (For example, dead people stay dead. Even magic has its limits [Natov 317].)

Like the Sacred, Rowling's wizarding world is structured in such a way as to point to a larger reality. It is here that the work of religious scholars becomes quite useful. For Eliade's *homo religiosus*, the Other is a place of awe and dread:

The numinous (from Latin *numen*, god) presents itself as something "wholly other"...something basically and totally different.... What will concern us is not the relation between the rational and nonrational elements of religion but the *sacred in its entirety*. The first possible definition of the sacred is that it is *the opposite of the profane*. (Eliade, *Sacred* 9, 10)

Similarly, in Rowling's world, the first possible definition of the magic is that it is the opposite of the Muggle. One key difference, however, is this: whereas in the presence of the sacred, "man senses his profound nothingness" (Eliade, *Sacred* 10), magic can be harnessed, and thus presents the effervescence of endless possibilities to one who wields it. It is empowering rather than belittling. In the presence of the Divine, the individual is negated; but face to face with powerful magic, the hero proves himself. We see these possibilities in enchanted objects such as Portkeys; in magical thresholds such as Diagon Alley and Platform Nine and Three-Quarters; and crucially in Hogwarts Castle itself. Each of these is conceived of in the physical world in such a way as to underscore its own relationship with the magical world. In this way they illustrate the nature of that world itself as a quasi-sacred Other.

In Rowling's world, Portkeys are seemingly ordinary objects which function as portals to the Secondary World.

"For those who don't want to Apparate, or can't, we use Portkeys. They're objects that are used to transport wizards from one spot to another at a prearranged time...."

"What sort of objects are Portkeys?" asked Harry curiously.

"Well, they can be anything," said Mr. Weasley. "Unobtrusive things, obviously, so Muggles don't go picking them up and playing with them... stuff they'll just think is litter." (*GoF* 70)

Clearly the true worth of the Portkey lies not in its external structure —the first one Harry encounters is a "manky old boot" (*GoF* 73)— but in its ability to provide access to the Other.

Harry felt as though a hook just behind his navel had been suddenly jerked irresistibly forward. His feet left the ground; he could feel Ron and Hermione on either side of him, their shoulders banging into his; they were all speeding forward in a howl of wind and swirling color; his forefinger was stuck to the boot as though it was pulling him magnetically onward and then—

His feet slammed into the ground; Ron staggered into him and he fell over; the Portkey hit the ground near his head with a heavy thud.

..."Seven past five from Stoatshead Hill," said a voice. (*GoF* 73–74)

Although Portkeys are not worshipped—they are entirely utilitarian, a means of transportation—still they bear a striking resemblance to sacred objects in archaic societies, for each provides access to another realm. Moreover, it is worth noting that in such societies the sacred object itself is never worshipped, but venerated for the sake of the Other which enters the world through it.

[W]hat is involved is not a veneration of the stone in itself, a cult of the tree in itself. The sacred tree, the sacred stone are not adored as stone or tree; they are worshipped precisely because they are *hierophanies* [i.e., revelations of the Divine], because they show something that is no longer stone or tree but the *sacred*. (Eliade, *Sacred* 12)

Much like Eliade's universe of sacred and profane, Rowling's physical world is pocked with magic. Like the sacred objects Eliade posits, the Portkey it is a point where the Other breaks into the ordinary world. Unlike Eliade's stones or trees, however, it gives physical rather than theological access. Furthermore, Portkeys are an instance in which the profane (or Muggle) does not merely point to the sacred (or magical); here, the profane literally becomes sacred, or

Other, as it is transformed to become something utterly unlike that which it was before.

This seeming contradiction is entirely in accordance with the religious mindset. Eliade notes, "By manifesting the sacred, any object becomes *something else*, yet it continues to remain *itself*, for it continues to participate in its surrounding cosmic milieu" (Eliade, *Sacred* 12). In other words, a sacred tree is still a tree, with roots and leaves and caterpillars chewing on its twigs. Yet it is also something entirely different and crucial in the revelation of the sacred to the profane universe. Similarly, a boot is a boot in the Muggle world, even if it is a Portkey. Its significance lies in its ability to take people to an entirely different reality.

This too finds a parallel in Eliade's description of traditional religions. In such societies, the presence of the sacred is the assumption on which all human activity is based.

The man of the archaic societies tends to live as much as possible *in* the sacred or in close proximity to consecrated objects. The tendency is perfectly understandable, because, for primitives as for the man of all pre-modern societies, the *sacred* is equivalent to a *power*, and, in the last analysis, to *reality*. (Eliade, *Sacred* 12)

Thus the member of an archaic society lives in constant contact with extraordinary objects that point the way to the Other. Since that Other is assumed to be more real and more significant than the physical world humans otherwise inhabit, the continuing presence of sacred objects is a comfort and reassurance against the vagaries of an impermanent Creation. Again, parallels with Rowling's universe are clear. Her magical realm is far more powerful than the physical world, and its forces can be wielded but not tamed.

By providing access to the realm of magic, Portkeys take the characters to locations where the main events of the stories occur. As in every myth, Harry's tale describes an existential journey through a symbolic world; and places in the mythological landscape are first and foremost symbolic points where the action unfolds (Virole 3). Once in the magical world, then, it follows that different parts of the realm have distinct properties and functions within the unfolding myth. In other words, the nature of a place is a template for the kind of action that will take place in it.

Again, we find useful antecedents in the religious mindset.

For religious man, space is not homogenous; he experiences interruptions, breaks in it; some parts of space are qualitatively different from others.... There is, then, a sacred space, and hence a strong, significant space; there are other spaces that are not sacred and so are without structure or consistency, amorphous. (Eliade, *Sacred* 20)

These breaks in the nature of physical space are very much a function of the *Harry Potter* universe.

[T]he sacred [is] a representation that runs through all of J. K. Rowling's work. The Muggle world and the magical world reproduce the fundamental cleavage between the profane and the sacred, between the secularized world of imbecilic commercial society (incarnated by the Dursley family) and a sacred world, which is certainly dangerous and ambivalent but where questions of meaning are not just central, but are also the only real questions. (Virole 7)

In Rowling's world, therefore, function follows form. Peripheral locations which are crosshatched with the profane world are not arenas for cosmic battles. They are points of access into that world, but not the heart of the world itself. Exemplars of this are the two alleys, Diagon and Knockturn, and Platform Nine and Three-Quarters.

Diagon Alley is a place that speaks its nature. It is not straight, clear and visible; instead, it runs diagonally (Colbert 181), weaving through the interstices of the ordinary world. Similarly, Knockturn Alley, the Dark Arts equivalent of Diagon Alley, is a place that lends itself to darkness of all kinds so that one would probably not want to visit there nocturnally (Colbert 183). The name also suggests violence, as the first time Harry visits there it is by accident and he is indeed knocked at every turn:

[S]omething hard knocked his elbow and he tucked it in tightly, still spinning and spinning—now it felt as though cold hands were slapping his face—...he closed his eyes again wishing it would stop, and then—
  He fell, face forward, onto cold stone and felt the bridge of his glasses snap. (*CoS* 49)

In Diagon Alley, interstitial though it may be, the air is full of light and the streets teem with friends. Schoolbooks are purchased and ice creams eaten. In Knockturn Alley, by contrast, all is dark and claustrophobic. Much of the action takes place in cramped, ill-lit stores where evil wizards make illegal dealings. Even outside menace lurks at every turn: Harry escapes the alley unscathed only because of the timely appearance of Hagrid (*CoS* 54).

The alleys are places where plot points are planted but not where they blossom. Lucius Malfoy places Tom Riddle's diary in Ginny Weasley's cauldron in Diagon Alley (*CoS* 63) and circumvents the law in Knockturn Alley (*CoS* 51), but these merely set the stage for later events. As peripheral spaces, the alleys are locations for minor action.

Somewhat different is the case of Platform Nine and Three-Quarters, which is a threshold between worlds. It physically separates the two realities while allowing passage between them. This is a device straight out of mythology the world over:

> The threshold that separates the two spaces also indicates the distance between two modes of being, the profane and the religious. The threshold is the limit, the boundary, the frontier that distinguishes and opposes two worlds—and at the same time the paradoxical place where those worlds communicated, where passage from the profane to the sacred world becomes possible. (Eliade, *Sacred* 25)

Indeed, situating the Hogwarts train between tracks nine and ten reinforces the central location of these stories between the earth-bound and magical worlds (Natov 318). When Harry first tries to find the track (with his supremely unhelpful Uncle Vernon), he looks at platforms nine and ten and sees "in the middle, nothing at all" (*SS* 91). As he hurtles himself toward what appears to be a solid barrier, his body braced for the shock of a crash, Harry must ignore the physical realities that deny the possibility of another world behind the visible.

> Harry walked more quickly. He was going to smash right into that barrier and then he'd be in trouble—leaning forward on his cart, he broke into a heavy run—the barrier was coming nearer and nearer—he wouldn't be able to stop—the cart was out of control—he was a foot away—he closed his eyes ready for the crash—
>
>   It didn't come…he kept on running…he opened his eyes.
>
>   A scarlet steam engine was waiting next to a platform packed with people. A sign overhead said Hogwarts Express, eleven o'clock. Harry looked behind him and saw a wrought-iron archway where the barrier had been, with the words *Platform Nine and Three-Quarters* on it. He had done it. (*SS* 93–94)

Harry has quite literally crossed the boundary between "two modes of being" (Eliade, *Sacred* 25). Gone is the world of brutal uncles who oversee drill bit manufacture and vile cousins who go to schools called Smeltings. Here photographs move, chocolate frogs leap, and true friendship flourishes in the crucible of adversity. The layering of realms that is to be found in Harry's world, and the sundry slippage between them, delineate a sacred and mythical symbolic geography (Neumann 173).

Thus the peripheral spaces are richly imagined and full of detail; but at first blush it would seem that Rowling's cosmos lacks a sacred center. There seems to be no clear *axis mundi*, no cosmic mountain, no Tree of Life; in short, no single point more magic, or sacred, than others which must be accessed to allow the requisite apocalyptic showdown between the forces of good and evil.

This is why one should always take a second glance, especially at writing as complex and thoughtful as Rowling's; for upon closer inspection we see that much of this is present but reconfigured. Rowling is too good a novelist to beat us over the head with leaden symbolism; literary Whack-a-Mole is simply not her style. Instead, she opts for an approach that is equal parts erudition and whimsy, so that many of the most profound symbols in the book are camouflaged with such dry absurdity that it is easy to dismiss them outright; until they return later in the book, or perhaps the book after that, and we see we have been lulled into a false sense of humor. Thus the good-for-nothing rat Scabbers turns out to be a murderous enemy in book three of the series, and not until book five do we find that the amusing old duffer Arabella Figg is in fact a spy sent by Dumbledore to watch over Harry in the Muggle world. It is decidedly worth our time to take a second look at some of the ostensibly innocuous or downright funny devices Rowling employs in delineating her world.

The seemingly absent Tree of Life is one such instance. A common motif in folklore, culture, and fiction, this symbol often relates to immortality or fertility. The tree, with its branches reaching up into the sky and roots plunging deep into the earth, can be understood as dwelling in three worlds simultaneously: it is a link between heaven, the earth, and the underworld, and with its very presence unites above and below ("Tree of Life" 2). This widespread symbol "came to express everything that religious man regards as *pre-eminently real and sacred*, everything that he knows the gods to possess of their own nature and that is only rarely accessible to privileged individuals, the heroes and demigods" (Eliade, *Sacred* 149).

In Rowling's able hands, the Tree of Life is re-imagined. The only tree with any bearing on the plotlines is the bellicose Whomping Willow; and though it may not unite the realms of heaven and earth, it does perform some of the functions of its cosmic antecedent. Its branches stretch high enough to ensnare flying Ford Anglias; and though its roots do not pierce the underworld, they do hide the entrance to a secret passageway that leads to the revelation of truths long hidden from the rest of the world. It is but one among many whimsical inversions of an expected archetype.

The model of the temple/cosmic mountain is similarly tweaked. In traditional societies both houses and temples are understood both to represent the center of the world, or *axis mundi*, and to reproduce symbolically the structure of that world itself, which is of course seen as the handiwork of the gods and therefore divine in nature. The house or temple is also an *imago mundi*, an image of the world.[1]

[B]oth the *imago mundi* and the Center are repeated in the inhabited world, [for] *the religious man sought to live as near as possible to the Center of the World.* He knew that his country lay at the midpoint of the earth; he knew too that his city constituted the navel of the universe, and, above all, that the temple or the palace were veritably Centers of the World. But he also wanted his own house to be at the Center and to be an *imago mundi.* And, in fact, as we shall see, houses are held to be at the Center of the world and, on the microcosmic scale, to reproduce the universe. (Eliade, *Sacred* 43)

Eliade then goes on to describe ceremonial houses in a variety of aboriginal cultures that are designed specifically to reproduce the created universe. In New Guinea the "men's house" stands at the center of the village; "its roof represents the celestial vault, the four walls correspond to the four directions of space." Similarly, in an Algonquin sacred lodge, "the roof symbolizes the dome of the sky, the floor represents earth, the four walls the four directions of cosmic space…. The four doors, the four windows, and the four colors signify the four cardinal points." He might as well have added that throughout medieval Europe cathedrals were at the centers of

---

1   Significantly, in some languages, such as Hebrew, "temple" and "house" are the same word.

their villages and had vaulted ceilings to resemble the sky. The symbolism is cross-cultural and uniform: the construction of such sacred spaces "repeats the cosmogony, for [it] represents the world" (Eliade, *Sacred* 46).

Hogwarts Castle is not a temple or a house, nor even, properly speaking, a palace; yet for all that it does enjoy "the prestige of the Center" (Eliade, *Myth* 12), for it is the heart of J. K. Rowling's ethical universe. The Great Hall at Hogwarts has a ceiling that is enchanted to resemble the sky; and indeed this is the first thing Harry sees in his new school:

Harry had never imagined such a strange and splendid place. It was lit by thousands and thousands of candles that were floating in midair over four long tables, where the rest of the students were sitting.... Harry looked upward and saw a velvety black ceiling dotted with stars. He heard Hermione whisper, "It's bewitched to look like the sky outside. I read about it in *Hogwarts, a History*."

It was hard to believe there was a ceiling there at all, and that the Great Hall didn't simply *open on to the heavens*. (*SS* 116–17, my emphasis)

It would be easy to dismiss this as simply a poetically lovely vision of what a school cafeteria could be under the best of circumstances. One does certainly get the impression that the ceiling's resemblance to the living sky is more for entertainment and weather reports than cosmic linkups, and thus that the Great Hall has none of the functions of a sacred center.

And yet the Hall's association with the sky is portentous, for the sky is by its nature transcendent. The traditional person "places himself at the Center of the World and by the same token at the source of absolute reality, as close as possible to the opening that ensures him communication with the gods" (Eliade, *Sacred* 65): It follows that the point of access would exist in or represent the natural world, for "the cosmos is a divine creation; coming from the hands of the gods, the world is impregnated with sacredness" (Eliade, *Sacred* 116). In all of Creation, the sky may be the most awe-inspiring facet:

Simple contemplation of the celestial vault already provokes a religious experience. The sky shows itself to be infinite, transcendent. It is pre-eminently the "wholly other" than the little represented by man and his environment. Transcendence is revealed by simple awareness of infinite height. "Most high" spontaneously becomes an attribute of divinity. (Eliade, *Sacred* 118)

Although Rowling is deliberately vague about physical space in Hogwarts,[1] the Great Hall does appear to be at the center of the building; we can reasonably suppose it to be roughly equidistant from each of the four dormitories, since everyone comes there several times a day. Thus the Great Hall is at the center of the four houses, a stand-in for the four cardinal directions; and each of the houses is represented by a table in the Hall itself, emphasizing the association and the centrality of the structure. Moreover, it is the place where all four houses gather to engage in that most basic of communal activities, breaking bread together. It is also the place where generations meet, as well as social classes: along with students, professors gather here to eat, as do visiting dignitaries. Finally, all school-wide celebrations take place here, from Halloween to Christmas to end-of-term Feasts. The Great Hall is unequivocally the social center of the school, and thus of Harry's world.

The Great Hall also represents a moral center. Each of the houses around it is further signaled within it by a table where students sit. Each house, and therefore each conglomerate of students, represents a human trait: Hufflepuff, industry; Ravenclaw, intelligence; Slytherin, ambition; and Gryffindor, courage. The Great Hall is the only place where all these passions mingle. They are what make up the student body. What the characters do with these traits, the choices they make, leads to the events that are played out in and around the school in the cosmic battles between good and evil. The Harry Potter series repeatedly emphasizes that choice is all; that free will leads to actions and actions have consequences for which the actor is fully responsible. Dumbledore himself makes this point throughout the series, but nowhere more clearly than when he tells Harry, "It is our choices, Harry, that show what we truly are, far more than our abilities" (*CoS* 333).

By making the Great Hall the social center of the school, and by making its ceiling a portal to the transcendent heavens, Rowling is

---

1   Staircases and doorways may or may not lead to the expected location, and they "move around a lot" (*SS* 132). At the end of a full year at Hogwarts, Harry and Ron realize they do not know the location of Dumbledore's office (*SS* 267), and they are well into their second year before they even begin to wonder where the Slytherin common room is—and forsooth, it is quite well hidden (*CoS* 217–18).

investing Hogwarts Castle with far greater meaning than is at first evident. In an ethical but completely secular universe, the castle is the stand-in for the temple, the dwelling-place of the gods, the center of the cosmos which is "always the meeting point of the three cosmic regions: heaven, earth, and hell" (Eliade, *Myth* 15). As the Great Hall is the social center of the school we may easily posit that it represents earth, and thus human society. Since it is at the moral center, the Great Hall represents humanity, for ethical decisions are the nexus of human activity in a fantasy.

As for Hell, it too is represented. In *Chamber of Secrets*, Harry, Ron, and Lockheart descend an "endless, slimy, dark slide" (301) to arrive "miles under the school" (302) to rescue Ginny Weasley from Voldemort, represented by Tom Riddle. The Chamber is replete with imagery of the Underworld: the tunnel leading to it is "quiet as the grave," the only sound being the crunching of rats' skulls underfoot (302). The entrance to the Chamber is guarded by two carved serpents (304). the Christian satanic symbol *par excellence*, and Harry must battle a Basilisk, the "king of serpents" (318). The Chamber itself is full of death and near-death, for Ginny is barely alive and Riddle exists only as a lethal memory. In this scene only Harry is alive in the usual sense of the word. Clearly, the roots of the castle descend to a hidden world of the dead. This is as grim a hellscape as any in literature. The castle truly does have its roots in the netherworld and its heart on earth with the living.

To function fully as a sacred center, however, the castle must also provide a link to the heavens along with its stations in earth and hell. This it does in two ways: first, as we have seen, via the enchanted ceiling of the Great Hall; and second, in the person and physical location of Albus Dumbledore. His stature is described as Harry faces Tom Riddle in the Chamber of Secrets:

"Sorry to disappoint you and all that, but the greatest wizard in the world is Albus Dumbledore. Everyone says so. Even when you were strong, you didn't dare try and take over at Hogwarts. Dumbledore saw through you when you were at school and he still frightens you now, wherever you're hiding these days—" (*CoS* 314)

Dumbledore is the force of puissant good that is strong enough to combat the evil incarnate in Voldemort. It is no accident that his first name, Albus, means "white" (Neumann 164), symbolizing purity; nor is it happenstance that his office is in a high tower overlooking the rest of the school. He is the force of moral rectitude that descends from above, the white lord on high.

Small wonder then that Voldemort is soundly defeated whenever he manifests at Hogwarts: he emerges at the center of the cosmic stage, typical for one of his bombast; but it is also the foothills of the cosmic mountain, with full access to the forces which exist chiefly to vanquish him.

Throughout the *Harry Potter* series, Rowling tweaks yet maintains the conventions of high fantasy. Mythology and its archetypes are the backbone of her narrative. Sometimes the expected symbols are altered in their meaning, as with the Portkeys; sometimes they are parodied, as with the Whomping Willow; and sometimes exalted places such as a sacred temple uniting three cosmic realms are simply camouflaged to resemble a school of wizardry and witchcraft. But the symbolic places and objects are always present. Cloaked in humor and whimsy, religious archetypes persist in Rowling's sacred landscape; and it is this painstaking construction of spaces large and small within her Secondary World that allow her to posit a deeper meaning in a realm that already dazzles us with its possibilities.

Works Cited

Colbert, David. *The Magical Worlds of Harry Potter: A Treasury of Myths, Legends, and Fascinating Facts.* New York: Berkley, 2004.

Eliade, Mircea. *The Myth of the Eternal Return; or, Cosmos and History.* Princeton, NJ: Princeton University Press, 1974.

—. *The Sacred and the Profane: The Nature of Religion.* New York: Harcourt Brace Jovanovich, 1959.

Natov, Roni. "Harry Potter and the Extraordinariness of the Ordinary." *The Lion and the Unicorn* 25.2 (2001): 310–27. 24 Apr 2007 <http://muse.jhu.edu/journals/lion_and_the_unicorn/v025/25.2natov.html>.

Neumann, Iver B. "Naturalizing Geography: Harry Potter and the Realms of Muggles, Magic Folks, and Giants." *Harry Potter and International Relations.* Ed. Daniel H. Nexon and Iver B. Neumann. Lanham, Boulder, New York, Toronto, Oxford: Rowman & Littlefield, 2006.

Rowling, J. K. *Harry Potter and the Chamber of Secrets.* New York: Scholastic, 1999.

—. *Harry Potter and the Goblet of Fire.* New York: Scholastic, 2000.

—. *Harry Potter and the Sorcerer's Stone.* New York: Scholastic, 1997.

Tolkien, J. R. R. *Tree and Leaf.* Boston: Houghton Mifflin, 1964.

"Tree of Life." *Wikipedia.* (2007): 9 May 2007 <http://en.wikipedia.org/wiki/Tree_of_life>.

Virole, Benoit. "Harry Potter's Cauldron: The Power of Myth and the Rebirth of the Sacred." *Queen's Quarterly* 111.3 (Fall 2004): p. 371(10). From Expanded Academic ASAP. 17 April 2007 <http://find.galegroup.com/ips/printdoc.do?&prodId=IPS&userGroupName=fst&docId=A1...>.

Haunted Castles and Hidden Rooms: Gothic Spaces and Identity in *Harry Potter*

Karen M. Bayne
Indiana University

"The house," writes Gaston Bachelard in *The Poetics of Space*, "is more than an embodiment of home, it also an embodiment of dreams" (15). The magical dwellings and interstices that lie beneath, between, outside, and behind the everyday spaces of the Muggle world in J. K. Rowling's *Harry Potter* novels represent in a very literal way the embodiment of dreams. When eleven-year-old Harry Potter moves from the tiny cupboard under the stairs at the Dursleys' oppressively normal, middle-class suburban house to the circular dorm room atop the Gryffindor tower of Hogwarts Castle, a space he soon comes to consider his real home, it sets in motion a classic coming-of-age story that is also about the confrontation between good and evil. The spaces of Harry Potter's world highlight the similarities and differences between the mundane and the magic worlds he inhabits. These spaces are where a seemingly ordinary boy is introduced to a larger world that is made accessible to him by his magical heritage and where he has the opportunity to reinvent himself as hero.

"Memories are motionless, and the more securely they are fixed in space, the sounder they are," Bachelard writes; "for a knowledge of intimacy, localization in the spaces of our intimacy is more urgent than determination of dates" (9). Gothic fiction, as Jerrold Hogle, David Punter, and other critics have noted, often explicitly associates various spaces to past events that continue to affect the characters. Memories provide a true link between spaces and identity, a theme that is gradually developed in *Harry Potter* as the events surrounding the deaths of James and Lily Potter at Godric's Hollow are carefully revealed. Harry witnesses important events as though he himself were experiencing them through Dumbledore's magical Pensieve, which allows Harry to access directly the memories of various characters. Harry's determination at the end of *Half-Blood Prince* to finish Voldemort by destroying the remaining Horcruxes is thus built not only from his own personal experiences of Voldemort's evil, particularly the deaths of Sirius, Cedric and his own parents, as well as his encounters with various incarnations of Voldemort, but also from experiences he has shared only through others' memories. Spaces such as the Chamber of Secrets, the Little Hangleton graveyard where Tom Riddle, Sr., is buried, the Shrieking Shack, and the Hall of Prophecies and courtroom at the Ministry of Magic are the sites of events that seem almost inevitably to shape Harry Potter into Voldemort's counter. Indeed, Dumbledore states this openly when he convinces Harry in *Half-Blood Prince* that it is Voldemort's belief in the prophecy that has "made [Harry] the person who would be the most dangerous to him" (*HBP* 309).

The memories associated with these spaces are for Harry both terrible and terrifying. "When thinking of the Gothic novel, a set of characteristics springs readily to mind," writes David Punter in *The Literature of Terror* (1). Gothic fiction places "an emphasis on portraying the terrifying" and insists on "archaic settings [and] a prominent use of the supernatural" as well as deploying "techniques of literary suspense.... Used in this sense, 'Gothic' fiction is the fiction of the haunted castle, of heroines preyed on by unspeakable terrors, of the blackly lowering villain, of ghosts, vampires, monsters and werewolves" (Punter 1). Critic Jerrold Hogle writes,

Though not always as obviously as in *The Castle of Otranto* or *Dracula*, a Gothic tale usually takes place (at least some of the time) in an antiquated or seemingly antiquated space—be it a castle,...a subterranean crypt, a graveyard,...a large old house or theatre, an aging city or urban underworld.... Within this space, or a combination of such spaces, are hidden some secrets from the past (sometimes the recent past) that haunt the characters, psychologically, physically, or otherwise at the main time of the story. (2)

Rowling draws upon the Gothic literary tradition in order to provide a suitably fantastic setting for a world in which, for some people, magic is real. Common spatial elements of Gothic fiction include caves, hidden rooms, haunted castles, dungeons, and secret passageways, all of which appear throughout the *Harry Potter* novels and which provide a suitably fantastic milieu for Rowling's magical world. Mysterious places like Knockturn and Diagon Alleys, Gringotts bank, the Ministry of Magic, and Platform 9¾ lie hidden between, behind, and beneath the spaces of Muggle London and can be accessed only by members of the wizard world. Far off in Scotland, the Hogwarts School of Witchcraft and Wizardry occupies a haunted castle with secret rooms, changeable staircases, turrets, and dungeons, and is surrounded by a dark, scary Forbidden Forest full of magical, dangerous creatures.

As part of an overtly magic world, Rowling's Gothic spaces are not generally as terrifying as those found in many literary Gothic sources. The Gothic spaces of Rowling's magic world can often be accessed through relatively mundane means—dial a phone number to get into the Ministry of Magic via elevator, or take the Hogwarts Express train to Hogsmeade, if you can get onto Platform 9¾. There is usually a magic portal or barrier that only people with magical knowledge and ability can pass. Hogwarts Castle itself is simultaneously a mysterious Gothic space and an everyday boarding-school, a genuine haunted castle rendered mostly unthreatening by familiarity. Hogwarts isn't scary in the true Gothic-terror sense, although Professor Snape's Potions class certainly terrifies Harry. Snape's classroom could be any Muggle chemistry lab classroom— but it *is* in the dungeon! While many of the Gothic spaces of Harry Potter exhibit elements of both the magical and the Muggle, Rowling generally uses these spaces in much the same way that traditional Gothic literature does; in them the hero confronts evil (as personified by Lord Voldemort), gains knowledge, overcomes adversity, and ultimately defines himself.

Novels provide insight into imagined worlds and selves. In this essay, I will examine the ways that Rowling's imagined Muggle and magical spaces influence the construction of her protagonist's identity. Through seven books we follow Harry Potter as he grows up and learns about the wizarding world and who he is—not just the Dursleys' unwanted orphaned nephew nor an all-powerful wizard who will single-handedly defeat Lord Voldemort, but instead a complex character whose identity formation must accommodate many aspects of personality, ability, experience, and desire. In the novels, Harry's explorations and personal experiences, both magical and mundane, contribute significantly to the development of his self-identity, as do the implicit assumptions of the wizarding world. Harry, after all, is the Boy Who Lived, and bears the identifying lightning-shaped scar on his forehead.

Philosopher Charles Taylor provides an approach to thinking about the "self" and "identity" as something that Harry Potter must shape and construct for himself by exploring his own Muggle and magic worlds and by interacting with the people in those two spheres. For Taylor these terms are not wholly identical to the "self" and "identity" of cognitive psychology or sociology; the sense of self or the conviction of identity, he writes, "is a definition of oneself, partly implicit, which a human agent must be able to elaborate in the course of becoming an adult and...must continue to redefine through his or her life" (139). Taylor's understanding of identity thus encompasses Harry's coming-of-age story; the real key to understanding who Harry Potter is, or will become, is located in his ongoing exploration of self and the formation of his identity as a young wizard. Harry is Sorted into Gryffindor when he arrives at Hogwarts, which establishes a set of initial character criteria: Gryffindors, sings the Sorting Hat, are "brave at heart / Their daring, nerve, and chivalry / Set Gryffindors apart" (*SS* 118). Dumbledore points out to Harry in *Chamber of Secrets* that "our choices ... show what we truly are" and adds that Harry's fervent wish while being Sorted *not* to be a Slytherin means that he is truly a Gryffindor (*CoS* 333). In *Goblet of Fire*, Harry's goal of becoming an Auror after Hogwarts represents a further redefinition of his identity and looks ahead to the next phase of his maturation. Of course, we have yet to see what will happen in *Deathly Hallows*— Rowling may take Harry's character in some other direction entirely.

Taylor also writes about identity as "something personal, potentially eccentric or original, and consequently to some extent something invented or assumed" (140). Vernon Dursley's preoccupation with drills and wizards' preoccupation with extravagantly magical tents at the Quidditch World Cup campsite show that Rowling's Muggle and magic folk represent perfectly the eccentricities of individual selves. Not incidentally, this dichotomy also deals with the important theme of being different. While the wizards and witches in their brightly colored cloaks and pointy hats may look odd to Muggle eyes, Rowling's Muggle characters are just as weird—look at the Dursleys' materialistic mania for maintaining the appearance of a perfect middle-class English suburban lifestyle.[1] This seems to drive their abusive treatment of Harry Potter, their significantly "different" nephew.

Harry's story is, of course, about growing up, and we can think of the novels as explicitly tracing his identity formation, a process that begins with Rubeus Hagrid's stunning assertion, "Harry—yer a wizard," a statement which forever alters the path of who Harry will become (*SS* 50). In *Harry Potter and the Sorcerer's Stone*, Harry's first contact[2] with the magical world takes place on his eleventh birthday in a "miserable little shack" perched on a "large rock way out at sea," where the Dursleys have fled in an effort to avoid the deluge of Hogwarts admissions letters (*SS* 43–44). In an entirely Gothic scenario, the door of the drafty, smelly shack is broken down violently by a hairy half-giant in the middle of the night. The cold, dank space of the Hut-on-the-Rock is where Harry first learns about his own heritage and suddenly perceives the tremendous possibility of a future very different from what he has always imagined. Harry

felt quite sure there had been a horrible mistake. A wizard? Him? How could he possibly be? He'd spent his life being clouted by Dudley, and bullied by Aunt Petunia and Uncle Vernon; if he was really a wizard, why hadn't they been turned into warty toads every time they'd tried to lock him in his cupboard? (*SS* 57)

Harry's world changes suddenly upon learning that he is a wizard, and as Hagrid lights a fire, cooks sausages, produces a birthday cake, and gives Dudley a curly pig's tail, the dismal shack is transformed into a magical space that hints at the wonderful possibilities yet to come.

---

1   The Dursleys' mania for excelling at being suburban—indistinguishable from their "normal" neighbors—is perhaps best exemplified by their willingness to head off to the fictitious All-England Best-Kept Suburban Lawn Competition, after being notified that they have been short-listed for a prize (*OotP* 48).

2   Although he has often met witches and wizards, Harry Potter has been kept in ignorance of his magical heritage and indeed of the entire wizarding world. Eleven-year-old Harry's meeting with Hagrid therefore represents the first real contact he has had with the wizarding world since the night his parents were killed by Lord Voldemort.

Harry and Hagrid travel to London the next morning, where another major shift in Harry's definition of self occurs when he begins to learn about his own place in the magical world. He's astonished to find that he's a celebrity. Harry Potter is not just another juvenile wizard about to enter school, but is famous among wizardkind for having survived Voldemort's attack. Harry also begins to perceive the separation of the familiar Muggle world from that of the magic world, as when Hagrid gets stuck in the ticket barrier on the Tube and has difficulty dealing with ordinary English (Muggle) money. Walking down the "ordinary street full of ordinary people," Harry wonders whether there are really "piles of wizard gold buried miles beneath them" in the Gringotts bank vaults and whether there are truly "shops that [sell] spell books and broomsticks" in London (*SS* 68). He notices that most people—those who are not magic—cannot even see The Leaky Cauldron because their attention slides right past it. Soon, however, Hagrid leads Harry into an unprepossessing courtyard behind The Leaky Cauldron, taps the appropriate brick three times with his umbrella-wand, and opens "an archway onto a cobbled street" called Diagon Alley, a completely magical space where all manner of wizarding items are available, from magic wands to broomsticks (*SS* 71).

While the magic spaces in *Harry Potter* are often squeezed between the spaces of the Muggle world, they are always connected to and part of it as well. The Muggle Prime Minister is kept apprised of important magical events through the portrait permanently affixed to his office wall. The Floo network provides instantaneous, if somewhat sooty, transport between any linked fireplace in the system, and is the preferred means of travel for underage wizards who cannot yet Apparate, a rite of passage reserved for those over 17. The Weasleys arrive at the Dursleys' fireplace via the Floo network, and Harry learns something of the dangerous dark side of the magic world when he mispronounces the address of Diagon Alley ("diagonally") and ends up in Knockturn Alley. Getting off one stop too late and ending up in a rather dodgy part of town parallels similar Muggle subway system experiences, but Rowling uses this unnerving occasion to introduce Harry to some darker aspects of the magic world, such as the Malfoys' prejudice against Muggleborn witches and wizards and several dangerous Dark artifacts. And although owl post provides superior distribution of written correspondence, in the absence of a Muggle telephone network Harry and Sirius Black have to converse via Floo network fireplaces as disembodied "talking heads." Indeed, the spaces of the magical world are dynamic and seemingly immune to the laws of Muggle physics. Paired Vanishing Cabinets link spaces and magically transport objects. The Knight Bus travels at breakneck speed through the streets of London and squeezes impossibly between double-decker buses, while Sirius Black's family house at number twelve, Grimmauld Place, fits somehow between the adjacent Muggle properties and is full of unpleasant reminders of Dark magic. Harry's sometimes frightening experiences in these new magical spaces further expand and complicate his development of self.

Portals like the Diagon Alley brick archway are another important element in Rowling's texts. They link the magic and Muggle worlds, yet keep the wizarding world separate and hidden. (As an aside, I've always wondered how a Muggle-born witch like Hermione Granger manages to get into Diagon Alley with her parents or onto Platform 9¾ after receiving her Hogwarts letter. Perhaps it included detailed instructions, but if so, why doesn't Muggle-raised Harry receive similar help?) Rowling also sneaks in certain elements of British culture: gold Galleons, which Harry first sees at Gringotts, are thinly-disguised British £1 coins, while the Hogwarts Express is, as Uncle Vernon points out, a "funny way to get to a wizards' school" (*SS* 89). Later books introduce Portkeys, ordinary-looking items that have been enchanted to transport everyone touching the object to a set destination instantaneously, although nearby Muggles must be protected from witnessing the sudden appearances of magical folk. In *Sorcerer's Stone,* Harry arrives at King's Cross Station with no idea how to get onto Platform 9¾ to catch the Hogwarts Express. Fortunately, Mrs. Weasley assists him with the directive to "walk straight at the barrier between platforms nine and ten. Don't stop and don't be scared you'll crash into it, that's very important," she says kindly (*SS* 93). The mental component of using these magical portals is apparently as important as inherent magical ability, whether from attentive concentration or specific knowledge of which brick to tap, wall to walk through, or phone number to dial.

Hogwarts Castle itself is the most important of the Gothic spaces in *Harry Potter.* "Perched atop a high mountain on the other side [of the lake], its windows sparkling in the starry sky," Harry sees "a vast castle with many turrets and towers" when he arrives for his first year at school (*SS* 111). Haunted castles are a stock item in Gothic fiction, and the more elaborate and terrifying they are, the better. Horace Walpole's *The Castle of Otranto* (1764) is commonly accepted as the first Gothic novel and features a suitably dramatic haunted castle. The novel's subtitle, "A Gothic Story," gave the entire genre its name (Clery 21), although as Hogle points out, "Gothic fiction is hardly 'Gothic' at all," being an "entirely post-medieval and even post-Renaissance phenomenon" (1). In *Otranto,* "an enormous helmet, an hundred times more large than any casque ever made for human being" falls into the castle's courtyard, crushing Conrad, the son and heir of Manfred, the prince of Otranto and setting up the novel's main plotline (Walpole 52). *Otranto,* Punter claims, "originates what was to become perhaps the most prevalent theme in Gothic fiction: the revisiting of the sins of the fathers upon their children" (46).[1] The castle of Otranto contains many of the key elements that characterize later Gothic-fiction castles,[2] such as battlements, towers, secret passages, ghostly apparitions, trap doors, hidden locks, subterranean caverns, and portraits that move and speak, surely precursors of the lively figures in the images in Rowling's wizard world. Clery writes, "The castle [of Otranto] is central to the fable and seems to have a life of its own. It traps and conceals; its walls frame almost all the main events.... Its alien modes of ingress and egress give rise to the prototypical scene of Isabella's desperate flight from the villain through the under-ground tunnel and to the display of chivalric pageantry when Prince Frederick arrives at its gates" (Clery 26). Hogwarts is similarly central to the action in *Harry Potter* and possesses many secret underground rooms and passages, most of

---

1   This is, of course, an important theme in *Harry Potter*, as evidenced not only in Harry's fervent desire to learn about his father, James Potter, but also in his growing awareness of his father as an individual who was flawed and human. Knowledge of James Potter's poor treatment of his fellow student Severus Snape becomes increasingly important as Harry forms his own identity. Tom Marvolo Riddle's metamorphosis into Lord Voldemort closely parallels the traditional Gothic in its emphasis on the sins of Voldemort's Muggle father.

2   Like Hogwarts, the castle of Otranto is also a residence. However, the spaces foregrounded in Walpole's novel are the castle's great public spaces, the battlements and courtyard, and the subterranean cavern and its secret passage. Although the women of the castle retreat to the comfort of their private apartments, the overall effect is of the castle as oppressive and terrifying.

which have been discovered by Fred and George Weasley; these figure prominently in Harry's battles with Voldemort as well as when he sneaks out to Hogsmeade to enjoy time with his friends and perhaps a butterbeer at The Three Broomsticks. In book six, Headmaster Albus Dumbledore falls to his death from the top of the Astronomy Tower, lending the castle's architecture a more sinister connotation.

J. K. Rowling wrote in an online interview that she visualizes Hogwarts as "[a] huge, rambling, quite scary-looking castle, with a jumble of towers and battlements. Like the Weasleys' house, it isn't a building that Muggles could build, because it is supported by magic." Harry soon learns that the castle is indeed a magical structure:

> There were a hundred and forty-two staircases at Hogwarts: wide, sweeping ones; narrow, rickety ones; some that led somewhere different on a Friday; some with a vanishing step halfway up that you had to remember to jump. Then there were the doors that wouldn't open unless you asked politely, or tickled them in exactly the right place, and doors that weren't really doors at all, but solid walls just pretending. (*SS* 131–32)

This castle almost has a personality of its own. Harry continues to discover new spaces within and under it throughout his years at Hogwarts.

In a unique twist on Gothic fiction, though, many of the rooms of this castle are turned into the familiar spaces of home and school. For all of its mystery, Hogwarts is also a secure and comfortable environment. Castle spaces like the Room of Requirement, where Dumbledore's Army meets, are the setting for an important phase in Harry's development of self. He discovers that he is, after all, pretty good at Defense Against the Dark Arts, and can teach the D.A. members these skills as well. The Great Hall with its enchanted ceiling is where most of the school's social activities occur, and it thus plays an important role as Harry develops lasting friendships with his fellow students. The Gryffindor common room is described as a "cozy, round room full of squashy armchairs," while the boys' dorm room is high atop a tower and contains comfy four-poster beds hung with red velvet curtains (*SS* 130). Harry soon thinks of Hogwarts as his true home and dreads returning to the Dursleys' during school holidays because the magical world is far more inviting and friendly than Little Whinging. Harry spends Christmases at school and finds that even the normal trappings of a Muggle Christmas are bigger and better at Hogwarts, where they are enhanced by Professor Flitwick's magic charms. Furthermore, Harry develops important friendships with Ron and Hermione and discovers for the first time in his life what it is like to be loved and accepted.

The process of constructing an identity is "partly implicit" because self-definition and the formation of identity are matters of negotiation with and recognition by others, and are not accomplished by the individual alone (Taylor 142). Hermione, Ron and the Weasley family, Dumbledore, McGonagall, Sirius, Lupin, Hagrid, and even Snape, Umbridge, and the Malfoys are thus important figures as Harry grows and develops as a person. Each of these individuals contributes friendship, antagonism, love, or guidance, influences that shape Harry's self-identity. Another example of how other people impact Harry's continuing identity formation can be seen in his success as the youngest Seeker on the Gryffindor Quidditch team in a century. For the first time in his life Harry is part of a team in which all members work together for success, and his Quidditch prowess also means acceptance and success in Gryffindor. While Quidditch is one of the most positive aspects of Harry's Hogwarts experience, his visions in the Mirror of Erised show that his most significant desire is to be part of a family. Eventually, this desire enables him to obtain the Philosopher's Stone and hide it from Voldemort because Harry can see the Stone in the Mirror but doesn't want to use it—its properties cannot fulfill Harry's hopes and dreams.

Finally, the Gothic spaces of Rowling's novels are brilliantly imagined places that allow Harry Potter to imagine a self within the story of his own life. "Narrative, a sense of then and now … [confirms] Charles Taylor's view that we make sense of our lives in narrative forms, as quests" (Taylor 1989, 51–52, qtd. in Amigoni 233). Harry's quest, then, is as much about finding himself as it is about defeating Lord Voldemort.

Works Cited

Amigoni, David. "Gothic Choirs and Gothic Fictions: Habitus, Moral Space and Identity in the Autobiographies of Ruskin and Newman." *Mapping the Self: Space, Identity, Discourse in British Auto/Biography.* Ed. and intro. Frédéric Regard. Pref. and epilogue Geoffrey Wall. Saint-Etienne, France: Publications de l'Université de Saint-Etienne, 2003. 231–46.

Bachelard, Gaston. *The Poetics of Space.* Trans. Maria Jolas. Fwd. John R. Stilgoe. Boston: Beacon Press, 1994.

Clery, E. J. "The Genesis of 'Gothic' Fiction." *The Cambridge Companion to Gothic Fiction.* Ed. Jerrold E. Hogle. Cambridge: Cambridge UP, 2002. 21–39.

Hogle, Jerrold E. Introduction. *The Cambridge Companion to Gothic Fiction.* Ed. Jerrold E. Hogle. Cambridge: Cambridge UP, 2002. 1–20.

Punter, David. *The Literature of Terror: A History of Gothic Fictions from 1765 to the Present Day.* 2nd rev. ed. Vol. 1. London: Longman, 1996.

Rowling, J[oanne] K[athleen]. *Harry Potter and the Chamber of Secrets.* Illus. Mary GrandPré. New York: Levine-Scholastic, 1999.

—. *Harry Potter and the Order of the Phoenix.* Illus. Mary GrandPré. New York: Levine-Scholastic, 2003.

—. *Harry Potter and the Sorcerer's Stone.* Illus. Mary GrandPré. New York: Levine-Scholastic, 1997.

—. Interview. Scholastic.com. 3 Feb. 2000. 15 May 2007. <http://www.scholastic.com/harrypotter/author/transcript1.htm>.

Taylor, Charles. "Modernity and Identity." *Schools of Thought: Twenty-five Years of Interpretive Social Science.* Eds. Joan W. Scott and Debra Keates. Princeton: Princeton UP, 2001. 139–53.

Walpole, Horace. *The Castle of Otranto. Three Gothic Novels.* Ed. Peter Fairclough. Intro. Mario Praz. Harmondsworth: Penguin, 1972. 37–148.

HARRY POTTER AS SOUTHERN GOTHIC?: NATURE AS SIGNIFIER IN FANTASY AND GOTHIC FICTION

Vincent Moore
Tiffin University

Early gothic literature made a bugbear of science. Works such as *Frankenstein* and *Dr. Jekyll and Mr. Hyde* showed how science can release the monstrous from the individual and into the world. In some ways, it's understandable that science was so fearsome; look at what it's created. We have super-viruses, weapons, and even terrifying everyday technology such as the Internet—there is a lot to fear. One of the early gothic devices was the mad scientist, and now a new gothic signifier is present, and it is dependent on our familiarity with science and technology. Nature, which once was seen as purifying and bringing one closer to the creator, is the bugbear of neo-gothic because of our lack of familiarity to it. Of course, this is nothing new, as it's been a trope in Southern Gothic for decades.

The *Harry Potter* series is neo-gothic in many ways. As Sherry Truffin pointed out in her presentation, *Harry Potter* is gothic in its use of the schoolhouse as the castle. Harry is caught between the technological world and the magical world. As an intelligent character, Harry is not frightened by the magical or the Muggle worlds. Nevertheless, Rowling, instead of making Harry master of technology and magic, makes him a student of the latter while coming from a world of the former. And since he's young, he's uninformed about the different milieu; therefore, both have their mysteries.

There are many aspects of gothic literature. There are many forms and many characteristics to each. Gothic literature is a type of fiction that developed in the eighteenth century with authors such as Horace Walpole, Ann Radcliffe and, later, Edgar Allan Poe and Charles Dickens. "It was characterized by horror, violence, supernatural effects, and medieval elements, usually set against a background of gothic architecture, especially a gloomy and isolated castle" (*Benet's* 417). We see this in *Harry Potter* from start to finish.

In addition, a distinction between horror and terror occurs in gothic studies. Horror, in modern entertainment, is explicit. It is the attack of the monster or the knife blade and the blood that follows. This is a common sight in splatter films from *Texas Chainsaw Massacre* (1974) to *Saw* (2004) and *Hostel* (2005). The horror there is of the knife piercing the flesh. The gothic is more about terror—the fear or dread of something about to happen. It is the moment before the monster attacks, when, in the mind of the audience, it could just as easily jump from the page or the screen and attack the audience as it could the characters in the fiction. Terror is created as a mood by the use of suggestion, shadows, and unrecognizable shapes. Alfred Hitchcock's film, *Psycho* (1960), shows this in the famed shower scene. There is the suggestion of both nudity and the stabbing, but all that is seen is Janet Leigh's shoulder and blood (chocolate syrup, actually) whirlpooling down the drain— nevertheless, the suggestion is so strong that the scene was sent back to Hitchcock to be recut. He did not touch it but sent it back as it was, and the film board allowed it the second time.

Terror, in the gothic, doesn't surprise the audience by being obvious, but is just around the corner, and we know it is coming— we just don't know what. Terror is the fear of the unknown, while horror is shock at something that is violent, gory, and all too obvious.

In *Harry Potter*, of course, there is no specific horror. We are given moments of terror as something unknown approaches, but not the gore and violence that is horror. An example of the unknown making its appearance is in *Sorcerer's Stone*:

But he hadn't walked five paces before a high voice spoke, though Quirrell wasn't moving his lips.
"He lies…. He lies…"

"Potter, come back here!" Quirrell shouted. "Tell me the truth! What did you just see?"

"Let me speak to him…face-to-face…"

…Petrified, [Harry] watched as Quirrell reached up and began to unwrap his turban. What was going on? The turban fell away. Quirrell's head looked strangely small without it. Then he turned slowly on the spot.

Harry would have screamed, but he couldn't make a sound.

The reader is put into Harry's point of view and finds out after Harry does what is on the back of Quirrell's head. Techniques such as this increase the suspense and thus the terror. The scene would have contained an emotional impact if the reader and Harry found out at the same time, but Rowling chose to give the reader an extra sentence to build up the suspense.

Southern Gothic is an American twist on the gothic. Incorrectly, "The term 'Southern Gothic' had become something very like a synonym—or a cliché—for modern Southern literature" (Donaldson 567). It is more than that. Southern gothic puts the focus on the South, incorporating much of the macabre that gothic fiction does but locating it in narratives that focus on regional and family history, including the Civil War, issues such as slavery and religion. It is best known from the work of Flannery O'Connor, William Faulkner, Carson McCullers, and Eudora Welty.

In addition to the subject matter, Southern Gothic has elements in common with Magic Realism. Magic Realism is a writing style that is often a product of hot, third-world countries and is characterized by when "contrasting elements—such as the supernatural, myth, dream, fantasy—invade the realism and change the whole basis of the art" (Harman & Holman 304). Examples can be found in the works of Gabriel García Marquez, Eduardo Galeano, and Salman Rushdie, to name a few.

The elements Southern Gothic shares with Magic Realism are the heat and a surreal view of the world. In Southern Gothic, just as in Magic Realism, everything looks as if it is seen through a hazy lens, or the heat of the deep South or many tropical countries. Nature in these places is more frightening and mysterious. From the dense jungles in tropical Third World countries to the shadowy bayous of the American South, nature is full of strange, mysterious, and dangerous beasts.

Southern Gothic and Magic Realism make use of several common attributes that are also found in *Harry Potter*. Both Southern Gothic and Magic Realism take advantage of the oppressive heat of the southern and tropical climes, which leads to a hazy, unreal atmosphere in which the unnatural can thrive. Both show nature to be dark and mysterious. The *Harry Potter* novels, while not set in a tropical climate, still use the same gothic and magic realism tropes of nature's being dark and mysterious and of oppressive heat leading to a hallucinatory ambience. Many scenes are seen through fog, and Harry himself is prone to visions in Professor Trelawney's overheated attic classroom.

While *Frankenstein* and *Dr. Jekyll and Mr. Hyde* show the terrors of science, establishing science as a gothic trope, contemporary literature is in a world that is more urban and suburban. The unknown, then, is not everyday technology (although Stephen King makes such things as a car, a word processor, or an exercise bike fit into the gothic mold); it is what we are unfamiliar with—nature.

For people used to the civilized world, the unfamiliar beasts and even plants found in nature can be terrifying. As an example, when I was teaching at a university in upstate New York, many students came from New York City. One day they were talking about the mysterious howls they'd heard the night before. It was likely a coyote, but the speculation was of a wolf and even werewolf—and none of the students was at all interested in going into the woods to see that there was nothing to fear, even in the daytime. They believed rattlesnakes, crazed hillbillies, and other monsters lived there. The local students thought this was funny, but I wondered how frightened they would be in Harlem after dark.

In *Harry Potter*, the wizarding world and the Muggle world show different aspects of nature, and their differences show the differences between reality and the gothic world. The Muggle world's use of nature is tight and controlled. Aunt Petunia (even her name is a cultivated flower) conforms her garden to her wishes, and at the beginning of *Order of the Phoenix*, the Dursleys are lured away from home with the promise of an award at a best lawn contest. The Dursleys, who represent the worst of the Muggle world, live on Privet Drive, and a privet, or privet hedge, is a species of evergreen shrub, the *Ligustrum vulgare*. Privet hedges are used for privacy (note the similarity to the word "private"). From the second page of

Sorcerer's Stone, we are shown the intrusion of nature, from a cat (McGonagall) to owls. And from there, nature conspires against the Dursleys and their attempts at control.

The boa constrictor in *Sorcerer's Stone* renders Uncle Vernon almost speechless in anger. The many owl-delivered letters force him to vacate his properly cared-for home and take his family to a shack on an island. This turns into a very bad idea, since it is under attack by nature in the form of a storm, and Hagrid finds Harry with the Dursleys.

Hagrid is another example of the connection between nature and supernatural that is so very apparent in the gothic. In a way, he is a hybrid between nature and something beyond human. He is, we are told, half giant and half human, but we also see him in his moleskin coat, and through his role as groundskeeper and later Professor of Care of Magical Creatures. His appearance to the Dursleys is terrifying, but he soon shows Harry that he's a friend. Hagrid continues in this liminal space between natural and supernatural in several ways, from his residence to his love for odd animals.

Other hybrids, such as centaurs, hippogriffs, werewolves, and Animagi, populate the series. Nature is not predictable, nor is it under human control, especially when it is part of unusual, supernatural hybrids, as Dolores Umbridge found when confronting centaurs in their forest.

In addition to the Dursleys and other humans, Harry must deal with nature being mysterious and threatening. At Hogwarts, from the Whomping Willow to the Haunted Forest, nature is at odds with the wizarding world. Hagrid is a human/nature connector, and Professor Sprout teaches the students to be cautious in the greenhouse, but when they must go to the Haunted Forest in *Sorcerer's Stone*, they find dark and scary things there. Later, when they enter the forest in *Chamber of Secrets*, they are almost killed by the spiders. In *Order of the Phoenix*, more chaos is introduced into the forest, as Grawp is kept there, and we find that the invisible Thestrals roam freely in the woods.

In a more mundane example of nature being terrifying even to the wizarding world, at the Weasleys' Burrow the children dispose of garden gnomes, which are a common garden problem; if one is not careful, one could get bitten by one. Mandrake roots scream and the children wear earplugs when transplanting them. And Blast-Ended Skrewts…well, Blast-Ended Skrewts.

Natural objects aren't the only things that are used as gothic devices as well, which is seen most explicitly in *Harry Potter and the Chamber of Secrets*. Technology becomes unstable in the enchanted car. The car is not gothic when all it does is fly, but when it becomes feral and rescues Harry and Ron from giant spiders, it displays the same unpredictability that the rest of nature does.

Locations other than the haunted forest and Hogwarts also have a connection to nature in a mysterious way. The Shrieking Shack, which stands at the edge of Hogsmeade, is another hybrid of the world-under-control and the chaos that is nature. It is a locus of great mystical energy, although not the hauntings that are its reputation. Instead, the secret passage to it is guarded by the Whomping Willow; it is a place where Professor Lupin would change to his werewolf self and where his unregistered Animagus friends would change as well.

These different perceptions of and reactions to nature not only show the difference between fantasy and reality, but they also show the world that is desired. In reality, outside of the books, humanity likes its nature kept in order—we mow our lawns, put up fences, and tear down forests. A moose or bear in a suburb is enough to make the local news. When most people are exposed to nature in the wild, it can be unnerving and even frightening. Southern gothic fiction depends on and is inspired by this fear. The world of Harry Potter likewise uses these same techniques to show the difference between the real (Muggle) world and the fantasy world of wizards.

The classic pattern found in gothic literature of the innocent person being trapped in a mysterious mansion, or incarcerated in a dungeon, or lost on the foggy moors, is found many times in the *Harry Potter* series. Harry is the epitome of the lost child. He is orphaned, beset by many evil forces, and ignorant of the rules of his world. Masse argues that the gothic stages, in her words, "what Freud calls the beating fantasy, in which a spectator watches someone being hurt by a dominant other" (3).[1] In *Harry Potter*, in

---

1   "A Child Is Being Beaten" (1919) deals with the theoretical problem of how pleasure and suffering become linked. Freud explores the childhood beating fantasy (which is often accompanied by sexual arousal), its transformational stages, the changing cast of protagonists, and the differences between boys and girls in the sequences and meanings of the fantasy.

addition to the people who are trying to hurt the young protagonist, the natural world is lined up against him, ready to kill.

Rowling's use of nature in the series creates a tone that is sometimes Southern Gothic, sometimes Magic Realism, and always fantastic. Her use of terror as a method to increase the tension of the story is supported by the gothic surroundings, from the natural to the wizarding world. Harry Potter is at the mercy of not only of He Who Must Be Named, but also of nature, which often has no name, merely a description.

Works Cited

Benet's Reader's Encyclopedia. 4th ed. Edited by Bruce Murphy. New York: HarperCollins, 1996.

Donaldson, Susan V. "Making a Spectacle: Welty, Faulkner, and Southern Gothic." *Mississippi Quarterly: The Journal of Southern Cultures*, 50(4) (Fall 1997): 567–83.

Harmon, William, and C. Hugh Holman. *A Handbook to Literature*, 7th ed. Upper Saddle River, NJ: Prentice Hall, 1996.

Hogle, Jerrold E. "Romanticism and the 'New Gothic'." *Gothic Studies* 3(1) (April 2001): 1–7.

Masse, Michelle A. *In the Name of Love: Women, Masochism, and the Gothic.* Ithaca: Cornell University Press, 1992.

HARRY POTTER AND THE
GOBLET OF COLONIALISM

Tracy Douglas

At the close of the millennium, J. K. Rowling's *Harry Potter* franchise burst onto the scene, immediately classified as children's fantasy fiction and marked as heir to J. M. Barrie and C. S. Lewis. *Potter* influenced culture by spurring Halloween costumes and feature films, introducing new slang into the lexicon, and inspiring entries on the free Internet encyclopedia, Wikipedia.org. While some critics study *Potter* in relation to popular culture, it should also be considered within the scope of the entire British canon and the societal implications of the novels. In Edward Said's framework,[1] postcolonialism exposes one part of the British canon's history and illuminates where the series rates in the canon, as it reveals the ideal of the hero's national identity and objectifies the foreigner. With postcolonialism in mind, an examination of *Harry Potter and the Goblet of Fire* illustrates colonialist underpinnings of British society, positioning Harry as the embodiment of the heroic British identity while contrasting him with continental European and non-European foreigners by exoticizing and demonizing the "other." In a social commentary on the British cultural and literary imagination, Rowling employs colonialist language and representations to contrast a construction of national identity connected with the Ministry of Magic's *status quo* white, aristocratic Britain against Dumbledore's vision of unity in an emerging British multi-cultural melting pot.

---

1 Edward Said, *Orientalism* (London: Routledge & Kegan Paul.,1978).

Decolonization and Postcolonialism: Theory in Historical Context

Postcolonialism concerns itself with examining representations of the dominant colonizer and powerless colonized, but in order to fully understand the theory and its relationship to *Harry Potter*, some historical context needs to be provided. Decolonization was a twentieth-century phenomenon across Europe after the end of the Second World War, which left the British Empire's public with a loss of identity because the nation's power on the international stage was limited by the loss of its colonial possessions.[1] Immigrants from former colonies came to the mother country to find work, which created fears of white British population decline because the formerly colonized had come to haunt the colonizer.[2] As the twenty-first century began in Britain with an emphasis on multi-culturalism, the Commission into the Future of Multi-Ethnic Britain published a report suggesting that the conception of British identity "is widely understood [to be] racially coded" to indicate that "non-whites do not belong."[3] Half a century after decolonization, some parts of the British cultural imagination remain colonized, and it was Edward Said's literary theory that exposed the colonialist tendencies of British writers.

Edward Said began postcolonial theory in the midst of decolonization in 1978 with the publication of *Orientalism*. According to Peter Barry in *Beginning Theory*, Said shows how Europeans imposed stereotypes upon non-European subjects.[4] Postcolonial theory exposes "representations of the non-European as exotic or immoral 'Other'" in Western literature, giving the colonial subject a sexualized or demonized identity.[5] Colonialism constructs an "other" to define against an idea of national identity. Barry writes that Said's reading of Jane Austen's *Mansfield Park* shows a latent colonialism that can be found in works that are not expressly about colonization. In Austen's novel, Sir Thomas owns an

1 Mark Mazower, "Democracy Transformed: Western Europe 1950–75," in *Dark Continent: Europe's Twentieth Century* (New York: Vintage Books, 1998), 292–93.
2 *Ibid.*, 323.
3 Alexander MacLeod, "What's in a name? Maybe a lot, if you're 'British'," *Christian Science Monitor* 92, no. 226 (2000).
4 Peter Barry, "Postcolonial Criticism," in *Beginning Theory* (Manchester: Manchester University Press, 2002), 193.
5 *Ibid.*, 194.

estate in the Caribbean that helps maintain his British estate, and this illustrates how colonialism appears in texts that are not typically considered to be colonialist.[1] Rowling's text can be viewed as similar to Austen's because fantasy literature is not usually associated with colonialism, yet representations reminiscent of colonialism are apparent in *Harry Potter*. The legacy of empire and Oriental representations remains in the British literary imagination. Rowling's status as an heir to colonialist Joseph Conrad comes shining through in the presentations of the dominant British hero against the exotic "other" as sexual and immoral in *Harry Potter and the Goblet of Fire*.

Enter the Boy Wizard Hero

The title character of *Harry Potter* is positioned as the embodiment of the British dominant hero, as demonstrated with his name and his actions, creating a hero to define against an "other." Harry's name is tied to British royalty because he shares his name with the current Prince Harry. His name is also the nickname of Henry V, who was part of the Tudor dynasty immortalized by Shakespeare. This connection gives the name a distinctly British flavor. The name, which originates from Middle English "Herry," is a nickname for Henry and was used as a character name by canonical British authors Geoffrey Chaucer, John Milton and William Shakespeare.[2] That Rowling chooses to name her central character "Harry" points to how she is following in the British literary tradition. With Harry's British identity established, he can step into the role of hero, defending the realm against evil outsiders.

It is Harry's actions more than anything that serve to identify him as a hero in the mold of British knights and kings and that set up the differences in nationalities. His heroics as he battles the dragon in the fourth novel illuminate ways in which the English hero is pitted against the outside invader, which is a common theme in the British canon reminiscent of early works such as *Sir Gawain and the Green Knight*.[3] The patron saint of England, St. George, is most famous for slaying a dragon, a feat so daring that many artists depict

---

1   *Ibid.*, 200.
2   "Harry," *Oxford English Dictionary* (Oxford: Oxford University Press, 2005). <http://dictionary.oed.com>.
3   J. K. Rowling, *Harry Potter and the Goblet of Fire* (New York: Scholastic, 2000), 353.

him as so doing.[1] Harry slays a dragon, marking him as equal with the patron saint of his land. His dragon is a Hungarian Horntail, forcing him to defeat a dragon that bears the name of a foreign country.[2] Harry's victory displays his heroic identity as dominant; he has power over the dragon and others. In addition, Harry's adventures are part of the Triwizard Tournament, which is a competition among the European schools of wizardry. It creates a confrontation between England and mainland Europe, but it is described as "a most excellent way of establishing ties between young witches and wizards of different nationalities."[3] However, the competition ends by causing conflict and supporting the *status quo* vision that British witches and wizards have cause to fear outsiders. The events ultimately serve to set Harry and the Hogwarts students against the colonized "others" in the novel.

Defining the Other

Unable to speak standard English, foreigners in the novel become "others" as a result of language barriers. The complication first appears at the Quidditch World Cup, an event attended by wizards and witches from all over the world. The British Minister of Magic, Cornelius Fudge, has difficulty in speaking with the Bulgarian Minister of Magic, resorting to crude sign language in the form of pointing.[4] Later, the Bulgarian reveals he can speak English after the game is over, but it is English with a distinct accent, reminiscent of Bela Lugosi in Universal's 1931 film *Dracula*, as he says, "Vell, ve fought bravely."[5] The British witch or wizard would have a mastery of the English language, whereas the "other" does not speak English at all or speaks with an accent. This characterization of the foreigner pervades the novel as the Headmistress of the French magic school, Madame Maxime, addresses Dumbledore in a similarly accented manner by calling him "Dumbly-dorr."[6] Elizabeth Heilman and Anne E. Gregory have claimed that the treatment of the European foreigner "serve[s] to normalize nationalistic disdain

---

1   Michael Collins, "St. George," *Encyclopedia Brittanica* Web site. `<http://www.brittanica.com/ history/stgeorge.html>`.
2   J. K. Rowling, *Harry Potter and the Goblet of Fire* (New York: Scholastic, 2000), 350.
3   *Ibid.*, 187.
4   *Ibid.*, 100.
5   *Ibid.*, 114.
6   *Ibid.*, 244.

among the British for other Europeans and serve[s] to justify dominance."[1] It is a correct assessment, as the inability to have mastery over language marks the mainland European foreigner as separate. British identity in the novel is superior to that of other Europeans in terms of language and the ability to speak it, which aids in defining the novel's continental Europeans against British characters.

Other Europeans are not the only objects of British disdain in the novels because within the hierarchy of British wizardry are human and non-human characters who sometimes find themselves objectified and judged. One of Harry's professors, Hagrid, does not have a great command of English, speaking in a distinct way as he says "Tha's next lesson... Yer jus' feedin' 'em today."[2] Someone with a completely British identity would not mispronounce words, and it is revealed that Hagrid is not fully human because he is half-giant.[3] Hagrid's English ability and heritage give him an inferior status, which is reinforced by the fact that Irish and Scottish characters, such as Seamus Finnigan, do not speak with accents. Hagrid's accent identifies him as half-giant and separate from other wizards.

However, Hagrid is not alone because house-elves are looked down upon by wizards for lacking a command of the language; they are legally treated as inferior. When the elf Winky speaks, she lacks proper grammar by telling Harry that "I knows Dobby too, sir." Also, house-elves are treated very poorly, which Mr. Diggory exemplifies when he addresses Winky by repeatedly calling her "elf" instead of using her name.[4] However, not everyone supports this treatment because Dumbledore pays Dobby while employing him and Hermione views the standard treatment as slavery.[5] In the course of research, Hermione discovers that elf enslavement "goes back centuries," proving that it is rooted in the community.[6] The *status quo* politics of the Ministry of Magic support the dominant view of treating non-humans and half-humans as inferior and serve to put Britain at the forefront of world affairs while asserting power

---

1   Anne E. Gregory and Elizabeth Heilman, "Images of the Privileged Insider and Outcast Outsider," *Harry Potter's World: Multidisciplinary Perspectives* (New York: RoutledgeFalmer, 2003), 255.

2   J. K. Rowling, *Harry Potter and the Goblet of Fire* (New York: Scholastic, 2000), 196.

3   *Ibid.*, 428.

4   *Ibid.*, 97, 134.

5   *Ibid.*, 125, 380.

6   *Ibid.*, 224.

over foreigners. These British "others" are similar in representation to the colonized and immigrants, and it paints a vision of Britishness where the white British look down upon everyone who is different. That vision of British identity is deeply connected to colonialism, which never left the British imagination. However, creating inferiors is only one part because colonialist representations often involved a sexualized object.

"Most beautiful women Harry had ever seen"

As Said noted, the "other" was often characterized as a sexual object in British and Western literature, which appears in *Harry Potter* in terms of the British male students' romantic gaze being turned upon the exotic "other" rather than the traditionally British school friend. This becomes evident at the Quidditch World Cup when Harry catches the gaze of Cho Chang, who smiles at Harry, who in turn "slop[s] quite a lot of water down his front as he waves."[1] Cho has a demonstrated effect on Harry, an effect white British female friends do not have on him. When the Yule Ball approaches, Harry instantly decides that he wants to ask Cho, who is British but presumably of Asian descent.[2] She and others are portrayed as sexualized objects for the enjoyment of men in this novel, a way in which Harry's British friends Hermione Granger and Ginny Weasley are not regarded. Harry's romantic gaze is turned upon one of the girls who has an identity affiliated with Eastern exoticism, which is particularly evocative of colonialist literature. The other Hogwarts Triwizard Champion, Cedric Diggory, beats Harry to asking Cho to the ball, casting Cedric in the same colonial mode. Cedric, Harry and other British characters engage in sexualizing students of foreign descent, and this objectifying action extends to all female students who are presumably of foreign descent.

Harry could have easily gone to the Yule Ball with a more traditionally British girl, but he does not, which serves to create an atmosphere where female students are objectified because of their ethnic origin. Harry is asked by other girls, but he refuses their offers for various reasons, such as the asker being "a foot taller than

1   *Ibid.*, 84.
2   *Ibid.*, 388.

me."[1] Ron engages in similar behavior with his romantic inclination by asking Fleur Delacour, a French student, but he is turned down.[2] British male students sexualize foreigners with an exotic flair. Objectifying the "other" creates a power structure where British men like Harry are empowered and foreign women are stripped of their power; it enables the creation of a British identity that has supremacy over foreigners, a supremacy reinforced by colonial ideals. After failing several times and resorting to Hermione and Ginny with no luck, Harry asks Parvati Patil to the dance, who is presumably of Indian descent, with another name evocative of the former dominance of the British colonial realm.[3] Parvati and her sister, Padma, are beautiful girls, which is evident after Dean Thomas remarks that he "still can't figure out how you two got the best-looking girls in the year."[4] Dean's comment joins exotic identities with an idea of beauty. Parvati, Padma, and Cho are all objectified and sexualized by British characters because of their ethnic identities.

The association between being good-looking and being an "other" is apparent in this novel, with the British gaze being turned upon European and non-European "others." The association makes being exotic the only part of their identity. The reader knows that Padma Patil and Cho Chang are in the intelligent house, Ravenclaw, but they are not shown to be especially smart by being at the top of their class.[5] The honor of being the top of the class is reserved for the familiarly British Gryffindor Hermione Granger, not the objectified ethnic "others."[6] The exotic students are apparently smart, but their characterizations are focused on their romantic ties, not intellectual pursuits. It furthers the representation of "other" as an object exclusively for romantic pleasure and for the British male to obsess over, which is continued in the form of the Bulgarian veela and female French students.

Women from foreign countries in this novel are portrayed as exotic, sexualized beings, especially the veela of Bulgaria. The veela are introduced at the Quidditch World Cup, described as "the most

---

1   *Ibid.*, 389.
2   *Ibid.*, 398.
3   *Ibid.*, 400–1.
4   *Ibid.*, 411.
5   *Ibid.*, 84, 402.
6   *Ibid.*, 315.

beautiful women Harry had ever seen"; they perform as the Bulgarian team's mascots.[1] Being from Bulgaria reinforces their status as outsiders who are stared at by British men. Arthur Weasley describes their act as "a bit of a show," which is what it is—a show for the pleasure of the exoticizing male gaze.[2] These women captivate the minds of British male characters because they are exotic, unlike the familiar British women, and are the "most beautiful," a description that suggests British women are not as pretty or captivating as the veela. This representation falls into the sexualization of the "other" that postcolonialism posits, and foreign women are represented in a manner reminiscent of the depiction of the Bulgarian veela.

The description of students and teachers from the French school Beauxbatons resembles the characterization of the veela, especially the treatment of Fleur Delacour and Madame Maxime. Fleur has the same hypnotic effect as the veela because "many boys' heads turned, and some of them seemed to have become temporarily speechless" as she walks.[3] She possesses the power to turn heads and cause British men to stare, a trait that would seem almost empowering except that it sexualizes her as an object of pleasure. The revelation that she is part veela furthers Fleur's depiction as exotic, a characterization that is reinforced by her status as a French student.[4] She possesses the power to turn heads, an effect on British boys that British girls apparently lack. Fleur is not the only French woman objectified by the British, as Hagrid finds his own romantic interest in the Beauxbatons headmistress, Madame Maxime. She has power over Hagrid, who is observed speaking to Maxime with "a rapt, misty-eyed expression."[5] It marks her as similar to Fleur and the veela with respect to the other characters, and it makes her identity the only part of her, just like the other women. The objectification illustrates how representations of exotic characters function in literature, even literature in the postcolonial era. The exoticization of foreigners is one facet of the representation of the colonized by the colonizer. What follows is the portrayal of foreigners as suspicious and immoral.

---

1   *Ibid.*, 103.
2   *Ibid.*, 99.
3   *Ibid.*, 252.
4   *Ibid.*, 308.
5   *Ibid.*, 266.

Linking Evil Monstrosity with the East

The monstrosity of evil manifests itself from the outside world in *Harry Potter and the Goblet of Fire*, giving evil the reputation of coming from foreign soil. A fear of the evil foreigner permeates the novel, with some wizards and witches refusing to name the evil that they fear, whom they call "You-Know-Who" but Harry calls "Voldemort." Harry, in his profoundly heroic British identity, is able to put a name on evil, whereas the less heroic are not able to name it. Most of the wizarding world, including Arthur Weasley and the employees of the Ministry of Magic, "flinch" when they hear Voldemort's name.[1] It gives Harry a dominance over monstrosity as he has the power to assign a name to it and defy evil's power. Harry may be in the position of supremacy, but even dominant British cultural identity is prone to fear of the outsider, including Harry's bird, which does not like the "flashy intruders."[2] The fear appears to be well-founded as Harry begins to dream about Voldemort, who is supposedly "far away in some distant country, in hiding alone… feeble and powerless."[3] Harry is frightened by this dream, and it serves to show that Harry may be in the position of hero but is also in the position of the hunted. From afar, Voldemort is coming after Harry, even invading his dreams, and Voldemort's evil is connected with foreigners.

There are several ways the association of evil with foreigners is created in the novel, such as the pairing of Voldemort with Albania and the Triwizard Tournament's creation of suspicion among rivals. Durmstrang, a European school in the tournament, has a reputation for teaching the Dark Arts, which separates it from the British Hogwarts because Hogwarts will not associate itself with the Dark Arts.[4] British wizards discuss the school's reputation, and Sirius tells Harry that Durmstrang's headmaster, Karkaroff, has been "teaching the Dark Arts to every student who passes through that school of his."[5] The reputation comes out of a xenophobic fear of this school and its pupils. Later, Hagrid tells Harry to remain suspicious of Durmstrang students, such as Viktor Krum, simply because they are

1   *Ibid.*, 142–43.
2   *Ibid.*, 24.
3   *Ibid.*, 284.
4   *Ibid.*, 165.
5   *Ibid.*, 332.

from Durmstrang.[1] The threat from Krum is two-fold—he is a competitor in the Triwizard Tournament, and he is in romantic pursuit of Hermione by taking her to the Yule Ball and asking her to come to Bulgaria in the summer.[2] Ron and Harry suspect Krum because of the romantic and competition threats he poses. Evil, in the form of the outsider, comes from without rather than within; Voldemort is the invader in this novel. This serves to depict the continental outsider in connection with the evil side of wizardry while keeping the British on the good side, demonstrating that evil comes from the East and causing a fear of the East.

With evil coming from foreigners, British characters are in turn suspicious of foreigners and their motives. Another witch, Bertha Jorkins, "went on holiday to Albania and never came back," and that is the country where Voldemort was "rumored to be last."[3] Albania and Bulgaria are both on the border of East and West. In this case, Rowling seems to be associating them with the East and a characterization that evil comes from the East, similar to that of Bram Stoker's 1897 novel *Dracula*. The East has become a place where people become lost and where they are evil. Hagrid tells Harry that he "can't trust any of 'em."[4] Those who are allied with Harry are suspicious of foreigners for this reason—they might be evil. Foreigners are not meant to be trusted because the Dark Arts are connected with them. Throughout the novel, when suspicious events occur, outsiders, not those connected with British identity, are immediately suspected of wrongdoing; it aids in painting a portrait of the evil outsider.

Characters cast in the mold of evil monstrosity are markedly different from their British counterparts, none more so than the ultimate villain, Lord Voldemort. When Voldemort manages to return to his body, he is distinct, with "vivid scarlet eyes and a nose that was flat as a snake's with slits for nostrils."[5] He cannot blend in with the other British characters because his appearance is less than human, and while he preaches purity of the wizarding race, he has completely shed any British identity he had. He has become the foreigner who returns to the mother country to haunt it.

---

1   *Ibid.*, 563.
2   *Ibid.*, 269, 414, 512.
3   *Ibid.*, 61, 333.
4   *Ibid.*, 563.
5   *Ibid.*, 643.

Voldemort's naming reinforces his newly foreign status because "vol de mort" in French means "flight of death."[1] Giving Voldemort a French name connects him to the fear of foreigners in the novel. Rowling certainly seems to be taking a page from Stoker's book in this characterization, as his Dracula came from Transylvania to Britain, in an almost reverse colonization. Indeed, Voldemort needed Harry's blood to return to a body, giving him a vampire-like quality.[2] The farther the story is removed from the safety of Britain, the more evil is associated with the East and colonialism. Describing evil as the outsider in comparison to the British hero of Harry draws a comparison with canonical British literature, a xenophobic characterization that *Harry Potter and the Goblet of Fire* follows in its depiction of evil. The xenophobic, colonialist elements of *Harry Potter* are contrasted with Dumbledore's creed of judging students on their individual merit and keeping international ties.

"Differences of language and habit are nothing"

Hogwarts Headmaster Albus Dumbledore defies politics as usual by standing up to those in the wizarding community who fear the loss of blood purity among British witches and wizards, meaning that they should not marry humans who lack magical powers. Since he is the wizard whom Harry trusts the most, the reader can assume that Rowling speaks through Dumbledore, especially when he calls out the tendency to fear outsiders and students who are not pure-blood. At the end of *Goblet of Fire*, Dumbledore and the Minister of Magic have a falling-out, mostly due to Fudge's refusal to admit that Voldemort has returned. Fudge's politics are called into question when Dumbledore tells him that he "place[s] too much importance…on the so-called purity of blood. You fail to recognize that it matters not what someone is born, but what they grow to be."[3] Fudge's politics as usual support strengthening Britain by defining wizarding national identity in relation to pure-blood politics. Dumbledore rejects Voldemort's philosophy, which happens to be the philosophy of many British wizards, but even Voldemort cannot truly support pure-blood wizards because he is a half-blood, the son of a witch and a Muggle father. Contrary to pure-blood

---

1 "Vol de mort," Word Reference site (2007), <http://www.wordreference.com/>.
2 *Ibid.*, 656–57.
3 *Ibid.*, 708.

dogma, Dumbledore and his allies want to judge students on their individual magical merits and talents, not just a distinction of inheritance. His insistence on rejecting pure-blood standards sets him apart, but his stance on international unity truly sets him apart from the colonialist, xenophobic elements at work in the novel.

The Headmaster tells students present at the Triwizard Tournament that its mission is to create closer international relations, a position that Dumbledore supports time and again. Dumbledore desires "closer international wizarding links," an effort to create ties and forget the differences that separate wizards and witches.[1] He uses his position of power to forge connections between British and foreign students and citizens, and he uses his position to get his ideas into the marketplace. After Voldemort's return, Dumbledore tells the assembled students that the tournament's aim was "to further and promote magical understanding...such ties are more important than ever before... Differences of habit and language are nothing at all if our aims are identical and our hearts are open."[2] His address signals that he wants unity among all wizards in the fight against Voldemort's ideology, and he demonstrates that there is more that unites wizards and witches than divides them. Dumbledore's speech sums up the argument against an ideology that preaches separation and fear of foreigners and outsiders. Rowling uses the representations of colonialism to contrast the ideologies at the heart of the battle between Harry and Voldemort.

Postcolonial theory concerns itself partly with an awareness of representations, which can be applied to *Harry Potter and the Goblet of Fire* with its depiction of Harry as distinctly British while giving the continental European and non-European an exotic or evil characterization. The representations of the "other" as exotic, sexual and perhaps evil continue in *Harry Potter* even though it is written in the postcolonial era. Ideas of the "other" appear throughout the fourth novel and the series as a whole, with foreigners, Dark wizards, and good wizards all opposed to each other. The novel continues in a colonial tradition of defining the "other" against a notion of heroic Britishness. However, Rowling's use of that tradition serves to expose the difference between two ideas of

---

1   *Ibid.*, 561–62.
2   *Ibid.*, 723.

Britishness—one where purity reigns supreme and another where multi-culturalism rules the day. Indeed, even the battle between Harry and Voldemort supports multi-culturalism because both are half-blood wizards, not pure-blood, making it a confrontation between a hero and a villain of similar descent. In doing so, Rowling provides a commentary on British society at the beginning of the twenty-first century where there is a tension between competing ideas of Britishness, but through Dumbledore, the author supports a multi-ethnic future of society.

An Ordinary Hero:
Neville Longbottom and the Hero's Path

Layla A. Abuisba
St. Louis Community College

Neville Longbottom, a character in J. K. Rowling's *Harry Potter* series, is portrayed as endearingly inept to readers and a pitiable nerd in the estimation of his fictional peers. As readers, most of us are pulling for Neville as he shakily stands up to Draco Malfoy, or more shakily still tries to make a potion under the vengeful eye of Professor Snape. We cringe as he silently endures his formidable grandmother's comments about his inadequacies. However, I can't help but find common ground with Neville as he encounters his challenges in the wizarding world, and I suspect that I am not the only one. Many of us have had some kind of clash with a schoolyard bully, and many others have doubtless had a teacher or mentor, or even a parent, who we felt overlooked our better qualities. So where should we turn when we confront our life challenges? Friends, family and therapists, of course, but stories can also play an important role in our understanding of ourselves and the world.

Stories offer children a glimpse of the world that they might not otherwise encounter until they are old enough to explore on their own. I realized the impact that books have on children one Fourth of July when my children and I were on our backyard deck watching fireworks. My two-year-old son pointed at the fireworks and asked, "Is that a shooting star?" I was puzzled by his question because I could not remember ever showing one or describing one to him. Several days later, I solved the mystery. We read books before bed every night, and I realized that one of his books had a picture of a shooting star in it.

Stories play a similar role in our ability as children and adults to understand the emotional complexity of the world we live in. Personal testimonials of those who overcame obstacles are useful when we are seeking answers to, or solace for, perplexing personal issues. Idries Shah, a noted scholar of Sufi folktales, defines fables, fairy tales, and any culturally relevant story as an important way to impart essential knowledge. He says that "we must approach [stories] from the point of view that they may on that level be documents of technical value: an ancient yet still irreplaceable method of arranging and transmitting a knowledge which can not be put in any other way" ("Teaching"). Joseph Campbell, another noted scholar and expert on mythology, says this: "Myths are clues to the spiritual potentialities of the human life" (*Hero* 5).

J. K. Rowling provides inspiration to her readers through her portrayal of Neville in *Harry Potter*. As Neville challenges himself, we who are lost in a sea of nervous anxiety are inspired to do the same. While Harry, although facing challenges of his own, has friends and supporters to comfort him, Neville apparently does not. And while we cannot all be Harry, the Boy Who Lived, who has a lightning bolt on his forehead to mark him as a chosen one, we can recognize ourselves in Neville because Neville is ordinary, yet heroic.

But how does the *Harry Potter* series relate to mythological themes, especially that of the hero? While Rowling uses many mythological themes in her series, one of the most important is that of the hero's path. Joseph Campbell defines the hero's experience this way:

We have only to follow the thread of the hero path. And where we had thought to find an abomination, we shall find a god; where we had thought to slay another, we shall slay ourselves; where we had thought to travel outward, we shall come to the center of our own existence. And where we had thought to be alone, we shall be with all the world. (*Hero* 25)

Here, Campbell alludes to the challenges that heroes of all stories endure and that inspire readers and listeners throughout the world. Neville, on a personal scale, is on a journey that is typical of any hero. True, as readers we are inspired to develop our abilities and display our better selves through Harry's example, but Rowling's portrayal of Neville provides a path for any child or adult hoping to overcome adversity, especially emotional adversity. The path that

Neville walks is that of the ordinary hero. He is an Everyman who has an inner strength awaiting his discovery. He displays determination, loyalty, and an innate talent in Herbology. As we watch Neville mature during the *Harry Potter* series, we see a person growing into knowledge of himself. His growth comes as he encounters challenges that test his faith and confidence in himself. Neville's path is a hero's path.

My favorite scene with Neville comes in book six, *Harry Potter and the Half-Blood Prince.* One day while heading to the Gryffindor dormitory, Harry, Ron and other students encounter Peeves the poltergeist. Peeves had "jammed the door on the fourth floor shut and was refusing to let anyone pass until they set fire to their own pants" (387). Harry and Ron, because of their adventures, are knowledgeable about Hogwarts passageways. They quickly turn and find a shortcut to their destination. Later, as they are in their bedroom, Neville comes in to change his pants, which are singed (388). The first time I read this scene, I laughed appreciatively at the humor of it and at the fine detail Rowling applies to her work. On the face of it, this small but funny moment in the series merely reinforces the surface personalities of the characters. Ron and Harry, daring and quick-thinking, are more knowledgeable about the passageways of the castle and are able to circumvent Peeves. Timid Neville displays gullibility and weakness at the behest of Peeves. Or does he? Throughout these years, each time I read the scene or heard it through Jim Dale's audio performance, an alternative point nagged at me. One day, as I read the scene, I realized that although Neville appears to display weakness during this scene, he actually shows a single-minded determination. Neville is not thwarted in his attempt to get back to his room. He is only slightly delayed and a bit singed, but he gets there. For all his apparent weaknesses, Neville is a determined individual. This is not the only example of Neville's determination we find in the books, but it is the most exquisitely drawn. It is a fine literary moment.

Joseph Campbell defines the "heroic life" as "living the individual adventure" (Osbon 22). Campbell defines three stages of the hero's path: departure, initiation and return. Within these three phases, certain events take place, such as the Call to Adventure and the Refusal of the Call. In Neville's departure, the call to adventure is delayed, and he experiences the effects of his refusal. Campbell defines the refusal of the call thus:

Often in actual life, and not infrequently in the myths and popular tales, we encounter the dull case of the call unanswered; for it is always possible to turn the ear to other interests. Refusal of the summons converts the adventure into its negative. Walled in boredom, hard work, or "culture," the subject loses the power of significant affirmative action and becomes a victim to be saved. (*Hero* 59)

Neville, at first glance, appears to be reluctant to answer his call to adventure.

When we meet Neville in *Harry Potter and the Sorcerer's Stone*, his status as a "victim" is readily apparent. He has lost his toad, Trevor, and his grandmother is sighing in apparent frustration. Toads, we have already learned from Hagrid, are out of fashion and toad owners "would be laughed at" (81). Later, as Neville leaves Ron and Harry's train compartment after asking about his toad, lost for the second time, Ron comments that that if he owned a toad, he'd lose it as quick as he could (104). Through the words and actions of Neville and those around him, and by his ownership of the toad, Rowling seems to intend for us to label Neville as a nerd. His reaction to his inability to control Trevor communicates a lack of confidence in himself. The fact that he has had to bring an unpopular pet, which might get him laughed at, demonstrates his wizarding family's lack of communication and understanding because it was his Great-Uncle Algie who bought him the toad. However, during a recent discussion at the Phoenix Rising conference, a participant pointed out that a toad is the appropriate symbolic pet for Neville because of his talent with plant life.[1] His best subject is Herbology. Toads need water to live, as do plants, and they are also helpful in keeping a bothersome insect population away from fragile plants. This is an excellent point, and it further emphasizes the fact that when we first meet Neville, he does not have the ability to connect with his basic self. He is has refused to (or is afraid to) answer his Call to Adventure.

Harry's journey on the train allows him to leave the Dursleys behind in the Muggle world. He is ready to define himself on new terms supplied by the wizarding world. Neville, like Harry,

---

1   Discussion Participant, "An Ordinary Hero: Neville Longbottom and the Hero's Path," Phoenix Rising Conference, New Orleans, 20 May 2007.

discovered that he can do magic in his late childhood, but Neville's self is still defined by his wizarding family, and he appears to have brought the influence of his family with him, symbolized by the escaping toad. Harry is cheerful and has accepted his Call to Adventure, while Neville's ability to define himself and accept his Call to Adventure is blocked. Guardians of the threshold stand between him and his acceptance of the call—his formidable and very critical grandmother, and by extension, his entire family.

Campbell says this about the guardian or guardians of the threshold:

One is bound by the walls of childhood; the father and mother stand as threshold guardians, and the timorous soul, fearful of some punishment, fails to make the passage through the door to come to birth in the world without. (*Hero* 62)

Neville struggles to get past the guardians of his threshold: his addled parents who are insane and cannot recognize him (giving him no positive sense of self), his grandmother and her criticism, and his distracted but well-meaning Great-Uncle Algie. Until he gets past them, he cannot "come to birth" or find confidence in himself in relation to the larger world (*Hero* 62). It is this predicament that many in the real world find themselves in. If it is not a critical authority figure standing as our guardian, perhaps it is a cultural assumption about our limitations, or another troubling experience, which we allow to prevent us from embarking on our own hero's journey.

Bellatrix Lestrange's escape from Azkaban solidifies Neville's call to adventure. It is Bellatrix, along with her husband and other Death Eaters, who tortured Neville's parents into insanity. Until their escape, which happens in the fifth book, *Harry Potter and the Order of the Phoenix,* Neville showed signs that he is made of sterner stuff, yet our glimpses are haphazard, and there is no sustained energy behind his acts. For example, in book one, Neville takes on Harry, Ron and Hermione and tries to stop them from leaving the common room at night (*SS* 273). In book two, he is a less visible character without a major role to play in the plot. His most memorable line comes when he expresses his fear of whoever has petrified Mrs. Norris and Colin Creevey: "'They went for Filch first,' Neville said, his round face fearful, 'and everyone knows I'm almost a Squib'" (185). In book three, with Professor Lupin's help, he faces his greatest fear and fights a boggart (*PoA* 137). In book four he is able to ask two girls to the ball before Harry and Ron can pluck up the courage to ask anyone (*GoF* 399). But it is in book five, when Bellatrix escapes, where we see Neville begin to focus his energies toward the same goal as Harry: vanquishing Voldemort and his Death Eaters.

Neville earns freedom from his grandmother's influence, and from the shadow of his parents, through his fight at the Ministry of Magic in book five. The events at the Ministry contribute to Neville's need to get past his guardians and reach atonement with his father and his family in general. Campbell describes atonement as when the hero "beholds the face of the father, understands—and the two are atoned" (*Hero* 147). Symbolic of his success in getting past his threshold guardians, Neville participates in the fight against Voldemort's Death Eaters with members of Dumbledore's Army (a defense group led by Harry) and the Order of the Phoenix (led by Dumbledore) at the Ministry of Magic. A Death Eater breaks Frank Longbottom's wand as he kicks Neville, and Neville encounters and attempts to fight Bellatrix, who performs the Cruciatus Curse on him just as she did to Neville's parents (*OotP* 792–801). The wand in this case signifies Frank Longbottom's abilities as a wizard. We are told in book one that "the wand chooses the wizard" so, clearly, Frank Longbottom's wand was never meant for Neville (*SS* 82). But Neville's relationship to his father's reputation is tragically significant to his self-image. Having been told that he "doesn't have his father's talent," he seems to accept this pronouncement and act accordingly (*OotP* 513). In addition, he entered Hogwarts knowing that his family had worried that he "might not be magic enough" for the school (*SS* 125). His involvement with the D.A. and Harry's coaching of Neville in Defense Against the Dark Arts have helped to shape Neville for his hero's journey. Fighting Death Eaters and experiencing the Cruciatus Curse allows Neville to understand his parents' experience in relation to his own.

Book six introduces us to a Neville who is ready to take steps down his own hero's path. Now that he has passed his threshold guardians, Neville finds that he can draw on the support of helpers that have been with him all along. Campbell says,

Once having traversed the threshold, the hero moves in a dream landscape where he must survive a succession of trials.... The hero is covertly aided by the advice, amulets and secret agents of the supernatural helper whom he met before his entrance into this region. (*Hero* 97)

Although Neville notes that his grandmother "wishes Harry were her grandson," Augusta Longbottom is clearly pleased with Neville's actions, and she buys him a new wand to replace his father's broken one (*HBP* 137–39). Professor McGonagall helps Neville break away from his grandmother's influence by encouraging him to take the courses he does best in. She says that she will drop his grandmother a line and tell her that she should be proud of the grandson she's got, not the one that she thinks she should have. McGonagall is one of many "supernatural" helpers who have been with Neville all along, but whose help he has not yet been able to tap. She helps him evaluate his O.W.L.s and recommends that he take courses based on his interests and abilities (*HBP* 174).

Neville's bond with male figures has also been clarified. It was his Great-Uncle Algie who first helped him discover his magical ability by accidentally dropping him out of a window (*SS* 125). He was more worried about Neville's magic ability than Neville's feelings. Later, Great-Uncle Algie bought him a toad, a well-meaning act that was supportive of Neville's basic self, but also indicated his lack of knowledge of the modern world that Neville was facing. Toads, as I mentioned earlier, are out of fashion. Great-Uncle Algie's generous act was symbolic of Neville's family living in the past. In comparison, Hagrid (Harry's father figure) advises Harry to get something other than a toad so that he would not be laughed at (*SS* 81). But it is also Great-Uncle Algie who, we learn at the beginning in book five, has tried to encourage Neville's talent in Herbology by bringing him a *Mimbulus mimbletonia* from Assyria (*OotP* 186–87). As Neville's talents and interests become clear, and as his story approaches the fight at the Ministry, he lays the groundwork for a breakthrough to enter a wider field of action. As he wins through, the guardians who once prevented him from acting, or who had been in the background, become supporters. We can assume that Great-Uncle Algie, like Augusta Longbottom, sees Neville in a new light.

A word or two must also be said of the special connection that Harry and Neville share. When they first meet on the Hogwarts Express, neither is aware of their mutual connection to a prophecy that has profoundly influenced their lives. In *Sorcerer's Stone*, they cross the lake in a boat together, along with Ron and Hermione, on their way from the train to Hogwarts Castle (111). Harry is another helper who has been with Neville all along and in fact has helped him define himself since their early days at Hogwarts. It is Harry and Ron who first help Neville stand up for himself against Draco. Harry tells Neville that he is "worth twelve of [Draco] Malfoy"; Neville repeats this to Draco and later joins a fight against Draco, Crabbe and Goyle (218, 223). Harry helps to replace the message of Neville's family, namely comparisons to the lost talent of Frank Longbottom, with an estimate of Neville's true capabilities.

Harry is in a sense a father and brother figure to Neville, as their stories are entwined with that of the prophecy. But although Harry encourages Neville, his opinion of Neville in book five is that he is not the right person to be sitting with on the Hogwarts Express, if Harry wants to impress Cho Chang (*OotP* 187–88). However, after the fight at the Ministry, just as Neville has crossed his threshold guardians, Harry has matured and realized that Neville is a true friend and collaborator. In book six, he is happy to have Neville beside him as they ride the train (*HBP* 139). They reach atonement, and Neville receives new respect from an important but till-now latent ally. From many corners, Neville receives the acceptance that he has earned as his strengths finally come to fruition.

In *Reflections on the Art of Living: A Joseph Campbell Companion*, Joseph Campbell says that

The heroic life is living the individual adventure. You enter the forest at the darkest point, where there is not path. Where there is a way or a path it is someone else's path. You are not on your own path. If you follow someone else's way you are not going to realize your potential. (Osbon 22)

Our experience of Neville and Harry's journey begins on the Hogwarts Express. Harry's journey is more that of the classic hero, and it is one that contains experiences inspirational to us all. But Harry has been blessed with good looks, an inner confidence, and curiosity that allow him to weather trials earlier than Neville. In contrast, Neville's trials are different from Harry's. They are more personal. His trials include a critical family, the burden of his parents' health, an apparent weight problem, social and physical awkwardness, and his own talents, which are more earthbound than Harry's. Harry's talent is flying. Neville's talent is in Herbology. One ability may be more glamorous that the other, but that does not mean that they are not equally valuable. Neville faces more mundane concerns, which are familiar to us all. These concerns grace many magazine covers in the grocery checkout line: unappreciated talent, family criticism and expectations, weight issues, and a parent's health.

Rowling has described Neville Longbottom as an "ordinary wizarding boy" who was "so nearly king" ("What Is the Significance?"). While Harry possesses many attributes of an archetypal hero, Rowling portrays Neville as a classic nerd, as mentioned. Yet her portrayal of Neville also illustrates that he walks his own hero's path. In describing an archetypal hero's triumph, Campbell says that "godly powers sought and dangerously won are found to have been within the heart of the hero all of the time" (*Hero* 39). Neville possesses many powers and talents, yet they are hidden by his lack of confidence. Because of Rowling's realistic portrayal of Neville, many readers may identify with Neville's personal struggle. At the end of book six, Neville appears to be overcoming his personal obstacles. And while Neville willingly joins Harry in the fight against Voldemort, he is not Harry's follower. His quiet, affable manner communicates a personal independence and dignity that is very different from the giddy admiration of Colin Creevey for Harry, or Peter Pettigrew's sycophantic adulation of James Potter. Neville may be timid at times, but he also displays a desire for self-improvement and a strong inner core of determination. He works against Voldemort for his own reasons. Neville independently pursues his own hero's path in order to fulfill his personal destiny.

So what is Neville's personal destiny? The hope of many readers must surely be that Neville vanquish Bellatrix Lestrange and go back to Hogwarts as a teacher, having reached to the end of Campbell's final phase of the hero's path: the return. At the return, the hero has earned what Campbell calls the freedom to live (*Hero* 238). However, as readers we are also well aware of Rowling's penchant to inject realism into her work. Will Neville die in book seven? I hope not, but it is a likely possibility. In *The Way of Art*, Joseph Campbell explains artistic depictions of destiny and fate as well. He says:

All of our lives are moving to limits but not many of us threaten the limit…. As Aristotle says, the hero of a tragedy is one of certain nobility.

With a certain fault. The fault is that he doesn't respect the limit. He goes to it.

Now the next thing about art is it doesn't say "no" to the thing it's talking about…. It's a totally different perspective from that of desire and loathing. It's that of getting through an instance, the real zing of what it is to be alive and what life is and what it's doing to us and what we are doing with respect to it. (Campbell, "Way")

Many of Rowling's main characters threaten their limits at times, and most would agree that Rowling has created a work of art. Campbell's theory on art reminds us that regardless of the outcome, whether it be Neville's destiny or someone else's, when a literary character challenges his or her limit, the character has succeeded regardless of how mundane the circumstance or flawed the endeavor. Neville does not perform perfectly at the Ministry as a typical literary hero would, but he does perform heroically and imperfectly as many real-world heroes often do. However, in terms of our own daily lives, our limits are not always as desperate. J. K. Rowling's portrayal of Neville inspires us to confront our own emotional challenges imperfectly. If we do, we may find our lives transformed.

Works Cited

Campbell, Joseph. *The Hero with a Thousand Faces*. Princeton: Princeton UP, 1973.

Campbell, Joseph. "The Way of Art." *Rawpaint*. 6 May 2007. <http://www.Rawpaint.com/library/jcampbell/jctwoa.html>.

Osbon, Diane K., ed. *Reflections on the Art of Living: A Joseph Campbell Companion*. New York: HarperCollins, 1991.

Rowling, J. K. *Harry Potter and the Chamber of Secrets*. New York: Arthur A. Levine, 1999.

—. *Harry Potter and the Goblet of Fire*. New York: Arthur A. Levine, 2000.

—. *Harry Potter and the Half-Blood Prince*. New York: Arthur A. Levine, 2005.

—. *Harry Potter and the Order of the Phoenix*. New York: Arthur A. Levine, 2003.

—. *Harry Potter and the Prisoner of Azkaban*. New York: Arthur A. Levine, 1999.

—. *Harry Potter and the Sorcerer's Stone*. New York: Arthur A. Levine, 1997.

—. "What Is the Significance of Neville Being the Other Boy to Whom the Prophecy Might Have Referred?" *J. K. Rowling Official Site FAQ*. 16 May 2005. <http://www.jkrowling.com/textonly/en/faq_view.cfm?id=84>.

Shah, Idries. "The Teaching Story: Observations on the Folklore of Our 'Modern' Thought." IdriesShah.Info. 25 Mar 2007. <http://www.idriesshah.info/Shah/ShahTea.htm>.

Fantasy's Rebirth: Reconciling the Hero's and Heroine's Journeys

Valerie Estelle Frankel
San Jose State University, California

Great heroes stride through all our epic legends, from Gilgamesh and Hercules to the beloved Harry Potter. But can we leave these legends only to heroes? Where are the warrior women and goddesses rescuing themselves? Though much has been written on the hero's journey, many famous folklorists—the celebrated Joseph Campbell among them—have neglected the story of the heroine, despite its frequency in literature. While *Harry Potter*, like *Star Wars*, *King Arthur*, and many other fantasies, offers the quintessential "boy story," with weaker female sidekicks allowing boys to dominate the action, more balanced tales, such as *The Lion, the Witch, and the Wardrobe*, follow both genders as they diverge. Just as the hero must defeat his father-figure and take his ordained place as king, the heroine battles the deadly witch to become a mother-goddess.

The hero quests to confront the ultimate enemy—a figure that represents his dark side, his evil and submerged half. This conflict also represents a war with the father figure and a struggle for dominance, appearing in works such as *Star Wars* ("Luke, I am your father") and *King Arthur*, where the son and opposite covets the father's place.

Not all heroines sing sweetly about marrying princes, leading passive, Cinderella-like existences. Many women throughout literature and myth actually battle seductresses and witches to establish a family and ascend to motherhood. Others rescue babies in danger or kidnapped husbands, questing to build their own family circle. Heroines dominate ancient myths in the guises of Antigone, Isis, and Demeter, and now enter the famous children's fantasy series of Oz and Narnia, as well as their overwhelmingly popular movies. Other books include *A Wrinkle in Time, The Golden Compass, Dealing with Dragons, Alice in Wonderland,* and more. Heroines from all these stories travel through fantasy worlds on the heroine's traditional journey, battling their shadow selves and protecting loved ones in order to ascend to goddesshood.

Comparison of Models

The Steps of the Journey

Campbell's Model	The Heroine's Journey Model
World of Common Day	World of Common Day
Call to Adventure	Call to Adventure—A Desire to Reconnect with the Feminine
Refusal of the Call	Refusal of the Call
Supernatural Aid	The Ruthless Mentor and the Bladeless Talisman
Crossing the First Threshold: Belly of the Whale	Crossing the First Threshold: Opening One's Senses
Road of Trials	Sidekicks, Trials, Adversaries
Meeting with the Goddess Woman as Temptress	Marriage to the Animus Sensitive Man as Completion Confronting the Powerless Father
Atonement with the Father Apotheosis	Atonement with the Mother Apotheosis Through Accepting One's Feminine Side
The Ultimate Boon	Reward: Winning the Family
The Refusal of the Return The Magic Flight Rescue from Within Return	The Magic Flight Reinstating the Family
Master of the Two Worlds	Power over Life and Death
Freedom to Live	Ascension of the New Mother

Call to Adventure

While the goal, enemy, and reward vary between genders, the path remains similar. The journey starts in the everyday world, whether it be Kansas, Hobbiton, or Privet Drive, before the hero or heroine can venture into the "otherworld" of magic and strangeness. In *The Lion, the Witch, and the Wardrobe,* Susan and Lucy suffer through a dull winter in the country, listening to radioed news of the London Blitz. This is the stage before leaving home, the childhood in which everything is secure and familiar. The protagonist exists in a state of innocence, but also has feelings of adolescent rebellion or misery. The time has arrived to leave home.

At once, a mysterious herald appears summoning the child to an adventure. You see he has...a destiny. The hero often rejects this call —it is too strange, too mysterious, but at last, he accepts.

Of course, this will mean a separation from the parents. This represents a traumatic moment in every person's life, craving the family's love and protection, yet desiring to grow up. One way myth often softens this separation is by substituting foster parents or insensitive relatives. Thus, leaving home becomes less terrifying for young readers. Harry's adoptive family is so nasty, they won't even let him have an imagination; book one states, "If there was one thing the Dursleys hated even more than his asking questions, it was his talking about things acting in a way it shouldn't" (*PS* 24). Both Luke Skywalker and Dorothy Gale live with an unsympathetic aunt and uncle. The children in the Narnia books, likewise, are staying with a cranky old man who requires them to be quiet all the time. He gives the children no hesitation in escaping.

As with many "chosen one" plots in juvenile fiction, Harry Potter outperforms adults over and over. He flees from the unsympathetic adult world to a world of fantasy, a dazzling dream for most readers. Children live in the normal world surrounded by restrictions and a lack of power, with adults telling them what to do. At Hogwarts, Harry resists Malfoy's bullying with magic, and Dumbledore assists Harry in breaking school rules by giving him an invisibility cloak. In the world of wizards, Harry saves the day in every book, while adults such as Cornelius Fudge foolishly dismiss the truth of Voldemort's return because Harry, a child, is the messenger. After living in an adult world where he's ordered around with no control over his life, Harry learns that everyone in the wizarding world regards him as a hero and expects him to do "great things" (*PS* 64). "The idea that we could have a child who escapes from the confines of the adult world and goes somewhere where he has power, both literally and metaphorically, really appealed to me," the book's author said in an interview (Scholastic).

This theme dominates children's fiction, since "the author's characterization of the child's emotions is a crucial factor" (Marshall 26). Dorothy Gale, the four Narnia children, and even Christopher Robin also have power in the worlds they travel to, simply because they're children from earth. In each volume of Lemony Snicket's *A Series of Unfortunate Events,* the children recognize their arch-nemesis, Count Olaf, but all the adults disbelieve them. Lyra of Philip Pullman's *The Golden Compass* works with children and outcasts, since the powerful Lord Asriel and Mrs. Coulter deceive her again and again. Thus all the children must save the day, even without adult support.

Once in the world of magic and acceptance, the protagonist receives a quest. Hagrid tells Harry about Lord Voldemort, setting him on the path to their final conflict. The children of Narnia battle to rescue Edmund and sit on the four thrones. Many critics note that boys do all the fighting and conquering of kingdoms, while characters such as Cinderella want nothing more than a ball dress and wedding. And let's not even consider Sleeping Beauty!

Young women are rarely destined to lead armies and swing swords, Jeanne D'Arc being a rare example. Cinderella and the Little Mermaid blatantly quest to acquire husbands. Does this make them weak and shallow? Part of the woman's quest is to become a mother by surpassing her own mother figure (the evil stepmother or the sea witch) to become an adult with her own family. Yet the road to this task can be as hazardous as any battle.

The man quests to conquer and rule, as with Jason, Perseus, and Theseus from Greek mythology. This, of course, reflects the archetypal search for a career that men have long embarked on. The best career available, of course, is king of the known world. Women, by contrast, have only recently started looking toward career goals. Hundreds of years ago, a perfect marriage was the goal for many women because a career was not even in their sphere of reference. Some heroines wed princes in their quest (as some modern women still do), but others rescue family or slay monsters, showing interest in a wider circle. The recurring theme is a completed family, a goal that heroines risk life and health to achieve.

Mentor and Talisman

At the beginning of the quest, the mentor arrives. In male stories, Dumbledore/Merlin/Gandalf/Obi-Wan teaches the hero to use his magical sword and battle evil. In fact, these quirky, bearded wizards are nearly interchangeable. Heroes must have appropriate role models; this image of the bearded wise man represents a king with a full arsenal of knowledge, the sort of ruler the hero longs to become. Dumbledore advises Harry on the Mirror of Erised, along with the dangers of pride and foolhardiness. Later, Dumbledore tutors Harry as they study Riddle's childhood in book six, *Half-Blood Prince*. As a traditional kindly mentor, he prepares Harry for the world ahead with support and thoughtful advice. Dorothy has Glinda, a dazzlingly beautiful protectress, who offers her the ruby slippers. Some heroines have crueler mentors, such as Ursula the Sea Witch, Snow White's evil stepmother, and Wonderland's Queen of Hearts. These mentors advise, but, like male mentors, die or vanish and leave the heroines to cope alone at the worst moment.

Harry also chooses a wand, representing the enchanted swords of so many legends. He duels with it, and defends himself at the most hopeless junctures. Though it's not a gift from Dumbledore, Fawkes significantly donates a tail feather (*GoF* 697). Thus, Dumbledore's gift and protection always guard Harry from harm. As Harry confidently states, even after Dumbledore's death, "He will only be gone from the school when none here are loyal to him" (*HBP* 649).

While the hero always carries a magic sword (wand, lightsaber, etc.), heroines almost never do. Dorothy has the silver slippers, though she must determine their use. Meg in Madeleine L'Engle's *A Wrinkle in Time* has Mrs. Which's spectacles. Lucy gets a bottle of healing elixir. A golden compass. A candle. A golden ball. A book of spells. Rings. This list does not even address all the Cinderella-type heroines who receive fine clothes and beautiful slippers to catch a Prince Charming's attention. What do these talismans have in common? They're everyday items, almost domestic ones. Is this the mentor's message, that each heroine should wield high-heeled shoes and electric mixers, while Arthur conquers the world with Excalibur?

The gift-giving scene from *The Lion, the Witch, and the Wardrobe* is quite telling:

> "Peter, Adam's son," said Father Christmas.
>
> "Here, sir," said Peter.
>
> "These are your presents," was the answer, "they are tools, not toys. The time to use them is perhaps near at hand. Bear them well." With these words he handed to Peter a shield and a sword. The shield was the color of silver and across it there ramped a red lion as a bright as a ripe strawberry at the moment when you pick it. The hilt of the sword was of gold and it had a sheath and a sword belt and everything it needed, and it was just the size and weight for Peter to use. Peter was silent and solemn as he received these gifts, for he felt they were a very serious kind of present.
>
> "Susan, Eve's Daughter," said Father Christmas. "These are for you," and he handed her a bow and a quiver full of arrows and a little ivory horn. "You must use the bow only in great need," he said, "for I do not mean you to fight in the battle. It does not easily miss. And when you put this horn to your lips and blow it, then, wherever you are, I think help of some kind will come to you."
>
> Last of all he said, "Lucy, Eve's Daughter," and Lucy came forward. He gave her a little bottle of what looked like glass (but people said afterward that it was made of diamond) and a small dagger. "In this bottle," he said, "there is a cordial made of the juice of the fire-flowers that grow in the mountains of the sun. If you or any of your friends is hurt, a few drops of this will restore them. And the dagger is to defend yourself at great need. For you also are not to be in the battle."
>
> "Why, sir?" said Lucy. "I think—I don't know—but I think I could be brave enough."
>
> "That is not the point," he said. "But battles are ugly when women fight." (Lewis 108–9)

Lucy and Susan receive gifts as magical as their brother's, but gentler, to reflect their role in the story. Susan is told to call for aid, and Lucy, to heal those already wounded. Only Peter is supposed to fight. At first glance, this seems horribly sexist and dismissive of our heroines. However, the gifts actually reflect the children's different journeys and goals. Slaying a wolf marks Peter's first test. From there, he ventures on his hero's journey through knighthood, war, and kingship, leading the troops into battle. Susan and Lucy, meanwhile, save Edmund, just as heroines throughout all of literature and myth defend lost family members.

Lucy, as a child still in touch with the world of magic, becomes the ultimate guide and guardian. Her instinctive comprehension of the feminine world of creativity and the unconscious ushers the children through Narnia, as her faith in the magical characters around her safeguards the siblings. Peter, the central hero, receives a powerful sword, but Lucy, the central heroine, saves the day: while all the children battle the heroine's dark side, the Terrible Mother, only Lucy can rescue Edmund and many others from the brink of death with her healing elixir (Lewis 179). Susan receives a horn to call for help, and uses it to protect herself *and her younger sister* (Lewis 130). Just as the battle turns ugly, Aslan, Susan, and Lucy ride up with reinforcements, again rescuing the people of Narnia. As future queens, Susan and Lucy finally expand their circle beyond their brothers to shelter the entire magical world.

Unlike Susan and Lucy, most heroines travel unarmed. Dorothy slays the witch with a bucket of water (after numerous protests that she couldn't possibly kill someone). The crone of "The Wild Swans" offers Eliza only a nettle, along with advice. Nancy Drew hates guns. Red Riding Hood has a cloak (which offers her no protection) and a basket of goodies. Tattercoats and the heroine of "East of the Sun, West of the Moon" don't fight; they bribe others with gold rings and spindles.

Gowns and gifts help the heroines to entice their princes and discover their own self-worth. But do all these clothes turn powerful heroines into Barbie dolls? Why doesn't Dorothy wield a silver dagger? What message are these stories passing to our children?

One message is that girls are not supposed to fight. Sexist, perhaps, but let us examine the topic more closely. Lucy is the smartest of the Narnia children, getting her siblings out of danger through her trust and faith. Psyche, Cinderella, and many others do tasks like sorting grain and befriending animals to prove their worthiness and earn a reward. Many, like Rumpelstiltskin's heroine, guess riddles. Eliza saves her swan siblings at great personal danger, knitting shirts and keeping silent. All the heroines accomplish their quests without violence, valuing cleverness and fortitude over Excalibur.

Perhaps in the days of tales by the fireside, the girls looked on wistfully as their brothers rode off to war. "There's magic in our lives, too," their grandmothers would say. "We can disguise ourselves as men and pick up swords, be warrior queens like Maeve and

Atalanta, or we can follow our own path." From there emerged stories of spinning (Rumpelstiltskin), gardening (Rapunzel), weaving (The Wild Swans), housework (Cinderella), washing clothes (East of the Sun, West of the Moon), holding a loved one (Tam Lin), caring for relatives (Red Riding Hood), child rearing (Electra), and marriage (nearly all of them).

In each story, actions in the so-called "women's domain" save the men and allow the heroines to accomplish their goals. Antigone heroically buries her brother, though death is the penalty. Alice sees through the card game that entraps her. Meg in *A Wrinkle in Time* restores her little brother through love, in a *Harry Potter*-like moment. The heroine of Gail Carson Levine's *Ella Enchanted* breaks her curse to protect the prince she loves. Janet must clasp Tam Lin in her arms—whatever shape he takes—in order to steal him away from the fairy queen. Magic and incredible heroism enter these everyday tasks as the women complete their journeys with skills they already possess.

Heroes wield their gifts in a more straightforward world: their powerful swords can kill antagonists and defend the helpless. Heroines live in a more treacherous, shifting world, where even their mentor can seek their death. Just as the outdoor world threatens the hero, the interior world of the home offers shocking dangers for the heroine.

The mentor has given the champion the path to destiny. From there, the protagonist travels through the magical world, encountering hardships and dangers, making friends, and having small adventures. Still, this is not just a quest; this is the story of adulthood, as the hero or heroine grows. To do this, the child must overcome both parents.

Confrontation

The male hero accepts his mother-figure into himself, using her insights of magic and creativity to reclaim his lost feminine side and absorb the power into himself. In this way he prepares to confront his deadly adversary—his father. Ginny has an intuition of magic, a joy even, that Harry lacks. She does excellently in Dumbledore's Army (*OotP* 394) and joins the Slug Club for her ferocious Bat-Bogey hex (*HBP* 146). Likewise, Luke learns from Princess Leia and

Frodo from Galadriel as they reclaim their spiritual sides and prepare for the battle to come.

Heroines symbolically encounter their fathers, but understand a different, harsher lesson. In the middle of the journey, heroines must understand (ironically enough) the feminine power they already possess by realizing their father's power has ended (Warner 275).

In Narnia, Susan and Lucy see Aslan shaved and killed, completely stripped of his majesty. Only then can they protect him through the night with their nurturing feminine strength and arrive to save the battle the next morning. When the last unicorn finally defends herself against the terrifying red bull in Peter S. Beagle's novel, the bull turns and flees in an instant. Dorothy returns to the Emerald City to find the wizard cowering in his office. He is not a wizard, merely a pasteboard head. Thus having faced down the animus of her life, the heroine prepares to defeat the overpowering anima, or feminine presence.

In Jungian psychology, the witch personifies self-consuming evil; she is the destructive power of the unconscious, opposite to the heroine (Murdock 18). Yet, at the same time, the witch (generally the story's villain) represents the heroine's dark side. She is her equal and opposite, with contrasting desires and powers. The heroine wants to save the world, so her enemy wants to destroy it. She is selfless and nurturing, so the witch is demanding and cruel. Jung writes: "The shadow personifies everything that the subject refuses to acknowledge about himself and yet is always thrusting itself upon him directly or indirectly—for instance, inferior traits of character and other incompatible tendencies" (285). In other words, the enemy is the part of ourselves we most dislike. We see the negative aspects of our mothers in ourselves and reject them, saying "That's as different from me as possible; that quality belongs to the enemy."

Harry likewise battles his own Dark Lord. This ruler is evil incarnate, a monster as Harry is human, tall as Harry is short, dominant in power and knowledge as Harry is a student. In short, he represents everything Harry has rejected. This struggle to conquer the overlord and become the hero (and in time, a better ruler) represents the son supplanting the father. As Ryan Weber observes in his essay, "Harry Potter's Quest: The Hero's Journey and the Shadow":

In order for a villain to function effectively as a manifestation of the shadow archetype, it must have a personal and psychologically irreversible connection with the hero… In the case of Voldemort and Harry, this is literally the case, for when Harry was attacked and scarred by Voldemort, the sorcerer permanently implanted a piece of himself within the mark. This forever binds the two, and causes Harry's scar to throb whenever Voldemort is near.

Though Rowling has stated the two aren't literally related (what a creepy thought), they're symbolically linked throughout the story, even before book five's prophecy binds them forever. From the moment Harry buys a wand that's the twin of Voldemort's, people around him comment on how much the two wizards have in common; the hero and the villain are more similar than we'd like to think. As Carl Jung describes, "The shadow is a living part of the personality and therefore wants to live with it in some form. It cannot be argued out of existence or rationalized into harmlessness" (20). Mr. Ollivander, the wand seller, says, "I think we must expect great things from you, Mr. Potter… After all, He-Who-Must-Not-Be-Named did great things—terrible, yes, but great" (*PS* 64). Both wizards are great, even though one is the villain and the other the hero. The Sorting Hat memorably offers to put Harry in Slytherin, leaving him to suspect he's Slytherin's heir (*PS* 91). All this culminates with book five's prophecy. Harry and Voldemort's destinies are interdependent: "Neither can live while the other survives" (*OotP* 841). Harry and Voldemort are indeed two sides: light and dark, good and evil, yet with an intrinsic bond that may destroy them both.

Innermost Cave

Just as Beowulf sinks under the water to battle Grendel's mother and Aragorn descends into the cave of the dead, each protagonist must make his or her descent into the unknown as the greatest obstacle to conquering the quest. These journeys into darkness represent death—only by completely surrendering to the unknown can the champion transcend, and learn enough to accomplish the quest and rule over the future community.

Susan and Lucy do not die, but they walk into dark places where the witch awaits them, disappearing from view and risking certain destruction. Yet, only in this way can they face the witch and defeat her, learning their own powers of motherhood by guarding Aslan through the night. Jung explains, "The meeting with oneself is, at first, the meeting with one's own shadow. The shadow is a tight passage, a narrow door, whose painful constriction no one is spared who goes down to the deep well. But one must learn to know oneself in order to know who one is. For what comes after the door is, surprisingly enough, a boundless expanse filled with unprecedented uncertainty" (21).

In ancient, matriarchal mythology, this descent was a desirable initiation made by female seekers of knowledge. The great goddesses Inanna and Ishtar descend bravely into the night in order to find enlightenment. (Perera 50–58). Once, this initiation ritual was sought out and desired, since young women craved their descent into the cave and the new wisdom it would bring. The power of the ancient feminine would guide a woman down to the world of the unconscious, with untold wisdom as a reward. Even the figure of the dark god was not menacing, but welcoming, as the young, questing anima sought its dark opposite, the wise and powerful animus (Estés 412). As the patriarchal Hellenistic religion took over, the woman's journey and archetypal eagerness for knowledge faded. From this shift in power came the legend of Persephone, an innocent flower princess who must be violently kidnapped to enter the realm of the dead (Estés 412). All eagerness to enter the underworld, filled with dark secrets, vanishes, and the heroine in this case must allow a man to drag her on the ultimate initiation.

Harry has plenty of symbolic deaths himself. In book one, *Philosopher's Stone*, he faces not only Voldemort and the defeat of his friends, but also the Mirror of Erised and his own repressed wishes. Weber explains:

In the inmost cave lies the sorcerer's stone, which is the power to fuel Harry's shadow, and the magic mirror that reveals the strongest yearnings of Harry's heart. Naturally, it is here that the climax between Harry and his shadow must take place, and since the shadow is the repressed qualities of Harry's own psyche, only his own positive attributes, his internal and inherited love, can be used to defeat it.

Still, the most memorable of Harry's descents is the deserted graveyard where Voldemort reincarnates himself from Harry's blood. Alone in the dark and surrounded by Death Eaters, Harry has lost all defenses. Only the unexpected magic of his link with

Voldemort, *Priori Incantatem*, saves him from inevitable destruction. (*GoF* 668). He encounters his first real death there (Cedric's) and can afterward see thestrals, indicating his growing understanding (*OotP* 446). Likewise, he journeys under Hogwarts at the climaxes of the first three books, then into the Ministry's cellar and the Horcrux cave. Why such a predilection for battling evil underground? The underworld offers only death and darkness: to truly grow, Harry passes a fearsome initiation and gains the wisdom of mortality.

Ascension

Susan and Lucy bring reinforcements to the battle, where Lucy rescues Edmund from death. Having thus proved themselves, the boys in battle and the girls in rescue, the children ascend to the four thrones of Narnia, sharing their wisdom with their subjects. In his own crucial final step of his first trial, the Philosopher's Stone, "Harry returns to his community, bringing renewal, wisdom, and treasures. The stone is destroyed, and his shadow, Voldemort, has temporarily dissipated" (Weber). Harry has faced his greatest desire, the Mirror of Erised and all it offers, along with his shadow-self. Now, he can return to Hogwarts, and even to the Dursleys, thanks to his new wisdom.

To achieve the greatest success, the protagonist becomes a divine ruler. Harry longs to be an Auror, battling Death Eaters with the same courage and selflessness as his parents, dispensing justice and protecting the innocent. Lucy and Susan become queens of Narnia forever. Just as importantly, Lucy guides the "next generation" of Eustace and Jill. Dorothy guides younger friends into Oz, while the Baudelaire orphans of *A Series of Unfortunate Events* adopt an orphan baby of their own. While heroes become warrior kings and sages, the greatest heroines achieve worldly power and motherhood while remaining wholly feminine throughout the journey.

The purpose of this journey, after all, is to achieve adulthood and balance. By embracing the dark side as part of the self, the hero and heroine find their way to the power and majesty of adulthood. It is this passage that defines who we are, regardless of gender.

Works Cited

Estés, Clarissa Pinkola. *Women Who Run with the Wolves*. New York: Ballantine, 1992.

Jan, Isabelle. *On Children's Literature*. London: Penguin, 1969.

Jung, Carl. *The Archetypes and the Collective Unconscious*. Trans. R. F. C. Hull. Bollingen Series XX. Princeton, NJ: Princeton UP, 1969.

Lewis, C. S. *The Lion, the Witch, and the Wardrobe*. New York: HarperCollins, 1978.

Margaret L. Marshall. *An Introduction to the World of Children's Books*. Aldershot: Gower, 1982.

Murdock, Maureen. *The Heroine's Journey*. Boston: Shambhala, 1990.

Perera, Silvia Brinton. *Descent to the Goddess*. Toronto: Inner City, 1981.

Rowling, J. K. *Harry Potter and the Goblet of Fire*. New York: Scholastic, 2000.

—. *Harry Potter and the Half-Blood Prince*. New York: Scholastic, 2005.

— . *Harry Potter and the Order of the Phoenix*. New York: Scholastic, 2003.

—. *Harry Potter and the Philosopher's Stone*. London: Bloomsbury, 1997.

Scholastic Official Harry Potter Site. Scholastic Books. Accessed 12 Mar 2000. <http://www.scholastic.com/harrypotter/home.asp>.

Warner, Maria. *From the Beast to the Blonde*. New York: Farrar, Straus, and Giroux, 1994.

Weber, Ryan P. "Harry Potter's Quest: The Hero's Journey and the Shadow." *Headline Muse* 23 (2002).

The Hero's and Heroine's Journey: Reading List
http://www.calithwain.com/

Heroine's Journey Children's Series

First Book	Series	Author
The Wizard of Oz	The Oz Books	L. Frank Baum
Dealing with Dragons	The Enchanted Forest Chroni	Patricia C. Wrede
The Lion, the Witch, and the Wardrobe	The Chronicles of Narnia	C. S. Lewis
Alanna: The First Adventure	The Lioness Quartet	Tamora Pierce
Wild Magic	The Immortals Quartet	Tamora Pierce
A Wrinkle in Time	The Time Quintet	Madeleine L'Engle
The Golden Compass	His Dark Materials	Philip Pullman
* Arrows of the Queen	The Heralds of Valdemar	Mercedes Lackey
* Sister Light, Sister Dark	The Great Alta Saga	Jane Yolen

Heroine's Journey Children's Novels

The Hero and the Crown	Robin McKinley
Mrs. Frisby and the Rats of NIMH	Robert O'Brien
Alice in Wonderland	Lewis Carroll
A Great and Terrible Beauty	Libba Bray
The Last Unicorn	Peter S. Beagle
Coraline	Neil Gaiman
Sabriel	Garth Nix

---

*   Designed for a young-adult audience.

Hero's Journey Children's Series

First Book	Series	Author
Harry Potter and the Philosopher's Stone	Harry Potter	J. K. Rowling
Eragon	Inheritance	Christopher Paolini
The Lion, the Witch, and the Wardrobe	The Chronicles of Narnia	C. S. Lewis
* *Over Sea, Under Stone*	The Dark Is Rising	Susan Cooper
* *Ender's Game*	The Ender Saga	Orson Scott Card
* *Seventh Son*	The Tales of Alvin Maker	Orson Scott Card
A Wizard of Earthsea	The Earthsea Cycle	Ursula K. Le Guin
The Book of Three	The Chronicles of Prydain	Lloyd Alexander
* *Pawn of Prophecy*	The Belgariad	David Eddings

Hero's Journey Children's Novels

* *The Princess Bride*	William Goldman
The Hobbit	J. R. R. Tolkien
The Neverending Story	Michael Ende

Movies

Star Wars	*Eragon*	*The Dark Crystal*
The Princess Bride	*The Lion, the Witch, and the Wardrobe*	*Labyrinth*
The Hobbit	*The Lion King*	*Spiderman*
Lord of the Rings	*The Wizard of Oz*	*Superman*
King Arthur (any version)	* *The 10 th Kingdom*	*Shrek*
Harry Potter	* *Mirrormask*	* *Hercules* (any version)

---

* Designed for a young-adult audience.

"I NEVER DO ANYTHING TWICE!"
—STEPHEN SONDHEIM[1]

"I ALWAYS DO EVERYTHING AT LEAST TWICE"
—ATTRIBUTED TO J. K. ROWLING

Diana Patterson
Mount Royal College

J. K. Rowling repeats herself. And yet she does not repeat as many another writer does owing to a lack of imagination, a limited repertoire of plots, or forgetfulness. Rowling uses repetition to increase our astonishment.

Genuine repetition must be distinguished from foreshadowing. To foreshadow is to hint that something is coming. Rowling uses these hints often, such as when Harry manages to make the glass disappear in chapter two of Philosopher's Stone.[2] That ability to make astonishing things happen foreshadows that Harry is going to be able to do magic. But it is not genuinely repeated later in the text.

Repetition as a serious subject of inquiry into narrative and poetics has been addressed by a number of critics, and we shall acknowledge that work without summarizing the findings more than to note, as Rommon-Kenan does, that "[w]e never go into the same river twice, and no pure repetition exists."[3] Rowling illustrates this point very well.

---

1 Song title from the film *The 7% Solution*. Appears in *Side by Side by Sondheim*, compact disc, disc 1, Original London Cast Recording, RCA Victor 1851-2-RG.

2 J. K. Rowling, *Harry Potter and the Philosopher's Stone* (London: Bloomsbury, 1997).

3 Shlomith Rimmon-Kenan, "The Paradoxical Status of Repetition," *Poetics Today* 1, no. 4 (1980): 151–59.

Rowling frequently uses repetition to make her fantastical world familiar and to create consistent characters. Possibly the first repetition we see of this kind in *Chamber of Secrets* is Hedwig's screeching.[1] Uncle Vernon describes the screeching, but then we experience it when Dobby sets Hedwig off. The important screech, however, is really when Harry is escaping in the Ford Anglia, and Harry has forgotten her.[2] She screeches, alerting Uncle Vernon. The repetition gives us two pieces of consistency: first that Hedwig screeches when left in her cage, and second that Uncle Vernon reacts violently and immediately to her screeches. Similarly, but more subtly, Harry dreams of Dudley rattling the bars of the cage he thinks he is in.[3] This is virtually a repetition of Dudley's behaviour when he has his father rap on the glass of the snake's enclosure in the reptile house in *Philosopher's Stone*: Dudley is consistently a disturber and a bully.[4]

An even subtler repetition that might be worth noting is tongue chewing. Aunt Petunia, at the start of *Goblet of Fire* chews her tongue rather than lunch, anticipating the arrival of the Weasleys to take Harry to the World Cup;[5] then, of course, Dudley eats the Ton-Tongue Toffee, when he appears to be eating something long and purple, but is in fact chewing and choking on his tongue.[6] This is not particularly useful in creating consistency or character: it is rather as if Rowling is simply incapable of introducing the tongue-chewing idea only once.[7] It is as if she cannot do without pairs, without twins, without mirror images, without two Barty Crouches, both under invisibility cloaks in woods, and so on.[8]

In the wizarding world, repetition occurs in the constant reminder of the oddity of the world, for instance in trick or squeaky steps, particularly in *Goblet of Fire*. First we see Neville get stuck in the trick step,[9] and then Harry gets stuck in the same fashion when

---

1   J. K. Rowling, *Harry Potter and the Chamber of Secrets* (London: Bloomsbury, 1998), p. 7.

2   *Ibid.*, p. 26.

3   *Ibid.*, p. 22.

4   *PS*, p. 25.

5   J. K. Rowling, *Harry Potter and the Goblet of Fire* (London: Bloomsbury, 2000), p. 40.

6   *Ibid.*, pp. 47–49.

7   Robert Rogers, "Freud and the Semiotics of Repetition," *Poetics Today* 8, nos. 3–4 (1987): 579–590, discusses Freud's repetition compulsion in a literary context. Although Freud sees the compulsion to repeat as a disease, Rogers manages to break this view and see repetition as meaning, because to repeat is to move forward as a wave does (p. 585).

8   *GoF*, pp. 115, 481–483, 595–599.

9   *Ibid.*, p. 168.

we need Harry to be trapped and invisible for the key scene in "The Egg and the Eye."[1] In *Philosopher's Stone,* we see Hermione use her fire charm: she can keep fire in a jam jar, first to keep the trio warm during a break,[2] and then to set Snape's robes on fire during the Quidditch match.[3] Part of the humour that releases tension in the final fight against Voldemort in that first book is Hermione's forgetting that she can conjure this fire when she is confronted by Devil's Snare.[4] Later, of course, she uses presumably the same flame in the toilet in Moaning Myrtle's bathroom, in *Chamber of Secrets.*[5] Presumably Lupin uses the same spell in *Prisoner of Azkaban* when he holds a handful of blue flames before the first Dementor appears.[6] The consistency creates a world from a series of incidents and also allows for humour when a Muggle forgets the consistency of the magical world.

But sometimes the repetition is not for consistency, but for revelation. One of the earlier of these incidents is Harry's talking to the snake in chapter two of *Philosopher's Stone* followed by his talking to a snake in book two, *Chamber of Secrets* (chapter 11).[7] The first time we listen to Harry talking to the snake, we are drawn into a world that is clearly fantasy. The second time we discover that this is highly unusual! What is common for Harry, and now seen as familiar behaviour by those of us who have read both books, is actually startlingly peculiar behaviour to Harry's classmates and teachers.

One of Rowling's peculiar uses of repetition is to create a bit of a twist and to compress explanation of one of the quirks of the wizarding world at a critical moment. Probably the very first repetition we notice in the series is one of these repetitions with a twist, the re-use of the spell *Wingardium Leviosa.* We watch the spell work in Flitwick's class,[8] when Ron cannot make the spell work but Hermione can. Then, later that very day, whilst Hermione is cowering against the wall of the girls' toilet in fear of the troll,[9] Ron performs a perfect *Wingardium Leviosa* charm and saves the day.

---

1   *Ibid,*. p. 406 ff.
2   *PS,* p. 134.
3   *Ibid.,* p. 140.
4   *Ibid.,* p. 202.
5   *CoS,* p. 138.
6   J. K. Rowling, *Harry Potter and the Prisoner of Azkaban* (London: Bloomsbury, 1999), p. 65.
7   *PS,* p. 25–26; *CoS,* p. 145.
8   *PS,* p. 127.
9   *Ibid.,* p. 129.

None of us missed that repetition. The wondrous effect is achieved precisely because we have seen Ron try this spell and be unable to do it, and Hermione, now helpless with fear, very capable of performing the spell in class, but unable to do the spell in the real world. The repetition makes the scene and creates the characters.

We also do not miss the series of mirrors in *Philosopher's Stone*. At Christmas Harry receives an invisibility cloak, and he dashes to look at himself in a mirror.[1] He then stumbles on the Mirror of Erised and wants to look into it to repeat the effect, but instead stumbles on his family.[2] Finally, the Mirror of Erised is the means to the Philosopher's Stone.[3] At this tense moment, no explanation of how the mirror works is required because we have met it before: the emphasis is on suspense, and the horror of Voldemort, not how this confounded mirror works.

A frequent use of repetition is one where a spell is rehearsed in class so that the students and we readers learn it before the spell is used in the moment of crisis. For instance, we watch Hermione perform the *Silencio* charm in *Order of the Phoenix* on a frog and a raven,[4] then perform it on a Death Eater,[5] who probably looked like a large raven in his black robes topped by a fixed mask. A variation on this method is the *Accio* charm in *Goblet of Fire*. The charm is used again, and again, and again. We first see Mrs. Weasley use it to get the Ton-Tongue Toffee from Fred and George's pockets and turn-ups,[6] then Hermione practices the spell on the Hogwarts Express;[7] next Harry is the only person who cannot do the spell in class and as a result is given it to practice for homework.[8] At last Harry uses the summoning charm to get his Firebolt for the first task.[9] The effect of the repetition is first satisfaction that Harry can do the charm, and then amazement that nobody else thought of doing such a thing. And yet *Accio* is not left there: the fake Moody saves much trouble by using the spell to get the Marauder's Map before Snape or Harry can discover that Barty Crouch is standing

---

1   *Ibid.*, p. 148.
2   *Ibid*,. p. 153.
3   *Ibid.*, pp. 210–12.
4   J. K. Rowling, *Harry Potter and the Order of the Phoenix* (London: Bloomsbury, 2003), p. 333.
5   *Ibid.*, p. 698.
6   *GoF*, p. 65.
7   *Ibid.*, p. 149.
8   *Ibid.*, p. 278.
9   *Ibid.*, pp. 302–3, 309.

before them (not that he knew that at the time!),[1] and Harry uses the spell to get the Triwizard Cup to Portkey back to Hogwarts just in the nick of time before Voldemort curses him.[2] As a teacher, I rather like the fact that Flitwick uses it to collect the O.W.L. papers at the end of the exam.[3] *Accio* is simply everywhere.

Only on rereading, possibly several times, do we see some of the other consistencies or explanations these repetitions bring to the Potterverse. One of these is the simultaneous cursing of Harry and Malfoy in *Goblet of Fire*.[4] Because the wands' spells are triggered simultaneously, they ricochet off each other. Harry's *Furnunculus* curse hits Goyle, causing his face to break into boils. Malfoy's *Densaugeo* curse hits Hermione, enlarging her teeth. What we are seeing are simultaneous spells hitting each other from wands that are not brothers. When Harry and Voldemort face each other, their simultaneous spells repeat the action, but not the result of the wands meeting each other. Instead of having ricocheted spells, we get the golden network and the *Priori Incantatem* effect, bringing Harry's parents out of Voldemort's wand tip.[5] The repetition of simultaneous curses shows us just how unusual the result is when wands share cores.

Likewise in the *Order of the Phoenix*, we see the repetition of Voldemort's possession.[6] In the "Eye of the Snake" chapter, Harry sees through the eyes of a snake that Voldemort was possessing at the time.[7] The culmination of the fight at the Ministry, in the chapter "The Only One He Ever Feared," is the repeated possession, but this time Voldemort possessing Harry directly.[8] Voldemort tempts Dumbledore to kill Harry so that he might kill Voldemort's soul or whatever is possessing Harry.[9] This ability to possess is unexplained, but its repetition enforces the idea that the

---

1 *Ibid.*, p. 410.
2 *Ibid.*, p. 580.
3 *OotP*, p. 566.
4 P. 262.
5 *Ibid.*, 575.
6 This is a most curious occurrence, and it deserves some explanation: how can Voldemort, who now has a body of his own, leave and yet not leave that body to possess another body? and where was Voldemort's body in the Ministry of Magic fight when he was possessing Harry?
7 *OotP*, pp. 408–9, 410. The explanation is given by Snape on p. 470.
8 *Ibid.*, pp. 719–20.
9 The cryptic "but in essence divided?"(*ibid.*, p. 416) answered by two snakes seems to explain this to Dumbledore, but not to the rest of us.

possession is not imaginary or a voice-throwing or vision-throwing trick.

There are many good examples of repetitions that occur within the same volume of the story, but, of course, Rowling is really writing a seven-volume novel, and repetitions occur intra-volume as well. Probably the grandest of these starts in *Chamber of Secrets*—the first occurrence of many repeated items that stay fairly quiet until *Half-Blood Prince*.[1] Here we arrive at Borgin and Burkes and see the cursed necklace, the Hand of Glory, giving light only to the beholder, and the one working Vanishing Cabinet of the pair.[2] Later we see the broken one—possibly we even see how it is broken—when Peeves drops it over Filch's office.[3] Here also we see Snape first suspected of reading minds,[4] and the first Howler.[5] Of course this collection of first hints in book two, connected with events in book six fits neatly into the theory that the books have a kind of correspondence of volumes from the inside out: 1–7, 2–6, 3–5, and 4 within itself. Repetition makes the correspondence. Several papers and theories on the web have dealt with these correspondences, so they are omitted here.

In *Philosopher's Stone*, all the tasks, except one, are understood by Harry because he has seen them before. The one new kind of task is the one undertaken by Hermione, solving a riddle. We do not see an important and formal riddle again until *Goblet of Fire*, where Harry faces the Sphinx. I suspect, however, that there are riddle qualities awaiting us in the interpretation of the prophecy, as well as in finding the horcruxes. No skill acquired in the books seems to be for nought, and so despite the thousands of pages of this narrative, the story ends up being very tightly controlled indeed—through repetition.

The repeated motifs within the confines of *Chamber of Secrets*, however, are the *Expelliarmus* charm, where Lockhart is "blasted off

---

1 J. K. Rowling, *Harry Potter and the Half-Blood Prince* (London: Bloomsbury, 2005).
2 *CoS*, pp. 42–44.
3 *Ibid.*, pp. 97–99. We do not see how broken the cabinet is, however, until *Order of the Phoenix*, when the twins forced Montague head-first into the Vanishing Cabinet (p. 552).
4 *CoS*, pp. 62, 141. The first of these says, "This wasn't the first time Snape had given Harry the impression of being able to read minds." *PS*, however, never explicitly mentions Snape seeming to read minds. Presumably the incident referred to is *PS*, p. 195, where Snape says that they should not hang around indoors, or people will think they are up to something.
5 *CoS*, p. 69.

his feet" in the Duelling Club,[1] as well as at the end when Harry and
Ron find him in his office and defend themselves against the
memory charm, where Lockhart is described as "blasted
backwards."[2] Nobody else seems to have such a violent reaction to
the disarming charm. In *Chamber of Secrets* we might also notice
some of the tiny, obscure repetitions that simply show how helpless
Rowling appears to be to avoid repetition: Ron throws Lockhart's
wand out the window just before the descent into the Chamber[3] in
the same way that the Cornish Pixies throws it out the window in his
classroom.[4] There is the phrase that Harry says to Professor Dippet
in the memory, "I'll just go."[5] He tries the same line with Aragog.[6]
And then it sounds as if Lockhart is going to use the same line just
as they are about to slide down the sunk sink in Moaning Myrtle's
bathroom, but Lockhart is never allowed to complete the sentence.[7]
There is also a repetition of Harry's misdirected gaze: in the first
instance Harry is looking at the petrified Hermione's hand in the
Hospital Wing whilst Ron is gazing at her face.[8] As a result, Harry
finds the torn page with the basilisk on it. Then later, when
Dumbledore is talking to Lucius Malfoy, obviously politely looking
at his face, Harry is looking at Dobby's dumbshow wherein Dobby
explains that the diary was provided by Mr. Malfoy.[9] Similar small
comparisons that are beyond *Chamber of Secrets*, but that illustrate the
same point, are the talking mirror in the Weasleys' house,[10] with a
similar, but cheekier version in The Leaky Cauldron.[11] And in *Half-
Blood Prince*, we see two house-elves who appear to be moving
tables.[12] In other words, tiny repetitions are ubiquitous.

Sometimes incidents are repeated particularly in order to show
contrast in character or in setting. For instance, in *Goblet of Fire*, we
are invited to compare two incidents of fathers seeing their sons in
situations of extreme danger. In one we see a generous, caring

---

1 *Ibid.*, p. 142.
2 *Ibid.*, p. 221.
3 *Ibid.*
4 *Ibid.*, p. 79.
5 *Ibid.*, p. 181.
6 *Ibid.*, p. 206— "We'll just go, then."
7 *Ibid.*, p. 222.
8 *Ibid.*, p. 214.
9 *Ibid.*, p. 246.
10 *Ibid.*, p. 37.
11 *PoA*, pp. 46, 55.
12 *HBP*, pp. 295, 408.

father, and in the other, a self-absorbed one, caring more for his reputation than his offspring. The Dark Mark appears in the sky above the copse where Harry, Ron, and Hermione are hiding. A group of 20 wizards, led by Barty Crouch, Apparates at that spot assuming that someone right there has cast the spell, and they start stunning all those in the clearing. "STOP! *That's my son*," says Mr. Weasley.[1] We see a father catching his son *seemingly* doing something wrong. Yet, Mr. Weasley protects his son. Later in the memory in the Pensieve, we see Mr. Crouch finding that his son is accused of doing something wrong. Crouch does not protect his son, but condemns him, and sentences him to prison in order that the good name of Crouch stand for something, ignoring the role of a father.[2] In fact, he disowns his son entirely. We have two sons, two fathers, and two accusations, but the repetition illustrates a contrast between the people and their characters.

In *Order of the Phoenix*, during Hagrid's first lesson back from his journey into the mountains tracking giants, Harry comments that Hagrid's cuts are still bleeding, when they seemed to have been fresh and bleeding the night before. Harry wonders if Hagrid could have been bitten by some beast whose cuts do not heal.[3] This leads us nicely to Mr. Weasley's cuts that do not heal in St. Mungo's—and we know he has been bitten by a snake with venom "that keeps wounds open."[4] The repeated beast bites suggest the same cause, but eventually we learn how different they are.

In *Order of the Phoenix*, and then *Half-Blood Prince*, we have a more enigmatic pairing of events.[5] In Grimmauld Place, Sirius and Snape are having a conversation alone, just as Harry is going to get his instructions to attend Occlumency lessons. Snape accuses Sirius of deliberately letting Lucius Malfoy see him in his Animagus shape so that he will not have to do any fighting with the Order. Sirius responds, "Are you calling me a coward?" And Snape replies, "Why, yes, I suppose I am."[6] Snape here is his usual supercilious self, and Sirius, as a true Gryffindor, is particularly touchy about having his

1   *GoF*, p. 116.
2   *Ibid.*, pp. 517–18.
3   *Ibid.*, p. 391.
4   *Ibid.*, p. 431.
5   The enigma may well be solved in Rowling's *Harry Potter and the Deathly Hallows*, which is not yet released.
6   *OotP*, p. 460.

bravery impeached. In a very similar incident, at the end of *Half-Blood Prince,* Harry calls Snape a coward.[1] Snape's anger is ever greater than Sirius's was, and is clearly there to tell us something vital about Snape, in so many ways the opposite of Sirius—but what?

The implication of the Snape-Sirius comparison is unclear because we do not yet know the end. This repetition for obfuscation is one of Rowling's masterful storytelling techniques. She sets up what appears to be a pattern and then undermines it. We see nothing sinister in Kreacher's being given the order, "OUT!" just before Christmas,[2] because he has been told, "Now go away, Kreacher," during the summer cleaning, when we first meet him. We assume he is always being told to go away, as he is utterly useless. Why, in our most far-fetched imaginings, would we foresee that that famous "OUT!" would lead to Kreacher's betraying the Order to Voldemort? But, of course, it does.

One of the more amusing patterns of repetition that fools us completely is the interpretation of a new teacher riding on the Hogwarts Express. In *Prisoner of Azkaban,* the trio are in a compartment with a sleeping adult.[3] Ron asks, "Who do you reckon he is?" Hermione reads his name from his suitcase label, and then interprets which teacher he will be with the phrase, "That's obvious…. There's only one vacancy, isn't there? Defence Against the Dark Arts." The pattern of losing the Defence Against the Dark Arts Teacher repeats each year. So, in *Half-Blood Prince,* the joke is that we, like the trio, make Hermione's assumption again about Horace Slughorn, but find that he is Potions Master.[4]

A couple of the repetitions amaze us, partly because in the first instance we do not recognize what is going on, and the repetition produces a different, or seemingly different effect. The first of these in the series, used in the mode probably most reminiscent of the mystery genre—and *Harry Potter* is most certainly a mystery—is the rereading of Dumbledore's Chocolate Frog Card.[5] The first time, we find out something about Dumbledore, but the second we suddenly find out about Nicholas Flamel and alchemy. The clue we need is in

1   *HBP,* p. 564.
2   *OotP,* p. 420.
3   *PoA,* pp. 59–60.
4   *HBP,* p. 158.
5   *PS,* pp. 77, 160.

plain sight, but only when it is repeated at the right time do we see it for what it is.

Probably the most amazing, absolutely repetitive, and most pleasing chapter in all the Potterverse in the retelling of the escape/ execution of Buckbeak in *Prisoner of Azkaban*. Word for word, scene by scene, we re-see the section and can only be incoherent with amazement at the ingenuity of the solution.[1]

These examples of repetition in the series have been far from exhaustive (although they may have been exhausting to take in). The question remains: how is it that Rowling gets away with so much repetition, usually without castigation by the critics, and often even without our noticing that she has done it? The key is the way in which Rowling tells her story. The reason we are gripped by the tale, almost from the opening words—"Mr and Mrs Dursley, at number 4, Privet Drive were proud to say that they were perfectly normal, thank you very much"—is that Rowling tells us very little about the world and about her characters.[2] Instead, she *shows* us people acting and speaking and moving around in her world. It is thus much more natural that things should repeat themselves, particularly within the rush of action. After all, children mimic their parents, and friends use similar expressions and gestures. We see visual similarities all the time, usually without commenting on them, for we find our world filled with consistency, symmetry, familiarity. And so Rowling has shown us these very facets of a natural world. Had she *told* us, as she does in the opening of *Chamber of Secrets* in order to remind us of things that happened in book one, just in case we did not read the first volume, the repetition would be boring.

This retelling does occur elsewhere, admittedly—often in the denouement when someone, as in a mystery, retells the events of the story that Harry has misinterpreted: Snape was muttering a counter-curse to save Harry, not trying to kill him;[3] the professor in the chair was not Alastor Moody—Harry had never known Alastor Moody;[4] Dumbledore would not look at Harry because he knew Voldemort

---

1   *PoA*, pp. 240–88; 288–305. These scenes need to be investigated in light of Edward Casey, "Imagination and Repetition in Literature: A reassessment," in "Graphesis: Perspectives in Literature and Philosophy," special issue, *Yale French Studies*, 52 (1975): 249–67. He discusses notions of absence in both repetition and imagination, but alas, there is no room here to explore this matter.

2   *PS*, p. 7.

3   *Ibid.*, p. 209.

4   *GoF*, p. 590.

could look out through Harry's eyes.[1] Telling is acceptable, but most often at the end of the story, not at the beginning. Telling rather than showing in the exposition is the reason that many people find *Chamber of Secrets* Rowling's least successful book. She learned from that work, and never delivered the necessary background exposition so ineptly again.[2] In fact, that glorious first chapter, in the Prime Minister's office, in *Half-Blood Prince* is one of the most charming chapters of all—and yet its purpose is entirely one of exposition. Being as we are present and seeing action and reading the inside of the Prime Minister's mind, all the background information has the charm of being both new and familiar. Instead of feeling that we have heard it all before, and that we wish the author would get on with the story, we feel rather smug in that we recognise things that are new to, or only vaguely known by, the Prime Minister. Thus, it is *how* Rowling tells her story that makes repetition not only tolerable, a technique of the mystery story, and a method of speeding up the action, but utterly delightful.

---

1   *OotP*, pp. 729–730.
2   Gary E. Raney, David J. Therriault, Scott R. B. Minkoff, "Repetition Effects from Paraphrased Text: Evidence for an Integrated Representation Model of Text Representation," *Discourse Processes: A Multidisciplinary Journal* 29, no. 1 (2000): 61–81, discusses how we remember only incidents, not detail, so that paraphrase appears to be full repetition, even when the repetition does not provide full facts. Raney *et al.* do not discuss telling rather than showing, nor Western cultural bias in their model, but the experiment does account for reader fatigue at this kind of exposition.

TRICKED OR FOOLED?: ROWLING'S MASTERY OF THE ART OF MISDIRECTION

Phyllis D. Morris

"Readers love to be tricked, but not conned."

—J. K. Rowling[1]

We are convinced that Scabbers is only an unimportant rat, until he transforms into the wizard who betrayed the Potters before our stunned eyes. We are sure that Mad-Eye Moody is working to assist and protect Harry through the tournament, until he is revealed as an imposter as the Polyjuice Potion wears off. Snape is surely the one who is seeking to steal the Philosopher's Stone, but Quirrell turns out to be the villain. While the entire wizarding world knows that Sirius Black has escaped from Azkaban prison to rejoin Lord Voldemort, he is actually one of Voldemort's chief adversaries. We assume Ginny's anxiety was due to the attacks on her fellow students, only to find out that she was the instrument Voldemort used to send the Basilisk after Muggle-borns.

Over and over, J. K. Rowling displays her mastery of the art of misdirection in the *Harry Potter* series. Yet when we read the books a second (or third, or fourth, or fifty-ninth) time, we find the subtle hints she has planted that, if we could only have recognized them for what they were at the time, would have kept us from being ensnared in the clever misdirection web she has so skillfully woven. This paper analyzes the ways in which Rowling employs misdirection in each of the *Harry Potter* books, and discusses why we almost

---

1 Quoted in Tim Boquet, J. K. Rowling: The Wizard Behind *Harry Potter*, *Reader's Digest*, December 2000, <http://www.accio-quote.org/articles/2000/1200-readersdigest-boquet.htm>.

always miss the hints that seem so obvious upon subsequent readings of the books.

The Heir(ess?) of Slytherin

We first hear of the existence of Ginny's diary when it is mentioned as the reason for the third return to the Burrow in the mad scramble to get to the Hogwarts Express on time. Because the return for the diary follows the return first for George's fireworks and then for Fred's broomstick, we are led to think that Rowling is using the forgotten diary as just another reason to make the Weasleys and Harry late and to set up the scene where Dobby seals the gateway and prevents Ron and Harry from entering Platform 9¾. However, in retrospect, we realise that if the Weasleys had not returned a third time for the diary, the Chamber of Secrets would not have been opened.

There are a number of references to dead roosters in the preceding pages that we miss because we do not learn until the sixteenth chapter of book two that "the Basilisk flees only from the crowing of the rooster, which is fatal to it."[1] When Harry, Ron and Hermione visit Hagrid's vast pumpkins, Hagrid mentions meeting Ginny, who "said she was jus' lookin' round the grounds,"[2] but Hagrid speculates she was really looking for Harry. Two pages earlier, Hagrid moves "a half-plucked rooster off his scrubbed table"[3] when he sets out tea, and it is only after we discover that Ginny has been killing the school roosters that we connect her encounter with Hagrid and his possession of the dead rooster. Sixty pages later, Harry runs into Hagrid carrying a dead rooster, the "second one killed this term."[4] We again do not connect the dead rooster with either Ginny or the Chamber of Secrets events, as at the time, Harry is preoccupied with Ernie MacMillan's accusation that he is the heir of Slytherin. Moreover, Hagrid attributes the death of the roosters to "either foxes or a Blood-Suckin' Bugbear."[5]

Rowling also provides numerous hints regarding Ginny's emotional distress throughout book two, all of which are attributed

1   J. K. Rowling, *Harry Potter and the Chamber of Secrets* (London: Bloomsbury, 1999), 215.
2   *Ibid.*, 90.
3   *Ibid.*, 88.
4   *Ibid.*, 150.
5   *Ibid.*

to reasons other than her culpability in the opening of the Chamber of Secrets. In Chapter Eight, we are told that Ginny "had been looking peaky,"[1] but we are led to think that she was just one of the many students with a cold being tended to by Madam Pomfrey. When Mrs Norris is petrified, Ginny is described as being "very disturbed," but because Ron says she "was a great cat-lover,"[2] we do not see that the real reason for her distress is that she knows she is responsible. Eight pages later, Percy tells Harry and Ron that he has "never seen her so upset, crying her eyes out," but Percy attributes this to Ginny thinking Ron and Harry were "going to be expelled."[3] After Colin Creevey is attacked, Ginny is "distraught,"[4] but her emotional state is cast in the context of her sitting next to Colin in Charms and a reference to the other first years moving in scared packs. After Hermione is petrified, Ginny watches Harry and Ron play Exploding Snap "very subdued in Hermione's usual chair,"[5] which we assume is due solely to her closeness with Hermione.

When Harry is falsely accused of being the heir of Slytherin, Fred and George make light of it, but Ginny asks them to stop every time they ask Harry "who he was planning to attack next."[6] In retrospect, we become aware that the attacks stop during the time when the diary is not in Ginny's possession. When the diary falls out of Harry's bag and Malfoy threatens to look through it, we are handed a huge clue when we are told that "Ginny was staring from the diary to Harry, looking terrified,"[7] although we are led to think that she is mortified by the outcome of her Valentine rather than by the realisation that Harry has the diary she thought she had disposed of.

In the end, our feeling of being tricked intensifies when we realise that Rowling gave us the answer to the question of the identity of the heir of Slytherin—when Harry wonders "how Riddle got an award for special services to Hogwarts" and Ron replies, "Maybe he murdered Myrtle, that would've done everyone a favour,"[8] which at the time we take to be just another one of Ron's

---

1   *Ibid.*, 94.
2   *Ibid.*, 111.
3   *Ibid.*, 119.
4   *Ibid.*, 139.
5   *Ibid.*, 201.
6   *Ibid.*, 157.
7   *Ibid.*, 178.
8   *Ibid.*, 173.

jokes.

A Rat Turned Wizard

Rowling skillfully lures us into thinking that Scabbers is only a rat through seemingly insignificant references that are dropped at strategically placed intervals throughout the first three books. We first meet Scabbers on the Hogwarts Express, where it is Ron's unsuccessful attempt to turn him yellow that commands our attention, rather than the rat itself.[1] Scabbers' insignificance is underscored by Ron's description of him as "Percy's old rat"[2] and that "He might have died and you wouldn't know the difference."[3]

Reminders of Scabbers' existence are found throughout the beginning of the series—just enough to keep us aware of his existence without making us suspicious that he is anything but a fat grey rat. We barely notice Scabbers chewing on Ron's sheets;[4] Harry shoving him off his pillow;[5] the rat "snoozing in a patch of sun"[6] the first time Harry visits Ron's room; Ron bending down to pick up the rat after the flying car ejects Harry and Ron;[7] Hermione shifting Scabbers so she can sit down on the end of Harry's bed;[8] Scabbers sitting atop Ron's shoulder in the cutting from *The Daily Prophet* that Ron sends to Harry to tell him of the Weasleys' trip to Egypt[9] and Scabbers poking "his nose out of the shelter of Ron's pocket to sniff hopefully at the air"[10] when the smell of cooking becomes strong on Christmas Eve.

When Ron takes an off-colour Scabbers to the Magical Menagerie in book three, the eyes of the witch behind the counter "moved from Scabbers's tattered left ear to his front paw, which had a toe missing."[11] The missing toe is not viewed as significant in the context of his overall dreadful appearance, and we therefore do not

---

1 J. K. Rowling, *Harry Potter and the Philosopher's Stone* (London: Bloomsbury, 1998), 79.
2 *Ibid.*, 75.
3 *Ibid.*, 78.
4 *Ibid.*, 97.
5 *Ibid.*, 157.
6 *CoS*, 35.
7 *Ibid.*, 60.
8 *Ibid.*, 158.
9 J. K. Rowling, *Harry Potter and the Prisoner of Azkaban* (London: Bloomsbury, 2000), 12.
10 *Ibid.*, 165.
11 *Ibid.*, 49.

make the connection when Ron later says that "Pettigrew's finger... was the biggest bit of him they could find."[1]

When Harry, Ron and Hermione join Lupin in the compartment on the Hogwarts Express in book three, the Sneakoscope Ron had given Harry begins to whistle and spin.[2] While Ron dismisses this by saying the Sneakoscope was a "very cheap one" that "went haywire just as [he] was tying it to Errol's leg to send it to Harry,"[3] we begin to wonder whether Lupin (as the only person in the compartment who is new to us at the time) triggered the Sneakoscope to go off. After we discover Scabbers' true identify, we realise that "the lump in Ron's pocket" that "trembled"[4] when Hermione let Crookshanks out of his basket was the actual trigger. The Sneakoscope goes off again to reveal Scabbers' untrustworthiness after Harry receives the Firebolt, but we think it is due to the potential for the Firebolt to be jinxed, and we fail to make the connection to Scabbers.[5]

Animagi are mentioned in the series for the first time in a passing reference that we completely miss because we, like Harry, are focused on Professor Trelawney seeing the Grim in his tea cup: Harry "*hardly heard* what Professor McGonagall was telling them about Animagi (wizards who could transform at will into animals)."[6] When Pettigrew is revealed to be an Animagus, we do not feel "conned" because we have in fact been told that wizards can change into animals—albeit in a parenthetical reference that was carefully planned by Rowling to be easily missed.

Crookshanks' unceasing pursuit of Scabbers is another key clue, although we think it is just the usual cat after rat rather than realising that Scabbers is not what he seems. When Hermione says, "All cats chase rats, Ron!", Ron responds, "There's something funny about that animal!... It heard me say that Scabbers was in my bag!" Hermione retorts, "Oh, what rubbish... Crookshanks could *smell* him, Ron, how else d'you think..." to which Ron angrily replies, "That cat's got it in for Scabbers!"[7] Through this interchange, Ron hands us a clue that Crookshanks may be hunting for Scabbers for a

1   *Ibid.*, 160.
2   *Ibid.*, 60.
3   *Ibid.*, 61.
4   *Ibid.*, 62.
5   *Ibid.*, 167.
6   *Ibid.*, 83–84. My emphasis.
7   *Ibid.*, 111.

reason unrelated to filling an empty belly, but Hermione's characterization of Ron's claims as "rubbish" lead us to discount this clue entirely.

In retrospect, we realise that key clues were also provided in the name of Pettigrew's Animagus and in Rowling's choice of his first name. "Scabbers" is presumably derived from "scab," which is a term used "to refer to people who continue to work when trade unionists go on strike action"[1]—in other words, a traitor. "Peter" is presumably a parallel to Simon Peter, the disciple to whom Jesus said, during the Last Supper, "Verily I say unto thee, that this night, before the cock crow, thou shalt deny me thrice."[2] Simon Peter does deny Jesus three times as Jesus had foretold, as Peter Pettigrew betrayed the Potters. Since Simon Peter then redeems himself by subsequently establishing the Christian Church in Rome and was eventually martyred, perhaps Peter Pettigrew will also turn to the right side by the end of the *Harry Potter* series.

The Vanishing Cabinets

The first time we see the first of the two vanishing cabinets is in book two, where Harry misspeaks in the fire and accidentally winds up in Borgin and Burkes. In looking for a place to hide from an approaching Draco Malfoy, "Harry looked quickly around and spotted a large black cabinet to his left; he shot inside it and pulled the doors to, leaving a small crack to peer through."[3] We do not give the cabinet another thought—it is just a place to hide; it is not described as a vanishing cabinet (note that Harry does not vanish when he enters it!); it is just described as "large" and "black"—nondescript.

A mere 56 pages later, we meet the second of the pair of vanishing cabinets, when Nearly Headless Nick persuades "Peeves to crash it right over Filch's office"[4] to divert his attention from punishing Harry for tracking mud into the castle. This is the first time we learn that the cabinet is a vanishing cabinet, as Filch tells Mrs Norris, "That *vanishing cabinet* was extremely valuable!"[5] We do

1 Wikipedia, "Strike Action." <http://en.wikipedia.org/wiki/Strikebreaker>.
2 Matthew 26:34.
3 *CoS*, 42.
4 *Ibid.*, 99.
5 *Ibid.*, 98. My emphasis.

not connect this cabinet at the time with the cabinet in Borgin and Burkes, as the cabinet in the shop is not referred to as a *vanishing* cabinet and is also described as large and black, while the Hogwarts cabinet is described as "large, black and *gold.*"[1] Moreover, because we assume that the dropping of the Hogwarts cabinet "from a great height" that has reduced the cabinet to "wreckage"[2] has effectively relegated the cabinet to the trash bin, we do not think it will reappear significantly later in the series. Our attention is also successfully diverted by the mystery of Filch's Kwikspell course and Harry's invitation to Nearly Headless Nick's deathday party.

The broken Hogwarts vanishing cabinet does not reappear until three books later, when Fred tells Harry, Ron and Hermione that the Captain of the Slytherin Quidditch team, Montague, was unable to dock points from the twins because "He never managed to get all the words out…due to the fact that we forced him head-first into that Vanishing Cabinet on the first floor."[3] While our attention is focused on the newly discovered injustice of Umbridge's Inquisitorial Squad's ability to dock points from students and the mayhem Fred and George are planning to implement next, this mention is significant because it is the first time that we learn that the vanishing cabinet can be used to transport people from one location to another. Fred says that Montague's reappearance "could take weeks, I dunno where we sent him."[4] However, even if we were to register this fact, since Montague is later found "jammed inside a toilet on the fourth floor"[5] rather than arriving through the second cabinet into Borgin and Burkes (presumably due to the fact that the Hogwarts cabinet was broken), we would not have been able to deduce that there was a passage between the two cabinets.

The Borgin and Burkes vanishing cabinet next appears in book six, when Harry, Ron and Hermione follow Draco Malfoy to Knockturn Alley and find Malfoy in Borgin and Burkes "with his back to them, just visible beyond the very same large black cabinet in which Harry had once hidden to avoid Malfoy and his father."[6] Note that the cabinet is once again described as "large" and "black"

1   *Ibid.*, 99. My emphasis.
2   *Ibid.*
3   J. K. Rowling, *Harry Potter and the Order of the Phoenix* (London: Bloomsbury, 2003), 552.
4   *Ibid.*
5   *Ibid.*, 563.
6   J. K. Rowling, *Harry Potter and the Half-Blood Prince* (London: Bloomsbury, 2005), 120.

and, once again, is not referred to as a vanishing cabinet. Moreover, when Malfoy tells Borgin to "keep *that* one safe, I'll need it," Malfoy "was blocked from view by the cabinet"[1]—carefully planned by Rowling to keep Harry, Ron and Hermione (and the reader) from seeing what Malfoy is pointing at by using that very object as the obstacle that keeps him out of view. Our feeling of being tricked is further enhanced when we later realise that the very object whose identity we are so keen to learn is prominently mentioned several times in that scene.

Moreover, Hermione hands us a huge clue when Harry and Ron are speculating that the cursed opal necklace was the object Malfoy told Borgin to keep safe. She says, "I think whatever he reserved at Borgin and Burkes was noisy or *bulky*; something he knew would draw attention to him if he carried it down the street."[2] Our feeling of being tricked intensifies when we remember seeing Harry take "a left at the broken Vanishing Cabinet in which Montague had got lost the previous year"[3] in his haste to hide the Half-Blood Prince's potions book in the Room of Requirement. We realise later that in needing the Room of Requirement to turn into "*a place to hide [his] book*," Harry actually found the place where Malfoy was working on fixing the broken cabinet. Since we (and Harry) are still reeling from the unexpected effect of the Sectumsempra spell and the fear of Snape's retribution, the cabinet becomes merely of one the many "objects hidden by generations of Hogwarts inhabitants"[4] that clutter the Room.

Buzzing Insects and Guttering Fires

Rowling also sets us up to disregard seemingly inconsequential background events which prove later to be important. Before Harry falls asleep in Professor Trelawney's class in book four, "He could hear an insect humming gently somewhere behind the curtain"[5]—an insect that turns out to be Rita Skeeter, lurking as a beetle Animagus on the window ledge. At the time, however, we think this is just another way of setting the scene for Harry's sleepiness—along with

---

1 *Ibid.*, 121.
2 *Ibid.*, 239. My emphasis.
3 *Ibid.*, 492.
4 *Ibid.*
5 J. K. Rowling, *Harry Potter and the Goblet of Fire* (London: Bloomsbury, 2001), 500.

the "heavily perfumed fumes" and "the breeze from the window."[1] Moreover, Harry has heard buzzing insects before that have been of no consequence: while waiting for his Divination exam in book three, Harry "settled himself on the floor with his back against the wall, listening to a fly buzzing in the sunny window."[2]

Similarly, when Harry leans out of the Owlery window after sending a food parcel to Sirius and observes the "treetops of the Forbidden Forest and the rippling sails of the Durmstrang ship," we take no note of his next watching an "eagle owl" that "flew through the coil of smoke rising from Hagrid's chimney; it soared towards the castle, around the Owlery and out of sight."[3] We think this is just another background description. However, this is the very eagle owl that brings Barty Crouch, Jr., the news of his father's escape and approach to Hogwarts, as we later learn when Harry rides "on the back of an *eagle owl*"[4] as the owl returns to Voldemort with the news that Crouch, Sr., has been killed.

After realising that there may well be something more to background descriptions after our experience of book four, we are ready not to be tricked again when Harry is taking his History of Magic O.W.L. examination in book five. Harry notices "a wasp buzzing distractingly against one of the high windows."[5] Moreover, we extend our heightened perception of the significance of background descriptions by becoming convinced that there is meaning behind when "a light night breeze rattled the windowpanes behind Ron, and the fire guttered"[6] in the Common Room, after Hermione suggests that Harry teach them Defence Against the Dark Arts. However, Rowling successfully tricks us again by having the buzzing wasp and the guttering fire come to nothing.

Since this will be my last opportunity to do so before the release of the seventh and final book in the series, I am now going to "leav[e] the firm foundation of fact and journey...through the murky marshes...into thickets of wildest guesswork."[7] Specifically, I would like to speculate on the ultimate fate of three of the

---

1   *Ibid.*
2   *PoA*, 236.
3   *GoF*, 469.
4   *Ibid.*, 500. My emphasis.
5   *OotP*, 639.
6   *Ibid.*, 291.
7   *HBP*, 187.

characters in the series—Snape, Ron and Harry—and how Rowling has sown the seeds to create controversy on their eventual outcome.

The Inscrutable Severus Snape

If we only had the following on which to base our assessment of which side Severus Snape is on, would there be such a controversy about whether Snape is good or evil?

Snape gazed for a moment at Dumbledore, and there was revulsion and hatred etched in the harsh lines of his face... Snape raised his wand and pointed it directly at Dumbledore. "*Avada Kedavra!*"[1]

Without the context of the complicated web Rowling has woven in the preceding pages of the first six books, these words alone would presumably make a straightforward case for Snape's evilness, especially when combined with Snape's answers to Bellatrix Lestrange's questions regarding his loyalty to Voldemort and his willingness to make an Unbreakable Vow to assist Draco Malfoy in his mission to kill Dumbledore. However, in the second of Scholastic's seven questions for fans to answer in anticipation of the release of book seven, "Is Snape Good or Evil," 39% voted "Good and still a spy for the Order of the Phoenix;" 32% voted "Good but in too deep with Voldemort;" 19% voted "Evil and has always been a spy for Voldemort" and 10% voted "Evil but only because Voldemort is back."[2]

It is the sequence of events preceding book six that has led to so much controversy among fans. We start in book one with Harry, Ron and Hermione being convinced that Snape is trying to obtain the Philosopher's Stone for his own gain, and trying to kill Harry in the process. Even when Quirrell is revealed to be the villain, our questions about Snape remain. When Dumbledore fails to expel Harry and Ron for crashing the flying Ford Anglia into the Whomping Willow, "Snape looked as though Christmas had been cancelled."[3] Later in book two, Snape suggests that Harry, Ron and Hermione were responsible for the attack on Mrs Norris, based solely upon their presence in the corridor where the petrified cat was

1   *Ibid.*, 556.
2   Scholastic, *Is Snape Good or Evil?*, 12 May 2007 <http://www.scholastic.com/harrypotter/activities/shriekingshack/>.
3   *CoS*, 64.

found. In book three, Snape is ready to deliver both Sirius and Lupin to the Dementors to satisfy a "schoolboy grudge"[1] without taking the time to hear the true story.

However, it is when we learn in book four that Snape was once a Death Eater that we start to question seriously which side he is on, rather than simply wondering how he can be so unceasingly cruel to Harry. Barty Crouch, Jr., says to Snape, "I say there are spots that don't come off, Snape. Spots that never come off, d'you know what I mean?" after which Snape "seized his left forearm convulsively with his right hand."[2] We learn later that Snape is clutching his Dark Mark, but if the Mark can never come off, does that also mean that Snape can never be redeemed?

When Voldemort ponders the absence of six of his Death Eaters in the graveyard in book four, he refers to Snape as "One, who I believe has left me for ever...he will be killed, of course."[3] However, as of the end of book six, Snape remains alive and well, with Narcissa Malfoy referring to him as "The Dark Lord's favourite, his most trusted advisor."[4] Presumably this means that Snape has successfully convinced Voldemort that he is back on his side, but is he really? At the end of book four, Snape shows Cornelius Fudge his Dark Mark to convince Fudge that Voldemort had returned,[5] which he presumably would not have done had he been on Voldemort's side at the time. Is this because Snape initially intended to spy for Dumbledore but decided to return to Voldemort's side after his first encounter with the reborn Voldemort? Is the "sudden movement"[6] Snape makes when Harry tells Fudge that Lucius Malfoy was in the graveyard an indication of Snape's surprise that Lucius has returned to Voldemort's side? We are also left to wonder whether Snape is trying to block or open Harry's mind to Voldemort during their Occlumency lessons.

Ron reminds us that he does not believe in Snape's innocence when he says, "*sagely*," "Poisonous toadstools don't change their spots."[7] Rowling's use of "sagely" to describe Ron's pronouncement

1   *PoA*, 263.
2   *GoF*, 410.
3   *Ibid.*, 565.
4   *HBP*, 38.
5   *GoF*, 616.
6   *Ibid.*, 613.
7   *OotP*, 212. My emphasis.

suggests that there may actually be some truth to this statement, and we are once again reminded that certain types of spots (in book four, the Dark Mark; in book five, toadstool spots) cannot come off. Moreover, Lucius Malfoy, who is revealed to be a continued supporter of Lord Voldemort at the end of book four, is hit in the eye by an *Encyclopedia of Toadstools* during his fight with Arthur Weasley in Flourish and Blotts in book two,[1] so perhaps Ron's reference to "toadstools" is also a clue that Snape as well as Lucius have rejoined Voldemort's side.

From Weasel King to Fisher King

Ron's eventual fate becomes clear through a significant clue planted in book five; however, it was not until the title of book seven was announced that the connection became clear. When Draco Malfoy discovers that Ron's goalkeeping ability suffers in direct proportion to humiliating distractions, he creates the "Weasley Is Our King" song for the Slytherins to sing during Gryffindor Quidditch matches, along with silver "crown-shaped badges" for the Slytherins to wear, engraved with "*Weasley is our King.*"[2] The song is incredibly insulting and starts with "*Weasley cannot save a thing / He cannot block a single ring / That's why Slytherins all sing / Weasley is our King.*"[3] The song has the desired effect, and Ron lets in all four Slytherin goals during the first match in which the song is sung.

At the time, we see the song as just another example of Slytherin cruelty and an illustration of Ron's deep-seated insecurity. However, the significance of the song becomes clear when Draco Malfoy later refers to Ron as "Weasel King."[4] In Rowling's usual style, this is a passing reference, easily missed and one of many derogatory nicknames Malfoy has used over the course of the series. For example, Malfoy refers to Harry and Ron as "Potty and the Weasel" on the Hogwarts Express in *Prisoner of Azkaban.*[5]

The announcement of the title of book seven as *Harry Potter and the Deathly Hallows* suggests that the events in the seventh book will in some way follow the Arthurian tradition. The four "hallows" in

1 *CoS*, 51.
2 *OotP*, 358.
3 *Ibid.*, 360.
4 *Ibid.*, 551.
5 *PoA*, 63.

Arthurian legend are the "broken sword, the silver serving dish, the Grail, and the bleeding Lance"[1] that surround the grievously wounded King of the Grail Castle, known as the Fisher King.[2] The Fisher King can only be healed by the hero who is able to achieve the Grail Quest. "The fisher is a North American marten,"[3] and "Martens are carnivorous animals related to wolverines, minks and *weasels*."[4] Malfoy's reference to Ron as "Weasel King" is therefore a clue that Ron will fill the role of Fisher King in the seventh and final book.

In Arthurian legend, Lancelot's son Galahad is the grandson of the Fisher King—also known as King Pelles, a descendant of Joseph of Arimathea and the father of Galahad's mother, Elaine. After a series of unsuccessful attempts by other knights, Galahad arrives at the castle where the Grail was located, and "was permitted entry to the Grail Chapel and allowed to gaze upon the great cup. His life became complete and together grail and man were lifted up to heaven."[5] Prior to his death, however, Galahad uses the power of the Grail to heal his grandfather of the sword wound inflicted many years earlier.

With this clue in hand, we can therefore speculate that the Weasel King of the Slytherin's song will become the Fisher King in the seventh book, with his life or death held in Harry's hands as he attempts to fulfill his final role as seeker. The change in the lyrics of "Weasley is our King" and the transition from the song being sung by Slytherins at the start of the final Quidditch match of their fifth year to the song being sung by Gryffindors by the end of the match suggests that the final quest of book seven will start with our feeling hopeless regarding the fate of Ron, the wounded Fisher (Weasel) King, and that it will end with Harry achieving his quest and healing Ron—thereby asserting the victory of the Gryffindor Harry over the Slytherin Voldemort as Ron transforms from Slytherin's hero to Gryffindor's king.

---

1 Erin Ogden-Korus, *The Quest: An Arthurian Resource*, <http://www.uidaho.edu/student_orgs/arthurian_legend/grail/fisher/>.

2 *Ibid.*

3 Wikipedia, "Fisher (animal)," <http://en.wikipedia.org/wiki/Fisher_(animal)>.

4 Wikipedia, "Marten," <http://en.wikipedia.org/wiki/Marten>. My emphasis.

5 David Nash Ford, *Britannia: The Holy Grail: A Discussion of the Holy Grail's Arthurian Connections*, <http://www.britannia.com/bhc/arthur/grail.html>.

Will Harry Survive?

One of the most intriguing and widely pondered questions is whether Harry will live or die when the series concludes. The first time Professor Trelawney reads Harry's tea leaves, she sees "The falcon...you have a deadly enemy... The club...an attack... The skull...danger in your path" and finally (and most dramatically), "The Grim...the worst omen—of *death*!"[1] Professor McGonagall dismisses their fears by telling the class that "Sybill Trelawney has predicted the death of one student a year since she arrived at this school. None of them has died yet."[2] While McGonagall makes it clear that she does not think that Trelawney is one of the rare True Seers, and Ron agrees with Hermione that Trelawney is a "right old fraud,"[3] we cannot help but wonder when Professor Trelawney tells Harry during a palmistry lesson that "he had the shortest life-lines she had ever seen."[4] Moreover, we realise that Trelawney is capable of making true predictions when Harry hears her predict Pettigrew's escape and return to Voldemort, although Dumbledore's comment of "Who'd have thought it? That brings her total of real predictions up to two"[5] leaves us wondering whether he is just joking or whether Trelawney really has made a significant, real prediction previously (which, of course, we learn she has, once we reach the end of book five).

Our fear that Trelawney's predictions will become reality is assuaged due to the regularity with which she continues to predict Harry's death, as well as Harry's reaction. Harry grows to find her predictions "extremely annoying,"[6] finally saying to Ron, "if I'd dropped dead every time she's told me I'm going to, I'd be a medical miracle."[7] Moreover, after Harry's interview of the night Voldemort returned is published in *The Quibbler*, Trelawney expresses her support by announcing that "Harry was *not* going to suffer an early death after all, but would live to a ripe old age, become Minister of Magic and have twelve children,"[8] which serves only to discredit her

1 *PoA*, 82–83.
2 *Ibid.*, 84.
3 *Ibid.*, 236.
4 *Ibid.*, 174.
5 *Ibid.*, 311.
6 *GoF*, 171.
7 *Ibid.*, 325.
8 *OotP*, 513.

pronouncements further.

The most intriguing and hotly debated clues regarding Harry's eventual fate are, first, the enigmatic "gleam of triumph"[1] that appears in Dumbledore's eyes when Harry describes how Voldemort used his blood in his regeneration potion and, second, that Voldemort said Harry's blood "would make him stronger than if he'd used someone else's."[2] The way in which the gleam is described is illustrative of Rowling's misdirection style. We are left to ponder whether Harry even in fact saw a gleam at all, given the way the paragraph is worded:

For a fleeting instant, Harry *thought* he saw a gleam of *something like* triumph in Dumbledore's eyes. But next second, Harry *was sure he had imagined it,* for when Dumbledore had returned to his seat behind the desk, he looked as old and weary as Harry had ever seen him.[3]

Note that the paragraph starts with "For a fleeting instant," which leads us to wonder whether this is significant due to its brevity. Moreover, because Harry "thought" he saw the gleam suggests that he may not have even seen it at all, and he is then "sure he had imagined it." And we are not even sure it is in fact triumph at all that Harry might have seen in Dumbledore's eyes, as it is described as "something like" triumph.

However, Rowling's attempts to make us doubt whether this is significant have been in vain this time, as we caught right on to this one, and when Rowling was asked, "Does the gleam of triumph still have yet to make an appearance?" she replied, 'That's still enormously significant. And let's face it, I haven't told you that much is enormously significant, so you can let your imaginations run free there."[4]

It would take more pages than I have to describe each and every time Rowling uses misdirection in the series, as it is difficult to read more than a page or two without finding such an instance. In some cases, there are multiple examples on a single page. However, I

---

1   *GoF,* 604.
2   *Ibid.*
3   *Ibid.* My emphasis.
4   Melissa Anelli and Emerson Spartz, *The Leaky Cauldron and Mugglenet Interview Joanne Kathleen Rowling: Part Three,* 16 July 2005, <http://www.accio-quote.org/ articles/2005/0705-tlc_mugglenet-anelli-3.htm>.

would like to end by briefly highlighting a few more examples where we have been tricked, rather than fooled or conned.

The Polyjuice Potion

Because Hermione tells Ron and Harry that "Once we've drunk [the Polyjuice Potion] we'll have exactly *an hour* before we change back into ourselves,"[1] we are led to believe that the Potion only works for one hour. As a result, it does not occur to us to think that Barty Crouch, Jr., could impersonate Mad-Eye Moody for an entire school year by drinking the Potion. Once we learn that Crouch Jr. was drinking the Potion "on the hour...every hour,"[2] however, we feel tricked rather than conned because we realise that Rowling never said the Potion could only be drunk once. Our feeling of being tricked is intensified when we realise that we were handed a huge clue when Snape accuses Harry of stealing boomslang skin, a key ingredient of the potion, from his private stores,[3] although since Harry then recalls Hermione stealing the boomslang skin in their second year, we are led to believe that Snape is referring to past, rather than current, Polyjuice Potion ingredient thievery.

Subtle Body Movements

Rowling also provides clues in the subtle body movements of her characters. When Dumbledore tells the Wizengamot at Harry's hearing that he does not "think any of us believe the Dementors were there by coincidence," "the witch sitting to the right of Fudge, with her face in shadow"—who is later revealed to be Umbridge, the person responsible for sending the Dementors to the alleyway —"moved slightly."[4] Umbridge also "leaned forwards" after Dumbledore says, "we must ask ourselves why somebody within the Ministry ordered a pair of Dementors into that alleyway on the second of August."[5] At the time, however, our attention is diverted by our curiosity as to the identity of this witch, as well as by our concerns about the fairness of Harry's hearing.

---

1   *CoS*, 161. My emphasis.
2   *GoF*, 592.
3   *Ibid.*, 448.
4   *OotP*, 133.
5   *Ibid.*, 134.

Moreover, when Mundungus, disguised as a witch, eavesdrops on the first meeting of Dumbledore's Army, "the veiled witch sitting alone shifted very slightly in her seat"[1] when Harry confesses that he does get quite enough attention as it is. It does not occur to us at the time that this could be Mundungus, due to the person under the veil being female and as a result of Harry asking Hermione, "Has it occurred to you Umbridge might be under that?"[2]

Aberforth and His Goats

In an attempt to cheer up Hagrid after Rita Skeeter informs the wizarding world that he is half-giant, Dumbledore says that his "own brother, Aberforth" did not hide when he "was prosecuted for practising inappropriate charms on a goat."[3] The first time Harry enters the Hog's Head, the bar "smelled strongly of *something* that *might have been* goats,"[4] which suggests that Aberforth may in fact be continuing his inappropriate goat charms in his bar, although Rowling cloaks this clue with uncertainty as to whether or not it is actually goats that Harry is smelling.

In addition, the Hog's Head barman had "a great deal of long grey hair and beard" and "was tall and thin and looked vaguely familiar to Harry,"[5] both of which suggest that the barman looks like Dumbledore. Moreover, when Harry views the Pensieve scene where Voldemort returns to Hogwarts to ask again for a teaching post, and Dumbledore is able to list the names of the Death Eaters with whom Voldemort has traveled, Voldemort says that Dumbledore is "omniscient as ever," and Dumbledore replies, "Oh, no, merely friendly with the local barmen."[6]

We know that the barman has been the same for at least the past twenty years, since Sirius says that the reason Mundungus was disguised as a witch was that "He was banned from the Hog's Head twenty years ago…and that barman's got a long memory."[7] While the books have yet to say whether the barman in the Hog's Head is indeed Dumbledore's brother Aberforth, Rowling confirmed this at

---

1   *Ibid.*, 305.
2   *Ibid.*, 300.
3   *GoF*, 395.
4   *OotP*, 299. My emphasis.
5   *Ibid.*, 300.
6   *HBP*, 416.
7   *OotP*, 329.

the Edinburgh Book Festival on 15 August 2004, saying, "I like the goat clue—I sniggered to myself about that one."[1]

Cats with Human Names

In retrospect, we see that we should have realized that Arabella Figg was not only Harry's batty old neighbour, but also a squib. Both Argus Filch and Mrs Figg have cats with names that begin with "Mr" or "Mrs" (Mr Tibbles is Mrs Figg's cat, while Mrs Norris is Argus Filch's cat). Moreover, both of their initials are "A. F.," although we are not given Mrs Figg's first name until the end of book four.

The Mournful Broderick Bode

On the elevators at the Ministry of Magic, when Harry meets Broderick Bode, who is later killed by the Death Eaters after he is forced to attempt to retrieve the prophecy, Bode is described as having a "mournful face" and as speaking in a "sepulchral voice," which are clues that he is not long for this world, but which we overlook because at the time, "Harry barely had emotion to spare for Bode."[2] Moreover, when Bode is later seen in St. Mungo's just prior to his murder, he is described as "a sallow-skinned, mournful-looking wizard,"[3] which we overlook in our amazement at meeting Gilderoy Lockhart again and in our sadness at seeing Neville's parents for the first time.

Hints of Dumbledore's Demise

We are given hints of Dumbledore's approaching death when Dumbledore bids farewell to the Dursleys with "Until we meet again" and the Dursleys "looked as though that moment could wait for ever as far as they were concerned,"[4] although we take this as just another example of the Dursleys' eagerness to be rid of anything connected with the wizarding world. In addition, in their encounter in Madam Malkin's robe shop, Narcissa Malfoy tells Harry that

---

1   J. K. Rowling, *J. K. Rowling Official Site*, <http://www.jkrowling.com/textonly/en/news_view.cfm?id=80>.
2   *OotP*, 124.
3   *Ibid.*, 452.
4   *HBP*, 58.

"Dumbledore won't always be there to protect you,"[1] which we overlook because Harry subsequently mocks Narcissa by pointing out that Dumbledore is not currently present in the shop.

The Identity of the Half-Blood Prince

When Harry sees Snape taking his Defence Against the Dark Arts O.W.L. examination in the Pensieve, Snape's writing is described as "minuscule and cramped."[2] Since the writing in Harry's copy of Advanced Potion-Making is described as "small" and "cramped,"[3] we are led to conclude that Snape is the Half-Blood Prince. However, doubt is cast on that conclusion when Harry thinks to himself that "the Prince had proved a much more effective teacher than Snape so far."[4] Moreover, when Lupin suggests that Harry see how old the book is, Harry discovers that it is fifty years old and concludes that the book was therefore not around during his father's (and therefore Snape's) time at Hogwarts.[5]

One Final Opportunity to be Tricked by the Master

Each time Rowling uses misdirection, she does it in such a way as to provide enough information so that when we reach the end of each book, we are able to look back and see that the clues were there all along, yet careful to not provide enough information to enable us to deduce accurately where she is leading us. She has done this in a way that is not accidental, but intentional, which has taken a great deal of work on her part, as she admits to having "sweated blood to create all my red herrings and lay all my clues."[6] In this way, she leaves us with the pleasant feeling of being "tricked" rather than the bitter taste of being "fooled" or "conned," and we look forward to happily succumbing to the tricks of the master for the very last time in book seven.

---

1   *Ibid.*, 111.
2   *OotP*, 565.
3   *HBP*, 183.
4   *Ibid.*, 224.
5   *Ibid.*, 316.
6   J. K. Rowling, *JK's OotP interview with Jeremy Paxman*, BBC Newsnight, 19 June 2003, <http://www.accio-quote.org/articles/2003/0619-bbcnews-paxman.htm>.

Bibliography

Anelli, Melissa and Emerson Spartz. *The Leaky Cauldron and Mugglenet Interview Joanne Kathleen Rowling: Part Three*, 16 July 2005. <http://www.accio-quote.org/articles/2005/0705-tlc_mugglenet-anelli-3.htm>.

Boquet, Tim. *J. K. Rowling: The Wizard Behind Harry Potter. Reader's Digest*, December 2000. <http://www.accio-quote.org/articles/2000/1200-readersdigest-boquet.htm>.

"Fisher (animal)." *Wikipedia.* <http://en.wikipedia.org/wiki/Fisher_(animal)>.

Ford, David Nash. *Britannia: The Holy Grail: A Discussion of the Holy Grail's Arthurian Connections.* <http://www.britannia.com/bhc/arthur/grail.html>.

"Marten." *Wikipedia.* <http://en.wikipedia.org/wiki/Marten>.

Ogden-Korus, Erin. *The Quest: An Arthurian Resource.* <http://www.uidaho.edu/student_orgs/arthurian_legend/grail/fisher/>.

Rowling, J. K. *Harry Potter and the Chamber of Secrets.* London: Bloomsbury, 1999.

—. *Harry Potter and the Goblet of Fire.* London: Bloomsbury, 2001.

—. *Harry Potter and the Half-Blood Prince.* London: Bloomsbury, 2005.

—. *Harry Potter and the Order of the Phoenix.* London: Bloomsbury, 2003.

—. *Harry Potter and the Philosopher's Stone.* London: Bloomsbury, 1998.

—. *Harry Potter and the Prisoner of Azkaban.* London: Bloomsbury, 2000.

—. *JKR's OOTP interview with Jeremy Paxman.* BBC Newsnight, 19 June 2003. <http://www.accio-quote.org/articles/2003/0619-bbcnews-paxman.htm>.

—. *J. K. Rowling Official Site.* <http://www.jkrowling.com/textonly/en/news_view.cfm?id=80>.

Scholastic. *Is Snape Good or Evil?* 12 May 2007. <http://www.scholastic.com/harrypotter/activities/shriekingshack/>.

"Strike Action." *Wikipedia.* <http://en.wikipedia.org/wiki/Strikebreaker>.

Understanding Prejudice Utilizing the *Harry Potter* Series: Education/Library Studies Presentation

Nancee Lee-Allen
Violence Intervention Program, Los Angeles, Calif.

The world of *Harry Potter* is full of prejudicial thoughts and ideas, though not the ones found in our world. In Harry's world, people are not discriminated against for the color of their skin, religious affiliation or sexual identity—it is all about blood (pure, half or Muggle).

Some witches and wizards feel that purity of blood makes for better people and that the non-magic, or muggle world, is less important than the magic world. "Muggle" is a term used freely and is not an insult, though "Mudblood" is the equivalent of such terms in our society as "faggot" or the "n-word." Good people just don't say these things, but do they think them?

The addition of a black Slytherin in *Half-Blood Prince* adds to the richness of the series. The Slytherins are often viewed as Nazi-like purebloods who hate anyone who is not exactly like themselves. The fact that a Slytherin could be anything but white shows that prejudice in Harry Potter's world is truly not about race.

The introduction of Horace Slughorn in *Half-Blood Prince* also shows that all Slytherins are not completely prejudiced, which opens a discussion as to whether or not a person can be partially prejudiced. Professor Slughorn sees value in Muggle-born witches and wizards as long as they possess exceptional talent, like Hermione.

Young teens easily identify with characters in the series and are able to relate to the idea of prejudice in the magic world. Using these books allows us to explore our inner feelings about people who are different without identifying anyone as a "real-world" racist. We can talk about pure-bloods and half-bloods without insulting anyone or showing any truly racist ideals. This can lead to a better understanding of ourselves and help build respect for those who are different. The attached curriculum can be a starting point for open discussion on tolerance and understanding for those who are different.

Many teens like the idea that both Harry Potter and Fred Weasley asked nonwhite young ladies to the Yule Ball. Girls with whom I have worked say that it confirms that beauty comes in many colors, and they are happy that Harry and Fred can see this. The inclusion of students of multiple races at Hogwarts—though they're all British—allows children of all backgrounds to relate to the characters.

I have found that the *Harry Potter* series contains a wealth of lessons on many topics and that helping teens to better understand prejudice and human nature is truly one of the most valuable.

Curriculum

Lesson title: Who would I be in Harry's world?

Objective: To become more aware of how our preconceived ideas about people based on their national origin affect our interactions with individuals from other cultures (religions, races *et al.*).

Suggested reading: One or more book in the *Harry Potter* series

Supplies: Post-it Easel Notes (or other poster paper with tape), five large markers

Teaching strategies:

a) After reading any of the *Harry Potter* books, ask the class to divide themselves into five groups depending on who they would be in the wizarding world: pure-blood, half-blood, Muggle-born, part-human or Muggle.

b) Ask each student to write a paragraph about their category and one about each of the other groups.

c)   When they are finished, ask them to share their ideas with the others in their group. As a group they should list the top five things about each of the other groups on a piece of poster paper. Then ask them to share these with the class. Hang the poster paper on the walls of the classroom. Note: the students will most likely list negatives and positives about each group.

d)   After each group presents their work, ask the class to focus on the positive traits of each group, as a tool to teach tolerance. Ask if they would like to have a friend from each group.

e)   Discuss what Harry's world would be like if people had friendships with not only with all types of magical people but with Muggles, goblins and house-elves.

f)   Homework assignment: A short essay about why you chose to be pureblood, half-blood, muggle-born, part-human or Muggle. Note: for those who are happy to be Muggles, many will say that they are content to have computers and iPods, things that would not work in the wizarding world. Those who wish to be magic might talk about how wonderful it is to have so much power, but would they be willing to give up TV and computers? For the half-bloods, ask which world they would live in, since it might be difficult to try to live in both.

Discussion Points from Specific Books

Sorcerer's Stone
The first time Harry meets Draco, Draco asks about Harry's parentage and says, "I really don't think they should let the other sort in, do you? They're just not the same; they've never been brought up to know our ways. Some of them have never even heard of Hogwarts until they get the letter, imagine. I think they should keep it in the old wizarding families." Ask students how they felt about Harry and Draco when they first read this.

Chamber of Secrets
When Draco calls Hermione a Mudblood for the first time—are Ron's actions justified?

Hagrid tells the trio that there aren't any true pureblood wizards left. Do you think people like the Malfoys believe this to be true?

Why would Slytherin's heir wish to rid Hogwarts of Muggle-born students? Has this happened in our history? Is it happening now (ethnic cleansing)? Where? What can we do to help?

Goblet of Fire
Hermione feels a need to help house-elves, so she knits hats and founds S.P.E.W.

Does she feel deeply for the elves because of the prejudice she has faced as a muggle-born witch?

Is S.P.E.W. degrading to house-elves? Why or why not?

Do you think race matters at all in the wizarding world? Do Cedric/Cho and Fred/Angelina consider their relationships to be interracial?

In what ways do the Death Eaters resemble the Ku Klux Klan?

Order of the Phoenix
The Weasleys are considered by some others to be blood traitors, as they do not have "proper respect" and pride in the purity of their lineage. Do you agree?

Professor Umbridge dislikes those she refers to as "part-humans." Do you think many other people share her views? Do you think the Minister of Magic would agree with her?

What is the division between humans, part-humans and nonhumans in the Wizarding world?

What does the Fountain of Magical Brethren really represent? Is there any truth to it?

Who is on the "Inquisitorial Squad"? What does this tell us about Professor Umbridge and possibly the Ministry of Magic?

How the centaurs feel about humans? Are they justified?

What do we now know about giants?

Half-Blood Prince
What does it mean to be a half-blood? Would it be difficult for the non-magic parent?

Do you think Professor Snape felt isolated in school because he was a half-blood Slytherin? How would being half-blood affect his attitude toward Muggle-born wizards?

Does Mrs. Weasley dislike Fleur because she is part Veela, or is there another reason?

Lupin's situation and explanation of life as a werewolf:
Tonks & Lupin—age and "part-human" status; can this relationship work?

Nancee Lee-Allen can be contacted at nanceeleeallen@aol.com.

MUGGLING THROUGH: MUGGLE-BORNS AND HALF-BLOODS, AND THEIR PLACE IN THE WIZARDING WORLD

Yolanda R. Carroll

In a discussion about Muggle-borns, half-bloods, and pure-bloods, one of the defining characteristics and sources of contention is how much Muggle blood you do or do not have in you. Therefore, we need to take a look at the wizarding world's attitudes toward Muggles, too.

"—packed with Muggles, of course," Mrs. Weasley says in *Sorcerer's Stone*. Why does she say "packed with Muggles" instead of "packed with people" or simply "packed"? I would like to bring attention to the fact that the way Mrs. Weasley says "packed with Muggles" sounds an awful lot like the way someone would refer to another race or social type. An example, albeit a derogatory one, would be the "have-nots" versus the "haves."

I'm focusing on Mrs. Weasley for a reason, as all *Harry Potter* readers know the Weasleys are a wizarding family with a more positive attitude than some others towards Muggles. However, they are not perfect. Mrs. Weasley—the same woman who welcomes a half-blood, Harry Potter, and a Muggle-born, Hermione Granger, into her home—has, according to George, always wished for a "house-elf to do the ironing."

To give another example, Mrs. Weasley doesn't have any problems associating with Remus Lupin. However, when she hears that there's a werewolf near Arthur in St. Mungo's, she wonders whether he shouldn't be kept away from the other patients: "Is he safe in a public ward? Shouldn't he be in a private room?"

To be fair, Mr. Weasley, injured and weakened, is in a less than ideal position to defend himself against an attack from a werewolf.

Mrs. Weasley's prejudice isn't malicious. Werewolves can be dangerous. They can also be as harmless as Lupin. Out of genuine concern for her husband, though, her prejudice shows:

"Are all your family wizards?" asked Harry, who found Ron just as interesting as Ron found him.

"Er—Yes, I think so," said Ron. "I think Mom's got a second cousin who's an accountant, but we never talk about him."

The Weasleys are, as I stated above, a family of wizards with a better attitude than most about Muggles. It says something that the Weasleys "never talk about" their "accountant" cousin who is not a wizard. I honestly believe that the Weasleys do not mean to be prejudiced. However, like all wizards, they see Muggles as being a separate group that, quite frankly, they don't always know what to make of. The Weasleys' attitude toward Muggles is at least partially founded on ignorance. As seen by their covering a letter with stamps and calling a telephone "felly tone", they do not seem at all familiar with Muggle culture. It is telling, however, that a family of wizards who have a fairly good attitude towards Muggles still has certain subtle prejudices.

Some wizards' attitudes towards Muggles are condescending and pitying. In the books, we commonly hear the sentiment, "How do they get on without magic?" Even the attitude, "How clever of them to find ways around not having magic and getting things done anyway," is condescending. It's like saying that Muggles are handicapped, which the wizarding world probably considers not having magic to be, and that Muggles have found work-arounds.

Part of the wizarding world does view Muggles as deaf, dumb, and blind, totally oblivious to what's really going on in the word around them. A perfect example of this is the Knight Bus:

"How come the Muggles don't hear the bus?" said Harry.

"Them!" said Stan contemptuously. "Don' listen properly, do they? Don' look properly ether. Never notice nuffink, they don'."

Muggles must be protected like children. When I say "like children", I refer to the fact that adults take on the responsibility for looking after them and that the children aren't aware of all of the dangers that the adults are protecting them from. The wizarding world has taken on the responsibility of protecting Muggles from the more malicious members of the magical community.

Muggles are never informed that there are threats that they are being protected from. For some examples of this attitude, look at the chat between the two ministers in *Half-Blood Prince* and the Muggle Protection Act. Of course, if we look at the Black family, we see that in some cases, we definitely need protection:

…and Araminta Meliflua…cousin of my mother's…tried to force through a Ministry Bill to make Muggle-hunting legal.

Despite Araminta Meliflua's efforts, Muggle-hunting is illegal. So is Muggle-baiting; however, we know that the latter goes on all the time. In fact, it keeps Mr. Weasley's office quite busy.

Why would wizards want to hunt Muggles and enjoying tormenting them? This attitude is probably a holdover from the days when wizards were persecuted. Those days aren't over. Wizards are in hiding. Hagrid says that the reason the wizarding world doesn't want Muggles to know they exist is that they would bother them constantly to use magic and help them out. I can see that as being part of it; however, given what we know of history, it also stands to reason that they're scared of us. Remember, Muggles have wizards outnumbered, and technology is quickly closing the gap between Muggles and wizards.

We know that attitudes towards Muggles and Muggle-borns differs throughout the magical community. However, the official attitude doesn't appear to be too negative:

Harry knew exactly what was making Mr. Malfoy's lip curl like that. The Malfoys prided themselves on being pure-bloods; in other words, they considered anyone of Muggle descent, like Hermione, second-class. However, under the gaze of the Minister of Magic, Mr. Malfoy didn't dare say anything.

Officially, perhaps, the prejudice doesn't exist, but Slughorn's words say a lot about people's attitudes:

"Your mother was Muggle-born, of course. Couldn't believe it when I found out. Thought she must have been pure-blood, she was so good."

"One of my best friends is Muggle-born," said Harry, "and she's the best in our year."

"Funny how that sometimes happens, isn't it?" said Slughorn.

"Not really," said Harry coldly.

Slughorn looked down at him in surprise. "You mustn't think I'm prejudiced!" he said. "No, no, no! Haven't I just said your mother was one of my all-time favorite students? And there was Dirk Cresswell in the year after her too—now Head of the Goblin Liaison Office, of course."

Note that he says, "You mustn't think I'm prejudiced!", and then goes on to give examples of other talented Muggle-born students he has had. Slughorn's saying that he had other favorite students who are Muggle-born is not unlike someone saying, "I'm not prejudiced! I have friends who are African-American, Jewish, etc."

Many of us probably have the same reaction to Slughorn that Harry has:

Harry wasn't sure whether he liked Slughorn or not. He supposed he had been pleasant in his way, but he had also seemed vain and, whatever he said to the contrary, much too surprised that a Muggle-born should make a good witch.

Being surprised that a Muggle-born would make a good witch is not unlike being surprised that someone from a particular background could be well-spoken. It has been noted that saying, "He's so well-spoken," is actually an insult, because it implies that by rights the person in question shouldn't be and that the person who made the comment is surprised that they are.

The examples above show that some wizards, while not necessarily against Muggle-borns, do think that they are inferior to pure-blood and half-blood wizards. Even when Muggle-borns aren't being looked down on, they are treated as different. This quotation is from *Goblet of Fire*:

Harry has at last found love at Hogwarts. His close friend, Colin Creevey, says that Harry is rarely seen out of the company of one Hermione Granger, a stunningly pretty Muggle-born girl.

And here's another one, also from *Goblet of Fire*:

Deprived of love since the tragic demise of his parents, fourteen-year-old Harry Potter thought he had found solace in his steady girlfriend at Hogwarts, Muggle-born Hermione Granger.

Why mention that she's Muggle-born? The way it is phrased reminds me of how people say things like, "the lovely Brazilian model" or "French-Canadian born Jean-Paul Beaubier." It is similar to someone being described as being from somewhere else or of a different nationality or race. Then again, having been born outside of the wizarding world, Hermione is a foreigner. This attitude isn't necessarily bad, unless you count the fact that Muggle-borns are seen and treated as outsiders.

How do Muggle-borns see themselves? From what we've seen through Harry's point of view, Hermione Granger, Colin Creevey, Dennis Creevey, and Justin Finch-Fletchley all show positive attitudes about having been contacted and inducted into the wizarding world. With the exception of Hermione's hurt feelings at being called "mudblood" and Justin's fear of Harry, the assumed "Heir of Slytherin," we haven't seen any of them show discomfort about being Muggle-born. However, it must be noted that the only Muggle-borns we've really seen through Harry's eyes are still students. At Hogwarts, they are being indoctrinated into the wizarding world, but they have not spent much time in it. Trips to Diagon Alley, Hogsmeade, and the Quidditch World Cup notwithstanding, they haven't seen the wizarding world beyond Hogwarts.

Now let's move on to half-bloods and how they see themselves. The wizarding world's obsession with purity shows in the fact that Harry Potter, a son of a pure-blood wizard and a Muggle-born witch, is considered a half-blood. By rights, Harry should be a full-blood. His mother is a Muggle-born witch, not a Muggle.

Seamus Finnigan is a half-blood. His dad's a Muggle and his mum's a witch. The same applies to Tom Riddle and Severus Snape. Each is considered a half-blood, but so is Harry, whose mother was a witch. So, if you have a parent or grandparent who is a Muggle, then you're a half-blood. We don't know what constitutes full-blood. I haven't even seen that term used in the books, at least not in the U.S. editions. We also do not know what officially or socially constitutes a pure-blood.

In *Chamber of Secrets*, Ron informs us that "Most wizards these days are half-blood anyway. If we hadn't married Muggles we'd've died out." If most wizards are half-bloods, then why are Snape and Riddle so ashamed of being what most wizards are? One reason is pure-blood rhetoric. Riddle and Snape felt that their Muggle blood made them inferior to pure-blood wizards. Another reason is that they both wanted to be special, elite. Here are a few quotes from *Half-Blood Prince*:

His legs were trembling. He stumbled forward and sat down on the bed again, staring at his hands, his head bowed as though in prayer.
"I knew I was different," he whispered to his own quivering fingers.
"I knew I was special. Always, I knew there was something."
"Well, you were quite right," said Dumbledore, who was no longer smiling, but watching Riddle intently. "You are a wizard."

I will omit part of this scene and pick up below:

"Yes, Riddle was perfectly ready to believe that he was—to use his word —'special'," said Dumbledore.

Again, I will omit part of this scene:

Riddle gave an irritable twitch, as though trying to displace an irksome fly.
"You dislike the name 'Tom'?"
"There are a lot of Toms," muttered Riddle.

After the above Pensieve scene, Dumbledore discusses Riddle's behavior with Harry:

"Firstly, I hope you noticed Riddle's reaction when I mentioned that another shared his first name, 'Tom'?"
Harry nodded.
"There he showed contempt for anything that tied him to other people, anything that made him ordinary. Even then, he wished to be different, separate, notorious. He shed his name, as you know, within a few short years of that conversation and created the mask of 'Lord Voldemort' behind which he has been hidden for so long."

Tom Riddle chose to change his name completely and become someone else. This decision shows Riddle's issues of self-identity and self-worth. Riddle never learned to accept or appreciate his bicultural heritage. He chose instead to revel in part of who he was and to hate the other part. His attempt to rid Hogwarts of Muggles and Muggle-borns shows his self-hate. This is not an uncommon attitude for a person with a mixed, diverse background who has been told that part of their heritage is "inferior." Such people sometimes come to hate both the part of themselves that they see as "inferior" and other people who belong to the "inferior" group.

Tom Riddle isn't the only half-blood wizard who felt the need to create a more desirable identity:

"You dare use my own spells against me, Potter? It was I who invented them—I, the Half-Blood Prince!

The above quotation shows Severus Snape announcing with pride the title he'd given himself, "the Half-Blood Prince." Below is Harry Potter's view of Snape after discovering his other "identity":

"Yeah, that fits," said Harry. "He'd play up the pure-blood side so he could get in with Lucius Malfoy and the rest of them... he's just like Voldemort. Pure-blood mother, Muggle father...ashamed of his parentage, trying to make himself feared using the Dark Arts, gave himself an impressive new name—Lord   Voldemort—the   Half-Blood   Prince—how   could Dumbledore have missed—?"

As far as I can tell from my reading, Harry is correct about Snape. I can't think of a different reason for him to have given himself that particular title. Snape was ashamed of his parentage and tried to deny part of it. He also tried to overcome his feelings of inferiority by making "himself feared using the Dark Arts."

Of course, not all half-bloods are that obsessed with purity and trying to "play up the pure-blood side":

"Yeh know what I'd love, Harry? I'd love yeh ter win, I really would. It'd show 'em all... yeh don' have ter be pure-blood ter do it. Yeh don' have ter be ashamed of what yeh are. It'd show 'em Dumbledore's the one who's got it righ', lettin' anyone in as long as they can do magic."

Hagrid's words show pride in being a half-blood; however, they also point out a struggle for acceptance by half-bloods not to be seen as inferior to pure-bloods.

Speaking of them, we will now look at pure-bloods and their attitudes toward themselves and non-pure-blood wizards. These elitist pure-bloods' attitudes include not wanting Muggle-borns to go to Hogwarts and wanting to "purify" the wizarding race and have pure-bloods in charge:

"There are some wizards—like Malfoy's family—who think they're better than everyone else because they're what people call pure-blood."
"I mean, the rest of us know it doesn't make any difference at all."

Some pure-bloods see themselves as being superior to half-bloods and Muggle-borns.

Knowledge is power. Salazar Slytherin didn't want Muggle-borns to have the knowledge and training that they could obtain at Hogwarts—with good reason; after the separation was a dangerous time. Children from Muggle families would have been seen as a threat due to the fact that they might have divided loyalties. However, elitist pure-bloods have gone beyond worries about wizarding world security and taken on a very negative attitude toward anyone with Muggle blood in their veins: "*Filth! Scum! By-products of dirt and vileness! Half-breeds, mutants, freaks, begone from this place! How dare you befoul the house of my fathers—*" Mrs. Black, who was actually a portrait by the time we're introduced to her in *Order of the Phoenix*, has some definite views on the matter of blood purity. The above quotation contains only some of the obscenities that Mrs. Black shrieks at the "defilers" who have dared to besmirch the house of her fathers simply by being in it.

Speaking of obscenities, there is one I'd like to specifically point out:

"Mudblood's a really foul name for someone who is Muggle-born—you know, non-magic parents."

"It's a disgusting thing to call someone," said Ron, "Dirty blood, see. Common blood."

Mudblood: the word defines itself, "dirty blood." Elitist pure-bloods seem to equate being Muggle or Muggle-born with being "common" or "dirty." In *Chamber of Secrets*, Draco demonstrates this exact sentiment:

"Father says to keep my head down and let the Heir of Slytherin get on with it. He says the school needs ridding of all the Mudblood filth, but not to get mixed up in it.... I wish I knew who it is," said Malfoy petulantly. "I could help them."

I'd like to focus a moment on the fact that some pure-bloods are averse to the idea of being "common."

If something is common, then it is routine, the usual, mediocre, or average. We can easily contrast this with something that's special. "Special" brings to mind things that are exceptional, above average, and unique. As mentioned earlier, Tom Riddle wanted to be "special." He couldn't even stand the fact that his name is "common":

"You think I was going to use my filthy Muggle father's name forever? I, in whose veins runs the blood of Salazar Slytherin himself, through my mother's side? I, keep the name of a foul, common Muggle, who abandoned me even before I was born?"

The word "common" has other meanings. It can also refer to the political group or estate consisting of commoners. Commoners are the "common" people not of noble rank. In *Goblet of Fire*, Voldemort refers to them and others whom he considers inferior to him:

"And I answer myself, perhaps they believed a still greater power could exist, one that could vanquish even Lord Voldemort... perhaps they now pay allegiance to another.... Perhaps that champion of commoners, of Mudbloods and Muggles, Albus Dumbledore?"

It is telling that Voldemort lumps commoners, Mudbloods, and Muggles together. To him they are the same thing.

Voldemort using the word commoners is another insight into pure-blood attitudes. In a feudal society, "commoners" would have comprised a large part of the peasantry. These peasants were legally and judicially subject to a hereditary landholding elite made up of nobility and royalty. Another reason that I decided to bring up the subject of nobility and royalty is Sirius' words in *Order of the Phoenix*: "Because I hated the whole lot of them: my parents, with their pure-blood mania, convinced that to be a Black made you practically royal."

The tapestry in the Blacks' house does say, *"The Noble and Most Ancient House of Black."* "There are no Wizarding princes," says Lupin in *Half-Blood Prince*. This can't always have been the case. I might have missed that part of Professor Binns's lecture; however, given what we know of Muggle history, it's a safe bet that there once was wizarding royalty. Wizards could have had their own royal and noble families. *"The Noble and Most Ancient House of Black"* may not be an exaggeration. The Blacks have been around since at least the fifteenth century. The fact that at least some pure-blood families are able to trace their bloodlines back through several centuries and that, if you went back far enough, you might find nobility or even royalty, would also add to their feelings of superiority.

To summarize, the wizarding world is made up of Muggle-borns, half-bloods, and pure-bloods. All three of these similar yet disparate groups have particular views towards themselves and others. One rather outspoken attitude is superiority or inferiority based on one's bloodline. pure-bloods' attitudes of superiority come from attitudes toward blood purity and possibly social class.

Despite the negative attitudes of some elitist pure-bloods, many members of the magical community are not so overtly prejudiced. However, many wizards exhibit a form of subtle prejudice that they may not be consciously aware of towards Muggles, Muggle-borns, and half-bloods.

COLEOPTEROLOGY

Amanda Pommer

How lovely of all of you to be here! We are of course discussing a very fascinating subject, me, myself, and I! Rita Skeeter. Wretched, enchantingly nasty, horrible, foul.

My name is Amanda Pommer, a.k.a. Generalmanda or PyrateM, and I've been cosplaying Rita Skeeter since the release of *Half-Blood Prince*. She was introduced in *Goblet of Fire* as a sort of side villain and plot mover, and perhaps a bit of creative release for Jo, who may have had her fair share of run-ins with morally devoid reporters. She can be both cursed for laying the groundwork for the public shunning of Harry and Dumbledore and thanked for finally reporting the rebirth of Voldemort.

- So, my first question to you is, "Love or loathe, and a short reason why?"

- How did Miranda Richardson meet your expectation for the character?

- Do you think that her job ambitions drove her to learn the skill of becoming an Animagus? Or was it because of the form she took that made her realize it could be an asset in the world of journalism?

- Did her interference in *GoF* distract Hermione from the true danger of the false Professor Moody—whereas if she were on top of her game, she might have deduced what Harry was really up against?

- Do you think the Slytherins figured out how she was getting her stories, or do you think she told them outright?

- Is this a strong indicator of which House she belonged to?

- Does she support a side in the war?

- Is she pushing her own agenda or is she a tool of higher powers?

- Why do her stories work so well to sway public opinion?

- What can we tell about her past?

- What did she do with herself during the time she swore off writing to keep her Animagus self a secret?

- Did the stories she wrote in *GoF* benefit anyone? Who?

- Do you believe she is J. K. Rowling's characterization of real-life press she's had to deal with?

- How did writing the article for *The Quibbler* affect her career?

- Is her style of finding out information unethical?

- What purpose does she serve the reader?

- Does she serve any sort of positive role for the trio?

- How does she manage to keep those nails so very long and lovely?

- Do you think she wears a wig?

- What is her motivation? What drives the character?

- Can she be blamed for the general feelings toward Harry at the onset of book five?

Selected interviews with J. K. Rowling concerning Rita Skeeter's characterization which were used for discussion:

"About the Books: Transcript of J. K. Rowling's live interview on Scholastic.com," Scholastic.com, 16 Oct 2000. <http://www.scholastic.com/harrypotter/books/author/interview2.htm>.

Ballard, Nigel. Interview, BBCi Bristol, 12 Nov 2001. <http://www.bbc.co.uk/bristol/content/features/2001/11/12/ jk.shtml>.

Carrell, Severin. "Media: *Harry Potter* and the Horrible Hackette; Which Interviewer Inspired the Venomous Portrait in J. K. Rowling's Latest

Bestseller? Severin Carrell Rounds Up the Likely Suspects." *The Independent* (London), 5 Sept 2000. <http://www.accio-quote.org/articles/2000/0900-independent-carrell.html>.

"Harry Potter and Me" (*BBC Christmas Special*, British version). BBC, 28 Dec 2001. <http://www.accio-quote.org/articles/2001/1201-bbc-hpandme.htm>.

"J. K. Rowling at the Edinburgh Book Festival, Sunday, August 15, 2004." <http://www.jkrowling.com/textonly/en/news_view.cfm?id=80>.

Lockerbie, Catherine. "All aboard the Hogwarts Express." *The Scotsman*, 11 July 2000. <http://www.accio-quote.org/articles/2000/0700-scotsman-lockerbie.html>.

CROSSING AGE LINES IN FANFICTION: A ROUNDTABLE

Veronica Atkins (LupinTonks85)

We open with introductions and favorite cross-generational pairings. This is a roundtable on cross-gen pairings in fanfiction.

1   What is cross-gen?

2   Why do we like cross-gen pairings? Is it the age difference, a personal preference for older or younger partners in your life—or is it just easy, kinky smut?

3   When reading/writing cross-gen fanfiction, how old do you have the younger character? How large is the age difference?

4   If you read/write other non-cross-gen fanfiction, does your cross-gen fanfiction affect the story? (Example: a secondary pairing that is cross-gen.)

5   Is it easier to find taboos such as BDSM, dubious/non-con, et cetera, in cross-gen fanfiction?

6   Is cross-gen itself a taboo?

7   Do you read cross-gen that involves a Time Turner? Is it cross-gen if both parties are the same age, such as Hermione / Sirius in the 1970s?

8   Is cross-gen found in canon?

9   Where does Tonks fall in the generation gap?

10   Is there a line delimiting what we will read?

But Mom and Dad, It's Only Harry Potter

Alison Luperchio

Boy wizard Harry Potter, with his distinctive scar and glasses, has become as recognizable as any Hollywood star, and early readers are known to practice their budding reading skills on J. K. Rowling's series. As Harry matures, so do topics and themes within the texts. How can a parent or caregiver prepare for and answer the questions that are raised in the books, including prejudice, bullying, use of illicit substances, stealing, cheating, lying, and perhaps most frightening of all, Harry's Chest Monster? Join other parents, caregivers, and teachers who read the books to or for children to discuss tips and experiences for navigating the wizarding world and using it as a springboard for opening dialogue between youth and adults.

Roundtable Questions

To start off, we'll brainstorm some of the major controversial topics that J. K. Rowling raises and discuss the age groups that first address these issues in real life.

Topic suggestions include prejudice, bullying, use of illicit substances, stealing, cheating, lying, attraction and jealousy.

Then to the questions, starting at the youngest ages and moving up.

1   At what ages are the youngest independent *Harry Potter* readers? At what ages (earlier or later) do they hear it from adults who read to them?

2 At these early ages, when their questions tend to be more literal than philosophical, what do they ask, and what have you particularly noticed that they miss?

3 What topics do you wish the youngest readers would miss, but they pick up on anyway? How do you direct that conversation so that you don't overwhelm them with information they're not psychologically prepared to deal with?

4 What about Harry's chest monster? Do the youngest readers ask about it, and if so, do they have any understanding at all? Or does this go right over their heads?

5 Moving into the preteen/tween ages, do readers in this age bracket directly associate issues in the books with issues in their own lives? Or do they acknowledge the issues but not directly admit that the issues relate to them?

6 Which topics are most relevant to the tween/preteen crowd, and do you like the way Rowling has addressed them in the books?

7 Given that tweens as an age group are slightly notorious for evading sensitive issues, how can you use a question from a tween about these topics to open a discussion with them without scaring them off?

8 Are there "transitional" issues from tweenhood to teenhood that are addressed by Rowling?

9 What are teenagers' major questions and concerns? How do pressures from social and school settings influence what teens can learn from the books?

10 How do teenagers see the romances that Rowling has written into the books? Do they resonate with teens? Why or why not?

11 Are teens likely to relate what they read in the books directly to their own lives, or do they distance themselves from relevant issues? How can adults help them bridge the gap when they struggle with it?

12 What are the biggest hot buttons that Rowling pushes, and how are they different for different age groups?

Do You Want to Go to Hogwarts?: How Living in Literature Brings it Into Reality

Jessica Zebrine Gray
Louisiana State University

Do you want to go to Hogwarts? I know a lot of children and adults who dream about going to this magical castle filled with mystery and wonder. When we open the pages to J. K. Rowling's books, we are given the opportunity to travel to this English boarding school in our imaginations…but what if we could create a "Hogwarts" environment right here in Louisiana? Would anyone want to go to Hogwarts here? This will be our third summer offering Hogwarts School of Magic and Fun at the Unitarian Church of Baton Rouge. Our camp is similar to Vacation Bible School (VBS), but since the Bible is not considered to be the authority in UU churches, we decided to host a Vacation "Magic" School. Unitarian Universalism (UU) prides itself on being non-creedal and open to all people and life-affirming ideas.

Our version of the magical school of "Hogwarts" includes a three-dimensional theatrical environment in which adult volunteers invest tremendous time and energy so that children can learn spiritual and social values. We offer the day camp in July, and we already have full registration with a waiting list. We have children and adults who talk about this summer camp all year long. In the past we have only offered a one-week camp, but this year we have expanded to two weeks leading up to the release of the fifth film and the seventh book. I have been asked to speak at several conferences about how we run the camp, and several other churches are now working off of our model. So what makes this experience so different, so unique? By bringing the world of *Harry Potter* to life, we allow children to live inside the literature. This brings it into a reality. Some issues inherent in the books have played out in real life, such as an inversion of the normal social order, class distinctions, and dynamic power structures. Ultimately, the camp provides its participants with an opportunity to bond as a community and strongly affects the culture of the church congregation.

The *Harry Potter* books and spirituality are often pitted against each other. The most common message of Christian conservatives is that the books teach children witchcraft, or at least that they give children an impression that witchcraft can be positive. Harry has become the poster child for the American Library Association, based on the attempts to ban the books in schools. While these books are often cited as the most controversial books of the current media, in reality the conservative critics seem to have calmed down during the past few years, while the fan base has continued to grow. While most Christian churches still do not endorse the books, some have come out strongly in favor of them. Unitarian Universalist Churches, who have no inherent bias against witchcraft, have accepted the *Harry Potter* books quite readily and adapted them for religious education. A UU Church in Kent, Ohio, began holding *Harry Potter*-themed day camps over five years ago, and hundreds of churches have followed the tradition based on the idea that the books teach valuable moral lessons that fit well within religious education.

According to James Fowler, a psychologist whose theories of faith development are highly influential in religious education, stories are a fundamental part of early categorization of meaning. The stage he marks "Intuitive-Projective" usually lasts from ages two to seven, and includes a reliance on fantasy and narrative to give meaning to their experiences of the world. Fairy tales are encouraged because they allow children to make early intuitive connections between their own experiences and the experiences of others. According to Scholastic, distributor of the *Harry Potter* books, the first book is recommended for ages seven and up. As the characters in the books mature, the recommended minimum age is increased to ten. Thus, the books are a good fit for children in the intuitive-projective stage. Yet, if children in this stage have parents or older siblings who read the books, they want to be a part of it.

For this reason we opened our day camp to children as young as five years old. Some of these young children had the early books read to them, but many had only heard of the stories. The camp provided a rich and fertile fantasy-land for children in the Intuitive-Projective stage to make their own connections and narrative before their encounter with the books themselves.

Most of the students at our Hogwarts camp fit within the second stage of faith development, which Fowler calls "Mythic-Literal." This stage usually begins in elementary school and may last through adolescence or even adulthood. With the foundation of stories and beliefs from the Intuitive-Projective stage, the Mythic-Literal child begins to test those stories to develop concrete "reality" from "make-believe." J. K. Rowling insists that her readers know the difference between fantasy and reality, as she says in a CNN interview: "It is a fantasy world and they understand that completely." Fowler also explains that this stage of faith development is when a child "begins to take on for him- or herself the stories, beliefs and observances that symbolize belonging to his or her community" (149). Sometimes this translates to a literal interpretation of stories that are taught to be true, such as the stories in the Bible or in history, and a person in this stage will argue vehemently for the literal truth of the story (150).

One challenge in UU Religious Education are that children in the Mythic-Literal stage long for something concrete on which they can rely, but the denomination is built on a postmodern sense of relativism. The only concrete guidelines offered to UU children are the "Principles," a basic agreement about how we treat each other and act in the world.

1   The inherent worth and dignity of every person;

2   Justice, equity and compassion in human relations;

3   Acceptance of one another and encouragement to spiritual growth in our congregations;

4   A free and responsible search for truth and meaning;

5   The right of conscience and the use of the democratic process within our congregations and in society at large;

6   The goal of world community with peace, liberty, and justice for all;

7   Respect for the interdependent web of all existence of which we are a part. ("UUA Principles and Purposes")

These principles provide positive guidelines for children and adults, but they are quite abstract. According to Fowler, stories are the best way for children at this stage to learn ethical guidelines, whether taken literally or metaphorically. In a traditional VBS, the Bible stories are taught as necessarily true, giving the children no opportunity to develop their own mythic-literal interpretations. At our camp, the stories of *Harry Potter* gave us a structure and framework to present the UU principles. We never taught the stories as "literal" truth, but the books became like a Bible to us, providing a point of departure for the spiritual and social messages we wanted to teach.

The overall theme of UCBR's Hogwarts in 2005 developed out of a quotation from the second book in the series, *Harry Potter and the Chamber of Secrets*. In the book, when young Harry is questioning his motivations, his mentor Professor Dumbledore says, "It is our choices, Harry, that show what we truly are, not our abilities" (333). This quotation was printed on posters and brochures and emphasized throughout the week. The primary conflict in the books between Harry and Lord Voldemort is essentially about making positive choices. In relating this to the students' lives, first they must recognize their own inherent worth and then their ability to make a difference in the world. Teamwork is essential in the books, as each character brings his or her own strengths to the confrontation. Our theme for 2006 was "Indivisible," with the quotation, "Differences of habit and language are nothing at all if our aims are identical and our hearts are open," again by Professor Dumbledore. We used this as a point of departure, finding the many ways that we are alike as well as the ways that we are different. In each of the Hogwarts classes and in the basic structure of the camp, we help the children explore their questions and how they can make their own unique, positive choices, facing the darkness that confronts them. The children are given tools to explore possibilities rather than answers.

We begin the camp by sorting the children into four "houses," just as they are in the books. However, since the "houses" in the

Figure 1: Waverider House at the Peace Pole

books have definite negative and positive connotations, we chose our own house names of Stonedragon, Waverider, Phoenixfire, and Windhorse. Each house has its own color and animal mascot and is associated with one of the qualities of Faith, Peace, Hope, and Love. During house time each day, the multi-aged groups work together to perform service projects. In the past, Waverider, whose quality is peace, planted a flower garden around the peace pole (Figure 1), while Stonedragon, whose quality is faith, assembled a small rock meditation area they called the "Junior Peace-stones," imitating an adult meditation area on the property. Windhorse, whose quality is Love, made care packages for the local battered women's shelter, while Phoenixfire, whose quality is hope, made recycled flowerpots to give to people in the hospital. This year we are bringing in a quilting specialist to teach the children how to make quilts together with their house. We will then donate the quilts to Project Linus, an organization that gives homemade quilts to terminally ill children. The purpose of the service projects is to teach that the "real" magic we can make in the world is helping others. The houses are intended to be small communities within the larger Hogwarts community. They each have their own specific common room with a password to enter and an adult leader called their "Head of House." The houses also form teams to play Quidditch, the flying broomstick game that is quite popular in the books. Through an imitation of the houses in the books, each house has an opportunity to experience hands-on service while getting to know each other. These small communities eat together, work together, and play together for a significant portion of each day, forming a group identity that crosses the boundaries of age.

Then the students are divided by age into classes, all based on the classes in the books. Transfiguration and Charms are arts and craft classes where the students take ordinary materials and turn them into something else. Potions is basically a science experiment class, though the students also make edible potions like "Positivity Potions" with soda and pop rocks, emphasizing the idea that they had the choice about whether to think positively or negatively. They explore different types of Magical Creatures and learn about the medicinal properties of herbs in Herbology. In History of Magic, they discuss the *Harry Potter* books and the themes within, including how the books teach us to treat one another and to make positive choices. In Defense Against Dark Arts, which I teach, we talk about how any darkness must be counteracted with light, such that the darkness of fear and depression can be counteracted with a positive

Figure 2: Fighting fear with humor

outlook and laughter. It is basically a drama class where we enact our protectors. We enacted the spells taught to defend against Boggarts and Dementors in the third book of the series, *Harry Potter and the Prisoner of Azkaban*. Boggarts are physical manifestations of a person's fears, which are overcome by making the situation humorous. I paired the students and had one act out the "fear" while the other thought of a way to make it funny (Figure 2).

Dementors are creatures that cause misery and depression, and they are fought by summoning a "Patronus" or protector. The children were encouraged to think of something positive and act it out as their own Patronus to send the Dementors away. Divination is taught as a type of storytelling, using images to tell stories. Incantations is a music class. We try to use all of the multiple intelligence types in the various classes. Overall, the message that students were taught in these classes is that each person has the power to choose to face any situation with a positive attitude.

The structure of the camp is necessarily performative, as it involves creating three-dimensional scenery, characters in costume, and an improvised "script" that we enact throughout the week. Though we plan for months in advance, the actual "scenery" cannot be set up until the Sunday before camp begins. For hours we work to transform ordinary classrooms into extraordinary spaces. Christmas lights and ornaments, fabric, artificial plants, Halloween decorations, and more go into creating these environments. A similar process happens at the end of the camp, when all of the decorations have to be taken down in a short period of time. The time between is marked as sacred, the "liminal" phase described by anthropologist Victor Turner in which transfor-mation can take place. In an initiatory rite of passage, the first step according to Turner is separation, which "demarcates sacred space and time from profane or secular space and time" (24). We emphasize this moment of separation each day as the students arrive. In the *Harry Potter* books, Harry and his

Figure 3: The Journey

friends travel to Hogwarts on a special train, and they also travel to

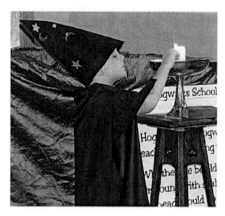

Figure 4: Lighting the Chalice

other places in the wizarding world through magical means like Floo powder, which allows them to journey through fire-places. In our camp, each student makes a journey by tossing Floo powder (bird-seed) on the lawn, walking into a fireplace to go through a tunnel to the Great Hall for morning assembly (Figure 3). This journey marks a separation from ordinary reality, a time and place where "special" things could happen. Once in the assembly, one of the students "lights the chalice," a tradition unique to Unitarian Universalism (Figure 4). These actions mark the time and space as sacred.

Figure 5: Iris Imaginoria

Each adult is required to choose a name and "character" and develop his or her own costume. Though we use the structure of the books, we do not try to imitate the characters of the books. As Headmistress, I chose the name Iris Imaginoria to reflect the many facets of the rainbow and the possibilities of the imagi-nation. My costume included a lot of purple velvet and a witch hat with faceted prism beads rimming the edge (Figure 5). Most of our characters choose their names according to the job they have chosen to do; Professor Queequeg Freewilly is the head of the watery Waverider house, and Madame Paprika Brulee is teaching Edible Transfiguration, a cooking class. Some of the costumes are quite extravagant, and we offer simple costumes to any adult volunteers who cannot provide their own. The children receive their own costumes on Monday morning in "Diagon Alley," a space we created to imitate the magical shopping area described in the books. Each student is fitted for a very simple cape at the Wizard Wear Shop, can decorate their own hat at the Magical Hats Store, and at the wand Emporium is measured for a filled, thin plastic wand with glittering unicorn hairs (tinsel) and dragon heartstrings (chenille stems). As of this year they also receive a camp T-shirt and a tote bag to help carry their many magical items. The costumes and environment help to reinforce the "special" nature of the camp.

This change of space and character through costuming prepares the students for an unusual "inversion" experience. Each of the books begins with Harry Potter at home with his Muggle aunt and uncle until his "normal" life is inversed by his journey to Hogwarts. This inversion is related to Mikhail Bakhtin's theory of the carnival, which "celebrated temporary liberation from the prevailing truth and from established order; it marked the suspension of hierarchical rank, privileges, norms, and prohibitions" (45). In the first book, *Harry Potter and the Sorcerer's Stone,* Harry knows nothing of the wizarding world, so everything is an inversion of the hierarchy of his foster family and the rules of reality as he knows them. Though Hogwarts has its own hierarchy, structure, and social dynamics, the shift from his Muggle existence makes every school year an inversion for Harry Potter.

Our students also experience an inversion of reality as they knew it through the Hogwarts camp. The situation of a day camp, transformation of the space, and the costumes invert the normal order, much as Mardi Gras and similar festivals invert normal order for a society. Bakhtin claims the inversion of hierarchy allows a "special type of communication impossible in every day life" (46). The children in this camp were in a completely new situation, allowing for them to develop connections they never had opportunity to make before. Approximately 75% of the students at our Hogwarts are regular attendees of Religious Education classes that take place Sunday mornings, 11:15 a.m. to 12:15 p.m. Before we began these summer camps, most of these children had never been to the church at any other time. While some of the children have known each other for years, many of them had never spent any extended time together. Also, the regular classes are separated by age, so having the children in multi-age houses changed the usual order. They also were allowed to inhabit spaces usually off-limits from them, such as the rooms usually used for adult and senior youth meetings.

The most dramatic space that children do not usually inhabit is the sanctuary. For the weeks of camp we set up half of the sanctuary as the "Great Hall" for assemblies, and the other half as the "Quidditch Field" for an indoor version of the high-paced broomstick game played in the books. In the books and movies Quidditch takes place outside, but this indoor Quidditch was one of the concessions we had to make due to the extreme heat of a Louisiana summer. It actually turned out to be an excellent exchange of space, using the sanctuary for the most active part of the camp. During these weeks, the sanctuary, the heart of the church, belongs to the children.

The costumes and characters also invert traditional order, since the children relate to adults as different "characters." Even the children whose parents teach call their parents by their character names. The result of this inversion is a crossing of boundaries that has allowed the children to relate more to the spaces, adults, and children of other age groups in the church. Several of the children began attending regular religious education classes after the camp, some adults became regular volunteers, and several families have since joined the church. Just as Harry is transformed through his inverted experiences at Hogwarts, forming alliances and friendships he never would have imagined before, so the students in our camp have opportunities to do the same thing.

One of the primary features of each year at Hogwarts in the book is the competition between houses for points that eventually leads to the House Cup. Throughout the week the students compete for "points," and whichever house has the most at the end of the week wins. Points can be given for good behavior, correct answers in classes, winning Quidditch games, and good sportsmanship, but points can be taken away for misbehavior as well. In the books, the points are magically tallied through huge hourglasses filled with precious gems representing the four houses. Taking a cue from the local Louisiana culture, we decided to use Mardi Gras beads in the four house colors to tally the points. During the camp, students who win points for their house get a strand of beads worth fifty points. They wear their points until the assembly at the end of the day, when they add their points to their "House Goblet." Some students receive as many as ten strands of beads each day, while others have only a few. However, any misbehavior costs points, so the students have to give back beads. Troublesome students often do not have any beads themselves, so they actually have to get beads from one of their housemates to give back. This seems harsh, but it teaches a lesson of accountability, as the points are for the house, not the individual. The students all sign a behavior agreement at the start of camp, stating they would not act with violence or disrupt activities.

The House Cup competition is an essential part of the Hogwarts experience, but it has presented some challenges for our Baton Rouge Hogwarts. The most competitive part of the camp, the Quidditch game, causes very few problems, but it does favor athletic children, so we decided in our second year to add a "knowledge bowl" so that non-athletic children could have an opportunity to shine. Also, despite our best efforts the overall house competition has played out some subtle power dynamics. As in the books, there has been great inequity amongst the staff about what qualified as disruptive and about what deserved to win or lose points. Some houses had more difficult students than others, and some professors gave more points to their own house than others. The beads became much like a commodity, being bought and sold with behavior. The exchange was not unlike Mardi Gras, where beads become the focus of an exchange of power. Like any hegemonic system, the students' longing for the commodity of beads kept them from crossing behavioral boundaries. In some ways, this is a drastic variance from the books, which do not really support "staying within the boundaries." Harry and his friends are constantly getting in trouble for breaking rules, though he usually faces some sort of consequences. In our camp, none of the students have attempted to seriously step outside the boundaries as they were given. However, there is also no serious threat like Voldemort. The boundaries inherent in the House Cup competition give the students a reason to strive towards positive behavior, and overall the system works.

Though we did not anticipate this ahead of time, Pierre Bourdieu's class distinctions also came to play in our camp, just as they do in the books. Harry's friend Ron Weasley is from a large, less financially successful wizarding family, so Harry and Ron have a constant tension about money. Ron's robes are always worn, and his books are always used. In our camp we provide very simple capes as part of the registration fee, but we allow students to wear their own robes from home if they wish. Some students wear store-bought robes, and others have very nice homemade robes. Our first year we also had different types of hats, some store-bought right after Halloween the previous year and some homemade out of felt. They were distributed on a first-come, first-served basis. The conflicts this caused were not usually overt, but some children clearly felt slighted. Ironically, the homemade hats were actually more expensive to make than the hats bought on clearance, but the students strongly preferred the store-bought hats. The variation in robes caused a more overt conflict. Towards the end of the first camp, one of the younger boys with only a cape asked one of the girls with a homemade robe to switch with him. When she refused, he proceeded to argue and might have started a physical fight if teachers had not intervened. Thus, even in our "make-believe" world of Hogwarts, some of the social distinctions described in Rowling's Hogwarts became very real.

Despite these inequities, the students who attended and adults who worked on Hogwarts: Baton Rouge seemed to really bond through this experience. Richard Schechner calls a performance that changes its performers "transformations," while performances that return participants back to where they began are "transportations" (125). The former is more common of initiatory rites and religious rituals, while the latter is characteristic of traditional theatre. However, he describes a process by which a group could "workshop" a performance, thus transforming into a group; then that group could transport the audience during the time and space of the performance (148). It may seem that the camp is only a transportation, as we take down the decorations at the end of the camp and ordinary life resumes. Yet, through this process the social dynamics of the Religious Education program shift each year. Children who come to the camp have the opportunity to "own" the church in a way that children never had before. They share this liminal, "insider" experience. New friendships have formed between children and adults, and many of the students recall aspects of lessons learned months later. The students and faculty of Hogwarts transform each year into a bonded community. We then invite the church congregation to take an abbreviated journey with us. Sunday morning we share stories, pictures and songs, inviting the audience to experience in part the work that we have done. The services are some of the highest attended in the summer, as so many want to see the "magic" for themselves. Many of the adult congregants are quite inspired by the children's service projects and by seeing their enthusiasm for helping others. After the service, the congregation is encouraged to "tour Hogwarts," as we keep all the rooms other than the sanctuary exactly as they are during the week. The "transformed" community of Hogwarts School "transports" the congregation of the Unitarian Church, and boundaries dissolve. The children's programming is no longer entirely separate from the adults, and thus the church community is stronger as a whole.

In her article "Performance, Utopia, and the 'Utopian Performative'," Jill Dolan expresses her interest in teaching students "to use performance as a tool for making the world better, to use performance to incite people to profound responses that shake their consciousness of themselves and the world" (456). She suggests that art can be used to evoke a response in life. We use performative techniques in creating our Hogwarts camp, and the results of that artistic effort brings the ideas inherent in the *Harry Potter* books into reality for the students, encouraging them to take action in helping make the world a better place, much like Dolan's utopia. We frame the experience as living art, based on the art of J. K. Rowling's literature, and then that art becomes a part of people's lives.

Works Cited

Bakhtin, Mikhail. "Rabelais and his World." *Literary Theory: An Anthology.* Ed. Julie Rivkin and Michael Ryan. London: Blackwell, 1998. 45–51.

Dolan, Jill. "Performance, Utopia, and the 'Utopian Performative'." *Theatre Journal* 53 (2001): 455–79.

Haines, Becky, and Mac Goekler. "Harry Potter and the Magic of Children," UUA General Assembly. Boston, MA: June 26–30, 2003. Available online at <http://www.uua.org/ga/ga03/4027.html>.

Rowling, J. K. *Harry Potter and the Sorcerer's Stone*. New York: Scholastic, 1997.

—. *Harry Potter and the Chamber of Secrets*. New York: Scholastic, 1998.

—. *Harry Potter and the Prisoner of Azkaban*. New York: Scholastic, 1999.

—. *Harry Potter and the Goblet of Fire*. New York: Scholastic, 2000.

Schechner, Richard. *Between Theater and Anthropology*. Philadelphia: University of Pennsylvania Press, 1985.

"Scholastic: About the Books." available online at <http://www.scholastic.com/harrypotter/books/stone/index.htm>.

"Success of *Harry Potter* bowls author over." Interview on CNN. com, 21 Oct 1999. Available at <http://www.cnn.com/books/news/9910/21/rowling.intvu/index.html>.

Turner, Victor. *From Ritual to Theatre: The Human Seriousness of Play*. New York: PAJ Publications, 1982.

"UUA Principles and Purposes." Available online at <http://www.uua.org/aboutuua/principles.html>.

SALAMANGKA: A LOOK INTO THE FILIPINO POTTER FANDOM EXPERIENCE

Cherie M. del Rio

Magic—this is the English translation of the Filipino word "salamangka." Before the novels of J. K. Rowling made their way onto Filipino bookshelves, "magic" was a word seldom used, sometimes popping up on poker cards, in the performances of clowns and so-named magicians during birthday parties, in exhibitions by illusionists, in very few literary materials that schools required their students to read. But when the *Potter* phenomenon hit the Pearl of the Orient Sea, "magic" or "salamangka" ceased to become merely a word. It has evolved into a lifestyle, a term that most aptly described the passion of Filipinos who have come to love the hero in Rowling's books. That magic is no longer of handkerchiefs turned to doves. That magic is no longer of a deck of playing cards which comes with manuals on how to trick audiences. That magic is now associated with wands and cauldrons, with spells and unforgivable curses, with bushy-haired nerds and redheaded best friends. And that magic, of course, is that of the Boy Who Lived.

Since the books were released in the country, the magic of *Harry Potter* quickly blended with the Filipino culture. It is no wonder, then, that an organization devoted purely to the fandom later emerged. In 2001, the "Pinoy[1] Harry Potter" Community (otherwise known as "Hogwarts Philippines") was born. Structured very much like the Hogwarts in Rowling's novels, "Hogwarts Philippines" is the first and only wizarding school for the Filipino witch and wizard. And for almost six years, the community has been spreading magic all over the Philippines: converting skeptical Muggles to diehard Potterheads, orphans to witches and wizards who find family in the

---

1 "Pinoy" is a slang term for "Filipino."

company of Potter geeks, indifferent relatives to supportive clans—
basically sharing the Potter love one magical day at a time.

Hogwarts Philippines: A History

I became a fan only in the year 2001. In that same year, I heard
of a *Harry Potter* trivia game contest sponsored by a bookstore. I
joined and later qualified for the championships. I met and made a
friend with another one of the contestants—Inez Ponce de Leon.
Inez and I were both undefeated during the elimination rounds, but
when we reached the finals, we both lost. We were both saddened
that we failed to bring home the *Harry Potter* merchandise that the
sponsors gave away as prizes. Little did we know that such loss only
meant something much more grand—that the friendship we have
formed would later lay the first brick of the castle of Hogwarts
Philippines.

Yahoo! Club was the trend back then, and so I sent Inez a text
message a couple of days before Halloween. I told her we should
start a club for Filipino *Harry Potter* fans. And so we did; I set up the
club and Inez invited her students as she was then working as a
professor in the University of the Philippines. We wanted to get in
touch with the other contestants who joined the Trivia Game
challenge, but sadly, we did not have everyone else's contact
information. Up to this day, Inez and I never found out who truly
won that contest. However, I—for one—believe that the honor,
prestige, and the prizes that those winners may have garnered will
never be as wonderful and as magical as the prize we have won in
the birth of a Filipino *Harry Potter* community—because in losing,
we have won not only a fan base of fellow Potterheads but also a
family whose members share a distinguished passion for The Boy
Who Lived.

Because the members come from all walks of life and from all
over the country, the internet was the quickest, easiest, and cheapest
way to gather the magical Pinoy folk. From the Yahoo! Club, we
evolved into a Yahoo! Group and later launched our very own Web
site, <http://www.pinoyharrypotter.org/>—which, unfortunately, fell
prey to countless hackers. And as we struggle to "renovate" our
main castle, the Pinoy *Harry Potter* community has taken refuge
under a new domain, <http://www.hogwartsphilippines.org/>. Later

on, the members have come to refer to the community as PHP—short for Pinoy *Harry Potter.*

While PHP is not officially endorsed by J. K. Rowling, Warner Bros., and all the other legal publishers of *Harry Potter,* this lack of official recognition from the aforementioned entities does not hinder our continuous growth, bringing together fans regardless of class, age, or profession. Hogwarts Philippines hopes to promote *Harry Potter* further and to foster a strong bond of friendship among its members while doing so.

Following the format of the real "Hogwarts," Hogwarts Philippines has its own set of administrators, faculty, staff, and student leaders. At first, the positions were awarded by means of appointment due to the small number of members. More than a year later, the school began to hold elections to determine who among the members are to be Prefects, who will be the school year's Head Boy and Head Girl. Each year, students would advance to the next level based on the house points they have earned. The graduates are usually offered a teaching post. They may choose to hold their own online classes, or perhaps help out as school staff, or maybe settle for the designation of a lurker.

To date, there are over a thousand registered members in our mailing list, and hundreds more are signing up at our Web site. We have about a hundred members who regularly show up for conventions, conferences, and a multitude of other *Harry Potter*-related meet-ups and gatherings. In the Philippines, the magic starts once a Potterhead gets enrolled and sorted.

Enrollment and Sorting: Where the Magic Begins

At Hogwarts Philippines, enrollment is free. Internet access is all that is required. Once you have accessed our Web site, you may sign up to be sorted. The sorting questions have been adapted to the Filipino culture. For instance, we used Filipino heroes as models for the primary traits each House prides itself in: national heroes who represent bravery, loyalty, intelligence, and cunning. And to avoid instances of having members re-take the sorting quiz with the hope of getting into the houses they prefer, we sort students manually. We go through every single username, profile, and e-mail address to make sure that there are no duplications. True enough, we would find some members using several names but only a single e-mail address, attempting to be "re-sorted." This is a process which requires an ample amount of both time and effort; but as most of the founding members have come to realize, we would do anything for the love of PHP, from shouldering Web site subscription expenses to conducting online classes for free. This brand of devotion is another definition of Filipino *Potter* fandom.

"I think that fandom is really about people," Mary Ann Ortiz, PHP's Web Administrator and Gryffindor Head of House, states:

> It's about interacting with people who share the same passion for things like *Harry Potter*. I show my love for the fandom by working for the fandom, helping to make sure everyone will have a place to go to to interact, make sure that information is always available to fellow fans, make sure fans will have something to work for and celebrate. I get my energy from fellow fans, especially fellow PHP members, who have proven to me that they are worth all the work that PHP has been doing for them.

Online Classes: An Evolution of Potter Magic

The structure of Hogwarts and the subject titles subsequently inspired the appointed professors of Hogwarts Philippines to come up with their own sets of online classes. These classes take after the subjects presented in the books. In Hogwarts Philippines, the magical classes have been modified to meet Pinoy fans' needs and wants in light of the given space of interaction in an online message board or forum. These classes are held online, and every registered member is welcome to sign up for their preferred courses. However, due to the large number of members, "enrollment" is on a first-come, first-served basis.

A number of members from Hogwarts Philippines are professionals who are not only talented in their field but also magnanimous when it comes to sharing these talents with their fellow Pinoy Potterheads. These "faculty members" now use their respective fields of expertise in teaching subjects born from the classes in the *Potter* universe; these subjects, of course, are now molded to suit the Filipino *Potter* fandom's unique style and culture.

PHP's Defense Against the Dark Arts Professor, Anne Frances Sangil, is Professor of Literature at De La Salle University. Professor Sangil, or DADAProf as PHPers know her, also attended the Nimbus–2003 symposium. In her introduction for the DADAFIL

101 (which stands for Defense Against the Dark Arts—Philippines) syllabus, she wrote:

No one subject can hope to prepare you to cope with all the challenges of the times as well as the challenges of a magical career. This course is a gateway course for those who intend to work for the Ministry of Magic as Aurors, Obliviators, or officers in charge of the regulation and control of magical creatures. If you do well in this subject, you can embark on a more serious study of DADA in your succeeding years at PHP. Hogwarts Philippines has proven itself to be an institution not only devoted to all things *Harry Potter* but also committed to excellence vis-à-vis the values the Four Founders highly prize, those of courage, patience, ambition and intelligence. It goes without saying, then, that students enrolled in this course are expected to develop and nourish these values throughout the school year.

Professor Sangil's course on a Philippine counterpart of Defense Against the Dark Arts

aims to introduce students to the basic elements and creatures in Philippine magic and traditions. The subject will also try to delve into, clarify, and debunk certain notions in our so-called Philippine "mythology" as propagated by Muggle historians and folklorists (is there really a tikbalang? Are sirenas and syokoys mere sailor-tall tales? Was there really a Pepeng Agimat? And what about the late Lizardo? Was he really one of the old friends and supporters of Voldemort before his encounter with the Boy Who Lived? What do you do when you see a manananggal flying overhead?).

In DADAFIL101, PHPers enter a wizarding class born from the *Potter* universe, but what they discuss inside is a magical world that is uniquely Filipino—where local mythical creatures meet Rowling's fantastic beasts.

Other courses which Hogwarts Philippines offers to its student members are Charms, Muggle Studies, Dark Arts, and Arithmancy. A lesson in grammar is what Charms students conjure with every swish and flick of their wands in class—with Professor Abigail Santos (a.k.a. Prof. A) teaching the members the proper spells for correct spelling. With this free grammar class, student members charm their way into improving their command of the English language. With *Harry Potter* as topics for essays and grammar exercises, the students are inspired to better their grammar skills with their wizarding hero at the heart of their compositions.

Professor Mary Ann Ortiz leads the Pinoy witches and wizards in studying the Filipino Muggle under wizarding microscopes. We look at our culture from the vantage point of a magical community, identifying the uniqueness of Muggle culture in doing so. "Salamangkultura," which is a survey of magic and Filipino Muggle culture, is Hogwarts Philippines' version of Muggle Studies. In her course description, Professor Ortiz writes:

"Salamangkultura" is a survey of specific aspects of Filipino Muggle culture and how magic relates (or does not relate) to them. Some topics may deal with Muggle culture in general. The objectives of this course is to be aware and learn more about Pinoy Muggle culture, promote Muggle tolerance, and increase appreciation of wizarding culture.

Professor Gary Mayoralgo, a comic book artist and a talented wizard, teaches art and drawing to the students of Hogwarts Philippines. Heading the House of Slytherin, Prof. Mayoralgo calls his subject "Dark Arts." Professor Edwin Madera, an engineer, offers math tutorials in his Arithmancy course—preparing problems and solutions for the eager student, teaching tips and techniques in solving equations.

While these courses prove to be truly helpful to the members in their Muggle lives—education- and/or entertainment-wise—it cannot be denied that these subjects are rooted in the universe of *Harry Potter*, and therefore their elements will always be tainted with that same culture of Harry's world, with that same unreality, with that same magic. Even if we do discuss Filipino mythical creatures, tackle Muggle Filipinos' idiosyncrasies, or draw Philippine-themed artwork—we do so in a manner that leaves us tied to the fantasy of *Harry Potter*. That magic is kept alive in role-play, where each participating individual lives two distinct yet merged identities: one of a Potterhead and one of a Filipino.

House Points: Learning and Earning

The efforts, contributions, and all other manifestations of magic, skill, and talent will never go unnoticed in Hogwarts Philippines. Participation in the online classes, activities, and events is a chance to earn house points. At the end of every school year, all the house points are tallied, much like what is done in the novels. Since 2001, the Gryffindor House has always won the House Cup. And since

2001, the remaining three houses have also put up quite a good fight in earning for their respective houses a handful of points.

The professors have the power to award and deduct points, as do the student leaders (Head Boy, Head Girl, and the prefects). From the simple act of posting pictures to the trying task of setting up a booth for the convention, efforts exerted for the love of the organization are rewarded with house points. Likewise, misbehavior in the forums or during events warrants deduction of house points from offending members.

Over the years, we have gotten quite a number of unique ideas from our members—young and old—on how we can keep that burning *Potter* passion aflame: suggestions on what to discuss both online and during meet-ups, where to celebrate Christmas parties, which activities to hold during movie premieres and book launches, which booth design should be adopted for conventions, and many others. For these bright ideas, the members are awarded their well-deserved house points. Moreover, PHP is proud to grant house points to students who come up with excellent compositions—from Valentine greetings to speculative essays, from shipper filks and poetry to full-length fanfictions. PHP has collected quite a number of great fanworks, and now that the release of the last installment is fast approaching, our own wizarding school is bound to receive more of these magical output from the wizarding Pinoy geniuses.

Events and Activities: Sharing the Magic, Sharing the Love

Like many other Potter fan communities, PHP has had its share of meet-ups, parties, and conventions. What better way to enjoy the Potter magic than to share it with fellow fans? However, we do take the most pride in the activities that we share with the Muggle world, for as we reach out to non-fans, we open to them the doors of a universe, a fandom, a magic which has bonded us so tightly…a magic which we wish to continually share with Filipino wizarding and non-wizarding folks alike.

There are many types of Filipino *Potter* fan (or Pinoy Potterhead), and one will find these types evident in the events and activities that PHP both organizes and joins. The average Filipino fan might be seen at a book launch donning a black Hogwarts robe. Underneath the robe would be Muggle clothing. Some fans do not even bother with costumes. A single reading of all the books would suffice—unlike for those obsessed Potterheads who maintain a twice or thrice minimum when it comes to reading and re-reading the books. Other Pinoy Potterheads are labeled "obsessed" primarily from their long list of "crazy things done for the love of *Harry Potter.*" One of our members, a Gryffindor named Felice Nicole Del Rosario, has even had her car painted with Harry Potter chasing the golden snitch. I, for one, have been regarded as addicted to the fandom, what with flying thousands of miles just to attend The Witching Hour in 2005 and this year's Phoenix Rising. I have my own *Harry Potter* collection, and I must admit that I don't see myself ceasing to add *Harry Potter* items to my prized possessions. I collect because I am happy to see these items around me; I am glad to be reminded of the fandom which has changed my life in so many ways—from inspiring me to choose the focus of my graduate degree to meeting people I now cannot imagine to be out of my life. But there are other Filipino fans who are just as obsessed as I am, yet their display cabinets are almost free of *Harry Potter* collectibles.

Mary Ann Ortiz, our Muggle Studies Professor, relates her choice to be a non-collector:

At first it really was a matter of my not being able to afford to collect. But I realized that if there's something I really want, I actually have the patience to wait and save up for it. But the compulsion to buy just isn't there, apart from occasional items that really catch my fancy. A book is more likely to induce compulsive buying in me than a collectible. I think the very essence of fandom means you should reach out to other fans, and not shut yourself up in your room, reading books you will not discuss with anyone, surfing the internet for pictures or video or news you won't share with anyone, collecting merchandise you won't show to anyone.

Magic Works in the Muggle World

In April 2006, Hogwarts Philippines—in cooperation with McDonalds—organized "Magic Works," an outreach activity with the orphans from the "Jesus Loves the Little Children Foundation" in Pinagbuhatan, Pasig City, Philippines. PHPers spent the day with the orphans, teaching them how to play UNO and Quidditch, singing and dancing with them, sharing books, and basically just having magical fun.

It is in events like "Magic Works" that PHP sees the broader horizons of the magic that has glued the community together, and as the members join each other in the organization's activities, the bond grows stronger and the magic grows even bigger and brighter. After only six years of existence, the magic of Harry Potter has shone so brightly on the friendships formed within the PHP community that it has ceased to become a mere organization. The Pinoy *Harry Potter* community has become a family.

Hogwarts Philippines: From Fan Club to Family

I asked my fellow Pinoy Potterheads what they thought made our organization different from other fan clubs.

Professor Mayoralgo relates back to "Magic Works" with his answer:

Filipinos view magic differently. Others may think of the occult first and foremost: wiccans, spells, and stuff like that. Some others go for the bunny-out-of-the-hat kind of magic, while others go for the Merlin and Gandalf type of magic. We, however, believe that extraordinary experiences and miracles are works of magic...and our experiences with our fellow fans in and out of PHP are magical. When you consider our events, none of them focuses on the magic that the other countries celebrate. Our magic comes from seeing orphans play Quidditch using rubber balls and plastic hoops tied to trees. Magic comes from the look on a child's face knowing that his last card is a "Draw Three." Magic comes from seeing a little girl point at a costumed member, imitating the swish-and-flick. Magic is when a four-year-old boy blurts out, "Expecto Patrolguard!" That's what sets Filipino fans, and PHP in particular, apart from the rest of the fans elsewhere.

Giselle Goloy, a faculty member who is a geologist by Muggle profession, answers: "The way I see it, what sets PHP apart is that fact that we feel we are family and not just an organisation. And the greatest rule that we follow is to always respect others." In many ways, PHP is regarded as a role-play where the members take on identities existing in Harry Potter's world, mainly because we desire for such escape and because Muggle life forces us sometimes to search for that escape from reality. "It's an escape from reality, but in a good way," Prof. Giselle recounts. "For us, it's still a form of escape, but it also transcends fantasy, and we are able to apply in our Muggle lives the good values we get from the books."

I have yet to meet a Pinoy Potterhead who will refute the validity of the statements made by Prof. Mayoralgo and Prof. Goloy. After all, these statements were made in a setting that will rival that of a Veritaserum-induced confession: these statements were made from the heart.

The Pinoy *Harry Potter* community has truly outgrown its nature of a mere fan group. We have forged such strong friendships that our Muggle lives are very much influenced by the relationships born out of the fandom.

Last January, I found myself spending a weekend out of town with eight other people who came into my world by way of *Harry Potter*'s magic. We spent a two-day vacation no longer under the confines of the Hogwarts Philippines castle: we were there as great friends, as a loving family. We were, of course, still enveloped in the bond that *Harry Potter* made for us—but looking at their faces, I knew my relationship with these people transcends that of a mere "group mate" or "co-member" in a *Harry Potter* fan club. These are people who have become such an indispensable part of my life. These are people I turn to in my most trying times, and I have *Harry Potter* to thank for that. If not for the existence of a Filipino *Potter* fandom, I would not have such great people in my life. Had I taken one wrong turn and decided not to be a Potterhead, I wouldn't have found people who constantly inspire me, people who are there when I am in need, from heartbreaking family split-ups to silly discussions of non-existent love-lives. It is a scary path, one I am happy to have avoided—one road PHP has blocked for me. And this is only one testimonial from a Pinoy Potterhead—there are hundreds more: hundreds of other Pinoy Potterheads, all of whom have testimonials of their own, all of whom are grateful for the influence *Harry Potter* has had on their lives, all of whom have felt the uniqueness of a Filipino *Potter* fandom experience. I, for one, can say today without batting an eyelash that the Pinoy *Potter* fandom is the best thing that has ever happened to me.

This is a reality which I truly believe is "salamangka." With just one wizard, one fandom, my life—my choices, my realities—have changed...and that, in itself, is magic.

FLAMES OR EMBERS: THE FUTURE OF FANDOM ON THE INTERNET

Katherine Calore, Katherine DelGiudice, and Michelle K. Gardner

Proposed congressional legislation and restructured proposals from telecommunication companies have the potential to restrict access to Internet-based classroom tools and popular culture Web sites, and also change how information is transmitted on the Internet. Tim Berners-Lee envisioned the World Wide Web as a virtual round-table discussion (Berners-Lee, 1999). Current users have taken his idea literally by utilizing social networking Web sites, chat rooms, Web logs (blogs), and Web site forums to analyze books, films, television shows, graphic novels, and other forms of popular culture. The Internet and the World Wide Web are crucial for the development and continuation of these fan communities. To allow these fan communities to grow, it is critical that the Internet remain unaltered by commercial entities or unnecessary restrictive legislation.

Network Neutrality and Fandom

Telecommunication companies are considering alteration of how data is transmitted over the Internet to increase revenues. Their proposed changes may greatly alter how fan communities communicate over the Internet.

As a network, one of the best things about the Internet is that the everyday user can use it without knowing how it works. However, to understand the necessity of Network Neutrality, a brief explanation of two essential components of how the Internet currently works is critical. These two components are an Internet-like network composed of three basic pieces, and the end-to-end principle.

Three basic pieces form the network necessary for transmission of information on the Internet. These pieces are a computer, a line or wire, and another computer or server. A computer sitting on your home or office desk is the first component, and the wire or line is what you use to connect to the Internet. Typically, the line is either a coaxial cable if you use cable-based Internet service or a phone line if you use Digital Subscription Line (DSL) service. To access the Internet, you pay an access fee to either the cable or phone company for the use of their line. The third component is a computer or server at the other end of the line that receives your request for information. This relationship is diagrammed in Figure 1 below.

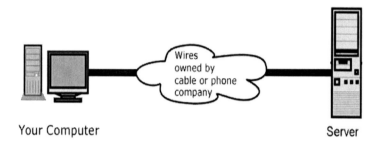

Your Computer   Server

Figure 1: The three basic components of a network

To demonstrate this relationship, consider the process of checking e-mail. First, you make a request for information using the computer. This request travels along the line and reaches the server at the other end of the line, which receives and processes this request. After the server processes the information request, information flows back over the wire to your local computer. This conversation continues for each bit of information requested from the computer while it is connected to the Internet.

In addition to basic network structure, an understanding of the end-to-end principle is important to comprehend the impact of Network Neutrality. Simply stated, the end-to-end principle places the power of innovation at the ends of the network (Saltzer, Clark, and Reed, 1984). (An end on the network is anything that is connected to the network's lines; for example, your personal computer and the server in Figure 1 are ends on the network.) This principle allows computers (such as your personal computer or a server) using the network's lines to employ various technologies, new or old, to create new services.

The key to innovation using the end-to-end principle is that the creation of services over the network is not limited by the lines that will carry the information. Instead, the lines themselves are not aware of what types of information are being sent over them, only where the bits of information are supposed to go. The lines in a neutral network are essentially "dumb." This allows those with computers attached to the ends of the network to create new technologies without hindrance from the network itself or the network's operators. In the fandom world, the end-to-end principle has spurred the development of software for forums, blogs, podcasts, digital art galleries, fan music videos and many of the activities in which fans participate daily over the Internet.

The end-to-end principle enforces one of the key components of the Internet as it exists today, Network Neutrality. Under Network Neutrality, all information sent over network lines, from computer to server and back, is treated the same (Network Neutrality, n.d.). Past evidence of the Internet's performance suggests that keeping a network neutral is crucial for allowing innovation to occur (Lessig, 2006).

Several CEOs of telecommunications companies have made public statements indicating their desire to remove neutrality restrictions on their networks in order to increase revenue (Krim, 2005; O'Connell, 2005). The aim is to create a tiered-access structure for their piece of the Internet by charging content providers access fees to send content over the network with a higher quality of service, i.e., faster service. At the basic level, this process would create two lines for Internet content providers: a fast line and a slower line. Any content providers who do not have the ability to pay for faster content delivery, including many fan-run Web sites, will have their content effectively discriminated against because the information will be delivered more slowly across network lines to individual computers.

The telecommunications companies' proposed action reverses the end-to-end principle by creating a smart network that is aware of what information is traveling over it. The end-to-end principle is one of the basic principles that the Internet was founded on and that has generated much of its growth. Tiered access to the Internet would stifle innovation and hurt the fandom community. In response to the proposal, Congress has proposed several pieces of legislation to secure a neutral, unbiased network. This legislation would effectively sign into law the founding principles of the Internet's design and eliminate the possibility of information discrimination (Internet Freedom Preservation Act of 2006).

On the other hand, some opponents of network neutrality legislation believe that any legislation at all, even when designed to protect core components of the Internet's design, has the potential to be detrimental to the network (Farber and Katz, 2007). In their view, information on the network should not be unfairly discriminated against, but they doubt the ability of the network to act in an entirely neutral manner without being discriminatory in some fashion. Instead, they feel the best option is to have no legislation at all concerning neutrality on Internet networks.

Telecommunication companies have announced plans to enact a tiered-access structure on their network. We must act to prevent active discrimination of information. Network Neutrality is critical to the future of fandom on the Internet to ensure that fan content is not discriminated against by being pushed to the "slow line" of the Internet. It will further ensure that the Web sites and services that survive on the Internet do so by the quality of their content, not through active information discrimination.

Protecting Our Children or Limiting Their Freedom?

Introduction of the Child Protection Act of the 21st Century (DOPA Jr.) into Congress in January of 2007, combined with the Deleting Online Predators Act 2007 (DOPA) in February 2007, is evidence of a nation's concern with the safety of our children while they are online (Library of Congress, 2007). DOPA and DOPA Jr. aim to protect our children from unsolicited online sexual propositions, but instead will drastically limit their access to knowledge, restrict their right to free speech, and potentially block their access to web sites such as <http://www.librarything.com>, <http://www.flickr.com>, <http://www.myspace.com>, <http://www.facebook.com>, <http://www.wikipedia.org>, and many others.

DOPA restricts specific federally funded, public-access computers from accessing social networking Web sites, forums, chat rooms and any other Web sites that include an interactive element.

Critics ranging from the American Library Association to media guru Dr. Henry Jenkins claim that the bill potentially encompasses mailing lists, video and photo sharing sites, and any educational sites that include forums or blogs (Boyd and Jenkins, 2006).

Both of these legislative proposals are rooted in the shocking result of an Internet study, *Online Victimization: A Report on the Nation's Youth*, which concluded that "approximately one in five [children] received a sexual solicitation over the Internet in the last year" (Finkelhor, 2000). This study, conducted through the National Center for Missing and Exploited Children, surveyed 1501 children aged 10–17. Here is a breakdown of some of the conclusions from this survey taken in 1999–2000:

- One in five children surveyed received a "sexual solicitation" online in the last year. Based on 1501 surveyed children, this translates to 300 children.

- Of the 300 children who received a sexual solicitation, 75% were "not very upset or afraid": 75 children had a reaction to the solicitation.

- Of the 1501 children interviewed, 70% of the children accessed the Internet from home, not from schools or libraries (1051 out of 1501). Of the 75 children above who were offended by the online content they received, 53 of those children would have accessed the Web from home. (Finkelhor, 2000)

This survey found that one child was involved in an incident that needed the attention of proper authorities and had the potential to damage the child. No discredit is meant to this child or the emotional and/or physical harm that might have occurred (the study does not go into detail), but to restrict access to such a vital tool as the Internet in classrooms and libraries throughout the country based on an interesting interpretation of a survey conducted in 2000 is simply ludicrous.

Education, Not Legislation

Both DOPA and DOPA Jr. are based on the numbers broken down above and represent a poor interpretation of the study. Clearly stated in this survey is the fact that it is the first-ever study of its kind and that further investigations into this area is necessary. Another vital conclusion drawn is:

Probably the best approach, based on the findings here, is simply to remind youth that people they meet may have ulterior motives and hidden agendas. The caution to first meet someone from the Internet in a safe, public, or supervised place and to alert others (family or friends) about such a meeting, seems something that teens may be more likely to actually put into practice.... It may be important for prevention educators to acknowledge this as they try to be a credible source of useful information about safety practices. (Finkelhor, Mitchell, and Wolak, 2000)

One terrifying conclusion of this study was that a majority of children who were offended by the sexual solicitation they received did not report the incident to their parents or another authority. Clearly, the point of this study and the best assurance for their safety while online is for parents, teachers, and librarians to educate our children. We teach our children to recognize situations and scream phrases like "stranger danger" while in public places; these lessons should now include the Internet. The environment is different, but the trained reaction should be the same. Our children need to be safe, and protecting them is our job as parents and educators. Restriction of their access to the vast amount of knowledge that is available online is not the proper way to exert control in this situation. We should educate our children about the dangers facing them in the world at large and not legislate their access to information.

The Reality of Restrictive Internet Legislation

A personal account from Katherine Calore, a teacher

DOPA and DOPA Jr., if passed, will limit Internet access for students who rely on public access computers in schools and libraries. As an instructor of non-traditional students for a rural community college, I can say that this will not work.

We have two ethnic groups in our area. One group consists of Hispanics, many of whom are migrant workers whose children are now are trying to go to college and raise the family's quality of life. We also have rednecks (I mean that in a good way)—white, Christian, blue-collar, hard-working, pickup truck-driving, born-and-bred-in-the-same-small-town Americans. These students are full of hard-won wisdom, and they respect the chain of command, which means they are actually willing to do what I tell them in the classroom.

Our campus does not have a library. When students have research to do, they are limited to our poorly funded, antiquated public library. Luckily, our campus has a fantastic computer lab. Although it is rare to have a student with a personal computer, they all have access to the lab's computers.

Computers and the Internet play a vital role in my classroom. In my Speech class, I play clips from the twentieth century's greatest speakers. We watch Martin Luther King's "I Have a Dream" speech, and we watch John F. Kennedy's inaugural speech. We even watch a speech by Hitler to show how easily public speech is misused. I get those clips from <http://www.rmericanrhetoric.com>, and we watch and analyze them in class.

When it is time for the students to give speeches, they utilize Internet resources to connect to the larger outside world. One student gave a speech on the history of the White House. As part of the presentation, the student used the in-class computer and gave us a virtual tour of the White House. We got to see Olympic volleyball and different types of fishing lures. Students called up graphs on gun violence in Missouri, the growing rate of cosmetic surgery among people under eighteen, and the detrimental effects of chocolate.

Probably the most interesting and effective use of Internet technology happens in my World Religions class. I had a student who used the Internet to prepare a presentation on the Hindu festival of Divali. Along with her PowerPoint presentation, she researched traditional Divali recipes and prepared Divali foods for the whole class.

Another student did a presentation on Native American funeral rites. He was able to find a Shawnee tribal elder online. The student was invited to do research at the library on the Shawnee reservation. Because of the relationships that the Internet makes possible, this student was able to conduct primary research—that is, seeing the things used in the rites, and listening to first-hand accounts from people whose role it is to guide the tribe through death rituals. He would never have been able to walk in and ask to see these things and talk to these people, but because of his Internet-based research, he was able to form a relationship and was then offered access.

My students are becoming smart, savvy, insightful and multiculturally aware through the use of the Internet. There are no Shinto, Taoists, Jews, Muslims, Hindus, Jains, Buddhists, Zoroastrians or Baha'i in Cassville, Missouri. But my students can reach out to any of those people and have intelligent conversations about their cultures. Some of this is a reflection of my teaching, but I think mostly it is because the Internet expands our borders in ways that previous generations could never have dreamed.

I want to stress that very few of these students have a computer at home. Computers are a great equalizer. The world inside our computers is as close as human beings come to Dr. King's dream that we judge each other solely by the content of our character.

I do not want those opportunities taken away from my students. I will oppose any legislation that limits their access to the world outside of our little corner of Missouri. DOPA and DOPA Jr. will not keep children safe but will instead hurt the people who truly need unbiased and open access to the Internet.

Conclusion

The conclusions to be drawn from the above information are evident: a neutral network and free and open exchange of information—while alerting our children to potential dangers—are the components needed for the Internet's continued success. Fandom will also benefit from this arrangement, ensuring that the Internet remains a non-discriminatory space where fans can meet and share their works. Any successful new technology produces challenges and potential abuse that cause alarm for parents and the general public alike. However, we believe that turning a blind eye to information discrimination or legislating access to information is not the correct way to solve the many dilemmas we must face in the new information society. Instead, fandom and the world at large will greatly benefit if the Internet continues to operate as it does today, as a free and open forum.

References

Berners-Lee, T. (1999). *Weaving the Web: The original design and ultimate destiny of the World Wide Web by its inventor.* New York: Harper.

boyd, d. and Jenkins, H. (2006). MySpace and Deleting Online Predators Act (DOPA) MIT Tech Talk. May 26. <http://www.danah.org/papers/MySpaceDOPA.html>.

Farber, D. & Katz, M. (2007, January 19). Hold off on network neutrality. *Washington Post*, A19.

Finkelhor, D., Mitchell, K., & Wolak, J. (2000). Online victimization: A report on the nation's youth. National Center for Missing & Exploited Children.

Internet Freedom Preservation Act of 2006, S. 2917. (2006, May 19). Retrieved May 30, 2007, from <http://frwebgate.access.gpo.gov/cgibin/getdoc.cgi?dbname=109_cong_bills&docid=f:s2917is.txt.pdf>.

Krim, J. (2005, December 1). Executive wants to charge for web speed. *Washington Post*, D05.

Lessig, L. (2006, March). Testimony of Lawrence Lessig on "Network Neutrality".

Network Neutrality (n.d.). Retrieved 30 May 2007 from <http://en.wikipedia.org/wiki/Network_neutrality>.

O'Connell, P. (2005, November 7). At SBC, it's all about "scale and scope". Retrieved 30 May 2007 from <http://www.businessweek.com/@@n34h*IUQu7KtOwgA/magazine/content/05_45/b3958092.htm>.

The Library of Congress H.R., 1120 (2007). Deleting online predators act. Retrieved 30 May 2007 from <http://www.govtrack.us/congress/billtext.xpd?bill=h110-1120>.

The Library of Congress s.49 (2007) . Protecting Children in the 21st Century Act. Retrieved 30 May 2007 from <http://thomas.loc.gov/cgi-bin/query/z?c110:S.49>.

Saltzer, J. H., Reed, D. P., & Clark, D. D. (1984, November). End-to-end arguments in system design. *ACM Transactions on Computer Systems*, 4(2), 277–88.

Katherine DelGiudice can be contacted at ktdid2000@gmail.com.
Michelle K. Gardner can be contacted at enelya.oronar@gmail.com.

ACQUIRING A MAGICAL LITERACY: *HARRY POTTER* CHARACTERS' TRANSITION INTO THE CULTURAL LITERACY OF THE WIZARDING WORLD

Robin Martin
Texas A&M University–Corpus Christi

The *Harry Potter* novel series has undoubtedly reached the status of "phenomenon" in its level of world-wide attention, success, and popularity. Dismissed by some as inconsequential pop-fiction, the novels are now beginning to garner serious academic attention and criticism. My intention here is to add to that criticism by looking at how literacy functions within the magical world created in the books by J. K. Rowling. This culture created by Rowling within the books presents an excellent fictitious environment—meticulous in its detail and perhaps bested in its precision only by the likes of J. R. R. Tolkien's *Lord of the Rings*—in which to explore the function of literacy and the literacy functions practiced by the characters. In this essay I will point out the different approaches to literacy of certain characters within the books and their acquisition of a magical literacy, or rather a cultural literacy of the magical world to which each has been introduced. Specifically, I will address how the characters Harry and Hermione approach the appropriation of a magical cultural literacy in two different ways—orally and textually. In order to better explain how Harry and Hermione make this transition into a new cultural literacy, I will first provide a brief overview of some of the literacy theories and scholars who lay the foundation for this look at Harry and Hermione's literacy acquisition.

Discourse of Cultural Literacy in Academia

The concept and explanation of literacy has been volleyed among academics for some time now. Its many definitions have bounced back and forth between scholars in the discourse to little avail if our intent is to nail down one simple definition of literacy. Most commonly, literacy is associated with a person's ability to read and write in a given language, though this only scratches the surface of the matter. Despite the fact that scholars tend to speak pontifically about each of his or her own explanations of literacy (as though it were the one and only explanation), in truth, there cannot possibly be only one approach to the concept of literacy. However, for the purpose of our discussion within this essay, we will address only three types of literacy—cultural, text-based, and oral—focusing mainly on the concept of cultural literacy.

Although cultural literacy can be considered a specific type of literacy within the broader concept of literacy, it remains difficult to define precisely. In his book *Lives on the Boundary*, Mike Rose recounts the struggles and achievements he faced in assimilating to the unfamiliar culture of academia while on the road to educational self-actualization. Within his personal narrative Rose mixes pragmatic socioeconomic pedagogy and a first-hand view of someone in the midst of appropriating a new cultural literacy. Rose emphasizes the importance of recognizing a cultural literacy and defines it as "systematically inspecting a document, an issue, or an event, synthesizing different points of view, applying a theory to disparate phenomena, and so on" (Rose 188). He goes on to state that most seemingly remedial students would normally be considered literate by societal standards except for the fact that, in the university, they have entered a new and unfamiliar "society"—a society of the educational elite. Rose further contends, "To understand the nature and development of literacy we need to consider the social context in which it occurs—the political, economic, and cultural forces that encourage or inhibit it" (237). With this in mind, the question is not about a student's written literacy but about his or her cultural literacy—the cultural literacy of academia.

E. D. Hirsch, Jr., outlines his concept of the term "cultural literacy" in his book of the same title. Though his misapplication of cultural literacy in this book has received much criticism because of the Anglocentric approach he takes, his overarching concept of cultural literacy still has definite merit. Hirsch states that being "culturally literate is to possess the basic information needed to thrive in the modern world" (xiii). He emphasizes the fact that for people to be literate in a given society and the world, they must possess certain facts and certain information generally known to mainstream culture. Hirsch's concept here, at this point, has value. However, Hirsch applies his views to disastrous effect. His attempt to catalogue and organize a list of facts and knowledge that a person in American society needs in order to be considered literate in American culture is where his fault lies. There is no way to fairly and effectively outline a list of things one should know in order to function successfully in mainstream society without leaving out this cultural group or that cultural group. However, I reiterate that Hirsch's general concept of cultural literacy is denigrated and overlooked as a result of his foolhardy attempt to compile this list of general knowledge for American culture.

Aside from his culturally insensitive catalog of knowledge, Hirsch's points have merit. Hirsch speaks of the disenfranchisement of members of society who have not had ready access to the basic knowledge that comes with regular exposure to mainstream cultural literacy, such as minorities, immigrants, and lower socioeconomic classes. He suggests that these marginalized groups are hindered from gaining a successful role in society by their lack of the factual knowledge that surrounds mainstream culture. Hirsch states that "the civic importance of cultural literacy lies in the fact that true enfranchisement depends upon knowledge, knowledge upon literacy, and literacy upon cultural literacy" (12). Therefore, according to Hirsch, to be fully functional and successful in a culture, one must possess the general knowledge, facts, and information that are connected with the mainstream group within that culture.

Many literacy scholars tend to take a Marxist view of literacy and the power structures that surround the disbursement of literacy skills. Brian Street could be said to fall into this category. He introduces the concept of looking at literacy within the context of specific cultures. Moreover, he emphasizes the concept of the power structures surrounding literacy and how those structures influence the acquisition of literacy. With his ideological model, he views "literacy practices as inextricably linked to cultural and power structures in society" (Street 433). He stresses the need to recognize that literacy in the context of different situations can effectively change the aspects of the definition of literacy within that given context. More specifically, he states that "an understanding of literacy requires detailed, in-depth accounts of actual practice in different cultural settings" (430). In short, Street suggests that literacy cannot and should not be taken out of its cultural context, as the culture from which it originates has a significant effect on the shaping of that same literacy.

Like Street, Deborah Brandt highlights with Marxist flair the power structures surrounding literacy acquisition. She refers to literacy as a "resource" or a "valued commodity" and stresses the value that literacy has as a resource in society (Brandt 558). In her article, "Sponsors of Literacy," Brandt presents us with the concept that literacy learners are introduced or "sponsored" into a literacy discourse or culture through literacy sponsors.

> Sponsors, as I have come to think of them, are any agents, local or distant, concrete or abstract, who enable, support, teach, model, as well as recruit, regulate, suppress, or withhold literacy—and gain advantage by it in some way. (556)

Therefore, according to Brandt, our sponsors can manipulate our literacy learning by helping or hindering the acquisition process.

Harry Acquires a *Magical* Literacy

Harry, the main character of the *Harry Potter* series by J. K. Rowling, is a boy thrust into a culture completely new and unfamiliar to him in the first book, *Harry Potter and the Sorcerer's Stone*. Almost from the instant that he is made aware of the magical culture which he is about to enter, he begins his literacy "sponsorship," as Brandt would call it. Hagrid, the older and emotionally sensitive half-giant who informs Harry of the magical community, becomes Harry's first positive literacy sponsor in the wizarding world. Hagrid assumes that Harry, unknowingly a famous wizard within the magical community, is already a literate member of the culture of the wizarding world. As Harry begins asking questions to which any literate member of the magical community would already know the answers, Hagrid shifts his approach with

Harry from that of equally literate member to knowledgeable
sponsor:

> "Call me Hagrid," he said, "everyone does. An' like I told yeh, I'm
> Keeper of Keys at Hogwarts—yeh'll know all about Hogwarts, o' course."
> "Er—no," said Harry.
> Hagrid looked shocked.
> "Sorry," Harry said quickly.
> "*Sorry?*" barked Hagrid, turning to stare at the Dursleys, who shrank
> back into the shadows. "It's them as should be sorry! I knew yeh weren't
> gettin' yer letters but I never thought yeh wouldn't even know abou'
> Hogwarts, fer cryin' out loud! Did yeh never wonder where yer parents
> learned it all?"
> "All what?" asked Harry. (*SS* 49)

From here, Hagrid begins his sponsorship of Harry by informing
him of Hogwarts, a school for young wizards and witches, and of
James and Lily Potter, a famous wizarding couple and Harry's
deceased parents. Here we see Harry's illiteracy quite pronouncedly
in the fact that he does not even know the role that his family and
he himself play in the culture of the wizarding world. In her article
"Harry Potter and the Acquisition of Knowledge," Lisa Hopkins
discusses the fact that certain aspects of Harry's personal life are
knowledge that he must acquire upon entering the magical
community: "He knows nothing about the magical world, not even
what he himself is—a celebrated wizard" (Hopkins 25). This
meeting with Hagrid begins a literacy sponsorship between Harry
and Hagrid that continues through all the books to date. In his
article "The Seeker of Secrets: Images of Learning, Knowing, and
Schooling" which discusses aspects of learning and schooling at
Hogwarts, Charles Elster points out that Harry is sponsored by at
least five adults (Elster 214). This literacy sponsorship, or
mentorship, on the part of Hagrid is only one of several for Harry.

Through Harry's interaction with the Dursleys, we can see
Brandt's concept of literacy sponsorship exhibited in a way that is
detrimental to Harry's cultural literacy development. As mentioned
earlier in the discussion of Brandt's theory of literacy sponsorship,
literacy sponsors can "enable, support, teach, [and] model," but, as
we see by the actions of Harry's only living relations, sponsors can
also "regulate, suppress, or withhold literacy" (Brandt 556). We see
this literacy regulation on the part of the Dursleys—comprised of

Harry's uncle, aunt and cousin—on several occasions. Initially, the Dursleys withhold from Harry all literacy information relating to the wizarding world. Harry's aunt and uncle are both literate enough in the culture of the wizarding world to know of its existence and to know that Harry was born into that culture; however, the Dursleys withhold any information relating to the wizarding world in order to keep Harry illiterate of this magical culture to which he should rightly belong. In order to accomplish this suppression of his literacy, the Dursleys feed Harry false information relating to his birth, his parents, and his parents' death. In one specific instance, Harry is sent mail from Hogwarts, a school in the wizarding world. Before Harry has a chance to read this letter and thus begin his transition into the literacy of this culture, the Dursleys intercept his letter and all of the subsequent letters he receives from Hogwarts. This intentional hindrance of Harry's literacy development in relation to the wizarding world is done, as the Dursleys reasoned, in an effort to keep Harry "normal"—or rather, non-magical. The Dursleys, as literate sponsors of Harry to wizarding culture, recognize that by restricting Harry's exposure to any information about the wizarding world, they will be able to accomplish their collective desired goal to remain "normal" in the eyes of their own culture. With this behavior of the Dursleys, Brandt's conclusion that "Most of the time,…literacy takes its shape from the interests of its sponsor" is supported even in the realm of literature (558).

Harry's eagerness to enter into these particular types of sponsorships is our first indication of Harry's predilection towards oral learning. In his definitive book *Orality and Literacy*, Walter Ong highlights key aspects of oral learning. One of these aspects focuses on the importance of "those wise old men and women who specialize in conserving [knowledge], who know and can tell the stories of the days of old" (Ong 41). Hagrid, and later several other characters, serve this function for Harry, passing along their knowledge to him as wise, old members of the magical culture.

Additionally, Ong stresses the need for repetition in oral learning in order to help with memorization and retention of knowledge (34–36). This comes to Harry in the form of repeating what he has learned from his sponsors to his friends, Ron and Hermione. With this regular retelling to and discussion with his friends, Harry is further advancing his oral learning by cementing firmly in his memory the knowledge passed to him via his magical literacy sponsors, thus allowing him to call on this knowledge easily as he needs it.

Furthermore, Ong points out that in an oral culture—or in this case, oral learning—knowledge is kept within its context (49). In other words, knowledge is situational rather than abstract. This relates to Harry in that he is often seeing information only in the limited context of his surroundings, opinions, or knowledge. For example, in *Harry Potter and the Sorcerer's Stone*, Harry sees that Professor Severus Snape, Harry's Potions instructor, has been injured by what appears to be a bite from an animal. Harry takes this information and applies it to the information he has regarding the large, three-headed dog guarding a precious stone within the school. Applying his limited knowledge to the situation, Harry assumes that Snape is trying to steal the stone. He is wrong in his assumption, but this act on his part shows, again, his tendency towards oral learning. He applies information within his context and, as a result, is unable to think abstractly and see the larger picture.

Hermione Acquires a *Magical* Literacy

Hermione, the bookish Muggle-born witch, acclimates into the magical culture with a much more text-based approach. Reading everything she possibly can that relates to the wizarding world before even setting foot in the culture, Hermione validates textual literacy as a form of appropriating cultural literacy within the magical community. Conversely, in relation to Harry and because of her reliance on text-based knowledge, Hermione is able to view things abstractly and objectively in a way that Harry is not able to do. This ability of Hermione's to view things abstractly and objectively is, according to Ong, a quality of print culture (45–46).

Because of Hermione's predilection towards text-based learning, the various books and texts that she so often references function as Hermione's literacy sponsors. Rowling herself recognizes the obvious significance that books have on Hermione, in that Rowling believes that readers see Hermione as a credible source of information. According to Rowling, she uses Hermione to relay important information to the readers because readers just assume "that Hermione has read it somewhere," and according to Ong, this is a mark of a literate society (Ong 78–79, 96; Mzimba). Ong states that "a present-day literate usually assumes that written records have more force than spoken words"; therefore, Hermione is seen as a credible source of information because she cites all of her knowledge as having come from one book or another (96).

This concept of Hermione as a bibliophile, and as a reliable source of facts in general, begins in the first book as she references the fictional text *Hogwarts: A History*, and continues to grow in the minds of characters and readers as the series progresses. Even with Harry and the reader's first encounter with Hermione, we see her reference texts and the knowledge that she has acquired from them when Harry introduces himself:

"Are you really?" said Hermione. "I know all about you, of course—I got a few extra books for background reading, and you're in *Modern Magical History* and *The Rise and Fall of the Dark Arts* and *Great Wizarding Events of the Twentieth Century*." (*SS* 106)

Ong states that "writing separates the knower from the known and thus sets up conditions for 'objectivity'" (46). Furthermore, he also states that "without writing, human consciousness cannot achieve its fuller potentials" (14–15). Additionally, Ong argues that "writing establishes in the text a 'line' of continuity outside the mind. If distraction confuses or obliterates from the mind the context out of which emerges the material I am now reading, the context can be retrieved by glancing back over the text selectively" (39). With these things in mind, it would be logical to argue that Hermione, the objective, text-based learner, is more capable of reasoned and objective thought than is Harry, the oral learner who does not function with the same "'line' of continuity" upon which Hermione has become reliant. We can see this objective, reasoned thought exhibited by Hermione in the first book when the three friends, Harry, Ron and Hermione, are forced to grapple with what Hermione discovers to be Devil's Snare. Ultimately, her practiced ability to use a continuity of logic outside of herself, allowed her to save the lives of her friends in the face of impending, man-eating-plant danger.

In the final chapter of his book *Orality & Literacy*, Ong states that the field of literary studies "has begun, but only just begun, to exploit the possibilities which orality-literacy studies open to it" (157). By looking at the methods of cultural acquisition of the characters Harry Potter and Hermione Granger in the *Harry Potter* novels, scholars and readers alike are able to follow Ong's prompting and use theories of orality and literacy to broaden their understanding of these exquisite novels and the characters within them. By applying these orality and literacy theories to character analysis, we are able to take a new look at character analysis, in general, and how characters develop throughout a given series, specifically. In the case of the *Harry Potter* series, these theories not only provide character analysis as to how the story's hero eventually gains all of his magical knowledge, but these theories also provide the novel's readers with a firmer understanding as to why Hermione will forever remain "an insufferable know-it-all" (*PoA* 172).

Works Cited

Brandt, Deborah. "Sponsors of Literacy." In Cushman, 555–71.

Cushman, Ellen, Eugene R. Kintgen, Barry M. Kroll, and Mike Rose, eds. *Literacy: A Critical Sourcebook*. Boston: Bedford/St. Martin's, 2001.

Elster, Charles. "The Seeker of Secrets: Images of Learning, Knowing, and Schooling." *Harry Potter's World: Multidisciplinary Critical Perspectives*. Ed. Elizabeth E. Heilman. New York: RoutledgeFalmer, 2003. 203–20.

Hirsch, E. D., Jr. *Cultural Literacy*. Boston: Houghton Mifflin, 1987.

Hopkins, Lisa. "Harry Potter and the Acquisition of Knowledge." *Reading Harry Potter*. Ed. Giselle Liza Anatol. Westport: Praeger, 2003. 25–34.

Mzimba, Lizo. Interview with J. K. Rowling and Steve Kloves. *Harry Potter and the Chamber of Secrets*. Dir. Chris Columbus. Perf. Daniel Radcliffe, Rupert Grint, Emma Watson. 2003. DVD. Warner Brothers.

Ong, Walter. *Orality and Literacy: The Technologizing of the Word*. 1982. London: Routledge, 1999.

Rose, Mike. *Lives on the Boundary: A Moving Account of the Struggles and Achievements of America's Educational Underclass*. New York: Penguin, 1989.

Rowling, J. K. *Harry Potter and the Sorcerer's Stone*. New York: Scholastic, 1997.

— *Harry Potter and the Prisoner of Azkaban*. New York: Scholastic, 1999.

Street, Brian. "New Literacy Studies." In Cushman, 430–42.

WHERE DID *SHE* COME FROM?: THE NOT-SO-NEW GINNY WEASLEY

Yolanda R. Carroll

Some see Ginny as wonderful and the girl for Harry. Some see her as not so well-written and her characterization forced. I vote for well-written. Readers need to be aware that Ginny is simply written differently from the other characters. She is not written in the same manner as Harry, Hermione, and Ron.

Some readers have complained that in *Order of the Phoenix*, we learn lots of important facts about Ginny secondhand and in retrospect—for instance, Ginny's having given up on Harry, how Ginny learned to play Quidditch so well, and her Bat-Bogey Hex.

One well-accepted rule of writing is "show, don't tell." I will now give you an example of Rowling showing instead of telling us about a character. I'll use two quotations from *Sorcerer's Stone*:

By the end of the lesson, only Hermione Granger had made any difference to her match; Professor McGonagall showed the class how it had gone all silver and pointy and gave Hermione a rare smile.

Here is the second quotation:

Harry turned to Hermione.
"Do something," he said desperately.
Hermione stepped forward.
"Neville," she said, "I'm really, really sorry about this."
She raised her wand.
"*Petrificus Totalus!*" she cried, pointing it at Neville.
Neville's arms snapped to his sides. His legs sprang together. His whole body rigid, he swayed where he stood and then fell flat on his face, stiff as a board.
Hermione ran to turn him over. Neville's jaws were jammed together so he couldn't speak. Only his eyes were moving, looking at them in horror.

413

"What've you done to him?" Harry whispered.

"It's the Full Body-Bind," said Hermione miserably. "Oh, Neville, I'm so sorry."

The above two quotations from *Sorcerer's Stone* demonstrate Hermione Granger's talent and power as a witch. Now contrast that with the following two quotes about Ginny from *Order of the Phoenix*:

"Yeah, size is no guarantee of power," said George. "Look at Ginny."

"What d'you mean?" said Harry.

"You've never been on the receiving end of one of her Bat-Bogey Hexes, have you?"

Here is the second quotation:

"How did you get away?" asked Harry in amazement, taking his wand from Ron.

"Couple of Stunners, a Disarming Charm, Neville brought off a really nice little Impediment Jinx," said Ron airily, now handing back Hermione's wand, too. "But Ginny was best, she got Malfoy—Bat-Bogey Hex—it was superb, his whole face was covered in the great flapping things."

The above quotations tell us about Ginny's Bat-Bogey Hex. We never actually see her use it. Rowling knows how to write "show," as my example of Hermione above demonstrates. Rowling deliberately does not do this with Ginny. The idea is for us to be as surprised as Harry at Ginny's transformation from Ron's little sister to Harry's possible love interest.

After *Order of the Phoenix*, Rowling was accused of using "tell" (versus "show") regarding Ginny. Actually, Rowling has done this all along. In *Chamber of Secrets*, Ron mentions that she is usually a lot more talkative and that she's been talking about Harry all summer. Also in *Chamber of Secrets*, Percy tells Harry, Ron, and Hermione how upset Ginny was about Mrs. Norris and Colin Creevey's petrifications. In *Prisoner of Azkaban*, during the Dementor attack, Harry blacks out. He wakes up and people tell him that Ginny was "shaking like mad, though," when he asks whether any one else fell off their seat.

Part of the reason why we don't see more of Ginny is that she isn't part of the trio. By not having her closer to the trio and incidentally, not in Harry's line of sight, we don't see her. She's there, but Harry's not focused on her. Harry's lack of interest makes her characterization seem inconsistent. Harry and the reader turn around and find that she's older and has changed.

Actually, Rowling does show us some of Ginny's growth and change. Ginny was simply growing up in the background. We do see her. She simply isn't the center of the action or of our attention. Why does Rowling handle Ginny in that manner? Why doesn't the trio become a foursome sooner?

In *Sorcerer's Stone*, Rowling writes, "There are some things you can't share without ending up liking each other, and knocking out a twelve-foot mountain troll is one of them." With that in mind, why don't Ginny and Harry become fast friends after the basilisk incident? There are a few reasons for this. One is that in *Prisoner of Azkaban*, Ginny still has a crush on Harry and is embarrassed by having been saved by her would-be love interest. Also, Ginny is still seen as Ron's little sister. The trio see her as younger than they— perhaps even younger than she is.

In *Chamber of Secrets*, Mrs. Weasley holds Ginny's hand while they shop in Diagon Alley. We know that Mrs. Weasley needs to buy Ginny's things. However, it must be noted that all the other kids take off in other directions. Percy has his own thing to do, whatever that is, as do the twins. Harry, Ron, and Hermione have their own shopping to do and don't wait around trying to include Ron's little sister. If Ron had needed new robes, Harry and Hermione would have stayed nearby or agreed to meet up a bit later. Admittedly, Mrs. Weasley gives everyone the meeting place and time, but you do see that Ginny never has any time to wander around with her peers on that shopping trip.

Also, if you remember Ron's letters to Harry at the beginning of *Prisoner of Azkaban*, we see more of Ginny being treated "younger" than the others:

Mum wouldn't let Ginny come in the last one. There were all these mutant skeletons in there, of Muggles who'd broken in and grown extra heads and stuff.

Bill is obviously good at what he does, and like all Weasleys, he looks out for his family. Would he have taken the kids in if he thought they were in any danger? No. Molly was being overprotective of Ginny. It is important to note that Mrs. Weasley was being overprotective only of Ginny. Ron goes in and sees everything, and he's only about a year older than his sister.

Those are some of the reasons why Ginny has been written the way she has. Now we'll look at Ginny's character and her relationship with Harry. I'm going to start in book one, then take us through to book four, and hopefully show you enough support for my view of Ginny. Admittedly, Ginny doesn't get a lot of page time in the earlier books. However, one thing we always see is her greeting to Harry. Through her greetings to Harry, we can see her changing character and their changing relationship.

At the end of *Sorcerer's Stone*, Harry has just finished assuring Ron that he's not famous where he's going…namely, home with the Dursleys. The next thing we read is:

> "There he is, Mom, there he is, look!"
> It was Ginny Weasley, Ron's younger sister, but she wasn't pointing at Ron.
> "Harry Potter!" she squealed. "Look, Mom! I can see—"

At that point, Mrs. Weasley cuts her off. At the end of book one, Ginny sees Harry as "The Famous Harry Potter." To her, he's a celebrity that her brother actually went to school with.

I'm going to do something different with the greeting in *Chamber of Secrets*. You'll see that I nearly have to:

> At that moment there was a diversion in the form of a small, redheaded figure in a long nightdress, who appeared in the kitchen, gave a small squeal, and ran out again.
> "Ginny," said Ron in an undertone to Harry. "My sister. She's been talking about you all summer."
> "Yeah, she'll be wanting your autograph, Harry," Fred said with a grin.

She doesn't actually speak to him, so I'll try again. Here's the second time they meet in *Chamber of Secrets*:

> On the third landing, a door stood ajar. Harry just caught sight of a pair of bright brown eyes staring at him before it closed with a snap.
> "Ginny," said Ron. "You don't know how weird it is for her to be this shy. She never shuts up normally—"

She still hasn't actually greeted him. Let's try this one more time. The third time they meet in *Chamber of Secrets*—

> "Oh, are you starting at Hogwarts this year?" Harry asked Ginny.

She nodded, blushing to the roots of her flaming hair, and put her elbow in the butter dish.

—they finally have a conversation. Harry talks. Ginny nods. At this point, she has a fierce crush on Harry. She can't speak at all and feels clumsy when he's around her.

That was *Chamber of Secrets*. Let's continue on to *Prisoner of Azkaban*:

Ginny, who had always been very taken with Harry, seemed even more heartily embarrassed than usual when she saw him, perhaps because he had saved her life during their previous year at Hogwarts. She went very red and muttered "hello" without looking at him.

Now at least she can speak to him. She simply can't look him in the eye while doing it. Remember that the events at the end of *Chamber of Secrets* and the beginning of *Prison of Azkaban* are only about three or four months apart. I'll move on to *Goblet of Fire*:

Then two girls appeared in the kitchen doorway behind Mrs. Weasley. One, with very bushy brown hair and rather large front teeth, was Harry's and Ron's friend, Hermione Granger. The other, who was small and red-haired, was Ron's younger sister, Ginny. Both of them smiled at Harry, who grinned back, which made Ginny go scarlet—she had been very taken with Harry ever since his first visit to the Burrow.

Hang on a bit. Now, she may have blushed; however, if you keep reading you'll see:

"What are Weasleys' Wizard Wheezes?" Harry asked as they climbed.
Ron and Ginny both laughed.
"Mum found this stack of order forms when she was cleaning Fred and George's room," said Ron quietly. "Great long price lists for stuff they've invented. Joke stuff, you know. Fake wands and trick sweets, loads of stuff. It was brilliant, I never knew they'd been inventing all that..."
"We've been hearing explosions out of their room for ages, but we never thought they were actually *making* things," said Ginny. "We thought they just liked the noise."

I will omit part of this scene and pick up below:

"And then there was this big row," Ginny said, "because Mum wants them to go into the Ministry of Magic like Dad, and they told her all they want to do is open a joke shop."

Ginny in *Goblet of Fire* is still blushing; however, she can now laugh and speak in front of Harry. In fact, she speaks to him, helping Ron tell the story of Weasleys' Wizarding Wheezes. We immediately see a more talkative and outgoing Ginny than in book two and even book three. Also, in *Goblet of Fire*, at least she can speak in front of Harry now. For instance, she tells her mom that Bill's hair is fine. She says this with Harry at the table with them. By *Goblet of Fire*, she's had two years at Hogwarts, including a "normal" year for a change—well, more normal than her first year—and she's also a bit older.

So far the changes have been consistent and gradual. Then comes book five. In *Order of the Phoenix*, Ginny greets Harry thus:

"Oh, hello, Harry!" said Ron's younger sister, Ginny, brightly. "I thought I heard your voice."

She then turns to speak to Fred and George about the Extendable Ears. Now she can speak to Harry and in front of him without blushing. I immediately noticed that Ginny isn't shy and acts normally in front of Harry. Now let's look at the greeting in *Half-Blood Prince*:

"I know someone who's worse than Umbridge," said a voice from the doorway. Ron's younger sister slouched into the room, looking irritable. "Hi, Harry."

"What's up with you?" Ron asked.

"It's her," said Ginny, plonking herself down on Harry's bed. "She's driving me mad."

We then get into Ginny's feelings about Fleur, which she has no problems expressing in front of Harry. By now Ginny's earlier shyness is a moot point; she's now a talkative, opinionated young witch, and I for one can see how she and Hermione would be friends.

The Ginny in *Order of the Phoenix* and *Half-Blood Prince*—to me, at least—aren't that disparate from the Ginny in *Goblet of Fire*. Some fans found the Ginny in book five to be a huge change. However, the change isn't that big when you consider how she behaves in book four. I'll set the scene. Ron and Harry have been laughing at Neville for trying to ask Hermione to the Yule Ball. In other words, Neville should have known Hermione wouldn't have said yes to him:

"Why weren't you two at dinner?" she said, coming over to join them.

"Because—oh shut up laughing, you two—because they've both just been turned down by girls they asked to the ball!" said Ginny.

That shut Harry and Ron up.

"Thanks a bunch, Ginny," said Ron sourly.

The Ginny in *Chamber of Secrets* can't speak in front of Harry. In *Prisoner of Azkaban*, she can share a laugh at Percy with Harry, something *Chamber of Secrets* Ginny can't do; however, she still can't speak to him. Ginny in *Goblet of Fire* can shut Harry and Ron up at the same time. However, there is still a part of Ginny in *Goblet of Fire* that is the same as Ginny in *Sorcerer's Stone* and *Chamber of Secrets*:

"She's part veela," said Harry. "You were right—her grandmother was one. It wasn't your fault, I bet you just walked past when she was turning on the old charm for Diggory and got a blast of it—but she was wasting her time. He's going with Cho Chang."

Ron looked up.

"I asked her to go with me just now," Harry said dully, "and she told me." Ginny had suddenly stopped smiling.

I will omit part of this scene and continue below:

"Right," said Ron, who looked extremely put out, "this is getting stupid. Ginny, *you* can go with Harry, and I'll just—"

"I can't," said Ginny, and she went scarlet too. "I'm going with—with Neville. He asked me when Hermione said no, and I thought...well...I'm not going to be able to go otherwise, I'm not in fourth year." She looked extremely miserable. "I think I'll go and have dinner," she said, and she got up and walked off to the portrait hole, her head bowed.

I admit that there is a difference between book four and book five Ginny. There is a reason why all of a sudden we're seeing more of her and learning more about her:

"Ginny *used* to fancy Harry, but she gave up on him months ago. Not that she doesn't *like* you, of course," she added kindly to Harry while she examined a long black and gold quill.

Harry, whose head was still full of Cho's parting wave, did not find this subject quite as interesting as Ron, who was positively quivering with indignation, but it did bring something home to him that until now he had not really registered.

"So that's why she talks now?" he asked Hermione. "She never used to talk in front of me."

"Exactly," said Hermione.

Now we've gotten to the difference between Ginny in books four and five. We're seeing more of Ginny's character because Harry is. Harry's seeing her now that she can act normally around him.

Add to the above explanation the fact that Ginny has joined Dumbledore's Army and the Gryffindor Quidditch team. Both affiliations bring her into more contact with Harry. One more reason is that the twins leave Hogwarts in *Order of the Phoenix*, and Rowling started moving Ginny into position to take their place.

Now it is time for me to switch gears a bit. Let's look at Harry's view of Ginny. Over the course of the first five books, Harry laughs and smiles with Ginny. In *Order of the Phoenix*, she is able to talk to him, to calm him down and make him think logically. She tells him that his "lifelong ban" from Quidditch lasts only while Umbridge is at Hogwarts, not forever. She also helps him to understand that he wasn't being possessed by Voldemort because he hadn't been blacking out and waking up somewhere different than where he should be. She experienced that with Tom Riddle, so she has some experience in the matter. Now, in *Half-Blood Prince*, we see her making Harry laugh:

> "'E is always so thoughtful," purred Fleur adoringly, stroking Bill's nose.
> Ginny mimed vomiting into her cereal behind Fleur. Harry choked over his cornflakes, and Ron thumped him on the back.

Here is another example:

> "I wouldn't go in the kitchen just now," she warned him. "There's a lot of Phlegm around."
> "I'll be careful not to slip in it." Harry smiled.

Harry thinks she's funny. They've gone from sharing laughs and smirks to actual jokes. In *Half-Blood Prince*, we see Harry trying to spend some time with her:

> "Fancy trying to find a compartment?"
> "I can't, Harry, I said I'd meet Dean," said Ginny brightly. "See you later."
> "Right," said Harry. He felt a strange twinge of annoyance as she walked away, her long red hair dancing behind her; he had become so used to her presence over the summer that he had almost forgotten that Ginny did not hang around with him, Ron, and Hermione while at school.

Things have changed. In *Prisoner of Azkaban*, when Harry needs to talk to Ron and Hermione about Sirius, Ron tells Ginny to go away. Of course, she was in Dumbledore's Army, so Harry isn't trying to get rid of her so that he, Ron and Hermione can talk about Sirius Black. The above quotation isn't the last time Harry tries to talk to Ginny:

> "Want to join us in Hogsmeade, Ginny?" he asked.
> "I'm going with Dean—might see you there," she replied, waving at them as she left.

Here is what happens on the Hogsmeade trip:

> Harry's thoughts strayed to Ginny as they trudged up the road to Hogwarts through the frozen slush. They had not met up with her, undoubtedly, thought Harry, because she and Dean were cozily closeted in Madam Puddifoot's Tea Shop, that haunt of happy couples. Scowling, he bowed his head against the swirling sleet and trudged on.

So, now we have Harry envious of Dean and Ginny. However, does he really understand how his feelings toward Ginny have changed yet? When Harry smells Amortentia, the "love" potion, this is what happens: "it reminded him simultaneously of treacle tart, the woody smell of a broomstick handle and something flowery he thought he might have smelled at the Burrow." After class, while Harry is at the Gryffindor table having dinner, the flowery smell makes another appearance:

> "Hang on," said a voice close by Harry's left ear, and he caught a sudden waft of that flowery smell.... He looked around and saw that Ginny had joined them.

So, we see that subconsciously he is associating Ginny with love. Eventually, Harry understands consciously that he wants to be with Ginny:

> they found themselves looking at Dean and Ginny, who were locked in a close embrace and kissing fiercely as though glued together. It was as though something large and scaly erupted into life in Harry's stomach, clawing at his insides: Hot blood seemed to flood his brain, so that all thought was extinguished, replaced by a savage urge to jinx Dean into a jelly.

I will omit part of this scene and continue below:

Dean was looking embarrassed. He gave Harry a shifty grin that Harry did not return, as the newborn monster inside him was roaring for Dean's instant dismissal from the team.

After the scene behind the tapestry, Harry tries to convince himself that he feels this way because she is Ron's little sister and that his feelings for her are brotherly concern:

Harry hardly noticed the sound of shattering glass; he felt disoriented, dizzy; being struck by a lightning bolt must be something like this. It's just because she's Ron's sister, he told himself. You just didn't like seeing her kissing Dean because she's Ron's sister....

Here's another quotation along the same lines:

Harry lay awake for a long time, looking up at the canopy of his four poster and trying to convince himself that his feelings for Ginny were entirely elder-brotherly. They had lived, had they not, like brother and sister all summer, playing Quidditch, teasing Ron, and having a laugh about Bill and Phlegm? He had known Ginny for years now.... It was natural that he should feel protective...natural that he should want to look out for her... want to rip Dean limb from limb for kissing her... No...he would have to control that particular brotherly feeling.

He doesn't get very far with that lie. He admits to himself pretty quickly that his feelings aren't brotherly:

But unbidden into his mind came an image of that same deserted corridor with himself kissing Ginny instead.... The monster in his chest purred.

He does hesitate to pursue a relationship with her at first, because he thinks that this could ruin his friendship with Ron:

She's Ron's sister, Harry told himself firmly. Ron's sister. She's out-of-bounds. He would not risk his friendship with Ron for anything.

Here's a quotation about what Harry thinks Ron's reaction would be:

but then he remembered Ron's expression when he had seen her kissing Dean, and was sure that Ron would consider it base treachery if Harry so much as held her hand.

However, Harry's fear of Ron's reaction is soon resolved:

At last he found him, still clutching the Cup and wearing an expression appropriate to having been clubbed over the head. For a fraction of a second they looked at each other, then Ron gave a tiny jerk of the head that Harry understood to mean, Well—if you must.

The creature in his chest roaring in triumph, he grinned down at Ginny and gestured wordlessly out of the portrait hole. A long walk in the grounds seemed indicated, during which—if they had time—they might discuss the match.

Ginny and Harry are now together and Harry for one is quite pleased about that:

The fact that Harry Potter was going out with Ginny Weasley seemed to interest a great number of people, most of them girls, yet Harry found himself newly and happily impervious to gossip over the next few weeks. After all, it made a very nice change to be talked about because of something that was making him happier than he could remember being for a very long time, rather than because he had been involved in horrific scenes of Dark magic.

So now we have Ron giving his blessing, Ginny and Harry together, and Harry being happier than he's ever felt. This is important, because Rowling wants the readers to feel that being with Ginny is this wonderful thing for Harry. His relationship with Ginny, which represents his being able to have a relationship with a girl, period, is simply another thing that he can't have while Voldemort is still a threat. Harry has to defeat Voldemort so that he and Ginny can be together and so that he can be happy.

In summary, I hope my presentation has shown you that Ginny is a well-written character who is simply written differently than the major characters. She does grow consistently, if in the background, and yes, she is the girl for Harry, if for no other reason than that Harry thinks she is.

WHERE YOU'LL MEET YOUR TRUE FRIENDS

Sister Magpie

In *Harry Potter and the Order of the Phoenix*, Sirius Black tells Harry, "believe me, [my family] thought Voldemort had the right idea, they were all for the purification of the wizarding race, getting rid of Muggle-borns and having pure-bloods in charge. They weren't alone, either, there were quite a few people, before Voldemort showed his true colours, who thought he had the right idea about things" (*OotP* 104).[1]

In today's presentation I'm going to expand on Sirius's remark by offering a reading of Draco Malfoy as a typical follower of Voldemort. Not everyone buys the idea that Draco is a morally serious character, but I hope to show that J. K. Rowling, even in the early books, uses him to tell us a lot of subtle things about how Voldemort's influence works.

Voldemort will be vanquished physically by Harry Potter, but that fight won't mean much in the long run if there are still people who believe he had the right idea about things. Just like in the real world, prejudice exists first at the personal level. A figure like Voldemort takes advantages of feelings that already exist. If Rowling wants to show the death of Voldemort-the-idea, she needs a bigot poised to carry his beliefs into the next generation, and she has one in Draco. Through him she can show bigotry at work in one individual: what it provides for him, how it hurts him, what he's missing in himself that he tries to fill with it. Once she has established these things, she can let bigotry destroy him, or show how he grows beyond it.

Is this what Rowling is doing with Draco? If so, we should be able to see why he has and why he needs the beliefs he has, and then see him challenged to overcome them.

---

1   All citations are to the UK editions.

If Rowling is true to her style, all the key elements of Draco's character should be present in his very first scene, where he meets Harry at Madam Malkin's robe shop: what he wants, how he goes about getting it, why he fails, and what he does in response. We all remember what this scene means for Harry, and how badly Draco comes off from Harry's perspective. But if we look past Harry's perspective, the scene packs a lot of information about Draco, and I want to understand what Draco is actually up to in terms of his own personality, his own psychology.

Rowling often uses Harry's point of view to hide things that will later come into play. It's a trick that is very well suited to a book about personal development, about how we revise our takes on things as we grow up. And it makes a close reading of Rowling very rewarding. We'll see lots of examples of this as we go through the argument. The things we learn about Draco in this scene will apply in many later scenes, too, whether or not Harry notices. So I'm going to use the robe shop scene to establish a pattern for what's going on inside Draco's head, and then apply it to some other canonical Draco scenes.

What Does Draco Want?

In his first scene Draco initiates a conversation with another boy, asks him questions and talks about himself. Draco doesn't feel very friendly to Harry, but Harry may be confusing a poor effort to make friends with no effort at all. At the end of the scene it's Harry who hops off the stool "not sorry for an excuse to stop talking to the boy," and Draco who more hopefully says "Well, I'll see you at Hogwarts, I suppose" (*PS* 61). Later, it's Draco who holds out his hand to shake and Harry who rejects it.

There's never any ulterior motive revealed for Draco in either of those scenes besides wanting to be friends. Even in the robe shop, where he doesn't know who Harry is, his lines taken by themselves are almost Colin Creevey-eager to connect with him:

"Hullo. Hogwarts too? My father's next door buying my books and mother's up the street looking at wands. Then I'm going to drag them off to look at racing brooms. I don't see why first years can't have their own. I think I'll bully father into getting me one and I'll smuggle it in somehow. Have *you* got your own broom? Play Quidditch at all? I do—Father says it's a crime if I'm not picked to play for my house and I must say, I agree.

Know what house you'll be in yet? Well, no one really knows until they get there, do they, but I know I'll be in Slytherin, all our family have been—imagine being in Hufflepuff, I think I'd leave, wouldn't you?" (*PS* 60)

How Does Draco Go about Getting What He Wants?

Thrusting himself at Harry like this is a bad way to get Harry to want him as a friend, but if we accept that it is what Draco is trying to do, what do these lines say about what he thinks he needs to be to make a friend? Judging by his words here, he thinks he has to prove he's worthy based on his social status and references. He tells Harry his parents totally love him and prove it by buying him whatever he wants; his dad says he ought to be on the Quidditch team. His family are Slytherins, so he will be; he knows Hufflepuffs are lame.

There's never any point in this conversation where just being Draco is good enough, and his own bragging immediately shows how much he relies on things outside of himself to validate him—his family, his house, his circumstances of birth. Even being on the Quidditch team is validated by what "Father says."

All this talk about his House connections, Quidditch chances and parents means that Draco reveals very little of himself. His actual personality—which, from what we'll see, is goofy and energetic—is hidden under a bored-sounding drawl. He doesn't talk about his family like Ron does, as a way of revealing himself, his personal hopes and his fears. Even the opinions Draco gives in the scene can't be his own, because he lacks the experience to have developed them. He can't know how Muggle-borns adapt to Hogwarts or what Hufflepuffs are like. He has to be parroting someone else. All he's telling Harry is that he is the right sort, because he knows who the wrong sort is: Hufflepuffs, gamekeepers, Muggle-borns, and later, Weasleys and poor people.

Why Doesn't Draco Get What He Wants?

We know Harry will never be friends with this boy from the moment Harry is "strongly reminded of Dudley" (*PS* 60). But what reminds Harry of Dudley is very specific—Draco wasn't fat like Dudley, he wasn't intimidating or violent. What reminds Harry of Dudley is: "I think I'll bully father into getting me [a broom]" (*PS* 60).

All Dudley's power over Harry came from the fact that Dudley was beloved and wanted, while Harry was hated and unwanted. That imbalance is so central to Harry's place in the Muggle world that Harry is introduced into his own story through it:

Ten years ago, there had been lots of pictures of what looked like a large pink beach ball wearing different-coloured bobble hats—but Dudley Dursley was no longer a baby, and now the photographs showed a large, blond boy riding his first bicycle, on a roundabout at the fair, playing a computer game with his father, being hugged and kissed by his mother. The room held no sign at all that another boy lived in the house too. (*PS* 19)

Draco tells Harry that he is that beloved child who is wanted and "fits" in ways some children—like Harry—never could. So Draco becomes the symbol of all Harry's fears of rejection in the wizarding world. Even though he doesn't like Draco, when he leaves the robe shop Harry is gloomily betting he'll be in Hufflepuff and sure he doesn't fit in.

Draco's weaknesses reflect Harry's insecurities in a dark way. This guarantees that Draco is going to get under Harry's skin. It also means that Harry could potentially learn something by understanding him instead of just fighting him. Harry will never be drawn to Voldemort, as Draco is, but since Draco is built around insecurities Harry himself has, his struggle with Voldemort has meaning to Harry in ways that, for instance, Barty Crouch's fall to Voldemort would not.

Along with pushing Harry's own insecurity buttons, there's another important impression that Draco makes on Harry: Harry thinks he's a fake. When Draco says he is sorry to hear Harry's parents are dead, Harry thinks Draco "doesn't sound sorry at all." When they meet later on the Hogwarts Express, Harry again marks Draco as false by saying that now that Draco knows he is Harry Potter, Draco is "looking at [him] with a lot more interest than he'd shown back in Diagon Alley" (*PS* 81).

Now, Harry could be projecting some of his own issues here. Many boys at eleven aren't mature enough to truly sound sorry about a stranger's death. Ron doesn't "sound sorry" about Harry's life either—he's eager to hear about how he became the Boy Who Lived. But it's Draco who has been marked as insincere in his first scene, and we must read further to understand what's underneath the insincerity. So far, everything about Draco has suggested this character is lacking substance underneath the façade.

What Does Draco Do When He Doesn't Get What He Wants?

When Harry makes it clear he doesn't like Draco's conversation, that's when Draco introduces blood prejudice:

> 'I think [Hagrid's] brilliant,' Harry said coldly.
>
> '*Do* you,' said the boy, with a slight sneer. 'Why is he with you? Where are your parents?...they were *our* kind, weren't they? I really don't think they should let the other sort in, do you? They're just not the same, they've never been brought up to know our ways. Some of them have never even heard of Hogwarts until they get the letter, I imagine. I think they should keep it in the old Wizarding families. What's your surname, anyway?' (*PS* 60–61)

Draco is still jockeying for social position, using bigotry to place himself above Muggle-borns who "don't belong" and trying to link himself to Harry as a non-Muggle-born, even if Harry doesn't like it. Rather than actually discuss Hagrid—rather than meet Harry halfway as one individual to another—Draco retreats into blood distinctions. He has avoided real social interaction in favor of dealing with group generalizations. He even asks for Harry's surname, which tells to whom Harry belongs, rather than his first name, which says who he is as an individual. This is the pattern Draco follows in the robe shop, and that pattern continues throughout the story.

What Does Draco Want?

Just as Draco is introduced trying to make friends with Harry, once at Hogwarts he continues to work harder than any other character in canon at getting attention from his peers—he's still a boy who wants friends. He tells jokes, does impressions, and takes pratfalls. He sings, he clowns, he writes songs. He exaggerates, strikes poses and tells long, wildly improbable stories. He draws the eye physically when he's in a scene, making faces, snickering or juggling wands. He makes grand entrances, talks loudly, turns conversations into performances, and is often described with a growing "crowd" of Slytherins with whom he "holds court." Harry thinks Draco was "acting" in the robe shop, and indeed performing turns out to be a major part of his characterization.

Even after he's declared himself Harry's enemy, Draco compulsively forces interactions with him so that Harry can reject him again:

> Draco Malfoy, who was passing the Gryffindor table, snatched the Remembrall out of [Neville's] hand.
> Harry and Ron jumped to their feet. They were half hoping for a reason to fight Malfoy. (*PS* 108)

> Fred and George had hardly disappeared when someone far less welcome turned up: Malfoy flanked by Crabbe and Goyle. (*PS* 114)

> They left the hall quickly, wanting to unwrap the broomstick in private before their first lesson, but half-way across the entrance hall they found the way upstairs barred by Crabbe and Goyle. Malfoy seized the package from Harry and felt it. (*PS* 122)

Dudley was dangerous and physically intimidating. Draco is just not welcome and not wanted.

How Does Draco Go about Getting What He Wants?

At no time is Draco more of a pest than when he discovers that the Trio is secretly trying to help Hagrid with his illegal dragon. Instead of using the information to get Harry in trouble, Draco keeps the secret, and "performs" this fact by smiling ambiguously in class and visiting Ron in the infirmary to remind him that he could tell, but making no demands for his silence. When he gets written proof of when and how the kids are going to send the dragon away, instead of passing it to Filch or Snape, he sneaks out to "catch" the Trio by himself. He only spills the beans to McGonagall when his chance to join the party himself is ruined.

Harry assumes Draco would use this information to get what he wanted, and that seems to be exactly what Draco is doing. He's tried to use the information to get himself included.

Why Doesn't Draco Get What He Wants?

Despite all his effort, Draco still remains insincere in Harry's eyes, never showing us a "true self" underneath the false one. When we think of a character who is false, we usually think of someone like Moody in *Goblet of Fire*, who pretended to be Harry's friend, but then revealed himself actually to be Death Eater Barty Crouch. Barty Crouch was not insincere. Once the Polyjuice wore off, we saw a man with very strong personal convictions.

Draco, on the other hand, has no secret convictions to uncover. His insincerity, unlike Barty's or Peter Pettigrew's, is not just a means to an end, but a fundamental part of his character. The most common advice Harry is given about Draco is not to listen to him because he only talks to get a reaction out of the listener: "He's making it up...he's trying to make you do something stupid." "He was just showing off for Parkinson." "Of course he provoked you...he'd just lost, hadn't he?"

It's not that Draco is covering up the truth of how he really feels; it's that there is no truth, only the reaction he hopes to get from his words. Nothing Draco does is ever to be taken seriously because there's nothing there. He's always oriented towards his audience. Even when the Trio comes across Draco alone in the woods at the Quidditch World Cup, he seems to have been doing nothing at all besides waiting for a cue.

Harry cannot completely follow this advice to ignore Draco because Draco still reflects his own insecurities. Whenever he doubts himself, it's Draco's laughing face that rises before him. When Harry fears no House will want him for a member at the Sorting:

Malfoy swaggered forward when his name was called and got his wish at once: the hat had barely touched his head when it screamed, 'SLYTHERIN.' Malfoy went to join his friends Crabbe and Goyle, looking pleased with himself. (*PS* 90)

A few weeks later Harry hates him even more than Dudley, even though Draco is not actually doing anything to Harry at all:

'Just what I always wanted. To make a fool of myself on a broomstick in front of Malfoy.'

He had been looking forward to learning to fly more than anything else...

[Ron said reasonably], 'I know Malfoy's always going on about how good he is at Quidditch, but I bet **that's all talk**.'

Malfoy certainly did talk about flying a lot. He complained loudly about first years never getting on the house Quidditch teams and told long, boastful stories which always seemed to end with him narrowly escaping Muggles in helicopters. (*PS* 107; emphasis added)

Readers can gauge how insecure Harry is feeling by how smug Malfoy looks. If Malfoy looks happy, Harry is feeling like an outcast or worried about being found publicly unworthy. If Harry is feeling confident, Malfoy's spite and jealousy will be ugly and repulsive.

What Does Draco Do When He Doesn't Get What He Wants?

Both Harry and Draco may fear rejection, but they deal with it in opposite ways. Draco, as always, looks for outside validation in bigotry or superficial markers of social success. His effectiveness as a bully is based on his ability to spot where other people are insecure, what they wish they weren't or what they hope others don't see about them. He remains an uneasy combination of the bully who makes others feel rejected, and the kid who really wants to be accepted. Harry, on the other hand, faces and masters his fear, gains confidence from within and learns to trust his abilities in defiance of public opinion.

This difference is so fundamental to their personalities, it's even reflected in their talents. Harry is a natural at throwing off the Imperius curse. He can instinctively tell the difference between his own will and someone else's trying to undermine it. Meanwhile, Draco is a natural at repressing and erasing himself with Occlumency, hiding that which he doesn't want other people to see.

Once again, we're back to something lacking in Draco that makes him need to look outside himself for strength, and makes him weaker than Harry even when they ought to be evenly matched. Look, for instance, at Draco as a Quidditch player. Although Ron says his bragging is all talk, Harry objectively notes that Draco does fly well. So it's not surprising that in *Chamber of Secrets*, Draco makes the Slytherin team as the Seeker.

This is the moment in canon when we see Draco at his most accepted, surrounded by his team, in uniform and "smirking all over his pale, pointed face" (*CoS* 85). When Marcus Flint shows off Lucius Malfoy's gift of Nimbus Two Thousand Ones, Draco's smirk becomes so broad "his cold eyes were reduced to slits" (*CoS* 86). You need a really big grin to do that on a pointy face.

Everything's coming up Draco until Hermione cuts in:

'At least no one on the Gryffindor team had to *buy* their way in. *They* got
in on pure talent.'
The smug look on Malfoy's face flickered. (*CoS* 86)

This scene isn't about revealing that Draco bought his way onto
the team. That story goes nowhere. If he were untalented, it should
show up on the pitch, and it doesn't. There's no suggestion of
frustration on the Slytherin team at being stuck with a weak Seeker,
and Draco always gives Harry a run for his money, even when
Harry's on a Firebolt. Yet even in a situation where Draco should be
reasonably confident in his abilities, he's unable to defend himself.
He retreats into bigotry again: "No one asked your opinion, you
filthy little Mudblood" (*CoS* 86). He's not prepared to defend his
own abilities, even when he has abilities to defend.

Draco doesn't only use bigotry to dismiss people who don't like
him. He also uses it to assure himself and show others that other
people do like him. He never misses a chance to hint to Harry that
he's in on the plans of Death Eaters, that they include him in things.
Basilisk in the school? Draco makes sure everyone knows it's going
after who he thinks it should. Somebody murdered at the Triwizard
Tournament? It means his side's coming to smite Draco's enemies
for him. Heir of Slytherin? Would totally want Draco helping him
and is totally not Harry Potter. Harry rejects his handshake? He's
picked the losing side. Draco is not a boy on his own; he has an
army of pure-bloods, Dark wizards and Voldemort behind him.
Draco might not be so pleased with Voldemort as a friend as he
claims to be, but he's stuck with him once his bluff is called:

'I s'pose Lord Voldemort's just a warm-up for you three—what's the
matter?' [Harry] added, for Malfoy, Crabbe and Goyle had all looked
stricken at the sound of the name. 'He's a mate of your dad, isn't he? Not
scared of him, are you?' (*OotP* 750)

Talking about Draco's bigotry as an expression of his desire for
connection to others risks sounding too sentimental. The Draco
who "just wants to be friends" might call to mind certain fanon
portrayals where just under the racist veneer, Draco is—to quote
Blackadder—"a soft little marshmallowy, pigletty type of creature."
But that's why it's so important to remember that at this point, we've

not yet been told there is anything underneath Draco's façade at all, so the façade really can't be said to suggest positive things underneath it. Not yet.

What it can tell us is what Draco might want, what he's willing to do to get it and what he thinks is important. Making friends is most important as a theme in *Philosopher's Stone*, because that's the book where the kids are first establishing themselves in the social world at Hogwarts. In that book Hermione, too, acts like a superior know-it-all who's better than everyone else when she tries to make friends. When she's vulnerable she cries, hidden in the bathroom. Draco, too, will be found crying in the bathroom one day.

Hermione and Draco are very different people "underneath" their superior acts, but they both show us that the person who is ashamed of showing weakness is the person who's going to go to great lengths to hide it. Draco is wounded by rejection. He is affected by criticism. He does care what people think. Perhaps too much.

Still, we can't avoid it forever: if Draco is all talk, what is he underneath the talk? Why is his sense of self so undeveloped to begin with? Rowling has said, looking over her series, "I realize that it's kind of a litany of bad fathers. That's where evil seems to flourish, in places where people didn't get good fathering."

Draco did not get good fathering. But it doesn't mean that he's a racist Death Eater because his father is. Rowling is far more specific about her fathers and sons. The weaknesses of the one combine with the weaknesses of the other, sometimes in unexpected ways. Barty Crouch's obsession with hunting Death Eaters contributed to his son's becoming one, and rebel Sirius Black reacted to his unhappy pro-Death Eater home by joining the Order of the Phoenix.

We know that Lucius is very important to Draco. Draco invokes his father's opinion so often in *Philosopher's Stone* it's easy to forget that we don't actually meet him until the second book. Knowing that Draco thinks his father's opinions carry great weight, and that outside validation is important to Draco, what opinions does Lucius express about his son? Lucius has all of five lines spoken to Draco in canon so far, and every one of them is in conflict with Draco himself:

'Touch nothing, Draco.'

Malfoy, who had reached for the glass eye, said, 'I thought you were going to buy me a present.'

'I said I would buy you a racing broom,' said his father, drumming his fingers on the counter. (*CoS* 42)

The first thing Lucius does in canon is show us that the father Draco referred to back in the robe shop, the one who could be bullied, was just talk. That was the relationship with his father Draco thought he should have, the one he wanted Harry to think he had, not the one he really has.

Lucius then tells Draco what he thinks of his son's complaints that Harry doesn't deserve the admiration and popularity he gets at school:

'You have told me this at least a dozen times already,' said Mr Malfoy, with a quelling look at his son, 'and I would remind you it is not—prudent—to appear less than fond of Harry Potter, not when our kind regard him as the hero who made the Dark Lord disappear.' (*CoS* 43)

Any parent might get tired of hearing their child complain about a hated classmate, but what we're also seeing here is Draco telling his father about something we know is a really big deal to him. Lucius's response to his son's feelings is, and seems to always have been: cover them up. (Ironically, Lucius expects Draco to take his own personal battles seriously, sending him newspaper clippings about Arthur Weasley.) He doesn't reassure Draco or help him see things more clearly. Even if Lucius considers Harry the enemy, it's on his own terms, not Draco's. Draco should "appear" fond of Harry. Appearances, unsurprisingly, are important to Lucius, who is as "slippery" as they come.

Lucius also comments on Draco's grades:

'I hope my son will amount to more than a thief or a plunderer, Borgin.... Though if his school marks don't pick up, that may indeed be all he is fit for....'

'I would have thought you'd be ashamed that a girl of no wizard family beat you in every exam.... Come, Draco.' (*CoS* 44)

Harry assumes that Draco's arrogance comes from the same place Dudley's does: from parents who tell him everything he does is good. But here we see the opposite. Lucius does not use bigotry to praise his son, but to put him down. It's Draco the pure-blood, not

Hermione the Muggle-born, who ought to be ashamed in this scene. Lucius dangles the idea of an elite circle of superior pure-bloods but uses words like "shame" and "fit for nothing" to refer to Draco himself.

Lucius gives Draco no advice about Harry or Hermione that can strengthen him as a person or help him deal with the world. Nor does he give him any advice about improving himself. He says anything Draco might do right is due to his circumstances of birth, and anything he does wrong is due to inferiority of character. It's just too consistent with the way Draco presents himself to be a coincidence that Lucius spends the scene shaming, criticizing and dismissing Draco as a boy while telling him he's superior as a pure-blood.

If Draco were another boy, these lapses in logic might lead him to rethink the ideology. But Rowling has already established that Draco is a character motivated by the desire for positive attention. He looks outward for validation, not inward for the truth. Where Harry responds to personal criticism by stubbornly asserting himself even more (remember his resistance to the Imperius curse again), Draco willingly represses parts of himself and adjusts his behavior for others. No wonder he's a fake with such a conflict between what he's supposed to be and what he is. Look, too, at the way Draco imagines paradise under Voldemort:

'When the Dark Lord takes over, is he going to care how many O.W.L.s or N.E.W.T.s anyone's got? Of course he isn't…it'll be all about the kind of service he received, the level of devotion he was shown.' (*HBP* 145)

That little speech of Draco's where he lays out the great world under Voldemort shows just how much he's willing to rely on outside validation. He talks about a world where grown adults live or die based on the level of devotion they show to a father figure, as if it's perfectly normal. In this world, all that matters is making an effort for positive attention.

Meanwhile, personal accomplishment becomes meaningless. People aren't judged on their abilities or individual worth. It's tempting, therefore, to say that Draco is jealous of others. He has been beaten by Harry and by Hermione, and even Ron has won the Quidditch Cup when he hasn't. Therefore, he wants a world where people aren't judged on personal accomplishments because he has none.

But if Rowling's point were that Draco is jealous of people with actual talents because he has none, why give him the actual talents he has? Draco is no superstar, but he is good at things. He can compete with Harry at Quidditch. He isn't a bad student—he's at least capable of beating Harry and Ron in one subject. He's not dull-witted or sluggish.

Draco doesn't lack abilities; he lacks the ability to appreciate those he has in a healthy way. Healthy self-confidence, as opposed to arrogance, is an essential quality for a wizard. Ron and Neville worry that their personal abilities are worse than they are. Draco doesn't understand the importance of personal abilities for their own sake rather than just a way of getting praise.

Draco has done fairly well with his O.W.L.s, from what we see, yet he's willing to trade that for being rewarded for shows of devotion to the Dark Lord. In fact, Draco has blurred the line between personal achievement and random favoritism throughout canon. He's claimed Hermione does well because she's the teachers' favorite, that O.W.L. grades depend on "who you know." And Harry Potter is the worst example of all:

'Harry Potter got a Nimbus Two Thousand last year. Special permission from Dumbledore so he could play for Gryffindor. He's not even that good, it's just because he's *famous*…famous for having a stupid *scar* on his forehead…. Everyone thinks he's so *smart*, wonderful *Potter* with his *scar* and his *broomstick*—' (*CoS* 42–43)

It may sound a bit frightening to suggest that a braggart like Draco needs more appreciation of his abilities, but realistic confidence is portrayed as a source of strength in canon. Ron plays better Quidditch when he's not insecure. When Neville knows he's right, he has courage he might have lacked otherwise. Hermione is more likable when she stops over-asserting herself.

By the beginning of *Half-Blood Prince*, Rowling has established how Draco relies on his bigoted beliefs, but where will they lead him? Are they stronger than he is, or does he have a chance of learning to live without them? The task Draco is given in *Half-Blood Prince* is built around this very challenge.

First, by giving Draco a task that's isolating and anti-social, by having the Death Eaters encourage him while his family and friends try to hold him back, Voldemort helps Draco start to distinguish between false connections based on thinking pure-bloods are superior, and the true, flawed human connections he really has.

Draco is also forced for the first time to see what he's able to live without. Petty social advantage like the Slug Club falls away first, then glory, until he is left with only the people he actually cares about and who care about him in return.

To understand Draco's development in *Half-Blood Prince*, it helps to return to Harry again. Harry knows what matters to him, and he's always true to himself. So the challenges he faces strengthen his character and resolve from within. Draco, on the other hand, needs to be broken down, the false layers and inefficient ways he deals with the world peeled away. He has to lose the things he's tried to define himself with in the past: his name, his father—perhaps most of all, his audience. It's the only way he'll be forced to rely on and get to know himself, and have a chance to build a stronger person from the inside out.

Only after all that is peeled away can we—and he—get a glimpse of what might be hiding underneath. When Draco faces himself in a cracked mirror at last, the person he sees is crying like a baby. In fact, when Myrtle first tells Harry about someone crying in the boy's room, Harry draws the same conclusion: 'There's been a boy in here crying?' said Harry curiously. 'A young boy?' (*HBP* 433).

Draco is taking his first unsure steps as a sincere person—he is, in some sense, like a baby. And just as Harry is the first person to recognize Draco's false nature back in *Philosopher's Stone*, Harry's the first one to see Draco differently in *Half-Blood Prince*. This Draco, the one who is devoting himself to something he cares about, is someone Harry can imagine being valued by others, from fangirls Myrtle and Kreacher to scared, frustrated Snape to Crabbe and Goyle, who for the first time are glimpsed disagreeing with Draco as well as helping him. This Draco is worth paying attention to.

And then, just like that, the book ends. The Draco picked up by the scruff of his neck like a kitten by Snape on the Astronomy Tower isn't redeemed or triumphant, pledging himself to the Order and rejecting bigotry forever. But he has begun to address everything brought up in that robe shop. Instead of chasing after friends, he's had to consider what friends he wants and how friends should be treated. He's been left alone with his own opinions and feelings. He's learned the harsh difference between performance and action, between fantasy and reality. He's tested his own abilities and found "comfort and courage"—courage!—in his success. It's only once he fights his way up to the Astronomy Tower that he is even able to listen to the lesson Dumbledore's waiting to give him there.

If Draco never went any further than this, it might still be an improvement. But he might have it in him to go further than that. When the Death Eaters appear on the Tower, Draco does not fall back into his old habit of playing to the crowd. Instead of siding with the Death Eaters, he keeps his eyes on Dumbledore. He can now distinguish real strength when he sees it. Instead of returning to empty Death Eater bragging, he continues giving honest answers:

> [Dumbledore said,] 'I am a little shocked that Draco here invited [Fenrir], of all people, into the school where his friends live…'
> 'I didn't,' breathed Malfoy…. 'I didn't know he was going to come.' (*HBP* 554)

That's Draco's last line in canon, speaking up in front of a room full of armed Death Eaters to agree with Dumbledore about his own true intentions and about what is decent behavior.

Draco's development has already had an effect on Harry. He still dislikes Draco in *Half-Blood Prince*, but for the first time he's moving towards him instead of always trying to get him out of his sight. When Harry looks more closely at Draco, and so looks more closely at what Draco represents to Harry about himself, he is not so hopeless after all. Draco's true colours are not Voldemort's.

No Wizard Left Behind: A Comparison of the No Child Left Behind Legislation and *Harry Potter and the Order of the Phoenix*

Hilary Pollack
Northland College, Wisconsin

At first glance the magic and delightful fantasy of *Harry Potter* has little to do with the serious federal legislation that governs much of what transpires in the schools of this nation. A closer look, however, reveals some ominous similarities between the role that the Bush administration has taken to attempt to insure quality education for all children and the efforts of the Ministry of Magic to control the teachers and students of the Hogwarts Academy in J. K. Rowling's mythical land, where students take classes and are tested in *Ancient Runes, Arithmancy, Astronomy, Care of Magical Creatures, Charms, Defense Against the Dark Arts, Divination, Flying, Herbology, History of Magic, Muggle Studies, Potions,* and *Transfiguration*, rather than math, reading, language arts, science, and social studies.

The principles which the U.S. federal government has outlined in No Child Left Behind (NCLB) are ideals which have defined public education since Horace Mann planted the roots of compulsory education as a cornerstone of democracy. Mann laid the groundwork to institutionalize education and to make it the domain of the public sector as he actualized his beliefs that "a human being is not attaining his full heights until he is educated," and "education then, beyond all other devices of human origin, is the great equalizer of the conditions of men, the balance-wheel of the social machinery" (Mann). In setting specific guidelines for public education, the Bush administration is attempting to protect and strengthen the educational system and assure that democratic values are preserved as "no child" is overlooked and all children have equal access to the educational process.

Similar intentions direct the government intervention in public education in the *Harry Potter* books. This relationship becomes very apparent in *Harry Potter and the Order of the Phoenix*, the fifth book in the series, which directly addresses the complex dynamic between the government and the educational system. The Ministry of Magic, according to Professor Umbridge, a ministry infiltrator at Hogwarts, takes a vital interest in Education, analogous to that of the Bush administration:

"The Ministry of Magic has always considered the education of young witches and wizards to be of vital importance. The rare gifts with which you were born may come to nothing if not nurtured and honed by careful instruction." (212)

President Bush expressed a comparable interest in education, as legislated by NCLB when he stated:

These reforms express my deep belief in our public schools and their mission to build the mind and character of every child, from every background, in every part of America. (Bush, 2004)

The basic tenets of No Child Left Behind are inarguable. However, the ways in which these tenets might be implemented are ambiguous, and educators are concerned about possible consequences (Metz, 2005). The frenzied behavior and arbitrary educational policies which characterized Hogwarts when Professor Umbridge replaced Professor Dumbledore as Headmaster and further increased her power when she was appointed to the role of High Inquisitor could forecast possible effects of NCLB. The failure of schools to make Adequate Yearly Progress (AYP), as defined by standardized test scores "has the potential to create chaos that will systematically undermine the faith of the populace in public education" (Metz 6). This scenario is analogous to the chaos that reigned at Hogwarts when Headmaster Dumbledore's powers were usurped, and administrators like Professor Umbridge and parents like Lucius Malfoy were allowed to use their influence and financial power to determine the Hogwarts curriculum and teaching methodology. As soon as Professor Umbridge took over, pandemonium prevailed at Hogwarts; the fireworks that Fred and George Weasley unleashed are a metaphor for the disruption that can evolve from federal control of education:

Dragons comprised of green-and-gold sparks were soaring up and down the corridors, emitting loud, fiery blasts and bangs as they went. Shocking-pink Catherine Wheels five feet in diameter were whizzing lethally through the air like so many flying saucers.... Fireworks were exploding like mines everywhere Harry looked, and instead of burning themselves out, fading from sight, or fizzling to a halt, these pyrotechnical miracles seemed to be gaining in energy and momentum the longer he watched. (*OotP* 62)

Disruptive fireworks have not yet resulted from NCLB, but educators predict that in 2014, when it will be required that all children reach levels of proficiency or above in reading and mathematics that there will be confusion and turmoil in the schools, such as Hogwarts experienced. The failure of the federal government to provide adequate resources for the mandates could pave the way for continuing problems. As schools scramble to achieve AYP, they are forced to make sacrifices in curriculum and personnel that detract from the quality of the education that children are receiving under NCLB (Saulny, 2006).

Mississippi State Superintendent of Education Henry Johnson blithely predicts that "'if you have high standards, kids will learn what you teach them. The goal is for 100 percent of students to be proficient'" (Spellings 2). Optimistic though his statement may be, it shows no recognition of the individual differences that characterize student learning and the widely disparate rate at which children learn. Most educators understand that "one can expect...differences in developmental needs from one child to the next...related to each child's physical, cognitive, language, social, and emotional growth (Meece 316). Indeed, the concept of universal achievement of a proficiency level on standardized tests is antithetical to the premise of statistical analysis, which predicts a bell curve distribution for the educational achievement of a large, representative population. According to statistical research, "many of the important characteristics we wish to study (including all inherited characteristics) are normally distributed," which means "50 percent of the population will be below the arithmetical average (the mean)" (http://www.mala.bc). Only in Garrison Keillor's Lake Woebegone are "all children above average."

Standardized testing is one of the major tenets of NCLB. The federal government has established annual assessment requirements which specify in what school year students will be tested and what content areas will be covered. Similarly, at Hogwarts, students are required to take O.W.L.s (Ordinary Wizarding Level) and N.E.W.T.s (Nastily Exhausting Wizarding Tests), the achievement tests which measure what they have learned in their classes. As standardized test scores are used to measure students' growth and schools' effectiveness under NCLB, so do the results of the O.W.L.s reflect on Hogwarts because, as Professor McGonagall explains, "your examination results will reflect upon the headmistress's new regime at the school" (*OotP* 709). Harry and his friends suffer from the anxiety that often accompanies the "high stakes" standardized testing mandated by NCLB. When Harry and his friend Hermione are preparing for one of their exams, Hermione "was very agitated and kept snatching the book back from him to check that she had gotten the answer completely right, finally hitting him hard on the nose with the sharp edge of *Achievements in Charming*" (709). Educators predict that the impact of the mandated testing that is at the core of NCLB will have profound and dramatic effects on the public education system. According to James Horn, Professor of Education at Monmouth University:

the spread of the testing hysteria, into high schools and even now into kindergarten, threatens an intellectual and emotional genocide against minorities that could leave future generations more devastated by the remedy than by the awful schools that the current reform frenzy supposedly intended to fix. (Horn 1)

Rather than enhancing education, many educators feel that the shadow of annual standardized testing can significantly detract from students' learning, and teachers will "teach to the test," focusing only on concepts that they know will be assessed and ignoring important subjects like art, music, and history that will not be assessed (Metz). This practice is institutionalized at Hogwarts when Professor Umbridge in her role as High Inquisitor decrees that "teachers are hereby banned from giving students any information that is not strictly related to the subjects they are paid to teach" (*OotP* 551). Professor Flitwick, in preparing his students for the O.W.L. in the Summoning Charms class, announces that everyone should be capable of passing the exam, and he intends to ensure that all of his students could do so. With many of the students "panicking slightly about the amount of homework they had to do" (257), the students at Hogwarts are immersed in preparing for their exams, although that may ultimately be at the expense of their actual learning. "So you've got your exams coming up, haven't you?" Fred Weasley asks. "They'll be keeping your noses so hard to that grindstone they'll be rubbed raw." His brother George adds, "Half our year had minor breakdowns coming up to O.W.L.s. Tears and tantrums…nightmare of a year" (226).

Umbridge further emphasizes the disconnect between the testing and the curriculum and students' futures when she prohibits students from practicing magic in their Defense of the Dark Arts class, informing them that "theoretical knowledge will be more than sufficient to get you through your examination, which, after all, is what school is about" (243). There is little room for application of knowledge when it is not part of standardized examinations. President Bush would support the testing policies at Hogwarts, as he asserts "that in order to know, in order to diagnose a problem, you have to measure it in the first place" (Bush). His reliance on this single standardized measure reflects an ignorance of the commonly accepted understanding that valid assessment requires the use of multiple measures of evaluation to document student learning (Kellough and Roberts 342). The federal government will use standardized test scores alone to assess students' learning and impose standards of Annual Yearly Progress which will require proficiency level achievement by all students (subtracting a small fraction for students with exceptional needs) in 2014. According to NAEP trend data, testing expert Robert Linn estimates that "it would take 166 years for all twelfth graders to attain proficiency in reading and math" (http://fairtest.org).

No Child Left Behind also requires that all classrooms in the nation be staffed by "highly qualified teachers." Although requirements differ from state to state, "highly qualified" teachers are defined generally as capable of passing a standardized test and having a college major which supports the content that they are teaching. This requirement sounds reasonable, but it does not consider the reality of recruiting and retaining teachers, especially in low-income districts. Gloria Ladson-Billings, Professor of Urban

Education and Curriculum at the University of Wisconsin, asks, "Who can argue against a federal provision that requires there to be a highly qualified teacher in every classroom? However, the simple logic of the provision ignores the conditions under which teachers do their work and the uneven distribution of good teachers in districts and schools" (Metz 6). The narrow definitions of "highly qualified" that states adopt can have the effect of eliminating very competent teachers from the classroom. Professor Umbridge articulated a similar policy enacted by the Ministry of Magic when she explained to Hagrid, the gamekeeper and instructor of *Care of Magical Creatures* that in her role of High Inquisitor, she exercised her responsibility to "inspect my fellow teachers and…weed out unsatisfactory teachers" (*OotP* 438). Hagrid tells Hermione, Ron, and Harry that he wants to make his class "really special" "interestin'" and "impressive" (439), but Hermione warns him that he should just give his students dull information that will appear on their exams if he wants to keep his position. Umbridge's high-handed policies also result in the relieving of Professor Trelawney of her teaching duties although she has been at Hogwarts for sixteen years. In the attempt to staff classrooms with "highly qualified teachers," it is announced that "the Ministry's really determined to crack down on substandard teaching in this place" (260).

No Child Left Behind promises that schools will employ research-based teaching methodology that has been proven to work (Reutzel and Cooter xx). According to guidelines, only teaching strategies that are scientifically based and proven to be effective will be eligible for federal funding. In her introductory speech to the students of Hogwarts, Professor Umbridge reinforces this principle when she states that "the treasure trove of magical knowledge amassed by our ancestors must be guarded, replenished, and polished by those who have been called to the noble profession of teaching" (*OotP* 212). She adds that "our tried and tested traditions often require no tinkering" (213), affirming the principle of "best-practice teaching" that underlies NCLB. The result of the focus is "a carefully structured, theory-centered, Ministry- approved course of Defensive Magic" (239) that has very little to do with students' needs and life applications. Hermione interprets Umbridge's remarks as a foreboding of "the Ministry interfering at Hogwarts" (214), a clear parallel to many educators' apprehension regarding the consequences of the federal government's increased role in education under NCLB. Indeed, several states have initiated lawsuits against the federal Department of Education for "federal intrusion into an area long considered the domain of the states" (Dillon, 2005). In her role as High Inquisitor at Hogwarts, Umbridge plans to address the "falling standards" (*OotP* 307) at the school thus involving the Ministry of Magic in designing and delivering the Hogwarts curriculum. Headmaster Dumbledore warns Cornelius Fudge, the Minister of Magic, that "the Ministry has no authority to punish Hogwarts students," nor is it empowered to "expel Hogwarts students" (149). Dumbledore implies that the government is overstepping its boundaries when he observes sarcastically to Fudge that "in your admirable haste to ensure that the law is upheld, you appear, inadvertently I am sure, to have overlooked a few laws yourself" (149). This blurring of responsibilities is also characteristic of NCLB as it attempts to reach its goal "to ensure that all children have a fair, equal, and significant opportunity to obtain a high-quality education" (http://www.ed.gov).

The fourth major tenet of NCLB provides opportunities for parents to participate in the education of their children. In fact, under NCLB, many parents actually feel disenfranchised as far as their children's education is concerned (Saulny). For example, NCLB requires consistently failing schools to offer tutoring services to academically deficient students, but in reality "the program is allotted too few federal funds, is poorly advertised to parents, has too much complicated paperwork for signing up, and...has not fully penetrated the most difficult neighborhoods where there are high concentrations of poor, failing students" (Saulny 2). Parents of students at Hogwarts are reportedly enthusiastic about the edicts from the Ministry of Magic, but the reality is that only parents like Lucius Malfoy, who is wealthy and well-connected with Ministry officials, are happy with the ministry's enhanced role at Hogwarts. His judgmental remark about "concerns voiced by anxious parents who feel the school may be moving in a direction they do not approve" (*OotP* 307) does not reflect the opinions of parents such as the Weasleys, the Grangers, the Longbottoms, or the Lovegoods, but rather speaks to Malfoy's questionable relationship with Cornelius Fudge and the Ministry of Magic; it is more indicative of the larger community being excluded from educational decisions rather than included. This trend is mirrored in U.S. schools as affluent, prosperous families are well-connected to the schools, while families that are struggling financially, often ethnic minorities, are becoming increasingly disengaged from the education of their children.

There is turmoil in schools all over the world. Particularly in the U.S. do we see the rage of young people explode as students respond to the social and academic pressures that characterize their world. One of the assumptions that emerges from NCLB is that all children are the same and they should all achieve at parallel levels. This characterization leads to frustration, stereotyping, and a cookie-cutter curriculum that requires all students to act the same. And contributes to the rage. In their musical interpretation of the institution of education "Another Brick in the Wall," the musical group Pink Floyd vehemently objects to the concept that each child is just another brick in the wall, a product of thought control. This depiction of the consequences of this "one size fits all" educational value that emerges from the principles of NCLB and the domination of Hogwarts by the Ministry of Magic is consistent with many educators' interpretation of No Child Left Behind.

J. K. Rowling is British and probably had no intention to compare the political situation at Hogwarts with the intentions and results of No Child Left Behind. Somehow, the distance that she has from American public education and the Bush administration that spawned No Child Left Behind renders her message even more powerful, as she examines a totally separate scenario of the relationship between government and education. In the song of the Sorting Hat, one of the major traditions at Hogwarts, she echoes some of the ominous forebodings that critics of No Child Left Behind voice in their response to the legislation that governs much of what is happening in public education in this country:

> Oh, know the perils, read the signs,
> The warning history shows,
> For our Hogwarts is in danger
> From external, deadly foes
> And we must unite inside her
> Or we'll crumble from within. (*OotP* 206–7)

Works Cited

Bush, G. W. (2004). `<http://www.ontheissues.org/2004/georgewbush/education.htm>`. Retrieved Jan. 21, 2006.

Dillon, S. (April 20, 2005). "Teachers' union sues over *No Child Left Behind*," *New York Times*.

Horn, J. (July 7–9 2005,). "NCLB Testing Hysteria at Full Maturity: Ideological Blindness, Color Blindness, or No Blindness at All?" Research presented at the CREATE's 13th National Evaluation Institute. Memphis, Tenn.

Kellough, R and Roberts, P. (1991). *A resource guide for elementary school teaching*. New York: Macmillan.

Mann, H. (n.d.). Retrieved 2 Feb 2006. `<http://en.wikiquote.org/wiki/Horace_Mann>`.

Meece, J. (2002). *Child and adolescent development for educators*. New York: McGraw-Hill.

Metz, M. (May 2005). "Conferees analyze No Child Left Behind." *Campus Connections*. UW Madison School of Education alumni newsletter, 6–9.

O'Hanian, S. (n.d.). Retrieved 2 Feb 2006. `<http://www.susanohanian.org/shownclb/stories.html?id=250>`.

Reutzel, R. and Cooter, R. (2005) *The essentials of teaching children to read*. Upper Saddle River, NJ: Pearson.

Rowling, J. K. (2003). *Harry Potter and the Order of the Phoenix*. New York: Scholastic.

Saulny, S. (12 Feb 2006). "Tutor program offered by NCLB is going unused." *New York Times*, 1–5.

Spellings, M. (April 7, 2005). "Raising achievement: A new path for No Child Left Behind." Mount Vernon, VA.

`<http://www.fairtest.org/nattest/Reality_TestingNCLB.html>`. (n.d.). Retrieved 13 Jan 2006.

`<http://www.ed.gov/print/policy/elsec/leg/esea02>`. (n.d.). Retrieved 18 May 2005.

`<http://www.mala.bc.ca/~johnstoi/maybe/maybe5.htm#oneb>`. (n.d.). Retrieved 21 Mar 2006.

Hilary Pollack can be contacted at hpollack@northland.edu.

Marketing "Fast Food" Curriculum: Scholastic's Foray into Reading Instruction

Martha Young-Rhymes
Northwestern State University of Louisiana

Early in my teaching career, I implemented the tenets of reader response and transactional theories within a whole-language setting because those approaches supported my belief that *real* books are more relevant to children and, thus, hold more value for reading instruction than basal anthologies. A large part of my instructional program relied on popular trade book content in the form of class read-alouds.[1] These chapter books provided opportunities not only for me to model fluency and strategies for comprehension building, but they also spurred my students to explore open-ended questions through written responses in their reading logs. My fifth graders were involved in the selection of the books we read throughout the year, remained motivated to study the content, and clamored for the next installment each day; in short, they were engaged both with the text and in the process of reading.

Though I deliberately presented a variety of genres as part of the trade book selection process, fantasies were consistently preferred by the students as evidenced by their annual vote for favorite book of the year. Winners from past classes had included Roald Dahl's *The BFG* (1998) and Lois Lowry's *The Giver* (1994). However, with these two exceptions, no class read-aloud approached the level of

---

1   Class Read-Aloud is a widely used term that specifies a book read to the entire group. More recently this approach has been dubbed a Focus Unit. The process, as I used it, allowed all children—no matter their reading level or ability—to enjoy more difficult reading material and initiated transactional response dialogue for journals and group discussions. I used the oral delivery to model fluency and comprehension strategies. Students were involved in book selections.

student (and teacher) enthusiasm awarded J. K. Rowling's initial fantasy, *Harry Potter and the Sorcerer's Stone* (1998).

Leaving the classroom a year later to complete my doctoral coursework, during semester breaks I read the second and third books in Rowling's series, *Harry Potter and the Chamber of Secrets* (1999a) and *Harry Potter and the Prisoner of Azkaban* (1999b). Hermione's involvement with the plight of the oppressed house-elves suddenly connected to my growing understanding of Paulo Friere's critical theory; in *Pedagogy of the Oppressed* (1998) Freire suggested reading against the text—to disrupt, to question, to act, and to transform social injustices toward equity. I reflected on how Rowling represents issues of gender, class and race throughout her books and began to "practice" the questioning process. My interest piqued, I purchased two of Scholastic, Inc.'s literature guides to determine the reading approach proffered by the publisher to accompany the books. Upon first inspection the reading activities in the guides revealed a surprisingly superficial study of Rowling's rich content. Friere's hopes for a critical pedagogy were dashed, and there were too few open-ended opportunities for student response to please me.

Thinking back to my own presentation of the book to my fifth graders, I was relieved that I had not followed the rather close-minded approach presented in the guides. Nevertheless, I, too, had stopped short of providing my students the opportunity to perform a deeper reading—to explicate and challenge the author's so-called correct ways of being. In this omission had I sent the message that some children are valued over *others*? This oversight was especially troubling as I, in the role of teacher, had unerringly used my authority to reify the messages presented within the text of children's books that I regularly incorporated into my class curriculum without providing the necessary tools for delving deeper into the authors' sociocultural representations.

Since at this point my own "theoretical underpinnings" were a bit shaken, I harkened back to *Literature as Exploration* written by the highly acclaimed theorist Louise Rosenblatt (1995), whose important contribution to "the literature" is her reader response theory—the belief that the reader is a participant in the reading process, who brings personal experiences and knowledge to the author's message —thus, the reader is involved in meaning-making. Rosenblatt also suggested two bases from which to view reading comprehension for instructional purposes—the efferent (informing) and the aesthetic (entertaining) stances. More recently, a third perspective has been added for consideration—one that is cogently described by Maureen McLaughlin and Glenn DeVoogd (2004) as the "critical stance." It is from this third vantage that the reader explores the author's ideological implications (52–54), troubling and disturbing the text for its messages of power and for the purpose of analyzing and judging the subtleties and connotations of its sociocultural content. For me, this was the missing element, a crucial additive to the instruction of reading comprehension—one that can provide a more meaningful experience for the student who is grappling with the text.

Though this autobiographical glimpse into my past teaching experience is important to situating this work within the context of the classroom, the endeavors of critical theorists fill volumes, and the intricacies involved in political, cultural, and corporate machinations that surround their efforts are difficult to clarify in one brief paper. The hope here is merely to heighten both teacher and student awareness for the cultural and political factors that are involved when the *Harry Potter* books, and others like them, are brought into the classroom. Also crucial for educators is the awareness of the problematic relationship between the corporate publisher and how it influences classroom reading curriculum when a teacher selects and purchases literature guides and implements their suggested reading instructional approach. Toward these fundamental goals the remainder of this work addresses the following assertions: 1) Children's identities are currently corporatized and conventionalized through the establishment of the author's *ideal* within the text of highly popular books, such as the *Harry Potter* series; 2) when these blockbuster books are adopted as textbooks and their literature guides are implemented as curriculum materials, the author's portrayals of the conventional *ideal* are strengthened by their association with school; 3) the content of the *Harry Potter* literature guides, curriculum reduced to commodity by their creator Scholastic, Inc. further reinforces the author's messages through their reliance on questioning techniques that omit critical literacy development; and 4) teachers with heightened awareness of the presence of ideology in highly popular literary texts and in their literature guides can expose the corporatized *ideal* by engaging student readers in critical dialogue—thus, challenging the dominant voices in the text.

Image Building: Representations of the Conventional Ideal in Rowling's Text

Conclusions drawn by a variety of theorists position an author's ideology as an unavoidable part of the writing endeavor (Friere, 1998; Giroux, 2000; Williams, 1977; Zipes, 2001). Thus, an initial step toward analyzing any text is the attempt to locate the author's socio-cultural and political backgrounds (Apol, 1998; Kohl, 1995; Rosenblatt, 1995). In *Should We Burn Babar* Herbert Kohl (1995) asserts that an author is likely to propagandize the text, based on personal political beliefs which, in turn, reflect the author's stance regarding issues of gender, race, and class (4). Through this process the author privileges certain characters and ways of being over others, modeling the culturally acceptable—the way things are—as defined from her personal perspective. According to Elizabeth Heilman in *Harry Potter's World* (2003), children's identities are currently corporatized and conventionalized when situated within the corporate machinations inherent to the publishing industry. The widely marketed book content found in the astoundingly popular *Harry Potter* series may specifically affect a young reader's perceptions of the author's representations of these ways of being as they become the familiar and the acceptable to her readers. Heilman posits,

When narrative text and images become such a pervasive part of the cultural environment they also become part of the identity of people who read and consume the images and narratives. *Harry Potter* then is not just books we read or movies we see or things we buy. The text and images of *Harry Potter* become part of who we are. (2)

In support of Heilman's position, Tammy Turner-Vorbeck (2003) adds that the *Potter* series is as pervasive and worrisome as the Disney Corporation and deserves the same serious attention of concerned educators and parents because childhood represents a "site of enculturation" (16). Childhood, then, is a timely opportunity for corporate advertisers to indoctrinate children with a consumer mentality and for adults to reproduce the ideological codes necessary to carry on the accepted, dominant views of society within the upcoming generation. Turner-Vorbeck also asserts that children who are exposed to the heavily marketed techniques surrounding the blockbuster books are indeed more susceptible to their messages because "cultural values and practices are constructed to appear normal and natural, rendering them beyond question" (16).

Equating Rowling's works to those of Disney, based on their massive appeal and hidden ideological agendas, reveals them as sources of conventionality that perpetuate the status quo, forming a kind of cultural hegemony (Giroux, 1999; Turner-Vorbeck, 2003; Zipes, 2001). Harry Potter, like Disney's heroes, stands as a formidable white, male hero for the good against, in his case, the dark Lord Voldemort, who is predictably the very essence of evil. Potter and the denizens of his magical world—friend and foe alike —could easily inhabit a Hogwarts School of Witchcraft and Wizardry that is comfortably nestled within the hyperreal borders of Disneyland, where Disney fantasy characters—*The Sword and the Stone's* Arthur to Mordred, *The Lion King's* Simba to Scar, *Peter Pan's* Peter to Hook, *The Black Cauldron's* Taran to the Horned King, and other assorted princes to their individual nemeses—have taken on the burdens of heroism and good deeds as they defeat evil with each viewing—virtual Davids facing down their Goliaths.

Potter's cohabitation with such an august group has become a corporatized fairy tale of its own, establishing Rowling and the books' characters as popular cultural icons irrevocably woven into the fabric of Western society (Heilman, 2003; Turner-Vorbeck, 2003; Zipes, 2001), while expanding the notions of that society to the global community.

Understanding the maneuverings found within the construct of assumed cultural power structures reveals its hegemonic nature and unearths the ideological assumptions that are interred in the author's text. When multiple works by the author are investigated, power positions become embedded into the fictive societal schema, replicating the author's cultural views and political positions. Locating these replications is then revelatory to the values and images perpetuated throughout the author's writing. A worrisome consideration surfaces with the realization that when these blockbuster books are adopted as curriculum materials, they take on the role of textbook, and the author's views are legitimized by their association with school.

Rowling's Blockbusters Become Textbooks and Scholastic's Literature Guides Become "Fast Food" Curriculum

In *Understanding Curriculum* authors William Pinar, William Reynolds, Patrick Slattery, and Peter Taubman (1996) address the issues of power implicit within this construct and turn the conversation from the ideological content of the books themselves to their new role as textbook and the significance of this classification:

> The essence of schooling revolves around what young people do in school [which is to] work with curriculum materials.... More than any other curriculum material in school classrooms the textbook tends to represent the totality of the school curriculum for many parents and other lay observers such as politicians.... Debates over textbooks are debates over power. (616–17, 780)

Thus, control of textbook content ultimately determines which societal meanings and practices are to be privileged and which are to be ignored. In *Critical Pedagogy and Cyberspace*, theorists Colin Lankshear, Michael Peters, and Michele Knobel (1996) extend this troubling concept and suggest that textbooks present, reinforce, and maintain the dominant ideology:

> In the text-dominated school curriculum...reality is represented as fixed, transcendent and "given," immutable and "natural," rather than as contingent, historical, constantly in the process of being made and remade and, as such, capable of being remade in quite different forms from those which currently prevail. (166)

With the socio-political stakes so high, it is unsurprising that discourse generated around the establishment of the best reading textbooks for children in the United States is ongoing between traditional-minded positivists and more broad-minded critical theorists (Apple, 1998; Apple & Christian-Smith, 1991). Reading researcher Alan Block (1995) discussed this same issue over a decade ago in his important work *Occupied Reading*, in which he asserts that the central issue continues to involve the sociopolitical struggle for *who* defines knowledge via the control of the ideological messages presented in children's reading books. In the introduction to Block's book, critical theorists Joe Kincheloe and Shirley Steinberg (1995) point out that most reading instructional styles in this country have evolved through "empirically based scientism and play a supporting role in the establishment of an expert-guided, patriarchal social order" (xii).

Block, Kincheloe, and Steinberg rightly envision reading as a liberating act in which meaning is multiplicitous and negotiated through the world of the reader. However, the favored approach to reading instruction currently takes a more positivist position reducing the act of reading to a linear, skills-oriented process in which segmented and disconnected bits of information are tested and retested to prove the test taker can or cannot read. Tests are often based on one-answer questions, giving little credence to the social context in which a child produces meaning through a reflective process involved in what Kincheloe and Steinberg (1995) call "a dynamic dance between reader and text" (xiv). Searching for the main idea of a long absent author is placing priority on knowledge discovery over knowledge production. Block (1995) charges that by controlling the "how of reading," one manipulates "what is being read," and transports the purpose of reading from "meaningful thought" to "a means to achieve thought" (6). Thus, the dispute among theorists concerns more than text content and the format in which the text is published; contention also arises as to which instructional approach will be privileged over another. These vital questions implicate publishers as purveyors of knowledge and partners in curriculum making.

Seemingly unfazed by such weighty issues, publishers have long seen schools as consumer sites through the marketing of their textbooks (Apple & Christian-Smith, 1991), and in recent years, they have expanded the education market by packaging and selling class sets of children's books. By marketing easy-to-follow teaching guides that reinforce the author's messages more directly to students through their adherence to a linear and less reflective teaching style (Apple, 1998; Block, 1995), publishers enlist teachers as unsuspecting participants in the complex story of cultural politics that currently surrounds reading instruction (Apple & Christian-Smith 15).

Scholastic, Inc. is in the business of selling traditional textbooks, but it also has made millions of dollars selling trade books to teachers and to school systems. Taking a path of *more* resistance, some teachers gladly take on the extra planning burden because of a strong belief in the power and the importance of *real* books to motivate children to read. Time-beleaguered, they look for easy-to-follow "teacher instructional guides" to enhance their book teaching and solve the learning dilemmas posed by using multiple titles of books in one school year. If there is a need, the publisher will fill it,[1] and Scholastic, Inc. unhesitatingly blunders into the realm of reading instructional methodology, adopting an un-credentialed role as curriculum writer and peddling its "fast-food" curriculum to well-intentioned classroom teachers.

A final concern becomes evident once the teacher selects the book and purchases the instructional guide. The student's choice is suspended, and three agendas are served—the teacher's personal motivation for inclusion of the book, the publisher's incentive for producing the book, and the author's motivation for representations of her own biases and prejudices in the content. Thus, the decisions made by a long line of adults are privileged over the interests of the child reader who becomes a member of a command audience—one that is, in effect, captive to the classroom environment. As the author's message, perpetuated by the commercialization of the blockbuster books, is validated to a greater extent through its connection to the institution of schooling (Apple & Christian-Smith, 1991), and the instructional approach, presented in the accompanying guides, is sanctioned only by the publisher (McGinley, Conley, & White, 2000), in my estimation, the vulnerability of the child reader—individually or collectively viewed—is intensified by the manipulations of corporate enterprise that has expanded rapidly from the child's private life into the broader venue of her/his school environment (Giroux, 2000; Steinberg & Kincheloe, 1995).

---

1   According to a report posted at their Web site and produced by Quality Education Data, Inc. (2007), teachers directly select and spend over $1.8 billion dollars of their personal and professional funds per school year on classroom materials, with 81% purchasing workbook materials and 98% purchasing materials for lessons, making them an attractive consumer target.

Critiquing the Reading Instructional Approaches Presented in the Guides

As both products and producers of literate culture, the conceptual frames put forth by book guides...represent a sort of new kid on the literature-reading block...[one that] has the power to persuade readers [and their teachers] to see the approaches endorsed by the book industry as the natural way of proceeding with books. (McGinley *et al.*, 2000, 213)

Critique of the *Harry Potter Literature Guides* directly questions the instructional approach put forward by Linda Ward Beech and Scholastic, Inc. as the "right way" to teach Rowling's content. Because a work cannot be detached from its author, it was crucial to begin any critical analysis by establishing the author's voice. However, Scholastic, Inc. has successfully obfuscated the search for Linda Ward Beech. All efforts to locate biographical information through the company, including her academic or professional credentials for writing reading instructional curriculum, have been denied. Initial e-mails to Scholastic, Inc. resulted in one brief response from an employee named Virginia Dooley, who replied to my written request for information in 2003 with this statement:

Beech is a New York City-based writer who writes for both teachers and children. Linda volunteers to lead a reading club in a New York City public school. She has written more than 30 books for teachers and more than 20 books for children.

To this reply I sent a second e-mail to Ms. Dooley specifically requesting information as to the academic credentials of this author; this appeal resulted in an additional copy of the above statement. More recent contact efforts have produced a generic address for "Scholastic Authors" with a suggestion to write to Scholastic, Inc. in care of Ms. Beech; the letter will then be forwarded to her. According to an employee named Amy, there is no guarantee that Beech will answer the letter; so far, she has not. The worrisome result of these rather odd communications is that academic or educational credentials are, in effect, denied the booklets because Scholastic, Inc. refuses to provide either university affiliation or professional background information related to their rather prolific author.

In fact, it is as if Scholastic, Inc. has deliberately set out to divorce Ms. Beech from her own work, since her name is listed once in the "small print" at the bottom of the inside title page, while the front cover of each guide boldly features the familiar *Harry Potter* book cover art immediately followed by the words "by J. K. Rowling," leading consumers to believe that Rowling is the author of both her books and the study guides created to accompany them. Not only capitalizing on her name recognition, the assumption that Rowling wrote the guides may also lend pedagogical credibility to the works based on Rowling's past career as an English teacher.

Aside from the eye-catching art and the attempt to present the internationally known Rowling as their author, Scholastic concludes the cover design by providing an emboldened list of contents that comprise educational buzz words, such as "Assessment Strategies, Reproducibles, and Cross-Curricular Activities for Students of All Learning Styles"—perfect for plugging into lesson plans that are regularly surveilled by principals and system supervisors. The back covers of the booklets are used as advertising sites to hawk the additional *Harry Potter Literature Guides*.

Overall, the small package is particularly appealing to teachers who may be put off by a more complicated or overlong presentation of written material, the slim 16-page booklets (24 pages for the *Goblet of Fire*) also come with a "colorful teaching poster" and a relatively inexpensive price ($5.95). In the final assessment of their outside appearance, the attractive cover art, the promises expressed in teacher-friendly jargon and the highly recognizable names "Harry Potter" and "J. K. Rowling" ensure that these manuals will stand out among other published guides on the retail shelves of local teacher stores.

Inside the booklets their appearances change dramatically to a drab monochromatic look incorporating a black, gray, and white design with the print arranged in text boxes, placed under headings, and enumerated into lists presumably to facilitate the teacher's quick perusal of the material. Beech provides a table of contents that reveals four activity-driven sections dedicated to pre-reading, reading, summarizing, and completing reproducibles. In the first section, titled "Before Reading the Book," she delineates the following: Summary (a short synopsis of the entire book), Characters (People, Ghosts, Elves, Animals), About the Author (a biographical sketch of Rowling), Literature Connections (other books by Rowling), Vocabulary (extensive lists from 45 to 60 words), Notes about Genre (definition of fantasy), and Getting Started (strategies for introducing the book). Under the heading "Exploring the Book," Beech sorts a dozen additional sets of instructional practices to be implemented during the actual reading of the book and accompanies them with a plethora of basic recall and fact-related questions.

Far too brief to offer any valuable information to the teacher, the plot summaries ("What Happens") are perhaps unintentionally misleading, as Beech attempts to summarize 400- to 1200-page books with intricate plot lines in less than a half page of print. In this sentence Beech sums up what Rowling took seventeen chapters and 309 pages to tell in *Sorcerer's Stone*:

Harry Potter lives in the cupboard under the stairs at his relatives' home until he receives letters inviting him to the Hogwarts School of Witchcraft and Wizardry. (2000d, 3)

A similar problem arises for Beech regarding the specificity of her answer key for the many short answer questions ("Questions to Talk About"). By demanding the one *correct answer* Beech disregards the complexities inherent to Rowling's works and minimizes the child's possibly broader understanding of the context within which the query is based. Examples of this limiting and narrow approach are plentiful:

Why is the Fat Lady so upset?
Answer: *Sirius Black slashes her when she won't let him in.* (2000c, 8)

In fact, there are several reasons for this character's actions, some of which involve stereotypical gender issues that would perhaps be far more significant to a discussion than the shallow response couched by Beech. In another missed opportunity:

Why can't Harry control himself in front of Aunt Marge?
Answer: *She says mean and untrue things about his parents.* (2000c, 6)

Taking a broader view this question could initiate discussions involving class issues because Aunt Marge assumes an elitist position when dealing with Harry, who she sees as a lower-class individual due to his parentage; to Marge's calculations he should work to overcome his inherited flaws and conform to the "right" standards —hers.

For critically thinking teachers there are two particularly significant opportunities for turning Beech's questions "inside out" to better interrogate critical issues residing within. In the section marked "Personal Response" the following samples are particularly relevant to dialogic interaction:

1. Is Hermione right to try to liberate the house-elves when they don't really want to be liberated and are happy as things stand? (Beech, 2000b, 11)

This topic offers the chance to look at socio-political positions, regarding both historical and current events: Are the house-elves happy? Should we who are free foist our love of freedom on those who are not? What makes us think that they are happy unliberated? These more relevant questions can move discourse from the fantasy world set in the book to a more serious yet timely discussion of America's role in present-day, real-world events.

2. Slytherin wanted Hogwarts to be a school for Purebloods, a school that excluded those who weren't like him. How does his attitude compare with real prejudices people have had throughout history? (2000a, p. 9)

Certainly, a teacher who desires to elevate discussions through the use of critical reading strategies might easily build upon the points raised here and move them toward historical exploration of slavery and the Civil Rights Movement in this country; or, taking a different tack, students could explore issues of race relevant to World War II and Hitler's Germany.

Unfortunately, Beech stops short of offering any guidance or suggestions toward extending these questions into broader areas, thus missing important opportunities for teaching and learning.

Extended projects aimed at the exploration of Rowling's works and intended to culminate the study of the books are also minimal and equally disappointing. Immediately following the overused comprehension checks suggested by Beech, the teacher finds two additional pages dedicated to "Summarizing the Book, Putting it All Together," in which there are ideas for class, group, partner, and individual activities. Assigned tasks are followed by a set of four questions that can be used by the teacher to format a generic rubric for assessing any or all of the recommended completed projects. Among the more suitable suggestions accumulated from the four guides are creating a yearbook for the Hogwarts School, making the book scenes into a comic strip, making brochures for Hogwarts Academy, designing a class schedule for Harry, interviewing book characters, making calendars of Hogwarts events, and illustrating dramatic scenes.

In addition, the promised Cross-Curricular Activities include ideas for logic, drama, art, and music projects added to the more usual activities involving social studies, language arts, and math. Finally, reaching the end of the guides, the "Student Reproducible" activity sheets offer teachers an easy lesson for filling a day's class time—one that can be notated directly into their lesson plans and keyed to the curriculum guides. In large part, the reproducibles' activities support the kind of teaching that allows students to explore story elements and use graphic organizers in cooperative groups. These reproducibles, mostly graphic organizers using compare and contrast type activities, offered one of the few bright spots in the guides; however, the activities continue to fall short of a critically informed understanding of the books' content.

In final assessment the packaging, format, size, cost, and use of professional terminology that is easily penciled into waiting lesson plan forms make the guides attractive to teachers who are focused on meeting goals and objectives set by many state public school education departments and assessed through national standardized testing procedures. However, by emphasizing a linear, skills-based response to literature, the Scholastic guides, crafted by Linda Ward Beech, completely deny a critical approach to the *Potter* books and take on an odd mix of positivist and response theories. Though the guides fail to critically analyze or question Rowling's ideological representations, as tie-in commodities dependent on a direct connection to the name *Harry Potter* they are a marketing success.

Adopting a Critical Literacy and Mitigating the Corporatized "Ideal"

My own view of good practice involves a critical style of reading pedagogy—one that arms students with the power to read disruptively—to question—to doubt—to reach a deeper level of understanding from which they are better equipped to deny privileged voices dominating most text. As an educator I believe that highly popular children's fantasy, like that found in Rowling's engaging *Harry Potter* books, holds an especially strong appeal for children in the classroom environment, delighting them in its novel approach, encouraging them to explore and deconstruct basic human conditions. The incorporation of such fantasy, when joined with the dialogic process, inherent to critical literacy, offers a promise of abatement from ideological hegemony through the awareness of the reader's political, economic, and social "situatedness" in the world; it also offers the freedom for developing critical strategies to oppose messages in printed text while demystifying their validity and questioning their views of the culturally accepted model of the corporate idyllic. To disorder the norm is to engage with the fantasy in an active form of readership —a refusal of the passive role. It is not destructive to those aesthetic powers enlivened through literature, but rather approaches it fully aware.

Critical literacy then brings this opportunity to children in the classroom through the incorporation of popular text, refocusing the rather beleaguered interruptions toward multicultural and gender education to a place of assumed existence—one that usurps former dependencies on the monocultural, dominant views, replacing them with an embedded assumption of diversity. Envisioned here is what Lisa Delpit (1995) calls for in her landmark book *Other People's Children*—not just a tolerance for diversity but an acceptance of diversity—the development of a generalizable process in which the author's words are accepted or discarded based on their validity after weighing in on critical scales.

In adopting this view, multicultural and gender education are subsumed seamlessly into the context of curricula in its entirety and not limited to a month to celebrate women or Black History, or to a day set aside to recognize a Hispanic battle. These issues do not belong on a shelf packed away in the January, February, or May theme boxes. Since multicultural and gender concerns are evident within our daily teaching environments, it is reasonable to conclude that they *ought* to be present within our teaching materials and teaching practices as well. Meeting these important issues head on through popular literary text is one way to ensure our approach remains relevant, and our attention remains constant.

A Final Thought...

Through continued efforts to investigate the effects of consumption on a young reader's identity formation, the most pertinent question may be who will champion children against the dark lord of advertising? Who will guard against the Death Eaters of a child's acceptance of *self*? Ironically, Harry Potter may stand once again as that hero, backed up by classroom teachers, joined in a just cause of heightened awareness through the use of dialogue. Elizabeth Heilman (2003b) contends that "We can talk back to Harry Potter" (9); I would add that we can also talk back to corporate enterprise, through critical engagement with Rowling's text and others like it.

References

Agee, J. (2000). What is effective literature instruction? A study of experienced high school English teachers in differing grade-and ability-level classes. *Journal of Literacy Research* 32, 303–48.

Allington, R. (2002). *Big brother and the National Reading Curriculum: How ideology trumped evidence.* Portsmouth, NH: Heineman.

Apple, M. (1998). The culture and commerce of the textbook. In L. Beyer & M. Apple (eds.), *The curriculum: Problems, politics and possibilities* (2nd ed.) (pp. 5–32). Albany, NY: SUNY Press.

Apple, M., & Christian-Smith, L. K. (eds.) (1991). *The politics of the textbook.* London: Routledge.

Apol, L. (1998). But what does this have to do with kids: Literary theory and children's literature in the teacher education classroom. *Journal of Children's Literature*, 24 (2), 32–46.

Beech, L. (2000a). *Scholastic literature guide: Harry Potter and the Chamber of Secrets by J. K. Rowling.* New York: Scholastic.

Beech, L. (2000b). *Scholastic literature guide: Harry Potter and the Goblet of Fire by J. K. Rowling.* New York: Scholastic.

Beech, L. (2000c). *Scholastic literature guide: Harry Potter and the Prisoner of Azkaban by J. K. Rowling.* New York: Scholastic.

Beech, L. (2000d). *Scholastic literature guide: Harry Potter and the Sorcerer's Stone by J. K. Rowling.* New York: Scholastic.

Block, A. (1995). *Occupied reading: Critical foundations for an ecological theory.* New York: Garland.

Block, A. (1997). Reading children's magazines: Kinderculture and popular culture. In S. Steinberg & J. Kincheloe (eds.), *Kinderculture: The corporate construction of childhood* (pp. 153–64). Boulder, CO: Westview.

Freire, P. (1998). *Pedagogy of the oppressed* (M. B. Ramos, trans.). New York: Continuum.

Giroux, H. (2000). *Impure acts: The practical politics of cultural studies.* New York: Routledge.

Heilman, E. (2003). Introduction: Fostering critical insight through multidisciplinary perspectives. In E. Heilman (ed.), *Harry Potter's world: Multidisciplinary critical perspectives* (pp. 1–12). New York: RoutledgeFalmer.

Kohl, H. (1995). *Should we burn Babar: Essays on children's literature and the power of stories.* New York: The New Press.

Lankshear, C., Peters, M., and Knobel, M. (1996). Critical pedagogy and cyberspace. In H. Giroux, C. Lankshear, P. McLaren, & P. Peters (eds.), *Counternarratives: Cultural studies and critical pedagogies in postmodern spaces* (149–88). London: Routledge.

McGinley, W., Conley, K., and White, J. W. (2000). Pedagogy for a few: Book club discussion guides and the modern book industry as literature teacher. *Journal of Adolescent and Adult Literacy* 44 (3), 204–14.

McLaughlin, M. and DeVoogd, G. (2004). Critical literacy as comprehension: Expanding reader response. *Journal of Adolescent and Adult Literacy* 48 (1), 52–62.

Pinar, W., Reynolds, W., Slattery, P. and Taubman, P. M. (1996). *Understanding Curriculum: An introduction to the study of historical and contemporary curriculum discourses.* New York: Peter Lang.

Quality education data. Teacher buying behavior. Retrieved 15 May 2007. <http://www.qeddata.com/MarketKno/ResearchReports/TeacherBuying.aspx>.

Rosenblatt, L. M. (1995). *Literature as exploration* (5th ed.). New York: The Modern Language Association of America.

Rowling, J. (1998). *Harry Potter and the Sorcerer's Stone.* Jefferson City, MO: Scholastic.

Rowling, J. (1999a). *Harry Potter and the Chamber of Secrets.* Jefferson City, MO: Scholastic.

Rowling, J. (1999b). *Harry Potter and the Prisoner of Azkaban.* Jefferson City, MO: Scholastic.

Rowling, J. (2000). *Harry Potter and the Goblet of Fire.* Jefferson City, MO: Scholastic.

Rowling, J. (2004). *Harry Potter and the Order of the Phoenix.* Jefferson City, MO: Scholastic.

Rowling, J. (2006). *Harry Potter and the Half-Blood Prince.* Jefferson City, MO: Scholastic.

Steinberg, S. and Kincheloe, J. (eds.). (1997). *Kinderculture: The corporate construction of childhood.* Boulder, CO: Westview.

Turner-Vorbeck, T. (2003). Pottermania: Good, clean fun or cultural hegemony. In E. Heilman (ed.), *Harry Potter's world: Multidisciplinary critical perspectives* (pp. 13–24). New York: RoutledgeFalmer.

Zipes, J. (2001). The phenomenon of Harry Potter, or why all the talk. In J. Zipes, *Sticks and stones: The troublesome success of children's literature from slovenly Peter to* Harry Potter (pp. 170–90). New York: Routledge.

The *Harry Potter* World as Existential Inspiration for Gifties

Paula Christensen
Northwestern State University of Louisiana

Gifted students are often referred to as the *brightest and best* and the best natural resources of the state. This can put a tremendous burden on gifted students. Gifted students often feel alienated from the rest of the world, and then to be told that they must be the best in all areas increases this alienation. It is also a myth to believe that gifted students can be left to their own devices to succeed in the world just because they are smart. Just like any other child, gifted children need guidance. I have a passion for working with gifted students because I would rather that they grow up to be Dumbledore than Voldemort. Of course, as will be explained later in this paper, I actually hope each gifted child will not become either Dumbledore or Voldemort but rather find her own purpose in life, grow up to reach his potential, find her passion, and be a productive citizen of the world (i.e., do good and fight evil).

Although gifted students are not the only students who have become fans of the *Harry Potter* books, because the gifties think and feel in ways different from others, they may find existential inspiration from the *Harry Potter* world. This paper will delineate gifted students and their educational needs, briefly describe major tenets of existentialism, and provide information related to how the *Harry Potter* world may be existential inspiration for gifties.

Who Are the Gifties?

"Gifties" is a term applied to many students identified as gifted in school. But before they receive the label of gifted, gifties often recognize their differences. Gifted students commonly have characteristics that distinguish them. Specifically, gifted students often think and feel in ways that are different from other students; therefore, they also require educational programs that are different than offered in general education classrooms. As one giftie noted:

We are not *normal* and we know it; it can be fun sometimes but not funny always. We tend to be much more sensitive than other people. Intensive self-analysis, self-criticism, and the inability to recognize that we have limits make us despondent. In fact, most times our self-searching leaves us more discombobbled than we were at the outset. (American Association for Gifted Children as cited in Silverman, 1993, p. 17)

The quotation above illustrates how gifties recognize their differences, especially in the realm of feelings and identity development. The self-analysis that gifted students engage in is a natural part of identity development for all adolescents, but what sets them apart is that their analysis happens at a younger age or in more depth than the average student. The gifties' manner of thought and feeling may be even more in-depth than many adult patterns of thinking and feeling. This, of course, contributes to the gifted students' being misunderstood and not being provided with educational programming that meets their needs (Silverman, 1993).

Think Differently

There are many characteristics that describe how gifted students think differently. Not every gifted student has every characteristic. Primarily, gifted students think more abstractly and, again, at an earlier age than average students. Their thought processes are often very complex; they acquire sophisticated understandings with ease in learning. Gifted students think divergently, problem-solving by generating numerous and unique solutions. Divergent thinking is part of the creative process. Some gifted students are adept in creative thinking, whereas others may be more proficient in critical thinking, and some may be very capable in both types of thinking. Creative thinking relies on a tolerance for ambiguity, risk-taking, problem-finding, and working with analogy, in order to develop creative products. On the other hand, critical thinkers seek reasons, try to be well-informed, consider the total situation and look for alternatives. Critical thinking is part of the analytical process. Gifted students may be more analytical in their thinking, which includes gathering facts, comparing and contrasting ideas, researching issues, and making decisions (Maker & Nielson, 1996).

Feel Differently

The ways that gifties feel differently include their intensity, sensitivity, excitability, entelechy. The behaviors that arise from these traits are what set gifted students apart. The gifted students' intensity probably affects their different thinking and feeling more than anything else. Gifted students approach learning and life with an intensity or passion. The intensity trait may be manifested in a behavior in which the giftie becomes preoccupied with an interest to the exclusion of everything else until they have learned everything they possibly can about that interest (i.e., live, eat, sleep, and breathe that particular interest). The intensity in feeling means that behaviorally they are *very sad* or *very happy*; feelings are extreme. Depth of feeling characterizes their sensitivity. Sensitivity is closely related to intensity, as gifted students may think with their passions and feelings. Excitability includes an intensity that includes a high energy level and high arousal of the central nervous system. These students have a high need for stimulation and novelty; they may appear hyperactive but are actually able to concentrate incredibly well when appropriately challenged. The trait of entelechy relates to the gifted students' inner strength and self-determination. They are highly motivated to achieve self-actualization and make their own destiny (Lovecky, 1993).

Educational Needs of the Gifted

Based on the characteristic descriptions of the gifties, it should be evident that they may require programs that are different from those offered in general education classrooms. The gifted should be helped to reach their potential, and there may be expectations that they will be the leaders of tomorrow, but education for the gifted should be appropriate for each student such that the learning environment is a safe haven for exploration and facilitates development of student-directed learning. The process of learning should match the ways that gifted students think and feel differently. Because gifted students think more abstractly, creatively, divergently, critically, and analytically, the process of learning should include content that is abstract, varied, complex, and interdisciplinary. Their thought processes are already complex, so their learning should be presented in a complex manner across disciplines. Learning should encompass higher levels of thinking, open-endedness, discovery, creativity, critical thinking, and group interaction. The process should also include appropriate variety and pacing for the individual learner. The process of learning should match the characteristics of the gifted student. The end products that students develop should include addressing real problems for real audiences and indicate transformation and evaluation. Real problems for real audiences indicate that students should develop products that would be evaluated by experts in the field. For example, if a student produces a play, a drama critic should evaluate the play (Maker & Nielson, 1996).

While it is important to meet the needs of gifted students related to their cognitive traits, at the same time, the learning environment should address the social and emotional needs of the gifted. The gifted students' feelings push their passions. They have a fire under them to learn but many educational systems put out the fires. If Harry were told not to capture the Snitch or Angelina not to score in a game of Quidditch because it might hurt the self-esteem of the other team, it would be laughable. But every day in school, gifted students are told not to move forward academically because they might hurt the self-esteem of the other students in the class; to hold back until the other students catch up. This type of environment often squelches the gifted students' natural passion for learning and may lead them to unhealthy, destructive behaviors instead of healthy, constructive behaviors. With the appropriate educational environment, ultimately, gifted students will become responsible for their learning which will lead them to discover their own direction and purpose in life.

Existentialism

Although scholars have debated whether existentialism is truly a philosophy or a theoretical basis for psychotherapy because of some attitudes that there is no unifying concept related to existentialism, existentialist writers and thinkers do share some views or beliefs related to the human condition. Specifically, a brief summary of the concepts related to existentialism would indicate that existentialism addresses finding purpose and deals with issues of discovering meaning in life and dealing with death. Reality consists of living based on choices and being responsible for one's life. Finding meaning regardless of your life circumstances, taking responsibility for the purpose and direction of your life, and dealing with your and others' mortality is no easy endeavor, but life cannot be fully lived unless these issues are faced (Frankl, 1963; Yalom, 1980). Existential philosophy can be one way to direct gifted individuals to reach their potential.

Literature as Existential Inspiration

Literature provides inspiration for readers to find meaning and purpose in life through a connection with the story and relationship with the characters. Literature provides opportunities to relate to characters in two ways: identification and disassociation. Identification means that the reader wants to be like the character and/or is like the character. Disassociation means that the reader does not like the character and/or would not want to be like the character. Literature also allows readers to link specific themes in stories to their lives.

The *Harry Potter* world provides rich content and context that can provide inspiration for gifties. Many readers find inspiration in the *Harry Potter* novels; however, unique revelations may be offered to the gifted student. Specifically, a group of middle-school gifted students shared about how the *Harry Potter* world helps them in making choices, finding purpose, and being responsible for their lives.

First, in relation to identification and disassociation to characters in the *Harry Potter* books, gifted students have indicated identification with Harry, Hermione, Ron, Neville, Luna, Ginny, Fred and George, and Cedric. They have indicated identification with the adults Hagrid, McGonagall, and Dumbledore. The gifted students have also indicated identification with Dumbledore's Army. The gifted students have indicated disassociation with "He Who Must Not Be Named" or Voldemort, Malfoy, Crabbe, Goyle, Wormtail, and Dolores Umbridge.

The gifted students shared the reasons they liked the *Harry Potter* books and what the books provided for them. The *Harry Potter* books provide a reluctant hero, suspense, the element of surprise, advanced language, fantasy and imagination, and wonderful characterization. The students indicated that they felt they understood some of the characters as well as they understood some of their friends. The reluctant hero status of Harry Potter and some of his friends was especially cogent to some of the gifties, as they related feeling like reluctant heroes based on being identified as gifted or, worse, called the *brightest and best*, with the intended expectations that went along with that phrase.

The gifted students related specific themes from the *Harry Potter* stories that held the most meaning for them, related to what was important for each of their lives, and that were the most inspiring to them. Although there are many more themes to the stories, the following themes were the most referenced by the students: (a) being helpful is important; (b) everything written is not always true, learn how to judge right; (c) believe in yourself, have a positive mindset, have confidence; (d) you need to fight against that which is harmful or evil, be brave; (e) stand up for what is right; (f) friends will have your back; and (g) face your problems.

The themes were not listed in any order of importance because the students indicated that all of the themes were equally important. The students revealed that these themes represented for them the existential inspiration that would help them in making choices, finding purpose, and being responsible for their lives. Of particular importance to the gifted students was Dumbledore's recurring message about "choices not ability," which makes the difference in a person's life. Based on these inspiring themes, there are attitudes and conduct that would help the gifted students reach their potential.

Potential of Excellence

Existentialism is about finding purpose, and for the gifted students part of their purpose and passion is the striving for excellence—to do and be their best based on choices, not just their ability. They will not become Dumbledore; they will each become their own person. The *Harry Potter* world as existential inspiration for the gifties to reach their potential includes (a) engaging the power of imagination; (b) embracing values as the cornerstone to decision-making; (c) finding passion; (d) making choices; (e) being responsible for self and others; and (f) following your star.

Of course, the information shared by this particular group of middle-school gifted students cannot necessarily be generalized to the gifted population at large nor to the greater *Harry Potter* fandom. However, the insights offered by these gifted students do indicate how the *Harry Potter* world can provide existential inspiration to gifties.

References

Bassham, G. (2004). The prophecy-driven life: Foreknowledge and freedom at Hogwarts. In D. Baggett & S. E. Klein (eds.), *Harry Potter and philosophy: If Aristotle ran Hogwarts* (pp. 213–26). Peru, IL: Carus Publishing Company.

Frankl, V. E. (1963). *Man's search for meaning: An introduction to logotherapy* (rev. ed.). New York: Simon & Schuster, Inc.

Kern, E. M. (2003). *The wisdom of Harry Potter: What our favorite hero teaches us about moral choices.* Amherst, NY: Prometheus Books.

Kierkegaard, S. (1940). *For self-examination* (trans. from Danish to English by E. & H. Hong). Minneapolis: Augsburg Publishing House.

Lovecky, D. V. (1993). The quest for meaning: Counseling issues with gifted children and adolescents. In L. K. Silverman (ed.), *Counseling the gifted & talented* (pp. 29–51). Denver: Love Publishing Company.

Maker, C. J., & Nielson, A. B. (1996). *Curriculum development and teaching strategies for gifted learners* (2nd ed.). Austin, TX: PRO-ED, Inc.

Silverman, L. K. (1993). The gifted individual. In L. K. Silverman (ed.), *Counseling the gifted & talented* (pp. 3–28). Denver, CO: Love Publishing Company.

Yalom, I. D. *Existential psychotherapy.* (1980). New York: Basic Books.

RISING ABOVE SITUATIONAL ETHICS: RAISING PHOENIXES IN A WORLD OF CROWS

Gina Burkart
University of Northern Iowa

While reading the *Harry Potter* stories with my children, I became amazed at the deep and moral discussions that developed in the middle of our reading. As the characters struggled with tough choices, made the wrong choice, and suffered the natural consequences, my children would stop me and share their insights. Often, their reactions to the characters led to stories of their own struggles. In the characters, they saw themselves. And through this, I gained a better understanding of my children and their daily struggles, and gained an opportunity to guide them in their moral decisions and development. The depth and complexity of the characters in the *Harry Potter* series provides us with many opportunities to discuss ethical situations. Lawrence Kohlberg has concluded that discussing such ethical situations with each other and our children advances us through the levels of moral development. In essence, in a society where our role models make pragmatic decisions based on the situation, we can help our children to rise to a higher level of moral reasoning and become Phoenixes in a World of Crows.

Lawrence Kohlberg based his stages of moral development on Jean Piaget's *Stages of Cognitive Development* (1965). In looking at Piaget's studies, we gain a picture of how children progress in their cognitive thought processes. Piaget's stages show that in the span from birth to eleven years of age, children grow from identifying objects to abstract thought. Since Harry Potter has his eleventh birthday in the early chapters of *Sorcerer's Stone* (book one), we can think of him in the later stage of cognitive development and thus in

472

the early stages of abstract reasoning. From my experiences in working with children in the elementary and middle-school classrooms, I would also generally say that eleven is the age when most children begin reading the *Harry Potter* series. So, according to Piaget, like Harry, they are also beginning to grow in abstract thought processes.

By abstract thought, I mean an attempt to make sense of non-tangible concepts and emotions such as love, anger, and fear. For example, at the end of the first book, Dumbledore tells Harry that he was saved by and continues to be protected by the love of his mother. This becomes pivotal to the plot of the books, and in book six, we see that Harry still struggles to understand how love protects him, as he responds to Dumbledore, "I have love. Big deal!" But this is a big deal, as Lawrence Kohlberg (1975) builds his *Stages of Moral Development* on Piaget's *Stages of Cognitive Development*. According to Kohlberg, one needs abstract reasoning and thought to reach the highest level of moral reasoning.

Kohlberg (1975) breaks down the stages in the following manner:

Level One: Pre-Conventional Stage

Stage 1: Punishment/Reward

Physical consequences determine good and bad behavior. Rewards indicate good; punishments signify bad. Adults are seen as judges and enforcers of good and bad.

Stage 2: Self Interests

Thinking and decision making is pragmatic and businesslike. For example, "You do this for me, and I will do this for you." I call this *situational ethics*.

Level Two: Conventional Morality

Stage 3: Peer Approval

Good behavior earns group approval; thus, behavior is guided with the question, "What will others think of me if I do this?"

Stage 4: Law and Order

Behavior affects the larger society; thus, decisions should and behavior should be governed by the law. Law takes precedence over family and friends.

Level Three: Post-Conventional Morality

Stage 5: Personal Values and Opinions

Behavior adheres to laws and rules only if they are good for everyone. The rights of the individual must be protected, and laws should be evaluated and changed for the good of society. One should not follow blindly.

Stage 6: The Golden Rule/Categorical Imperative

Behavior follows abstract, self-chosen principles that seek justice, equal rights, and respect for human life and dignity.

In mapping out these stages, Kohlberg (1975) also made the assumption that most children progress through the stages sequentially. None of the stages can be skipped. He also found that few adults ever advance beyond stage four. Additionally, he concluded that discussing and considering ethical situations helps children and adults to progress and advance through the stages of moral development. I have found literature such as *Harry Potter* to be the fertile ground that parents and educators need for helping children consider ethical and moral situations.

In discussing Harry's decisions and dilemmas with my own children and with children in elementary and middle school classrooms, I have found windows into our children's lives. When they begin talking about Harry, they begin talking about themselves. In talking about what Harry should do or should have done, they discover what they should do or might do in a similar situation. Additionally, it provides parents and educators the opportunity to see how our children are thinking, struggling, and progressing in moral development. By understanding and recognizing the cognitive and moral stages, we can use the character's dilemmas as we guide them and provide opportunities for them to advance to the higher levels of moral development. Rather than staying stagnant at stage four, adults and children can help each other push toward stage six —the highest level of moral development.

I shared one of my most memorable experiences with this type of moral exploration in my book *A Parent's Guide to Harry Potter* (Burkart, 2005). While I was reading *Harry Potter and the Chamber of Secrets* aloud, my daughter stopped me in the scene where Malfoy calls Hermione a mudblood. In an agitated voice, she remarked, "Why can't people get along? Why do they care if people are different?" (54). From there we began a moral discussion about racial discrimination (documented more thoroughly on p. 54 of my book), where my daughter eventually shared what was really troubling her. In her daycare, one of her friends was being ridiculed because of her race. I would not have learned about nor had a chance to help my daughter work through that tough situation had we not been reading *Harry Potter* that night.

In helping her decide the best way to handle the situation, we worked through Ron's handling of the situation. In defense of Hermione, he acted violently out of anger and turned his wand on Malfoy. As a result, Malfoy's attitude never changed, and Ron received the negative consequence of belching up slugs. This showed my daughter that verbally or violently lashing out in defense of her friend would not solve the problem. We decided that if she calmly ignored the remarks and continued to play with her friend, her actions might speak louder than any retaliating words. Additionally, I encouraged her to privately share the situation with an adult in charge.

Through the ethical situation presented in the *Harry Potter* book, I was able to help my children understand and deal with the moral issue of racial discrimination. As Kohlberg suggested, considering the ethical situation of the book led to a higher level of moral reasoning. In many occasions, I have found the *Harry Potter* series to provide these necessary ethical situations.

In classroom situations where children may not feel comfortable stopping to discuss ethical situations, discussion can be facilitated by breaking the children into small groups and asking them to reflect on various passages that present such situations. In addition to providing opportunities to reflect on and work through moral issues, this also allows them to reflect internally on their level of moral development. It also fosters critical thinking skills as they make connections between moral development and the *Harry Potter* characters. It forces them to go beyond reading for content and to begin reading for an understanding that recognizes how the many themes of our lives are mirrored in literature.

For example, you could have students reflect on and identify Harry's stage of moral development at the beginning of the series in *Harry Potter and the Sorcerer's Stone*. One such simple, initial passage that might be used occurs when Harry begins receiving letters:

> "Get out, both of you," croaked Uncle Vernon, stuffing the letter back inside its envelope.
> Harry didn't move.
> "I WANT MY LETTER!" he shouted. (*SS* 35)

After identifying and reading the passage, provide students with a copy of the stages of moral development. Break the students into small groups, and have them decide which stage Harry is in here and support their conclusions. Additionally, have them identify Uncle Vernon's stage of moral development. After 10–15 minutes, encourage them to share their conclusions with the large group. To move the conversation to a more personal level that invites personal sharing and reflection of the situation, share an experience when you felt like Harry. Encourage students to share their similar situations. Then discuss why Harry reacted as he did and alternative ways that Harry might have reacted with more success.

Another useful tool for discussing moral development is Hogwarts' use of House points. Clearly, the professors of Hogwarts are showing an understanding of and appealing to most children's early pre-conventional, stage one level of moral development. Remember, in this stage decisions are made on the basis of punishment and reward. Adults are seen as enforcers and judges of behavior. At Hogwarts, good actions receive points and bad actions result in a deduction of points. A good scene to help students understand and identify this stage also occurs in *Harry Potter and the Sorcerer's Stone*. In the following passage, Professor McGonagall deducts 150 house points from Harry, Ron, Hermione, and Neville for putting themselves in danger by roaming around the school at night:

"nothing gives you the right to walk around school at night, especially these days, it's very dangerous—and fifty points will be taken from Gryffindor… I've never been more ashamed of Gryffindor students." (*SS* 244)

After sharing the passage, ask students to identify in small groups what stage of development Professor McGonagall is in. Also ask them to determine if she is justified in her punishment. Then, move on to the following passage that shows Harry's reaction to the punishment:

From being one of the most popular and admired at the school, Harry was suddenly the most hated…. Everywhere Harry went people pointed and didn't trouble to lower their voices as they insulted him…. Only Ron stood by him…. Harry swore to himself not to meddle in things that weren't his business from now on…. He went to Wood and offered to resign from the Quidditch team. (*SS* 245)

Have students identify which level of moral development Harry is in here. They will likely relate to his desire for peer approval. Explore these feelings by moving to a more personal level of discussion. Share some of your personal experiences as a student and educator. This will help them to see both sides of the situation. Then ask them to share their own experiences with questions, such as:

• When have you felt like Harry?

• What did you do?

• Why is Harry resigning?

• Should he?

• What would you do?

Once all students have had a chance to share, broaden the discussion further by introducing the following passage where Wood responds to Harry's decision:

"Resign?" Wood thundered. "What good'll that do? How are we going to get any points back if we can't win at Quidditch?"

Ask the students once again to discuss in their small groups. Have them discuss Wood's reaction and identify Wood's stage of moral development. In large groups, have them share their findings, and then evaluate Wood's reaction by asking: Does Wood offer good advice to Harry? Why or why not? What advice would you offer Harry? How would you respond to him? Why?

This discussion could then be concluded by showing how Dumbledore uses House points to move the children beyond the pre-conventional stage of moral reasoning where punishment and reward dictate actions. In the passage on page 305 at the end of *Harry Potter and the Sorcerer's Stone*, Dumbledore reinstates the lost points and then some. The result is that Gryffindor wins the house cup. However, he reinforces abstract concepts and discusses good choices made in ethical situations, in an attempt to move the students to a higher level of moral reasoning. In other words, he meets the Hogwarts students at their level of development (punishment and reward) and reinforces choices and behaviors that are of a higher level of moral development. A breakdown follows of Dumbledore's awarded points as they appear on page 305:

Ron (50 points): "best-played game of chess." Remember, he sacrifices his own life. Stage?
Hermione (50 points): "cool logic in the face of fire." Her knowledge and ability to stay calm saves Ron's life. Stage?
Harry (50 points): "pure nerve and outstanding courage." He goes on to face Voldemort alone and keeps the stone safe. Stage?
Neville (10 points): "standing up to friends." Neville wisely tells Ron, Hermione, and Harry that their actions are wrong and dangerous. Stage?

Ask the students to discuss in small groups the awarding of points. Ask them to identify each of the characters' stage of moral development. Then, have them consider the difference in how Professors McGonagall and Dumbledore use the House point system. How does Dumbledore reinforce moral development in this scene? At what stage of moral development is Dumbledore? Why?

As educators and students, we can learn from how Dumbledore reinforces and interacts with students. You will notice that he always remains calm and leads students to greater understanding through a series of questions resembling the Socratic method. This is particularly true with Harry. For example, in book six, when Harry becomes livid with anger after finding out that Snape delivered the prophecy information to Voldemort, Harry lashes out at Dumbledore. Dumbledore calmly defends his stance that Snape can be trusted. He lets Harry vent, but he also lets him know with a calm and firm "Enough" that Harry has stepped over "an invisible line" (*HBP* 550).

Additionally, in the same book on page 509, when Harry continues to struggle with the abstract concept of love, Dumbledore patiently leads him through a series of questions that results in a deeper understanding. He repeats the same calm Socratic method again on page 512 to help Harry understand the concept of free will. As a result, Harry realizes "that it was the difference between being dragged into the arena to face a battle to death and walking into the arena with your head held high."

As a teacher, Dumbledore takes the time to understand each of the students' individual strengths and weaknesses. Whether the student is good or evil, he still accepts the student and seeks to understand him or her. We see this when he rescued Voldemort from the orphanage and mentored him in the early years, and we see it again when he faces death at the hands of Malfoy. Rather than showing a concern for his own suffering and imminent death, Dumbledore carries on a lengthy conversation with Malfoy, in which Dumbledore reveals that he knew of Malfoy's actions all along. He also reveals that he kept his knowledge hidden to keep Malfoy safe from Voldemort. He asserts that he knows Malfoy is "not a killer" (*HBP* 585), and ultimately he offers Malfoy an out and protection. More profoundly, even in the midst of death, Dumbledore wisely tells Malfoy and us, "It is my mercy, and not yours that matters now" (592).

In all of these situations, Dumbledore portrays the highest level of moral reasoning. He operates under the principals of the golden rule and remains a phoenix in even the toughest situations. In reflecting on these situations with others, we come to see how we could better handle ourselves in similar tough situations. As a parent facing an angry teenager several times a week, I know that I do not always stay calm and cool. In reflecting on how Dumbledore helps diffuse Harry's anger and leads him to understanding, I find better ways to parent. In watching Dumbledore take the time to intimately know his students, I find better ways to teach. Dumbledore rises above situational ethics to lead and guide us. From him, we can learn how to raise phoenixes in a world of crows.

References

Burkart, G. (2005). *A Parent's Guide to Harry Potter.* Downer's Grove, IL: InterVarsity Press.

Kohlberg, L. (1975). "Continuities and Discontinuities in Childhood and Moral Development." In *Moral Education: Interdisciplinary Approaches.* New York: Newman.

Piaget, J. (1965). *The Moral Development of the Child.* New York: Free Press.

Rowling, J. K. (1997). *Harry Potter and the Sorcerer's Stone.* New York: Scholastic.

—. (1999). *Harry Potter and the Chamber of Secrets.* New York: Scholastic.

—. (2005). *Harry Potter and the Half-Blood Prince.* New York: Scholastic.

Gina Burkart can be contacted at ginaburkart@mchsi.com.

RISING ABOVE SITUATIONAL ETHICS:
RAISING PHOENIXES IN A
WORLD OF CROWS II

ROUNDTABLE DISCUSSION:
DISCUSSING THE SENSITIVE ISSUES
IN HARRY POTTER

Facilitator: Gina Burkart, author of *A Parent's Guide to* Harry Potter (InterVarsity Press, 2005)

Public Concern

1 What have your experiences been with negative reactions to *Harry Potter*? What fears and concerns have you heard expressed? How did you respond? React?

2 *Harry Potter, Huckleberry Finn, Tom Sawyer, To Kill a Mockingbird,* and Judy Blume's series always top the list of the most-banned books. It seems that the most popular books become the banned books. Why do you think this is the case? How should we respond as parents, educators, and citizens? Are these books harmful to our children?

Sensitive Issues

3 What have you found to be the most objected-to scenes and topics of the books? Why? How should these be handled? Are they dangerous?

4 How have you shared some of the scenes and situations with children reading the books? With adults?

5   I have found the books to be rich with real-life issues that provoke stimulating discussion—opening doors for guidance and relationships. I also have found myself relating to and healing with Harry. What experiences have you had with the issues presented in the books?

6   Which scenes and situations have the most potential for discussing life's issues with children and other adults?

Moral Examples

7   Some believe that Harry Potter and his friends act as though they are above a moral law; do you find this to be true? Should protagonists of children's books be expected always to make the right choice? Can it be beneficial that they don't?

8   Do fictional characters have as much influence over our children as public role models? Peers? Parents? Do fictional characters mirror our children? Public role models?

9   What moral decisions have the characters faced that we can also relate to?

10   Is there a moral voice in the *Harry Potter* series? If so, whose voice is it? How does it affect our children? How can we use it?

11   Which characters seem to operate by a higher moral code?

12   Do the male and female characters have different moral standards (as discussed by Kohlberg/Gilligan?) Is this a reflection of our society?

Gina Burkart can be contacted at ginaburkart@mchsi.com.

O.W.L.s and Knuts: Playfulness and Its Translation in *Harry Potter*

Nancy K. Jentsch
Northern Kentucky University

J. K. Rowling's *Harry Potter* series has become a global phenomenon. Even before the movie rights were sold to Warner Brothers and all the movie-related products came on the market, the books themselves were selling worldwide and being translated into many of the world's languages.

Translators of these works face many challenges, among them the neologisms with which the stories abound, the strong and important sense of place in the novels and the playful use of language which has endeared the books to readers across the generations. It is this final challenge—the translation of playful language—that is the subject of this paper. My examination of playful language is organized by the function of that language in the books. First, I will look at puzzles, riddles and other passages in the books whose purpose it is to engage the reader to become an active participant in the text. Next, I will examine the parodies present in the stories which have linguistic significance. Finally, I will present examples of fun for fun's sake in J. K .Rowling's works. I will take examples from the Czech, French, German and Spanish translations of books one to five.

There is no lack of puzzles in this series. Philip Nel, in his reader's guide to the *Harry Potter* novels, compares Rowling's use of puzzles to give expression to a certain joy in learning to that of Lewis Carroll. He comments that many of Rowling's puzzles "suggest...an intellectual playfulness characteristic...of Carroll" (31). Rowling's puzzles do indeed intrigue and engage readers, adding intellectual stimulation to sheer enjoyment. In book

one, a mirror named Erised and its inscription which looks like
gibberish are introduced. Nowhere is a clue given, but it doesn't take
most readers long to realize that "Erised" is the word "desire"
spelled backwards, i.e., as in a mirror. The mirror, in fact, does not
reflect the image of the onlooker, but rather that person's heart's
desire. The inscription around the mirror of Erised describes the
properties of the mirror in backwards prose. The German and
French translators translated the name of the mirror to mean
"desire" in their languages, and the inscription was also translated
and then rendered from back to front. But what happens if the
translator doesn't get the puzzle? The Spanish translation uses the
name Erised for the mirror, though there is no cognate of "desire"
in Spanish, and then goes on to render the inscription in backwards
English for the Spanish reader. This detracts greatly from Rowling's
intention, which I believe is to involve readers actively in the stories,
even to the point of having them solve puzzles as they read.

When I read the fifth book in the series in English—*Harry Potter
and the Order of the Phoenix*—I couldn't wait to see what the
translators would do with the section where Ron Weasley talks with
his mouth full. The significance of this is that Ron grew up in a
family of seven Weasley children, where there was never an
abundance of money and food. When he attends the Hogwarts
feasts, he puts away large amounts of food quickly. In Chapter
Eleven of this book, Ron says, "Ow kunnit nofe skusin danger
ifzat?" Hermione translates his question as, "How can it know if the
school's in danger if it's a Hat?" (189). Later, though, Ron speaks
with his mouth full again, and the sentence is never translated in the
text. This is unequivocally a puzzle addressed to the reader. It goes
"Node iddum eentup sechew" (189). Ron is telling Nearly-Headless
Nick that he didn't mean to upset him. The Spanish, French and
German translations of this passage show that the translators "got
it" and were able to present the puzzle to their readers. "Nunfa me
gío fon ga boga gena" (220) "I never make fun with my mouth full,"
"Pa d'tou v'lu ou 'xer" (238) "I certainly didn't want to annoy you,"
and "Nö isch wollschi nisch feraaschn (248) "No, I didn't mean to
make a fool of you."

Another passage that encourages the reader to solve a puzzle is in
the fourth book, *Harry Potter and the Goblet of Fire*. Harry is presented
with a riddle as he comes to the end of a maze he has been fighting

his way through. He wishes his friend Hermione could be at his side to help him with this mental puzzle and needs to have it repeated before he can solve it. The construction of this riddle presents the translator with a few interesting problems. In English, the riddle goes like this:

> First think of the person who lives in disguise,
> Who deals in secrets and tells naught but lies.
> Next, tell me what's always the last thing to mend,
> The middle of middle and end of the end?
> And finally give me the sound often heard
> During the search for a hard-to-find word.
> Now string them together, and answer me this,
> Which creature would you be unwilling to kiss? (546)

The translator must obviously start with the answer and then compose a riddle. The original riddle first gives three clues, which when guessed can be strung together to form a word. That word is the name of a creature one would likely rather not kiss. The French, German, Spanish and Czech translators stuck to the form of the original, with the answer being the word "spider" in translation. The Spanish translation goes with two clues rather than three, and uses more of the rhyme as introductory material.

> Y no es fácil la respuesta de esta adivinanza,
> porque está lejana, en tierras de bonanza,
> donde empieza la región de las montañas de arena
> y acaba la de los toros, la sangre, el mar y la verbena. (548)

The French translation of this riddle follows the original in style, and as the clues get strung together, they need to be looked at phonetically to come up with the solution.

> D'abord, pense au premier de ce qu'il faut apprendre
> Lorsque l'on ne sait rien à l'âge le plus tendre.
> Ensuite, dis-moi donc ce que fait par naissance
> Celui qui, au palais, a élu résidence.
> Il suffit de la prendre à la fin de l'année.
> Tu connaîtras ainsi la créature immonde
> Que tu n'embrasserais vraiment pour rien au monde. (561–62)

The solution is a-règne-ée, or "araignée." In both the English and the French versions, Harry has trouble with the clue which points to the place in a word to take the letters from, and in the French version, he starts out thinking that the clue is leading him to something to do with the word "Noël," being at the end of the year, rather than the letters that appear at the end of the word "année."

The Czech version of this riddle demonstrates two interesting aspects of translation. First, it illustrates how a translator can use elements specific to and common in the target language in making the translation sound natural, and second, how a translator to a language not related to English faces even more challenges than the translators to related European languages. The Czech rhyme first describes a peacock, but then tells us that we can take off the čárka, a Czech diacritical marking that lengthens vowel sounds. The second clue indicates a sound which will stop a horse and the third describes a syllable that is the difference between a big star and a little star—the diminutive ending -ka. Diminutives are extremely common in the Czech language. By using descriptions of anomalies of the Czech language, the riddle hardly seems like a translation! And there's more to come. The word "spider" is "pavouk," but the clue has to lead us to the accusative (direct object) form of the word. Czech is a highly inflected language, which does not use definite or indefinite articles, but inflects the nouns themselves. The result is the word "pavouka," which would be the answer to the question of what the reader wouldn't like to kiss.

> Nejdřív si vzpomeň, kdo nejvíc se honosí,
> a i když pozbyl čárku, se jako duha skví.
> Hned nato doprostřed to slůvko najít zkus,
> na které zastaví koně a pak i vůz
> Nakonec poslouží ti jediná slabika:
> když zbledne velká hvězda, zůstane hvězdinka.
>
> Spoj ty tři navzájem a zvíš, zda dál smíš jít:
> kterého z živých tvorů bys nechtěl políbít? (492)

One final puzzle J. K. Rowling likes to present her readers with is the puzzle of what meaning her names and neologisms have that are not readily visible. While children can easily read the books not knowing that Minerva was the Roman goddess of wisdom, those who do know that get a smile at Minerva McGonagall, the deputy headmistress of Hogwarts. The student of German literature who has suffered through works written during the period *Sturm und Drang* nods in recognition of the name of the wizarding school

Durmstrang. Whereas the Spanish translations tend to leave many of the names in the original, the French translator has chosen to translate most proper names in the books. Neither solution is satisfying, as one makes it impossible for readers to appreciate much of the humor of the original, and the other destroys the sense of place so important to the stories. The German translator has done a remarkable job in choosing which names to translate and which to leave in the original. For example, the acid-green-ink-pen-toting reporter Rita Skeeter first appears in book four of the series. Her name may derive from skeet-shooting, with the idea being that she takes aim at those she interviews. The German translator worked under this assumption and came up with the name Rita Kimmkorn. In German, the *Kimme* and the *Korn* are the two sights one lines up when aiming a rifle. In colloquial German, it is common to use the expression *jemanden aufs Korn nehmen* to express the idea of taking aim at a person. In addition, the name is flashy with its internal alliteration. This translation is an example of one where the reader is encouraged to make the connection between the name and the character, just as in the original.

Different languages have different tolerances for foreign words used in their language and for the creation of new words (neologisms). Spanish and French are two languages that maintain language academies and, at least officially, have the goal of maintaining linguistic purity. In particular, the French language is viewed as having little need for synonyms, as the language strives to express things precisely. Today the trend is for French to borrow a concept from English but very quickly coin a term for it that is essentially French (Nadeau 379). Perhaps the adherence to the ideal of language purity has led to the retention of many of Rowling's original names and titles in the Spanish translations and the translation of many of the same in the French version. The Czech version of the books also translates many proper names. Czech and English share few cognates (words that are recognizable from one language to another). Translations of many of Rowling's words bring their meaning to readers in languages which do not share the Germanic and Romance roots that have shaped the English language.

J. K. Rowling uses language to poke fun at our world. Her magical creation parallels the world we live in and as we look at this distant world, we see parodies of our own lives. The names of the Ministry of Magic's many offices parallel and ridicule modern bureaucracies. Percy Weasley, for example, graduates from the Hogwarts School of Witchcraft and Wizardry and gets a job at the Ministry of Magic. When asked what he is doing, in *Harry Potter and the Goblet of Fire*, Percy replies, "'A report for the Department of International Magical Co-operation,' said Percy smugly. 'We're trying to standardize cauldron thickness. Some of these foreign imports are just a shade too thin—leakages have been increasing at a rate of almost three per cent a year—'" (53). Translators easily find a solution for the titles of these ministries, as a simple literal translation sounds just as real and pompous and at the same time as bizarre in the target language.

In book four, Hermione begins a campaign to better the lives of house elves. Karin Westman sees this as a parody of British "left-wing fringe movements" and even of "the nineteenth-century tradition of well-to-do liberals speaking for the lower classes whom they have never met" (325). The challenge here is for the translator to create just as unappealing an acronym as Hermione has for her group—S.P.E.W. The German translator's B.ELFE.R. (Bund für ELFEnRechte) is just as awkward, or even more so than the original, and Harry and Ron even make fun of it by pronouncing at as a word and not letters. The acronyms O.W.L. (Ordinary Wizarding Levels) and N.E.W.T. (Nastily Exhausting Wizarding Tests), which refer to testing levels at Hogwarts, parallel the British school system's exit exams. The translators call them funny and sometimes pompous things in their own languages. In German they are ZAG and UTZ (Zaubergrad and Unheimlich Toller Zauberer) and in French BUSE and ASPIC (Brevet Universel de Sorcellerie Elementaire and Accumulation de Sorcellerie Particulièrement Intensive et Contraignante). In Spanish the tests are called TIMO (Título Indispensable de Magia Ordinaria) and ÉXTASIS (Exámenes Terribles de Alta Sabiduría e Invocaciones Secretas).

Another jab given our modern world is the use of slick advertising slogans and product names designed to make sales in Rowling's magical world. The reader encounters racing brooms named "Comet," "Firebolt" and "Cleansweep," for example. The German translator has come up with a good translation for the latter. A Cleansweep 7 becomes a Sauberwisch 7. The slick alliteration in the German version makes up for the fact that a winning streak is not implied in the word *Sauberwisch*. *Sauberwisch*, though, incorporating the words *sauber* (clean) and *wisch* from *wischen* (wipe), does continue the cleaning image of the Cleansweep. When, as in the Spanish translation, this proper name is not translated, the comparison with our market-driven society is lost. The French translator changes the name of this broom from book to book, from *Astiqueur* to *Brossdur 7*, which complicates understanding and can only be viewed as an error.

There is also much humor for humor's sake in Rowling's writing. Word plays such as Diagon Alley, Knockturn Alley, Spellotape, Which Broomstick and Blast-Ended Skrewts abound. The translator must decide what is worth translating and what is best left in the original. If translated, the humorous sections of the book present the unique challenge of finding equivalents that will further the enjoyment of the text as was the case in the original. In Chapter Four of book one, the reader is introduced to Albus Dumbledore by name and titles. Among his titles is "Supreme Mugwump, International Confederation of Wizards" (42). The German translation is superb "Ganz hohes Tier, Internationale Vereinigung der Zauberer" (59), while the Spanish translation shows much less creativity. Dumbledore has already been given the title of *Jefe de Magos*, when the mugwump translation appears simply as "Jefe Supremo, Confederación Internacional de Magos" (50). This illustration shows the range of solutions that translators find for specific situations. Equally as important as this micro-example is the question of how well the translator captures the flavor of the original text. Early in the series the reader becomes acquainted with the Sorting Hat, a hat which speaks and places pupils in the house of the Hogwarts school in which they would be best suited. *Sorting Hat* is in itself not a playful term, but the French translator captured the quality of Rowling's overall bent toward playful language in naming it "le choixpeau magique" (118). *Chapeau* means hat, and *choix* is the word for choice. Put them together, and voilà, we have *choixpeau*! Another ingenious translation is found in the German version of book three. The wizard's bus is the Knight Bus, whose seats are beds. I thought the German *Fahrender Ritter* (driving knight) was a lame translation until I realized that it was also the German for *knight errant.* Now it seems ingenious! It's a bus, so it drives, but it's also an adventure-seeking vehicle, like the knights it was named for!

Rowling's choice of names for her characters presents the translator with challenges. First of all, the translator must decide whether or not to even translate the name. There is no doubt that Millicent Bulstrode and Madam Hooch are meant to be humorous. Is it best to leave the names in the original, or should the translator try to come up with something equally humorous in the target language? This is complicated even further when the origin of a name is obscure. There is, for example, a teacher at Hogwarts named Professor Binns. He is a ghost, and his character parodies the academic profession—the supreme absent-minded professor, since he has ceased to exist. Philip Nel, in his article "Harry Potter and the Transfiguration of Language," theorizes that Binns's name is a pun derived from the British "dustbins" and implies that his classes are little more than rubbish (281). This being the case, a translator might do well to come up with a name for this professor which conveys a similar meaning. In 2001, though, an article in the Exeter *Express and Echo* appeared under the headline "I'm Harry's Professor." In it, an over eighty-year-old former professor of Rowling confirmed that he had served as her prototype for Professor Binns. Hugh Stubbs pointed out the "etymological derivation: Stubbs, tubs, bins, Binns" (Sapiens 95). In this case, the name has no intrinsic meaning to the reader and can just as easily be left in the original.

As in the previous example, it is often open to discussion, whether a name or a word play has significance worth being rendered in the target language. An example from the German version shows the playfulness possible in creative translation. The card game Exploding Snap is enjoyed by the Hogwarts students. It is obviously based on the British card games for children like Number Snap, Alphabet Snap, etc. The German translator either misread the original or decided to create more humor in his version of the books by naming the game Exploding Snape, Snape being the dreaded Potions Master of Hogwarts. The name makes so much sense that fans have even created an online demo of Exploding Snape!

J. K. Rowling's playful use of language is engaging, thought-provoking and sometimes just plain fun. Translators face challenges in rendering playful language appropriately and their solutions range from failures to strokes of genius. Examining how translators have dealt with these challenges is a magical journey well worth taking.

Works Cited

Nadeau, Jean-Benoît, and Julie Barlow. *The Story of French*. New York: St Martin's Press, 2006.

Nel, Philip. "Harry Potter and the Transformation of Language." *The Ivory Tower and Harry Potter*. Ed. Lana A. Whited. Columbia, MO: University of Missouri Press, 2002.

Nel, Philip. *J. K. Rowling's Harry Potter Novels*. New York: Continuum, 2001.

Rowling, J. K. *Harry Potter à l'école des sorciers*. Trans. Jean-François Ménard. Paris: Gallimard Jeunesse, 1998.

—. *Harry Potter a Ohnivý pohár*. Trans. Vladimír Medek. Prague: Albatros, 2001.

—. *Harry Potter and the Goblet of Fire*. London: Bloomsbury, 2000.

—. *Harry Potter and the Order of the Phoenix*. London: Bloomsbury, 2003.

—. *Harry Potter and the Philosopher's Stone*. London: Bloomsbury, 1997.

—. *Harry Potter et la Coupe de Feu*. Trans. Jean-François Ménard. Paris: Gallimard, 2000.

—. *Harry Potter et l'Ordre du Phénix*. Trans. Jean-François Ménard. Paris: Gallimard, 2003.

—. *Harry Potter und der Orden des Phönix*. Trans. Klaus Fritz. Hamburg: Carlsen, 2003.

—. *Harry Potter und der Stein der Weisen*. Trans. Klaus Fritz. Hamburg: Carlsen, 1998.

—. *Harry Potter y el Cáliz de Fuego*. Trans. Adolfo Muñoz García and Nieves Martín Azofra. Barcelona: Salamandra, 2001.

—. *Harry Potter y la Órden del Fénix*. Trans. Gemma Rovira Ortega. Barcelona: Salamandra, 2004.

—. *Harry Potter y la piedra filosofal*. Trans. Alicia Dellepiane. Barcelona: Emecé, 1999.

Sapiens, Petrus. "At Figulus... J. K. Rowling and the Ancient World." *The Classical Outlook* 79 (2002): 93–96.

Westman, Karin. "Specters of Thatcherism: Contemporary British Culture in J. K. Rowling's *Harry Potter* Series." *The Ivory Tower and Harry Potter.* Ed. Lana A. Whited. Columbia, MO: University of Missouri Press, 2002.

Are the Patients Running St. Mungo's?: Usability and *Harry Potter* Fandom Web Sites

Alison Luperchio

"Great Web experiences don't happen by accident. They're the product of a solid design process that focuses both on business objectives and user goals."[1]

This is true whether your Web site sells books, markets a designer drug, publishes fanfiction, or keeps people up-to-date on the latest *Harry Potter* news. "But my fan site doesn't have business objectives!" you might say. I disagree. They're the "number of hits per day" or "number of published authors and stories" or the "percentage of readers who review." Even if these aren't written down, site owners pay attention when they break a previous record or pass a milestone. These are the same numbers that an e-commerce site uses ("number of hits per day," "number of registered users," and "conversion ratios"), just in different terms. And you want your Web site to break those records or hit the next big milestone. Today, I'm going to talk about tips for making a great Web experience. I can't make you a usability expert in an hour and a half, but I hope to give you something to think about.

Definitions

- *Usability* is a quality attribute that assesses how easy user interfaces

---

1 Kerry Bodine, "The State of the Web in 2006: Usability Luminaries Weigh In," Forrester Research (2006), <http://www.forrester.com/Research/Document/0,7211,40040,00.html>.

are to use. The word "usability" also refers to methods for improving ease-of-use during the design process.[1]

- *Usability testing* is a method by which users of a product are asked to perform certain tasks in an effort to measure the product's ease-of-use, task time, and the user's perception of the experience.[2]

- *Interaction design* is the process of defining product behavior based on observed and analyzed user behavior.[3]

- *Web design* is the process of creating a complete visual image exactly representing what a Web site will look like. It may extend to converting that image into the actual HTML and individual buttons, logos, etc. that are needed for it.

- *Web development* is the process of taking HTML and graphical buttons, logos, etc. and converting it into the actual programming code that is necessary to run a Web site.

Top Ten Mistakes:[4] Fix These First

- Bad search
- PDF files for online reading
- Not changing the color of visited links
- Non-scannable text
- Fixed font size
- Page titles with low search engine visibility
- Anything that looks like an advertisement
- Violating design conventions
- Opening new browser windows
- Not answering users' questions

---

1 Jakob Nielsen, "Usability 101: Introduction to Usability," *Alertbox* (25 Aug 2003), <http://www.useit.com/alertbox/20030825.html>.
2 Multiple sources (origin unknown).
3 Dave Cronin, "RUP & Goal-Directed Design: Toward a New Development Process," *Cooper Interactive Journal of Design* (2003), <http://www.cooper.com/insights/journal_of_design/articles/rup_goaldirected_design.html>.
4 Jakob Nielsen, "Top Ten Mistakes in Web Design," *Alertbox* (updated 2007), <http://www.useit.com/alertbox/9605.html>.

I'm going to have to skip a discussion of search, as that's an entire day—days or weeks, really—in and of itself. I am happy to say that in my fan site searches I didn't encounter any PDFs that were expected to be used in on-line reading. Visited links are more miss than hit (that is, not meeting the guideline), but the concept is straightforward; use a standard change in link color to let people know where they've already been, so that they don't keep going there just to find out it wasn't what they wanted—again. Search engine visibility is also an entire talk on its own. When you open new browser windows, some people still don't realize it's happened and then become confused when the "Back" button is grayed out. It doesn't fit their expectations of how the Web works. Not answering users' questions: Nielsen says one of the most common failures is business-to-business (B2B) sites not publishing prices, just to give a quick example.

Unfortunately, I don't have time today to do an in-depth analysis of each of these, but I'd like to go through the ones I haven't yet mentioned in a bit more detail, with examples that both meet and fail the criteria. I want to state up front that I am making assumptions about their goals and objectives of these sites. I also want to state that I have nothing personal against any of the sites that I'm going to reference today. They were chosen out of many, many more that I looked at—and they were chosen simply because they illustrate the points I'm making. I actually had to exclude some of my biggest dislikes simply because they didn't fit with the topics I'd chosen.

Violating Design Conventions

If you asked me to give you one word that you should always keep in mind while working on a Web site, that word would be "consistency." Use the same terms all the time—and preferably the same terms that your competitors use (unless your competitors use a lot of jargon and lingo—but I'll get into that later). Use the same colors to mean the same thing on every page—don't let your link colors be different depending on what section you're in. And consider breaking your content into the same sections that your competitors' sites do. In the same Jakob Nielsen article that this mistakes list came from, he reiterates one of his big catchphrases: "users spend most of their time on *other* Web sites." That means that they don't spend a lot of time learning how to use yours, so if it looks and acts like other sites they've been to, they're more likely to be able to navigate your site easily. Therefore, they're more likely to use it.

Let's take a look at a few *Harry Potter* news sites. In this case, my assumption is that all of them can be seen as competitors.

Figure 1 is our first site—one of my favorite news feeds, The Leaky Cauldron. Notice that it has a left navigation bar with key topics as well as information about the site itself. It also has headlines on the front page.

Figure 1

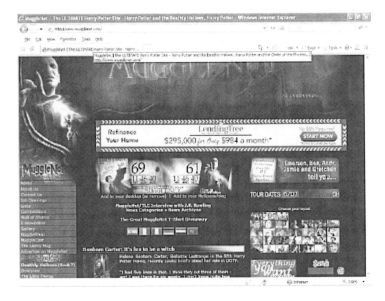

Figure 2

Figure 2, MuggleNet, also has a similar navigation bar on the left-hand side, and headlines on the front page.

Figure 3

HPANA (Figure 3), however, doesn't. It has navigation across the top. Is this wrong? No, not necessarily. But TLC and MuggleNet have menus on the left that expose all their second-level navigation, which is a good practice, and HPANA doesn't. It also seems to have news on the home page as well as an entirely different section called the News Browser. It's not consistent with TLC and MuggleNet, which is something HPANA should be aware of and consider.

Fixed Font Size

Most Web designers are young, and therefore are more likely to have good eyesight. Assuming that the attendees of Phoenix Rising are a reasonable representation of *Harry Potter* fans, not all *fans* are young with good eyesight! In order to appeal to a wider audience, it's best to allow a user to adjust the font size using their browser controls. I realize that some sites have page-specific font controllers —which is tolerable, but annoying because it violates the last rule that I mentioned, consistency across Web sites. Specifically, I should mention that a corollary to that rule is that if the browser can do something, let it—don't rewrite the functionality into the page. In that way, the Web site always works the same as every other one.

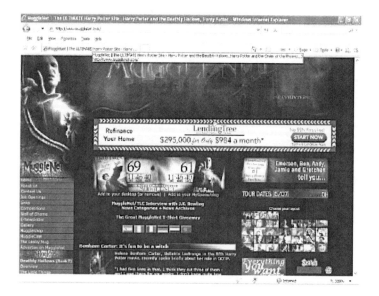

Figure 4

I'm going to go back and look at MuggleNet (Figure 4) again. As far as I can find, MuggleNet does not have anything within their homepage that lets you change the font size. This is the default that you see with Internet Explorer set to a medium text size—pretty small. Keep your eye on the bottom left as I show you what happened when I changed my browser setting from medium to largest...

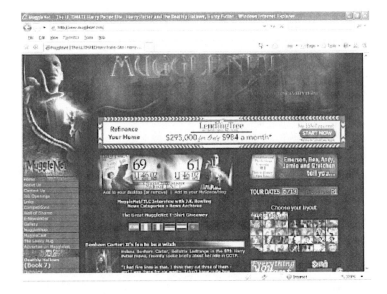

Figure 5

In Figure 5, can you see what changed? The only thing that changed is the phrase "Book 7" in the left nav. Not only does the site not let me change the text size of the main content for easier reading, but it also changes the nav bar text size inconsistently.

Let's look at another example.

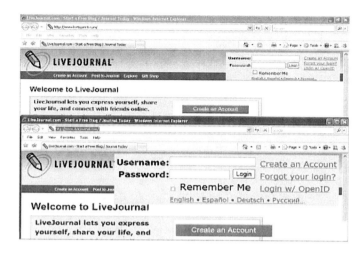

Figure 6

For comparison, I've combined two screenshots of LiveJournal into Figure 6. The top is text size medium, the bottom is text size largest. Here we have the opposite problem; it lets you resize the

Figure 7

text but doing so messes up the layout to the point where you can't see all the navigation options.

Figure 7 is The Petulant Poetess, a fanfiction site, set to the default medium text size in my browser. It looks lovely.

In Figure 8, I've changed the text size setting to largest, and it still looks lovely—so it's definitely possible to create layouts that work with multiple text sizes. Doing so is a best practice. If you're not doing so, ask yourself why not.

Figure 8

Non-scannable Text

People do not read on-line the same way they do a book—so don't write content as if you're writing a book. Web users scan things looking for noticeable subheaders, bulleted lists, and highlighted links and keywords. Beyond actually providing easily digestible content, this helps to assure users quickly that they're in the right place. And short, easily digestible paragraphs are equally important—very few things on a Web site are a bigger turn-off than a huge wall of text.

Most of the Web sites I looked at were good about this—though to be fair, I only looked at the home pages and maybe one level deeper. It's quite possible that going deeper into the site would turn up issues. Nevertheless, I do have an example.

Figure 9

The home page for Hobbie's House of Wizard Wear (Figure 9) has two glaring problems.

Problem number one: the ads are in a typical place where users scan for content.

Problem number two: the "School Uniform" that's underlined is not a link to a page about school uniforms that Hobbie's sells; it's some sort of advertising link. I had to scroll down to the third screen of textual content to find the bulleted list of what Hobbie's offers. Not only is this home page a wall of text, it also misleads you into thinking that the underlined words will get you somewhere useful on the site, when they actually take you away from it.

On the other hand, WizardTies.com (Figure 10) has a short, concise introduction. All the highlighted words are links and go to useful places.

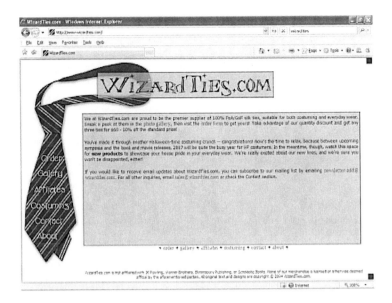

Figure 10

Content That Looks Like Ads

Any content that looks like an advertisement is asking to be ignored. Most users have developed the skill of tuning out banner ads, animation, and pop-ups—so if you use those as a way to navigate your site or present critical content, your readers are likely to miss it.

I love the Lexicon (Figure 11). I've long since lost track of how often I look things up there. But I never, ever go to their home page, and here's why. The first time I visited the site, I had absolutely no idea where any of the content was. Why? Because the content links look like banner ads. Any time you have to tell readers how to navigate your site—see the bit in the middle right, about "click on the covers to explore each book"?—you need to rethink what you're doing.

Figure 11

Here's another example. Figure 12, Whimsic Alley, is also rather

Figure 12

confusing. It looks like there are ads down the right side of the page —typical ad placement. But those are actually subsections of the site. Not the best option. (To make matters worse, they each open a new browser window—but we already covered that.)

Three Traps[1]

Moving to a different source, here are three traps you should avoid: starting with technology, having an end goal of being first to market, and worrying about having the most features.

First off—technology is pointless if it doesn't specifically address a user goal. More on that in a minute.

Being the first to market, in this case, means being the first to roll out new ideas, Web site sections, etc. The point is, being first isn't necessarily a long-term advantage—being *best* is, and more importantly, *meeting a real need* is. So don't rush something out the door because you hear that someone else is doing it. Rolling out a substandard feature will cause users to abandon it and not return, even after you've fixed it.

Less is more. Or at least, simple is more. Really. You don't have time to do everything, and if you try, you'll fail. If you try to meet the needs of everyone, you'll end up meeting the needs of no one. So make sure you know what your site's focus is. If you see yourself straying away from it because "someone might want to know X" or "Y would be a cool feature"—call it off. Spend your time making sure that the most critical and popular features are easy to use but comprehensive. Make sure they're easy to find, as well. Mr. Greenwood states that "in terms of user satisfaction, a genuinely useful product will beat an awkward product with more features every time." And I believe he's right.

Starting with Technology: RIAs

Back to the bit about starting with technology. Podcasting aside, the most common "technology" that Web sites are looking at these days are RIAs, or Rich Internet Applications. They're the shiny new toy that looks like so much fun. It must be better than plain old

---

1 Wayne Greenwood, "Three Traps," *Cooper Interactive Journal of Design* (2001), <http://www.cooper.com/insights/journal_of_design/articles/three_traps.html>.

HTML, right? Mmm—well, maybe. Do you remember when Flash was first introduced? At one point Jakob Nielsen went so far as to call it "99% Bad." Was there something inherently wrong with it? No—but the early reasons people used it were. Splash pages. Putting all the content into it just because we could—and then the search engines couldn't find it. Not a useful addition to a Web site. RIAs— and the two leading contenders are Ajax and Adobe's Flex/Flash combination—should enhance functionality and/or improve the user experience.

When can they help? When they allow you to accomplish a goal in less time, with fewer clicks, with better response time. When there is a need to cycle through iterations or levels of data, but it would be nice to have it all on one screen (for example, a drop-down menu choice triggers the options in the next drop-down menu on a form). When you want to do something interactive—like http://www.jkrowling.com. When you want to have a richly-featured application in a web browser—like Gmail.

When won't they help? I'm going to be absolutely honest here, and I'm sure that some of you will disagree with me. I have yet to see a compelling reason to have an RIA on any fan site. Why? Because fan sites are inherently about browsing *content*, and inherently, a user's mental model for doing so is by clicking between pages. One implementation red flag is when a feature doesn't add anything to the user experience but slows down the perception of site speed; the page is retrieving content but not reloading, so it appears slow. Another clear implementation failure: when the RIA doesn't react in an expected manner to leaving the page and returning by way of the back button. RIAs should have a *purpose*; they shouldn't just appear because a developer thought it was fun to program them.

And yes, I know that there are fan sites out there that use them for navigating content. I'm thinking I might get some flak for having said this, but I will extend further by saying that I don't support it, and that I believe that those Web sites are not giving users the best experience possible.

Some Additional Best Practices

I have some additional best practices that I'd like to mention. These seem pretty straightforward but still trip people up.

Logical, memorable URLs: I still don't understand why TLC and HP Lexicon have dashes in their URLs. And Hobbie's House is actually `http://www.wizardknits.com`. I do understand that by now, some people have those URLs memorized and wouldn't be able to find them if they changed. However, for optimal usability, alternate likely URLs should be registered and used to redirect users to the "official" one.

Optimize for a 1024 x 768 screen size—the most common screen size at the moment—but make sure it works at both higher and lower resolutions. Not everyone is in the same place as far as monitors go, and not everyone keeps their browser maximized; the best option is to use a liquid layout.

Make sure all your language is clear and consistent. Use layman's terms, so to speak, not jargon. Make sure that your site's content is readable and comprehensible to someone who has never been there before and who hasn't ever been to any site like yours before.

I want to talk a bit more about understandable navigation.

Understandable Navigation

Like your content, you need to use easily understood language in your navigation, not jargon. Yes, Warner Bros. uses catchy phrases. Does that mean it's right? No, but in their case, it's part of the entertainment value.

Expose subcategory links if they exist, or flatten the navigation structure if that works for you. But do make sure you categorize the links; long lists without any hint of where to find something within them are just as bad as that wall of content text. If you remember the first set of Web sites I showed you, I criticized HPANA for not having the left nav structure that TLC and MuggleNet did. One of the reasons that I used this comparison is that all three sites have content divided up by each book and each movie. One of the things that HPANA loses with its navigation structure is the ability to foreground links that go directly to that content. On TLC, it took me one click to get to information specific to book seven—on HPANA it took me three.

Feedback: I don't mean user comments, or other ways that users give feedback to the site owners; I mean the opposite, in a way. I mean having clear page titles that reflect the navigation links. Using breadcrumbs if appropriate. Highlighting the section you're in on the nav bar. This is feedback to the *user* that they have arrived in the place they were looking for.

This is something that HPANA is very clear about (Figure 13). You can see you're in the news section, and though it took me three clicks to get to this page, I can clearly see where I am in the Web site. And I can use the breadcrumbs to navigate back up.

Figure 13

The Other Mistake: but But BUT!

There's one last mistake I want to talk about. I call it the "but But BUT" mistake. It's when the people working on a site look at a usability best practice and say, "that's nice, but I don't need to do it that way because…"

Don't rationalize a design that doesn't help your users accomplish their goals. Fix it.

Best practices are named as such for a reason. Top ten mistakes are named as such for a reason. Take that into consideration, and don't assume your site is above them. Here are a few examples of how this sometimes plays out:

But I need to get more text on that page above the fold, so we need to shrink the font…

Do you? Do you REALLY? Maybe you need to chunk it up better instead. Or find someone who can write more concisely.

But we want our site to feel special, so we want to use our own verbiage...

It doesn't make it special. It makes it confusing. How does someone who is new to your site understand? Don't get me wrong—I'm not saying you can't use *Harry Potter* terms here and there. But don't pick the name of a spell to represent each section and then use those spell names as your navigation links. Just don't.

But we want to keep users on our site, so we open outside links in a new window...

By providing the link, you are inviting people to click on it. If you don't want people leaving your site, don't provide outside links. Otherwise, by not letting them leave, you're interfering with the way they want to use the Web.

There are very few times when flouting the rules actually helps.

What Is Scenario Design?

Scenario design is a process, a collection of strategies and practices, if you will. It is a concept built on a simple assumption: No experience is inherently good or bad, it can only be judged by looking at how well it helps customers achieve their goals.[1]

Scenario design is a method of discovering how to help your users achieve those goals.

Who Are Your Users?

First things first—who are your users? Who are you designing for?

I always like to start off by identifying who you're not designing for. You (the Web master, developer, designer, or editor) are not designing for yourself or the other people who work on the site. You may be a member of your target audience, but you are too close to the site to be considered "typical" or "average."

---

1   Bruce D. Temkin, "Scenario Design: A Disciplined Approach to Customer Experience," Forrester Research (2004), <http://www.forrester.com/Research/Document/0,7211,35020,00.html>.

This is a case of the patients running St. Mungo's, or, in more conventional terms in the usability arena, a case of the inmates running the asylum. (The phrase came into use because it is the title of a book by Alan Cooper. Anyone who deals with a Web site should read it.) It's what can happen when the people who know how the existing system works—or know what development tools they want to play with—design the next iteration of the system. The result ends up being a new design that is limited by existing "rules" of the system, or has lots of bells and whistles that are showy but don't help users achieve their goals.

How do you know who to design for? Ideally, you'll have personas.

What is a persona? A representative user with representative behavior, based on direct observation. The persona has aspirations, goals and tasks, and a personality. You'll know whether your persona is a late-night user or a lunchtime user, and whether he or she can tell the difference between Dementors and Lethifolds. You may have more than one, representing different classes of user behavior.

What *isn't* a persona? A description of a user segment or a collection of tasks that a user might do. It specifically represents user behavior, not user demographics. You may have a handful of them, but you need to pick one as being primary. You design for that user, but keep the others in mind. Yes, you design for *one* user. Like search and search engine optimization, though, personas are a topic that need far more time to cover. I recommend Alan Cooper's book, or *The User Is Always Right* by Steve Mulder.[1]

In the absence of personas, try at least to have a target audience —user segments, if you will. They're not a substitute for personas, and they won't work as well, but if that's the best data that you have, make the best of it.

What Are Their Goals?

Let's say we have a casual *Harry Potter* fan who shuns the movies but loves the books.

What do they want to achieve?

---

1   Alan Cooper, Robert Reimann, and David Cronin, *About Face 3.0* (Wiley, 2007); Steve Mulder and Ziv Yaar, *The User Is Always Right: A Practical Guide to Creating and Using Personas for the Web* (New Riders Press, 2006).

Perhaps their general aspiration is to stay up-to-date about rumors regarding book seven.

What are the most common tasks they want to perform?

They want to check the latest news headlines, and read new essays. But they don't want to get bogged down with movie news.

What is the most complicated task they need to perform?

Registration? Submitting their own essay for consideration?

Now take that user and task and weave them together with some context. This fan checks *Harry Potter* news sites on his lunch hour, so he's crunched for time. He's at work, so he doesn't want the site to draw the attention of people walking by his cubicle. He wants to check the latest news, but he also hopes to re-find an essay he read a while back that he really liked.

That's a scenario.

How Can You Help Them Succeed?

Unlike the scenario I just pulled out of nowhere, your scenarios should represent common, important tasks and the people who need to carry them out. Once you've figured out what those scenarios are, you should use them during development to create screen flows that optimize for these scenarios. You should make sure your writers are creating content that is actually relevant to those users.

And you should use those scenarios to evaluate your existing design. Don't assume that everything you've done in the past contributes to fulfilling them.

Evaluating a Site

There are many ways to evaluate a site. Surveys, field observation, and usability testing provide detailed and thorough information, but they're time-consuming and require significant resources—either in people and time, or in money. Or both.

Reviewing your data can give you some quick wins: monitor your inbound e-mail questions and comments for trends. If possible, do some log analysis: see what your top search terms are, see which pages are most popular. Also, look for "drop-off" or "abandoned" pages—which is to say, pages that are the last page a person visits. If you see a trend there and it's not supposed to be an exit page, take a good look at that page and see what's going on.

Another option is the heuristic evaluation, and this is the kind of evaluation that I want to discuss here.

Heuristic Evaluation

A heuristic (expert) evaluation of a Web site is a systematic inspection of a site design measured against recognized usability principles. The purpose of a heuristic evaluation is to identify a majority of the usability problems in a Web site.[1]

Yes, a heuristic evaluation is typically done by experts. And yes, that will obviously get you the best results. But if you have no other way of doing usability testing—and let's face it, volunteer-supported Web sites are pretty lacking in resources for lab testing—then heuristic evaluations can still provide insight even if you use people who are less than expert.

Who Should Evaluate?

When finding alternatives for usability experts, take these points into consideration.

They definitely should not be anyone who works on the Web site in any capacity, nor should it be a frequent user. Both these groups have detailed knowledge of how to navigate the site and won't provide optimal feedback, no matter how much they try to distance themselves and be objective.

Preferably, they won't even be domain experts—which is to say, they won't have comprehensive knowledge of the topic of the Web site. But if possible, they should have a strong Web background.

But, absolutely above everything else, they should empathize with the users and want to make sure they get the best experience possible. Who does that mean you should draw on? Perhaps the Web staff of other fandoms, though that does skirt close to the domain knowledge issue. In reality, though, it always depends on who you know. The person I know might have a very different background than the one you do.

---

1   Multiple sources (origin unknown).

Using a handful of evaluators is particularly important when they aren't experts in doing evaluations. Be sure each of them evaluates separately first. If you want them to do so, they can then discuss and help you pull their opinions together afterwards, but you want each to have the chance to analyze based on their own opinions before they do that.

What Should They Evaluate?

First and foremost, evaluators should take a few minutes and just look at the home page. Make sure it conveys a clear message explaining what you'll find on the site, and provides a good jumping-off point for any further exploration.

Use two to three key scenarios and have them approach the site to fulfill the goals of those users. Here are two possible scenarios for a fanfiction archive:

1. A writer who's been reading fanfiction for two years wants to post their first story.
2. A reader, completely new to fanfiction, wants to find a story about Harry and Ginny.

Why did I pick these two? I'm guessing—and this is something I can't substantiate and wouldn't want to recommend without looking into—that most fanfiction writers spend time reading it first. I'm guessing also that fanfiction newbies are likely to start with canon pairings before branching out. Are those accurate? I have no idea. But for the purposes of my presentation, they're good examples.

How Should They Evaluate It?

Evaluators should have a list of questions that are not specific to the site or the scenario. They should be generic enough that you could use them on pretty much any site at all. To get ideas, search the Web for "web site heuristic evaluation questions."

Make sure the evaluation scale is clear before you start. I would recommend no more than four scale "levels." Each level should have not only a score or name but also a more detailed description. The levels can be as simple as Pass or Fail, or they can be more detailed, such as Critical Failure, Causes Frustration, Acceptable, and Best Practice.

For example, "critical failure" might mean something to the effect of "causes the user to be unable to complete a task." These are frequently page errors, browser incompatibility issues, or simply not having the content a user needs to make a decision. Let's say I need a new refrigerator. It needs to fit in the same space—if the Web site I'm looking to buy from doesn't have dimensions listed, I won't make a decision; I'll go and find one someplace else.

Example

Let's go through an example—I'll use just a few sample questions to do this, since a comprehensive review takes a couple of hours.

I'm going to pretend I'm—well, me. Let's say someone has recommended The Burrow to me because while I've been reading fanfiction for several years, I've just recently developed an interest in reading fanfiction about Fred and George. I'm not interested in romance, I just want to read some funny stories. Let's try finding some on this site.

Figure 14: the home page. Yes—the tagline tells me this is all about the Weasleys, implying all of them, not just Ron or Ginny.

Figure 14

Perfect. The font's rather small, and using my browser's resize option doesn't work. At least there's a font change option in the top right.

I'm an existing fanfiction reader, so I'm going to jump right to Categories.

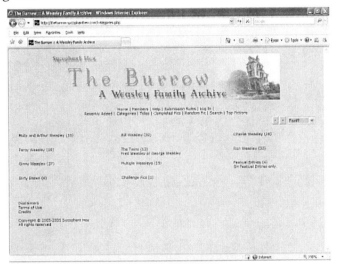

Figure 15

Figure 15. It looks like I'm at the categories, though it would be nice if it confirmed it with a header or a highlighted navigation link. Look—I see an option for "The Twins." Wonderful.

Clicking on that gave me a list of presumably all the stories about Fred and George, along with some drop-down menus to refine my search (Figure 16). On the left, I only want general stories. (A note about the word "general"—it's not always very friendly to new users, as they don't know what "general" might mean. But in a list like this, they can at least typically determine that it's basically none of the rest of the options—assuming that's what the word is being used to mean!)

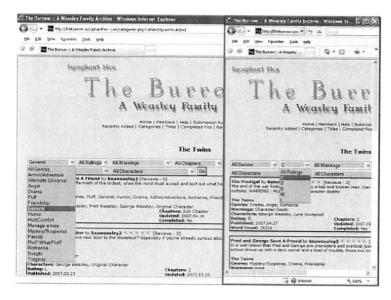

Figure 16

Just to be on the safe side, I want to pick only G-rated fiction, so I go to the rating drop-down. And I don't know what the letters stand for. Since I've been to the Ashwinder site, run by the same group, I have a vague idea, but it would really be nice to get some confirmation. And I'd have to leave this page to get to the help section. (I checked it later and found that C stands for Conservative.) That said, it's reasonable to assume that the ratings are in order, from least likely to offend anyone to most likely to be explicit. So I'll just choose the first one. Not a show-stopper, but it held me up.

And yes, I've arrived (Figure 17). The drop-down menus still show my choices so that I can remember what filter I used. The story listings are easy to read and easy to spot where one ends and the next begins. My only comment on this is that the very first one seems to list nine different genres! How can any one story really fit so many? And especially, if it's everything else, how is it "general"? Well, so be it—the second option sounds just perfect.

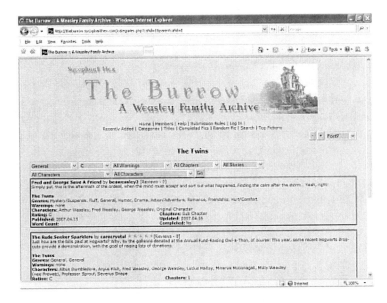

Figure 17

Heuristic Questions

Let's review The Burrow with a small cross-section of heuristic questions, using the scale of Critical Failure, Frustration, Good, and Best Practice.

Looking at the home page, does it appear that the user can find what they want?
> Yes, the tag line on the header graphic is useful, and there's a "categories" link in the navigation section. I'd like to see the categories right up on the home page, though. (Okay, they are there, but they're at the bottom of the second screen of content—not very prominent.) I'd give this a Good.

Was the language clear and understandable at all times?
> No, I didn't understand the ratings and had to guess. I'd rate this a Frustration.

Are the pages easily scannable?
> Yes, titles and key phrases are in boldface on the home page. The boxes around each item in the results list are good, with criteria names bolded as well to make it easy to

see a summary of the content at glance—though it would be very nice if the title were larger or the links weren't black. Again, a Good.

Does the site give feedback during navigation?

Yes, when I adjusted my search, my selected options remained selected in the drop-down menus. Best Practice.

Is the text legible?

The text is very small. I do see that there's a place to change the font size, but it's preferable to allow the user to do that via the browser, and that feature was disabled. Frustration.

I hope that gave you an idea of how to evaluate your Web site with limited money and time.

We Have Problems—Now What?

You've evaluated and found problems. Now what? Start by categorizing the problems.

Figure out which problems have been well-studied and have known, nearly surefire solutions. Text size, links to privacy/security policies, helpful error responses, consistent and understandable navigation, and scannability come to mind.

Then there are problems that can be analyzed using established, straightforward methodologies. If names of navigation links are unclear, grab a few non-*Potter*-expert friends and ask them to do a card-sorting exercise. Can't figure out your users or scenarios? Use a conference like Phoenix Rising to find volunteers to interview so that you *can* create personas. If you're feeling generous, you might give them a mug or a t-shirt! But one nice thing about something that's as community-oriented as fandom: people are actually interested in doing things just to make the on-line experience better. Don't abuse it, but don't ignore that, either.

Finally, if there are problems that you just can't figure out, make a list so that you can move onto step two: prioritize. Rank each thing to fix by a guesstimate of impact and a guesstimate of time and effort to fix. Your first pass should be fast fixes that make a big difference. Last should be things that few people will notice and that will take a lot of effort. Now, the stuff in the middle gets fuzzy and requires judgment calls, and that's where you need to insert your problems that you can't figure out. Try to decide when and if it's a good idea to pursue investigation.

To Conclude...

Fandom Web sites are typically volunteer-run and lacking in monetary resources to implement any sort of comprehensive usability testing methods. However, that doesn't mean that these sites need to drop all thoughts of good usability. By referencing some publicly available research, site owners can easily follow the most common Web usability guidelines. Right now, fandom Web sites are all over the map in their adherence to best practices. Site owners should take a look at their sites, try to fix the easy mistakes, and plan for more major redesigns. Specifically, recruiting help to complete a heuristic evaluation on an existing site can provide a good starting point for planning these changes.

I hope that this analysis has sparked your interest in usability and good user experience!

Selected Resources

Cooper, Alan. *The Inmates Are Running the Asylum: Why High Tech Products Drive Us Crazy and How to Restore the Sanity.* 2nd ed. Sams, 2004.

Cooper, Alan, Robert Reimann, and David Cronin. *About Face 3.0.* Wiley, 2007.

Cooper Interactive. <http://www.cooper.com/>.

Forrester Research. <http://www.forrester.com/>.

Human Factors International. "Usability consulting and training with Human Factors International: Ensuring user satisfaction through user-centered design, human factors, and software ergonomics." <http://www.humanfactors.com>.

Mulder, Steve, and Ziv Yaar. *The User Is Always Right: A Practical Guide to Creating and Using Personas for the Web.* New Riders Press, 2006.

Nielsen, Jakob (Nielsen Norman Group). "Jakob Nielsen on Usability and Web Design." <http://www.useit.com/>.

User Interface Engineering. "User Interface Engineering—Usability Research, Training, and Events—UIE." <http://www.uie.com/>.

When Wands Become Brushes: Painting the Magical Real

Marjorie Cohee Manifold
Indiana University

Introduction

The walls of Hogwarts School of Witchcraft and Wizardry are richly decorated with art.* Sir Cadogan's portrait, for example, hangs in an upper corridor challenging all who pass; in a tapestry, Barnabas the Barmy foolishly attempts to teach ballet to a gaggle of trolls. The Fat Lady and Violet move from their respective frames to visit one another and, of course, there are portraits of former headmasters and mistresses in Dumbledore's office. Characters of these portraits are not only able to move, but to talk, gossip, offer comfort, reveal secrets, and carouse with one another, the students, and professors. We are not told who painted these pictures or how they were created. Since the Hogwarts' curriculum includes no art classes, however, one might assume they were conjured from the minds of wizard-artists and the sorcery of wands. Perhaps there is no need for art education in a world where any ordinary witch or wizard may craft art with the wave of a wand.

In the Muggle world, however, art-making is not effortless. Artists must not only clearly visualize the object to be depicted, but also go through lengthy learning processes in order to master the skills necessary for transforming media into art. Brushes must be *made* to function as wands. Whereas the magical art images and objects of Harry Potter's world are seamlessly and unremarkably

---
* Special thanks to Karen Bayne, Donna Lafferty, and Josephina Manifold for providing information and/or feedback pertinent to this paper.

integrated with the cultural lives of the Potterean witches and wizard, art in the Muggle world is often subject to categorization. In formal art classrooms, the *high art* of the elite, acclaimed artists, and/ or the avant-garde may be given precedent over popular culture (i.e., those arts created as commodities for consumption by the masses, and the arts and crafts made by ordinary people as hobby, pleasure, or escape from mundane experience). Nevertheless, there seems a commitment among some Muggle *fans*[1] of popular culture phenomena to access or reclaim the magic of art. In this paper, I will look at two spontaneous art activities of adolescents and young adults who are fans of *Harry Potter*, and I will suggest that art teachers of traditionally taught art education have much to learn from the expressive activities of these youth.

Exploring Fandom Phenomena

Jenkins' (1992) assertion that the manipulation of popular culture into new expressive forms marks fans as creators of culture challenged me to wonder what new visual-cultural forms fans might be conjuring from the inspirational "stuff" of Rowling's fairy-tale. I was particularly curious as to *why* fans created these forms and *what* they meant to the people who made them. Additionally, as an art educator, I wanted to know *how* fans learned to create expressive visual forms of popular culture and what implications these culture-creative behaviors might have for formal art education.

To satisfy my curiosity on these topics, I engaged in an examination of the visual clues inherent in two expressive manipulations of popular culture, *fanart*[2] and *cosplay*.[3] These *fan*-based activities were chosen for study because they clearly take place outside formal art classrooms, yet call upon skills and knowledge that are typically taught in art classes. During a four-year study,[4] I perused websites of fanartists, read their blogs, and exchanged

---

1　A fan is a person who has an intense liking for some phenomenon of popular culture, seeks to know all manner of significant and trivial information about this interest, and may enter with other fans of the phenomenon into a loose social network known as a fandom.

2　Fanart is art that is based directly or indirectly on characters or settings from specific pop-culture phenomena.

3　Cosplay, a term that combines the words "costume" and "play," refers to dressing as and posing or performing as a character derived from pop culture.

4　The study was funded in part by a Proffitt Research Grant from Indiana University, School of Education.

online communications with dozens of youth who were identified
via their contributions to Web-based fanart galleries and cosplay
sites, such as deviantArt.com,[1] Elfwood,[2] Fanart Central,[3] and
Cosplay.com.[4] Fannish activities and expressions were observed and
photographed, and young fanartists and cosplayers were engaged in
conversations at public events such as film openings, book release
parties, and conventions. *Harry Potter* fans were observed and
interviewed at AnimeExpo 2004 (Anaheim, CA), Convention Alley
2004 (Ottawa), Comic-Con International 2005 (San Diego, CA), and
The Witching Hour (Salem, MA, 2005).

In order to collect first-hand accounts of what fanart and cosplay
might mean to fans who engaged in these expressive activities, and
to determine why and how they created these forms, I prepared a
questionnaire to be distributed via e-mail to 350 fanartists and
cosplayers. The people selected to receive the emailed questionnaire
were chosen from two online fanart sites (deviantArt and Elfwood)
and one cosplay site (`cosplay.com`), and included fans of various
literary popular-culture phenomena, such as anime/manga, science-
fiction and fantasy stories, films, television shows, and computer
games. More than 100 fans responded by answering the questions
put to them. For purposes of this paper, only the responses of
those twenty-seven fanartists and seventeen cosplayers who engaged
specifically with Potterean themes in their work are considered and
discussed.[5] The demographic of the Potterean fan group was similar
to that of the larger study group; all but four of the Potterean fans
were between the ages of fourteen and twenty-four, and all but two[6]
were female. While the larger sampling included respondents from
seventeen countries, the selective group of Potterean fans included
adolescents and young adults from eleven countries. These were: the
United States, Canada, Australia, the United Kingdom, France,
Belgium, Chile, Mexico, the Philippines, Puerto Rico, and Spain. The
answers given by the fans of the *Harry Potter* saga were statistically
similar to those of fans of those other popular texts or media works

---

1   <http://www.deviantart.com>.
2   <http://elfwood.lysator.liu.se/elfwood.html>.
3   <http://www.fanart-central.net>.
4   <http://www.cosplay.com>.
5   It should be pointed out, however, that fans of the *Harry Potter* texts also frequently
    created works based on stories or characters of other popular texts.
6   Statistically, 96% of the fanartists/cosplayers of *Harry Potter* were female. Overall, 86% of
    the total fanartist/cosplayers of the study were female.

included in the sample. Data were analyzed using content analysis methods suggested by Strauss and Corbin (1990).

The twelve questions of the research instrument encouraged open-ended responses. Three of the questions and their responses being addressed in this paper are:

- What of this art expression appeals to you, and why do you create it?
- Could you describe how you learned the techniques of this art form?
- What professional hopes or expectations do you have for the future in terms of your artistic activity?

What of This Art Expression Appeals to You, and Why Do You Create It?

What is it in the stories of *Harry Potter* that so fascinate the fan as to compel him or her to create *fanart*? Why would cosplayers wish to dress and act as characters from the Potterean saga? When these questions were put to fanartists and cosplayers of this study, they described the pleasures of engaging with great stories and fascinating characters, viewing images that were aesthetically pleasing, exploring and understanding human psychology or their own inner lives, and entering the real experience of a fantasized world. Fanart and cosplay engagements added a richer dimension to the fans' lives and, for more than two-thirds of the respondents, provided escape from boring, humdrum, or stressful everyday lives.

It was the story or, more specifically, the unique characters and character interactions of Rowling's saga that attracted adoring attention from fans. Respondents of the questionnaire reported that they were drawn to complex plots and subplots peopled by characters with intricate psychologies in complicated relationships. It became the fanartist's or cosplayer's task not only to depict the action of a storyline, but also to describe those emotions within each character that motivated the character to act or react in one way or another. Every respondent of the study identified character personality as both the most difficult to convey and the most important effect to master in an image. As one explained,

"Personality shapes…how [the characters] relate with one another and how they react to their world."

Nearly 80% of respondents indicated that fanart and cosplay interests helped them understand other people.[1] Creating fanart became a way of figuring out "how the world works"—not by reading how Rowling might have interpreted interactions[2] but by personally manipulating the interactions and understanding or "seeing" these relationships. In this way the fans began to decode some of the mysteries of human experience.

In spite of the volumes of academic research that suggest youths' attraction to characters of fairy-tales and other fictive children's literatures[3] reflect their internal quests for self-knowledge, only 25% of the study's respondents described their fanart or cosplay activities as helping them develop a holistic sense of self or come to terms with deep personal problems. This would lead one to believe that the majority of fanartists and cosplayers do not rely on fanart or cosplay as a process or tool of self-discovery or healing. Yet, the online comments made by fanartists and cosplayers about specific works they created confirms the positive, therapeutic psychological affects of these creative activities. Fanartist Kathryn Crenshaw (Figure 1), for example, explained that a "rougher treatment" than was generally characterized in her work, which had been used to create a scene showing Sirius's response to James Potter's death, could be attributed to the fact that she had created that illustration during "a particularly bad moment" in her life. Many fans are familiar with the intensely self-reflective cosplay images of Nathalie Mineault, a.k.a. Professor S. (Figure 2). Fanartists' and cosplayers' statements about specific works suggest that, although the overarching intent of fanart and cosplay may not be self-understanding *per se*, this may be a potent secondary or side effect of these creative experiences.

---

1   The major reason for interest was the pleasure they received from this activity; it had little to do with either self-discovery or exploration of others. This suggests that the interactions of individuals (i.e., social interactions) are in and of themselves inherently fascinating to fans.

2   Rowling has made it clear that she neither interprets nor condones interpretations of Potterean characters in erotic or homoerotic interactions, for example, yet these relational interactions flourish in the writings and art of fans.

3   Scholars of folklore, developmental psychology and child development, as well as education make these claims. Among these theorists are Bettelheim (1976), Winner (1985), Egan (1989, 1992).

Figure 1. Too Late (detail).
Kathryn A. Crenshaw.
Pencil and Photoshop airbrush. 2002.
`<http://oshinchan.com/main.htm>`

Figure 2. *The River Session* ~
Loss and Hope #3,
Nathalie Mineault a.k.a. Professor S.
Photographed by Diane Blanchard.
`<http://www.logospilgrim.com/>`

Potterean fanartists and cosplayers also were enthusiastic about meeting fans from other parts of the world. They enjoyed the social connections, and seeing their favorite characters and storylines depicted in the diverse aesthetic styles of fans from different parts of the world. Fans did not always agree about how a character should be represented; however, they prided themselves on their abilities to recognize visual cues and decode layers and subtexts of symbolic meaning that were hidden within the visual representations of their favorite stories. As members of the Potterverse fandom share their passionate interests online with fans from many different countries and cultural backgrounds, an appreciation for many different styles of fanart is cultivated. Styles of fanart presentation range, for example, from Japanese manga-inspired chibi to realistic illustrations reminiscent of the Brandywine School to decorative or abstractive works—and all manner of styles in between. On the other hand, cosplayers, regardless of their national, ethnic, or cultural backgrounds, strive to create works that are exact replications of the canon models. Differences between one cosplayer's presentation of Draco Malfoy and another, for example, rely upon the individual cosplayer's skill in crafting the costume, posing the body, or creating a subtly affecting gesture. Therefore, while fanartists of many cultures share, learn about, and celebrate one another's aesthetic traditions, cosplayers of many cultural traditions set aside these aesthetic differences and collectively apply the fan culture-specific visual language to explore an archetypal form.

Describe How You Learned the Techniques of this Art Form: Self-Learning, Peer Teaching, and Tutorials

More than one-third of the respondents of this study insisted that their fanart or costume making skills were "self-taught" because their art-learning and -making skills had been developed through self-motivated interests and practices. Fanartists studied and relentlessly copied images by other artists whose works they appreciated as well as photographs of actors from the *Harry Potter* movies. These character studies were then arranged and composed into scenes suggested by the books. In the privately situated environment of the fandom community, novice and experienced fanartists submitted their work for critique and asked advice of peer fanartists. Constructive critiques and comments from other fanartists were mentioned as the most valued aid to learning by 80% of the respondents.

Novice cosplayers studied the costumes of more skilled cosplayers at fan conferences, pored over magazines of cosplay images, and turned to relatives (especially mothers, grandmothers, and aunts) or other women in the community for instruction in sewing and dressmaking techniques. They appropriated materials from thrift shops, craft stores, and online sites, and shared information about how these ready-made materials could be worked into costumes and how props might be made. Online tutorials, how-to books, and craft instructional materials also were used to assist with specific technical problems related to costume-making. Although nearly every cosplayer appreciated how-to materials and tutorials, nearly one-fourth of the fanartists did not recommend these printed materials as appropriate for fanart learning because they perceived these as dictating specific processes that could be detrimental to the fanartist's discovery of a personal style or way of working.

Formal Art Education

The pervasive belief among art teachers that fanart is merely copied imagery made acquisition of art knowledge through formal instruction problematic. Over 35%[1] of the fanartist respondents indicated that although useful techniques, such as perspective, foreshortening, or shading, were learned in formal art classes, this knowledge was acquired *in spite of* the prejudices of their instructors. Youth who were discouraged from sharing their fanart work with their classmates were denied an opportunity to seek and receive classroom critiques of this work. In a few cases (10%), fanartists described the reactions of art teachers to their interests as being so adverse the fan was discouraged from taking *any* art courses in either high school or college.[2]

Several fanartists (about 18%) expressed a belief that art teachers *mis*understood fanart works as being juvenile, immature, or naïve. The negative view of Potterean fanart was exacerbated by the fact that Rowling's books are marketed to children and considered popular (rather than high) culture. Art teachers understandably were concerned that fanart constituted plagiarism of copyrighted intellectual property, but respondents believed the disdain some art teachers expressed toward fanart was attributable more to those teachers' lack of appreciation for the instructional benefits of copying from original models, than to genuine concerns regarding intellectual property rights. Two respondents commented on the "hypocrisy" of art teachers who ask students to "copy *styles* rather than *compositions*." According to these respondents, art teachers convey a double standard and put emphasis on an inappropriate aspect of art learning when they ask students to, for example, "paint a composition of the student's choice in the style of Cubism, Impressionism, or Post Impressionism," while prohibiting the

---

1   Although the 35% percent mentioned have received some benefit from formal art education, only two of the respondents were complimentary about the knowledge acquired through their formal art training. A staggering 65% were either altogether condemning or dismissive of art education as a learning resource.

2   In a single example of teacher support, Mara, a Puerto Rican high-school student, related that she and her art teacher became "best friends" after she discovered that they shared an interest in fanart.

student from rendering a compositional arrangement of a great artist in the student's personal style. Helénè, a fanartist living in France, describes the benefits of the latter approach:

> I made a *Harry Potter*-themed version of Picasso's *Bullfight: The Death of the Torero*,[1] which became the death of the wizard Sirius Black.[2] It made me look very closely at the painting. [I learned a lot] about Picasso and about composing a painting.

The fanartist respondents of this study overwhelmingly agreed that copying serves the need of beginning fanartists to learn important drawing skills and assists the more technically skilled fanartists' desires to develop personal styles that set them apart from all other fanartists who create images based on the same source.[3] The copy of a canon form may be likened to the function of a utilitarian object that is intended for a specific purpose but yields to the expressive manipulations of the artist or craftsperson. A similarity may be drawn between fanartists (or cosplayers) of popular-culture literatures and folk artists who create quilts or construct violins. The quilt pattern may be formulaic and the violin must conform to absolute standards as to shape, use of materials, and production of sound. Yet each quilt-maker or violin-maker seeks to leave a stamp of personal style and craftspersonship as part of the finished artifact. Likewise, a goal of every fanartist and cosplayer is to have his or her work immediately recognized in terms of content and form, then recognized and applauded based on his or her demonstration of distinctive personal styles.

Cosplayers may benefit more from this comparison than fanartists. Cosplayers reported that they gained from lessons in sewing and costume construction in home economics classes when the option to enroll in these courses was available to them. Art and home economics teachers, family members, and others of the local community seemed willing to teach the skills of costume-making without the judgmental encumbrances that discouraged fanartists. The ingenuity required in order to make impossible costumes or

---

1   *Bullfight: Death of the Torero* (1933), Pablo Picasso, The Musée Picasso, Paris. Oil on wood panel, 324 x 40 cm.

2   Sirius Black is a favorite character from J. K. Rowling's *Harry Potter* series.

3   In fact, fanartists' biggest complaint against other fans is the improper behavior of copying the styles of other fanartists. On the other hand, replication of original source material is not seen as copying—because the true fanartist attempts to reproduce the images in an original style.

body appurtenances appear "real" rendered costume-making acceptable as *craft* and allowed teachers of costume-making to sidestep issues related to originality versus the copy.

What Professional Hopes or Expectations Do You Have?

In spite of the high degree of skill and sophistication evidenced in many of their fanart and cosplay creations, only half of the fanartist respondents of this study indicated that they expected or aspired to pursue careers as artists. Furthermore, even those who described themselves as desiring to pursue professional careers in art, or who were artists involved in what they described as "legitimate" forms of art (i.e., as portrait or landscape painters, illustrators, graphic designers, photographers, or interior designers) experienced the creation of fanart and cosplay as qualitatively different than the creation of other types of art. Fanart-making activities were seen as kinds of pleasurable resistance to mundanity (de Certeau, 2002). Cosplayers also described costume play and performance as a hobbyist pursuit. Interestingly, however, a higher percentage of cosplayers did aspire to careers as clothing or costume designers. Perhaps because the creation of costume was more likely to be accepted or (at least) tolerated by teachers and family members, cosplayers were able to see themselves in careers that might support both their financial needs and desires for experiences in fantasy.

Nearly 70% of the respondents in this study described their fanart-making or cosplay activities as escapist in nature. Those who had no intentions of becoming professional artists indicated that they did plan to continue creating and improving their art- or costume-making skills because they "would rather live in the make-believe world" than the real one. "It adds meaning to my real life," stated one fanartist, who indicated that during periods of escape into the Potterverse, she could imagine "new possibilities." Fanart creation contributed to Mary's ability to find balance in her life. She stated:

I used to want to go into animation or illustration as a career, but lately, I've realized I'm much happier when I draw for myself. There's no expectations, I work at my own pace, and in the end, I've only got myself to please—and I am always my toughest critic. I don't ever see myself doing this for a living, Art is my way of dealing with life; I don't want to turn it into my source of living.

The life-enhancing benefits of fandom participation and fanart-making were described by persons whose careers were devoted to creating "legitimate" forms of art. For example, Charlene, a twenty-one year old graphic designer in Great Britain, writes, "It's a hobby, it's relaxing and fun; it's not another bloody boring piece of graphic design done for another person; it's a tiny personal bit of art drawn only for one person, me!"

Knowing and Being Known in Fandom

Fanartists and cosplayers who are members of a fandom know one another through the mediation of a narrative, which is the phenomenological focus of fans' interests but reveals nothing of participants' real-life histories or experiences. Initially, fans are known to one another only insofar as they express knowledge of a shared popular phenomenon and post data about themselves and their interests online. The "real" self is hidden from others in the public display of cosplay at fan conventions and behind catchy online pseudonyms that allude to the fan's interest or suggest that he or she bears similar characteristics to those of a known (or archetypal) character—for example, PaawPrintz, Ginny-Potterer, or MoonyLuna. Yet in online blogs, fans who disguise their real-life identities behind masks of adored Potterean characters reveal the most intimate details and private thoughts of their lives. These incongruencies suggest conflicts—struggles between public and private identities, real and virtual experiences, and the Muggle versus magical lives of adolescent and young adults.

Teaching and Learning Art at Hogwarts School for Wizardry

Why should art educators pay attention to these extracurricular art-making activities? What implications for formal art education can be drawn from an examination of how and why fans manipulate narratives of popular culture into new visual-cultural forms? One reason focuses on the recognition that many youth who create art based on fannish interests do not see themselves as pursuing careers in art. This suggests a large audience of creative individuals who may be missing from the formal art studio or academy. It cannot be assumed that those who eschew art as a valued subject of formal education devalue art's importance in their lives. Art for many individuals may, in fact, be too precious or special to be shared with those who may not value it as dearly. For these people, art-making may present "sacred possibilities" of vitality and dynamism that could not be enhanced, but potentially could be threatened or demeaned by academic applications. For others, fanart and cosplay are simply pleasurable hobbies that are not the central focus of their lives, but give balance and offer intrinsic rewards. For a few, fanart and cosplay may grant entrée to self-knowledge or emotional healing. The needs and purposes for which a variety of people may desire or need to learn art information and skills should be reassessed, and the notions of why and to whom we teach art reconsidered.

The way art is taught in formal classrooms is also called into question. Prohibitions against copying compositional models are challenged, even as problems of intellectual property and copyright infringements are highlighted. Traditions of teaching art in incremental, sequential steps grounded in the elements and principles of art as discrete building blocks are seen as potentially detrimental to art understanding. Fanart and cosplay are not about the elements and principles of design so much as the elements and principles of *aesthetic meaning* (Manifold, 2005; 2006). This suggests studio-based approaches that focus on instructing skills and techniques when art-making "problems" arise, rather than according to ordered lessons of art curricula.

The content of art might be drawn from stories and themes from popular culture that are known, enjoyed, and shared in the real experiences of youths' lives. These narratives, peopled by fictive archetypes, could present engaging foci for deep, meaningful self-expression and local and global discourse. Art teachers in one locale might collaborate with art teachers in distant geographic areas to design art programs that permit small group interactions *online* between students of diverse nations and cultures. The groups would be based on the students' shared pop-culture interests. The role of each teacher, in this regard, might be to invite students of his or her classroom to draw upon aspects of the local culture and the students' unique life experiences, in exploring personal styles worthy of contribution to the global discourse.

The fact that there are no formal art classes at Hogwarts does not imply that art is unimportant to the wizarding world. Rather, it highlights the value of art as integrated and indistinguishable from the essential nature of magic. This might inform art educators of the Muggle world. The whole milieu of stories, mythic archetypes, and cultural ideas—the stuff of the environment in which youth live —has magical potential. When youth are encouraged (or when they take it upon themselves) to manipulate these elements of the everyday into personally or collectively meaningful forms, they wield magic. When brushes become wands, wands paint reality with magic and that which is magical becomes real.

References

Bettelheim, B. (1976). *The uses of enchantment.* New York: Knopf.

de Certeau, M. (2002). *The practice of everyday life.* Berkeley, CA: University of California Press.

Egan, K. (1989). *Teaching as story telling: An alternative approach to teaching and curriculum in the elementary school.* Chicago: University of Chicago Press.

Egan, K. (1992). *Imagination in teaching and learning: The middle years.* Chicago: University of Chicago Press.

Jenkins, H. (1992). *Textual poachers: Television fans and participatory culture.* New York: Routledge.

Manifold, M. C. (2004). Imaged voices—envisioned landscapes: Storylines of Information-Age girls and young women. *Journal for Social Theory in Art Education, 24.* 234–56.

Manifold, M. C. (2005). Life as theater-theater as life: Spontaneous expressions of Information-Age youth. *Journal of Cultural Research in Art Education, 23.* 1–16.

Strauss, A. and Corbin, J. (1990). *Basics of qualitative research: Grounded theory procedures and techniques.* Newbury Park, CA: Sage Publications.

Winner, E. (1985). *Invented worlds: The psychology of the arts.* Cambridge, MA: Harvard University Press.

Printed in the United States
204525BV00001B/142/P